SUPERVISION

DIVERSITY AND TEAMS IN THE WORKPLACE

TENTH EDITION

Charles R. Greer

NEELEY SCHOOL OF BUSINESS, TEXAS CHRISTIAN UNIVERSITY

W. Richard Plunkett

EMERITUS, WRIGHT COLLEGE, CITY COLLEGES OF CHICAGO

Prentice
Hall

Upper Saddle River, New Jersey 07458

Library of Congress Cataloging-in-Publication Data

Greer, Charles R.
    Supervision : diversity and teams in the workplace / Charles R. Greer, W. Richard
Plunkett.—10th ed.
        p. cm.
    Plunkett's name appears first on the earlier editions.
    Includes bibliographgical references and index.
    ISBN 0-13-097290-8
    1. Supervision of employees. 2. Diversity in the workplace. I. Plunkett, W. Richard
(Warren Richard) II. Plunkett, W. Richard (Warren Richard) Supervision. III. Title.

HF5549 .P564 2003
658.3'02—dc21

                                                                                    2002070430

Editor-in-Chief: Stephen Helba
Director of Production and Manufacturing: Bruce Johnson
Manufacturing Buyer: Cathleen Petersen
Executive Editor: Elizabeth Sugg
Editorial Assistant: Anita Rhodes
Managing Editor: Mary Carnis
Production Liason: Denise Brown
Full Service Production: Gay Pauley/Holcomb Hathaway
Photo Research: Teri Stratford
Compositor: Aerocraft Charter Art Service
Design Director: Cheryl Asherman
Design Coordinator/Cover Design: Christopher Weigand
Cover Illustration: David Bishop
Cover Printer: Phoenix Color
Printer/Binder: Courier Westford

Pearson Education Ltd.
Pearson Education Australia Pty. Limited
Pearson Education Singapore Pte. Ltd.
Pearson Education North Asia Ltd.
Pearson Education Canada, Ltd.
Pearson Educación de Mexico, S.A. de C.V.
Pearson Education–Japan
Pearson Education Malaysia Pte. Ltd.
Pearson Education, *Upper Saddle River, New Jersey*

Photo Credits: Chapter 1: p. 6: Bob Daemmrich/ Stock Boston; p. 15: Wyatt McSpadden Photography; p. 24: Michael Heron/Woodfin Camp & Associates; p. 26: David Joel/Tony Stone Images. **Chapter 2:** p. 44: Jeff Zaruba/The Stock Market; p. 53: Mark Richards/PhotoEdit; p. 60: Jim Pickerell/Tony Stone Images. **Chapter 3:** p. 74: Don Bosler/Tony Stone Images; p. 78: Barbara Alper/ Stock Boston. **Chapter 4:** p. 106: Peter Yates/SABA Press Photos, Inc; p. 117: Alan Carey/The Image Works; p. 124: Walter Hodges/Tony Stone Images; p. 127: B. Mahoney/The Image Works. **Chapter 5:** p. 157: Cristy DiDonato/Ore-Ida Foods, Inc.; p. 158: F. Pedrick/The Image Works; p. 163: Photo-Disc, Inc. p. 174: Bruce Ayres/Tony Stone Images. **Chapter 6:** p. 183: Walter Hodges/Tony Stone Images; p. 189: Bruce Ayres/Tony Stone Images; p. 198: Hemera Technologies, Inc.; p. 200: Robert Severi/Woodfin Camp & Associates; p. 210: Andy Freeberg Photography. **Chapter 7:** p. 218: Xerox Corporation; p. 234: William Hubbell/Woodfin Camp & Associates; p. 245: Bob Daemmrich/The Image Works. **Chapter 8:** p. 262: Laima Druskis/ Stock Boston; p. 265: Billy E. Barnes/Stock Boston; p. 269: Bob Daemmrich/Stock Boston; p. 279: Andy Sacks/Tony Stone Images. **Chapter 9:** p. 293: Jon Feingersh/The Stock Market; p. 298: Chris Jones/The Stock Market; p. 305: General Motors; p. 314: PhotoDisc, Inc.; **Chapter 10:** p. 342: Telegraph Colour Library/FPG International LLC; p. 343: Maggie Steber/The Stock Market; p. 344: John Sohm/The Stock Market; p. 346: Tom Tracy/ Tony Stone Images. **Chapter 11:** p. 377: Donald Smetzer/Tony Stone Images; p. 382: Blair Saitz/ Photo Researchers, Inc. **Chapter 12:** p. 403: Hank Morgan/Photo Researchers, Inc.; p. 409: Chip Henderson/Tony Stone Images; p. 420: Joe Lynch/ Liaison Agency, Inc. **Chapter 13:** p. 434: Chuck Savage/The Stock Market; p. 447: Bob Daemmrich/ The Image Works; p. 450: Gabe Palmer/The Stock Market. **Chapter 14:** p. 467: Cary Wolinsky/Stock Boston; p. 474: Michael L. Abramson/Woodfin Camp & Associates; p. 479: Tom & Dee Ann McCarthy/The Stock Market. **Chapter 15:** p. 501: PhotoDisc, Inc.; p. 506: PhotoDisc, Inc.; p. 507: D. E. Cox/Tony Stone Images. **Chapter 16:** p. 533: William Edward Smith/The Stock Market; p. 550: Alon Reininger/Contact Stock Images.

10 9 8 7 6 5 4 3 2 1
ISBN 0-13-097290-8

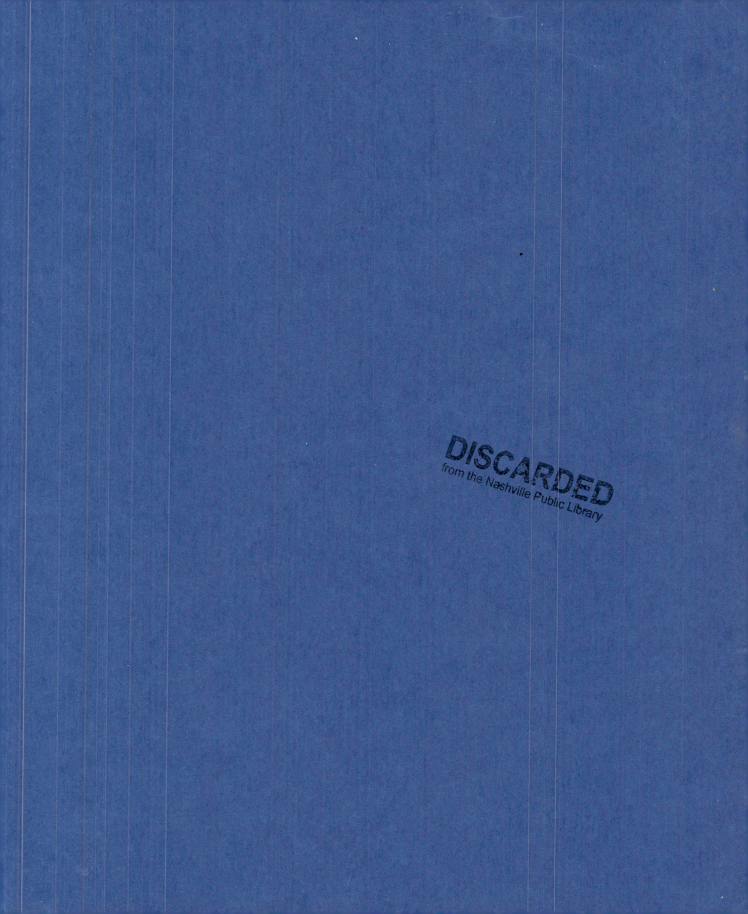

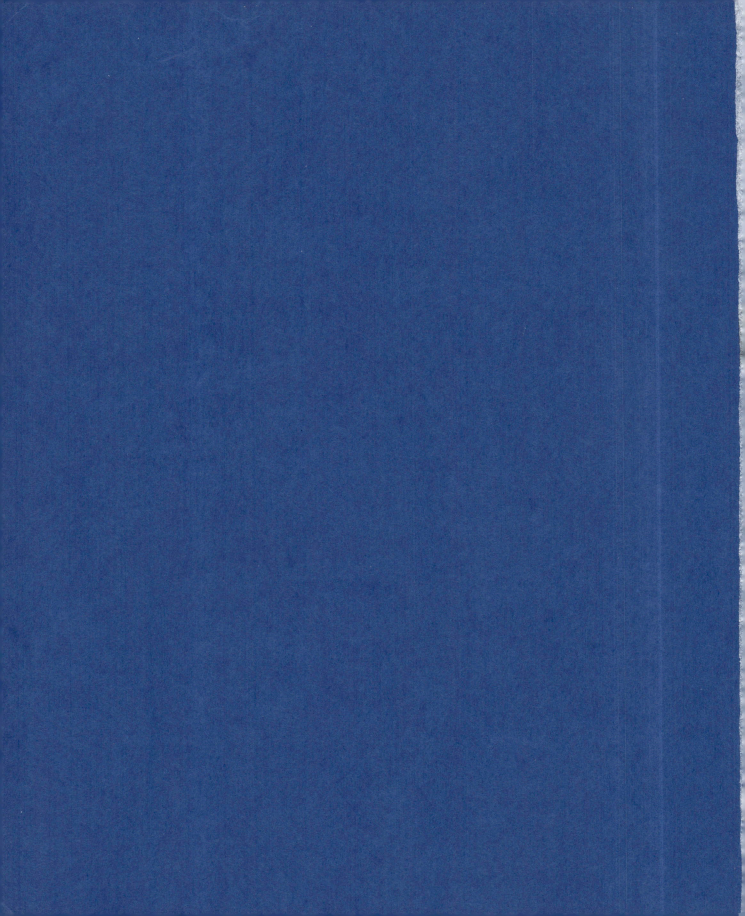

CONTENTS

Chapter 3

Chapter 4

PART II

YOU AND YOUR PEOPLE   143

Chapter 5

COMMUNICATION   145

Chapter 6

MANAGING CHANGE AND STRESS   181

Chapter 7

Chapter 8

PART III

SHAPING YOUR ENVIRONMENT   363

Chapter 11

SELECTION AND ORIENTATION   365

Chapter 12

TRAINING   401

Chapter 13

THE APPRAISAL PROCESS 433

Chapter 14

DISCIPLINE 465

PREFACE

This tenth edition of *Supervision: Diversity and Teams in the Work-place* has been thoroughly updated. Special care has been taken to preserve the "how to" and the "you" approaches of the previous editions, while enriching these features with current application materials. As before, the text emphasizes how a supervisor can apply the major concepts introduced.

INTENDED READERS

This edition is intended to be used as a primary instruction tool for those who want to become supervisors or want to improve the present levels of their supervisory skills and knowledge. Users will find this text to be an excellent introduction to management functions and principles as they apply to the supervisory level of management. It is designed for use in community colleges, in universities, in various in-house industry and trade association courses, and in supervisory management programs. The text's primary goals are to engage the students' interest; to explain management principles and theories with terms, examples, and situations that are understandable to beginners; and to translate these principles and theories into everyday managerial applications.

NEW AND IMPORTANT FEATURES

The major revisions in this tenth edition are as follows:

- There are many **new company examples**—more than 200 companies are now mentioned. These examples involve well-known U. S. companies as well as international companies and should help students see the real world applicability of the material while stimulating class discussion.

- Several of the special features on **supervising teams, supervisors and quality,** and **supervisors and ethics** are new. In addition, all chapters have these features.

- Updated, expanded, or new **topics** include:

ethics	planning	career management	theories of motivation
attitudes	work values	facilitating change	information technology
MIS	control	virtual teams	computer applications
appraisal	leadership	communication	Internet/World Wide Web
software	health issues		

- Icons (see below) highlight discussions related to the themes of this book. Look for these icons throughout the text:

Teams   **Diversity**   **International Perspective**   **Quality**   **Ethics**

- Several photographs included in each chapter show application of the major concepts. The **photographs illustrate realistic work situations** and reflect upon the diversity of the current and future workforce.
- The book is presented in a **visually pleasing two-color format.** The color has been used to maximum effect on all visuals, headings, icons, and marginal notes.
- Selections from the **JWA Video Library** are available to professors who use this textbook in their classrooms. Professors select from dozens of topics including: supervision, motivation, communication skills, coaching, and much more!
- We have changed from in-text **referencing** to the use of endnotes, which is less distracting for the readers.

In addition to the above features, each chapter continues to include the following pedagogical tools to aid students in the study and retention of the chapter's major concepts:

- *Learning objectives:* aid the student in identifying and mastering the chapter's key concepts.
- *Key terms:* define new vocabulary within the chapter and are contained in an end-of-book glossary.
- *Introduction:* briefly highlights the chapter's theme.
- *Exhibits:* visually represent data, eliminating the confusion between figures and tables.
- *Instant replay:* lists the chapter's key concepts for review and study preparation.
- *Incident:* asks students to apply their knowledge and experiences to the chapter's key concepts.

- *Cases:* ask students to apply each chapter's major principles based on supervisor's experiences.

SUGGESTIONS TO THE STUDENTS

We envy all of you for the fun and challenge you are about to experience. We congratulate you on your ambition and foresight in choosing a fascinating course of study: the management of people.

Do not hide your talents. Share your experiences with your class, and soon you will realize how valuable your personal experiences have been to yourself—and how valuable they may be to your classmates.

Expect to find a frequent and almost immediate use for almost everything you learn in the management course. If you are already a manager, apply the lessons at work. If not, study your boss. If your boss is highly qualified, you will soon be able to see why this is so. If he or she is not, you will learn what is wrong with his or her performance. More important, you will also know what mistakes you should not make. Often the example of a poorly qualified boss can provide an excellent learning experience.

Never seek to conceal your own ignorance about the task of being a supervisor. Admit to yourself that you have a lot to learn, as we all do. Only by recognizing a void in your knowledge can you hope to fill it. And the proper way to fill it is by studying and expanding your work experience. If you ask questions in class as they occur to you, you will avoid the old problem of missing out on important pieces of information. Take the initiative. Quite possibly, some questions that you are pondering might also concern others in the class. The more you contribute to the course, the more you will receive from it.

From now on, think of yourself as a supervisor. Throughout this book, we will be talking to you as one supervisor to another. In the following pages you will find many tools—the tools of supervision. Their uses are explained in detail. A skilled worker knows his or her tools and knows which ones are right for each task. When you complete this course, you will have the knowledge you need to be a successful supervisor. Put this knowledge to use as soon as possible. During the course, you may have a chance to present one of the case problems to your classmates. This will be a fine opportunity to test yourself on how to apply the principles of supervision to a concrete situation in the world of work. You also may find other applications of these principles, at home and on the job. Do not overlook them.

SUPPLEMENTARY MATERIAL

- **Instructor's Manual** includes chapter outlines, three additional cases for each chapter with suggested solutions, answers to the text's questions for class discussion and its cases, and a vocabulary review for each chapter's key terms. Each chapter has a separate test bank containing true/false and multiple-choice questions, with answers. Those test questions are also available in electronic format.

- **JWA Video Library** This library of videos has one video for training in each of the core skills a supervisor must develop.
- **Prentice Hall Test Manager** Organizes and delivers a complete, electronic bank of test questions in any format that suits your needs.

Acknowledgments

We would like to acknowledge the help of the following people on this and previous editions: Ray Ackerman, East Texas State University; Thomas Auer, Murray State University; Richard Baker, Mohave Community College; Raymond F. Balcerzak, Jr., Ferris State University; Gregory Barnes, Purdue University; James Baskfield, North Hennepin Community College; Lorraine Bassette, Prince George's Community College; Charles Beavin, Miami-Dade Community College; James Bishop, Arkansas State University; Frederick Blake, Bee County College; Raymond Bobillo, Purdue University; Arthur Boisselle, Pikes Peak Community College; Jerry Boles, Western Kentucky University; Terry Bordan, Cuny-Hostos Community College; Joe Breeden, Kansas Technical Institute; Robin Butler, Lakeshore Technical Institute; Leonard Callahan, Daytona Beach Community College; Donald Caruth, East Texas State University; Donald S. Carver, National University; Joseph Castelli, College of San Mateo; Joseph Chandler, Indiana-Purdue University at Fort Wayne; Win Chesney, Saint Louis Community College–Meramac; Jackie Conway, Lenoir Community College; Gloria Couch, Texas State Technical Institute; John C. Cox, New Mexico State University; Roger Crowe, State Technical Institute at Knoxville; E. Jane Dews, San Jacinto College–South; Michael Dougherty, Milwaukee Area Technical College; M. J. Duffey, Lord Fairfax Community College; C. S. "Pete" Everett, Des Moines Area Community College; Lawrence Finley, Western Kentucky University; Ethel Fishman, Fashion Institute of Technology; Jack Fleming, Moorpark College; Randall Scott Frederick, Delgado Community College; Daphne Friday, Sacred Heart College; Olene Fuller, San Jacinto College–North; Alfonso Garcia, Navajo Community College; John Guebtner, Tacoma Community College; Edwin A. Giermak, College of Dupage; Tommy Gilbreath, University of Texas at Tyler; Cliff Goodwin, Indiana University-Purdue University; Edward Gott, Jr., Eastern Maine Vocational Technical Institute; Luther Guynes, Los Angeles City College; Ed Hart, Elizabethtown Community College; Joann Hendricks, City College of San Francisco; Steven Herendeen, Indiana-Purdue University at Fort Wayne; Ron Herrick, Mesa Community College; Karen Heuer, Des Moines Area Community College; Larry Hill, San Jacinto College; Larry Holliday, Southwest Wisconsin Vocational Technical Institute; Eugene Holmen, Essex Community College; David Hunt, Blackhawk Technical Institute; Tonya Hynds, Purdue

University–Kokomo; Jim Jackson, Johnston Technical College; William Jacobs, Lake City Community College; Joseph James, Jr., Lamar University–Port Arthur; Debbie Jansky, Milwaukee Area Tech; Carl F. Jenks, Purdue University; F. Mike Kaufman; George Kelley, Erie Community College–City Campus; Billy Kirkland, Tarleton State University; Steve Kirman, Dyke College; Jay Knippen, University of South Florida; Thomas Leet, Purdue University; James Lewis, Gateway Technical Institute; Marvin Long, New River Community College; Doris Lux, Central Community College–Platte; Cheryl Macon, Butler County Community College; Joseph Manno, Montgomery College; Manuel Mena, Suny College At Oswego; Michael Miller, Indiana University-Purdue University at Fort Wayne; Jerry Moller, Frank Phillip's College; Sherry Montgomery, Saint Philip's College; Charles Moore, Neosho County Community College; Herff Moore, University of Central Arkansas; Jim Mulvihill, South Central Technical College; Jim Nestor, Daytona Beach Community College; Gerard Nistal, Our Lady of Holy Cross College; Smita Jain Oxford, Commonwealth College; Carolyn Patton, Stephen F. Austin State University; Jean Perry, Contra Costa College; Donald Pettit, Suffolk County Community College; Jerome Pilewski, University of Pittsburgh at Titusville; Sharon Pinebrook, University of Houston; Peter Randrup, Worwic Technical Community College; Ed Raskin, Los Angeles Mission College; Jim Rassi, Paradise Valley Community College; William Recker, Northern Kentucky University; Robert Redick, Lincoln Land Community College; James A. Reinemann, College of Lake County; Tom Reynolds, Southside Virginia Community College; Harriett Rice, Los Angeles City College; Ralph Rice, Maryland Technical College; Shirley Rickert, Indiana University-Purdue University at Fort Wayne; Charles Roegiers, University of South Dakota; Lloyd Roettger, Indiana Vocational Technical College; Pat Rothamel, Iowa Western Community College; Duane Schechter, Muskingum Community College; Robert Sedwick, Fairleigh Dickinson University; Sandra Seppamaki, Tanana Valley Community College; David Shepard, Virginia Western Community College; David Shufeldt, Clayton State College; David Smith, Dabney Lancaster Community College; Carl Sonntag, Pikes Peak Community College; Frank Sotrines, Washburn University; William Steiden, Jefferson Community College Southwest; Greg Stephens, Kansas Tech; John Stepp, Greenville Technical College; Lynn H. Suksdorf, Salt Lake Community College; Marge Sunderland, Fayetteville Technical Institute; George Sutcliffe, Central Piedmont Community College; H. Allan Tolbert, Central Texas College; Daniel R. Tomal, Purdue University; Wes Van Loon, Matanuske-Susitan Community College; Peter Vander Haeghen, Coastline Community College; Mike Vijuk, William Rainey Harper College; W. J. Waters, Central Piedmont Community College; Hal Ward, Temple Junior College; Willie Weaver, Amarillo College; George White, Ohlone College; Ron Williams, Merced College; Willie Williams, Tidewater Community College; Bob Willis, Rogers State College; Ira Wilsker, Lamar University;

Paul Wolff II, Dundalk Community College; Richard Wong, Olympic College; Robert Wood, Vance-Granville Community College; and Charles Yauger, Arkansas State University.

We would also like to acknowledge the editorial assistance of Elizabeth Sugg, Todd Ulrich, Gay Pauley, and Patricia Colarco.

Charles R. Greer
W. Richard Plunkett

THE BIG PICTURE

art I of this text contains four chapters designed to introduce you to the supervisor's (team leader's or team facilitator's) special place in management and the concepts and functions that are essential for all managers.

This part introduces three features that appear in every chapter: *Supervising Teams, Supervisors and Ethics,* and *Supervisors and Quality.* Each introduces you to various concepts and principles that will help you effectively manage your subordinates, team members, or associates—both individually and in groups.

Chapter 1 focuses on the unique challenges and opportunities connected with being a supervisor in any kind of organization. It examines the skills, roles, and responsibilities required of supervisors in detail.

Chapter 2 helps you assess your strengths and weaknesses and plan for the evolution of your career. It gives guidelines for personal growth and a strategy for seeking employment.

Chapter 3 defines management as a process through which supervisors, team leaders, and team facilitators accomplish organizational objectives by utilizing the skills and efforts of their associates. The chapter defines and illustrates the concepts of authority, responsibility, accountability, and power, as well as the three levels of management and the steps for rational decision making.

Chapter 4 concludes Part I with a brief look at the functions common to all levels of management. It examines the basic principles and tools that apply to each function, along with the ways in which supervisors put them to use.

CHAPTER 1

THE SUPERVISOR'S SPECIAL ROLE

Objectives

After reading and discussing this chapter, you should be able to do the following:

1. Define this chapter's key terms.

2. List and define management skills every supervisor must possess and apply.

3. List the groups to whom the supervisor is responsible and what responsibilities exist toward each group.

4. Explain the concepts of *effectiveness* and *efficiency* as they apply to a supervisor's performance.

5. Discuss the possible effects on supervisors of current trends in U.S. business.

6. Describe the sources of supervisory personnel.

Introduction

A **supervisor** is an employee (and member of the group called managers) who is responsible for the welfare, behaviors, and performances of non-management employees—called workers. (Throughout this text, the terms *worker, team member,* and *associate* will be used interchangeably with the term *subordinate*.) The supervisor is a person in the middle, positioned between the workers and higher-level managers. Supervisors' managers and subordinates differ in attitudes, values, priorities, and in the demands they make on supervisors. Workers and managers often make conflicting demands. The supervisor must cope with conflicts while gaining a sense of job satisfaction and identity in the process.

Major changes throughout both the private and public sectors of our economy are reshaping the traditional behaviors of supervisors. Organizational efforts to become more cost-effective, get closer to customers, and tap

supervisor

a manager responsible for the welfare, behaviors, and performances of non-management employees (workers) into the creativity of all employees have created self-directing teams and pushed decision-making responsibilities into the hands of supervisors and their associates. As a result, supervisors are moving away from giving orders and commands, planning subordinates' work, making all decisions, and inspecting subordinates' output. Instead, they are leading by example, coaching, counseling, guiding, consulting with, and meeting subordinates' individual and collective needs.

team leader

a supervisor working in a team who is responsible for its members

In many organizations, supervisors are being rapidly transformed into team leaders and team facilitators. **Team leaders** serve on and lead a team, and **team facilitators** nurture one or more teams of their subordinates. Both are expected to determine the human, financial, material, and informational resources needed by their associates and to make certain that necessary support is provided. Supervision entails getting work done through the effective utilization of subordinates and other resources. Team leaders and team facilitators should support their associates by helping to create and nurture a committed, trained, competent, and enthusiastic workforce. As William Bridges, the author of *Job Shift,* puts it: The value of supervisors "... can be defined only by how they facilitate the work of teams or how they contribute to it as a member."[1]

team facilitator

a supervisor in charge of teams but who is working outside them

Some companies have been disappointed with their application of teams. While we present examples of supervisors in team settings and stress that the use of teams is increasing, we point out in later chapters that there are limitations of teams. The primary requirement for effective teams is that the team members share a compelling purpose. Without such a purpose teams can be ineffective.[2]

Governmental regulations, while not providing the most meaningful definition, also define the supervisor. The Taft-Hartley Act of 1947 says that any person who can hire, suspend, transfer, lay off, recall, promote, discharge, assign, reward, or discipline other employees or recommend such action while using independent judgment is a supervisor—a member of management. For the purposes of the Fair Labor Standards Act of 1938, commonly referred to as the minimum wage law, supervisors are distinguishable from regular employees only if (1) they spend no more than 20 percent of their time performing the same kind of work that their subordinates perform and (2) they are paid other than an hourly wage.

foreman

a supervisor of workers in manufacturing

You may be familiar with the term **foreman.** While the term is used less frequently today, in some organizations it is used interchangeably with the word *supervisor* and usually refers to a supervisor of workers performing manufacturing activities.

Three Types of Management Skills

management skills

categories of capabilities needed by all managers at every level in an organization

No matter how supervisors are defined, they routinely must apply basic skills. The basic **management skills** required of all managers at every level in an organization can be grouped under three headings: interpersonal, technical, and conceptual.[3] Managers at different levels in an organization use

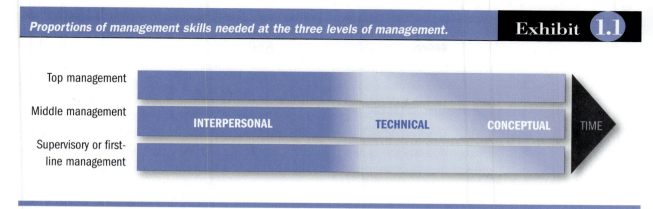

Exhibit 1.1

Proportions of management skills needed at the three levels of management.

Top management

Middle management

Supervisory or first-
line management

INTERPERSONAL · · · TECHNICAL · · · CONCEPTUAL · · · TIME

one or another of these skills to a greater or lesser degree, depending on the manager's position in the organization and the particular demands of the circumstances at any given time. As Exhibit 1.1 illustrates, the supervisor's role requires less conceptual skill than does higher-level management. On the other hand, supervisors require more technical skill.

INTERPERSONAL SKILLS

Interpersonal, human, or people skills determine the manager's ability to work effectively as a group or team member and to build cooperative effort within the group or team she leads. The manager also uses interpersonal skills to coordinate the interaction between that group and all the other groups with which it comes into contact.

Consider the lessons learned by team leaders in the Colorado-based XEL company. This maker of communications equipment wanted to create a quality-obsessed environment "to become a model of workplace efficiency, dedicated to quality and teamwork."[4] The process began with a needs assessment in which team leaders asked associates what they wanted to learn and how. After trying ready-made courses and evaluating them, team leaders decided to design their own "XEL University [offering] 30 classes, on topics from soldering to problem solving."[5] Associates volunteered to participate, and spent, on average, nearly five hours each month in class. Major improvements and some dozen new patents were the result.

Supervisors who have developed interpersonal skills know themselves well. They are tolerant and understanding of the viewpoints, attitudes, perceptions, and beliefs of others and are skillful communicators. People with interpersonal skills listen to others, are honest and open, and possess personalities that are pleasing to others. They create an atmosphere in which others feel free to express their ideas, and they make every effort to determine how intended actions will affect others in the organization. Supervisors who once held their subordinates' jobs have empathy for them—that is, supervisors have the ability to relate to what subordinates are experiencing and feeling. Managers at every level need interpersonal skills, but such skills are particularly important to supervisors. They must create and maintain an atmosphere of cooperation and harmony within and among the diverse individuals so often found in worker groups.

TECHNICAL SKILLS

Supervisors with technical skills understand and are proficient in specific kinds of activity. Their expertise may be in computer programming or repair, in utilizing precision equipment and tools, or in design. Technical skill involves specialized knowledge, analytical ability within that specialty, and facility in the use of the tools and techniques of the specific discipline.[6] Technical skills are the primary concern of training in industry, in public and private technical schools, and in community colleges. For example, Intel worked with community colleges in the design of two-year programs to train technicians to work in its microprocessor fabrication plants.[7]

Germany has a highly developed dual system that provides extensive technical training through apprenticeships with employers and classroom instruction. Its technical apprenticeship programs, which take from three to four years, make it the world's leader in some areas of technology. The typical German supervisor has a highly technical background, often obtained through an apprenticeship, and views this expertise as the foundation for his or her authority.[8] It is no surprise that many other countries have studied Germany's technical training system.

Technical skills are more important for supervisors than for mid-level and upper managers because the latter have responsibilities less closely related to the production, operations, service, and maintenance activities of the organization. Such skills are essential to supervisors for several reasons. Supervisors' influence over subordinates comes to them in part because of their technical competence. They must thoroughly understand the work they supervise, and they must be able to train others to do it. Without an understanding of their unit's machinery, equipment, procedures, and practices, they cannot adequately evaluate performance. As with human skills,

As a supervisor, you will need good people skills to help your workers realize their full potential. Here a supervisor at Glastron Boats takes time to assist a subordinate.

technological skills can be learned and developed. Moreover, supervisors can be expected to supervise a growing number of technical workers. Projections of the fastest growing jobs through 2008 have included several technical jobs in the highest growth category such as computer support specialists, systems analysts, desktop publishing specialists, data processing equipment repairers, and respiratory therapists.[9]

Practicing technical skills requires that you first possess them at a level sufficient both to apply them and to pass them along to others. Many supervisors are promoted from highly skilled jobs and then must turn around and supervise others who apply those same skills. If you are such a person, you have sound experience in skill applications. Such experience will prove quite useful to you when you are directing others who use those skills. But you will no longer have to execute your skills on the job as you had to when you were a worker. Your task is to help those you supervise to become as proficient as they can be in the execution of their skills.

CONCEPTUAL SKILLS

Managers with conceptual skills view their organizations as wholes with many parts, all of which are interrelated and interdependent. Supervisors must be able to perceive themselves and their associates, teams, and sections as part of and contributors to other sections and the entire organization. Every decision made by every manager can create a ripple effect that may influence others outside the particular decision-maker's control.

Consider the lessons learned by Randy Kirk, president of AC International in California. Kirk and his partner, Terry Brown, created a company specializing in bicycle accessories with only themselves as employees. They relied on outside suppliers for parts and felt that they had an ideal arrangement. Nonetheless, they soon began to receive customer complaints because their suppliers were unable to meet commitments. Quality and quantity of bike helmets became a problem even before the supplier had a fire and stopped production for several months. A second supplier of a key product went bankrupt. A third product was made in part by two different suppliers. This led to problems in shades of color and mating the different parts. The two entrepreneurs soon learned that if they made the parts themselves they would be less vulnerable to such shocks and in control of their products. With the help of several dozen associates, they began to make most of what they sold, used outside sources for a few services and raw materials, and reaped improvements to both quality and profits.[10] These entrepreneurs initially failed to anticipate and develop alternative plans for handling the shocks and ripple effects that they experienced. Their experience points out the need for conceptual thinking.

Acquiring a conceptual point of view becomes increasingly important as you climb higher on the management ladder. An employer must provide ways for you as a supervisor to know what is happening in other parts of the company and must inform you before changes are implemented. Internet sources, e-mail, official memos, reports, meetings, and workshops will also help keep you informed. Keeping in touch with fellow supervisors and reading the official correspondence that flows across your desk will make you a team player and help you and your people avoid unpleasant surprises.

The Supervisor's Responsibilities

Supervisors have responsibilities to three primary groups: their subordinates, their peers in management, and their superiors in management. They must work in harmony with all three groups if they are to be effective supervisors.

RELATIONS WITH SUBORDINATES

The responsibilities supervisors have to their subordinates are many and varied. To begin with, supervisors must get to know their subordinates as individuals. Each subordinate, like his supervisor, has specific needs and wants. Each has certain expectations from work, certain goals to achieve through work, and fundamental attitudes and aptitudes that influence work performance. When supervisors get to know each subordinate as an individual, they are able to tailor their approach to each. One of the first principles of good communication (see Chapter 5) is to keep your audience in mind when you attempt to communicate. If you are to be effective in your dealing with another person, you should know as much about that person as you can before you attempt to communicate any message.

Subordinates want to know that their supervisors care about them and are prepared to do something about their problems. As Lee Ledbetter, a team leader at the Fremont, Calif., GM/Toyota plant, puts it,

> Back when I worked in [another] GM [plant], I worked in the group for three months, and the foreman still didn't know my name. He'd come by and show me (my paycheck), and say "Hey, is that you?" Here, everybody knows everybody by their first name, right from the plant manager on down.[11]

A sure sign that supervisors care about their subordinates is common courtesy—using a person's name, a respectful tone of voice, personalized greetings, and sincere inquiries about the subordinate's health and well-being.

Getting to know subordinates well can be difficult. Some people are more open and outgoing than others. In addition, high levels of turnover or organizational reorganizations may change the members of work groups. These obstacles, however, should not be used as excuses to avoid trying to know your subordinates. Rather, such difficulties should be viewed as barriers that can be overcome through your sincere effort.

You will get to know your subordinates well only if you spend time with them and become familiar with their problems. If contacts with your people are informal, use the time for some casual conversation with them and find out what is going on in their lives. Your showing a sincere interest usually results in open responses from them. If contacts are formal, start out with a personal greeting, get through the formal communications, and then end on a friendly note. Only after you have a good understanding of your subordinates can you expect to be successful in your dealings with them.

Your major responsibilities to subordinates include the following:

- Getting to know them as individuals
- Giving them the respect and trust they deserve
- Valuing their uniqueness and individuality
- Assigning subordinates work that fits their abilities
- Listening to their concerns
- Treating them as they want to be treated
- Providing them with adequate instruction and training
- Enabling them to do and give their best
- Encouraging them to be lifelong learners
- Handling their complaints and problems in a fair and just way
- Safeguarding their health and welfare while they are on the job
- Praising and providing constructive criticism
- Providing examples of proper conduct at work

Among the most important of these is the last one. Team leaders and team facilitators must "walk the talk"—make their actions match their words. If these obligations are met, then subordinates will perceive their supervisors as leaders. Such supervisors gain the trust and respect of their subordinates—the keys to effective supervision and personal achievement. Your subordinates represent the most important group to whom and for whom you are responsible. Keep in mind that when a sports team does not perform, its owners fire the coach.

Supervisors fail when they exempt themselves from the rules, fail to make sacrifices asked of subordinates, or obtain extravagant perquisites. Such behavior can easily lead to an "us versus them" mentality that destroys teamwork and diminishes the role of subordinates. As an example of what *not* to do, on the same day that General Motors obtained concessions from its unionized workers, it announced a more lucrative bonus program for executives. The resentment aroused by this action was a factor that led to a strike in 1998, some 16 years later, that virtually shut down the entire company's production facilities.[12]

RELATIONS WITH PEERS

Managers on the same level of management and possessing similar levels of authority and status are **peers.** As a supervisor, your peers are your fellow supervisors throughout the company. When you serve as a team leader,

peer
a person with the same level of authority and status as another

your peers are other team leaders; when you serve as a team facilitator, your peers are other team facilitators. Peers are the individuals with whom you must cooperate and coordinate if your department and theirs are to operate in harmony.

Your peers normally constitute the bulk of your friends and associates at work. Your peers represent an enormous pool of talent and experience that will be yours to tap and contribute to if they view you in a favorable way. For this reason alone, it is to your advantage to cultivate their friendship. Your peers can teach you a great deal about the company, and they are often a fine source of advice on how to handle difficult situations that may arise. They can do more to keep you out of trouble than any other group in the company. In so many ways you need each other, and both you and they stand to benefit from a partnership or alliance based on mutual respect, trust, and the need to resolve common problems. If you share your expertise with them, you can expect them to share theirs with you.

Your responsibilities to your peers include the following:

- Getting to know them as individuals
- Valuing their uniqueness and individuality
- Giving them the respect and trust they deserve
- Treating them as they want to be treated
- Fostering a spirit of cooperation and teamwork

As a supervisor, team leader, or team facilitator, you will be asked or assigned to serve on peer-group teams. In such cases, you will shape your reputation by the ways in which you foster a spirit of cooperation and teamwork. Your ability or inability to contribute and cooperate with peers can mean either success or failure in your career. Teams of peers are common at all organizational levels.

Linda Hill, a Harvard University professor, has noted the importance for supervisors to establish relationships with peers. She has found that supervisors need to develop peer relationships or peer networks for several reasons. These include obtaining information through peers, obtaining an additional means for getting things done, relying on peers for emotional support, and obtaining feedback. Interestingly, the supervisors she studied sometimes sought advice and feedback from peers in other parts of the organization who were on different career paths. These supervisors realized that it was better to receive criticism from peers than their bosses. Furthermore, any weaknesses revealed by their request for assistance were less likely to be used against them since these peers were in different career paths. In addition, in Hill's study the importance of developing peer relationships was highlighted when some supervisors received instructions from their bosses to spend more time developing peer relationships.[13]

General Motors has recognized the value of teaming peers. The company uses vehicle launch center teams consisting of middle management specialists from engineering, design, and marketing to "evaluate car and truck proposals for cost, compatibility with other GM products, and marketability."[14] At the supervisory and worker levels, "GM is moving away from traditional assembly lines into smaller working units known as cells, where workers get more opportunity to design their own processes and thus improve output."[15] GM's Saturn division is famous for its self-managing teams and the inclusion of customers on its teams at every level.

Supervisors who are off in their own little worlds and unwilling to share their know-how are labeled uncooperative and antisocial, a reputation that jeopardizes their careers. Managers in higher positions in business have no need for withdrawn or isolated supervisors. In addition, most higher-level managers do not appreciate supervisors who are concerned about only their own units and who pursue their own units' objectives at the expense of the whole organization.

RELATIONS WITH SUPERIORS

If you are a supervisor, the person you report to is a **middle manager** who is accountable for your actions. Your boss is similar to you in being both a follower and a member of management. She executes all the functions of management and is evaluated on the basis of the performance of her subordinates. Like you, your boss must develop and maintain sound working relationships with her subordinates, peers, and superiors. Moreover, your boss has probably served an apprenticeship as a supervisor, so you can probably count on her understanding of your own situation.

middle manager
a manager of other managers or supervisors who reports to executives

Your responsibilities to your superiors, both line (having direct operational authority) and staff (having an advisory role to line managers and functional authority), can be summarized as follows:

- Valuing their uniqueness and individuality
- Giving them your best effort and the support they require
- Transmitting information about problems, along with recommendations for solving them
- Operating within company policies
- Promoting the company's goals
- Striving for constant improvement
- Seeking their counsel and using it
- Using the organization's resources effectively
- Keeping them informed about the unit's status

To your boss, you owe allegiance and respect. You must be a loyal follower if you intend to be a successful leader. To the company's team of staff specialists, you are the person through whom their recommendations are implemented. Chapter 8 has more to say about how you can get along with and cooperate with your peers and superiors in management.

BEING EFFECTIVE AND EFFICIENT

Managers at every level are expected to perform their tasks with effectiveness and efficiency. Managerial effectiveness is defined as *accomplishing stated goals*.[16] Accomplishing stated goals means meeting deadlines. Effective managers think ahead and schedule work so that enough resources will be available to complete it on time. Those who accomplish stated goals carefully plan their work (set goals, priorities, timetables) and stick to their plans. An ineffective supervisor fails to meet deadlines, falls behind on projects, and receives poor performance ratings.

Efficiency is defined as doing things with a minimal expense of time, money, and other resources. The efficient supervisor avoids waste of all kinds. The inefficient supervisor spends too much of any resource while executing tasks. The inefficient supervisor also receives poor performance ratings and places future operations in jeopardy because the needed resources may not be available.

Clearly, a supervisor must be both effective and efficient. Effectiveness is probably the more important of the two because it means that at a minimum essential tasks will get done. Effectiveness with inefficiency can often be tolerated by organizations, at least in the short run. But efficiency without effectiveness is intolerable, even in the short run. Essentials remain undone and vital work is left incomplete.

Supervisory Roles

Like actors who have to learn their roles well, all supervisors are expected to learn and play specific roles in order to execute their duties successfully. The precise role of individual supervisors depends on their understanding of the job, as well as on the pressures, rewards, and guidelines brought to bear on them from inside and outside the organization. What follows is a brief but important discussion of the ways in which roles are assigned to, designed for, and perceived by each supervisor in a business enterprise. The authors are indebted to Robert L. Kahn and his associates and to Prof. John B. Miner for much of this discussion.[17]

ROLE PRESCRIPTIONS

role prescription
the collection of expectations and demands from superiors, subordinates, and others that shapes a manager's job description and perception of his or her job

The subordinates, peers, friends, family, and superiors of supervisors help shape and define the kinds of roles the supervisors play and the way in which they play them. Demands made on the supervisors by these groups and their business organizations prescribe the roles (called **role prescriptions**) for them to follow. Through the expectations and demands placed on the supervisors, people help shape each supervisor's perception of his or her job. Organizational influences—such as policies, procedures, job descriptions, and union contracts—also exert influence on the roles of each supervisor. Of course, these multiple demands can and do create conflicts in

SUPERVISORS AND ETHICS

Patrons of Sotheby's Holdings and Christie's International, auction houses for very expensive artwork, were shocked recently by revelations of a price-fixing scandal. Federal prosecutors charged that high-level executives of the two firms colluded on the commissions they charge for sales. The former chief executive for Sotheby's pled guilty and testified at the trial that she was directed by her boss, the chairman and controlling shareholder of the firm, to engage in price-fixing with Christie's. Prosecutors also charged that Christie's previous chairman gave the same instructions to his subordinates. A lack of personal accountability was evident as executives testified that they engaged in illegal behavior because their bosses told them to do so. As with many failures in ethics, the price for their mistakes was high, as Sotheby's former chief faced a three-year sentence.

Not surprisingly, this incident of flawed behavior has become the subject of a Home Box Office film with actress Sigourney Weaver playing the role of the former Sotheby's chief executive. While the film was expected to generate viewer interest because it provides a view of the flaws and lifestyles of some of the world's most wealthy and influential people, the moral lesson is the same for supervisors and production workers. The consequences of lapses in business ethics can be professionally and personally devastating to individuals and the organizations that employ them.

Source: Kathryn Kranhold. "Auction Scandal Will Come Back As a TV Movie," *Wall Street Journal* (November 21, 2001), B11.

the minds of supervisors: What should their roles be and how precisely should they play them?

Henry Mintzberg, a noted management researcher, developed a classic description of all management behavior with 10 roles (see Exhibit 1.2). Mintzberg developed the 10 roles through close observations of chief executives. He found that different managers emphasized different roles and spent varying amounts of time on each, depending on their personalities, the job at hand, and the situation. All supervisors play these roles on a day-to-day basis as they interact with higher-level managers, peers, associates, and people outside their organization.

ROLE CONFLICT

When conflicting and contradictory demands are made on supervisors, they may find themselves in awkward or difficult positions. How they react to such pressures and precisely what they do to cope with such conflicts depend on their own values and perceptions and on the circumstances of the **role conflicts.** Consider the following incident that happened in a suburb north of Chicago. Two paramedics discovered a conflict between the instructions in their medical manual and the provisions of Illinois law about the proper method of treatment for heart-attack victims. If the paramedics followed their manual, they believed they would be in violation of state law. If they followed the law, however, they believed they would be giving incorrect or

role conflict
a situation that occurs when contradictory or opposing demands are made on a manager

Exhibit 1.2 — Mintzberg's management roles.

ROLE	DESCRIPTION	IDENTIFIABLE ACTIVITIES
INTERPERSONAL		
Figurehead	Symbolic head; obliged to perform a number of routine duties of legal or social nature	Ceremony, status, requests, solicitations
Leader	Responsible for the motivation and activation of subordinates; responsible for staffing, training, and associated duties	Virtually all managerial activities involving subordinates
Liaison	Maintains self-developed network of outside contacts and informers who provide favors and information	Acknowledgments of correspondence, external board work; other activities involving outsiders
INFORMATIONAL		
Monitor	Seeks and receives a wide variety of special information to develop thorough understanding of the organization and environment; emerges as a nerve center of internal and external information of the organization	Handling all correspondence and contacts concerned primarily with receiving information
Disseminator	Transmits information received from outsiders or from subordinates to members of the organization; some information factual, some involving interpretation and integration	Forwarding mail into organization for informational purposes; verbal contacts involving information flow to subordinates
Spokesman	Transmits information to outsiders on organization's plans, policies, actions, results, and so forth; serves as expert on organization's industry	Board meetings; handling correspondence and contacts involving transmission of information to outsiders
DECISIONAL		
Entrepreneur	Searches organization and its environment for opportunities and initiates projects to bring about change	Strategy and review sessions involving initiation or design of improvement projects
Disturbance Handler	Responsible for corrective action when organization faces important, unexpected disturbances	Strategy and review involving disturbances and crises
Resource Allocator	Responsible for the allocation of organizational resources of all kinds—in effect the making or approving of all significant organizational decisions	Scheduling; requests for authorization; any activity involving budgeting and the programming of subordinates' work
Negotiator	Responsible for representing the organization at major negotiations	Negotiation

Source: Slight adaptation of Table 2 from THE NATURE OF MANAGERIAL WORK by Mintzberg, H. © 1973 Addison Wesley Longman. Adapted by permission of Pearson Education, Inc., Upper Saddle River, NJ.

outmoded treatment to their patients. Perplexed, they asked their hospital administrator for clarification of the treatment procedures. To their surprise, they received in reply a letter that called them incompetent and suspended them from their duties as paramedics! This example highlights a common job situation, in which an employee's training in organizational procedures contradicts the demands of the immediate boss. Role conflicts can and do occur, and when they do, they may create tensions and job dissatisfaction.

ROLE AMBIGUITY

Whenever a supervisor is not sure of the role he is expected to play in a given situation or how to play it, he is a victim of **role ambiguity.** Role conflict results from clearly contradictory demands. Role ambiguity results from unclear or nonexistent job descriptions, orders, rules, policies, or procedures. When role ambiguity exists, supervisors may do things they should not do, may fail to do things they should do, and may find it hard to distinguish where one manager's job begins and another's ends.

role ambiguity
uncertainty about the role that one is expected to play

General Electric, a global company with 270,000 employees spanning several industries, provides a challenge for anyone attempting to eliminate role ambiguity. The company's former CEO, Jack Welch, who is widely recognized as one of the best business leaders in the world, emphasized the importance of communication. Welch's ability to communicate clearly and to gain enthusiasm for his ideas was legendary. He understood that effective communication requires repeated efforts to convey ideas to others. He also understood the importance of keeping things simple. One of the major differences between GE under Welch's leadership and many other companies was that its leaders and employees shared a common sense of direction. Welch was also legendary for his use of stretch targets as goals to eliminate ambiguity, set direction, provide clarity, and energize the company's workforce.[18]

Employees love to work for Southwest Airlines, saying that "It's a blast to work here." Southwest Airlines was chosen in 1998 as *Fortune's* Best Company to Work for in America. The company is known for its individuality and creativity.

ROLE PERFORMANCE

All organizations need their members to play their roles as prescribed. Exhibit 1.3 lists the "top 10 people strategies" at Southwest Airlines. Southwest Airlines, which is unconventional and creative, has a reputation as

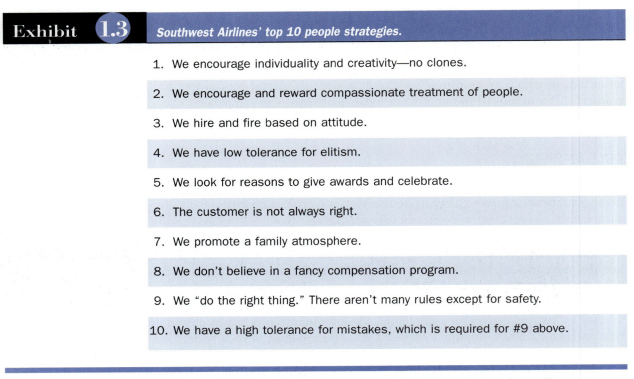

Exhibit 1.3   *Southwest Airlines' top 10 people strategies.*

1. We encourage individuality and creativity—no clones.

2. We encourage and reward compassionate treatment of people.

3. We hire and fire based on attitude.

4. We have low tolerance for elitism.

5. We look for reasons to give awards and celebrate.

6. The customer is not always right.

7. We promote a family atmosphere.

8. We don't believe in a fancy compensation program.

9. We "do the right thing." There aren't many rules except for safety.

10. We have a high tolerance for mistakes, which is required for #9 above.

Source: Presentation by Libby Sartain, Vice President of People, Southwest Airlines to the Human Resource Management Roundtable, Texas Christian University, February 6, 1996.

being one of the best-managed companies in the United States. Southwest's superior management and unique culture led to its selection by *Fortune* magazine in 1998 as the best company to work for in the United States. Furthermore, after the September 11, 2001 attack on the World Trade Center, in contrast to many other airlines, Southwest did not lay off employees and was the only airline in the U. S. that had a profit for the quarter.[19] The strategies in Exhibit 1.3 provide a good set of guidelines for supervisors in many organizations. Point number 3 indicates that having employees with good work attitudes is critical at Southwest; the company looks first for a good attitude. It feels that as long as an employee has a good work attitude she can be trained for her job and role. Point number 4 can be illustrated by several examples. Southwest's officers do not have big offices, and they give out their home phone numbers. They also perform the lowest-level jobs, such as handling baggage, one day every quarter. It is obvious that arrogant people do not fit in at Southwest. Point 6, which states that the customer is not always right, means that Southwest does not let its employees be abused by customers. This point is particularly relevant for supervisors in service industries. Keven Freiberg and Jackie Freiberg point out that Southwest Airlines feels that the manner in which employees are treated will be reflected in how employees treat customers.[20]

Current Trends Affecting Supervisors

One thing is certain: The demands being made on today's supervisors are growing in complexity. Great changes are taking place in both our work-force and our places of work. A brief look at some major trends will indicate a few of the problems and opportunities they represent for all of us.

INFORMATION AND TECHNOLOGY

Our economy is experiencing dramatic and fundamental changes in the ways in which business is conducted and in the ways in which people are employed. For example, information technology enables a human resources team leader for American Express, who is based in London, to work on a virtual team with other specialists based in such distant locations as Buenos Aires or Tokyo.[21] While there are disadvantages to virtual teams, such as interrupted meals and weekends, information technology enables team members to meet the mandate of being able to "work together not only across oceans but across the some-times deeper divides of corporate boundaries and corporate cultures."[22]

The power of computers is now at our fingertips. Notebook comput-ers, Internet e-mail, wireless e-mail, smart phones, personal digital assistants (PDAs), cellular telephones, scanners, laser printers, and fax machines are the hallmarks of a modern office. E-mail links people within a building and their counterparts in different states and countries. Even automobiles can be equipped with voice-activated cellular telephones, computers, printers, and fax machines. The portability of technology frees managers from their desks and provides them with greater mobility. Meetings can take place as teleconferences in which television signals are transmitted over telephone lines and through communication satellites. Other electronic links have an even greater impact, as indicated in the fol-lowing description of electronic data interchange (EDI):

> An order placed in Spain with an order-entry computer in France triggers man-ufacturing planning software in New York to place items into a manufacturing schedule in Dallas, which requires chips from Japan to be built into circuit boards in Singapore, with final assembly in the robotic factory in Dallas and computer-controlled shipment from a warehouse in Milan. . . . It does not make sense for a computer in one enterprise to print purchase orders and send them to another corporation to be entered (with errors) into another computer.[23]

EDI data transfer of business-to-business (b-to-b) transactions allows for instantaneous transfer of electronic data between points, eliminating com-munication delays between suppliers and purchasers or retailers, engineers and product design teams, and professionals and clients. Wal-Mart is recog-nized as the EDI innovator in retailing, which allowed just-in-time store replenishment and lower distribution costs. The Limited, which established EDI links to Asian suppliers, is an EDI innovator in the retailing of clothing. Flexible data formats, such as XML and VCML (value chain markup language), offer potential for greater use of such data transfer systems in more industries and smaller firms.[24] The most competitive manufacturers have put the power of computers to use through computer-aided design (CAD) and computer-aided manufacturing (CAM), which offer their best hope for future increases in quality, competitiveness, productivity, and profits.

CAD allows draftspeople and engineers to design, analyze, and test products entirely by means of computers and their video displays. Without putting pencil to paper, researchers can put new products through the rigors of testing, thus saving great amounts of time and money that would otherwise be invested in building and testing a prototype. In building the 777 jetliner, Boeing and its worldwide network of suppliers used the same CAD software to exchange information. Boeing and its suppliers also used computerized virtual reality systems to test aircraft components before actual assembly.[25]

CAM has come to mean computer control of production tools and machines. Both can be programmed and reprogrammed to work at a variety of tasks, providing users with dependable, predictable output at speeds no skilled person can match. Robots are CAM machines that are capable of working every hour of every day with great speed and reliability. They have been used for work that is toxic, dangerous, repetitive, boring, or extremely precise. Robots have become our nation's "steel-collar workers," demanding sophisticated supervision by a new breed of supervisors and workers with the latest in high-tech education and skills.

Flexible manufacturing—producing a variety of products and product variations (customization) simultaneously and in sequence with computer-integrated manufacturing (CIM)—is the current goal for many manufacturers. CIM links all the activities, materials flow, and machinery involved in manufacturing to a centralized computer control system, allowing for maximum efficiency and coordination. A good example of flexible manufacturing is provided by Honda America's plant in East Liberty, Ohio. The flexible system has improved worker satisfaction, increased safety, and reduced the amount of repair work needed before cars can be released from the factory. "The heart of the flexible system is a body-weld line that allows Honda to switch from vehicle to vehicle with the flip of a switch. It also shortened subassembly lines in the factory and installed quality assurance points at several spots through the assembly process."[26]

Along with being flexible, manufacturing is becoming lean—using fewer workers and adding temporary help during peak load periods. Just-in-time delivery systems eliminate expensive inventories of components needed for manufacturing products. Sophisticated information systems indicate times when components will be needed, and the components are delivered from suppliers "just in time." This drive to take the fat out of operations has led many companies to outsource—to allow more cost-effective businesses to provide needed work. When just-in-time companies expand their operations to new geographical areas, their suppliers follow. For example, OSI Industries, which supplies hamburger to McDonald's, also supplies OSI's global chain of restaurants and OSI's other partners throughout the world. The food processing and distribution firm has over 60 food processing plants in its global operations. Interestingly, OSI's successful use of cross-functional teams has been a key to the company's success.[27] These trends have led to better service for customers.

QUALITY AND PRODUCTIVITY IMPROVEMENT

Businesses in the United States exist and compete in a global economy. Their products and services must compete with the best that the world community has to offer. To be competitive, businesses must be lean and constantly strive to improve their efficiency and effectiveness. But it is not enough simply to produce efficiently. Products and services must have quality as good as, or better than, those provided by the competition.

Productivity may be defined as the measurement of the amount of input needed to generate a given amount of output. It is the basic measurement of the efficient use of resources and processes. By calculating how many products are produced by the investment of hours of human labor or by the use of machines over time, an organization can compare these measurements to those from the past and determine gains or losses.

Quality means different things to different people. Its result is a satisfied customer. Throughout this text, we define quality as the totality of features and characteristics of a product or service (or process or project) that bear on its ability to satisfy stated or implied goals (requirements of producers and customers).[28] To possess quality, products and services must be designed with the customers' needs in mind. Companies such as Motorola and Toyota consult with customers throughout the design phase of their product development to ensure that their customers' needs will be met.

Customers are the receivers and users of what is produced; they exist inside and outside the organization. *Internal customers* are employees who receive output from other employees. It is common practice today in major companies to assess employees' performance through what is called a 360-degree performance review or 360-degree feedback. Each manager or team member is evaluated by her boss, associates, and peers—all users of any outputs generated by the manager, team member, or her associates.

As a direct result of organizations' drive toward quality and productivity improvement, a movement and philosophy called *reengineering* emerged. Two pioneers in reengineering, Michael Hammer and James Champy, define **reengineering** as follows: "The fundamental rethinking and radical redesign of business process to achieve dramatic improvements in critical, contemporary measures of performance, such as cost, quality, service, and speed."[29] Through a reengineering approach, managers at every level ask some fundamental questions and make no assumptions. "Reengineering takes nothing for granted. It ignores what is and concentrates on what should be."[30] As Richard Sullivan at Home Depot puts it: "Companies must burn themselves down and rebuild every few years."[31]

productivity
the amount of input needed to generate a given amount of output

quality
the totality of features and characteristics of a product or service (or process or project) that bear on its ability to satisfy stated or implied goals (requirements of producers and customers)

reengineering
the total rethinking of what an organization should be doing and how it should do it

SUPERVISORS AND QUALITY

The 3M Company, based in St. Paul, Minn., has created the Scotch family of tapes, Post-It notes, and a host of other products. For years, it consistently attained its corporate "goal: deriving 25% of its revenues from products introduced within the past five years." It prides itself on a corporate culture that encourages all employees to become product champions—to spend part of their time each day trying to create new products. The company's earnings had flattened out, creeping along well below the CEO's target of an annual 10 percent growth. New products were too similar to existing ones, and too much time was needed to translate new discoveries into new products. Something was needed to shake up the troops. CEO L. D. Desimone "unveiled a stretch target: accelerate innovation to the point where 3M generates 30% of its sales from products introduced within the past four years. . . . Since new products grow far faster and generate higher [profits] than old ones, . . . the higher innovation rate would add the necessary octane to 3M's performance." This goal scared nearly everyone. If it were to be attained, all would have to commit to doing things in radically different ways. The company focused its initial efforts on identifying the products under development that had the greatest chance for financial success. A year later 50 candidates emerged, and more than half of them have been brought to market. Two years later both sales and profits increased: the former by 6 percent, and the latter by 12 percent.

What caused the turnaround? The stretch target and shakeup in research and development helped, but these were not the whole answer. One product, Never-Rust scouring pads, illustrates the remarkable reengineering that has overtaken 3M. The pad includes fibers of plastic containing fine abrasives and represents "the fastest new product introduction in company history." 3M set a one-year introduction schedule for Never Rust, a far more ambitious schedule than it had reached in the past. While manufacturing facilities were being built, marketing teams were preparing advertisements, promotional activities, and TV spots. "Workers started installing production equipment before the windows, bathrooms, or heating. When engineers hit a roadblock, they called on colleagues from all over 3M. . . . The plant hit full production right on schedule." Currently, the new pad has gained 22 percent of the market that had been dominated by Brillo and SOS.

Source: Shawn Tully. "Why to Go for Stretch Targets," *Fortune* (November 14, 1994): 148, 150.

Nonetheless, reengineering is not something that companies should go through without serious consideration, as the following statement indicates:

[Reengineering] is strong medicine, not always needed or successful, and almost always accompanied by pain—or at least unpleasant side effects, such as [causing] executives' hair to fall out. By one estimate, between 50% and 70% of reengineering efforts fail to achieve the goals set for them.[32]

While the results of reengineering are often disappointing and some view the concept as a management fad, reengineering has value in limited applications. The essence of reengineering is to eliminate the inefficiencies of numerous handoffs in the flow of work between individuals and between organizational units. Reengineering provides the advantage of combining the tasks of specialists so that one worker, supported with a powerful information system, can handle an expanded set of activities with greater efficiency. When the concept is applied in services, the worker can provide service similar to the notion of one-stop shopping.[33]

Because past reengineering efforts have altered career opportunities for supervisors and their associates, the subject will be discussed again in Chapter 2, where a more specific definition will be provided.

EDUCATION

According to the U. S. Census Bureau, over 84 percent of Americans over 25 years of age currently have completed high school and more than 25 percent have completed four or more years of college. College enrollments continue to be high: almost 63 percent of high school graduates from the class of 1999 enrolled in college. Women appear to be taking a significant lead in higher education as more women from this class enrolled in college (64.4 percent) as compared to men (61.4 percent).[34] The growing educational level of the U. S. workforce has brought brighter, more demanding employees to the ranks of both workers and management. Increasingly, people want a voice in planning and executing their work. They bring competence and skills to the workplace, and they desire growth through challenging work and meaningful tasks. They want to be listened to and respected as individuals with their own specific needs and goals.

Countering the influx of more highly educated people is a substantial influx of people who lack adequate reading skills. According to the National Institute for Literacy, "50 percent of the U. S. population reads below the eighth-grade level, and about 90 million adults are functionally illiterate."[35] The problem of illiteracy cuts into U. S. productivity, with the costs being estimated as high as $60 billion per year. Furthermore, the problem has been exacerbated by a decline in the percentage of employers who provide remedial training from 24 percent in 1993 to 13 percent in 2000.[36]

As a supervisor, you may find both highly educated and illiterate adults in your subordinate mix. Both groups present challenges that you and your organization must be prepared to deal with if you are to create quality products and productivity improvements.

Increasingly, we are becoming a lifetime learning society. No longer can any of us rely on one employer or one career during our working lives. Because of downsizing and mergers, people are expected to make several job and career changes within their lifetimes. "According to a survey . . . by the executive search firm of Robert Half International Inc., [it isn't until] a worker [makes] five job changes in a 10-year period [that he or she] is at risk of being labeled a job-hopper."[37] Today's younger workers are demanding opportunities to learn new skills that will make them employable in the future. They recognize that it is unlikely that they will be employed by one organization for their entire career. Instead of demanding lifetime job security they want employability.[38]

FOREIGN OWNERSHIP OF AMERICAN BUSINESSES

Each year foreign businesses invest billions of dollars both to acquire existing companies and to establish their own in the United States. U.S. businesses follow the same approach, investing billions of dollars to acquire companies in other countries. Examples of foreign investment in the United States include the UBS (Switzerland) merger with Paine Webber, the Daimler-Benz (Germany) merger with Chrysler, the Bayer Chemical (Germany) acquisition of Locktite, the acquisition of CompUSA by Grupo Sanborns (Mexico), the Bimbo (Mexico) acquisition of Mrs. Baird's Bread, and the acquisition of Ralston Purina by Nestle (Switzerland). In addition, BMW (Germany) built a plant in Alabama to make sport utility vehicles, Cemex (Mexico) has built plants in Texas to produce cement, and Nokia (Finland) has built plants in the United States to produce cellular telephones and telecommunications infrastructure.

Consider Japanese automobile manufacturers and their suppliers for a moment. Japan's Bridgestone company acquired Firestone's tire business. When Hitachi, Toyota, and Mitsubishi built their manufacturing facilities in the United States, their Japanese suppliers followed, building their facilities nearby to offer reliable delivery of needed parts. In the early 1990s, Japanese companies owned 10 percent or more of nearly 1,600 manufacturing facilities in the United States that employed about 350,000 American citizens. Today, companies from the United Kingdom and Germany are the largest investors. According to federal government estimates, approximately five percent of U.S. workers owe their jobs to a foreign-owned company, more than at any time in the past. Industries in which foreign-owned firms account for high employment include mining, manufacturing, and information-related areas.[39]

Foreign owners often bring different philosophies, methods, and traditions to the workplace. Supervising in a foreign-owned business may require changes in the attitudes, roles, and skills derived from training in the United States or abroad. Supervisors may have to adapt to different methods and values that come from a different cultural background. However, despite important cultural differences, many management practices of large multinational corporations are similar.

VALUING DIVERSITY

diversity
differences among people and groups that serve to both unite and separate them from others

Nearly every nation today is a mix of peoples with different origins, values, and traditions. Americans differ in race, age, gender, sexual orientation, religious belief, language, nation of birth, education, physical characteristics, and more. This **diversity** in individuals can both unite and separate. Organizations also have cultures: systems of shared values, beliefs, experiences, habits, norms, and expectations that give them a distinct identity. An organization usually has a dominant culture that shapes and is shaped by its members' attitudes and behaviors. The greatest influence comes from the people in charge—their values, norms, and beliefs. But an organization has subcultures as well, shared by groups of employees that influence and are influenced by the organization's culture. Thus organizations nearly always have diverse cultures. **Cultural diversity** exists when two or more cultures co-exist within an organization.

Motorola has an outstanding reputation for world-class products and is truly a global business. "But the key to Motorola's success is a culture that fosters candid internal debate, the vigorous competition of ideas and individual business autonomy."[40]

Valuing diversity in people and their diverse cultures is a relatively recent development in business. Today, businesses such as Motorola, Du Pont, Avon, and Levi Strauss are realizing that employees have a right to their own identity, within and separate from that of the organization. Diversity is increasingly viewed as a source of strength—providing pools of people with different and complementary skills, competencies, and beliefs that should be valued and can be drawn on to provide what an organization needs. At Levi Strauss diversity means that the company "values a diverse workforce (age, sex, ethnic group, etc.) at all levels of the organization. . . . Differing points of view will be sought; diversity will be valued and honestly rewarded, not suppressed."[41]

Nonetheless, examples such as Home Depot's $65 million settlement for discrimination against female employees and Texaco's $176 million settlement remind us that supervisors must be vigilant to eliminate racism or sexism.[42] In addition, although much progress has been made, supervisors must prevent discrimination against the aged and disabled. The software industry has been criticized recently for age discrimination. Despite shortages of programmers, software companies have been reluctant to hire older workers. For example, "a year-and-a-half search has netted Alan Ezer, 45, just one job interview, despite 10 years' experience and a nifty demonstration on the Internet of his self-taught virtuosity."[43]

Businesses—like the United States as a whole—now realize that they are not melting pots through which people and cultures fuse and lose their identities. They are mosaics, tapestries, and salad bowls in which individuals and groups retain their identities but work with others to yield something greater than the pieces could yield on their own. The supervisor's role in valuing diversity is discussed in each of this text's remaining chapters.

cultural diversity
the co-existence of two or more cultural groups within an organization

WORK SCHEDULES

By the year 2005, women will account for over 47 percent of the workforce.[44] African Americans, Hispanics, and Asians will account for over one-fourth of employed Americans by that year. Today's workforce is mobile, middle aged, and increasingly made up of other than full-time workers. In addition, between 2.7 and 6 million workers are contingent.[45] Furthermore, a growing number of contingent workers are accounting, engineering, and health care professionals.[46] Even the chief information offi-

Your job as a supervisor is to help all of your people reach their potential. Allowing your biases to rule your judgment will not only hurt your subordinates' performance, it will also reflect badly on you as a supervisor.

cer at Burlington Northern Santa Fe was hired to fill the role for a limited time period.

Several other trends are in evidence: flextime, job sharing, job splitting, permanent part-time workers, telecommuting, and employee leasing. Companies are increasing their use of these flexible approaches to work. For example, Merck has reported increased use of flextime, telecommuting, and job sharing. The composition of Merck's workforce is also illustrative of trends for the future, as women make up 52 percent of its U.S. employees while minorities account for 24 percent. More significantly, in its U.S. operations 32 percent of the company's managerial positions are held by women while minorities account for 16 percent.[47] All of these trends present unique challenges and opportunities for supervisors.

flextime
a work schedule with flexible starting and ending times

Flextime allows people to vary their starting and ending times. A company may specify a core time, requiring all employees to be on the job from 10:00 A.M. until 1:00 P.M., but some may start as early as 6:00 A.M. or as late as 10:00 A.M. Some may go home as early as 1:00 A.M. Flexible scheduling appeals to working parents with school-age children and to a growing number of self-managing information workers. But such work schedules make it difficult for one supervisor to manage people who work over a span of 10 or more hours. **Compressed work weeks** of four 10-hour days also help organizations meet the needs of employees.

compressed work week
a work week made up of four 10-hour days

The Bechtel Group, a construction and engineering firm, has 27,800 employees worldwide. It offers a flexible schedule to its employees in Houston, Texas. Under the plan, employees work nine-hour days, Monday through Thursday each week. Each Friday, about half the employees work eight hours, and the other half have the day off. All employees work 80 hours in nine days. Management initially feared that longer work days would mean lower productivity, but productivity has improved. Employees seemed to be scheduling more of their personal business for their off time.

job sharing
splitting the hours of a job between two or more employees

Job sharing allows two or more people to work at one full-time job. A growing number of people want to work part time, and a growing number of businesses want more part-time employees. The employer benefits in several ways. It gets double the creativity for each shared job. It may also cut benefit costs, which often add 30 to 40 percent to an employee's salary. People come to work refreshed and eager to perform and experience less fatigue and stress. Boring jobs can be more attractive when performed for fewer than 40 hours each week.

Permanent part-time workers usually work for small companies that do not have enough work for a full-timer to perform. Part-time work may be for any number of hours and days per week, up to 35 hours. Older individuals, such as those who may have retired from other jobs, provide a source of reliable employees who may be interested in permanent part-time work.

permanent part-time workers
employees who wish to work less than 40 hours per week

Temporary workers or contingent workers fill millions of jobs in the United States each year. The U. S. Bureau of Labor has estimated, using a broad definition of "contingent workers," that 4.4 percent of the employed population consists of contingent workers.[48] A somewhat lower estimate is provided by the CEO of Manpower Inc., who has estimated that 2.5 percent of the U. S. workforce is made up of temporary workers.[49] Temporary work agencies provide people to work part time for clients who need temporary help. Most come well trained for their jobs and work in skilled areas such as computer services, secretarial services, manufacturing, and accounting.[50] Another view of the broad presence of temporary workers in the workforce is provided by the president of a temporary help firm that provides temporary employees to such employers as Sun Microsystems and Silicon Graphics: "There's not a single major company in the United States that doesn't have a substantial percentage of the work force as contingent workers."[51]

temporary workers
workers employed by a temporary work agency to provide labor for other employers

Telecommuting allows a full- or part-time employee to work at home while remaining connected to the employer by telecommunications devices such as computers, e-mail, the Internet, and fax machines. Estimates of the number of telecommuters in the United States vary widely, with numbers ranging from 9 million to 24 million. More than half of the Fortune 500 companies reported that 1 to 5 percent of their employees are involved in telecommuting, and some companies have large numbers of telecommuters. For example, Merrill Lynch has 3,500 telecommuters.[52] Nortel, one of the pioneers in this area, had 3,600 telecommuters at one point.[53] In addition, AT&T has announced a telecommuting day, encouraging and making arrangements for any worker who can to telecommute. Telecommuters can increase their quality of life by living in geographic areas that are long distances from their offices and combining work at home with child care arrangements. In addition, major disasters quickly isolate people from their jobs and places of employment. The terrorist attack on the World Trade Center on September 11, 2001, earthquakes, floods, and hurricanes have highlighted the value of telecommuting—within hours, companies whose physical plants were in ruins were making alternative arrangements to meet their customers' needs, thanks to cellular communications.

telecommuting
working at home through telecommunications

UTILIZATION OF TEAMS

Increasingly, businesses are turning to the use of teams—some self-managing, others not. It is common in many different types of organizations to find teams "that recommend things, teams that make or do things, and teams that run or

Workers commonly meet to discuss issues such as quality.

manage things. . . . Teams are a means to an end. And that end is performance superior to what team members would achieve working as individuals."[54] As discussed in Chapter 9, many times teams are *cross-functional,* meaning that workers from such areas as marketing, production, and accounting may work on a team to solve a problem.

As was stated in this chapter's introduction, when supervisors work with and through teams of subordinates, they become team facilitators. They share responsibility with a team for "cost, quality, and on-time delivery of the product. So [supervisors] must train their teams to manage the production process, including work assignments, and to solve problems that crop up along the way, rather than provide solutions themselves."[55]

Team facilitators make certain that the team has the resources it needs when they are needed, arranges the meetings where information is passed along and ideas are put to use, represents the team's views and concerns to outsiders, and helps resolve disputes between and within teams. To be an effective team facilitator, you must be skilled at presenting your ideas in a group setting, at running different kinds of meetings, at sharing your skills and knowledge willingly, at turning decision making into a learning experience for all team members, and at taking control in a crisis.[56]

empower
to equip people to function on their own, without direct supervision

To work in teams effectively, people must be trained and empowered. Supervisors **empower** their subordinates when they equip them to function on their own, without direct oversight and constant supervision. Empowering others requires supervisors to give their people opportunities to contribute knowledge and expertise, and to encourage them to take on new tasks and to improve their capabilities. It means allowing people to participate in planning their work, making decisions, and solving problems. In short, empowering others means sharing the traditional roles and responsibilities of the supervisor with subordinates. More will be said on the subjects of teams and empowering subordinates in the *Supervising Teams* features, throughout the book.

Sources of Supervisory Personnel

In most companies the person who aspires to become a supervisor—to move from worker to management—must take on the responsibility of preparing

SUPERVISING TEAMS

SEI Investments is all about teams and performance. The financial services company provides back office services to mutual fund firms and trust departments of banks. The firm, which has a culture vastly different from most others in the industry, has been a success story with revenue growth as high as 30 percent in recent years. A key to SEI's success is its dynamic environment and heavy utilization of teams. The firm accomplishes its work through the use of approximately 140 self-managed teams ranging in size from two to 30 members. A distinguishing feature of the teams is that there are very few rules. A number of the teams are relatively permanent, such as those serving large customers. Others are ad hoc teams formed to solve specific problems and then disbanded after the completion of the task.

Employees typically have one relatively permanent team and are members of three to four ad hoc teams. These ad hoc teams help create an impression of perpetual motion. Leadership rotates among team members at different phases of projects as their expertise comes to the fore. Employees also move from team to team depending on the need for their expertise and their interest in the team's project. Team members change locations so often that the work environment is designed for frequent movements, with furniture on wheels and colorful spirals of telephone, electric, and Internet cable hanging down from the ceilings for flexible connections. Because moves are so frequent the firm uses software to track the locations of employees' desks.

Source: Scott Kirsner. "Total Teamwork—SEI Investments," *Fast Company* (April 1998): 130.

---

himself for such a promotion. Exhibit 1.4 lists the changes that have occurred in the skills requirements for a supervisor in an example supervisory position in the textile industry. Take a few minutes to study it. Aside from the technical features that are unique to the textile industry, think about whether you possess some of the more general skills, such as the people, reasoning, and administrative skills. If you need to improve on various skills, schools can help and a job change may be a good step you can take to improve a skill or gain an attribute.

Many employers prefer to hire some or all of their supervisory personnel from the ranks of community or four-year college graduates. After some preliminary training and understudy, these people are installed as functioning supervisors. The practice of hiring supervisors from outside the company may infuse new ideas and approaches into the organization. Nonetheless, some well-managed companies such as ServiceMaster, Whole Foods Markets, Southwest Airlines, Hewlett-Packard, AES, and Lincoln Electric promote only from within their ranks and hire only at entry level.[57]

A major disadvantage of the practice of going outside the organization for new supervisors fresh from college is that they may lack the firsthand experiences and technical skills needed to supervise the company's workers.

Exhibit 1.4 — *Changing supervisory skill requirements: Line supervisors in the textile industry.*

OLD PROGRESSIVE BUNDLE SYSTEM	NEW FLEXIBLE MANUFACTURING TEAMS
PEOPLE SKILLS	
• Acts as messenger for the manager	• Accepts initiative for decision making
• Supervises individuals	• Coaches teams
• Represents power and control as an authority figure	• Shares power and control as a communicator, motivator, coordinator
PRODUCTION/TECHNICAL SKILLS	
• Thoroughly understands selected operations but has little understanding of overall operations	• Understands methods and techniques used in all operations and how each affects the final product
• Has basic sewing skills	• Understands work measurement and techniques used
• Is an experienced production operator	• Understands cost control
• Has limited production responsibility	• Understands quality control
• Is a recorder of daily production	• Knows operator training techniques
• Polices equitable work distribution	• Administers safety regulations and ergonomics
• Is a bundle handler	• Assigns work fairly
• Repairs defective garments	• Is an expert in line balancing
• Has knowledge in line balancing	• Ensures proper productions are being used
• Ensures that proper production methods are being used	• Has knowledge of various garment styles, fabrics, and machine adjustments
• Verifies that work meets quality standard	• Can calculate production and payroll
	• Understands industry terminology
REASONING SKILLS	
• Is limited to following instructions	• Must have problem-diagnosing skills
	• Must have problem-solving skills
ADMINISTRATIVE SKILLS	
• Has little control over hiring, orientation (works with human resources department)	• Has a more direct role in employee hiring, orientation, training, and discipline
• Has little control in policy making	• Must handle absenteeism
• Has little control over labor cost (management's job)	• Participates in policy making
	• Has more control over labor cost

Source: Slight modification of materials from "Supervisors Must Face Changes," *Apparel Industry* (October 1995): 72.

They may also be resented by more experienced workers not promoted to supervisor. "At Union Pacific . . . all new employees who aspire to a management position must first become a data integrity analyst. . . . Why the hurdle? Union Pacific carries 13,000 shipments a day on 700 trains running on 19,000 miles of track. Coordinating that massive traffic flow poses a huge data management challenge. . . ."[58] As Jim Damman, national customer services vice president, puts it, "We saw that the company's future growth would depend more on the ability of our managers to be masters of technical data rather than overseers of the hourly workers."[59] The railroad's operational difficulties associated with its merger with Southern Pacific, highlight the critical importance of managing traffic flow. Similarly, at Nordstrom, all new employees—including those with advanced degrees—must begin by working on the sales floor.[60]

Some of your associates may not wish to be promoted to the ranks of management. Several may be convinced that the extra prestige is not worth the extra time, problems, and responsibilities that go along with a supervisory position. In addition, the attitude of the company toward supervisors may make many workers shy away from a supervisory role. In far too many companies, supervisors are given lip service as managers but are not treated with the respect, pay, and benefits that employees in other levels of management receive.

Instant Replay

1. The three most important types of skills for any manager to possess are interpersonal, technical, and conceptual. All are required for success, but different levels of management need them to different degrees.

2. Supervisors are responsible to three groups: their peers, their subordinates, and their superiors. Each group represents a source of support, demands on the supervisor's time, and potential problems or challenges for the supervisor.

3. Each organization attempts to define a supervisor's role through the creation of a job description and through the demands that various groups and individuals place on the supervisor. Problems can result from role conflict and role ambiguity. The supervisor can be "caught in the middle" between the demands of her managers and the workers she supervises.

4. Current trends that affect supervisors include changes in information and technology, the drive for improvements in both quality and productivity, the growth in both highly educated and illiterate adults in the workforce, increasing international ownership of American businesses, the growing effort to value diversity, shifts in the traditional scheduling and performance of work, and the growing use of teams.

5. Supervisors emerge from two sources: from inside and outside the organization. Organizations prefer to hire those who are ready to move up; this places the burden for training on the individual who aspires to move into management.

Questions for Class Discussion

1. Can you define this chapter's key terms?
2. What are the essential management skill areas that supervisors must have and apply? Give an example illustrating the application of each skill area.
3. What are the three groups to whom supervisors have responsibilities? Give an example of a responsibility to each group.
4. How do the concepts of effectiveness and efficiency apply to a supervisor's performance?
5. What are the current trends in the U.S. economy that affect the supervisor?
6. What are the sources of supervisory personnel for a business?

Incident

Purpose: To discover how many trends discussed in this chapter are part of your current work environment.

Your task: Answer each of the following as completely as you can using your current or most recent job environment as your model. Where parenthetical choices are given, choose one. In all other questions, written responses are required. Share your results with your class.

1. I work/have worked in a team. (yes) (no)
2. My team has/had the following basic duties:
3. I am/have been a team leader. (yes) (no)
4. As a team leader my duties are/were:
5. I am/have been a team facilitator/supervisor. (yes) (no)
6. As a team facilitator, my duties are/were:
7. My company employs contingent workers. (yes) (no)
8. The contingent workers perform the following duties:
9. My job requires/will require technical skills. (yes) (no)
10. My company cares about quality. (yes) (no)
11. My company cares about productivity. (yes) (no)
12. It shows it cares about quality and productivity by:

13. My company is foreign-owned. (yes) (no)
14. The foreign ownership has required me to change by:
15. The dominant culture in my organization stresses:
16. The subcultures existing in my company are based on:
17. Subcultures are (tolerated) (welcomed) at work.
18. My employer offers these nontraditional work options:

Southwest Microwave Communications, Inc.   CASE PROBLEM 1.1

Carla Martinez, a senior electronics technician, was filling out the forms to obtain reimbursement for last month's travel expenses. Her job as a senior electronics technician required her to be out of the office about 90 percent of the time on jobs installing transmitters in microwave towers. While in the office, the technicians usually use the time to read technical bulletins, to work in the electronics lab on repairs to the specialized testing and calibration equipment, to go through technical training, or to make travel arrangements. Carla was working in a common area the electronics technicians use as an office while not in the field. It was about 20 minutes to five, and she was almost finished with the last form.

Carla looked up from her paperwork to see Faye Griffin, her new supervisor, rush in with several file folders. Faye looked around the office and then spotted Carla and said, "I'm in a hurry and need you to complete these unit staff utilization forms for the regional office. The forms are self-explanatory, and you shouldn't have any trouble figuring out what to do. I'm just too overloaded with work and my schedule is a nightmare. Just leave the forms on my desk and I'll have them faxed to the regional office the first thing in the morning." Before Carla could say anything, Faye had turned and walked out of the office.

Carla couldn't believe that Faye had just asked her to do part of the work for which Faye was personally responsible. Faye had been the supervisor for six months, but Carla had little contact with her because she had been in the field so much. Carla and the rest of the technicians were so busy with installations that for the past six weeks they regularly put in 55- to 60-hour work weeks. After getting herself composed enough to sit down and look over the files, Carla began to figure out how to complete the forms. Two hours later, when she discovered that she didn't have all of the information she needed, she went down the hall to Faye's office to ask her some questions. To her surprise, she found that Faye was not in and that the janitor was cleaning her office. The janitor said that Faye had gone home at five o'clock and volunteered that he always cleaned Faye's office first because she was seldom in after five. Carla returned to the work room and filled out the rest of the forms the best that she could. She then wrote a note to Faye explaining that she didn't have the information to complete everything but that 90 percent of the forms were complete. She then put the forms in Faye's mail slot as she left for the evening at 7:45.

The next day as Carla was working in the electronics lab, she saw Faye come in a couple of times to talk to technicians or check on the progress of repairs. To her surprise, Faye never thanked her for her work or even mentioned it. Later in the afternoon, Carla told a couple of her technician friends, Tim Kelly and Ivan Ward, about what had happened. Tim just shook his head and said that the same thing had happened to him last month. He too had needed to stay until 8:00 to do some of Faye's scheduling. Ivan then recounted his experiences with Faye on his last installation job. When he and two other technicians arrived at the job site and started installing the transmitter, the customer's project engineer told them that they needed different equipment specifications. The engineer had called Faye three weeks before, and she said that she would make sure that the technicians ordered the right components. When Ivan called Faye at the office, she told him that he should have coordinated with the customer himself, that he needed to take on more responsibility, and that she couldn't be expected to handle details for him.

The next week, Carla and several other technicians were attending a technical training session. During the breaks in training, Faye was a common topic of discussion. Most of the technicians had similar experiences to Carla, Tim, and Ivan. One of them said that he had even confronted Faye about the fact that she gave him work to do that was obviously supervisory paperwork. Faye told him, "I'm responsible for the performance of this unit and routine paperwork is low on my priority list. You technicians will have to learn to help out when you're in the office. We all have to work as a team here."

Another technician said that he had gone in to see Faye about changes in purchasing policies. She told him that she was too busy to talk to him because she was frantically preparing for a presentation the next day that she had volunteered to do for the regional director. He then wrote out three proposed approaches for dealing with the changes and left the proposal on her desk. After a week, he tried to talk to her again, but she put him off again. Last Thursday, when he had to have an answer, he went in to see Faye, but her secretary told him that she was off for a long weekend. Because he could wait no longer to order components, he contacted purchasing and resolved the situation the best way he knew how. The next week Faye stormed into the equipment lab where he was working with three other technicians. She told him, "Don't ever go over my head again. I was going to handle the problem with purchasing and now you've let them dictate the rules."

Questions

1. Which of the attributes from Exhibit 1.4 has Faye failed to exhibit? Give examples from the case to support your choices.

2. Do you think Faye's subordinates need to change to adapt to her supervisory style? Why or why not?

3. How will Faye need to change if she is going to be a successful supervisor? Do you think she will be able to make these changes? Why or why not?

Walnut Grove Inn	CASE PROBLEM 1.2

Shelby Taylor had started her new job supervising desk clerks, housekeepers, and the bookkeeping staff for the Walnut Grove Inn. The Inn, which had 60 guest rooms, was in an attractive location in a medium-sized city. Unlike many hotels and motels, the Inn was independently owned. Because of its location and the attractiveness of the Inn, the business had been profitable, although not at the level expected by its owner. Shelby was excited about the opportunity to improve the performance of the Inn and looked forward to her first opportunity to be a supervisor. During her initial days on the job, she soon realized that she would have to develop an effective supervisory style for dealing with employees. In discussions with the owner about her first experiences on the job, the owner made several recommendations about how she should supervise the staff. He suggested what he called a "no-nonsense" approach. With this approach, employees would be treated impersonally and without regard for their feelings. Employees would be reminded regularly that they could be easily replaced if their performance was not up to standard. Furthermore, employees were to be motivated by the use of contests that placed them in competition with each other.

Although Shelby had not been a supervisor before, she had some very different views about the type of supervisory style that should be used. She wanted to adopt an approach that placed emphasis on respect for each employee. Shelby also wanted to utilize teamwork and to instill a spirit of cooperation among employees. She believed that by helping each other, employees could increase the quality of service and make each guest's stay at the Inn more enjoyable. Furthermore, it was clear to Shelby that the previous supervisor's approach was essentially the "no-nonsense" approach described by the owner. Shelby examined the Inn's employment records and found that turnover was higher than the average for the hotel industry. After looking through employee files and talking to some of the more experienced staff, she found that there were several problem employees. She also found out that a number of employees had low expectations of an acceptable level of performance. It appeared to her that the "no-nonsense" supervisory approach probably had a de-motivating effect on the staff.

Shelby began to implement her supervisory approach by meeting with small groups of employees. At these meetings, she told employees about her ideas for teamwork. She told employees that their tasks were interdependent like the spokes in a wheel. Without communication and coordination among the staff, there would be missing spokes and the wheel couldn't carry a load. Then she told the employees that they were important to the organization. "Without effective housekeepers, helpful desk clerks, and careful bookkeepers the Inn won't survive. We have to work as a team and depend on each other to make each guest's stay an enjoyable experience." She then outlined increased performance expectations and expressed confidence that each employee could perform at these levels. In addition, she explained to employees that she wanted them to make more decisions on their own. She stressed the importance of doing quality work in which they could take pride. Shelby also started the practice of holding birthday parties and celebrations of national holidays in order to make the work atmosphere more family-like and to make employees feel more accepted. In addition, she implemented a reward system based on accomplishment of performance goals.

At the end of the first three months there was an increase in employee productivity, and Shelby was gratified that her approach seemed to be working. Nonetheless, Shelby began to see problems, as some employees seemed to be taking advantage of her. Only a few employees were meeting their performance goals. Some employees began to ask favors, such as making exceptions to work schedules. After she would make an exception for one employee, other employees would then demand the same exceptions and claim that Shelby was being unfair when she denied such requests. She also found that some employees were not doing quality work and that they were not performing all of their duties. In some instances, rooms were not being cleaned as carefully as they should be, and housekeeping supplies began to disappear. In addition, when employees could not come to work, some called in too late for her to make accommodations in work assignments. When she confronted some of the worst offenders, they offered numerous excuses for their late call-ins, absenteeism, and poor performance. Many told her that she was just being two-faced about her managerial style. In essence, they told her that if she really had respect for them as she claimed, she wouldn't be confronting them about performance and would accept their excuses.

As Shelby sat in her office one day, she wondered what she should do to get things back on track. She wondered if her supervisory approach would work or whether she should adopt the "no-nonsense" approach suggested by the Inn's owner.

This case is based on a management brief written by Stoney White.

Questions

1. What mistakes do you see in Shelby Taylor's approach?
2. Do you think that housekeepers, desk clerks, and bookkeepers will be responsive to the supervisory approach Shelby used? Why or why not?
3. What does Shelby need to do to solve these problems? What should she retain from her initial approach?

References

1. Bridges, William. "The End of the Job," *Fortune* (September 19, 1994): 62–64, 68, 72, 74.
2. Katzenbach, Jon, and Smith, Douglas K. *The Wisdom of Teams*. New York: HarperCollins Publishers, 1994.
3. Katz, Robert L. "Skills of an Effective Administrator," in "Business Classics: Fifteen Key Concepts for Managerial Success," *Harvard Business Review* (1975): 23–25.

4. *Inc.,* "Asking Workers What They Want" (August 1994): 103.

5. Ibid.

6. Katz. "Skills of an Effective Administrator."

7. Marrelo, Pete. "Intel's Staffing Plans," presentation to the Fort Worth Human Resource Association (November 1997).

8. Glunk, Ursula; Wilderom, Celeste; and Ogilvie, Robert. "Finding the Key to German-Style Management," *International Studies of Management & Organization* (Fall 1996): 93–99.

9. U. S. Census Bureau, *Statistical Abstract of the United States, 2001.* Washington, D.C.: www.census.gov/statab/www/, 2002.

10. Kirk, Randy. "It's About Control," *Inc.* (August 1994): 25–26.

11. Nauman, Matt. "Job Well Done," *Chicago Tribune* (September 18, 1994): sect. 17, 3.

12. Ingrassia, Paul. "A Long Road to Good Labor Relations at GM," *The Wall Street Journal* (June 30, 1998): A18.

13. Hill, Linda. *Becoming a Manager.* Boston: Harvard Business School Press, 1992.

14. Taylor III, Alex. "GM's $11,000,000,000 Turnaround," *Fortune* (October 17, 1994): 54–56, 58, 62, 66, 70, 74.

15. Ibid.

16. Daft, Richard L., and Marcic, Dorothy. *Understanding Management,* 2nd ed. Fort Worth, Texas: Dryden Press, 1998.

17. Kahn, R. L.; Wolfe, D. M.; Quinn, P. R.; Snoek, J. D.; and Rosenthal, R. A. *Organizational Stress: Studies in Role Conflict and Ambiguity.* New York: John Wiley & Sons, 1964. Miner, J. B. *Management Theory.* New York: Macmillan, 1991.

18. Slater, Robert. *Jack Welch and the GE Way: Management Insights and Leadership Secrets of the Legendary CEO.* New York: McGraw-Hill, 1999.

19. Feldman, Joan M. "Southwest Keeps Moving," *Air Transport World* (November 2001): 48–49. Colvin, Geoffrey. "What's Love Got to Do With It?" *Fortune* (November 12, 2001): 24.

20. Freiberg, Kevin, and Freiberg, Jackie. *Nuts! Southwest Airlines' Crazy Recipe for Business and Personal Success.* Austin, Texas: Bard Press, 1996.

21. Katzenbach, Jon, and Smith, Douglas. "Virtual Teaming," *Forbes.com* (May 21, 2001): 48–51.

22. Katzenbach and Smith, "Virtual Teaming," 48.

23. Martin, James. *Cybercorp: The New Business Revolution.* New York: American Management Association, 1996.

24. Bacciocco, Dana. "EDI Fit to Survive in Competitive Retail Energy Markets," *Electric Light and Power* (October 2001): 24. Borck, James R. "Say Goodbye to EDI," *InfoWorld* (October 22, 2001): 57. *Economist,* "Stores of Value," (March 4, 1995): 5–8. Meehan, Michael, "Aerospace Group Backs New EDI-to-XML Bridge," *Computerworld* (October 2001): 14.

25. Martin, James. *Cybercorp.*

26. Chappell, Lindsay. "Honda's New Elasticity Has Reduced Costs," *Automotive News* (August 13, 2001): 6.

27. Serwer, Andrew. "McDonald's Conquers the World," *Fortune* (October 17, 1994): 103–104, 106, 108, 112, 114, 116. Young, Barbara. "Global Marketing Pursuits," *National Provisioner* (September 2000): 18–25.

28. Johnson, Ross, and Winchell, William O. *Management and Quality.* Milwaukee, Wisc.: American Society for Quality Control, 1989.

29. Hammer, Michael, and Champy, James. *Reengineering the Corporation.* New York: HarperBusiness (1993): 32, 76–77.

30. Ibid.

31. Peters, Tom. "Nobody Knows Nothin', So Go Ahead and Take Those Risks," *Chicago Tribune* (August 29, 1994): sect. 4, 3.

32. Stewart, Thomas A. "Reengineering: The New Management Tool," *Fortune* (August 23, 1993): 41–48.

33. Ibid.; Hall, Gene; Rosenthal, Jim; and Wade, Judy. "How to Make Reengineering Really Work," *Harvard Business Review* (November–December 1993): 1119–131. Nadler, David A., and Tushman, Michael L. *Competing by Design: The Power of Organizational Architecture.* New York: Oxford University Press, 1997.

34. U. S. Census Bureau, *Statistical Abstract of the United States, 2001.* Washington, D.C.: www.census.gov/statab/www/, 2002.

35. Baynton, Dannah. "America's $60 Billion Problem," *Training* (May 2001): 50.

36. Baynton, Dannah. "America's $60 Billion Problem," 50–54.

37. *Chicago Tribune.* "How Many Switches It Takes to Be Viewed As a Job-Hopper" (September 19, 1994): sect. 6, 5.

38. Kanter, Rosabeth M. *When Giants Learn to Dance: Mastering the Challenge of Strategy, Management, and Careers in the 1990s.* New York: Simon & Schuster, 1989.

39. Zeile, William J. "U. S. Affiliates of Foreign Companies," *Survey of Current Business* (August 1, 2000).

40. Lee, William. "The New Corporate Republics," *The Wall Street Journal* (September 26, 1994): A12.

41. *Business Week.* "Managing by Values."

42. *Fort Worth Star Telegram.* "Home Depot Discrimination Lawsuit Settled for $1 Million" (December 6, 1997): A5. *The Oil Daily.* "Judge OKs Texaco Settlement" (March 27, 1997): 59.

43. Lardner, James. "Too Old to Write Code?" *U. S. News & World Report* (March 16, 1998): 39–45.

44. Edmondson, Brad. "Work Slowdown," *American Demographics* (March 1996): 4–7.

45. Novack, Janet. "What Exploitation," *Forbes* (February 24, 1997): 161.

46. Bloom, Jennifer Kingston. "'Portable Executives' Find Top-Level Work as Temps," *American Banker* (January 28, 1997): 1–2.

47. Merck & Co., Inc. *1997 Annual Report,* 1997.

48. Hipple, Steven. "Contingent Work: Results from the Second Survey," *Monthly Labor Review* (November 1998): 22–35.

49. *U. S. News & World Report.* "Meet the 'New Economy' Temps" (August 30, 1999): 50.

50 Brownstein, Vivian. "As the Job Market Heats Up, Can Inflation Stay Cool?," *Fortune* (August 22, 1994): 23.

51. *U. S. News & World Report.* "Meet the 'New Economy' Temps."

52. Wells, Susan J. "Making Telecommuting Work," *HR Magazine* (October 2001): 34–45.

53. Morrissey, "Switching on Telecommuting," *PC Week* (June 15, 1998): 135.

54. Katzenbach, Jon. "The Right Kind of Teamwork," *The Wall Street Journal* (November 9, 1992): A10.

55. Klein, Janice A., and Posey, Pamela A. "Good Supervisors Make Good Supervisors—Anywhere," *Harvard Business Review* (November–December 1986): 126.

56. Ibid.

57. Pfeffer, Jeffrey. *The Human Equation: Building Profits by Putting People First.* Boston: Harvard Business School Press, 1998.

58. Richman. "The New Worker Elite."

59. Ibid.

60. Pfeffer, Jeffrey. *Competitive Advantage through People: Unleashing the Power of the Work Force.* Boston: Harvard Business School Press, 1994.

YOU AND YOUR FUTURE

Objectives

After reading and discussing this chapter, you should be able to do the following:

1. Define this chapter's key terms.

2. Explain how managers can avoid personal obsolescence.

3. List the steps involved in preparing oneself for advancement.

4. List the steps involved in planning a career.

5. Explain the importance of a personal code of ethics.

Introduction

Workers no longer expect to work for one company for decades and retire from there at age 65. "The new compact between company and worker dismisses paternalism and embraces self-reliance. . . . The key difference: shared responsibility. Employers have an obligation to provide opportunity for self-improvement; employees have to take charge of their own careers."[1] The economy and industries are changing so rapidly that no company can really know what it will be doing one or more years into the future. The emphasis is on gaining a competitive edge and on reinventing fundamental work processes and organizations.

Downsizing, reengineering, empowering, outsourcing, telecommuting, teaming, decentralizing, and globalizing are all changing the complexion of work and the workplace. All these efforts bring sudden and often painful changes to employees and their careers. Many companies have outsourced several activities, such as payroll functions, benefits administration, training, and information services. **Outsourcing** is a process in which companies contract with outside vendors to perform activities that were previously performed within the company. While outsourcing typically has an adverse effect on employees, firms outsource activities for a number of important reasons, such as the desire to focus on a smaller set of core activities or to

outsourcing

contracting with outside vendors to perform services previously handled within the organization by company employees gain efficiencies that specialized outside service providers can provide. Recent research indicates that the outsourcing of payroll activities and training is associated with increased firm performance.[2] According to Dunn and Bradstreet, the volume of outsourcing has increased at an estimated annual growth rate of 26 percent and expenditures on outsourcing now exceed $85 billion per year. **Reengineering,** which was introduced in the previous chapter, has also had a major impact on careers and work. Key thrusts of reengineering are to reduce the number of "hand-offs" between workers or units and to combine jobs in order to allow individual employees to perform larger numbers of tasks.

reengineering
fundamental changes in how work is performed that eliminate unnecessary activities, minimize hand-offs between employees and units, and combine jobs

Another reengineering technique involves redesign of the work to eliminate unnecessary activities. For example, reengineering efforts at the Banca di America e di Italia reduced the number of activities in check-deposit transactions from 64 to 25 and the number of forms from 9 to 2.[3] Reengineering also takes advantage of new information system capabilities. For example, a major telecommunications company reengineered customer service and repair functions by creating a new job called "front-end technician." Front-end technicians now use new information systems, testing equipment, and switching equipment to handle calls from customers who have questions or are experiencing telephone service problems. They also perform such functions as testing lines and answering billing questions. Whereas previously they were clerks who only took calls from customers and referred them to repair specialists or various departments, now these same employees handle a high proportion of all calls by themselves. The result has been a 10 to 30 percent productivity increase.[4]

As a result of such activities as outsourcing and reengineering, many employees' jobs have been eliminated. In addition, workers often need new skills for reengineered jobs. According to a Pitney Bowes Management Survey of 100 major U. S. companies, "Workers at three-fourths of firms that have carried out reengineering actions were more fearful about losing their jobs. . . . Likewise, 55 percent of the firms said their employees felt overburdened by their assignments after the changes. [But] 71 percent of the companies said their initiatives led to greater employee productivity, 61 percent reported cost-efficiency increases and 40 percent saw profit increases."[5] According to *Business Week*, such management actions have several effects:

> In companies that are flattening hierarchies and, bit by bit, decentralizing decision-making, workers are gaining greater control over what they do; self-direction has superseded the doctrine that workers do only what they're told. High performers are rewarded with higher pay. And flexible human resource strategies can free workers to pursue more fulfilling combinations of varied work, family life, and other interests.[6]

Many companies are stressing flexibility training. The aim is to prepare the company and its employees for rapid changes—both planned and unplanned. Michael Dell, the CEO of Dell Computer Corp., stresses the need for management flexibility and credits this characteristic as a key to his company's success. For example, his company changed its market strategies after encountering different market conditions in the mid-1990s. His background indicates how quickly companies evolve and change today, as he started Dell in 1984 while he was a student at the University of Texas in Austin.[7]

Diversity in Our Workforce

Researchers and government statisticians have predicted a number of substantial changes in the future workforce:

- *More female workers.* In contrast to lower representation in the past, the proportion of the labor force accounted for by women has steadily increased. In 2005, women are expected to account for 47.8 percent of a labor force of 147,100,000 people.[8]

- *More working mothers with preschoolers.* About two-thirds of all working women will have children under the age of six. This indicates a need for quality child care programs provided by employers in many cases.

- *More single-parent families.* Data from the 2000 Census reveal that traditional families with married parents and children account for only 24 percent of U. S. households and that 27 percent of all children are being raised in single-parent households.[9]

- *More dual-career couples.* Dual-career couples now account for 60 percent of all couples, an increase of 80 percent in the past decade. A recent survey of dual-career households found that 49 percent of the wives categorized their careers on the same level of importance as their husbands'.[10]

- *More nonwhites entering the workforce.* In 1997, African Americans and Hispanics accounted for 19 percent and 21 percent, respectively, of the growth in employment above the previous year.[11]

- *More older Americans.* The number of Americans in the labor force age 55 or older will increase to more than 22 million by 2005. Relative to 1994 levels, this represents whopping increases of 62.8 percent for women and 42.5 percent for men.[12]

Companies and industries are focusing on total quality management and are changing as never before. Increasingly, American businesses of all sizes are challenged by the uncertainties of a global economy. These changes mean that you will face a more demanding and stressful work environment in the future. Your career investments today will determine your options in the future. You must work to guarantee your employability, not job security with only one company. Your primary goal should be to commit to a lifelong program of continuous learning, while mastering the newest technologies in order to be ready for future job and career opportunities. This chapter focuses on your future and how you can avoid personal obsolescence by planning for your advancement and career.

Obsolescence

obsolescence

a state or condition that exists when a person or machine is no longer able to perform to standards or to management's expectations

Obsolescence exists when a person or machine is no longer capable of performing up to standards or to management's expectations. What choices does management have when confronted with an obsolete person or machine? Exhibit 2.1 highlights the alternatives. A person can become obsolete in attitudes, knowledge, skills, and abilities. Obsolescence in any of these areas marks a person as a potential candidate for the scrap heap. Exhibit 2.2 is a short quiz to help you determine if you are, or are in danger of becoming, obsolete.

Personal obsolescence can happen quite suddenly. Overnight changes can render an individual's performance inadequate or unnecessary. Corporate reengineering efforts and the shift from vertical layers of management to cross-functional teams have had this impact on workers as well as supervisors and other managers. When a company decides to outsource, often "the best and the brightest employees who did the work often are hired by the outside agency, but the others lose their jobs."[13]

According to Tom Peters, the supervisor's role is changing. In many companies Peters and others have studied, the traditional first-line supervisor's job has become obsolete. In companies where teams dominate, the supervisor has become a coordinator, facilitator, trainer, coach, and adviser. Candidates for supervisory positions and practicing supervisors receive training in working with and through teams, problem-solving techniques, statistics, participative management, and communications. Their primary duty is to empower others—team members—to do what they do to the best of their ability. Their primary focus is horizontal—working to improve the

---

Exhibit 2.1 *Alternative ways of dealing with obsolescence in a person or a machine.*

PERSON	MACHINE
Invest in the person through training and development, and offer incentives for efforts at self-improvement.	Keep the machine and modify it, when economically feasible to do so, to improve its efficiency and longevity.
Tolerate the person and his limitations and inefficiencies.	Keep the machine and live with its limitations and inefficiencies.
Tolerate the person, but reduce her role in the organization by deletion of duties or demotion.	Keep the machine but reduce its role in production, relegating it to backup or temporary use.
Discharge the person and replace him with a better-qualified individual.	Scrap the machine and replace it with a more up-to-date model.

Exhibit 2.2

20 questions to help you assess your degree of personal obsolescence.

Ask yourself the following questions to determine your degree of personal obsolescence.

Note that these questions put the burden to avoid obsolescence on you. For every "no" response, you highlight an area where you need a change in behavior. Your "yes" responses pinpoint areas that are keeping you current and growing.

ATTITUDES

1. Is my mind free from anxiety over personal matters while I work?

2. Do I believe in myself—my knowledge, skills, and abilities—and in my associates?

3. Am I open and receptive to advice and suggestions, regardless of their sources?

4. Do I look for the pluses before looking for the minuses?

5. Am I more concerned with the cause of management's action than with its effect?

SKILLS

1. Is what I am able to do still needed?

2. In light of recent developments, will my skills be required one year from now?

3. Do I practice my skills regularly?

4. Do I regularly observe how others perform their skills?

5. Do I have a concrete program for acquiring new skills?

KNOWLEDGE

1. Am I curious—do I still seek the "why" behind actions and events?

2. Do I read something and learn something new every day?

3. Do I question the old and the routine?

4. Do I converse regularly with my subordinates, peers, and superiors?

5. Do I have a definite program for increasing my knowledge?

ABILITIES

1. Do my subordinates, peers, and superiors consider me competent?

2. Do I consistently look for a better way of doing things?

3. Am I willing to take calculated risks?

4. Do I keep morally and physically fit?

5. Do I have a specific program for improving my performance?

flow of work from the beginning to the end of a process or project while working across functional lines.[14] Exhibit 2.3 contrasts the old traditional role of the supervisor with the new emerging role in team environments.

Again, according to Peters, "There is no more difficult transition in a career than the one from non-boss to boss; the second toughest is to boss of bosses. These passages should be marked by programs commensurate with

Exhibit 2.3 *Differences between the old and the new supervisor.*

OLD—TRADITIONAL ROLE	NEW—EMERGING ROLE
1. 10–20 subordinates	As many as 75 people reporting directly or through teams
2. Scheduling work	Coach, leader, coordinator, and trainer focusing on empowering team members to schedule
3. Enforcing rules	Creating bonds of mutual trust, enabling others to set and follow their own rules
4. Planning others' work	Enabling others to plan their work
5. Focusing downward	Focusing horizontally, working to speed the flow
6. Transmitting and translating middle-management needs and demands	Transmitting and selling teams' needs upward
7. Issuing orders and giving instructions	Facilitating: getting expert help as required by teams
8. Creating and instituting changes and innovations	Assisting others to be creative and to strive constantly for improvements

their significance."[15] Since many organizations lack adequate programs to aid these transitions, you have the primary responsibility for preparing yourself to move into a supervisory position.

To avoid obsolescence, just as corporations are reengineering themselves, you will have to reengineer yourself and your career periodically. The key, say many authors, is flexibility. According to statistics from the U. S. Department of Labor, 75 percent of today's employees will require some form of retraining to fit into the 21st-century workforce. Throughout your working life, you can expect to change jobs about six times and have at least three careers.

Students also need to prepare themselves to recognize business challenges, opportunities, and interrelationships. They need to be able to see the various functional implications of business decisions. For example, a problem may have production and finance elements as well as human resource management and legal implications. The traditional business school approach of studying situations solely from the unconnected perspectives of accounting, finance, management, management information systems, marketing, and production is inadequate in today's world.

Walter Kiechel III adds that managers also need to be "specialists—you must be an expert in something, [and] generalists—you must know enough of different disciplines to be able to mediate among them."[16] In the future, there will be a need for both specialists and generalists. Supervisors will need to manage people from different specialties and help integrate the expertise they

SUPERVISORS AND QUALITY

A key to the eventual success of business leaders is often the influence of experiences with their supervisors or managers early in their careers. For some, their bosses set good examples and stressed the importance of delivering a quality product, while others stressed the necessity of getting the job done with the resources that are available. For some others, the flaws or weaknesses of their bosses resulted in their developing a strong commitment to do things differently. The following are some accounts from business leaders about experiences with their bosses.

Naveen Jain
Chairman, Infospace.com

I remember a meeting when Bill Gates asked, "What do you think of Windows NT?" Everybody said it would be the best product. I said it will be a fat, slow system. Instead of getting upset, Bill's response to me was, "Good. Go fix it."

I learned from that. When a search engine comes to a site, it shows up as a page view, not an actual customer, impacting advertising prices. An engineer at InfoSpace told me he wanted to change the way that's done in the industry—a huge task. I could have received that badly but I said, "Fine. Fix it," and we have.

Lewis Campbell
Chief Executive, Textron

He was a dyed-in-the-wool, traditional, tough manufacturing manager. He was 55 years old, 6-foot-2, 200 pounds, hard-jawed, of German background. His name was Ed, and he was the general manufacturing manager at General Motors. I was a young design engineer assigned to air bags. Ed needed a manager, so he took me and another guy, divided up the plant and said, "One of you guys is gonna be plant manager in six months, and one of you isn't. Good luck."

I was bemoaning the fact that Ed had given me the run-of-the-mill choice of the available management team, so I said, "Ed, you've given me a bunch of average guys." He turned to me and said, "What the hell you think you're going to be dealing with for the rest of your life? This is what leadership's all about." I won the horse race.

Albert H. Gordon
Former Chairman, Kidder, Peabody

At my first job, as an analyst at Goldman Sachs in 1925, I got a deal for $2 million in bonds for National Dairy Products [predecessor of Kraft Foods]. I would have gotten a very substantial commission, but my boss took all the credit.

I had to stick with Goldman for the time being, because jobs then were very scarce. But after six years at Goldman, I took over at Kidder, Peabody with two partners. I never forgot the important lesson I learned from my first boss—that you can't retain employees if you don't spread credit around.

Source: Specific accounts from executives are excerpted from *Forbes*, "On Your Mind: The Worm Turns," (February 7, 2000): 36.

Continuing education programs help you improve your chances for advancement and avoid becoming obsolete.

have. They will also need to manage generalists, as the following comments from Bruce Harreld, senior vice president of strategy at IBM, indicate:

> We're going to place an increasingly high premium on the ability of people to be integrators—seeking out people who are a mile wide and an inch deep in a lot of different things. Right now, we've got a lot of people who are a mile deep in this industry, and we're teaching them to broaden their communication and collaboration skills. At the same time, we're reaching into the incoming work force, and other places in the company, and finding people who feel as comfortable in a manufacturing environment as they do working with customers or working with a software development team.[17]

Westin Hotels identified "14 key attributes employees from housekeepers to hotel managers must have. Besides technical competence, these include a capacity to demonstrate initiative, an ability to communicate clearly, and a commitment to quality."[18] Through careful screening, the hotel chain found people capable of managing themselves and reduced employee turnover while increasing customer satisfaction.[19] Employees at European Collision Center, an auto repair shop in Massachusetts, constantly learn new skills by returning to school and cross-training. They "take 'ownership' of a car while it's in the shop, staying with it [from] start to finish. No one looks over their shoulders." Customers love what they get, and "traffic has doubled every year for five years."[20]

Perhaps all this is best summarized by author William Bridges when he states that to survive in the new world of work one must have four essentials ("D.A.T.A."):

> The new qualifications are that you really want to do the work (desire), that you are good at what the work requires (ability), that you fit [a specific] kind of situation (temperament), and that you have whatever other resources the work requires (assets).[21]

The Importance of Education

In general, the more education one has, the more income and employment security one achieves. According to average earning data from the Census Bureau, high school graduates earn only 54 percent of bachelor's degree recipients and only 44 percent of holders of master's degrees.[22] Average starting salaries for 2001 bachelor's degree graduates were as follows: management information systems, $45,585; finance and economics, $40,776; accounting, $39,720; marketing, $35,194; computer science, $52,473; civil engineering, $40,979; electrical engineering, $52,092; and mechanical engineering, $48,588.[23]

According to MIT economist Lester Thurow, investments in education are a "defensive necessity"—without such investments one's earning power will fall faster than for more highly educated workers.[24] As the economy changes, manufacturing jobs requiring only low levels of skill in the United States and other high-wage countries are being shifted to low-wage countries, and those without skills are being left behind. In addition, with the shift to service and information analysis jobs in the United States, greater skills are needed. As a result, lower-skilled workers are encountering more difficulty finding good jobs.[25] Manufacturing jobs in the United States, as a percentage of the workforce, declined from 17.4 percent of employment in 1990 to 14 percent in 2000. Nonetheless, because of overall growth in employment, manufacturing still accounted for almost 18.4 million jobs in 2000.[26]

SOURCES OF EDUCATION

Education is achieved through various sources: community colleges, colleges and universities, professional associations, and on-the-job training, to name but a few. In addition, the courses that can be taken in individual industry associations are quite valuable. By joining certain professions and professional associations, you may become eligible for their various training programs. For information on how they can help you, look at their Web pages, such as the following.

Academy of Management, www.aom.pace.edu
Pace University, 235 Elm Road, Briarcliff Manor, NY 10510-3020

American Management Association, www.amanet.org
1601 Broadway, New York, NY 10019-7420

American Society for Training and Development, www.astd.org
1640 King Street, Box 1443, Alexandria, VA 22313-2043

Institute for Supply Management (formerly National Association for Purchasing Management), www.napm.org
P.O. Box 22160, Tempe, AZ 85285-2160

National Association for Female Executives, www.nafe.com
P.O. Box 469031, Escondido, CA 92046-9925

Society for Human Resource Management, www.shrm.org
1800 Duke Street, Alexandria, VA 22314

According to a survey of 100 college recruitment offices by the Hanigan Consulting Group, a student's "grade point average is the most important factor in determining hiring decisions and salary level. . . ."[27] On the other hand, a high grade-point average is insufficient to guarantee a good job upon graduation. Increasingly, employers are demanding that college graduates have gained knowledge from internships or other significant work experience before they will be hired. Students need experience working in real organizations and opportunities to learn and apply new skills that will be valued by potential employers.

The commitment to learn and to keep learning must be acquired so that you can continually seek what you need to grow and survive. Job success in the 21st century will require an increased emphasis on the continual acquisition of new skills. "In the 21st century, demand in the labor market will shift from those with know-how to those with learn-how. Job security will fade in importance and will be replaced by the goal of employability."[28] Each of us must make a commitment to continue our education and to work toward steady improvement.

PLANNING FOR ADVANCEMENT

Your future must be planned if you wish to control it. The seven steps in planning for advancement are as follows:

1. Decide what you want to accomplish.
2. Take a personal inventory.
3. Analyze your present situation.
4. Set your objectives for self-improvement.
5. Develop your program.
6. Set your program in motion.
7. Evaluate your progress periodically.

Decide what you want to accomplish. The first step is an important one. While it is sometimes difficult to visualize life goals at a younger age, it is important to think through what you want to accomplish in life. In what manner do you want to make a contribution? As people become older, they frequently feel that their early goals did not focus enough on building relationships, obtaining a proper balance between work and family life, and giving something back to society. Professor Douglas T. Hall provides the following valuable advice:

> The ultimate goal of the career is psychological success, the feeling of pride and personal accomplishment that comes from achieving one's most important goals in life, be they achievement, family happiness, inner peace, or something else. This is in contrast to vertical success under the old career contract, where the goal was climbing the corporate pyramid and making a lot of money. While there is only

one way to achieve vertical success (making it to the top), there are infinite ways to achieve psychological success, as many ways as there are unique human needs.[29]

Take a personal inventory. This second step is designed to give you a realistic understanding of your interests, values, and aptitudes. Exhibit 2.4 provides a guide for assessing interests and values—those states or conditions in life that are important to you. Rank each work characteristic listed in order of its importance to you, numbering them from 1 to 15. Use your preferences to evaluate your present and potential jobs and employers throughout your job search. All the listed factors were ranked as very important by 50 percent or more of the workers surveyed in a Gallup Poll. They are listed in the order of their importance to those surveyed—good health insurance and other benefits ranked number 1, interesting work ranked number 2, and so on.[30]

Interests and values assessment checklist.	**Exhibit 2.4**
Rank each of the following in order of its importance to you.	**Rank**
Good health insurance and other benefits	1
Interesting work	
Job security	
Opportunity to learn new skills	
Having a week or more of vacation	
Being able to work independently	
Recognition from coworkers	
Regular hours (no weekends, no nights)	
Having a job in which you can help others	
Limiting job stress	
High income	
Working close to home	2
Work that is important to society	
Chances for promotion	
Contact with a lot of people	

Along with your interests and values, you should assess your aptitudes—your ability, talent, or capacity to perform certain mental and physical processes. You should also learn more about your personality by completing personality inventories, such as the Myers–Briggs Type Indicator (MBTI), which is used extensively in industry today for career counseling.[31] By taking a battery of aptitude, interest, and personality tests through your college's counseling office, you will discover which aptitudes you possess and what kinds of jobs you would be most capable of handling. Through proper interpretation of the test results, you will learn the kinds of jobs for which you are best suited. The *Supervising Teams* feature provides an example of the type of instruments that are used to assess characteristics required for team leaders. The tests given by counselors will typically be longer. Counselors should be able to tell you about the validity (predictive ability) and reliability (consistency) of their tests.

In addition, students who may have decided that they want to pursue a career in business often do not have clear ideas about which specific areas of business are right for them. Fortunately, a comprehensive online career

SUPERVISING TEAMS

If you haven't already, you soon will find yourself a member of one or more teams and be expected to be a team player. The following quiz is designed to determine if you have the characteristics needed to be a good team member. After taking it, grade yourself with the answer key that follows.

A = Always,   S = Sometimes,   N = Never

Characteristics:

Ⓐ Ⓢ Ⓝ 1. I am a good listener.
Ⓐ Ⓢ Ⓝ 2. I enjoy the give and take of negotiating.
Ⓐ Ⓢ Ⓝ 3. I like working with and through others.
Ⓐ Ⓢ Ⓝ 4. I have good communication and interpersonal skills.
Ⓐ Ⓢ Ⓝ 5. I trust others.
Ⓐ Ⓢ Ⓝ 6. I respect and value the uniqueness in others.
Ⓐ Ⓢ Ⓝ 7. I am open to criticism.
Ⓐ Ⓢ Ⓝ 8. I can accept responsibility for the behavior of others.
Ⓐ Ⓢ Ⓝ 9. I enjoy continual learning.
Ⓐ Ⓢ Ⓝ 10. I like to solve problems.

Key: Give yourself two points for every *Always* response and one point for each *Sometimes* response.

Scoring: 15-20 points—team leader potential
10-14 points—team member potential
Under 10 points—loner

Each *Sometimes* and *Never* response indicates areas in which you should seek improvement.

Source: John A. Byrne, "Paradigms for Postmodern Managers," *Business Week,* January 19, 1993: 62.

self-assessment tool is available to help individuals discover the areas of business that are most consistent with their interests. The assessment tool, which is called CareerLeader, is used by leading business schools in the United States and was developed by James Waldroop and Timothy Butler, who have been involved in career development at the Harvard Business School. This integrated expert system enables individuals to gain insights into how well they match up with 27 different career paths in business.[32]

Analyze your present situation. Your present situation consists of the developmental resources that are available to you, and your view of your present state in life. How strong is your commitment to improve on what you have? How happy are you with your present job, income, education, and quality of life? The more you desire to change, the easier it will be to do so. Consider the advice of Sandy Rowe, editor of *The Oregonian* in Portland: "If you don't have genuine passion for what you're doing, don't do it. Passion for your work helps you through the most difficult times."[33]

Set your objectives for self-improvement. As clearly and precisely as you can, prepare a written list of the qualities you wish to obtain and the skills and abilities you wish to develop. Determine which of these you need most urgently, make them objectives for the short run, and set a time limit by which each is to be procured. Set the remainder of your needs as long-term goals—goals to be achieved within a year or two. Do not take on too much at once, you will only be setting yourself up for a letdown and frustration. Start with the goals you need most urgently, and select the one that appears easiest to achieve. As with a diet, early success is important to both commitment and continuation.

Develop your program. The program you formulate should contain the answers to who, what, when, where, why, how, and how much. Break it down into phases, each with specific goals and time limits. Keep it in writing and in front of you so that you constantly remind yourself of the targets you wish to hit. Share its contents with your loved ones—they can boost your willpower. Check on your progress regularly and when you reach one goal, add another.

Set your program in motion. Begin your execution of the program as soon as it is formulated. If you meet heavy resistance in one or another of its phases, leave that phase and divert your attention and efforts to another. Then come back to that phase and try again.

Evaluate your progress periodically. If certain goals you have stated appear to be impossible, you may have to replace them. Remember that the program is a continuing effort at improvement and personal growth. Check your progress against the time limits you established. Were you realistic? Are you on course? Share your successes and setbacks with your husband or wife, or with a good friend.

Most large companies offer supervisors and associates many opportunities for growth and development. Programs range from reading materials to college degrees underwritten by company funds. Find out what options are available to you and what the requirements are for taking advantage of each of them. Be selective, and do not overcommit yourself. It is better to do one or two things splendidly than to do several only adequately.

Planning Your Career

career

a sequence of jobs that takes people to higher levels of learning and responsibility

career path

a route chosen by an employer or employee through a series of related horizontal and vertical moves to jobs of ever-increasing responsibilities

A **career** for our purposes consists of a sequence of jobs that takes people to higher levels of learning and responsibility, usually in a specialty area. As a career progresses, one acquires new skills, skill levels, experiences, and competencies. This series of jobs is often called a **career path.** Fast-growing small businesses offer some of the best career opportunities. Many offer employees less pay and benefits but "greater opportunities for individual growth. . . . [A]n employee is likely to have more responsibilities in the first three to five years at a smaller company than at a larger one. That's because smaller firms have fewer employees and, thus, typically need workers to take on many tasks."[34] Fortunately, a large share of new jobs created in recent years has come from smaller to medium-sized companies. Over 56 percent of all working Americans are employed by companies with fewer than 500 persons.[35] Small businesses are excellent places to get a career started.

SELF-RELIANCE

You may find that no clearly defined path has been designated by your employer. If so, the burden will be yours to determine a path with your current employer or with another. As we have stated, you can expect to have several jobs and careers during your lifetime. Increasingly, employees are finding that they must take responsibility for their own career management. Professor Douglas T. Hall says that a 21st-century career will be "driven by the person, not the organization, and . . . will be reinvented by the person from time to time, as the person and the environment change."[36] The decline of careers with only one employer is a factor driving the need for career self-reliance. Companies that operate in rapidly changing industries with fierce competition for talent, such as computers and other high technology, seem to place most emphasis on supporting the transition to employee self-reliance for career planning. Specific examples of companies that emphasize self-reliance include Hewlett-Packard, IBM, Intel, Monsanto, Motorola, and Sun Microsystems.[37] Sun Microsystems has taken the following actions:

> Sun Microsystems implemented the first career program where self-reliance was the stated goal. At Sun, human resources leaders estimate that skills of engineers become outdated within three years. Employees are told that they own the main responsibility for their careers, and Sun provides them with the tools to keep up with fast-changing business needs. These tools include a career services center and career counseling offered on five campuses.[38]

Monsanto provides another example of company encouragement of self-reliance:

> A secretary at Monsanto's St. Louis headquarters attends a workshop on "career self-reliance." A battery of self-assessment tests and discussion with a career counselor confirm her interest in human resources. Coincidentally, recent structural changes at Monsanto have pushed HR responsibilities out to work groups; no one in her group has yet stepped forward to take on hiring and training. . . . She approaches her boss about taking on some of the department's [HR] work. She winds up expanding her job to fill the void. Within a few months, she has enrolled in a master's degree program in human resources at a nearby college.[39]

STEPS IN A CAREER PLAN

Like your future, your career must be planned if you are to control it. Five recommended steps for you to take in planning your career are:

1. Determine your career objectives.
2. Investigate jobs and career paths.
3. Label likely employers.
4. Seek employment.
5. Assess your situation periodically.

Determine Your Career Objectives

Write a mission statement for yourself, just as any business does. State in writing what you want to achieve and where you want to be over the next one, two, and three years. Start by listing your career goals. State as clearly as you can just what you want from work and what kind of work you want to specialize in over the next few years. Now work backward: List the short- and long-term steps you must take to get what you want. You will then know what steps are needed to reach your career goals. Many potential careers are only emerging at this time. Exhibit 2.5 lists some of these new careers. Workers in these new careers will need supervisors, who in turn will need to understand the underlying technology base of the area.

Investigate Jobs and Career Paths

You may wish to begin this step by looking at the jobs that best match up with your interests and aptitudes. The *Dictionary of Occupational Titles*, published by the U.S. Department of Labor, lists hundreds of jobs and describes the tasks and responsibilities they require. (The dictionary is online at the U.S. Bureau of Labor Statistics website: www.bls.gov/oco/ocodot1.htm.) Your college career service office will have information on jobs and forecasts for future employment. Government publications, along with many privately published reports and periodicals, can help you assess the jobs and career fields that will be in demand in the long term. For exam-

Exhibit 2.5 *Emerging careers.*

SMART HOME TECHNICIAN

Technicians who install smart-home features such as climate control systems, home theaters, lighting controls, and computer networks

RETAIL CREATIVE DIRECTOR

Specialists who employ a combination of marketing, architectural, and design skills to attract potential customers into stores

E-COMMERCE ACCOUNTANTS

Accountants who help Web developers set up online payment systems and ensure that such systems are safe from hackers

WEB PROMOTIONS PRODUCERS

Specialists having marketing and sales expertise who create and develop promotions for Web application

BROADBAND ARCHITECTS

Skilled professionals who set, organize, and present content for dissemination via broadband technology, such as to homes

Source: Sandra Baker, "Dead-end Career Paths: Internet Sites Offer Advice on Professions to Shun," *Fort Worth Star Telegram,* Careers (February 13, 2000): M1, M15.

ple, the *Occupational Outlook Handbook,* published by the U.S. Department of Labor, Bureau of Labor Statistics, identifies occupations projected to have the largest growth. Many supervisory and management jobs are included in these projections. (The *Occupational Outlook Handbook* also is available online at the Bureau of Labor Statistics website: www.bls.gov/oco/home.htm.) The projected growth in management jobs, and increases between 1996 and 2006, are as follows:

General managers and top executives	467,000 (15 percent)
Clerical supervisors and managers	262,000 (19 percent)
Marketing and sales worker supervisors	246,000 (11 percent)
Food service and lodging managers	168,000 (28 percent)

The Bureau also predicts that total U.S. employment in 2006 will reach 150.9 million, up from 132.4 million in 1996. Among the occupations cited by the Bureau as having the largest growth between 1996 and 2006 are database administrators, computer support specialists, and computer scientists (118 percent) and systems analysts (103 percent).[40]

Although these publications provide useful information for longer-term career planning, they do not provide information that is useful for the immediate time period. Some of the best sources of immediate job information are the employment sections of newspapers from major cities and the Web pages of companies. Company Web pages often have employment sections that provide extensive information about the jobs for which they have vacancies. In addition, numerous sources of jobs are available on the Internet today, including those maintained by governmental agencies, volunteer organizations, and professional associations. The U. S. Department of Labor's Bureau of Labor Statistics maintains an extensive website at http://stats.bls.gov that lists an impressive amount of employment data useful for employment planning.

Meeting recruiters at job fairs is one avenue to pursue in your job search.

Various on-campus clubs offer help with job and career information. They often feature guest speakers from occupations that are related to the clubs' activities and may sponsor field trips to visit major employers' facilities. Another good source is campus recruiters, who represent many different employers and who interview applicants and share information about what it is like to work in different areas. Nonetheless, personal networking and internships now provide frequent access to jobs and have taken the place of some campus recruiting activity. **Networking** means talking with one's friends, family, and other people you know to obtain information.

There is no substitute for talking in depth with someone who does the kind of work you wish to do. Schools can often put you in touch with experienced people in various areas through their alumni offices. Family and friends can do the same. Private and public employment services can also help by informing you about the specifics of various jobs.

networking

finding employment or advancing one's career through one's friends, family, and work-related contacts

Identify Likely Employers

Once you have a specific kind of work and job in mind, you are ready to begin identifying likely employers. Your goal is to find the specific job that you would like to get with a specific employer. One way to start is to determine if the area where you live is right for you. Is it growing in population, especially in terms of new businesses and job opportunities? It may be that you should begin researching jobs in another city or state.

Sources to help you determine where the jobs are that fit your needs include help-wanted or employment ads, local colleges' career services or placement offices, friends, family, and contacts employed in various companies. Private and public employment agencies can also be of assistance. Since private agencies often specialize by occupation, level of experience, and salary, it is important to identify the ones that can be most helpful for entry-level personnel. Begin by networking with your closest friends and relatives; ask them for help in identifying possible sources of employment. Some companies pay a finder's fee for each new hire recommended by a current employee. You can also network by attending professional meetings and conferences, where you can meet people from areas and employers of interest to you. According to data from the U.S. Department of Labor, more than half of all job holders found their employment through person-to-person contacts. Keep expanding your professional contacts and do not expect instant results. As relationships progress, so will the payoffs.

Increasingly job seekers are finding jobs through Internet job sites, and companies are similarly using such sites, as well as their own sites, to identify potential job applicants. One of the best known is Monster.com. This site both provides job listings by occupation and geographic area and allows job seekers to post their resumes for use in searches by employers. Examples of other similar sites include BrassRing.com, CareerBuilder.com, AllJobSearch.com, and JobsOnLine.com. In addition, specialized job sites include those for public relations jobs (WorkinPR.com); for accounting, finance, and banking (CareerBank.com); and for engineering (Engineer500.com). Furthermore, college and university career centers operate job sites that post the resumes of their current students, and some also provide similar services for alumni. In addition, sites such as JobsourceNetwork.com feature career or job fairs and offer search capabilities for specific companies and locations. Finally, sites that specialize in internships include InternshipPrograms.com and Internships.com.

Once you have information about a specific job that appeals to you, investigate the company to determine what kind of environment it offers. As noted earlier, many companies have Web pages that list employment opportunities. In addition, their Web pages usually provide a wealth of information about their products, divisions, financial performance, and locations of facilities. They also often describe the process for applying for a job and to whom correspondence should be directed. A search of library resources, company annual reports, and Internet summaries of company news, such as the information provided on stock market Web sites, can tell you about the company's recent history. It is beneficial to know as much about an employer as you can before you attempt to apply for employment. Every employer has a community history and an image, and you should be familiar with these before you attempt to give a company a voice in your future.

Seek Employment

With your research in hand, you are now ready to make contact with a specific person at a specific place of employment. Mail a letter of application (see Exhibit 2.6) requesting a personal interview, and include your resume. Your **resume** should contain your personal data (name, address, and phone number); your employment goals; and relevant education, successes, and job experience. "It should be achievement- and action-oriented. . . . Don't overlook summer jobs, internships, volunteer activities and life experiences. . . . [E]mployers are looking for well-rounded individuals who will be able to

resume

an employment-related document submitted by the applicant, containing vital data such as the person's name, address, employment goals, and work-related education and experience

Exhibit 2.6

Letter of application to accompany the resume shown in Exhibit 2.7.

539 Tenth Avenue
Chicago, IL 60600
January 5, 2003

Mr. William R. Johnson
Human Resource Director
J & M Electronics
3872 South Wabash
Chicago, IL 60615

Dear Mr. Johnson:

Recently I learned, through the Wright College Placement Office, of the expansion of your company's sales operations and your intention to hire several managers for outside salespeople. If a position is currently available, I would appreciate your considering me for it.

I have had progressively more responsible and diverse experience in selling and customer service. I have sold your company's fine products at the retail level and currently manage a sales force of six people.

For your review I am enclosing my resume. I would appreciate a personal interview with you, at your earliest convenience, in order to discuss my application further.

Very truly yours,

John D. Jones

Enclosure [your resume]

succeed in various positions in an organization."[41] Use short phrases rather than long sentences: "Handled the finances for my fraternity"; "Raised productivity in my team by 45 percent in six weeks." In addition, it is almost mandatory that employees have some computer skills. List your computer skills, such as knowledge of database, spreadsheet, graphics, and word processing software, as well as any programming languages you know.

Try to keep your resume to one page, as shown in the sample in Exhibit 2.7. A good resume is short, neat, specific, focused, and composed in a consistent style. Capital letters, underlining, indentation, and italics should be used sparingly and the same way throughout. Remember that the person who receives your letter will probably spend less than a minute reading it.

The use of the Internet to seek employment is growing in popularity. As noted earlier, local, regional, and national professional associations, as well as governmental agencies, list both job offerings and personal resumes. Your college or university may maintain an Internet listing of student resumes. It may also subscribe to an Internet service that lists student resumes from many colleges and universities. Employers can search these sources using key words to find sets of job applicants who meet their specific needs.

The job interview. The employment interview is your chance to sell yourself and the employer's chance to sell you on a job and an environment. You can prepare for the interview by (1) reviewing your research, (2) dressing appropriately, and (3) rehearsing your answers to often-asked questions such as the following:

1. Why have you picked our company?
2. Why did you leave your last job?
3. What are your career expectations?
4. What salary and benefits do you require?
5. What are your personal goals for the next year? Three years? Five years?
6. What team and team-building experiences have you had?
7. What are your strongest points? Your weaknesses?
8. What specific kind of work would you like to do?
9. What psychological rewards do you seek through work?
10. Would you object to moving if your job were to require it?

You should have clearly thought out answers to these questions before you take the interview. When you are stating a weakness, let the interviewer know what you are doing about it. Another question you might encounter is to describe how you handled a difficult issue in the past, such as a mistake or a conflict with a coworker. If the interviewer asks you for your salary expectations, ask the employer what the job pays. Emphasize that you are interested in other things besides money, such as satisfaction and a chance to get your start in a promising career with a fine company.

John D. Jones
539 Tenth Avenue
Chicago, IL 60600
(312) 555-1345
E-mail: jdjones@thornet.com

Job Objective:	To manage salespeople in the electronics field at the wholesale level.
Education:	Two-year degree in marketing from Wright College, City Colleges of Chicago, 2002.
Work Experience:	Manager, retail sales staff, Electronics Venture, Northbrook store, 2001 to present.
	Retail sales in consumer electronics, Sears, Golf Mill store, 2000–2001.
Accomplishments:	Won "Best Salesperson Award" for my department 2000, 2001 at Sears, Golf Mill.
	Employee of the Month at Electronics Venture, May 2001.
	Youngest supervisor of retail sales department in Electronics Venture's history.
Skills:	Access, Word, Excel, fluent in Spanish.
References:	Furnished on request.

You in turn need to find out as much about the job and the employer as you can during your interview. Before you say yes or no to any job offer, you should have the answers to the following questions:

1. What has been the company's recent growth record?
2. What is its reputation, as a local employer, with the people in its community?
3. How do employees who have been laid off describe the company?[42]
4. Does it offer career tracks or promote from within?

5. What are its major products and markets and its long-term plans for growth?

6. What have been its greatest successes recently?

7. What is your future boss like as a person?

8. Is your boss likely to remain your boss after you begin employment with the firm?[43]

9. How does your boss act during a crisis or emergency?[44]

10. What, specifically, will be your working conditions in the job being offered?

11. What new challenges and opportunities will the job offer you?

You may be asked to interview with more than one person, or you may be asked questions by a group of people. This is especially likely if you are seeking a team member or team facilitator position. Teams often have a say in, or even the ultimate authority to hire, their members, facilitators, and leaders. (This chapter's *Supervising Teams* feature asks you to assess your abilities as a team member.) You should expect to be asked to solve problems that team leaders, members, and facilitators face and to deal with them quickly. Expect open questions that call for you to explain your thinking.

Various surveys show that the most common mistakes made by job candidates during interviews are as follows:

- Failing to research the company
- Failing to project enthusiasm for or commitment to one's career
- Failing to project strengths and skills
- Exaggerating or lying about one's qualifications and capabilities
- Presenting a poor personal appearance
- Being unclear about one's career goals and aspirations
- Failing to list and describe in detail one's specific achievements

Finally, be ready to relate specific anecdotes and experiences that illustrate skills you have acquired and lessons you have learned about such things as the value of customer service or the importance of quality. When possible, place a dollar value on any savings you made possible for an employer. Real-world examples stick with an interviewer and separate you from other applicants.[45] Norman Maskin, a senior human resources representative, provides the following insights:

> Relatively few people are in the mode of really trying to stress their accomplishments. . . . Our interview process is based on achievements, and some candidates struggle with that. . . . We're interested in a person's ability to learn, teamwork orientation and leadership ability. We want to know about circumstances in which candidates found themselves, what they did, and what the results of their actions were. . . . We want to know the whole story—the steps he took to achieve an outcome.[46]

Your job offer. If the job meets your approval in the following areas, you should probably accept it:[47]

- Does the company think as you do (are the employees your kind of people)?
- Do you like the people you have met and what you have seen of the work environment?
- Is this a high-profile job (one where you will be noticed)?
- Would you be willing to stay for at least several years?
- Are the pay and benefits what you want?

Before you accept a job offer, find out whether the salary is competitive. Specific salary information is often not readily available for comparison purposes. While you may be a bit uncomfortable in doing so, you will need to talk to fellow students and placement personnel in order to obtain enough data points to evaluate the competitiveness of an offer. Students sometimes accept job offers without doing their homework, only to find out later that the salary is lower than the market rate. Bear in mind that your experience and educational specialization will affect your value to the employer. Accordingly, you should take such differences into consideration when comparing salaries to those of fellow classmates.

Assess Your Situation Periodically

Every few months, look closely at your job situation. Ask yourself the following questions:

- Have my expectations become reality?
- Is this the job I thought it would be?
- Do I know where I am on a career path?
- Are the promises made to me being kept?
- Am I keeping the promises I made?

After your first two performance appraisals, you should know how your boss thinks and what she is looking for in your performance. Whatever your situation, commit yourself to your job for a minimum of one full year. This commitment gives you time to earn most benefits, to understand the company's niche and future plans, and to assess your future prospects adequately. It also offers the employer a return on the investment made in you; if you quit before this payback occurs, you are placing any referral and your reputation in jeopardy.

The time will come when you need to change jobs. The change may be necessary to your professional growth, or you may wish to move into a more appealing career. You know it is time to move on when doors are closed to you, you hate going to work each day, and your best efforts go unrewarded. But do not quit your job until you find another. It is better to bargain with a potential employer from a position of employment than from one of unemployment.

CAREER STAGES

Most of us find ourselves making several job and career changes before we find a true commitment for our lives. We will usually pass through several distinct stages during this search. Exhibit 2.8 summarizes these stages and the need for support that occurs with each stage.

The organizational entry stage includes getting a job, taking on job responsibilities, and learning to live with a boss. It is often stressful when organizational reality conflicts with our expectations. In the second stage, early career, we decide on whether to specialize or become a generalist. We also develop mastery of our jobs at the same time that we experience family and work conflict. During the middle career phase we take on more responsibility and develop a broader perspective of the organization. We also often experience mid-life crises as we realize that we are running out of time. By late career, we are more concerned with mentoring our successors, coping with reduced power, and planning for retirement.

You begin a career at the organizational entry stage. As you reach the midcareer stage, you will share what you have already mastered with newer members of the firm.

Professional Ethics

ethics

a discipline dealing with the rightness and wrongness of human conduct in society

Ethics is a discipline focused on the rightness and wrongness of human conduct in society in light of specific sets of circumstances. Managers must take ethics into consideration when contemplating actions that will affect others. Before taking an action, the ethical manager will think about the circumstances surrounding the intended action: his or her objectives, possible means available to achieve them, motives for taking the action, and its possible consequences. Our moral and ethical thinking is affected by our personal values and by our experiences. The ethical person will do his best to refrain from taking actions that will be harmful to others. Ethical perspectives—to act to provide the greatest good for the greatest number, to do unto others as you would have them do unto you, and to respect the individual rights of others—also provide ethical guidelines.

Ethics helps individuals and groups determine the most beneficial and the least harmful actions to take. All of us must, on occasion, decide whether to take actions that have negative consequences for some people

Common career phases. **Exhibit** **2.8**

CAREER PHASE	SELECTED WORK-RELATED NEEDS	NEEDS FOR SUPPORT
Organizational Entry (Ages 18–25)	Finding a job and employing organization Accepting responsibility Interacting with a boss	Dealing with organizational reality Dealing with unused potential
Early (Ages 25–40)	Developing increased technical competency Deciding on a specialist or generalist track Gaining visibility Mastering the organization	Having a mentor Managing work–family conflict Pressures of rivalry and competition
Middle (Ages 40–55)	Adopting a broader perspective Dealing with greater responsibility Continued skill development for specialists	Coping with mid-life crisis Dealing with the realization that one is running out of time Frustrations of a career plateau
Late (Ages 55+)	Dealing with reduced power and responsibility Maintaining self-esteem Contributing as a mentor	Preparation for retirement Coping with biases against older individuals

Sources: Adapted from Douglas T. Hall, *Careers in Organizations,* Santa Monica, CA: Goodyear Publishing Company, Inc., 1976; Edgar H. Schein, *Career Dynamics: Matching Individual and Organizational Needs,* Reading, MA: Addison-Wesley Publishing Company, 1978; Jeffrey H. Greenhaus, *Career Management,* Chicago: Dryden Press, 1987; and D. T. Hall and M. A. Morgan, "Career Development and Planning," in W. C. Hammer and Frank L. Schmidt, Eds., *Contemporary Problems in Personnel,* revised edition, Chicago: St. Clair Press, 1977.

and groups while they actually help others—an ethical dilemma. When a government taxes one group to help another, some people are harmed to benefit others. When a business decides to stop manufacturing one item to produce a more profitable one, some employees and suppliers are hurt, whereas others benefit.

Many professionals—including lawyers, doctors, and accountants—and many corporations have stated codes of ethics, which their members are expected to live up to or incur some penalty. Such codes create boundaries around individuals' freedom to act. The decisions that supervisors must make each day have to be considered in terms of some kind of ethical test or code. If they are not, serious personal and legal problems can and will arise for both the supervisor and the employer.

Many pressures in business environments make for difficult ethical decisions, and employees sometimes use these pressures as excuses to justify unethical behavior. One type of excuse is to pass responsibility on to a

SUPERVISORS AND ETHICS

One of the requirements of an ethics course for second-year MBA students at the University of Maryland is a trip to a prison, where they meet some of the school's graduates who, prior to their incarceration, appeared to be models of success. One, a lawyer who obtained a master's degree from the university and served on its board of visitors, had been a lobbyist earning $1 million per year. He is serving a 30-month sentence for fraud after he conspired with a legislator in a scheme involving a phony bill that was designed to panic people into seeking lobbying from his firm.

Another wealthy graduate who had obtained an accounting degree from Maryland was the president of the state's board of public accounting. He had run afoul of the law as the CEO of a property management firm when he fraudulently shifted money between buildings being managed for the Department of Housing and Urban Development and buildings that he owned. Another graduate, who was convicted of embezzlement, had been a pillar of the community; he had served on the board of the United Way and been president of an anti-crime group.

Because of such lapses in the conduct of highly educated and talented people, companies are beginning to place greater emphasis on ethics. For example, an ethics professor at Colorado State University states that compliance or ethics officers are employed by 75 percent of the 1,000 largest companies in the United States.

Source: James Cox, "Inmates Teach MBA Students Ethics," *USA.Com Today* (May 23, 2001), website: www.usatoday.com/money/bcouthu.htm.

supervisor who told the employee to do something unethical. Since the pressures to comply with supervisors are high, taking individual responsibility is a challenge for many employees. Indeed, the Milgram studies at Yale University during the 1960s and 1970s, in which subjects made decisions to administer potentially lethal electrical shocks, indicate that people will do terrible things to others solely because someone with authority directed them to do so. This excuse could apply to all directed behaviors, regardless of how reprehensible, but the underlying truth is that in the final analysis it is up to the employee to accept personal responsibility for her behavior. A second type of excuse is that everybody else is engaging in the same behavior, although such perceptions are seldom correct. While research has revealed that individuals are often strongly influenced by comparisons with others when looking for guidance in ambiguous situations, doing as the Romans do while in Rome does not excuse unethical behavior.

A third type of excuse involves situations in which individuals fail to fulfill ethical obligations to act by claiming that the problem is not their concern.[48] This excuse often fails to withstand close scrutiny when we apply the following guideline: "We cannot always count on others to do the right thing, and there will be times when we ought to be involved, even if it is inconvenient, time-consuming, or puts our jobs—or our lives—on the line." A final type of excuse is that behaviors that would not be tolerated in our personal lives, such as deception and bluffing, are permissible in business. Again, this type of excuse fails when we apply the idea that morality in business cannot rest on different principles from those that apply in everyday morality.[49]

For most managerial positions, no clearly defined codes of conduct exist to provide exact guidance for behavior. Consequently, supervisors who do not have a well-formed conscience or who lack a model for thinking ethically are liable to make unethical decisions that result in serious negative consequences for themselves, their employers, and others.

The collapse of Enron exemplifies the terrible consequences that occur when business leaders and others fail to adhere to fundamental ethical standards. In less than 12 months, shareholders saw the value of their stock drop from over $80 per share to less than one dollar when the firm declared bankruptcy. Thousands of employees lost their jobs as well as their retirement savings as the value of the Enron stock in their 401(k) accounts plummeted. Companies that dealt with Enron were left with tens of millions of dollars in losses. The firm's auditing firm, Arthur Anderson, which was also tainted by conflicts of interest, found itself in the unenviable position of having to defend why it failed to detect Enron's bad accounting and how Enron's accounting practices hid massive losses and grossly overstated earnings. The credibility of financial analysts reached rock bottom as their ratings advised investors to buy Enron's stock until just days before Enron's bankruptcy. In addition, politicians of both parties were tainted by their acceptance of large campaign contributions and the effects these contributions may have had on their failure to enact regulatory reforms that could have prevented some of Enron's practices.[50]

The scandal revealed ethical lapses at the highest levels of Enron's leadership as executives enriched themselves to the tune of tens of millions of dollars at the expense of shareholders through lucrative options and financial arrangements that posed severe conflicts of interest. As investigators closed in, documents were shredded and executives called before Congressional investigative committees exercised their Fifth Amendment rights against self-incrimination and refused to testify. Even the organizational culture of Enron appears to have contributed to unethical conduct as the company's "rank and yank" performance evaluation system, which quickly forced out employees who fell in the bottom 20 percentile, placed tremendous pressure on employees to achieve results regardless of the means by which results were obtained.[51]

Authors Solomon and Hanson offer the following guidelines for contemplating the ethical implications of intended actions:[52]

- Consider other people's well-being, including the well-being of non-participants.
- Think as a member of the business community and not as an isolated individual.
- Obey the law, but do not depend solely on it for ethical guidance.
- Think of yourself and your company as part of society.

- Obey moral rules.
- Think objectively.
- Ask the question, "What sort of person would do such a thing?"
- Respect the customs of others, but not at the expense of your own ethics.

Here is another series of questions that you can use to explore the ethical implications of intended actions:[53]

- Is it legal? Will I be violating either civil law or company policy?
- Is it balanced? Is it fair to all concerned in the short term as well as the long term? Does it promote win–win relationships?
- How will it make me feel about myself? Will it make me proud?
- Would I feel good if my decision were published in a newspaper?
- Would I feel good if my family knew about it?

One final question: Does one party make a needless gain at another's expense? For example, keeping too much change from a cashier at the checkout counter means that the keeper wins at the checker's expense. This is usually a certain sign that the action (keeping too much change) is unethical. As a supervisor, you have not only ethical concerns but legal ones as well. You are charged to act both ethically and lawfully. Just refraining from doing things that are illegal is not enough. It may be legal to fire a person you do not like for that reason alone. But is it ethical to do so? What may be the consequences to you, to your associates, and to your company if you do so?

Wetherill Associates, a small company of 480 employees, provides us with an illustration of the fact that high standards of conduct are not inconsistent with high profitability. The company has high standards of conduct, and its recent return on equity was 33 percent. The following provides an example of the company's ethical standards: "So seriously is righteousness taken that the firm refuses to make sales targets. That way employees won't be tempted to lie if they fall behind."[54] Another example of the company's application of ethics is provided by the following: "Recently a new salesman proudly announced: 'Wow! I came up with a whopper to get that customer off my back.' His office mates were not amused. They made him call the customer back and tell the truth."[55] This last example indicates that supervisors are not alone in their desire for ethical conduct. When employees believe in the ethics of the organization, they also help their supervisors enforce standards of ethical conduct.

Your reputation is far too precious to waste on hasty, ill-thought-out decisions that fail to consider both the law and ethics. Times will come when you are asked to act in a way that you believe is immoral or unethical. What will you say to a boss who makes such a request of you? Are you prepared to cover up for a derelict employee? Once you are caught in a lie, your integrity is gone, and it is almost impossible to retrieve. Without personal codes of conduct and values we will fight to defend, our own actions and the actions of others will compromise our integrity. It is better to leave an environment that is unethical than to remain and become so ourselves. This text's remaining chapters contain additional insights on ethics.

Instant Replay

1. You can expect to have several jobs and several careers in your working years.
2. Education, both in and outside college classrooms, is a supervisor's best defense against obsolescence.
3. The more formal education a person has, the greater his or her employability, promotability, and earnings become (on average).
4. Planning for personal advancement includes efforts aimed at determining strengths and weaknesses and at building a program for removing weaknesses.
5. Your career is largely in your hands and must be planned.
6. A supervisor must apply ethical guidelines in order to survive with integrity.

Questions for Class Discussion

1. Can you define this chapter's key terms?
2. How can you avoid personal obsolescence?
3. What are the steps this text recommends to help you plan for your own advancement?
4. What are the steps this text recommends to help you plan your career?
5. Why do you think it is important for each person to have a personal method for thinking ethically?

Incident

Purpose: To help you determine your personal ethics.

Your task: Answer honestly the following statements; think about your answers, and decide if you need to think about anything further.

Agree   Disagree

◯   ◯   1. I like to make decisions while considering their effects on others.

◯   ◯   2. If an action I intend to take is legal, I feel it will also be ethical.

Agree   Disagree

◯   ◯   3. If I am not certain about the ethical implications of my actions, I like to talk them over with others.

◯   ◯   4. If my decision will result in a personal gain at someone else's expense, I believe it is unethical.

◯   ◯   5. When I am asked to engage in an action that I believe is wrong, I let others know about it.

◯   ◯   6. If I take an action and then feel bad about it, I believe I have probably committed an unethical act.

◯   ◯   7. When I consider the fact that I am part of a community, I am starting to think ethically.

◯   ◯   8. When I am faced with a decision that has nothing but negative consequences, I try to choose the alternative that has the least serious negative consequences.

CASE PROBLEM 2.1   *Terry's Promotion Dilemma*

Terry has been working four to five hours each weekday night at the distribution center of a parcel delivery service. His job involves sorting and loading packages on trucks for delivery to customers. The work is hard and it is often very hot when he is working in the back of the trucks. However, the loaders and drivers are represented by a union, and wages are good for a part-time job. During the days he attends a local community college, and he will complete his associate's degree in business in two months. Terry has been trying to decide what to do after the next two months.

Last week, Phil Gordon, the manager of the distribution center, called Terry into his office to talk about a promotion. His performance ratings had been good, and his immediate supervisor recommended him for promotion to crew leader. Phil explained that Terry would be a crew leader responsible for five or six other loaders and that he would work 25 hours a week at a wage rate about 50 percent higher than his present wage. Phil said, "If you take the job you'll gain experience as a supervisor and you will still have time to take classes at the branch campus of the state university. And after you finish your bachelor's degree the company will put you in the management training program. After two more years they will assign you as an assistant manager of one of the parcel distribution centers." Terry estimates that while working nights in the new job, he can complete his bachelor's degree during days in about two and a half years.

Last week while at school, Terry talked to his friend Kevin about the company's offer. Kevin, who is taking only two or three courses a year at the community college, works as a camera operator at a local television station. Kevin said, "Is that what you are going to college for? To load trucks? Why don't you come to work at the television station with me? The money is good and the work is interesting. You would be amazed at the things that we get to see. You can learn how to operate a camera fairly quickly and the wage rate is about double the amount you'll earn with the promotion."

Terry thought about Kevin's comment, and it was true that his present job involved nothing more than a strong back and a willingness to work nights. He hadn't been able to apply any of the things he was studying in his classes, and the crew leader job would be little different. He knew what crew leaders did, but he didn't know what was entailed in the job of an assistant manager or distribution center manager. He thought that he might like to be a supervisor or a manager, but he was not sure whether the parcel delivery business was one in which he wanted a career.

On the other hand, Terry remembered the difficulties his sister Sharon had encountered in obtaining a job after she graduated from a university. Sharon sort of drifted through college and had changed her major several times. After five years, she had graduated with a degree in political science. It was only after she had graduated that she began looking for a job. Eventually, she obtained a job as a probation officer working with the state department of corrections. Unfortunately, she was not happy with the type of work she was doing.

Questions

1. What career stage is Terry in now?
2. Do you think Terry is ready to accept his employer's offer? Why or why not?
3. What advice do you have for Terry?
4. What differences exist between Terry, Kevin, and Sharon?
5. Which of the three is in danger of becoming obsolete? Why or why not?

The Delayed Job Search   CASE PROBLEM 2.2

It was the first week of August when Natalie walked in the door of the college's career counseling and placement office and asked to see Sue Hartman, the placement director. Sue knew that Natalie must be having trouble finding a job. Sue asked Natalie when she had started her job search. Natalie told her that she had waited until two weeks after graduation. Natalie said, "I was so focused on making good grades that there wasn't time to spend looking for a job. I graduated with a 3.4 GPA in my B.S. with a major in marketing. Aren't high grades supposed to count for something? Why am I having so much trouble getting a job?"

Sue asked Natalie what kinds of jobs were of interest to her. Natalie said that she was fairly flexible except that she did not want to work in retailing and that she did not want to start out in sales. Sue then asked Natalie what she had done in her job search, and Natalie said that she had sent her resume to about 200 companies. Natalie said that she had managed to obtain only two interviews, neither of which had resulted in a job. Natalie said, "I have tried to call for interviews at several of these companies. Why won't these people in the human resources departments take the time to talk to me over the phone? I know that I can perform well in the jobs they have."

After inquiring some more about Natalie's job search, Sue asked whether she had done any networking with friends and relatives about finding a job. Natalie said that because she did not have any friends or relatives in human resource management she thought networking was a waste of time.

Sue then asked to see Natalie's resume. Although it was typed neatly and had some of the information needed, there was no list of school activities and no description of internships or summer and part-time job experience. Natalie said, "I wasn't active in organizations such as the student chapter of the American Marketing Association. I was too busy with my sorority and spent a lot of time studying. Besides, I went to a couple of meetings of these organizations and they seemed like a waste of time. I did have a couple of part-time jobs on campus and I worked in several jobs as a waitress. What should I list for activities? And what should I list for skills?"

Questions

1. What do you think about Natalie's job search efforts?
2. How can Sue help Natalie?
3. What do you think Sue should tell Natalie?
4. What course of action would you outline for Natalie?
5. Do you know anyone who approached a job search like Natalie? What was the outcome?

References

1. *Business Week*. "The New World of Work" (October 17, 1994): 76–77, 80–81, 84–90.

2. Gilley, K. Matthew, Greer, Charles R., and Rasheed, Abdul. "Human Resource Outsourcing and Organizational Performance in Manufacturing Firms," *Journal of Business Research* (conditionally accepted).

3. Hall, Gene; Rosenthal, Jim; and Wade, Judy. "How to Make Reengineering Really Work," *Harvard Business Review* (November–December 1993): 119–131.

4. Stewart, Thomas A. "Reengineering: The Hot New Managing Tool," *Fortune* (August 2, 1993): 41–48.

5. *Chicago Tribune*. "Execs, Workers Clash Over Redefined Jobs" (October 11, 1994): sect. 3, 3.

6. *Business Week*. "The New World of Work."

7. Katz, Michael, ed. *Technology Forecast*. Menlo Park, CA: Price Waterhouse World Firm Services BV Inc., 1997.

8. Edmondson, Brad. "Work Slowdown," *American Demographics* (March 1996): 4–7.

9. Armas, Genaro C. "One-Parent Families on Rise Worldwide: Many Nations Face Questions of Support," *Pittsburgh Post-Gazette* (November 25, 2001): A-4. Eskenazi, Stuart. "One-Parent Homes Are on the Increase: Helping Them to Cope Is Critical," *The Seattle Times* (August 12, 2001): B1.

10. Olian, Judy. "Life after Layoff: Road May Be Rocky," *Pittsburgh Post-Gazette* (October 23, 2001): E-3. Koretz, Gene. "The Power of Power

Couples: They Give Cities a Competitive Edge," *Business Week* (July 19, 1999): 20.

11. Ilg, Randy E., and Clinton, Angela. "Strong Job Growth Continues, Unemployment Declines in 1997," *Monthly Labor Review* (February 1998): 48–68.

12. Edmondson, Brad. "Work Slowdown."

13. Kleiman, Carol. "Human Resources Gets Outside Help," *Chicago Tribune* (September 25, 1994): sect. 8, 1.

14. Peters, Tom. *Thriving on Chaos*. New York: Alfred A. Knopf (1987): 299–301, 329.

15. Ibid.

16. Kiechel III, Walter. "A Manager's Career in the New Economy," *Fortune* (April 4, 1994): 68–72.

17. Katz, Michael, ed. *Technology Forecast*: 23.

18. Richman, Louis. "The New Work Force Builds Itself," *Fortune* (June 27, 1994): 68–70, 74, 76.

19. Ibid.

20. *Business Week*. "The New World of Work."

21. Bridges, William. "The End of the Job," *Fortune* (September 19, 1994): 62–64, 68, 72.

22. U. S. Census Bureau. *Statistical Abstract of the United States, 2001*. Washington, D.C.: www.census.gov/statab/www/, 2002.

23. National Association of Colleges and Employers, "Salary Offers Rose for Class of 2001, But Finding a Job Got Harder" (September 17, 2001), Web page: www.naceweb.org/press/display.asp?year=2001&prid=111. National Association of Colleges and Employers, "New Salary Report Shows Many New College Graduates Continue to Command Top Dollar" (July 11, 2001), Web page: www.naceweb.org/press/display.asp?year=2001&prid=109.

24. Thurow, Lester. *The Future of Capitalism*. New York: William Morrow and Company Inc., 1996.

25. Edmondson, Brad. "Work Slowdown."

26. U. S. Census Bureau. "USA Statistics in Brief" (April 12, 2001), website: www.census.gov/statab/www/part3.html.

27. Kleiman, Carol. "Praise Works Wonders in Improving Morale," *Chicago Tribune* (September 21, 1994): sect. 6, 5.

28. Hall, Douglas T. "Protean Careers of the 21st Century," *Academy of Management Executive* (November 1996): 10.

29. Hall. "Protean Careers": 8.

30. Caggiano, Christopher. "What Do Workers Want?" *Inc.* (November 1992): 101.

31. Gatewood, Robert D., and Feild, Hubert S. *Human Resource Selection*, 4th ed. Fort Worth, TX: Dryden Press, 1998.

32. Website: www.careerleader.com (November 29, 2001).

33. Hanson, Cynthia. "What It Takes to Succeed: Advice from 10 Top Achievers," *Chicago Tribune* (September 11, 1994): sect. 6, 9.

34. Szabo, Joan. "Offering Careers, Not Just Jobs," *Nation's Business* (June 1994): 56.

35. Schor, Juliet. "Debunking the Small-Business Myth: Big Firms Still Dominate," *Working Woman* (November 1994): 16.

36. Hall. "Protean Careers": 8.

37. Griffith, Carolyn. "Building a Resilient Work Force," *Training* (January 1998): 54–58.

38. Epperheimer, John. "Benchmarking Career Management," *HR Focus* (November 1997): 9–10.

39. Griffith. "Building a Resilient Work Force": 54.

40. U. S. Department of Labor, Bureau of Labor Statistics. Website excerpts from *1998–99 Occupational Outlook Handbook*, 1998; Employment Projections, 1998.

41. Furore, Kathleen. "Accentuate the Positive," *Chicago Tribune* (July 3, 1994): sect. 19: 2.

42. Kennedy, Marilyn M. "Starting Before Day One, *Across the Board* 36(8) (September 1999): 69–70.

43. Ibid.

44. Shellenbarger, Sue. "Spotting Bad Bosses Before You Get Stuck Working for Them," *The Wall Street Journal* (September 29, 1999): B4.

45. Furore. "Accentuate."

46. Ibid.

47. Spencer, Jim. "Analyzing a Job," *Chicago Tribune* (March 18, 1987): 2.

48. Gibson, Devin. "Excuses, Excuses: Moral Slippage in the Workplace," *Business Horizons* 43(6) (2000): 65–72.

49. Ibid.: 70.

50. Serwer, Andy. "Dirty Rotten Numbers," *Fortune* (February 18, 2002): 74–81. "The Lessons From Enron," *Economist* (February 9, 2002): 9–10. Zellner, Wendy. "A Hero—and a Smoking Gun Letter," *Business Week* (January 28, 2002):

34–35. Sloan, Allan; Naughton, Keith; Peraino, Kevin; Ehrenfeld, Temma; and Foote, Donna. "Who Killed Enron?" *Newsweek* (January 21, 2002): 18–24. Gesalman, Anne Belli; Peraino, Kevin; Brant, Martha; and Lipper, Tamara. "The Gambler Who Blew It All," *Newsweek* (February 4, 2002): 18–24.

51. Ibid.

52. Solomon, Robert C., and Hanson, Kristine, R. *It's Good Business*. New York: Athenaeum, 1985.

53. Blanchard, Kenneth, and Peale, Norman Vincent. *The Power of Ethical Management.* New York: William Morrow (1988): 27.

54. Burger, Katrina. "Righteousness Pays," *Forbes* (September 22, 1997): 200.

55. Ibid.

MANAGEMENT CONCEPTS

Objectives

After reading and discussing this chapter, you should be able to do the following:

1. Define this chapter's key terms.
2. List and define the essential elements of any formal organization.
3. List and explain the steps involved in delegating.
4. Identify the levels in the management hierarchy and describe the activities of each.
5. Identify the major functions performed by all managers.
6. Explain the steps in this chapter's decision-making model.
7. Specify the kinds of decisions that require your group's involvement.
8. Explain the value to supervisors of a daily planner and a time log.

Introduction

Everyone needs to be able to take charge of his own life. Each of us must be able to plan our daily activities, control our use of resources, interact with others to get jobs done, and accumulate the resources necessary to accomplish tasks and to reach our goals. Management is both an art and the application of known, proven principles. Through the practice of management, we become better people. All that we share together in this book will help make you a better manager of your finances, social relationships, family, career, and advancement in life.

Defining Management

Management is an activity that uses the functions of planning, organizing, directing, and controlling to apply human, informational, and material

management
the process of planning, organizing, directing, and controlling human, material, and informational resources for the purposes of setting and achieving stated goals; also, a team of people making up an organization's hierarchy

resources for the purposes of achieving stated goals. The word *management* may also refer to a team of people that oversees the activities of an enterprise in order to get its tasks and goals accomplished with and through others.

A **manager** is a member of a team of decision makers that gets things done with and through others by carrying out management functions or activities. Managers occupy positions of trust and power in a formal organization such as a business.

The term **formal organization** is used here to make a distinction from other types of organizations—for example, social or informal organizations. A formal organization is one created by design and rational plan, such as a business or industrial union. A formal organization is basically the coming together of people for the accomplishment of stated purposes, in which the tasks to be performed are identified and divided among the participants and a framework for decisions and control is established.

The essential elements of any formal organization are as follows:

1. A clear understanding about stated purposes and goals
2. A division of labor among specialists
3. A rational organization or design
4. A hierarchy of authority and accountability

Each of these elements is related to the others. We will look at each separately in order to understand all of them better.

STATED PURPOSES AND GOALS

Every business enterprise is established to make a profit. How each organization intends to make its profit is stated in its **mission**. The mission states in words—backed up with both plans and actions—the organization's central and common purpose, its reason for existing. The mission acts as a unifying force, giving all personnel a common purpose and direction. To create a proper mission, top management needs two things: a recognition of what the organization does best—its core competencies—and a continuing focus on the future. According to professors and consultants Gary Hamel and C. K. Prahalad, "Our experience suggests that to develop a . . . distinctive point of view about the future, a senior management team must be willing to spend 20% to 50% of its time over a period of months. It must then be willing to continually revisit that point of view, elaborating and adjusting it as the future unfolds."[1] Both individuals and teams in all parts of the organization need their own missions as well. "A common, meaningful purpose sets the tone and gives teams direction, momentum, and commitment. A real team needs both a common purpose and specific goals."[2] The following example from Bristol-Myers Squibb provides a good example of a mission statement:

> The Mission of Bristol-Myers Squibb is to extend and enhance human life by providing the highest-quality health and personal care products.[3]

manager
a member of an organization's hierarchy who is paid to make decisions; one who gets things done with and through others, through the execution of the basic management functions

formal organization
an enterprise that has clearly stated goals, a division of labor among specialists, a rational design, and a hierarchy of authority and accountability

mission
the expression in words—backed up with both plans and actions—of the organization's central and common purpose, its reason for existing

Norfolk Southern's mission statement provides an example that recognizes the importance of employees in the company's success:

> Norfolk Southern's mission is to enhance the value of our stockholders' investment over time by providing quality freight transportation services and undertaking any other related businesses in which our resources, particularly our people, give the company an advantage.[4]

Each day, an organization's managers must ask two basic questions: What is our business? What should it be? As time progresses and circumstances change, an organization's managers must continually reassess where they are and where they want to be.

In addition to the mission statement, chief executives also continually communicate their *vision* of where the company will go, what it will be in the future, and how it will change. Professor John Kotter provides the following explanation of **vision**:

> *Vision* refers to a picture of the future with some implicit or explicit commentary on why people should strive to create that future. . . . [A] good vision serves three important purposes. First, by clarifying the general direction for change, by saying the corporate equivalent of "we need to be south of here in a few years instead [of] where we are today," it simplifies hundreds or thousands of more detailed decisions. Second, it motivates people to take action in the right direction, even if the initial steps are personally painful. Third, it helps coordinate the actions of different people, even thousands and thousands of individuals, in a remarkably fast and efficient way.[5]

vision
a statement of what kind of company the organization wants to be in the future and the direction in which it will go

The organization's chief executive establishes a vision for the entire organization. Top management sets specific goals and plans for its achievement. With these in mind, managers of each division and department establish for themselves both short- and long-range goals and plans for achieving the vision. Insight into the vision of the top management team at Intel is provided in the following communication:

> Our initiatives will focus on all major segments of the computing market. We will continue to deliver high-performance microprocessors that drive high-end PCs and workstations at competitive prices and will still offer powerful microprocessors for the basic PC market segment. Servers based on Intel microprocessors will provide the storage and connection points to corporate networks and the booming Internet. Our networking and communications products will deliver easier manageability and greater band-width for a richer experience on the network.[6]

A DIVISION OF LABOR AMONG SPECIALISTS

We live in a world of specialists. In government, the professions, and business, men and women are asked to choose areas in which to specialize so that they can become experts in their fields. Any formal organization is set up to make good use of the special talents and abilities of its people. Each

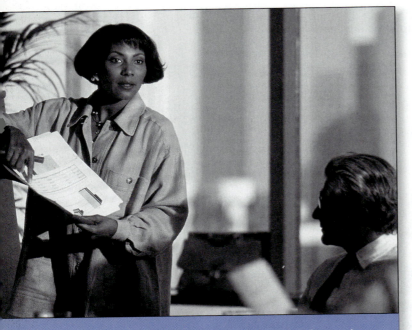

A team of supervisors meets to discuss goals for their firm. After agreeing on their overall goals, each supervisor must decide how her own workers will be utilized to meet the goals.

person is assigned tasks that he is best qualified to complete through the application of specialized knowledge. Through the coordination and teaming of these specialists—each of whom contributes a part to the whole job—the entire work of the organization is planned and then carried out.

In many of today's businesses, specialization is achieved by grouping individual experts into cross-functional teams that take ownership of a project or a process—such as designing a new product or improving customer billing. Highly educated specialists or knowledge workers, such as software engineers and market research experts, routinely work in cross-functional teams with other knowledge workers. The goals of cross-functional teams are to save time and money through both incremental and radical change.

A RATIONAL ORGANIZATION OR DESIGN

Formal business organizations must have designs that properly facilitate their missions and activities. Organizational designs or structures must be tailored to provide for the proper flow of needed information to all individuals, teams, and units. They must allow for the coordination and oversight of essential operations. Above all, they must be flexible enough to meet new challenges and opportunities. Chapter 4 has more to say about organizing.

A HIERARCHY OF AUTHORITY AND ACCOUNTABILITY

hierarchy
the group of people picked to staff an organization's positions of formal authority—its management position authority

The term **hierarchy** refers to the number of levels in an organization and the group of managers who occupy those levels and make the necessary plans and decisions that allow it to function. These people constitute the organization's management team. From the chief executive to team facilitators and team leaders, they must plan, organize, direct, and control the many activities that have to take place if the organization's goals are to be reached.

authority
a person's right to give orders and instructions to others and to use organizational resources

Authority. **Authority** is the right to give orders and instructions to others and to use organizational resources. Every manager needs authority in order to mobilize resources required to accomplish tasks. Authority allows team facilitators and team leaders to make a decision or take action that affects

SUPERVISING TEAMS

Although teams offer the potential for high performance, they often do not reach their potential because they suffer from various team diseases. Some of the diseases that afflict teams include the following:

Collective Amnesia. This disease occurs when top executives implement teams in work situations where there is no compelling need for teamwork. For example, when employees individually perform their work and the group leader integrates their individual contributions, there is no need for teams or teamwork. Inappropriate implementations of teams sometime occur in situations where executives have uncritically decided to use teams without having a good understanding of their limitations and inefficiencies. Furthermore, even when there is a need for teams they sometimes fail because instead of real teams there are only employee work groups. Teams differ from groups in that their members hold each other accountable for performance.

Chronic Cantankerousness. With this disease team members face recurring quarrels within the team, cannot agree on even the smallest of details about how the team should function, and have at least one member who does not follow the rules. It the team proceeds without dealing with such issues these disagreements can escalate into full-blown conflict. A preventive measure for this disease is for the team to write up a set of responses that it will use when members break the rules. An example of this preventive approach involves writing the responses on cards, which are then played when each rule is broken.

Leadership Phobia. This disease results from the absence of leadership within the team. Prevention of this disease involves making sure that the team has members that can play three different roles: team designer, team midwife, and team coach. Each of these roles is critical in different phases of the team's evolution. Designers help ensure that teams are set up correctly with clear tasks, responsibilities, and reward systems. Midwives assist with the development of team goals and work procedures as the teams make progress toward deadlines. Coaches begin to apply their skills after teams have reached their performing phase and are most effective when used sparingly at break points, such as when new projects begin or at various milestone points.

Source: Mark Fischetti, "Team Doctors, Report to ER," *Fast Company* (February 1998): 170.

the organization and its associates. All managers have the authority of their offices or positions. This kind of authority is often called *positional* or *formal authority* because it resides in a job or position and is there to be used by the person who holds that job or position.

Formal or positional authority is usually described in a formal written document, called a *job description*, that outlines the specific duties that the position holder is expected to execute. Managers' job descriptions usually give them the right to assign work to subordinates or team members, to oversee the execution of work, to appraise subordinates' and team members' performances, to use various kinds of capital equipment, and to spend specific amounts of budgeted funds. As a supervisor, team facilitator, or team leader, you must act within the limits of your authority.

Giving instructions and having them carried out in a satisfactory way are two different things. Have you ever wondered why two managers with the same authority often get very different results? The essential difference between such managers is their ability to influence others.

power

the ability to influence others so that they respond favorably to orders and instructions

Power. **Power** is the ability to influence others so that they will respond favorably to the orders and instructions they receive. Two managers may have the same authority but not the same power over others. One may be effective and the other ineffective. Power may come from several sources. In general, power comes to a person through his or her position (formal job description), personality traits and character (attractiveness to others), knowledge and experience base (expertise), and relationships with other powerful people. Power that flows to a manager from the position held is called *legitimate* or *position power*. It consists of the right to punish and reward—sometimes called *coercive power*. Your attractiveness to others is the basis for friendship and professional relationships. It is usually referred to as your *charisma*. Your influence over others because of what you know and are capable of doing is called *expert power*. Finally, you have influence over others because they see you as a person who is well connected—a person with powerful associates. All sources of power are important to you if you want to be a truly effective manager. Authority alone is not enough. You must be the kind of person others respect and want to follow. Authority and power make a manager a leader—a person others willingly follow. Chapter 10 has more to say on leadership and power.

responsibility

the obligation each person with authority has to execute his duties to the best of his ability

Responsibility. **Responsibility** is the name given to each employee's obligation to execute all duties to the best of her ability. Because all employees have the authority of their job descriptions, they all have responsibility. The concept of responsibility tells us not only that we must perform our duties but also that we must do so in line with the instructions and limits we receive from above. Failure to do our best may bring punishment, denial of rewards, and separation from our job.

accountability

having to answer to someone for your performance or failure to perform to standards

Accountability. **Accountability** is having to answer to someone (your superior or teammates) for your actions or failure to act. Suppose you have a job description that assigns you the duty to prepare a monthly report on the output of your department. Administrative routine dictates that this report be delivered to your boss on the first day of each month. Your authority is in your job description. Your task is the report. Your responsibility is to do the report properly to the best of your ability and to deliver it to your boss by the start of each month. If you begin the report but fail to finish it by the due date, you will have to answer for that failure to your boss. You will have to give an accounting of your progress and accept the credit or the blame. All employees in any organization have duties and, therefore, authority, responsibility, and accountability.

WORKFORCE FLEXIBILITY

Although job descriptions provide a basis for authority, power, responsibility, and accountability, many organizations recognize that job descriptions can also limit the **flexibility** of their workforce. When employees rigidly adhere to their job descriptions by performing only those tasks they enumerate, the organization's performance declines. Organizations need flexibility because work flows are often uneven. Where there are light work flows for some tasks and heavy flows for others, supervisors need the flexibility to move employees where they can be fully utilized. When unions represent employees, greater emphasis is usually placed on performance of only those tasks outlined in the job description. This is because different wage rates are negotiated for the various jobs, and the union does not want the employer to be able to assign lower-paid workers to perform higher-wage jobs. In order to obtain greater flexibility, some companies have limited the number of different jobs and have made their job descriptions very broad. For example, Chaparral Steel, which has very high workforce productivity, has only two job descriptions for its factory jobs—production worker and maintenance worker. Many employees respond favorably to broader job descriptions when they are linked with greater responsibility and empowerment.

flexibility
the ability of members of a workforce to perform different tasks

Delegation

Delegation is the act of passing part of one's authority to another. Only people possessing authority over others, such as managers, team leaders, and team facilitators, can delegate. When you accept a duty through delegation from your boss, you accept new authority and the responsibility for it, and you agree to be held accountable for your performance of the new duty. When you as a supervisor delegate authority, you agree to be held accountable for your decision to delegate (the way you have chosen to handle your responsibility) and for the execution of the delegated duty by your subordinate. The act of delegation, therefore, creates a duality of both responsibility and accountability related to the same task or duty and its execution. If this were not so, any manager could pass a tough job to a subordinate and escape from it entirely, with no adverse consequences. But the concept of accountability tells us that delegation is simply the manner in which a manager has chosen to execute a task—the way the manager has chosen to handle responsibility for the task. Delegation does not eliminate the supervisor's need to justify the decision.

delegation
the act of passing formal authority by a manager to another

Consider this example. Suppose you are going away from your job next Tuesday for personal business. You have one task that must be executed during your absence, and you decide to delegate it to a subordinate. You take your day off. When you return, you discover that the task was not performed. Your boss will want to know why, and you will be asked to answer for the failure to execute the task. You, in turn, will want to know what went wrong and why. Both you and your subordinate are accountable for the ways in which you chose to handle responsibility for the same task. But you, as supervisor, shoulder the primary burden of accountability in the eyes of your boss.

WHY YOU MUST DELEGATE

Delegation is a tool that allows you to train team members and associates. By introducing your most capable subordinates to bits and pieces of your job, you prepare them for advancement. Unless you have a trained successor to fill your shoes, it will be very hard for you to get promoted. Your boss will not want to create a hole in the operation by letting you move up if it means leaving behind a leaderless group.

Second, by delegating, you can free yourself from time-consuming routines and other duties that might be better performed by subordinates. Until you create some free time for yourself, you will not be able to accept delegation from your boss. Like yourself, your boss wants to meet your need to grow by letting you experience greater responsibilities, thereby grooming you for promotion.

Third, delegating empowers your associates. For the majority of people, empowerment adds interest, challenges, and opportunities for growth. By empowering your people, you are making a clear statement about your trust and faith in them. You are helping improve your operations by tapping into your associates' uniqueness and creativity. You also will be aiding their search for job satisfaction by giving them more say and control over their activities and decisions.

Some managers fear the delegation process because they do not want to give up any of their authority. They fear that a subordinate cannot do the job as well as they can or that they will lose control over the execution of their authority once it is in the hands of another. They may fear that once subordinates know their bosses' jobs, they will be a threat to their job security. But fearing the act of delegation is no excuse for not doing it. You must recognize that you will have no other choice. Your boss expects it, subordinates may demand it, and you will be away from your job at times because of illness and vacations. Keep

Part of delegating is making sure your subordinate understands the job. Although you may delegate the work, you are still accountable for its outcome. Decision making is an important time to involve subordinates. Ask for their opinions. When explaining the decision, take the time to explain why the decision was made.

SUPERVISORS AND ETHICS

Juanita Alvarez is a relatively new supervisor at the management consulting firm of Furman & Associates. She was promoted because of her expertise in computer programming—she was considered the best of seven department members—and is now overseeing the work of six former coworkers.

Juanita prides herself on her continuing efforts to stay current in her field, believing that maintaining her expertise is the best way to influence her associates. She is reluctant to delegate high-profile jobs to her associates because she fears they will not be able to do them as well as she can. She is afraid of the consequences that can result from a job poorly done, especially on projects assigned by top management.

Her subordinates are all young, well trained (by Juanita's predecessor), and eager to grow in their fields. All are specialists to some extent, but most recognize that they need a wide variety of programming experiences in order to advance their pay and careers. When asked by her associates for a role in the tougher assignments, Juanita usually turns them down. When asked for assistance on a project, she prefers to give her associates only as much as she feels they need to complete a project.

What are the ethical issues for Juanita and her associates? If you were her boss, what advice would you have for her?

in mind that delegation frees you from any task that your subordinates can do, helps you identify the subordinates that you can depend on, and lets you spend more of your time on things that only you can do or that you do best. This chapter's *Supervisors and Ethics* box deals with delegation.

HOW TO DELEGATE

Four basic steps are involved in the decision to pass some of your authority to another person:

1. *Decide on the task(s), limits, and support to provide.* Spell out in as much detail as is necessary exactly what you want your associate to do, the limits that you are placing on the execution, and the support you have to offer.

2. *Choose the subordinate.* The person you choose may be one in need of the experience, one who is capable of doing the job already, or one who wants exposure to the task. You may want to choose more than one person so that several people get the training or exposure. This will give your people more flexibility and will allow you to be less dependent on any one person.

3. *Give the assignment.* Let the person know what you want done, the limits, and the support. Explain why the task is necessary and the kind of results you expect. Ask the subordinate for feedback. Find out if

there are any misunderstandings. When the subordinate can restate the assignment and limits accurately and knows how to perform the task(s), you are ready for step four.

4. *Stay in touch*. Even so-called simple tasks are not so simple when an inexperienced person has to perform them. Keep track of the person's progress by checking with her periodically. You may ask for periodic reports of progress if the task is to stretch over several days or weeks.

When the task is accomplished, let the subordinate know how you evaluate her efforts. You may want to reward the person with praise and point out what went well and what could be improved.

WHAT YOU DO NOT WANT TO DELEGATE

In general, you should not delegate a task that you do not understand or know how to perform. If you do, you will be unable to offer any support when trouble arises, and you may not be able to evaluate the results fairly. As a supervisor, you should not delegate the authority to punish or reward. People work to please those who have this authority. Delegation should never strip you of these rights and duties. Finally, if you have no one who is capable of taking on the task, you must either prepare someone to take it or keep the task for yourself.

The Management Hierarchy

We have concluded that, among other things, managers make up a team of decision-makers charged with operating the formal organization of a business. You will recall that one of the characteristics of a formal organization is that it has a hierarchy of authority and accountability. We will now examine this hierarchy. The simple pyramid shown in Exhibit 3.1 is a basic model for a management hierarchy. In most organizations, this pyramid is divided into three levels: top management, middle management, and the supervisory or operating level of management.

As a result of downsizing during the 1980s and 1990s, the pyramid model has changed. Most organizations have a relatively smaller proportion of middle managers than in the past. In addition, in many organizations the pyramid has become flatter with fewer levels between top management and rank-and-file employees. Because computer information systems now handle much of the information dissemination and coordination performed by middle managers in the past, there is less need for such managers. In addition, in order to reduce labor costs many organizations have adopted lean staffing approaches in which smaller numbers of first-level managers each supervise a larger number of employees. This involves granting managers a broader **span of control**. We will discuss span of control in more detail in Chapter 4.

Steeper pyramids are typical of the traditional structure often found in large organizations in stable industries with stable competitive environments, and in government. Companies in less stable industries and environments

span of control
the number of employees over which a manager has direct supervisory control

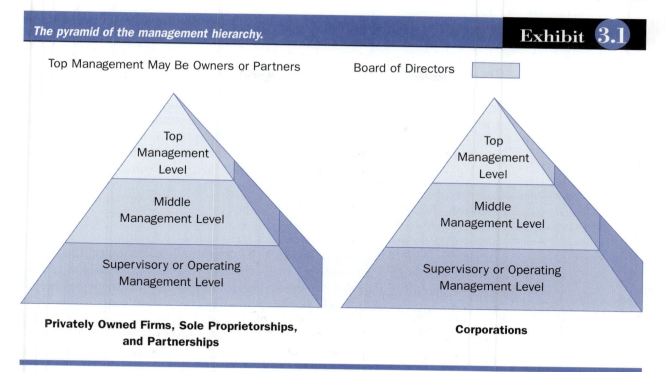

Exhibit 3.1

The pyramid of the management hierarchy.

Top Management May Be Owners or Partners Board of Directors

Top Management Level

Middle Management Level

Supervisory or Operating Management Level

Privately Owned Firms, Sole Proprietorships, and Partnerships

Top Management Level

Middle Management Level

Supervisory or Operating Management Level

Corporations

will need a different, more flexible structure. We discuss organizational structures in detail in Chapter 4.

Many sole proprietorships and partnerships have only one or two managers who must, out of necessity, direct more than one specialized area. Most sole proprietorships and partnerships are extremely small in terms of the number of people they employ. Their operations are usually not complex enough to require more than one or two levels of management. The examination that follows uses a business corporation as its model. Much of the discussion applies to sole proprietorships and partnerships as well. An exception is that a corporation is the only type of business organization to have a board of directors. The board of directors is outside and above the corporate management pyramid, and is represented graphically above the second pyramid in Exhibit 3.1.

THE TOP MANAGEMENT LEVEL

Occupying only the small topmost portion of the pyramid, the **top management** level is the location of the chief executive or president and immediate subordinates (vice-presidents or their equivalents). In a sole proprietorship, the owner is usually the chief executive. In a partnership, the role of the chief executive is usually shared between or among the managing partners, each of whom concentrates on his own specialty.

In a corporation, the top management is made up of the officers of the company: a president, one or more vice-presidents, a treasurer, and a secre-

top management
the uppermost part of the management hierarchy, containing the positions of the chief executive and immediate subordinates

tary. Any two (or more) offices may be held by the same person, except the offices of secretary and president.

The chief executive's role. The chief executive officer (CEO) has several major responsibilities. She must articulate a mission, vision, core values (quality, integrity, and employee participation, for example), and guiding principles for the entire company. This chapter's *Supervisors and Quality* box highlights the mission, values, and guiding principles of the pharmaceutical company Pfizer Inc. These become part of Pfizer's corporate climate and must govern the actions of its team leaders, facilitators, and associates.

The CEO must also sense when change is called for and initiate the change. This was the case when Dick Brown came to EDS. Shortly after he became CEO of EDS Brown "quickly laid off one-third of the sales force and cut $2 billion in annual costs, yet has landed $89 billion in multi-year contracts, double the previous sum."[7] By continually focusing on the future and reexamining organizational strengths and weaknesses, the CEO is able to develop and initiate major organizational objectives and strategies (grow the company by adding new products, increasing market share). The chief executive is the one manager who must be able to observe and comprehend the entire operation. Like the captain of a ship, the chief executive is responsible for his own decisions and is accountable for those of all other managers. Sometimes the CEO has to make very tough decisions, such as closing down a plant or laying off employees. Many companies also have a president, who takes on major responsibilities for the organization. The president reports directly to the CEO. In addition, companies in which operational responsibilities are significant may have a chief operating officer (COO) who reports directly to the CEO or president.

The vice-president's role. Vice-presidents are the immediate subordinates of the chief executive. In a typical bureaucratic–mechanistic organization, they are charged with the overall operation of the company's functional areas:

- Marketing—sales and all sales-connected activities
- Production—manufacturing and procurement of raw materials
- Finance—managing the company's financial resources and access to capital
- Human resource management—staffing, development, compensation, and employee relations duties

Other business activities, such as engineering, research and development, and procurement or supply chain management, may fall under one or another of these headings, or they may be led by their own specialized members of top management. Further, many companies combine this functional approach with other approaches such as organizing by product or customer groupings. In many companies, vice-presidents are in charge of strategic business units (SBUs). These are often autonomous and organized around product groups or customers served. Such is the case at IBM, Ford, and Xerox. The vice-presidents

SUPERVISORS AND QUALITY

Pfizer Inc.'s Vision

Mission

We will become the world's most valued company to patients, customers, colleagues, investors, business partners, and the communities where we work and live.

Purpose

We dedicate ourselves to humanity's quest for longer, healthier, happier lives through innovation in pharmaceutical, consumer, and animal health products.

Values

To achieve our Purpose and Mission, we affirm our values of Integrity, Leadership, Innovation, Performance, Teamwork, Customer Focus, Respect for People and Community.

Source: Pfizer Inc. Internet site, 2002.

must plan, organize, direct, and control the general operation of their departments, units, or divisions. Their subordinates are usually middle managers.

THE MIDDLE MANAGEMENT LEVEL

Middle management occupies the middle area of the pyramid. The middle management level is the location of all managers below the rank of vice-president and above the operating level. Each functional area has many specific tasks to be performed. Exhibit 3.2 illustrates the hierarchy of a retailer with branch stores. The store's divisional merchandise and branch store managers are not specialists, but all of their subordinate managers are. Each must carry out the operation of a specific part of the store's activities. Like those of all managers, the middle manager's functions are to plan, direct, control, and organize.

middle management
the members of the hierarchy below the rank of top management but above the rank of supervisor

THE OPERATING MANAGEMENT LEVEL

Shown at the bottom of the management pyramid, the **operating management** level is the home for supervisors. Managers or supervisors direct the work of non-management **workers,** individually or in teams. If a manager directs the work of other managers, he does not belong on this level.

In many organizations the supervisor is evolving into a team leader or facilitator, aiding the efforts of the group she heads. Typically, both the leader and the facilitator assist teams by providing training and support to team members. A team leader may even rotate on a regular basis, allowing other members of the team to gain managerial experience. Pindar Set, a small company in the United Kingdom that typesets Yellow Page directories, is an outstanding example of a company that utilizes teams very effectively. The company's award-winning application of teams was prompted by pressures for shorter delivery times, desire for greater responsiveness to customers,

operating management
the level of the hierarchy that oversees the work of non-management employees (workers)

worker
any employee who is not a member of the management hierarchy

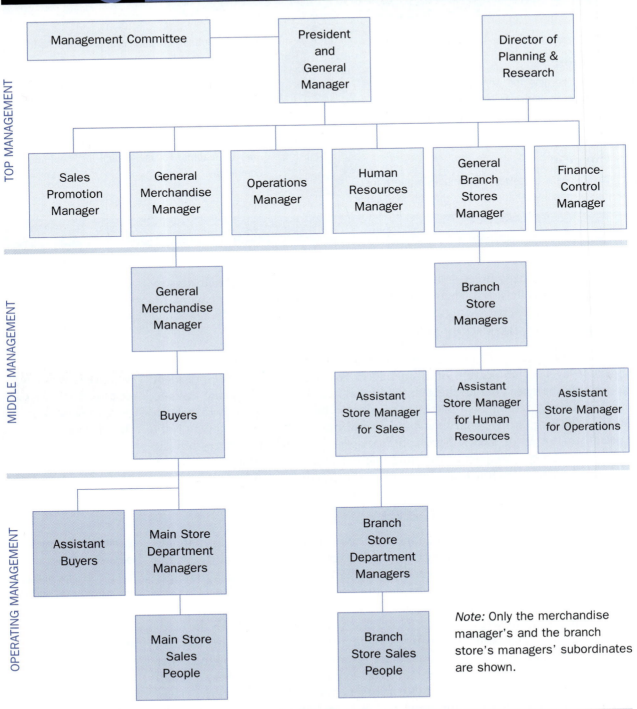

TOP MANAGEMENT

MIDDLE MANAGEMENT

OPERATING MANAGEMENT

Management Committee

President and General Manager

Director of Planning & Research

Sales Promotion Manager

General Merchandise Manager

Operations Manager

Human Resources Manager

General Branch Stores Manager

Finance-Control Manager

General Merchandise Manager

Branch Store Managers

Buyers

Assistant Store Manager for Sales

Assistant Store Manager for Human Resources

Assistant Store Manager for Operations

Assistant Buyers

Main Store Department Managers

Branch Store Department Managers

Main Store Sales People

Branch Store Sales People

Note: Only the merchandise manager's and the branch store's managers' subordinates are shown.

Source: Courtesy of the National Retail Merchants Association, New York, NY. (Slight modifications included.)

and tighter margins. The company's approach to teams and the role of team leaders is described as follows:

> The company set about training all its unskilled staff to do skilled jobs, phasing out unskilled text-inputting jobs completely. All the unskilled workers upgraded as planned, despite some initial wariness of the new accreditation process that was established to ensure consistent standards across the business. Remedial training was provided where necessary. Employees were also trained to follow a job through from start to finish, reducing the internal "pipeline" from 80 processes to one. And teamworking was introduced . . . This meant creating new team-leader roles. Previously senior operators had supervised work, but had still retained hands-on tasks. The company also recognized it needed a pool of new teamleaders to respond to future growth. Teamleaders were given more responsibility for financial operations and people management than before. They now run their sites as semi-autonomous businesses, with their own profit and loss accounts. This also required training and a team-leader programme was introduced.[8]

More will be said about team leaders and team facilitators throughout this text.

Exhibit 3.1 depicts only the management team. The majority of workers in an organization form the base of the pyramid, the group of people on whom managers depend to execute plans and to achieve goals. Exhibit 3.3 shows a more complete picture of a typical business corporation.

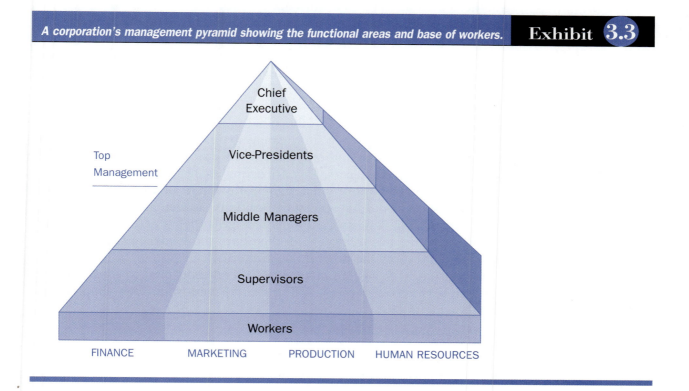

A corporation's management pyramid showing the functional areas and base of workers. **Exhibit 3.3**

Line and Staff Authority

line authority

a manager's right to give direct orders to subordinates and appraise, reward, and discipline those who receive those orders

Line authority allows its holder—a traditional manager, team leader, or team facilitator—to exercise direct supervision over his subordinates. Managers who have line authority can give direct orders to, appraise, reward, and discipline those who receive their orders.

The managers in the organization hierarchy who manage activities or departments that directly influence the success (profitability) of a business are called *line managers*. Their departments make direct contributions toward achieving the company's goals. Since line activities are identified in terms of the company's goals, the activities classified as line will differ with each organization. For example, a manufacturing company may limit line functions to production and marketing, whereas a department store, in which buying is a key element, will include the purchasing department and the sales department in its line activities.[9]

When an organization is small, all positions may be line roles; staff roles are added as the organization grows and as it becomes useful to devote specialists' time to assist the line members in doing their primary jobs.

staff authority

the right of staff managers to give advice and counsel to all other managers in an organization in the areas of their expertise

Staff authority, like line authority, is a kind of formal authority. It is distributed throughout the organization to various managers at any level who advise and assist other managers. Staff managers are specialists who supervise activities or departments that help others achieve the company's major goals. The staff managers' primary mission is to support all other managers who need their specialized knowledge.

The concept of staff is relevant only as applied to the relationships between managers. A manager is a staff manager if his job is to advise, counsel, assist, or provide service to another manager. You can tell if managers are staff or line managers by observing their relationships to the other managers. Since staff managers are linked to the top of an organization, they receive line authority also. If they have subordinates, they direct, appraise, and discipline those subordinates, just as any line manager does with her subordinates. When staff managers direct the work of their associates, they are using line authority. But when staff managers give advice or assistance to other managers, they are acting as staff managers.

Exhibit 3.4 is an abbreviated organization chart of a management hierarchy that shows both line and staff positions, as well as the relationships of authority. Note that staff and line managers appear at both the top and the middle of the hierarchy. The broken lines show advisory relationships. The solid lines show the flow of line authority.

Organization charts are just one of several tools used to show the part that each person or section plays in the entire enterprise. They should show the following things:

- Who reports to whom
- The flow of authority and accountability
- Formal positions of authority and their titles

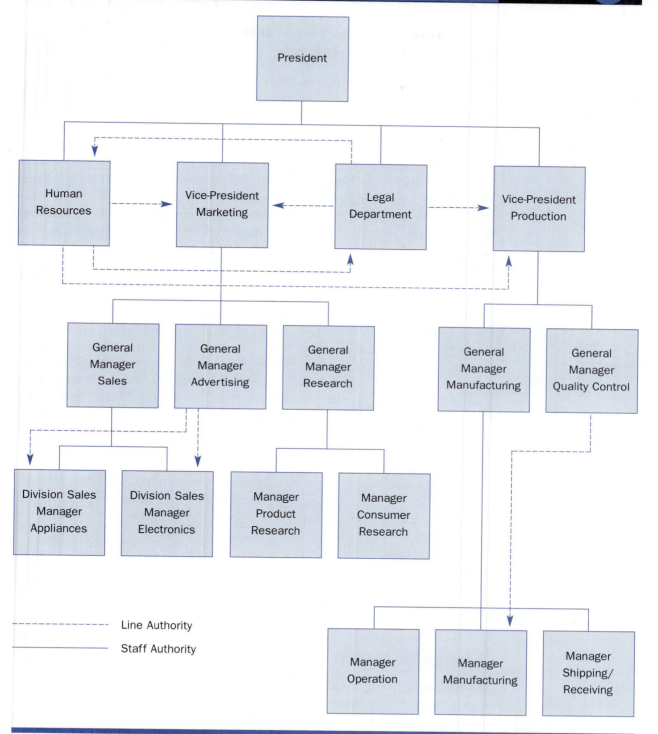

- Lines of communication
- Lines of promotion

Functional Authority

Functional authority is the right given to a manager of a department (usually a staff department) to make decisions that govern the operation of another department. Exhibit 3.5 illustrates the flow of functional authority from the staff managers to the other managers in an organization. The lines of functional authority indicate a measure of control by a staff manager over a line manager and her people and their activities.

The normal practice (where functional authority is not used) is for a line manager to have complete control over his area of responsibility and relative freedom to make his own decisions. Staff managers have been installed to help the line as well as other staff managers but usually only when called on to do so. Under this arrangement, a staff manager may never be consulted. Line managers must take full responsibility for their actions when acting on staff advice. After all, they could have ignored the advice of the staff manager.

For this and other reasons, many companies make use of the concept of functional authority. This concept holds that if a staff manager makes a decision about her functional area (such as marketing, finance, human resources, or legal affairs) that has application to the area of another manager, the manager of that other area is bound by the staff manager's decision. For example, the payroll department issues a directive stating that henceforth all payroll data from each department must be submitted electronically in a specific format by a certain date. If the managers throughout the business wish to get themselves and their people paid on time and in the correct amounts, they had better follow the directive.

Functional authority seems to subject a manager to the will of many bosses. But does it? Isn't a company merely removing many important, but nonessential, areas from a manager's concern in order to promote uniformity and efficiency? When many routine decisions about problem areas are made outside the department, each manager is freed of the responsibility for these matters. As a result, the manager has more time to devote to her specialized, essential tasks. The loss in autonomy is more than compensated for by an increase in efficiency and economy in the overall operation of the business.

The Manager's Functions

We will now briefly explore the four major functions of management. By major functions we mean the most important and time-consuming activities common to all managers. These functions consist of planning, organizing, directing, and controlling.

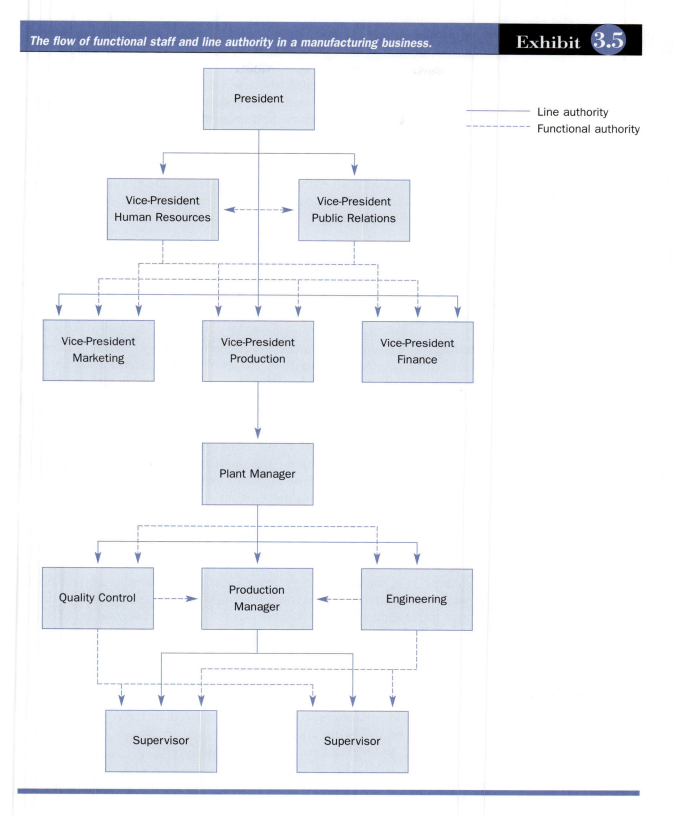

Line authority
---- Functional authority

President

Vice-President Human Resources ←---→ Vice-President Public Relations

Vice-President Marketing   Vice-President Production   Vice-President Finance

Plant Manager

Quality Control ---→ Production Manager ←--- Engineering

Supervisor   Supervisor

Planning. Planning is the first and most basic of the management functions. Through planning, managers attempt to prepare for and forecast future events. Planning involves the construction of programs for action designed to achieve stated goals through the use of people and other resources. Planning is also a part of the other functions of management: organizing, directing, and controlling. It is the first thing you must do, before executing any of these functions.

Organizing. The organizing function determines the tasks to be performed, the jobs or positions required to execute the tasks, and the resources needed to accomplish the organization's goals. Organizing is directly related to and dependent on planning.

Directing. The directing function includes the activities of overseeing, facilitating, coaching, training, evaluating, disciplining, rewarding, and staffing. Staffing is concerned with adding new talent to an organization, promoting or transferring people to new jobs and responsibilities, and separating people from the organization. Chapter 11 discusses the supervisor's staffing duties.

Controlling. The controlling function is concerned with preventing, identifying, and correcting deficiencies in all phases of an organization's operations. Through controlling, standards of performance are established, communicated to those affected by them, and used to measure the operation and performance of individuals and the entire organization.

These four functions apply to all managers, but each level of management spends different amounts of time performing each (see Exhibit 3.6). Although top management spends most of its time on planning, supervisors (operating management) spend most of their time on directing. Chapter 4 explores these functions in more detail from the supervisor's perspective.

Three other sets of activities are related to each of the four major management functions. First, it is impossible to consider any of the functions without recognizing the need to communicate. Communicating (the subject of Chapter 5) is the ability to get your ideas across to others by means of the spoken or written word. Second, it is impossible to carry out your duties without interacting with others. This fact tells us that a second set of activities is needed to coordinate what you do with others in your organization. By coordinating, teams and team members attempt to synchronize their activities with other groups and individuals. By working to maintain good relationships and through regular communication with subordinates, peers, and superiors, you promote cooperation and facilitate coordination. Along with being good communicators, supervisors need to have good interpersonal skills. The following comment about Jacques Nasser before he was forced out as CEO of Ford stresses this point.

> Jacques was less able to tolerate and overcome conflict at Ford Motor, where he was ousted last month as CEO. Mr. Nasser's sometimes abrasive and insular style

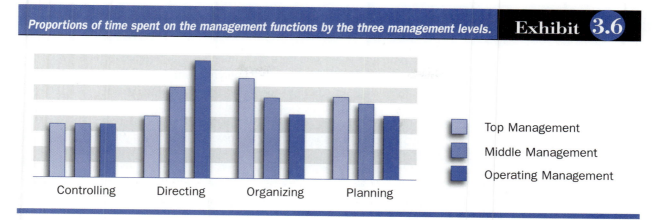

Proportions of time spent on the management functions by the three management levels. **Exhibit 3.6**

of management . . . alienated employees and dealers, whose support he sorely needed in his campaign to overhaul Ford's bureaucracy and lead the company through the crisis surrounding defective Firestone tires on Ford Explorers.[10]

Finally, decision making is part of every function as well. Chapter 4 examines coordinating and all four management functions in more detail.

Decision Making

You have been making decisions all of your life. You have already made many today. As a supervisor, team facilitator, and team leader, you are paid to make them to the best of your ability. As we have already seen, you have a responsibility to make them and are accountable for the results. A decision in its most essential form is a conclusion that you reach by making judgments. Most of us have a decision process, but we may never have put it in writing. It's simply there in our minds and serves us each time we try to answer questions and make a decision. The approach described below can help you make difficult decisions rationally. This approach will remove a great deal of uncertainty and will give you a method for problem solving that will help you avoid making many bad or mediocre decisions.

A RATIONAL MODEL

The rational model in Exhibit 3.7 has six steps. None of them is really new to you, but all are essential. They simply put what you have been doing all of your life into a systematic framework that will help you make better decisions. We will work through the sequence of steps by using an example.

Define the problem. A problem exists when a situation is not as it should be. Symptoms are usually the first signs of a problem. Your toaster keeps burning your bread or your television's channels are all snowy.

Exhibit 3.7   *Steps in the rational decision-making process.*

1. *Define the problem.* The effort here is to define the difference between what is and what should be. Avoid the pitfall of defining symptoms. Dig beneath the symptoms to make sure you have identified the underlying cause.

2. *Identify your restraints.* Your restraints are such resources as time, money, and talent. Anything that limits your ability to solve a problem as you would like is a restraint.

3. *List your alternatives.* Alternatives are possible solutions. List as many as you can without regard for their good and bad points. Involve the ideas of others if they can be of assistance.

4. *Evaluate your alternatives.* Go back to step two and consider each alternative with your restraints in mind. List the advantages and disadvantages of each course of action.

5. *Decide on the best alternative(s).* Pick one or a combination of two or more that have the fewest serious disadvantages and the most important advantages.

6. *Implement the decision and follow up.* This is the action step that tries out your solution. Learn from the application, and be prepared to fall back to another solution if the one you have chosen does not give positive results.

Ed, the supervisor of data control, has noticed several analysts sitting idle. All should be working. What is the problem? Lazy workers? Local area network (LAN) is down? Without further investigation, Ed will not be certain. He first talks with the operators to discover the source of their idleness. His investigation tells him that a necessary set of figures from the accounting department has not arrived on schedule. What is the problem now? Missing data from accounting? Ed calls the accounting supervisor and discovers that the data were sent over two hours ago. Ed conducts a search and his secretary discovers the data attached to an e-mail message on her computer buried among other messages that arrived later.

Ed started with symptoms and moved to an investigation that led him to the discovery that vital information was getting lost in his own department on his own desk. This discovery tells Ed that his problem is related to the way in which information from outside his office is received and filed. Ed now frames the problem as a question: "How can information flowing to us from the outside be properly handled to avoid losing it?" Having defined his problem, Ed is now ready to proceed to step two.

Identify your restraints. Restraints are limiting factors that affect your efforts to make a decision. Restraints generally fall under several headings, such as *who, what, when,* and *where.* Who will be involved in the decision? Is it a decision that needs the group's support and input? If so, the group must be involved in the process. "Who" also asks us to consider who is affected by the problem and whether or not the affected people have a role to play in solving it. What is involved? What resources may be affected and may have to be committed in order to implement the decision? Money, time, and other resources will surely be involved in some way. When must a solution be delivered? By what date must a decision be made? Finally, where is the solution needed and best implemented?

Ed has decided that he must make the decision and that the others will simply be informed about it after they give him their ideas about handling the problem. Ed has further decided that few resources will be needed. Time is the primary resource he and others must expend to make a decision. Ed thinks that the "when" is best answered with "as soon as possible." He assigns the highest priority to dealing with the problem. Ed is now ready for step three.

List your alternatives. Alternatives are the courses of action that may solve your problem. Lists of alternatives should be developed without criticism, as they are offered. The merits and drawbacks can be dealt with in step four. In developing the list, be as creative as you can, and seek counsel from others. All of your alternatives should represent possible ways to correct the difficulties you are experiencing.

Ed consulted his workforce, and over a period of several hours put together a list of four solutions:

(a) Do little since this is the first time the problem has occurred. Ed should merely instruct his secretary to check her e-mail more often.

(b) Have all incoming work e-mailed directly to Ed.

(c) In Ed's absence, have all work e-mailed to his secretary.

(d) Have all data sent directly by e-mail to the analysts with information copies to Ed and his secretary.

Ed is now ready to evaluate his alternatives.

Evaluate your alternatives. This step asks you to look critically at the list of alternatives and to focus on their relative merits and disadvantages. In doing so, you must consider the restraints you have identified in step two. For some merits and disadvantages, you may wish to assign a relative point value to give either a higher or a lower importance to each.

Ed evaluates his first alternative as follows. The problem is new but could recur. It resulted from the fact that through habit, people have always e-mailed their items to Ed's secretary, not to Ed. She checks her e-mail regularly, but there are blocks of time when she is out of the office. For this reason, the first alternative, (a), is rejected.

Ed realizes that the alternatives require cooperation from people in other departments if they are to work. The last alternative, (d), is advantageous in that neither he nor his secretary need be present for the system to work.

However, its major disadvantage is that all analysts would have to check their e-mail regularly for their work instead of getting it directly from Ed as in the past. The major disadvantage to the second and third alternatives, (b) and (c), is that a person must be present. If Ed and his secretary were absent, the current problem might then recur. Ed is now ready to move to step five.

Decide on the best alternative(s). At this step, the best alternative or combination of alternatives is chosen. The relative merits and disadvantages of each are considered, and the alternative offering the fewest serious disadvantages and the most merits is chosen. Keep in mind that after deciding and implementing, you may find that the problem still persists or that a new problem has arisen. For this reason, you may want to set up a contingency plan and be ready to implement other methods.

Ed has decided to go with his fourth alternative, (d). It overcomes what Ed feels is the biggest disadvantage of the other two alternatives—that the physical presence of either himself or his secretary is required for them to work. Even though he will have to get outsiders to change their routing procedures, Ed feels that they will cooperate with little opposition. It will take little adjustment on their part.

Implement the decision and follow up. Without implementation, a decision helps no one. Everyone involved in the decision must be informed in advance of his individual roles and responsibilities. People must know what is expected of them and what is new and different. In addition, they must be committed to their roles if the solution is to work. After the decision is enacted, the results must be monitored.

Ed has contacted the heads of the various departments that supply his work and has been assured that the new procedure will be made known. Ed has instructed his analysts to check their e-mail for data files. Both Ed and his secretary will make it a habit to check on the analysts' receipt of e-mail data attachments. Ed sets the time when the new procedure will be implemented and arranges to monitor the results.

COMMON ELEMENTS IN DECISION MAKING

Most supervisors are new to formal decision making. Before you become a member of management's team, you have specific goals and orders, resources provided by your boss, and a problem solver represented by the boss. You may or may not be consulted when decisions have to be made. But once you become a manager, you soon realize the need to consult with others before, during, and after the period when a decision is made.

Most decisions share the following common elements:[11]

- A situation that demands action
- Time pressures created by things getting steadily worse
- Incomplete information

- Some uncertainties that force you to take some risk
- The likelihood of costly consequences if your decision is wrong
- The likelihood of benefits from an effective decision
- The existence of at least two alternatives

Given these elements, you have to gather what input you can from whatever sources are available in the time allotted for your decision. Keep in mind that others may have been down this path before you. Your boss, your peers, and your associates may have the experience and ideas that you lack. Use whatever help you can to avoid as many traps as possible. Your aim is to make the best decision you can given the resources and restraints that exist.

SHARING THE DECISION PROCESS

You should involve members of your work group in a decision if they have valuable input to give, if they are going to have to implement it, or if their commitment to the decision is essential to make it work. Probably the easiest way for a supervisor to get in trouble is to make decisions without the input of people who will be affected by the decision or who have expertise on the matter. This is a common mistake that causes a great deal of grief for both supervisors and subordinates. Exhibit 3.8 offers some additional insights into when others should be involved in decisions. Note that the exhibit makes no recommendation to involve others when the problem stems from the behavior of a person and only that person's corrective action will solve the problem. Chapter 9 looks in detail at decision making with groups.

When to involve others in decisions that you have to make.	**Exhibit 3.8**

Involve others in the decision under the following conditions:

1. There is time for discussion and analysis; the decision does not have to be made immediately.

2. The decision affects the personal or business lives of the employees; their input and feedback will help you make a mutually acceptable decision.

3. Collective discussion would yield a better solution than simply mulling it over on your own.

4. The group should share responsibility for the decision with no individual being blamed if the decision produces an unsatisfactory result.

5. Others have information needed to solve the problem or their expertise will help you solve the problem.

6. Implementation requires group commitment and effort.

7. The members of the group need to develop their decision-making skills.

DECISIONS ABOUT VALUING DIVERSITY

Most of us work in a culturally diverse workforce. To prosper in such a workforce, you must prepare yourself by valuing your own uniqueness and the diversity in others. Supervisors, managers, and the organizations in which they work value diversity when they treat everyone fairly and with dignity, and utilize their skills and abilities to the fullest extent. Diversity is given more than lip service when people from all races and genders feel accepted and are included at all levels in the organization's social and managerial hierarchy. Such treatment of all people who work in the organization satisfies ethical, moral, and performance rationales. In regard to the performance rationale, it is helpful to find evidence showing where diversity efforts have led to increased revenue or decreased costs.[12]

Here are five guidelines to help you with your efforts to value diversity:

1. *Know yourself and your own cultural background.* Identify any preconceived notions you hold about others, where these notions came from, and how they affect your interactions with others who are different from yourself.

2. *Work to identify negative stereotypes*—inflexible sets of beliefs about groups of people, usually obtained through the hearsay of others rather than gained through your own experiences. Once they are identified, work to release yourself from the constraints these beliefs place on your thinking and interactions with others.

3. *Get to know your associates at work as individuals.* Learn from them about their cultures—their values, customs, and traditions. Attend workshops and seminars on cultural diversity. Read all that you can on the topic. Note the differences as well as the similarities between your culture and those of others with whom you work.

4. *Avoid being judgmental.* Approach each person as an individual, and seek an understanding of what that person values and why. If you are uncertain about how to approach someone, ask her how best to do so. In everyday matters, the new golden rule is simply—treat people as they want to be treated. As a team facilitator and team leader, your job is to get the most from all of your associates and team members.

5. *Remember the Pygmalion effect.* The essence of the Pygmalion effect (which is discussed in more detail in Chapter 6) is that the subconscious performance expectations a manager has for subordinates will often affect the subordinates' performance. Accordingly, when supervisors have expectations that their subordinates will perform at a high level, the supervisors are likely to treat their people in a manner that facilitates high performance. Conversely, when supervisors have expectations that their subordinates will not perform well, they will probably treat them in a manner that causes poorer performance.[13] In the context of diversity some supervisors may have performance expectations of new subordinates based solely on race or gender.

Because such supervisors may feel that a female or minority employee will not perform as well as others, it is important for them to develop and periodically conduct a mental review of profiles of individuals from the stereotyped group who are outstanding performers.

Managing Your Time

We all have the same amount of time in each day. We vary only in how we use that time. Studies have indicated that most of us waste time on the job in a variety of ways. We may make or accept personal phone calls. We may regularly stretch breaks by several minutes. We may fail to plan our work, reacting to things as they come, without giving the work to be done a timetable or priority. If you often find yourself working late, taking work home, and rushing to meet deadlines, you have a time management problem. People who use time well have enough time for their tasks, are able to train subordinates and delegate, can take on additional duties, and have time for themselves. Using time well gives us a sense of pride, whereas wasting it gives us a sense of guilt and frustration.

A good way to improve your use of time is to start keeping a record of how you use your time at present. Record your use of time at work by stopping each hour (or after each task is completed) to record how much time you just spent and on what you spent it. This record will let you know very quickly at the end of each day where you wasted time and where you used it productively.

KEEPING A TIME LOG

A daily time log provides an easy way for you to list the activities you perform each day, to record the time each activity took, and to classify each activity as regular, recurring, or one that is unexpected or unusual. The regular activities routinely make up a part of each working day: evaluating associates, planning your work schedule, attending planned-for meetings, and preparing regular reports. The unexpected activities include unscheduled visitors (drop-ins), unexpected telephone calls, and crises—problems that could not have been foreseen. After a few days, some interesting patterns will emerge. You will have a clear understanding of how you are using time, and you will then be ready to start planning in a realistic way for using it more efficiently.

CATEGORIZING WORK

By dividing your work into categories, you can more effectively execute tasks and assign priorities to them. For example, consider the pile of work on your desk each morning. There is probably work left over from preceding days; the mail; e-mail; memos and work generated by others; and various notes that you have left for yourself. Divide this work into three categories: read (then file or discard), to be delegated, and must do. Each task on your desk will fall into one of these categories. Memos sent to keep you informed belong in the first category. Work you want others to act on belongs to the second. Work only you can do belongs to the third. For the work to be assigned to others, determine a due date based on when it must be completed. Assess your third category from two points of view: how much time each task will take and by what date it must be completed. Then block out the time you will need on your calendar, working ahead as time allows and planning early completions where possible.

ELIMINATING INTERRUPTIONS

Your time log will list the unnecessary interruptions that have taken place. Consider what to do about them. For most supervisors, unexpected phone calls are among the most frequent sources of interruption, second only to unplanned-for visitors who drop by to shoot the breeze or seek your assistance. If you have a secretary, let him screen your calls. Calls can be classified in three ways: deal with now, I'll get back to you, or leave your message. Ask people to leave brief memos in writing or on your voice mail or e-mail instead of using the telephone. Drop-in visitors can be asked, courteously, to book an appointment, at a mutually acceptable time and place, so that you will have enough time to deal with their concerns. Social visits can wait for breaks and lunch.

USING DAILY PLANNERS, PERSONAL INFORMATION MANAGERS, AND PERSONAL DATA ASSISTANTS

The use of a daily planner can help you start getting your time at work under control. In addition to paper planners, various computer software packages can also help you manage your time. Pocket-sized computers called personal information managers (PIMs), personal data assistants (PDAs), and smart phones (combinations of cellular phones and PIMs) can perform a variety of tasks, such as automatic scheduling of appointments, maintaining address lists, sorting lists, establishing priorities, displaying task lists, providing access to e-mail and stock market reports, storing telephone numbers, and printing calendars.[14] They can also remind you of duties with a beep or an on-screen display. Some also offer e-mail, Internet features, and phone dialers. Others combine PIM features with more complex contact managers, such as those used by sales people. Smart phones, which have enhanced memory and applications, can allow users to obtain information from corporate databases and synchronize with applications such as Microsoft Outlook and Lotus Notes, in addition to their other features.[15] Examples of operating system and application software for these devices include Palm OS,[16] Microsoft Windows CE,[17] Microsoft Outlook,[18] Lotus Organizer,[19] and Wisdom OS.[20] Reviews of electronic devices and software products are published in computer magazines such as *PC Magazine, Computer Shopper, Macworld,* and *MacWeek,* as well as on these magazines' Internet sites. By keeping your time log and reviewing it each day, you will learn how realistic your planning of time and activities has been and how you can make it more accurate in the future. It won't be too long before you are blocking out time in your head, as well as on paper, and making better use of it. Then you can eliminate the log and rely on your choice of planning tools to manage your time.

USING SPARE TIME

Use your previously unproductive time productively. You can employ time spent traveling to and from work in your car or on a train to catch up on essential, work-related tapes or reading. You can make notes with a notepad and pen, on a portable tape recorder, or with a PIM. Some computerized devices allow you to write on a handheld computer and may offer a pager, address book, fax, and phone. Capture and store your good ideas as they occur to you. When you anticipate having to wait for an appointment, take work with you. By doing these things, you will become more accomplished and will look good to others as well as to yourself. These suggestions will also help you preserve sufficient time for your life away from work and achieve a balance between work and family life. An anthropologist studying work behavior in the Silicon Valley has reported an example of poor balance. In a play on words, he reported the actions of an executive who "quit his family to spend more time at work."[21]

Instant Replay

1. Management is an activity that uses the functions of planning, organizing, directing, and controlling human and material resources for the purpose of achieving stated goals.

2. A manager is a member of a team of paid decision-makers who gets things done with and through others by executing the four management functions. Managers occupy positions of formal authority in an organization.

3. Managers work for formal organizations, which have clearly stated purposes and goals, a division of labor among specialists, a rational structure or design, and a clearly defined hierarchy of authority and accountability.

4. Power flows to a person from two sources: the job she holds and the skills, experience, and personality she possesses.

5. The management hierarchy consists of three levels inherent in most businesses: top, middle, and supervisory or operating.

6. Staff managers may exercise functional authority over many other managers.

7. Managing time is as important to a supervisor as managing a career. Time, like other resources, must be used effectively and efficiently.

Questions for Class Discussion

1. Can you define this chapter's key terms?
2. What are the essential elements of any formal organization and the definition of each element?
3. What are the steps you should take to delegate?
4. What are the levels of the management hierarchy and the activities performed by each level?
5. What are the major functions performed by all managers?
6. What are the steps in this chapter's decision-making model, and what happens in each step?
7. In general, what kinds of decisions require the involvement of your subordinates?
8. How can you use a time log and a daily planner to help you improve your use of time?

Incident

Purpose: To assess the need for diversity training in your organization.

Your task: Take the following quiz by agreeing or disagreeing, based on your own experiences in your organization, with each statement:

Agree   Disagree

⚪   ⚪   1. There is a high turnover among diverse groups.

⚪   ⚪   2. There is a lack of diversity at all levels of the company's hierarchy.

⚪   ⚪   3. Some associates feel isolated from their peers because of their diversity.

⚪   ⚪   4. One or more diverse groups are the subject of inappropriate behavior and ridicule.

⚪   ⚪   5. Diversity is not reflected in those with powerful positions.

⚪   ⚪   6. The company seems to be demanding that diverse individuals conform to the dominant culture.

⚪   ⚪   7. No programs currently exist that encourage people to share and celebrate their differences.

⚪   ⚪   8. There have been/are charges of discrimination.

CASE PROBLEM 3.1   *Welcome to KVM*

Carl Foster looked forward to starting his new job as director of the headquarters systems support department at KVM Snack Foods. He was excited about the job because he had finally made it into the managerial ranks. In his previous company, REM Investments, he had been in a similar department but had been unable to advance beyond a senior systems coordinator position. He told several of his old colleagues about getting the job and said, "I think I'm going to like being a director at KVM. I'll have a big office, a reserved parking place, and my own secretary."

On his first day as manager at KVM, Carl met with his boss, Wes Taylor, the vice-president for Corporate Information Services. One of the things Wes told him was, "We need to place more emphasis on introducing leading-edge systems here. Your predecessor, Betty Carson, did a good job, but we need to move forward. I like the ideas you talked about during your interview for introducing new technology. You're going to have to get the word out that our priorities have shifted a bit."

In the following weeks, Carl met with all of the members of departments using the systems his unit supported. After telling them how delighted he was to be on board and a bit about his background, he told them that fewer services would be offered by his department because it would concentrate on more important activities. While the people who attended the meetings were happy to have Carl on board and wanted to make him feel welcomed at KVM, they were not pleased to hear that his department would be supplying fewer services. No one actually voiced a complaint at the meetings, but after Carl made the announcements about changed priorities and his department's intention to provide fewer "hand-holding services" the meetings generally became unusually quiet.

A few days after the last of his meetings with the departments, Carl was walking down the hallway when Gil Smith, one of the more experienced members of the marketing group, approached him. Gil said, "I'd like to talk to you about getting some support for adapting software. We want to use this software on laptop computers in focus groups that need to be run over the next few weeks." Carl said, "Just call my secretary for an appointment and I would be happy to meet with you." Gil was fuming as he returned to his office and passed Bill Kelly in the suite. He said to Bill, "Can you believe this one. I just told Carl Foster that I needed to see him about getting some help with software for focus groups and he told me to make an appointment!" Bill said, "This is not good news. It's not like they're overwhelmed with people walking in down there. I wish Betty Carson hadn't retired."

A couple of weeks later, on Tuesday, Luis Ortiz, another member of the marketing staff, went down to see Carl. Luis was worried about a problem in setting up the group decision support system (GSS) for some supermarket executives the next day. Carl's secretary was not in and Luis walked into Carl's office. Luis said, "Carl, the GSS isn't working like it should. I made prior arrangements for support from your department but the system isn't working right. It has to be working tomorrow morning for the meeting with the supermarket executives." Luis was surprised when Carl responded, "I'm too busy preparing for a briefing for the Executive Committee on Friday. Have Jim help you." Unfortunately, Carl's assistant, Jim Frazier, was out and did not return to the office until almost 5:30. Jim was able to help for only 30 minutes before he had to leave for the airport. Luis and two other non-technical people from marketing worked until 11:30 that night. Fortunately, they were able to get most of the features of the GSS working for the 8:00 A.M. session the next day.

After the session with the supermarket executives, Luis was fuming as he walked into the office of his boss, Sharon Armstrong, the vice-president of marketing. Sharon said, "What's wrong?" Luis said, "We were really lucky. The GSS held together until the last task. I'm absolutely exhausted. What are you going to do about Carl Foster? We need help and he's not providing it." Sharon replied, "I understand. I've been hearing from others about him as well. We've got a real problem with him. He's going to have to change how he deals with other units. I don't know why he didn't help you. Carl only has five people to manage and one of them is his secretary! Wes told him three weeks ago that he would be making a briefing to the Executive Committee. Unfortunately, Wes seems to think only about the needs of information services, and Carl appears to be heading in the same direction. I'm going to talk to Carl today."

Questions

1. Evaluate Carl's performance and his approach to supervision.

2. How could this situation have been avoided? Identify any actions of others that may have contributed to the problem.

3. If you were Sharon Armstrong, what would you do? What authority issues are involved here?

4. How do you think Wes Taylor will react after Sharon visits Carl?

CASE PROBLEM 3.2 *It's Not Easy Riding on the MTA*

Ellsworth Carpenter, the new director of the Metropolitan Transit Authority (MTA), thought about what he should do next to turn things around. He had been a star performer for the city and had succeeded in turning around bad situations, the most recent being the Water Line Maintenance Department. As a result of his past successes, the city manager asked him to take over the MTA. Ellsworth had just returned from a meeting with Greg Williams, the MTA's operations manager; Pat Dowling, the head of MTA's maintenance unit; Trisha Moore, the head of MTA's accounting and purchasing section; Jennifer Ho, the assistant city manager; and Harvey Jones, the business agent for the Bus Driver's Union.

Right from the start the meeting had been acrimonious. The subject had been low morale among the MTA's bus drivers and the increasing complaints by customers about discourteous drivers. Early in the meeting, Harvey Jones said, "If things don't get better quickly the drivers will picket at several locations throughout the city, including in front of City Hall. We're also going to demand 10 percent raises!" Greg Williams, the operations manager, fired back that the drivers were to blame for much of the situation. He felt that the supervisors should be stricter with the drivers, that they needed to put in more controls, and that they should fire the discourteous drivers. In response Harvey Jones said, "Haven't you guys here at MTA learned that organizations that treat their drivers well find that the drivers then treat the customers well? This is not rocket science we're dealing with here. Why don't you try treating the drivers better?"

Jennifer Ho then said that the city manager was getting lots of complaints about driver discourtesy and bus breakdowns. At that point, Pat Dowling became defensive and said, "The drivers are too hard on the buses. If they would be more careful the buses wouldn't break down! Besides, my guys can't get repair parts quickly enough because of all the red tape imposed on us by accounting and purchasing." Trisha Moore then shot back, "The maintenance people never file reports on time and sometimes their papers are so smudged with grease that we can't read them. Furthermore, their requisitions are usually incorrect and everything is submitted as a rush job. Don't you guys ever plan ahead?" Pat Dowling countered by saying, "My guys are too busy supervising repairs. They don't have time for paperwork. You ought to come out of your office and see what it's like in the shop." The bickering continued for several minutes until Ellsworth called the meeting to a halt. He told the group that they would reconvene in three days.

Ellsworth knew there were problems with the MTA, but he was surprised by the magnitude of what he found. He had been in the job only two weeks, but he had spent most of the time walking around and talking to drivers, mechanics, schedulers, and supervisors. He found numerous symptoms of bad management. For example, one of the more irksome practices required drivers to show their driver's licenses to their supervisors each day before they left on their routes. There were no exceptions, even for bus drivers who had worked for the MTA for 25 years. Another driver showed Ellsworth the MTA rule book. He said, "Do you know that there are 156 rules in this book that tell us such things as not to spit on the floor, not to watch portable televisions while driving the bus, and to get the passengers off the bus if it catches on fire? They must think we're idiots! How would you feel if someone treated you like this?" Later, Ellsworth asked Greg Williams about the rules. Greg said, "Each one of the rules was put in the book because we've had drivers do exactly those things! Three years ago, a bus caught on fire and the driver just jumped off without trying to help the passengers. And during the World Cup last year one driver was watching it on his portable TV while he was driving!"

There was also a problem with overtime. The city's auditors and the local newspaper had found that approximately 25 of the 500 MTA drivers made over $60,000 last year because they worked so much overtime. Since this amount was far above the average driver's salary, Ellsworth knew that there were serious problems somewhere. In addition, the drivers felt that their supervisors acted more like police officers than managers. For example, supervisors regularly drove to points on the routes to check on whether the buses arrived and departed on schedule. Ellsworth had asked Greg Williams about this practice, and Williams said that every city bus operation does the same thing. He said that drivers tend to "run hot" (early) before quitting time if they are not monitored and that this is a particularly serious problem because passengers may arrive at the bus stops after buses have already departed.

Source: A few of the features of this fictitious case are based on conditions reported in an article by Curtis Howell, "Many Bus Drivers Are Unhappy with DART," Dallas Morning News (April 8, 1997): 1A, 4A.

Questions

1. How do you think the typical MTA supervisor views the bus drivers?
2. What supervisory and managerial deficiencies are likely causes of the MTA's problems?
3. How are the MTA's organizational structure and its line and staff authority contributing to the problems?
4. What do you recommend that Ellsworth do next?

References

1. Hamel, Gary, and Prahalad, C. K. "Seeing the Future First," *Fortune* (September 5, 1994): 64, 66–67, 70.
2. Katzenbach, Jon. "The Right Kind of Teamwork," *The Wall Street Journal* (November 9, 1992): A10.
3. Bristol-Myers Squibb Internet site, www.bms.com /statil/annual/94annu/data/mission.html.
4. Norfolk Southern Corporation Internet site, www.nscorp.com/nscorp/html/vision.html.
5. Kotter, John P. *Leading Change.* Boston: Harvard Business School Press, 1996: 68–69.
6. Intel Corporation, *1997 Intel Annual Report* (1998): 1.
7. Weinberg, Neil. "Scare Tactics," *Forbes* (March 4, 2002): 84.
8. Crabb, Steve, and Johnson, Rebecca. "Press for Success," *People Management* (November 9, 2000): 30.
9. Stoner, James A. F. *Management.* Englewood Cliffs, NJ: Prentice Hall (1982): 310.
10. Hymowitz, Carol. "In Times of Trouble, The Best of Leaders Listen to Dissenters," *The Wall Street Journal* (November 13, 2001): B1.
11. Uris, Auren. *The Executive Deskbook,* 2nd ed. New York: Van Nostrand Reinhold (1986): 66.
12. Gilbert, Jacqueline A., and Ivancevich, John M. "Valuing Diversity: A Tale of Two Organizations," *Academy of Management Executive* (February 2000): 93–105.
13. Thomas, David A., and Wetlaufer, Suzy. "A Question of Color: A Debate on Race in the U. S. Workplace," *Harvard Business Review* (September–October 1997): 118–132.
14. *Fortune,* "It's a Phone! It's a PDA! But Wait, There's More!" (March 5, 2001): 240. *InfoWorld,* "The New Shape of Mobile Communication" (April 23, 2001): 65–66.
15. *InfoWorld.* "The New Shape."
16. Orubeondo, Ana. "Handheld OSes Continue to Evolve," *InfoWorld* (July 23, 2001): 50.
17. *Electronic Engineering Times,* "Casio Rolls Out PDA for Drive to Automotive Market" (July 2, 2001): 18.
18. Plain, Stephen W. "Microsoft Corp: Microsoft Outlook 98," *PC Magazine* (May 5, 1998).
19. Haskin, David. "Lotus Organizer 97: Office Organizing Made Easier," *Computer Shopper* (November 1996).
20. *InfoWorld.* "The New Shape."
21. Kaplan, David A. "Studying the Gearheads," *Newsweek* (August 3, 1998): 62.

MANAGEMENT FUNCTIONS

Objectives

After reading and discussing this chapter, you should be able to do the following:

1. Define this chapter's key terms.

2. List and briefly explain the steps in the planning process.

3. List and briefly define the principles of organizing.

4. List and briefly explain the steps in the organizing process.

5. Contrast the bureaucratic/mechanistic organization to the organic organization.

6. List and briefly explain the specific activities that are part of directing.

7. List and briefly explain the essential steps in the control process.

8. List and briefly describe the kinds of controls used by managers.

9. Describe ways in which a supervisor can coordinate his operations.

Introduction

As we stated and briefly defined in Chapter 3, the four major functions of a manager are planning, organizing, directing, and controlling. These represent the major sets of activities performed daily by all managers and autonomous teams. In this chapter, we examine these functions in detail with an emphasis on how you as a supervisor, team facilitator, or team leader can execute each. Planning prepares for the future, whereas organizing establishes a structure through which the decisions you and your people make can be implemented. Directing and controlling activities put resources and decisions into action. These activities also involve monitoring performance and evaluating results.

Chapter 3 also mentioned three other sets of activities—decision making, communicating, and coordinating—that are part of every manager's and team's daily routines. Chapter 5 looks at communicating, and this chapter discusses coordinating. All activities are part of the four major functions. You do activities, simultaneously, as you perform each function.

Although our analysis treats each function separately, keep in mind that all the functions are interrelated and interdependent. For example, planning is at the heart of the other functions; you must think ahead, set objectives, and determine needed resources as the first step in planning, organizing, directing, and controlling.

Planning

planning

the management function through which managers decide how they will proceed toward future goal accomplishment

You must first decide where you want to go and what you want to achieve before you commit any of your resources to the journey or the quest. **Planning** is the management function through which managers decide what they want to or must achieve and how they are going to do so. The goals to be achieved may be set by individual managers or teams, or higher-level managers may set them. We will examine the flow and parts of planning in a formal organization next.

PHILOSOPHY OF MANAGEMENT

The ways in which the management of a company thinks about and acts toward people and business events are known as its philosophy of management. An organization's management philosophy is largely determined by the attitudes, values, and guiding principles held by the managers with the most influence—usually top management. The philosophy results in predictable approaches to executing each of the management functions. All managers have a philosophy that affects their thinking and behaviors. Exhibit 4.1 highlights guiding principles at MBNA, which is frequently on the lists of the best companies for which to work. The principles in Exhibit 4.1, which describe how employees expect to be treated, reflect MBNA's management principles and values.

Like organizations, you have a personal philosophy of management. You have developed, through your experiences, predictable patterns of behavior that are based on your attitudes toward people, your job, your company environment, and your per-

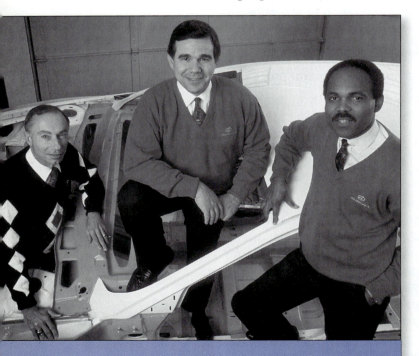

Development of a new General Motors vehicle involved cross-functional teams and a strong commitment to quality.

Principles and values.

Exhibit 4.1

MBNA is a company of people who expect to:

- Be treated fairly.

- Work hard in an environment absolutely committed to excellence and Customer satisfaction.

- Work with people who respect each other as important individuals.

- Have meaningful work to do and the education, equipment, and support to do it.

- Know what is required of them and be kept candidly informed of their performance and progress.

- Be judged individually by the quality and consistency of their effort, enthusiasm, honesty, and results.

- Have the opportunity to develop and advance.

- Be encouraged to offer suggestions and ideas with the understanding that each will be promptly considered and responded to; be able to reasonably speak their minds.

- Receive ample information about the company's plans, activities, and results.

- Be part of a company that recognizes each individual as absolutely fundamental to its overall success.

Source: Extracted from the website of MBNA America Bank, N.A., 2002, www.MBNA.com_peopleprecepts.html.

ception of your roles in your company. Your individual ways of approaching people, problems, and events make you unique as a person and as a manager. Your philosophy colors all of your judgments and, therefore, your decisions and their results.

Our values and beliefs about various individuals and groups, whose backgrounds are different from our own, form our philosophies and affect our ways of thinking about and interacting with them. Equal employment opportunity laws, business practices, and America's population mix bring diversity to the workplace. The job of team leaders and team facilitators then becomes one of creating pluralism—allowing each person to maintain identity and then finding ways to celebrate and effectively utilize the uniqueness of each person.

MISSION AND VISION STATEMENTS

As we mentioned in Chapter 3, every organization needs a mission: the formal statement about the central purpose behind its existence—its reason for being. Top management articulates the corporate vision of where the organization is headed and to what it wants to commit its resources in the short and long run. The following examples are the vision and mission statements, respectively, of Anhueser-Busch, Inc.[1]

> Our vision: Through all of our products, services and relationships, we will add to life's enjoyment.
>
> Our mission:
>
> - Be the world's beer company
> - Enrich and entertain a global audience
> - Deliver superior returns to our shareholders

Once these statements have been constructed, all the people in the organization must know about them and subscribe to them. Before you and your associates engage in any activities, make certain that what you plan to do conforms with your organization's vision and mission. Furthermore, supervisors and employees must understand how the mission should be translated for their units and circumstances. The following situation encountered by Norman Chambers, CEO of the marine construction firm Rockwater, is illustrative:

> Shortly after distributing . . . [the] mission statement, Chambers received a phone call from a project manager on a drilling platform in the middle of the North Sea. "Norm, I want you to know that I believe in the mission statement. I want to act in accordance with the mission statement. I'm here with my customer. What am I supposed to do? How should I be behaving each day, over the life of this project, to deliver on our mission statement?" Chambers realized that there was a large void between the mission statement and employees' day-to-day actions.[2]

Goals or objectives serve as the mechanism for translating the mission into day-to-day actions.

GOALS

goal
the objective, target, or end result expected from the execution of programs, tasks, and activities

From an organizational perspective, **goals** are defined as "a desired future state that the organization attempts to realize."[3] Thus, the outcomes that managers decide to work to achieve are known as their goals or objectives. A typical goal for a company might be to reduce expenses by 10 percent over the next two months. This goal meets important criteria of being both time-specific and quantifiable. The company-wide goal must be translated into divisional, departmental, team, and individual goals. Thus another criterion for effective goals is specificity. As goals are being formulated, the resources needed to achieve them should be determined. There is little point in setting goals that are beyond the capabilities of a company, group, or individual to achieve.

As a supervisor, many of your goals and those of your team are determined for you by higher levels of management. The other goals you set must not contradict those set at higher levels. Your goals determine the roles you and your associates will play in achieving upper management's goals. In addition, your unit's or team's goals must be coordinated with the goals set in other areas of the company to avoid duplication of effort. Once your goals have been determined, they should be precisely stated, communicated, and kept constantly in mind by all concerned until they are achieved.

Two goals on which you must constantly focus are quality improvement and productivity. A case in point relates to the quality and productivity achieved by auto industry suppliers. Ford Motor Company has been challenged by quality problems, recalling several vehicles for safety concerns, such as with the Ford Explorer. The company also had to recall the Ford Escape five times for safety reasons. Because of such problems Ford has imposed tougher quality standards on its suppliers and requires them to meet a monthly quality score. The company plans to raise these quality standards on an annual basis in the future.[4] In order to help its suppliers meet the new and tighter quality standards, Ford has sent its own engineers to its suppliers' plants to help with manufacturing processes, just as Toyota and Honda have done in the past.[5]

POLICIES

The broad guidelines for management action that have been formulated by members of top management are known as policies. They are based on top managers' philosophies and the company's mission and vision. **Policies** are used to coordinate and promote uniformity in the conduct of the business and in the behavior of associates. Policies tell managers what top management wants to encourage or what it hopes to achieve, such as promoting diversity and empowerment.

> Xerox, Johnson & Johnson, and MCI are all noted for their efforts to promote diversity of background and thought among their workers. Nike, Microsoft, and Federal Express [FedEx] are well known for pushing authority down through the ranks and allowing employees plenty of input when it comes to running the business. . . . Others are learning to give ethnic minorities, homosexuals, and women protection and respect . . . in an ever more litigious society, they fear being sued.[6]

Policies affect your role as a supervisor because you must act within their limits when carrying out your duties. For instance, the company policy on recruiting and hiring presented in Exhibit 4.2 requires supervisors to consider all applicants equally and seek a wide diversity in applicants.

RULES

Inflexible guides for the behavior of employees at work are known as the company **rules.** They are specific directions that govern the way people should act on the job. Many are prohibitions, such as no smoking while on the job or in certain locations; others are simply instructions, such as "turn lights off

policy
a broad guideline constructed by top management to influence managers' approaches to solving problems and dealing with recurring situations

rule
a regulation on human conduct at work

Exhibit 4.2   *A policy prohibiting discrimination.*

There shall be no discrimination for or against any applicant or for or against any current employee because of his or her race, creed, color, national origin, sex, sexual orientation, marital status, age, or handicap or membership or lawful participation in the activities of any organization or union or because of his or her refusal to join or participate in the activities of any organization or union. Moreover, the company shall adhere to an affirmative action program with each functional division's hiring, promotions, transfers, and other ongoing human resource activities.

when they are not in use." Rules promote safety and security; they are aimed at conserving resources and preventing problems from arising during the company's operations. Examples of rules that come from a labor agreement include those that cover assigning overtime and disciplinary procedures.

Supervisors find that employees tend to obey reasonable rules while they tend not to obey those that are unreasonable. In general, rules are reasonable when they are needed for safety or to promote operational efficiency. Unfortunately, organizations sometimes have unreasonable rules. They sometimes have too many rules as well—a condition that contributes to rule violations. Unnecessary rules result when managers are reluctant to confront individuals about unreasonable behavior. Instead of dealing with the individual, managers sometimes issue new rules prohibiting the behavior and then apply them to all employees. Employees who follow rules then have more rules to obey. Unfortunately, the individual whose behavior prompted the new rules may not follow them unless carefully monitored.

When there are too many rules employees typically learn that some are outdated and that others are simply not enforced. While supervisors sometimes deny that their organizations have too many rules, when asked if any rules are unenforced they generally agree. Upon reflection they often conclude that indeed, their organization has too many rules. When there are too many rules employees observe instances when rules are not enforced. Inconsistent rule enforcement leads to perceptions of unfair treatment and makes it difficult for employees to distinguish between important rules that should be obeyed and those that are unimportant.

Nordstrom has a reputation for good management. One of its distinctive management practices is that the company has few rules. In fact, its employee handbook consists of one small card. In addition to reaffirming that the company's "number one goal is to provide outstanding customer service," the card also specifies the rules. The company's only rule is the following: "Use your good judgment in all situations."[7] Nordstrom is able to rely on its employees' good judgment because the retailer is highly selective in its hiring practices, it invests heavily in training, and it has a strong organizational culture that serves to guide employee behavior in the absence of rules.

Mars Inc., the candy maker, is a $14 billion dollar business with factories in 28 countries and over 30,000 employees. The company is another example of a company that strives to minimize rules. It also has a strong organizational culture that provides guidance for appropriate behavior. In spite of its size, Mars has "only two human resources people at corporate headquarters. It has a culture of the utmost fairness, not because of corporate-wide rules, regulations and red tape, but simply because the division heads are expected to treat people with respect."[8]

In addition to company rules, various local, state, and federal laws determine rules for the workplace. Such is the case with the Occupational Safety and Health Act (OSHA) discussed in Chapter 16. It is the source of many rules related to both safe and healthful conduct at work.

PROGRAMS

Once goals are established for each department or for the entire organization, plans must be developed to achieve them. A **program** is such a plan. It starts with the goal to be achieved (the "what" of the plan); identifies the tasks required; and specifies the who, when, where, how, and how much that are needed. The required people, time allowed, methods to be employed, and dollars that are allotted are all pieces of a program. Most programs are single-use plans. Your budget is but one example. It is created to guide you for a specific period and is replaced by a new one when its time frame expires. Other programs, called *standing plans,* deal with ongoing activities such as hiring, payroll preparation, and customer service. These must be periodically evaluated and revised as circumstances dictate.

program
plan listing goals and containing the answers to the who, what, when, where, how, and how much of the plan

PROCEDURES

Procedures are the "how" in programs. They are the ways or methods chosen to carry out the tasks that a person or group must perform to reach a goal. Like programs, some procedures are for single use, whereas others are ongoing. Organizations often have sets of procedures that should be followed under different routine circumstances. These sets of procedures are often called **standard operating procedures (SOPs).** New programs may call for the creation of new procedures. Some procedures within your department are left to you and your associates to create and change as necessary. But before you change a procedure, consider who will be affected and consult with those people before you make the change. The people closest to a task or problem are often the best source of information about it. They can help you develop effective procedures. Well-designed and well-understood procedures can provide the basis for competitive advantage. For example, Marriott, one of the best-managed companies in the hospitality industry, has extensive procedures manuals that are described as follows:

procedure
general routine or method for executing day-to-day operations

standard operating procedure (SOP)
set of procedures providing guidance for decision making given different routine circumstances

We are sometimes teased about our passion for the Marriott Way of doing things. If you happen to work in the hospitality industry, you might already be familiar with our encyclopedic procedural manuals, which include what is probably the most infamous of the bunch: a guide setting out sixty-six separate steps for cleaning a hotel room in less than half an hour.[9]

As this example from Marriott illustrates, such procedures help ensure uniformly high quality. Detailed procedures may be needed for less-skilled employees, particularly in industries characterized by high turnover. Nonetheless, procedures or SOPs should not be unnecessarily rigid or burdensome.

Even the most maniacally detailed procedures can't cover every situation, problem, or emergency that might arise. . . . What solid systems and SOPs do is nip common problems in the bud so that staff can focus instead on solving the uncommon problems that come their way.[10]

Exhibit 4.3 shows a company's procedure for staffing a new position.

Exhibit 4.3 — *Procedure for staffing a new position.*

1. Develop a job description describing all major tasks to be performed.

2. Develop a job specification describing the minimum qualifications for the position.

3. Complete a request for authorization of staffing (Form 101-B).

4. Submit Form 101-B, the job description, and the job specification to the Division Vice President.

5. After obtaining the Vice-President's approval submit the approved Form 101-B, job description, and job specification to Human Resources.

6. After approval by Human Resources, advertise the position in appropriate media.

7. Acknowledge applications and keep records of all applications.

8. Screen applications for qualifications.

9. Conduct interviews of remaining applicants.

10. Conduct background check of remaining applicants.

11. Arrange for drug test of applicant selected.

12. Make offer of employment to applicant.

13. Inform Human Resources when applicant accepts offer.

14. Complete affirmative action documents (EEO-1 and Form 108).

OUTCOMES

The main reason for establishing procedures, programs, rules, and policies is to reach goals in an effective and efficient way. The results of efforts to achieve goals and execute programs are called *outcomes*. In large measure, teams and their facilitators are judged on how effectively they achieve outcomes.

Steps in Planning

Every manager has an approach to planning that has been developed over time and refined by experience. But just about everyone can improve his planning efforts. The five steps shown in Exhibit 4.4 can help you become a better planner. As you read about each in the sections that follow, consider how they are related to the steps in decision making discussed in Chapter 3. After all, planning involves a series of decisions, as do the other management functions.

STEP 1: SETTING OBJECTIVES (GOALS)

Your objectives or goals dictate your purposes and direction. Achieving them requires a commitment of resources. Each goal you set must be clearly stated, specific, achievable with available resources, measurable, and not in conflict with your other goals and the goals of others.

Steps in planning (the planning process).   **Exhibit 4.4**

Step 1: Setting Objectives (Goals)

Establish targets for both the short and the long term.

Step 2: Determining Your Alternatives and Restraints

Build a list of possible courses of action that can lead you to your goals and a list of the limits you must live within.

Step 3: Evaluating Your Alternatives

Measure each alternative's advantages and disadvantages in order to choose the alternative with the fewest serious defects.

Step 4: Implementing Your Course of Action

Place your plan in the hands of those who will carry it to completion.

Step 5: Following Up

Monitor progress toward accomplishment of the goal.

SUPERVISORS AND QUALITY

A critical process in obtaining high quality and performance is setting goals that are specific, relevant, capable of being monitored, and challenging yet attainable. Although the process of goal setting often appears relatively simple, it can be difficult to develop good goals that provide motivation for quality and performance. A number of practitioners have shared their views on goal setting. Establishing expectations of desired performance turns out to be critical: "'We want everybody to know what to expect, and that what we expect is measurable,' said Gary Geisel, president of Provident Bank in Baltimore. The use of measured performance based on specific goals helps create a climate where results are clearly expected, he adds. 'It makes you sit down and say 'define it'—to take management practices and identify them in a definable way.'"

A key to effective goal setting is the establishment of accountability. "The use of 'deliverables' in measuring performance makes everyone accountable, says Colleen O'Neill, practice leader for talent management at William M. Mercer in Atlanta. 'You see real, significant increases in financial returns for those organizations that have a formal system of communicating goals and expectations, and regular feedback,' O'Neill said. 'You see a difference on sales per employee, net revenue and other measures you can connect to shareholder value.'"

Other keys to effective goal setting are the clarity and the credibility of the process. "Clear goals and benchmarks stated in advance make reviews more cred-ible too, she [O'Neill] says. The rewards of going over and above those goals also motivate workers and managers to work smarter and harder." Providing a clear target for subordinates is absolutely critical: "The hardest thing is that companies still struggle with the 'I'll know it when I see it' approach rather than being clear about performance goals, O'Neill said. Rather than set goals, many firms still use open-ended reviews, she says. 'They wait until someone has performed, and then tell someone they didn't do their job well.'"

In addition, it is not enough to set good goals, as monitoring progress toward them is vital. "Carol Bartz, CEO of Autodesk, in San Rafael, Calif., is well known for monitoring results closely. She expects bad news at her software firm to come out quickly. That way, changes are made right away before any damage is done." Finally, using several different measures in goals is important. "Bartz uses a variety of gauges to see how her people deliver. Some are based on hard data, like revenue goals. Others are benchmarks based on specific projects. Geisel says Provident varies its goals based on an employee's rank and how much his or her job can directly affect bank profits. The seven positions that report to Geisel are graded against corporate objectives. Rank-and-file people are gauged on individual goals. For those in between, a ratio of corporate to individual goals is crafted, Geisel says. Where an employee can affect earnings more directly, corporate goals carry a higher weight."

Source: Quoted material from Antonio A. Prado, "Give Your People Specific Goals and They're More Apt to Deliver," *Investor's Business Daily* (October 31, 2001): A1.

Some of your goals and those of your team are set for you through the planning of others. Your boss may instruct you to reduce operating costs by 10 percent by the end of the month. How you do it may be left to you to decide. However, most of your goals will require consultation and cooperation with others, such as the union steward, fellow supervisors, subordinates, team members, or various staff managers.

Remember the concept of reengineering? Some companies are attempting to make major performance improvements by setting stretch targets: "gigantic, seemingly unreachable milestones . . . which require big, athletic leaps of progress on measures like inventory turns, product development time, and manufacturing cycles."[11] The alternative—incremental progress and gradual improvement—usually means things improve little by little. But in many industries, "companies now perceive that they must perform far better to prosper—or even, in the long term, to survive. . . . Companies conclude that traditional ways of doing business are no longer good enough. That's when they reach for stretch targets."[12]

> Four masters of what may be called the art of stretch management—Boeing, Mead, 3M and CSX—rely on varying degrees on a set of nuts-and-bolts techniques: (1) Set a clear, convincing, long-term goal. Example: earning the full cost of capital. (2) Translate it into one or two specific stretch targets for managers, such as doubling inventory turns. (3) Use benchmarking to prove that the goal—though tough—isn't impossible, and to enlist employees in the crusade. (4) Get out of the way: Let people in the plants and labs find ways to meet the goals.[13]

If you have not yet experienced the need to set or pursue stretch targets, you soon will.

STEP 2: DETERMINING YOUR ALTERNATIVES AND RESTRAINTS

Your alternatives are the feasible courses of action (sets of tasks) that enable you to reach your goals. Together, they make up a program for action. As with your goals, external factors can limit and influence the courses of action available to you. A course of action may be in violation of the union agreement or may exceed your budgeted funds. Company policies and your associates' capabilities can also restrict your choices.

When you know your limits and the restraints placed on you by others, you are ready to make a list of possible courses of action. As you construct your list, do not be afraid to ask others for their suggestions. Tap in to the diversity around you for new and unique suggestions for ways to deal with any issue. Your peers may have faced similar situations in the past, and you can benefit from their experiences. An excellent way to practice your human skills is to consult with peers and associates; you may need their assistance and commitment in order to execute your plans. Your associates also will appreciate your seeking their input.

STEP 3: EVALUATING YOUR ALTERNATIVES

Create a list of advantages and disadvantages for each of your alternatives. Consider what each alternative calls for in resources such as time, labor, and materials. Keep your company's mission, vision, values, and policies in mind as you evaluate alternatives. Consider combinations of alternatives. If no one best alternative—one with the fewest serious defects and best chance for success—emerges from your analysis, consult with your boss. Consider the second best alternative as a fallback position or contingency plan.

Finally, using your conceptual skills and personal code of ethics, consider the impact of your alternatives on your group, on other sections, and on your company as a whole. You will have to work with and through those other people and sections in the future, so avoid any loss of their goodwill. You do not want to incur any negative side effects that can be avoided.

STEP 4: IMPLEMENTING YOUR COURSE OF ACTION

Having weighed the relative merits and disadvantages of each of your alternatives and having chosen one that has the fewest serious problems, you are now ready to move from the thinking phase into the action phase of planning. Meet with those who will share responsibility for executing your program. Explain your course of action in detail, emphasizing the limits and means available. Set completion dates for various operations and establish checkpoints between the present and the completion dates. Explain the help available to all and stand ready to assist them in times of difficulty. Most important, let them know that you want to be kept informed of their progress.

STEP 5: FOLLOWING UP

You chose or helped to choose the goals and the courses of action to reach them, so you bear the primary responsibility for execution. Do not rely on your subordinates to come to you with problems. Check with them periodically, allowing yourself and them time to make adjustments and to avoid surprises. Keep track of the progress being made. Various kinds of computer software can help you do so. When you find that progress is ahead of schedule, establish new completion deadlines. Be sure to recognize good performances and demonstrate sincere concern for problems. Your reputation and success depend on your subordinates' efforts, and you will need them to execute your future plans.

We are now ready to examine the organizing function.

Organizing

Organizing consists of four primary tasks:

1. Determining and grouping the tasks to be performed.

2. Assigning work to people or people to work.

3. Establishing a framework of authority and accountability among the people who will accomplish the tasks.

4. Allocating appropriate resources to accomplish the tasks and reach the targets.

TYPES OF ORGANIZATION

What is the best way to organize a company in a specific industry and competitive environment? The answer may result in a pyramid-type structure (as discussed in Chapter 3) or a more flexible structure. Two contrasting types of organizations exist today: the *bureaucratic* (sometimes called *mechanistic*) and the *organic*. The bureaucratic/mechanistic organization usually looks like a pyramid or cone, with several layers of management. The organic is flatter by comparison and can change its shape more quickly to meet new challenges and opportunities (see Exhibit 4.5).

The bureaucratic/mechanistic organization makes use of vertical layers of narrowly defined jobs, usually within several functional areas such as production, marketing, finance, and human resource management. It usually concentrates decision making at the top, imposes severe constraints on risk taking, and unintentionally discourages innovation at the lower levels. It calls for reliance on specific vertical channels for communication. Such organizations usually find that it is quite difficult and time-consuming to respond to external changes or to change their structure.

The organic structure usually focuses horizontally and often uses teams when appropriate. (See this chapter's *Supervising Teams* box.) Organic structures facilitate cross-functional

Supervisors in all fields need good organizational skills. Movie directors must organize both the technical aspects of their operation and the actors' performances.

communications and encourage decision making, innovation, and risk taking at the lowest, most appropriate levels through various means of empowerment. Think of organic structures as living organisms capable of changing their shape and purpose as needed to respond to the new and different.

Bureaucratic and organic organizational structures have their place under differing sets of circumstances. In general, bureaucratic structures are

Exhibit 4.5   *Bureaucratic/mechanistic organization structure contrasted with the organic organization structure.*

BUREAUCRATIC/MECHANISTIC	ORGANIC
1. Focus on functions	1. Focus on process using cross-functional teams
2. Centralized decision making	2. Decentralized decision making
3. Tall structure, several layers	3. Flat structure, few layers
4. Distinctions between line and staff	4. Both line and staff represented in teams
5. Narrow job definitions	5. Broad job definitions
6. Heavy reliance on rules and procedures	6. Heavy reliance on innovation/reengineering
7. Emphasis on vertical communication	7. Emphasis on horizontal communication
8. Conformity to dominant culture	8. Cultural diversity
9. Emphasis on individuals	9. May place emphasis on teams
10. Focus on maintaining stability	10. Focus on change

appropriate in stable industries; gas and electric companies and governmental agencies are three examples. Organic structures work best in unstable, rapidly changing industries and competitive environments, such as those in consumer electronics and computer software. *Network* and *cellular* organizations provide maximum organizational flexibility and are likely to become prominent in the future. Exhibit 4.6 discusses such organizations and the managerial characteristics they will require. More will be said throughout this text about the different types of structures.

ORGANIZING PRINCIPLES

Six basic principles govern the execution of the organizing function: unity of command, span of control, chain of command, homogeneous assignment, flexibility, and centralization versus decentralization. Each of these principles will help prevent the designer of any organization from falling victim to the most common pitfalls of organizing. Keep them in mind as you plan an organization, evaluate an existing one, or attempt to redesign one.

Managerial requirements for 21st-century network and cellular organizations. **Exhibit 4.6**

Network Organizations—core organizations linked to other independent organizations throughout the world providing manufacturing, marketing, and other services. The core organization in the network often performs a broker function. Membership of non-core organizations in the network may be stable or dynamic.

Skills Required in Network Organizations
- Referral skills
  Directing problems to appropriate network components
- Partnering skills
  Conceiving mutually beneficial outcomes
  Negotiating solutions
  Implementing solutions
- Relationship management
  Sensitivity to needs of customers and partners

Cellular Organizations—loosely structured organizations made up of small companies employing technical professionals who also function as entrepreneurs. For a specific project, one company within the cellular organization provides project leadership in working with an external technology-based company and a customer company providing financial resources. Another company within the cellular organization may join the project to provide additional skills or to obtain knowledge. The cellular organization has characteristics of classical guilds and professional associations.

Skills Required in Cellular Organizations
- Technical knowledge
- Cross-functional experience
- International experience
- Collaborative leadership
- Self-management
- Flexibility

Source: Brent B. Allred, Charles C. Snow, and Raymond E. Miles, "Characteristics of Managerial Careers in the 21st Century," *Academy of Management Executive* (November 1996): 17–27.

Unity of command. Unity of command requires that there be only one individual responsible for each part of an organization. In each organization, each element of the organization should be under one chief. Each individual throughout an organization should have only one boss. This principle helps prevent conflicting orders and instructions and makes control of people and operations easier. At W. L. Gore & Associates:

SUPERVISING TEAMS

With today's business emphasis on decentralization and staying close to customers (both internal and external), the chances are that you and your people already serve on a variety of teams on and off the job. Membership in a functional group such as the advertising department or the second shift on the factory floor makes us team members in the loosest sense of that term. The most effective team, however, "is a small number of people with complementary skills who are committed to a common purpose, performance goals, and approach for which they hold themselves mutually accountable." Such "teams are collections of people who must rely on group collaboration if each member is to experience the optimum of success and goal achievement." They plan their work to some degree, usually by setting goals and priorities; have some measure of autonomy in deciding who will do what and how they will do it; and analyze the ways in which the team is functioning.

As a supervisor, you are a coach. Like any coach, you must be able to study your team's performance with a trained eye, note barriers to successful performance, and construct a program to overcome those barriers. It is essential to diagnose the conditions that affect a team—team members' abilities and the situation—before taking any corrective action. Each team, team member, and the challenges they face will be unique. In features on teams in future chapters, we will examine team-building activities and how to tell if your teams are functioning properly.

Sources: John R. Katzenbach and Douglas K. Smith. *The Wisdom of Teams.* Boston: Harvard Business School Press (1993): 45; William G. Dyer. *Team Building: Issues and Alternatives.* Reading, MA: Addison-Wesley, 2nd ed. (1987): 4.

A "product specialist" takes responsibility for developing a product. As it progresses, he or she creates a team, recruiting members from here or there until the team might become a whole plant. By that point the team has broken up into multiple teams, or manufacturing cells. Each member, who can perform most manufacturing processes, commits to performing certain tasks. Each cell has a leader, who evolves from within that cell. The leader is not appointed but achieves the position by assuming leadership which must be approved in a consensus reached through discussion—not a vote.[14]

Span of control. As noted in Chapter 3, the span of control concept recognizes that there is a limit to the number of individuals a supervisor, team leader, or team facilitator can manage effectively. Many variables can influence the span of control. Two of these variables are the complexity of the tasks performed by the subordinates and the degree of experience and expertise the associates possess. In bureaucratic structures, the highest levels of the management hierarchy contain the smallest number of subordinates. In organic structures, this principle is usually concerned with how many people should be in a team and how many teams a team facilitator should manage. Jon R. Katzenbach and Douglas K. Smith, consultants who have worked with many teams in numerous companies, offer the following counsel:

Virtually all the teams we have met, read, heard about, or been members of have ranged between two and twenty-five people. . . . A larger number of people, say fifty or more, can theoretically become a team. But groups of such size more likely will break into subteams rather than function as a single team. . . . Thus groups much bigger than twenty or twenty-five have difficulty becoming real teams.[15]

Chain of command. The chain formed by managers from the highest to the lowest is called the *chain of command*. Managers are the links in that chain. In bureaucratic structures, they must communicate through the links of the chain to which they are connected. Links may be skipped or circumvented only when superiors approve and there is real need to do so. In organic structures, command is usually vested in team leaders who head up process, project, or other types of autonomous work teams. These people run their own shows: they "own" their processes and projects and carry within their teams the functional expertise needed to do their tasks. The following description by the CEO of the predecessor of Boston Market provides an illustration:

Our 32 regional partners really run our business, . . . [T]hese executives are constructing a flat, antihierarchical company based on the power of information. . . . Using networking software tools such as Lotus Notes and IntelliStore, managers at every level collaborate on team projects like changing menus, solving distribution problems, and planning expansion—all on-line.[16]

We note that while the predecessor of Boston Market provides a good example of the use of teams, the company's state-of-the art information system has been criticized for the expenses it has added to the company's operations.[17] Thus the use of teams or other good management practices provides no guarantee that a company will be profitable.

Homogeneous assignment. Homogeneous assignment is the major reason companies organize by functions, as in the typical bureaucratic structure. Similar or related functions—advertising, selling, and sales promotion, for example—give rise to related problems and require coordinated efforts by teams and individuals with similar levels of experience and types of expertise. In organic structures, the focus is on a process such as billing customers or purchasing inventory. In such cases, homogeneous assignment means equipping a team with all needed expertise that bears on each process or project so that it can be managed from its beginning to its end.

The development of Hewlett-Packard's financial services center provides insights into the advantages that can be gained with networked and self-directed teams:

In 1990, HP was a $16.4 billion company spending over $60 million a year for processing financial transactions. At that time, it made a commitment to reduce these costs by 50 percent within five years. Using a unique blend of emerging technology, geographically dispersed partners, and self-directed teams, they succeeded. In fact, by 1998, they were able to reduce the cost of financial

transaction processing as a percentage of revenue by 75 percent while growing into a $47 billion company.[18]

Flexibility. Flexibility means that an organization, like Hewlett-Packard, is able to react quickly to changing conditions. It can change to take advantage of new challenges and opportunities. Organic organizations do both best. Paul Osterman, an expert on organizational development from MIT, says, "The market has become far too differentiated and complex for there to be one 'right' way to organize and manage employees."[19]

Once any organization is established, managers at all levels must regularly plan to embrace the new and review the organization's relevance and adaptability to changing situations. Most important, an organization's structure is dictated by the operations it was designed to accomplish. Attention should be given to the subtle changes worked out by an organization's autonomous units and teams. They often make changes that add greater efficiency and effectiveness to their units and might well do so for the organization as a whole when adopted by others.

Centralization versus decentralization. Everything an organization or manager does to reduce the importance of an individual subordinate's role leads to centralization of authority. *Centralized* organizations, like bureaucracies, place the responsibility for decision making at higher levels, concentrating both authority and power at the top.

In contrast, everything an organization or manager does to increase the importance of the individual is a move toward *decentralization,* which places decision authority in the hands of individuals and teams who are closest to a problem or who manage a process. Decentralization occurs through delegation of authority and empowerment. It speeds up decision making by reducing the number of people and hours needed to make a decision and usually results in an organic organization.

CEO Robert Frey at Cin-Made Corporation, a packaging maker in Ohio, knows the value of decentralization and delegation. His company was losing money and was racked by union–management conflict. When unionized workers at one of his plants went on strike, he vowed never again to grant another pay increase. Instead,

> he offered to set aside 30% of all pretax earnings as a bonus pool and delegated to the workers—most of them high school dropouts—authority to schedule production, control inventories, choose their own team leaders and screen every new hire. Some were sent out to learn such techniques as statistical process control, which they then taught to teammates. Frey also began giving everyone detailed updates on Cin-Made's finances at monthly meetings. Since 1989, workers' bonuses have added an average 30% to their annual compensation.[20]

The trend today in large organizations is to decentralize, to become organic in order to get closer to customers and become responsive to rapid changes that occur both internally and externally. Most companies with international operations have found it necessary to give some measure of autonomy to their overseas and specialized operations. Ford runs its European operations from headquarters outside London. Du Pont has shifted "its world-wide electronics operation from the United States to Tokyo, nearer its big base of Asian customers. Du Pont already manages its global agricultural-products operations . . . from Geneva."[21]

IBM uses both centralization and decentralization in its organization. The computer giant has partitioned itself into more than a dozen autonomous divisions. "Simultaneously, IBM created two centrally run entities that took over a host of staff and activities from the newly independent divisions. One . . . recruits and screens prospective employees. The other . . . handles benefits processing and other personnel-administration matters."[22]

STEPS IN ORGANIZING

The organizing process involves the five steps discussed here and listed in Exhibit 4.7.

The steps in constructing an organization (the organizing process).	Exhibit 4.7

Step 1: Determining the Tasks to Be Accomplished

Tasks are identified and included in programs, which then become the specific responsibilities of organizational units to accomplish.

Step 2: Subdividing Major Tasks into Individual Activities

Through analysis, tasks are broken down into specific activities, which can then be assigned in part or in total to individuals who possess the needed skills, knowledge, and abilities.

Step 3: Assigning Specific Activities to Individuals

The skills, knowledge, and abilities needed to execute specific activities are identified, and individuals who possess them are assigned activities. Where existing personnel cannot adequately handle the activities, training, new people, or outside assistance may be required.

Step 4: Providing the Necessary Resources

In order to accomplish their assignments, individuals and units may need additional people, authority, training, time, money, or materials.

Step 5: Designing Organizational Relationships

A hierarchy must be designed, or the existing one adapted, to provide the arrangement of authority and responsibility needed to oversee the execution and completion of assignments.

Step 1: Determining the tasks to be accomplished. The tasks (collections of activities) to be accomplished in your unit will be, in large measure, dictated by goals and responsibilities assigned by upper management and by the design of jobs in your unit. Your unit's goals will dictate the tasks your unit must execute. Step one illustrates the link between planning and organizing. Planning sets goals, both short and long term, and determines the programs needed to reach them. Programs constructed at various levels set forth what is to be done and by whom and determine what resources are to be expended. Tasks must then be broken down into the specific activities required.

Step 2: Subdividing major tasks into individual activities. Staff specialists can help individual unit supervisors break unit tasks down into specific activities. Existing and familiar tasks usually present no particular problem. Units and unit personnel are already equipped to deal with them. When new tasks are assigned or created, however, a job analysis must be done to determine what each task will require in the way of personal skills, knowledge, and abilities.

Step 3: Assigning specific activities to individuals. The specific skills needed to perform worker activities can generally be broken down into data processing, interpersonal, and technical skills. Once these skills are identified as being a part of an activity, individuals who possess the skills required can be assigned to execute the activity. Workers are matched by their particular skill levels to the activities that must be executed.

Step 4: Providing the necessary resources. Additional demands on people may tax them beyond their capabilities. If the existing workforce cannot absorb the activities, new people may have to be obtained, or the work may have to be outsourced. Where employees do not have the expertise or levels of skills required, additional training may be needed. Talent from other areas may be temporarily assigned to assist with the execution of specific activities. Additional funds and authority may be needed to accomplish all the tasks given to a particular individual or unit.

Step 5: Designing organizational relationships. The existing structure of management positions may or may not be adequate to oversee the execution of operations. When it is not,

As a supervisor, one of your most rewarding tasks will be training your subordinates to reach their potential. Just as your supervisor once gave you the training to get where you are today, you too have the opportunity to affect someone's career in a positive manner.

a new design—temporary or permanent—may have to be established. Enough authority must be in the hands of those designated to execute the various tasks. Everyone involved must have clear knowledge of who is to do what, by what time, and to what standards. The principles of organizing will help you design relationships that can function properly. The end result can be shown in graphic form as an organization chart.

Directing

Directing may be defined briefly as supervising or overseeing people and processes. It includes the specific activities of staffing, training, offering examples of appropriate behavior, evaluating performance, rewarding, coaching, counseling, and disciplining. One example of what it means to direct comes to us from theatrical and motion picture directors. These people remove obstacles that may stand in the way of individual and group performance. They attempt, through coaching and by giving examples, to bring out the best performances their actors have to give. Directors are teachers, facilitators, and cheerleaders. So should you be.

directing
the supervision or overseeing of people and processes

Directing subordinates individually and in teams is the most demanding and time-consuming function for all supervisors. The responses of your subordinates to your efforts to direct them will either make or break your career. This is why directing subordinates is the primary focus of this book. All the remaining chapters will help you become an effective director, team leader, and team facilitator.

STAFFING

Staffing involves adding new people to the organization, promoting people to higher levels of responsibility, transferring people to different jobs, and separating people from their employment. It is based on human resource planning—the analysis of the organization and its present and future needs for people with particular talents. An inventory of existing personnel is taken to determine who is now at work, what their skill levels are, how long they are likely to remain in the organization, and who among them is qualified for larger responsibilities. Existing personnel are matched to the organization's present and future needs in order to determine what kinds of people will be needed in the future. Specific staffing activities are defined as follows:

1. *Recruiting* is the search for talented people who might be interested in the jobs that the organization has. It occurs inside as well as outside the organization. Announcements about job opportunities may be posted on Internet websites and bulletin boards, or placed in newspapers or trade journals. Everyone who responds is considered a potential employee until the decision to hire is made. Chapter 11 has more to say about the supervisor's role in recruiting.

2. *Selecting* screens potential employees and job applicants to determine who among them is most qualified. Tests, interviews, physical examinations, and

records checks are used to eliminate the less qualified. The applicants are narrowed down to the most qualified. Selection is often considered a negative process because the people hired have the fewest deficiencies for the job opening. Chapter 11 discusses the supervisor's role in selection.

3. *Placement and orientation* follow as soon as a new employee is hired. It involves introducing the person to the company—its people, the jobs, and the working environment. The new employee is given the proper instructions and equipment needed to execute the job for which she has been hired. Once work rules are explained and coworkers are introduced, the break-in period begins. Chapter 11 has more to say about the supervisor's role in placing and introducing a new person to the job.

4. *Promoting* involves moving people from one job in the organization to another that offers higher levels of pay and responsibility. Promotions usually require approval by two levels of management and the assistance of the human resources department, where one exists. As a supervisor, your continual concern should be to qualify yourself for promotion and to prepare one or more of your subordinates to take your job.

5. *Transferring* moves people from one job to another, either temporarily or permanently. A transfer does not usually carry with it an increase in pay or responsibilities. Most transfers are lateral moves; they facilitate training and are often used to move people from one career path to another.

6. *Separating* people from their employment can be done on a voluntary or an involuntary basis. Voluntary separations include quits and retirements. Involuntary separations include firings (terminations due to disciplinary actions or unsatisfactory performance) and layoffs (terminations due to downsizing and economic slowdowns).

TRAINING

Training teaches skills, knowledge, and attitudes to both new and existing employees. It can be provided through classroom or on-the-job instruction. Although the supervisor of each trainee has the primary duty to train, the actual instruction may be done by any person who is qualified to train. Often the human resources department assists supervisors in training by providing training materials or by teaching them how to train their subordinates. In some cases, supervisors delegate the authority to train to an experienced subordinate while retaining accountability for the training. Chapter 12 explores the supervisor's training duties in more detail.

OFFERING INCENTIVES

Incentives are things that the company hopes will have a strong appeal to their employees. Those who desire incentives offered by their employer will be encouraged to give the kind and quality of performance required to earn them. The kinds of incentives most businesses offer include raises, bonuses, promotions, better working conditions, greater challenges and responsibilities, and symbols of status in the organization. Status symbols can be as small as a phone on the desk, as large as an executive suite, or anything in between. Which one, if any, appeals to a given employee at a given time depends on the individual—including such factors as his current level of job satisfaction and financial condition. Chapter 7 looks at human motivation in more detail.

EVALUATING

Evaluating requires each supervisor to make periodic appraisals of each subordinate's on-the-job performance. The primary purpose of performance evaluation is to improve job performance. Before supervisors can conduct performance evaluations, they must have precise guidelines and standards to follow. Employees must be evaluated on the performance standards for the job instead of on factors that are often irrelevant to the job, such as personal appearance.

Supervisors evaluate their subordinates informally each day through regular observations of their work. In contrast, formal appraisals are usually done only once or twice each year. Supervisors who lack intensive knowledge of their subordinates' performance will find it impossible to conduct fair appraisals. Chapter 13 explores the appraisal process in more detail.

DISCIPLINING

Disciplining requires supervisors to deal with subordinates' mistakes and shortcomings on the job. *Positive discipline* demands that employees be informed about and understand the rules that govern their behavior, the standards that guide their output, and the expectations their bosses have of them. The emphasis is on preventing trouble through the creation of an educated, self-disciplined subordinate. *Negative discipline* is concerned with handling infractions, usually through reprimands or more severe penalties. Chapter 14 deals with the supervisor's duties in this vital area.

Informal encounters with your subordinates are an important part of management. Sharing and spreading the enthusiasm of your subordinates is paramount to your own success.

MANAGEMENT BY WANDERING AROUND (MBWA)

management by wandering around (MBWA)

a leadership principle that encourages supervisors to get out of their offices regularly so that they can touch base with their subordinates and customers

Management by wandering around (**MBWA**) is a principle of management that encourages managers to get out of their offices regularly so that they can touch base with customers, suppliers, and others in their own organizations. MBWA encourages managers to listen, empathize, and stay in touch with people who are important to their operations and their mission.[23]

Most supervisors can practice MBWA each time they meet another person at work or make contact with outsiders during their business activities. When you meet customers, you should interact with them to find out how they like your products and services. If you uncover any complaints or criticisms, take them to the people who should know and can do something about them.

MBWA with suppliers is especially important if quality is uncertain. Before most purchasing agents decide on a supplier, they visit various suppliers' facilities and talk with those who will be responsible for creating what they need. If suppliers are making your life and the lives of your subordinates more difficult, practice a little MBWA with them.

Your most frequent use of MBWA will be with your associates. Casual and informal meetings, as well as formal encounters, create lots of opportunities to interact with them. You and they can then catch up on what is happening in your lives. You get a chance to see them in action—to watch and to listen. In addition, your subordinates want you to see them perform well. There is probably no better way to spend most of your time at work than with your people—those who make or break your own reputation and on whom you depend for the execution of your plans and instructions. Most of the activities we examine in later chapters depend on your practice of MBWA. A good example of MBWA is provided by J. W. Marriott Jr., the CEO of the Marriott Corporation:

> The time I spend on the road—actually, some 150,000 air miles a year—visiting Marriott locations is invaluable to me. One of the most important things it allows me to do is counter the notion that big corporations are faceless machines. If you're in the service business and your name is above the door, it's important for people to be able to link a face to the name. I want our associates to know that there really is a guy named Marriott who cares about them, even if he can only drop by every so often to personally tell them so. I also want to show our team in the field that I value their work enough to take the time to check it out.[24]

Some other important purposes are served by MBWA. For example, when managers practice MBWA late at night, on weekends, or during a difficult time, they often provide positive reinforcement and motivational boosts to heroics-in-progress. The impact of MBWA is important for all managers but is especially effective when practiced by high-level executives. An executive's visit to the workplace of a research and development team working late at night can send an invaluable message that the team's efforts are valued. Similarly, MBWA can reinforce the core values of the organization, such as when the former CEO of Southwest Airlines greeted passengers as they got on the planes, when Michael Eisner, CEO of Disney, takes time to help pick up trash at Disney World, or when Bill Marriott helps Marriott guests carry their luggage into one of the hotels. Likewise, MBWA enables leaders at all levels to demonstrate their humility. The former CEO of Harley-Davidson used MBWA for this purpose, which he felt was important in the organization's creativity and adaptability to change. In addition, MBWA enables leaders to provide important role modeling. Carl Sewell, the CEO of a large company of automobile dealerships, demonstrates the importance of customer service when he takes time to go to the service areas and get under the cars with his mechanics.[25]

Controlling

Controlling involves preventing, identifying, and correcting deficiencies in the performances of both people and processes. It begins with an assessment of the need for control, what types of controls are best (prevention efforts, monitoring ongoing operations, or after-action reporting on measures of outputs), and the establishment of various standards for measurement.

controlling
the management function that sets standards for performance and attempts to prevent, identify, and correct deviations from standards

STANDARDS

A **standard** is a device for measuring or monitoring the behavior of people or processes. Standards can be quantitative, qualitative, or a mixture of the two. Those for controlling people include policies, rules, and procedures. Standards set for the control of processes often include upper and lower control limits that form a boundary around acceptable output. Various measurements and observations are necessary throughout the performance of any operation to determine if standards are being met. Organizations sometimes use **benchmarks** for standards. Benchmarks are standards of performance, such as levels of defects, or practices that are characteristic of the best companies in a given industry. Companies often set benchmarks by studying the products or practices of the best companies in their industries, and sometimes in unrelated industries as well. Nonetheless, setting ambitious performance standards is insufficient for the attainment of outstanding performance. The company must also provide support systems, such as training and equipment that will enable employees and units to meet these standards. In addition, the company must consider how a standard or benchmark fits with other organizational priorities.[26]

standard
a definition of acceptable performance levels for people, machines, or processes

benchmarks
performance levels or best practices of the most exceptional companies in an industry

THE CONTROL PROCESS

Exhibit 4.8 summarizes the control process in any formal organization. Systems of controls should establish standards, measure performances against those expectations, detect deviations from standards, analyze causes for the deviations, and initiate corrective action.

Exhibit **4.8** *The control process in a formal organization.*

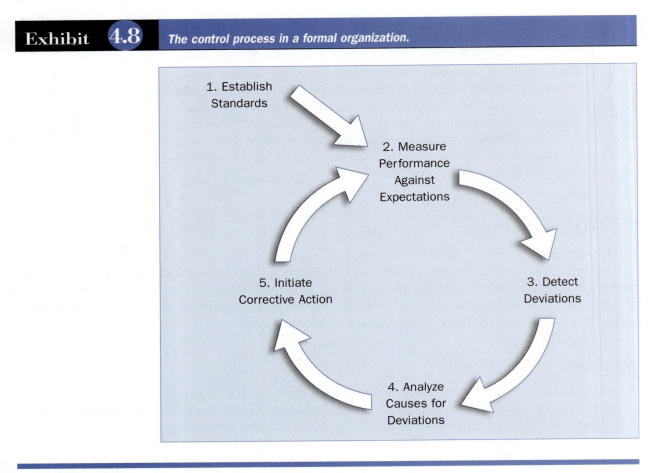

1. *Establish standards.* Standards provide the who, when, why, what, and how of a process. Qualitative and quantitative standards need to be established for all key activities (those directly affecting goal achievement). People must know their limits and what is expected of them.

2. *Measure performance against expectations.* If managers are going to prevent, identify, and correct deviations from standards, they must be able to compare performance to established standards. It is only through comparisons that the terms good or bad become meaningful. For example, the comparison of planned production levels to actual levels of production output will let a manager know if the actual is in line with the desirable.

3. *Detect deviations.* Through comparisons, managers can detect and note deviations. For example, a worker is supposed to generate 15 parts per hour for each of the last four hours. The supervisor compares output to this standard and discovers that the worker is five parts short of the goal. To do this, a supervisor needs accurate and timely information about each worker's production output. Both the worker and the supervisor need to know the standard and how it is applied.

SUPERVISORS AND ETHICS

In 1997 the HFS Corporation, owner of companies including Avis, Howard Johnson, Ramada Inns, and Coldwell Banker, merged with the CUC Corporation to form the Cendant Corporation. CUC had significant business operations selling memberships in clubs that offered discount travel and dining. CUC also owned other businesses such as credit reporting, software, and advertising firms. In April 1998, two managers notified top management at Cendant of fraudulent financial reporting practices that had occurred while they were still working for CUC prior to the merger. The two managers signed affidavits stating that "they had been instructed by CUC superiors to inflate revenue through bogus accounting. . . . They said they had been told to record millions of dollars of phony orders. . . . In short, the men alleged that they had cooked the books to order for CUC executives."

A subsequent investigation by Cendant alleges that the fraudulent financial reporting practices were a response to CUC's inability to increase the profitability of its club membership operations. Cendant and its auditing firm now estimate that "$500 million of revenue reported by CUC from 1995 to 1997 was simply invented. It says that 61% of CUC's 1997 net income was fake." Within a day after Cendant announced its discovery of the accounting problems, the company's stock dropped 46.5 percent. Further investigation has revealed that two executives "falsified entries themselves and ordered roughly half of CUC's 20 division controllers to do the same by increasing revenue or trimming expenses a few hundred thousand dollars at a time."

The aftermath of the falsified financial data has involved huge losses to investors, 71 investor lawsuits, terminations and resignations of executives, resignations of board members, investigations by the U. S. Attorney's office and the Securities and Exchange Commission, and criticisms of auditing firms.

How would you have handled the pressure if you had been one of the CUC managers or division controllers?

Sources: Emily Nelson and Joann S. Lublin, "How Whistle-Blowers Set Off a Fraud Probe That Crushed Cendant," *The Wall Street Journal* (August 13, 1998): A1, A8; Joann S. Lublin, "Scandals Signal Laxity of Audit Panels," *The Wall Street Journal* (July 17, 1998): B1, B9.

4. *Analyze causes for deviations.* When a supervisor notes deviation, such as poor quality, an investigation must be conducted to determine why the deviation has taken place. What is not functioning as planned? Through the decision-making process (Chapter 3), the supervisor determines possible remedies.

5. *Initiate corrective action.* Additional training or more explicit instructions and supervision may be needed. Problems with machines, equipment, supplies, or raw materials may call for changes in maintenance procedures, work flow, sources of materials, and more.

The control process may tell managers or an organization that its standards are inappropriate—either too loose or too strict. Further, the need for additional standards may be uncovered when a supervisor investigates the causes of deviations. New controls may be required to monitor other operations. The board of trustees for a Midwestern community college district discovered that its chief financial officer had invested $10 million of college funds in risky, speculative, long-term investments that earned no interest. The board had no control mechanism to prevent the poor decision, so the employee had full authority to do this without board approval.

TYPES OF CONTROLS

Preventive controls are familiar to all of us. Safety devices on a machine or firearm, a lock on a door to prevent unauthorized entry, safety locks on medicine containers to keep children from opening them, and the various checklists throughout this text are all examples of preventive controls. It is usually better to prevent trouble than to have to deal with it. If all of our problems could be foreseen, organizations would need no other types of controls.

Diagnostic controls attempt to identify trouble when it occurs. Ideally, they should do so immediately. Just as a physician cannot prescribe a treatment for an illness until its cause is identified, a manager needs to know why something has gone wrong in her department before taking corrective measures. Some familiar examples of diagnostic controls are warning lights, meters, and gauges. Personal observation and taking note of abnormal sounds and sights are daily routines that managers use to detect trouble. Once you detect problems, you must identify their causes and deal with them efficiently.

Therapeutic controls are usually automatic in their operation. They are designed to deal with and correct deficiencies once the causes are known. Thermostats that regulate the operation of heating and cooling systems are a good example. A safety valve that opens to release excess steam when the pressure reaches a certain level is another example.

All these controls are necessary for most operations and should form an integrated approach to controlling. No one type is completely adequate. Managers usually need to use combinations of controls to control resources and activities effectively.

A budget and the budgeting process effectively illustrate the three types of controls. A budget is a preventive control because it prevents (or helps prevent) unauthorized expenditures of funds. It is a diagnostic control because it helps monitor the funds as they are spent and matches actual expenditures against planned expenditures. When budgeted funds prove insufficient to meet required expenditures, an investigation should be made to determine why. If the budgeting process is at fault, changes can be introduced to make it more realistic. Budgets have a built-in therapeutic control. When more money is requested than has been authorized, it cannot be spent without higher approval.

CONTROL CHARACTERISTICS

Controls may have one or more of the following characteristics:

1. *Acceptance* by members of the organization who must enforce them and over whom they are enforced. That they are established and enforced in consultation with and with the consent of the governed is the hallmark of effective controls.

2. *Focus* on critical points that affect individuals' and the organization's ability to achieve goals. Critical points include essential areas of marketing, financial, production, and human resource activities.

3. *Economic feasibility.* Controls must be cost efficient—the benefit they provide has to be worth their cost of installation and operation. Too much control can be worse than too little. Appropriateness is the key.

4. *Accuracy.* Controls must provide information about operations and people in sufficient quantity and quality to enable managers to make meaningful comparisons to standards. Too much information can be worse than too little.

5. *Timeliness.* Information needed for comparisons has to be in a manager's hands in time for him to take effective action.

6. *Clarity.* Controls and their applicability to specific situations must be communicated clearly to those responsible for implementing them and to those who will be controlled by them.[27]

All these characteristics are important, but a control need not have all of them to do the job for which it is designed.

To illustrate these characteristics, we will look at a tool room situation. A supervisor wants to control the use of his department's tools. He starts by locking them up in a tool room. Next, he assigns to one person the task of issuing and accounting for each tool. Then he issues an I.D. card to each subordinate and sets up a procedure whereby tools are exchanged for these cards. Finally, he establishes records of the condition the tools are in and fixes responsibility for changes in their condition.

This may or may not be a good control system depending on the circumstances. It may be too expensive depending on the value of the tools he is safeguarding. It may be inadequate and impractical if, in the absence of the tool room supervisor, no one can get a tool. It may be inappropriate if only one or two workers ever need the tools. In short, all of the six control characteristics may be necessary; if any one of them is missing, the controls may accomplish something less than is desired.

Ricardo Semler, head of Semco in Brazil, has written about his experiences with the company in a book entitled *Maverick*. The company, in which control is based on mutual trust and respect between managers and workers, is radically different from the company he inherited—a traditional bureaucratic organization run by rules, procedure, and manuals. Essentially, the company moved to three levels of management and employs a set of concentric circles of coordinators and worker teams that execute most tasks. Controlling is everyone's job, and each person does what is necessary to control his or her own behavior and outputs.[28]

Because the company's performance was disastrous when Semler took over, he knew dramatic action was needed. Essentially, he gave control for all important decisions to the employees who worked in the company. Semler's approach was to create the most radically managed company in the western hemisphere. As he likes to say, he created an environment in which employees are treated like adults.[29] The following provides several examples of how Semler gave control to the company's employees:

> He fired most of the top managers and got rid of most management layers; there are now three. He eliminated nearly all job titles. There's still a CEO, but a half-dozen senior managers trade the title every six months, in March and September. Executives set their own pay, and everyone in the company knows what everyone else makes. All workers set their own hours. Every employee receives the company's financial statements, and the labor union holds classes on how to read them. Workers choose their managers by vote and evaluate them regularly, with the results posted publicly. Obviously it's all insane, except that it seems to work.[30]

Semler's approach has been very successful: his company has been growing at a rate of 24 percent per year since he wrote his book. In addition, Semco has expanded from industrial machinery manufacturing into some service businesses such as property management and equipment maintenance and has joint ventures with such well-established companies as Johnson Controls. Not surprisingly, Semler's unorthodox views of control and management have prompted the Harvard Business School and the Sloan School of Management at MIT to conduct case studies of Semco.[31] Semler's views about control are also reflected in his comments about the limitations of some of the world's most important leaders:

> Managers overrate knowing where they are going, understanding what business they are in, defining their mission. It is a macho, militaristic, and self-misleading posture. Giving up control in exchange for freedom, creativity, and inspired adaptation is my preference . . . Bad leadership is personified to me by the Pope, Fidel Castro, Bill Gates, and Lee Iacocca, all wonderful figures, brilliant strategists, and historic giants. They created enormous value and transformed the entities they led into some of the most important symbols of our age. But because they couldn't rise above their egos, they failed to create organizations that could flourish in spite of them, not because of them. Because they all overstayed their welcome, they have presided over declining creativity, freedom, innovation, and success.[32]

MANAGEMENT BY EXCEPTION

management by exception (MBE)
a management principle asserting that managers should spend their time on those matters that require their particular expertise

The recognized principle of **management by exception (MBE)** applies most directly to controlling. A manager should spend his time only on areas that demand personal attention. Routine matters should be delegated to others, and procedures should be established to deal with them. When exceptions occur, they are usually situations for which there are no precedents. Then the manager's attention is warranted. Where controls reveal exceptions for which there is no prescribed cure, the manager must take action. The theory underlying management by exception is illustrated in Exhibit 4.9, which identifies a few of the everyday demands on a supervisor's time and tells how the supervisor should handle each of them. Competent subordinates usually appreciate management by exception because it suggests that the manager has confidence in them.

An illustration of management by exception.			Exhibit 4.9
TASK	**KEEP**	**DELEGATE**	**OTHER**
Appraisals of subordinates	X		
Interviewing applicants for job vacancies	X		
Handling regular reports to higher-ups		X	Read before sending
Answering correspondence	Those only supervisors can answer	Those others can do as well or better	Read before sending
Attending meetings and conferences	When your expertise is needed	When your input is not required	Have substitute brief you

MANAGEMENT BY OBJECTIVES

Objectives are goals or targets to be achieved or reached within some specific time. **Management by objectives (MBO)** requires each manager (and sometimes each worker) to sit down periodically with her boss and work out goals on which they agree. These goals will, when achieved, result in a more efficient and economical operation for a section or department. Such goals can be set only after a clear understanding is reached about what a department's weaknesses are and what its capabilities seem to be. Goals set by any manager must be in line with—not contradictory to—those of his superiors and those of departments with which the manager must coordinate.

If MBO is to work efficiently, those participating in it must set clear, specific, and realistic goals for both the short and long run. Once goals are set, progress in reaching each goal is monitored by both the person who set the goal and her superior. The goal-setter's reputation and performance appraisals will be based in large measure on her efforts and success in reaching the established goals. MBO reduces the need for close supervision by involving subordinates in setting their own sights on specific targets and then having them work out the methods by which each goal is to be reached. In such a system, results are what really matter. Chapter 13 discusses MBO further.

management by objectives (MBO)

a management principle that uses performance objectives to guide, evaluate, and reward employee behavior

Coordinating

Coordinating is the managerial task of making sure that the various parts of the organization all operate in harmony with one another. It involves integrating all the details necessary for reaching the company's goals. Each activity must be executed without interference from other activities in order to have a unified effort in both the planning and the execution phases of every operation. The coordinating function should happen simultaneously with all the others. Through it, the manager attempts to foresee potential conflicts or to deal with existing ones. For example, the organization may have to be redesigned for better efficiency, or plans may have to be modified to include a better mix or balance between people and events. Lack of coordination means chaos.

KINDS OF COORDINATION

There are two kinds of coordinating: *coordination of thought* and *coordination of action*. A manager coordinates thought by making certain, through effective communication, that all parties involved in planning an operation have the same concepts, objectives, and overall understanding. He coordinates action by including in his plans for a project the steps to be taken in its execution, the sequence of those steps, the roles that each person must play, and how all the persons involved are to cooperate. As these definitions suggest, coordinating is both an aid to planning and an objective to be realized through planning.

Coordination of thought and coordination of action are best provided for by fixing responsibilities. Each person should have an up-to-date, clear definition of her duties in general, as well as of her particular role in each project in which she becomes involved. In this way, everyone's efforts are directed toward common purposes with as little wasted effort and overlap as possible. Coordination is the thread that stitches an entire operation together.

COORDINATION TECHNIQUES

Organizational units can coordinate their operations through programs, procedures, schedules, vertical feedback, and horizontal interaction. Horizontal interaction requires teamwork and occurs regularly when individuals and groups from different departments touch base with each other through a variety of means and for a variety of purposes. The larger the organization, the greater the need for these efforts at coordination. Chapter 5 relates these efforts to organizational communications.

As a supervisor, you can adopt the following measures to help coordinate your operations:

- Enforcing company policies
- Enforcing departmental procedures
- Regularly meeting with people who share responsibilities for projects
- Practicing management by wandering around—communicating regularly with those who feed you work, those who do your department's tasks, and those to whom you feed work or output
- Using the organization's established lines of authority and channels of communication

- Sharing information with those who need it through e-mail and regular routing of bulletins, newsletters, memos, and copies of pertinent documents
- Being available to those who need you; letting people know where you are and how they can reach you both on and off the job
- Rotating responsibilities in order to cross-train your people
- Playing your management roles of liaison, monitor, disseminator, spokesperson, disturbance handler, and negotiator
- Constantly focusing yourself and others on the mission

Instant Replay

1. Planning is often called the first management function because it is a part of every other function.
2. Organizing requires managers to determine tasks, break them into activities, identify the skills needed to perform them, and assign them to qualified people.
3. Directing requires managers to staff their operations and to train, offer incentives and examples, evaluate, and discipline their subordinates.
4. Staffing involves human resource planning, developing, recruiting, selecting, promoting, transferring, and separating people from their employment.
5. Controlling establishes standards to govern people's conduct and output at work, measures performance and conduct against those standards, detects deviations, finds the causes for the deviations, and implements appropriate remedies.
6. Preventive controls rely on methods to prevent problems, diagnostic controls signal the occurrence of deviations, and therapeutic controls deal with deviations as they occur.
7. Controls should be accepted by those who must use them and should be focused on critical points in vital operations.
8. The principle of management by exception tells a manager to spend time on only those matters that demand her personal attention and expertise.
9. Management by objectives requires bosses and subordinates to set goals that will become the standards by which their performance is measured.
10. Supervisors must take steps to coordinate the thoughts and actions of those who affect their operations so as to avoid confusion, waste, and duplication of effort.

Questions for Class Discussion

1. Can you define this chapter's key terms?

2. What are the steps in the planning process, and what happens in each step?

3. What are the principles that govern the organizing function, and what does each principle mean?

4. What are the steps in the organizing process, and what happens in each step?

5. What are the major differences between the mechanistic and the organic types of organization?

6. What activities belong to the directing function, and what is involved in each activity?

7. What are the steps in the control process, and what happens in each step?

8. What are the major ways in which supervisors can coordinate their actions and operations within and outside their work units?

Incident

Purpose: To encourage you to value the diversity in your teams and associates.

Your task: Perform the exercise described here with your team members and associates.

- Race—the result of inheritance
- Ethnicity—the result of upbringing
- Languages mastered
- Gender
- Sexual orientation—straight, bisexual, gay, or lesbian
- Place of birth—native born or immigrant
- Age—young, middle-aged, older, or elderly
- Physical characteristics—height and weight, able-bodied or physically challenged
- Education
- Religious affiliation and beliefs
- Mental characteristics—able or mentally challenged

Workshops in industry that focus on valuing diversity often begin by asking participants to introduce themselves to each other, using the preceding list. In one workshop, Juan starts the introductions by saying, "I am Puerto Rican by birth and of Spanish heritage; both my parents were born in Puerto Rico. I consider myself young at age twenty-eight and speak Spanish and English fluently. I am a straight male with a high school diploma and two years of college credit toward my bachelor's degree. I am hearing-impaired and a practicing Roman Catholic."

Imagine yourself in this workshop, and write out your own introduction to its participants. Then list the differences and similarities that exist between you and Juan. Which will draw you together? Which seem to form a barrier between you two? Ask yourself what additional information you would like to have from Juan in order to get to know him as an individual. Everyone in a workplace must do what you have just done if the goal of valuing diversity is to be realized. Next time you and your team or teams meet, consider performing this exercise, and make sure everyone participates. You will be surprised to discover that these are characteristics that bring people together more than drive people apart.

Balancing Work and Family Obligations	CASE PROBLEM 4.1

Stephanie Barr is a computer technician at Mercury Industrial Design. She is a specialist in computer-aided design (CAD) and produces computerized designs for Mercury's design engineers. Stephanie has an associate's degree in computer technology and is very knowledgeable about state-of-the-art CAD software. She works well with the engineers and is respected for her skills and the quality of her work. Stephanie enjoys her work, and market demand for her skills is strong. She occasionally receives job inquiries from other companies but likes her current employer and the proximity of the office to her home, her mother's house, and her children's school.

Until six months ago, Stephanie loved working at Mercury. She enjoyed her work, liked her supervisor, and had several good friends in the office. In addition, the pay and benefits package was very attractive. Unfortunately, things changed when her supervisor, Lucinda Ortiz, was transferred to one of the firm's other locations. Lucinda's replacement, Angelo Farris, began to make changes in the way work was scheduled. Because business was booming the company had several new contracts, and Angelo began asking Stephanie and the other CAD operators to work overtime when there was a rush job. After a couple of months Angelo began to schedule Stephanie for 50 to 60 hours of work every week. Overtime was no longer used only for rush jobs. It was simply built into the regular work schedule for each week.

After it became clear that the amount of overtime was not going to decline, Stephanie discussed the issue with Angelo. Stephanie said, "I don't mind working overtime on occasion when there is a rush project or an emergency. But I have two young children and obligations outside of work. My husband, Cliff, is a sales representative for an industrial products company and he's on the road at least two nights every week. So Cliff does not help much with the kids. Please don't schedule me for 10 to 20 hours of overtime every week." Stephanie was surprised by Angelo's response: "Stephanie, you have to understand that we have to get the work done that the engineers bring in here. I don't have any choice about overtime and I don't like to work a lot of overtime either. But the engineers like your work and the company is making a lot of money. Don't forget, the company's mission is to make money." Stephanie then said, "Well, why don't you hire more CAD technicians? We have more than enough work to justify more people." Angelo replied, "You know as well as I do that the market is so tight that we can't find good CAD technicians."

The situation continued for a few more weeks and Stephanie had one or two more conversations with Angelo about getting some relief from the amount of overtime. Finally, Angelo said, "Look, Stephanie, you have three options: work the overtime, transfer to another unit, or quit." Later, while Stephanie was talking with some coworkers about her conversation with Angelo, one of them said, "Angelo has been telling people that you are just trying to get more money." Stephanie was disappointed by this news and sought advice from friends away from work about her situation. All of them advised her to go to work elsewhere and said that she could find another job very quickly.

A few days later Stephanie inquired in the human resources office about getting a transfer. She was told that she could apply but that there were no guarantees that she would obtain one. Stephanie then went to see Angelo. Stephanie said, "Angelo, I've just talked to the people in HR and I'm going to request a transfer." Angelo then said, "Stephanie, we need you here. We have three major new projects coming in and the company is going to make half a million dollars on each one." Angelo then laid out the plans he had for Stephanie and the other CAD technicians. After listening a few more minutes Stephanie said once more, "Angelo, I'm going to request a transfer."

Questions

1. Why is Angelo handling the issue with Stephanie in this manner? What do you think about Angelo's planning skills?

2. How should a supervisor balance the demands of the company's mission of generating profits with an employee's family obligations? What do you think about Angelo's view of the company's mission?

3. What should a company be willing to do when an employee says that family obligations are interfering with work?

4. How much can a company reasonably expect from its employees? What would you recommend as a reasonable accommodation?

CASE PROBLEM 4.2   *Channel 66 Community Cable Television*

Channel 66 Community Cable TV is located in a large metropolitan area. Cable subscribers receive this community service channel as a part of their basic cable package. The station provides local public service shows such as city commission meetings, athletic events at local universities, high school football playoffs, minor league hockey games, and special events in the community. The station operates with a much smaller budget than commercial television stations, since its revenues come from the cities and the local cable TV company. Nonetheless, the station takes pride in the quality of its programming and does frequent shoots at remote locations. Joe Washington is the producer/director for most of the remote shoots. Part of his responsibilities involve staffing the audio and video crews for every shoot that he produces and directs. The majority of the crew members are freelancers. Because the pay for experienced professional freelancers is high, Joe hires people at lower rates who have only minimal experience to do the video and audio work on these shoots. Many of these video and audio people are motivated by the desire to gain television experience so that they can eventually obtain jobs at commercial stations. Unfortunately, a few months ago the city and cable company lowered their contributions to the station and most of Joe's more experienced crew members left for higher-paying jobs.

As a result of these staffing problems, the shoots sometimes lack quality and take more time than they should. Furthermore, some of the freelancers are unreliable and shoots sometimes have to be completed without a full crew. Joe says, "If we could raise our pay rates we could start requiring things like personal references and videotaped work samples. If my employees were getting really good pay I could treat them a lot differently. But since they're not, I have to be more accommodating with schedules and behavior." Furthermore, Joe has found that the varying experience and competency levels require him to adapt his supervisory style to the individual members of his crews. Joe says, "When you offer such low pay, you almost have to take people fresh out of college. A lot of them have never been on a sports crew before, and if they don't take the initiative to learn and help out, it can set everyone back. Some have worked out and some haven't." Joe also stated, "Sometimes I even find that these people are unfamiliar with our equipment and I have to drop everything and pitch in to get the work done. And a lot of the time when the crews arrive at the site of the shoot they discover that they don't have all of the equipment and I have to load up the van and make a special run." Although Joe tries to spend some time at every shoot, he says that he is spread too thin on other projects to be on site as much as he would like. He says, "When I have to leave I ask someone on the crew to make sure the job gets done. It usually works out, but we've had some real problems."

This case is based on a management brief written by Daniel Baham.

Questions

1. How can Joe improve his situation without more money to increase the pay for his crews? How would you evaluate his staffing practices?

2. What planning issues exist?

3. What directing issues exist?

4. What control issues exist?

References

1. Anhueser-Busch Internet site, 2002: www.anheuser-busch.com/misc/vision.html.

2. Kaplan, Robert S., and Norton, David P. *The Balanced Scorecard: Translating Strategy into Action.* Boston: Harvard Business School Press, 1996: 24–25.

3. Daft, Richard L. *Management,* 5th ed. Fort Worth: Dryden Press, 2000: 206.

4. Connelly, Mary. "Ford Suppliers Risk Losing New Business," *Automotive News Europe* (October 22, 2001): 12.

5. Connelly, Mary. "Ford Works with Suppliers to Ensure Quality Standards," *Automotive News* (April 30, 2001): 36.

6. Mitchell, Russell, and Oneal, Michael. "Managing by Values," *Business Week* (August 2, 1994): 46–52.

7. Nordstrom. *Nordstrom Employee Handbook* (undated card furnished to one of the authors in 1997).

8. Statistics: Mars Inc. website: www.mars.com, 2002. Quote: Cantoni, Craig J. "A Waste of Human Resources," *The Wall Street Journal* (May 15, 1995): A18.

9. Marriott, J. W., Jr., and Brown, Kathi A. *The Spirit to Serve.* New York: HarperCollins Publishers (1997): 16.

10. Ibid.

11. Tully, Shawn. "Why to Go for Stretch Targets," *Fortune* (November 14, 1994): 145–146, 148, 150, 154, 158.

12. Ibid.

13. Ibid.

14. Huey, John. "The New Post-Heroic Leadership," *Fortune* (February 21, 1994): 42–44, 48, 50.

15. Katzenbach, Jon R., and Smith, Douglas K. *The Wisdom of Teams.* Boston: Harvard Business School Press, 1993.

16. Serwer, Andrew E. "Lessons from America's Fastest Growing Companies," *Fortune* (August 8, 1994): 42–45, 48–51, 54, 56, 59–60.

17. *Forbes ASAP.* "America's Best Technology Users" (August 24, 1998): 63–86.

18. Hutcherson, Norman B. "The Power of Networked Teams (Book Review)," *Library Journal* (May 1, 2001): 102.

19. Richman, Louis S. "The New Work Force Builds Itself," *Fortune* (June 27, 1994): 68–70, 74, 76.

20. Ibid.

21. Lublin, Joann S. "Firms Ship Unit Headquarters Abroad," *The Wall Street Journal* (December 9, 1992): B1.

22. Ibid.

23. Peters, Tom, and Austin, Nancy. *A Passion for Excellence.* New York: Warner Books, 1985.

24. Marriott and Brown. *The Spirit to Serve:* 5.

25. Bell, Chip R., and Heerwagen, Judith H. "Managing by Wandering Around," *Journal for Quality and Participation* (Winter 2000): 42–44.

26. Kaplan and Norton. *The Balanced Scorecard:* 24–25.

27. Drucker, Peter R. *Management Tasks, Responsibilities, Practices.* New York: Harper & Row (1974): 489–504.

28. Semler, Ricardo. *Maverick.* New York: Warner Books, 1993.

29. Colvin, Geoffrey. "The Anti-Control Freak," *Fortune* (November 26, 2001): 60.

30. Ibid.

31. Ibid.

32. Semler, Ricardo. "Personal Histories: Ricardo Semler," *Harvard Business Review* (December 2001): 36.

YOU AND YOUR PEOPLE

Part II contains six chapters about topics that influence or bear directly on the routine relationships between supervisors, team leaders, team facilitators, and their associates.

Chapter 5 is concerned with understanding others and with being understood. Communicating is at the heart of all of your efforts and activities. It is the most basic process performed by every manager in every organization. It is a two-way process governed by specific principles and hindered by specific kinds of barriers—both are examined in detail.

Chapter 6 examines attitudes and how they can be changed. People's attitudes determine how they approach problems, situations, and other people. As a supervisor, your attitudes and your subordinates' attitudes directly affect the success of your unit and people.

Chapter 7 explores the most important theories and models for understanding why people do what they do. It presents the needs all people have in common and what supervisors can do to help their people become and remain motivated.

Chapter 8 is concerned with the supervisor's efforts to build sound relationships with individuals—associates, peers, and superiors—on the job. At the core of this effort are the need to know each person as an individual; the recognition and appreciation of differences in people; and the practice of the basic human relations roles of educator, counselor, judge, and spokesperson.

Chapter 9 focuses on the interaction between a supervisor and groups of subordinates. Formal and informal groups are examined along with how they form and how they affect their members.

Chapter 10 covers the various theories and principles that govern the complexities of leading and being perceived as a leader. It explores basic leadership and management styles and suggests when each is appropriate. Supervisors must be able to use each style as dictated by people or circumstances.

COMMUNICATION

Objectives

After reading and discussing this chapter, you should be able to do the following:

1. Define this chapter's key terms.

2. List the major goals of communication.

3. Describe the purposes of a management information system (MIS).

4. List the basic components in the communication process.

5. Outline the steps one should take in planning a communication.

6. Explain the barriers that can inhibit your efforts to communicate at work.

7. Explain ways to improve your listening skills.

Introduction

The importance of communication to you as a traditional supervisor, team leader, or team facilitator cannot be overstated. You must routinely give orders and instructions and relay information and ideas to and from your subordinates, associates, team members, superiors, and peers. Your plans can come to fruition only through effective communication.

Communication is the transmission of information and understanding from one person or group to another through the use of common symbols. **Information** is defined as facts, figures, or words in a usable form—the result of processing data. By **understanding,** we mean that all parties to a communication are of one mind as to its meaning and intent. The understanding that you should seek when receiving a communication is the exact perception of what the other person or group is trying to convey or transmit to you.

Communication can flow downward (vertically or diagonally), upward (vertically or diagonally), or horizontally (left or right). You will remember from our previous discussions of organization charts that the lines connect-

communication

the transmission of information and common understanding from one person or group to another through the use of common symbols

information

any facts, figures, or data that are in a form or format that makes them usable to a person who possesses them

understanding

all parties to a communication are of one mind regarding its meaning and intent

145

ing the various blocks of the management hierarchy indicate, among other things, formal and routine business communications. By using these lines of communication, managers help to plan, organize, direct, control, and coordinate their operations.

Goals of Communication

The goal of your communication is to produce one or more of the following responses:

- To be understood—to get something across to someone so that he knows exactly what you mean
- To understand others—to get to know their exact meanings and intentions
- To gain acceptance for yourself or your ideas
- To produce action or change—to get the other person or group to understand what is expected, when it is needed, why it is necessary, and how to do it

All these goals point out the two-way nature of communication. There must be a common understanding; that is, each person must know the other's meaning and intent. One or both parties may have to ask questions to determine exactly what the other person means. Whether you are the initiator of or the target for a communication, you have the duty to seek common understanding—to be understood and to understand.

When you initiate communication, you should attempt to give the other person or group your exact perception and meaning. Communicating requires a two-way effort. Ideally, all parties to the process should be active participants; unfortunately, this is not always the case. Before you can listen attentively to another person, the area surrounding you must be free of distractions. Both parties must concentrate on the ideas under discussion. After someone speaks to you, try rephrasing what the person has said. Put what you think the person said into your own words, and ask if that is an accurate restatement. Rephrasing is important because it forces you to listen for meaning as well as to words. Once you understand the words, try next to understand what the person intends as well. We examine techniques for effective listening later in this chapter.

Planning Communication

No matter to whom or why you feel the need to communicate your ideas, planning must precede the act of communication. The following checklist will serve you well as a sequential list of questions to answer as you prepare to communicate:

1. What are the objectives I wish to achieve by communicating? Do I want action? Understanding? Acceptance?

2. What are the essential facts? Do I know them, and am I able to express them properly?

3. Are my thoughts outlined? Whether your outline is mental or written, keep it brief and to the point.

4. Have I considered my receivers? What are their needs, and how can I sell my message to them? Do I know their backgrounds and frames of reference for this message?

5. Have I chosen the right symbols? Whether words, pictures, or some other symbols, are they correct for this communication? (Remember that words take on meaning both from the context in which they appear and in the minds of the people involved in the communication process.)

6. How should I communicate this message? Face to face? In writing? If in writing, should I use a memo? A letter? Is there time for formal channels, or should I go directly to my intended receivers?

7. When should I communicate? How receptive are my receivers? When will the environment be most free of anticipated disturbances?

8. Have I allowed for questions? Will I be able to judge my receivers' reactions, and will they be able to seek further information from me? How will I be sure my message has been received and properly interpreted?

The Communication Process

Six major components or variables compose the communication process: (1) the **transmitter** (sender), (2) the **message** (the sender's feelings, intent, ideas, and their meaning), (3) the **direction** (flow of the message), (4) the **medium** (the message carrier), (5) the **receivers** (intended audience), and the (6) **feedback** (efforts by either sender or receiver to clarify the meaning and intent of a message). The interaction and mix of these can result in effective or ineffective communications.

THE TRANSMITTER

As this chapter points out, the effort to communicate is quite complex. Before you attempt to engage in it, you must be certain of its intended purpose(s). Who should receive your message? What is the best way (in person or in writing) to communicate the message? Only after you answer these and related questions will you be ready to outline your thoughts and convey them to others. The emotional content and sense of urgency of your message are also important to the ideas contained in its content. Your attitudes reflect your predisposition toward a subject and will affect the tone of your message. Receivers will know by listening to or reading your messages how you feel about their content.

transmitter
the person or group that sends a message to a receiver

message
the ideas, intent, and feelings that you wish to communicate to a receiver

direction
in communication, the flow or path a message takes in order to reach a receiver

medium
a channel or means used to carry a message in the communication process

receiver
the person or group intended by a transmitter to receive the message

feedback
any effort made by parties to a communication to ensure that they have a common understanding of each other's meaning and intent

THE MESSAGE

Your message consists of your feelings, intent, ideas, and the meaning of all these that you want to communicate. The objective of your communication dictates, in part, your choices regarding the other five components. The choice of words will be influenced in part by your intended receiver's point of view with regard to the subject matter of your message. How much you have to include, as well as how you will phrase your message, depends in part on what your receiver already knows about the subject and its importance.

THE DIRECTION

As a traditional supervisor or team facilitator, you will most frequently send your communication in an upward or downward direction. You will be communicating most often with associates, team leaders, or your boss. You also will be using diagonal communication to communicate with staff specialists. Diagonal communication can occur outside formal channels, leaving your boss out of the flow. This is often the case when staff managers possess functional authority. It is wise, therefore, to keep appropriate records of such communication and to check with your boss before answering or reacting to staff orders or requests. A simple e-mail message or memo can keep your boss informed of actions that you eventually take.

As a traditional supervisor and team facilitator, you use horizontal paths to communicate with peers. As a team leader, you use them to coordinate your team's operations with those of other team leaders. Team members communicate horizontally on a regular basis. You also use horizontal paths to resolve conflicts and mutual problems between and among groups. The following advice applies to teams that rely heavily on electronic forms of communication:

> One of the key early lessons [of virtual teams with members in different locations] is that for collaboration to work well, it has to be between people, not just machines. Management experts say digital workspaces can't completely replace more traditional interactions, especially in the creative process. In-person communication is important for training, building relationships, and riding herd on a difficult project. Nistesvo [a software company] addresses that by mixing tech wizardry with old-fashioned meetings. Palacios of Land O'Lakes says companies participating in Nistevo's . . . project build trust and sort out their problems by meeting face-to-face every quarter.[1]

THE MEDIUM

Your choice of medium may be dictated by your choice of receiver. If the receiver is a team leader or team member, oral conversations in person with individuals and teams are usually adequate. Your boss, however, may require written correspondence. This is especially true when the contents have historical significance and relate to her evaluations of your unit's progress. Written communication provides specific evidence that can confirm later just what was communicated, when, by whom, and to whom. Complicated messages are best transmitted in writing.

Some information is best presented in tables, charts, graphs, or pictures. Such visual media can communicate ideas at a glance that would otherwise take many paragraphs to explain. Computer graphics provide a case in point.

> At . . . Boeing in Seattle, . . . researchers are developing head-mounted displays that put computer graphics to uses that are . . . helping workers do complex wiring or place the perfect rivet. . . . Cables connect the headset to a computer, which generates the image and changes it when the worker turns or proceeds to a new task; a magnetic or ultrasonic receiver on the helmet helps the system track its position . . . so the wearer sees a diagram superimposed on whatever he's working.[2]

Different media have different effects on receivers. Most people are used to seeing company bulletins, memos, and newsletters because they are routinely used to carry information. As a result, these media lose their ability to capture people's attention and gain their interest. They are read casually, if at all, and may be set aside during busy times to be read at a later date. Further, using two or more media either sequentially or simultaneously can add emphasis and help ensure that reception takes place. Unusual media should be used to carry only unusual messages.

Electronic communication technology. It is important to use the technology at hand in your organization as it best applies to your purposes and needs. Of particular note are e-mail, voice mail, voice messaging, networking, and **groupware** software packages. E-mail sends messages and documents instantaneously. However, both e-mail and voice mail must be used appropriately:

groupware
software enabling group members to work together without close proximity

> In e-mail, express sincere appreciation for the work of the group by using words that fit your character. If you're effervescent, use demonstrative words. If you're not, don't use words that are totally out of character. If you are sending a voice-mail, the right tone is more important than the words you use. If you get a voicemail that you must forward, hold on to it for review before broadcasting it to managers or staff. If the tone isn't right, you might want to recast the message in more appealing tones. Always remember this: Tone isn't simply part of the message; it is the message.[3]

Computer networks connect "people to people and people to data."[4] Through software such as Lotus Notes, users of networks share information from a common database—information is entered into a database that can be accessed by anyone in need of it. Filtering is eliminated. "Interdepartmental problem-solving teams form spontaneously [providing] easy links across functional boundaries."[5] Groupware allows for teleconferencing and networking between individuals and teams. All may focus on the same problem, information, or situation simultaneously and interact with one another directly. Of course, many Internet service providers (ISPs) now supply high-speed service, which makes such communication possible and affordable. By dialing up mass-market online services, such as America Online and Prodigy, or business-oriented services, such as Dow Jones News/Retrieval or Hoover's, users can access market data and obtain in-depth information about companies. They also can shop for office equipment and supplies, get free technical support from leading hardware and software vendors, and book travel arrangements.[6]

Virtual teaming. The global nature of business and advances in Internet and groupware technology have led to the development of virtual teams, which were noted earlier. *Virtual teams* are teams whose members are geographically dispersed, such as in different regions or countries. Although they have little face-to-face contact, members of virtual teams work together by communicating with one another through computer groupware, such as Lotus Notes, e-mail, and video conferencing. An example of a virtual team is provided by an engineering team at Lockheed-Martin in which members of the team work at the company's different plants in Palmdale, California; Fort Worth, Texas; and Marietta, Georgia. Members of virtual teams have discovered that they have to learn new skills before their teams can perform well. As with other teams, there must be a compelling purpose for the team to perform, clearly defined objectives, accountability, and commitment.[7]

A major difference between virtual and traditional teams is that some special rules are necessary. For example, the team needs to have solutions to problems when some members are not participating, the team should be small (no more than 12 to 16 members), and it should agree on "netiquette," such as the acceptability of some good-natured flaming. The team also has to resolve the issue of leadership, because a team leader is not present in real-time. In addition, it is important that the members of virtual teams have the opportunity to meet face to face in order to form stronger relationships. At such meetings the goals and purpose of the team can be clarified.

STMicroelectronics and American Express found that a benefit of such teams is that they can apply the best talent to the task instead of forcing the company to rely on the people who are at a particular physical location. In addition, virtual teams offer quality-of-life advantages in that team members do not have to travel as much and can be at home with their families at night.[8] Despite the advantages of virtual teams, team experts Jon Katzenbach and Douglas Smith point out that virtual teams do not provide as rich of a form of communication as personal contact:

> Note Katzenbach and Smith, "E-mail and threaded discussions, for all their virtues, cannot simulate a firm, friendly handshake, can't grin disarmingly and pat a colleague on a shoulder. Humans don't communicate by words alone." And, "Teaming only works with small groups, yet technology makes it too easy to keep adding members to the team."[9]

Telecommuting. Of note here also is the growing number of telecommuters (teleworkers) who work for governments and such businesses as IBM,

AT&T, Du Pont, American Express, and Pacific Bell. Telecommuting is growing because of quality-of-life considerations and environmental concerns about reducing work-related vehicle use.

> Telework centers—or telebusiness centers—have been established throughout the [United States] to keep workers closer to home, thereby reducing their commuting to and from distant offices. Telecommuters use the centers to hold client meetings, do paperwork, complete reports, or make telephone calls. Work space ranges from cubicles to private offices, which can sometimes be leased for as short as an hour. The centers are equipped with computers, modems, copiers, printers, and sophisticated phone services. Other services include videoconferencing and secretarial support.[10]

Based on teleworkers' experiences in Denver's city and county governments, teleworkers are "at least as productive at home as they were at the office. . . . Teleworkers abide by managers' rules . . . because they don't want to jeopardize their job situations."[11] Notebook computers have made many more people eligible for this role. And for many workers, a daily physical presence at work is really not necessary.

Surprisingly, many Silicon Valley technology firms have lagged other companies in telecommuting. Telecommuting is particularly attractive to employees of such firms because of the area's crowded highways and expensive housing. Because the average cost of homes in the area is $500,000, it is not possible for many employees to live within a short distance of their companies. Intel has recently opened satellite facilities that save on commuting time for employees. For example, one of its satellite offices in downtown San Francisco is equipped with 103 workstations. The company's recent support for telecommuting is in contrast to its previous view. "The old Intel mentality was that if you weren't in your cubicle, you weren't doing your work."[12] Not all Silicon Valley companies have been slow to adopt telecommuting; Hewlett-Packard and 3Com have longstanding telecommuting policies.[13]

THE RECEIVERS

Your own experience tells you that some subjects are received with more enthusiasm and interest than others. Some subjects touch off emotional responses and can inhibit reason and understanding. Try to determine your receiver's prior knowledge and predisposition toward the subject about which you wish to communicate before you attempt to do so. Delicate subjects, such as those requiring reprimands or punitive measures, are best handled in person, one on one, and in private. By anticipating how your receivers are likely to view your message, you can tailor your message's words, tone, and method of delivery to fit the circumstances.

Communicating with associates. Your associates want to know what you expect from them. They expect and need information from you on their progress, successes, and shortcomings. You should pass e-mail, memos, bulletins, and reports from others to them on an as-needed basis. Your practice of management by wandering around allows you ample opportunity to find out what is on their minds, what they are feeling, and what they are thinking about. Their activities and goals must be coordinated with those of your other subordinates.

open book management
sharing all financial information with employees so that they can make informed decisions and earn a share of increased profits

A new management approach called **open book management** addresses many communication issues. Essentially, open book management says there are no secrets. All employees are entitled to be informed about the company's financial status so that they will be able to make decisions that support the company's performance. The Bradshaw Group in Richardson, Texas, provides a good example of open book management.

> The 39-year-old founder and CEO of The Bradshaw Group Inc. has unlocked the financial secrets of his privately held office printer business to his employees, hoping that a company armed with knowledge will become a sleeker, smarter, more competitive beast. "Everybody makes decisions," he says. . . . "If they make them in a vacuum of information—or with what little information you eke out, or maybe even under a false impression of the truth—how can you expect them to make the right decisions for the result you want?" . . . Rather than go it alone he decided 55 heads were better than one. So everything has been laid out in black and white. The only info kept under wraps is individual salaries.[14]

Because most of its employees did not understand accounting and financial terms, the Bradshaw Group taught employees the basics of these subjects. Brown-bag lunches involving humorous presentation styles were used to teach these subjects. The incentive for employees is that they share 10 percent of the company's profits if it reaches its profit goal.[15]

Communicating with peers. Your peers consist of all managers who are on the same level of the company's hierarchy as you are. Touching base with peers regularly allows you to build friendships, share information, coordinate operations, and teach as well as learn. Open and honest communication with peers builds the teamwork and mutual commitment to values, goals, and strategies so essential to good working relationships.

Communicating with others. Others you must communicate with regularly include your boss, staff managers, and outsiders such as customers and suppliers. The boss wants to be kept up to date on your progress and on that of your section, without having to ask for updates. Staff people want to be consulted so that they can share their expertise. They need to know your progress on problems they have been asked to help you solve. They want to find you receptive to their suggestions and assistance.

You should recognize two principles in all of your communications: (1) that you have the right to be heard and understood and (2) that you must respect the same right for others. Self-esteem and respect for others are the most essential attitudes of supervisors, team leaders, and team facilitators.[16]

SUPERVISORS AND ETHICS

Supervisors sometimes ask their subordinates to lie for them or do something illegal or unethical. Such requests place subordinates in an extremely difficult position of wanting to be loyal to their bosses while they also want to behave ethically. This is a particularly difficult situation when there is a close working relationship such as between a supervisor and his or her secretary. The following examples describe situations in which secretaries have been asked to act unethically:

When Sharon Koehler was taking secretarial classes in high school, no one taught her what to do if her boss broke the law. But once she began working for a supervisor who, she says, lied, falsified time sheets and tried to trick people into taking drug tests, she quickly learned that loyalty had its limits. After confronting her boss repeatedly, losing sleep and worrying about whether she was being a good secretary, she finally decided to quit. 'I realized that my values and ethics were totally clashing with this person I was working for. . . . When you get to the point where it clashes so much, you're not productive.' . . . Secretaries everywhere routinely face a wide range of moral dilemmas that are rarely discussed in their training. Should they say their boss is out of the office when he's really sitting at his desk? Is it OK to fabricate the minutes of a meeting at the boss's request? . . . Some secretaries are supremely loyal, like Fawn Hall, who shredded documents for her boss, Lt. Colonel Oliver North. She later explained in court that her policy was 'not to ask questions and just follow orders'.

Others simply refuse to do what their bosses want. . . . Sometimes, secretaries become whistle-blowers, getting the government to protect them from being fired. . . . At the Three Mile Island nuclear power plant in Pennsylvania, a secretary with such protection exposed systematic violations of safety laws. . . .

Quoted material from Rochelle Sharpe, "What's a Secretary to Do When the Boss Asks Her to Lie," *The Wall Street Journal* (February 3, 1998): B1.

As you read this chapter's *Supervisors and Ethics* feature, think about the lack of respect some managers seem to communicate when they ask employees to support their unethical conduct.

THE FEEDBACK

Feedback allows both the sender and receiver to discover if they are of one mind as to the meaning and intent of a message. If the receiver does not engage in feedback, the sender must do so. Asking a receiver to restate a message in her own words is a good start. Anticipate where misunderstanding might take place, and quiz the receiver about those areas. Only when both sender and receiver have the same understanding has communication taken place.

The word *feedback* has other meanings in communications. Giving individuals and teams praise, constructive criticism, and measurements of their performance is often referred to as **scoreboarding.** More specifically, scoreboarding is an effort to:

scoreboarding
providing feedback on individual and team efforts to reach goals

SUPERVISORS AND QUALITY

The commitment to total quality in products, services, and processes has become a tradition in many companies, but it seems that some have lost their focus on the real purpose for their commitments: satisfying customer needs. A case in point is Varian Associates Inc. The scientific equipment producer focused on reengineering itself and achieved remarkable results. According to David Greising, improvements were made in nearly every area, but at a price:

Obsessed with meeting production schedules, the staff in [the] vacuum-equipment unit didn't return customers' phone calls, and the operation ended up losing market share. Radiation repair people were so rushed to meet deadlines that they left before explaining their work to customers. And Varian is not the only company to discover that obsessed employees, while achieving improvements to company operations, can alienate customers. . . .

[Q]uality that means little to customers usually doesn't produce a payoff in improved sales, profits, or market share. It's wasted effort and expense. . . . Instead, managers are trying to make sure that the quality they offer is the quality their customers want. Businesses are discovering that unless their customers perceive that they are benefiting somehow, there will be little financial payoff. The result of these revelations has taught companies to get closer and stay close to their customers. Some invite them to serve on product development teams. Others continually ask for feedback to identify failings and additional ways to meet their needs. Hampton Inns tried a money-back guarantee to customers who were unhappy with any product or service, regardless of the reason. "With everyone from maids to front-desk clerks empowered to grant refunds, employee job satisfaction climbed steadily. Turnover at the chain fell . . . and the program brought in an additional $11 million [in 1993].

Listening to customers is the easy part. Doing what they want without spending into oblivion can be difficult. The new focus: improving quality while satisfying customers at a reasonable cost.

Source: David Greising, "Quality: How to Make It Pay Off," *Business Week* (August 8, 1994): 54–59.

set up a game designed to change [a] situation. It has an easily measurable goal [usually quantifiable]. . . . It has rules that everybody understands. At the end there's some kind of payoff for a win. . . . Teach everybody to track [the] numbers. Show employees how what they do affects the figures. Then put up a big scoreboard and watch what happens. Oh, yes—pass out bonuses if employees hit monthly or quarterly targets.[17]

More will be said in later chapters about scoreboarding. It has the power to energize people and gain their commitment to a project.

Communication Barriers

The essential ingredients in the communication recipe are the transmitter, the message, the direction, the medium, the receiver, and the feedback. If any of these ingredients is defective in any way, clarity of meaning and understanding will be lacking. Communication barriers can arise that will spoil these ingredients and, therefore, the communication process. The following sections describe seven major barriers to successful communication.

UNCOMMON SYMBOLS

Words, such as "feedback," take on meaning only in the context of the message they compose. Similarly, facial expressions can be misinterpreted. Gestures viewed out of context can take on entirely different meanings than were intended. Every child knows the blank expression that his slang expressions can evoke on the face of a parent. Every employee knows the discomfort and confusion that can arise when the boss exhibits unfamiliar or contradictory behaviors.

Example: Sally, the supervisor of a data-processing section, has an established pattern of communication. Each morning on entering her section, she greets each of her seven associates warmly and inquires about their well-being and work. Today, she entered the office and went straight to her desk, ignoring all of her subordinates. What do you think might happen in the minds of her subordinates? What might the impact of her behavior be on today's work output?

Communication problems arise when a message in one language must be translated into another. Translating is becoming increasingly necessary for many team leaders, team facilitators, and their companies. Translating any language into another can create problems of interpretation. Consultant and author Robert M. March has identified several communications difficulties for Japanese managers working in American-based companies:

> The connotations of a number of words and phrases translated from Japanese into English can vary greatly and lead to misunderstandings and worse. . . . Moreover, although the Japanese may speak English, it is still a Japanized English, and their knowledge of local idioms or slang is likely to be minimal, especially in countries like the USA and Australia, where everyday male business speech is replete with local color.[18]

The European Community's translation service offers the following examples of literal translations of messages on signs that, after translation into English, did not come across exactly as their originators intended:[19]

- From a Swiss restaurant menu: "Our wines leave you nothing to hope for."

- From a bar in Norway: "Ladies are requested not to have children at the bar."

- From a furrier in Sweden: "Fur coats made for ladies from their own skins."

- From a doctor in Rome: "Specialist in women and other diseases."

Many companies that experience an influx of foreign-born employees have created English as a Second Language (ESL) programs. In tight labor markets temporary help agencies, such as Select Personnel Services in California, have entered into cooperative arrangements with important clients to provide language training for large immigrant groups such as Hispanics and Asians.[20] Interestingly, many Hispanics who become managers of newly immigrated Hispanic workers now need to learn to speak Spanish because they grew up in the U.S. speaking only English.[21]

IMPROPER TIMING

Unless the receiver is in the right frame of mind and tuned in on the proper channel, he will not hear your message. Likewise, the sender can be upset, agitated, or improperly prepared to communicate. We all know the regrets that go with speaking in haste while we are in the heat of emotion or not thinking clearly. And when we are distracted, we may hear words but not their intended meanings.

ENVIRONMENTAL DISTURBANCES

The communication environment should be as free as possible from *noise*—any thing or condition in the physical environment that interferes with the transmission and understanding of information. Such conditions as static on a cell phone, the din of machines on the shop floor, and the simultaneous conversations of people in groups create background noise that inhibits communication. When people must shout to be heard or receive too many messages at one time, they experience noise. When noise exists, you must either remove it or move to an environment more conducive to the communication process.

Example: A team leader had no sooner begun to interview a job applicant in her office when the phone rang. After handling the call, she resumed the interview. Five minutes later, a change in shift occurred, creating noise and confusion outside her office. How successful do you think this interview was for either person?

IMPROPER ATTITUDES

An unfavorable predisposition toward the subject, the sender, or the receiver will interfere with understanding. In fact, it may provoke emotional and harmful responses in place of the desired ones. Poor attitudes held by the sender or the receiver will confuse rather than clarify.

Example: One of your subordinates, Shirley, comes to ask you again today if she has gotten the pay raise you recommended for her two weeks ago. She has been asking you about it for the past five days, and you have told her that, as soon as you know, you will tell her. Since you have not heard anything yet, you answer her tersely, "No! Now don't bother me!" Have you created problems for yourself by such a response? How do you think Shirley will react?

BACKGROUND DIFFERENCES

A lack of similar backgrounds for the sender and the receiver may hinder receptiveness to a message and prevent a proper reaction to it. Deborah Tannen, author and professor, notes that the majority of men and women "learn to speak particular ways because those ways are associated with their own gender. And individual men or women who speak in ways associated with the other gender will pay a price for departing from cultural expectations."[22] When a newcomer attempts to give advice to the old-timer, the latter may react with irritation. These and many similar situations arise every day at work and often interfere with communication efforts.

Communication problems caused by language can be alleviated through education. Some companies offer on-site English as a Second Language (ESL) courses, like this one at Ore-Ida Foods. Ore-Ida Foods also offers tuition reimbursement for those willing to learn Spanish.

Example: Allen, age 25, is being trained by Arthur, who is about to retire. Arthur is teaching Allen his job. While certain established procedures are being discussed, Allen recommends a change he feels will speed things up. Instead of evaluating Allen's proposal, Arthur shuts him off by stating, "Who's the expert here, you or me? This is the way I have always done it, and it works." What do you think will be Allen's reaction? What are the potential negative effects for the company?

Communicating with people who differ significantly from you can be a challenge. One big problem is that most of us group people and use labels for them—Hispanics, blacks, whites, Asians, career women, handicapped, and so on. These labels can separate people and may be offensive to those to whom they are applied. The key to communicating with others is to determine what they want you to do and how they wish to be addressed—what they feel comfortable with—and to avoid generalizations and stereotypes.

Two examples serve to highlight the importance of personal communication with a boss, subordinate, or peer. When you ask a member of the Navajo people "How are you?" you are implying that the person has been sick. This question is not an everyday greeting. It is an inquiry about how a person is doing on the road to recovery. In like fashion, if you ask a disabled person if he or she needs help, that person may view your inquiry as an insulting expression of doubt about his ability to function independently. Most people with physical limitations will ask for assistance if they need it. They want to be treated like anyone else—on an individual and personal level.

Workshops with the physically challenged yield the following tips for communicating with handicapped subordinates or team members:

- Treat them with same respect and trust as any other employee or coworker
- Ask them what they need to succeed, and empower them with the needed items and assistance
- Don't expect anything less from them than you would expect from able-bodied subordinates in the same job
- Don't wait for them to experience problems in their physical environment; be proactive and seek to identify and remove barriers to their mobility and productivity

Educate yourself on the attitudes and problems typically encountered on the job by people facing physical challenges. One supervisor who had a subordinate with impaired hearing took the time to learn sign language and now communicates in this way or in writing with that person. Another supervisor quickly realized that her vision-impaired subordinate's productivity could be improved with the simple addition of a large magnifier lens affixed to a flexible arm attached to her desk. It greatly enhanced the readability of the text with which she had to work.

Communicating in a noisy environment interferes with the transmission and understanding of information.

SENDER–RECEIVER RELATIONSHIPS

Potentially conflicting functional relationships, such as between line manager and staff manager or between engineer and accountant, can hinder communication. Suspicion on the part of one about the other's intentions or doubt about her ability to communicate about the other's specialty can block the transmission of information. Unequal positional or status relationships, such as between supervisor and subordinate or between skilled worker and apprentice, can cause one to tune out the other.

Example: A production supervisor is told by the director of Human Resources that the production section will be reorganized into autonomous teams and that he is being assigned to training for a team leader position. Since the production manager resents being told by an "outsider" that he will have to learn to share authority with former subordinates, the supervisor resists the training assignment and begins to plot to sabotage the efforts at team building. What are the possible consequences? How could they have been prevented?

NON-QUESTIONING ASSOCIATES

Without conflict and discomfort, little meaningful change occurs in people and organizations. The saying "If it ain't broke, don't fix it" is often an excuse to maintain the old, familiar, and comfortable ways of doing things and may cause teams and their leaders to wait too long before reexamining their performance. A total quality management philosophy demands that all persons and their organizations commit to continual and often radical efforts to improve. It requires a commitment to a never-ending journey.

In everyday organizational life, there are those who promote and those who object to change. Resistance, no matter what its motivation, is to be expected and helps promoters become aware of any flaws in their thinking—anything they may have overlooked that could spell disaster. When you and your team members propose the new and different, you should welcome disagreement and arguments both for and against proposals. In addition, resistance is often a code for fear that the individual cannot successfully cope with the change.

> Often the first response people give you is not the true resistance. You need to explore their reactions deeply. For example, your plan to automate procurement procedures won't work because software development will be far too expensive. It could be that "costs too much" is a fact and that listening to the resistance may save you headaches and dollars. . . . Slowing down, going deeper lets you get at the real resistance. Perhaps people fear that they lack the skills to work sophisticated programs. Go deeper: perhaps they fear they are expendable. . . . To even hope to get people in sync with your plans, ideas, or dreams, you must listen and hear their concerns and fears—both rational and emotional. You must listen to the messages that come from their heads, hearts, and bodies. Let yourself be influenced by what you hear.[23]

When you don't receive any disagreement, you should suspect that "yes men and women" surround you. "If your [associates] haven't been disagreeing with you very much or very hard, you may need to do a bootlicking reality check. You may even need to reexamine your organization's incentive structure."[24] Beware, also, of those among your associates who make proposals that they believe will please you and agree with yours. Such people rarely report unpleasant developments and may act to hide them from your view. According to research by economist Candice Pendergast at the University of Chicago, "companies unwittingly create a culture of yes men [and women] when they rely on subjective performance evaluations of workers . . . the more the worker's pay is tied to the manager's opinion of [the worker], the more powerful [the worker's] incentive to say what the manager wants to hear."[25]

Example: This story is told about the founder of a company who held a meeting with his team facilitators to discuss a radical reorganization plan. The meeting went something like this:

FOUNDER: I trust all of you have read my proposal?

TEAM FACILITATORS: (Responses and nodding of heads in the affirmative.)

FOUNDER: Do you have any questions or objections?

TEAM FACILITATORS: (Silence and shaking of heads in the negative.)

FOUNDER: This meeting is adjourned and will reconvene when you all have both.

All barriers have the same effect on communication—they limit mutual understanding. Knowing that these barriers exist is half the battle. The other half is working to tear them down or to minimize their effects. The subject of resistance to change will be addressed in greater detail in Chapter 6.

Management and Information

All managers and their teams exist to make decisions. To make them, they need a steady flow of many kinds of information. Information originates with data (raw facts and figures) that are then gathered, analyzed, and placed into appropriate formats. This information can then be delivered to those who need it. Specialized departments and activities exist in most larger organizations to accomplish these activities.

MANAGEMENT INFORMATION SYSTEMS

In most large businesses, a systems approach is needed to manage the inflow, processing, and outflow of both data and information. A *management information system (MIS)* is a formal organizational effort to make information of the right quality available to all decision-makers. An organization's MIS should provide usable and needed information to the right people, at the right time, in the right amount, and at the right place. It may or may not use computers.

The first step in designing an MIS begins with a study or survey to determine who needs what kind of information, when, and in what quality and form. Information users help determine how the system will operate and what it will generate. Both users and data processors must cooperate to ensure that the system produces only what is needed—no more and no less—at a reasonable cost.

An example of a computer-based MIS is found in many supermarket chain stores. Their checkout lanes are equipped with cash registers and electronic sensing equipment linked directly to a central computer. Most items in these stores' inventories have data stored in universal product codes (UPCs)—the panels on the products that contain patterns of black lines and numbers below them. The UPCs are sensed at the checkout counter, and the data they contain are sent directly to a computer. In this example, the checkout system is only one part of the chain's MIS, but a vital one. It provides both data and information to the checker, the customer, and the store's and the chain's managers. The UPC data are needed to keep track of the store's inventory and sales, to assist in consolidated purchasing by the chain, and to carry out routine accounting activities for both the store and the chain.

The following describes a new and sophisticated form of MIS in which answers to questions about the buying patterns of retail customers can be found:

> Data mining . . . is the process of discovering interesting patterns in databases that are useful in decision making. Data mining is a discipline of growing interest and importance, and an application area that can provide significant competitive advantage to any organization by exploiting the potential of large data warehouses. The task of finding patterns in business data is not new. Traditionally, it was the responsibility of business analysts, who generally use statistical techniques. The scope of this activity, however, has recently changed. Widespread use of computers and networking technologies has created large electronic databases that store business transactions. Retailers, like Wal-Mart Stores, capture millions of sales transactions through their point-of-sale terminals. Transactions can be analyzed to identify buying patterns of individual customers as well as customer groups, and sales patterns of different stores.[26]

THE SUPERVISOR AND THE MIS

As a traditional supervisor, team leader, or team facilitator, you are part of your organization's MIS. Whether it is a formal, planned system using sophisticated computers and software or not, you send data to it and receive information from it. After you determine your information needs, you should consult with MIS specialists about meeting these needs. For example, are you receiving too much information, information in the wrong form, outdated information, or not enough information? If so, take action now to improve your situation. Stop the flow of unneeded information. Help create a flow of information you lack. Let those who generate your information know how well they are meeting your needs. If your organization lacks an adequate MIS, investigate what you and your peers can do to create one.

While the MIS has made massive contributions to improved operations in most organizations and is of substantial value to supervisors and managers, MIS has not made the same contribution to the jobs of top managers. While this text is concerned with the subjects of supervision and management, it is important to understand that MIS does not provide much of the

SUPERVISING TEAMS

Dean Smith, the legendary basketball coach at the University of North Carolina for more than 36 years, is the most successful coach in collegiate basketball history in terms of games won. During his coaching career at North Carolina his teams won 879 games and lost only 254. Coach Smith has always been known as a "class act" for the manner in which he treats his players as well as other coaches and their teams. His calm demeanor, even in the most intense moments of games, inspired his players' confidence. He stood out among competing coaches for the respectful manner in which he treated his players instead of screaming at them for mistakes. In addition, he was a developer of talent, with 51 of his players, such as Michael Jordan, going on to play in the National Basketball Association and Roy Williams becoming a highly successful and respected coach at the University of Kansas.

Smith's coaching provides many examples that are relevant to supervisors and work teams. One is that team members need to acknowledge each other's contributions and reinforce successful team behaviors: "To reinforce his teamwork message, Smith made sure morale stayed high. For example, he invented the practice of having a scorer point to the passer to thank him for the assist. It boosted the player making the assist and emphasized the importance of working together." Another of his practices was to instill discipline in his teams, as indicated in the following:

The younger Smith saw how his father [Alfred Smith, the high school basketball coach in his hometown of Emporia, Kansas] was a stickler for discipline. Alfred suspended four starters who stayed out past curfew the night before a big game . . . Alfred Smith pushed his reserves to work together. They came through in that game, leading Emporia to a one-point victory. The win reinforced Alfred's "long-held view that the only way to win consistently in basketball is to play as a team, a view that suffused my upbringing and my own philosophy of the game," Smith wrote in his book, *Dean Smith: A Coach's Life.*

His efforts to instill teamwork are exemplified in the following passages describing his concern over individual measures of performance:

If only one or two players gained the spotlight, he believed, their teammates would lose focus and a desire to win. Instead, Smith emphasized teamwork, requiring his players to pass the ball until they found the open man. The more players who touch the ball, the better chance a team has of finding a shot and scoring, he believed . . . Stressing unselfishness helped Smith become the all-time winningest coach . . .

Material in quotations from Michael Richman, "Basketball Coach Dean Smith: Emphasis on Teamwork Netted Him Record Number of Wins," *Investor's Business Daily* (January 8, 2001), A3. Statistics from the same source.

information top managers need. All managers, especially top managers, need information about the external environment.[27] Management scholar Peter Drucker provides an interesting perspective on the information needs of top managers:

All of the new information concepts . . . still provide inside information only. So, of course, does the existing MIS system. It can be argued that the computer and the data flow it made possible, including the new information concepts, actually have done more harm than good to business management. They have aggravated what all along has been management's degenerative tendency, especially in the big corporations: to focus inward on costs and efforts, rather than outward on opportunities, changes, and threats.[28]

COMPUTERS AND COMMUNICATION

Computer technology is making an immeasurable impact on managers' jobs. Leading-edge applications are affecting the work of managers in myriad ways. For example, Blockbuster Video maintains a sophisticated customer database that has allowed the company to increase same-store sales in a declining industry. Another example is Detroit Edison, which uses an information system to deploy its employees in advance of forecasted storms. The system is so precise that when a utility pole is knocked down by a storm, it signals the location so that repair crews can be dispatched. Duke Energy, which is pursuing an aggressive acquisition strategy, uses PeopleSoft to include the employees of acquired companies into its payroll and benefits systems quickly.[29] Keebler Foods provides another example of excellent information systems. The company has an information system to which its "five regional offices, 12 plants, 14 shipping centers, and 54 distribution centers are connected, allowing Keebler to efficiently manage inventory, sales, and costs and to maintain a two-day delivery cycle to grocery stores."[30]

Probably the best example of the impact of computerized information systems on managerial communications is provided by Wal-Mart, America's largest and most successful retailer. Before he died, Sam Walton saw to it that Wal-Mart's stores and managers were connected to his companies' suppliers. Through interfacing computer networks, store managers track sales by inventory item, keep in touch with suppliers, keep tabs on the progress of orders, and allow suppliers to tap in to their computer memories. Such instant communication and monitoring allows the organization to respond to any trends and changes in consumer preferences within a few hours. Stores can communicate with the home office, each other, and their suppliers with the touch of a few keys on

Laptop computers, PDAs, and other technology continue to improve employee flexibility, mobility, and efficiency.

their computer keyboards. Vendors stay on top of the trends that may be developing and are able to respond to the buyers' needs within hours. The company, which spends $500 million each year on information technology, now has a database that is exceeded in size only by the U. S. government.[31]

Computers can make work faster and more efficient. They can eliminate paperwork, make information flow more freely, put information into more useful forms, and reduce costs. Unfortunately, they can also create more stress for the people who use them. As with so many other things, the manner in which computers are used can mean either that work will be more efficient or that it will be more tedious. If people are not taught how to use their computer technology properly, they will fear and misuse it. If people see computers as another way that management can keep track of them and monitor their work, they may resent management.

Further indication of the role of computers in communication is revealed by the following example of what is called the next wave of connectivity.

> The X Internet is a net through which a user's computer takes a more active role in the communication process. Instead of just downloading files, computers on the X Internet download lots of little programs that tell the machine what to do . . . Rebol Technologies, Ukiah, Calif., is developing software for the X Internet. The product is like a virtual private network (VPN); it allows a group of individuals to have access to each other's information and share constantly updated files . . . "We knew this was going to happen sooner or later," said Carl Sassenrath, chairman and chief technology officer of Rebol. "Now it's getting interesting and exciting . . . we realized that a lot of folks needed to be able to work more closely together than they do with the Web. The Web's a really good technology for brochures and a lot of shallow relationships for brief information." But, Sassenrath added, the ability to view other people's work in real time allows for more efficiency.[32]

Many companies are now providing managers with a wider variety of computer-based communication devices including the following:

- Portable computers—laptops, notebooks, sub-notebooks, and palm-tops—allow telephone linkups. Furthermore, very small pocket or palm PCs allow managers to read their e-mail while on the road.[33] Many managers have portable offices in their cars that include computers, telephones, modems, fax machines, and printers.
- Teleconferencing through either cable, satellite communication links, or Internet II allows people in different locations to see, hear, and speak to one another. Xerox uses videoconferencing to link its research people to each other no matter where they happen to be.
- Computer voice recognition systems now allow people to converse with computers for a wide variety of tasks that previously required manual human interaction. Voice recognition software allows computers to handle routine interactions with exceptions being handled with

human interaction. The accuracy of voice recognition has been steadily improving and now has high accuracy even with strong accents. In addition, sophisticated voice recognition systems provide added security by making a record of the caller's voice. When a subsequent call occurs, the system verifies whether the caller is who he claims to be. Needless to say, such systems promote cost savings because they eliminate the need for human data entry via keypad.[34]

Do what you can now to become familiar with how you and your company can put these and many other innovative methods and tools to effective use in managing your tasks, people, and information.

Spoken Communication

All successful managers have two basic qualities in common: the ability to think logically (analyze and problem solve) and the ability to communicate effectively. The most frequently used form of communication for a supervisor is oral. The ability to express yourself effectively through the use of spoken words is the most important tool at your disposal.

Effective speaking is much more than knowing correct grammar. You must know your audience. Your way of talking to Juanita is probably different from your way of talking to Elle, even though your subject is the same with both. Elle requires key concepts cemented to several application examples (a kind of show and tell), whereas Juanita requires that you link your message to her experiences. Furthermore, the communication that takes places involves much more than speaking. Communication experts explain that words account for only 7 percent of communication, while tone of voice conveys 38 percent and body language conveys 55 percent.[35] Therefore, you should make sure your total approach to the conversation is appropriate for the information you wish to share.

As you speak, watch your listeners' facial expressions and body language. Give your listeners time to ask questions. If they do not, ask some of your own in order to check their understanding and keep their attention.

Tailor your message to your audience. Choose your words carefully. Use the minimum number of words possible to get your point across. Be honest and open, and your message will be welcomed. Stick to the facts, and leave out personal opinions. If your listeners ask for more information than you have, do not bluff. Tell them you will get it and give it to them as soon as you can; be sure to do so.

BASIC INGREDIENTS

An effective oral presentation to individuals or to groups usually contains three stages: the introduction, the explanation, and the summary. Each part has a definite purpose and specific ingredients.

The introduction. The introduction or beginning of your oral presentation should attempt to do three things: (1) get the listener's attention, (2) arouse interest, and (3) introduce the subject matter and purpose of the communication. The introduction can help you gain the listener's attention through a number of devices. These include a statement designed to startle or amaze, a quotation from a famous source, an anecdote, a story with a moral, or a question that will be answered later in the oral communication (see Exhibit 5.1). To convey the subject matter and the purpose of the communication, you as speaker can simply state what you intend to talk about, why the communication is necessary, and what goals and responses you have in mind. To obtain and keep the listener's interest, you need to say why the communication is necessary and how the message will affect your listener. Try to relate the oral presentation to your listener's experience, job, or special interests.

Exhibit 5.1	*Guide to planning your oral presentation.*

INTRODUCTION

- Gain the listener's attention

- Arouse the listener's interest

- Introduce your purpose

- Introduce your idea

EXPLANATION

- Develop your idea with logic and examples

- Link your idea to the listener's interests

- Use language your listener will understand

- Keep it brief and on track

- Use illustrations and graphics whenever possible

- Invite questions when and where appropriate

SUMMARY

- Restate your idea and its advantages to your listener

- Call for questions and be prepared to ask some of your own to check the listener's understanding of the topic

- State the specific actions you desire

The explanation. The explanation follows the introduction and should also be well organized. It should flow logically from one key point to another. To make sure that it does, you must (1) identify the key points or ideas, (2) group them in a sequence that makes sense, and (3) present them in that sequence to your listener.

Transitions from one point to another should carry your listener logically from one point or idea to the next. Use emphasis to help your listener define in her own mind what the key points are and why they are worth knowing and remembering. Some devices for adding emphasis include repetition, voice tone and inflection, specific wording such as "this is really important," visual aids, and specific questions. When speaking, use these devices to fix important ideas in your receiver's mind.

The summary. Use a summary at any stage in an oral presentation where it might be helpful to restate important points you have been making. Frequent summaries aid the memory and add emphasis. Any oral communication should conclude with a comprehensive summary of all the key ideas, as well as a statement of the responses expected from your listener. This final summary is your opportunity to reemphasize major points, to clarify the message through questions, and to leave a lasting impression with your listener. It should restate the goals and actions that you expect as a result of the communication, echoing how they were first stated in your introduction.

THE INFORMATIONAL MEETING

Informational meetings provide opportunities to disseminate various kinds of information to your people. Usually, you will use the lecture format to communicate information about such topics as status reports on work (scoreboarding) and new projects or programs in progress. You may also use the lecture format to explain changes taking place elsewhere in the company that will affect your department and its members. Many teams hold such meetings fairly regularly, since meetings provide a means for efficient communication and an excellent opportunity to relate to teammates.

Informational meetings promote cooperation among group members by fostering individual growth, keeping people informed, and conveying the reasons behind changes that will be necessary in the future. These meetings work best when they permit the supervisor and group members to accomplish the following purposes:

1. Keep informed about what is going on in all areas of the company and in their division, department, or section.
2. Obtain observations and information from people outside their group—for example, from higher management authorities, guest lecturers, or consultants.
3. Report on decisions and changes that have been made or will be handed down from a higher level of the hierarchy.

| Exhibit 5.2 | *Guide to planning your meetings.* |

- In advance, notify all who are invited of the meeting's purpose, starting time, ending time, and place

- Reserve facilities and equipment

- Prepare notes for the meeting, and rehearse your presentation

- Prepare and distribute a written agenda for the meeting

- Start the meeting on time

- Keep the meeting on its agenda

- Gather input from all attendees

- End the meeting once the purpose is achieved or at the scheduled ending time

- Record significant contributions

- Summarize the meeting's results before and after adjournment

- Make certain that all participants know their new roles or the changes that arise from the meeting

- Follow up on the results of the meeting

Informational meetings benefit employees greatly by helping them understand more fully how each part of the company contributes to the whole. They are reminded that they are members of a team and are kept informed and up to date on individual and group progress. Although the format is usually a lecture, time should be set aside for questions so that misunderstandings can be identified and resolved. Exhibit 5.2 points out a number of things to think about before you decide to hold such a meeting.

LISTENING

"From *listening* comes wisdom, and from speaking repentance."[36]

—CHINESE PROVERB

Nearly one half of your working day as a supervisor and about 90 percent of your class time as a student are spent in listening.[37] Your business and academic success depends as much on listening as it does on writing, speaking, or reading. Listening attentively will allow you to respond intelligently to what you hear, but this requires your conscious effort. As a listener, you should attempt to see the expressed idea and attitude from the other person's point of view—to sense how it feels to the speaker and to accept the speaker's frame of reference in relation to the subject.[38] Few people can do this well, and that is why so few people are good listeners.

Studies have shown that we operate at a 25 percent level of efficiency when listening to a 10-minute talk.[39] Pidgeon Savage Lewis Inc. of Minneapolis conducted a study of the communicative efficiency of 100 businesses and found that 37 percent of information passed from the board of directors to vice-presidents was lost. By the time the information had been relayed to supervisors, 70 percent had been lost. Workers ultimately got 20 percent of what had been initiated by the board.[40] A similarly depressing account of listening effectiveness goes as follows:

> In fact, research indicates that we hear half of what is said, listen to half of what we hear, understand half of it, believe half of that, and remember only half of that. That means in an eight-hour work day, you spend about four hours *listening*. You hear about two hours' worth. You listen to one hours' worth. You understand 30 minutes of that hour. You believe only 15 minutes' worth. And you remember just under eight minutes' worth.[41]

Most of us speak at a rate ranging between 100 to 125 words per minute, but most of us can think at between 400 and 500 words per minute. This difference allows us time to criticize and to let our minds wander off on tangents while listening.[42] Our criticisms can be of the speaker, the delivery, or the content. Being critical, judgmental, approving, or disapproving of a speaker's message takes us away from our primary goals: to perceive the other person's point of view, to know how that person feels, and to understand his frame of reference. Wandering off on mental trips during listening shuts down our hearing and perceptions.

Barriers to Effective Listening

Remember the following: "A wise man once explained, 'We never learn anything with our mouth open. We can only learn by reading, *by listening*, by observing, and by doing.'"[43] Many things (including our own attitudes and desire to talk) stand in our way when we attempt to listen to another person. Here are the major barriers to effective listening:

- Wanting to talk more than we want to listen
- Not being in the right (rested and alert) frame of mind
- Prejudging what the speaker is going to say, based on what we know about the speaker's knowledge of the subject, experience, and point of view
- Letting the speaker's less-than-perfect delivery turn us off to the ideas and words
- Taking exception to a speaker's remarks as they are made and thus not listening to the message that follows those remarks

- Allowing events and those around us to distract our attention from the speaker
- Labeling the speaker or the subject dull or boring
- Dealing only with the speaker's facts and not listening for the speaker's emotional content
- Tuning out the speaker because she disagrees with what we "know" is right
- Mentally preparing arguments to refute what the speaker is saying
- Making assumptions about anything we are not certain of—filling in the blanks with what we think the speaker or writer means

Exhibit 5.3 is a short quiz to help you determine the effectiveness of your listening efforts. In addition to taking this quiz yourself, you should encour-

---

Exhibit 5.3 | *Measuring your listening skills.*

Read the questions below and rate yourself according to the following:
Always = 3 points   Usually = 2 points   Rarely = 1 point

③②① 1. Do I let speakers deliver their messages without interrupting them?

③②① 2. Do I take notes, recording the most important points made by a speaker?

③②① 3. Do I try to connect the speaker's points with my past experiences to help me remember them?

③②① 4. Do I try to restate the speaker's points to make certain that I understand them?

③②① 5. Do I give the speaker my undivided attention, blocking out any noise or distractions?

③②① 6. Do I keep my emotional reactions to the speaker in check, not allowing them to distract me?

③②① 7. Do I keep my emotional reactions to the speaker's message in check, not allowing them to distract me?

③②① 8. Do I keep listening even if the message is boring or uninteresting to me?

③②① 9. Do I try to get at the speaker's intended meaning by listening "between the lines" of the speaker's words?

③②① 10. Do I formulate questions to ask about any unclear messages in the speaker's words?

age your subordinates or team members to take it. The maximum score is 30. A rating of 24 or more indicates that you are an above-average listener. A score of 18 to 23 is average. Below 18, your listening skills need improvement.

Active Listening

Active listening is "listening and responding in a way that makes it clear that the listener appreciates both the meaning and the feelings behind what is said."[44] Here are two examples of the process:[45]

EMPLOYEE: Don't you think my performance has improved since the last review?

SUPERVISOR: It sounds as if you think your work has picked up over these last few months?

EMPLOYEE: Just who is responsible for getting this job done?

SUPERVISOR: Do you think you don't have enough authority?

Active listeners leave the door open for a person to continue to tell what is on his mind. In the two instances just presented, the supervisor answered the employee's question with a question to draw the employee out and to get deeper insight into the problem or at least the employee's perception of it. Active listeners follow these guidelines:[46]

- They think with people and respond to their needs.
- They avoid passing judgment, either positive or negative.
- They listen for total meaning—both for content and for feelings.
- They respond to what a person is really saying.

Keep in mind that listening is not a passive activity. It requires mental alertness and skills. Use every opportunity to seek clarification of the speaker's subject, feelings, and frame of reference. Questions are the key, as they set the stage for listening.

Written Communication

Probably the most difficult form of communication is the written form. Yet nothing will mark you more clearly as a poor manager than an inability to write your thoughts effectively and correctly. A badly written, poorly constructed piece of writing can quickly discredit you.

Just what is good writing? It is writing that transmits an idea or information clearly to the intended reader in accordance with the rules of grammar and proper sentence construction. Effective writing, like effective oral presentations, must accomplish several things. It should especially be gauged to accomplish the following purposes:

- *Command the reader's attention.* Something in your writing or its appearance has to get the reader to read.

- *Arouse interest.* The writing's appeal must be aimed at the reader's specific interests. The "what's in this for you" should be up front. A benefit can be promised, or a potential loss or cost can be cited.
- *Specify the needed action.* The basic purpose of most business correspondence is to get a favorable response or an acceptance from the reader.

Written summaries and reminders make effective follow-ups to oral communication. The combination of the two forms of communication helps add importance and emphasis to key points, prevent misunderstandings, and provide evidence that communication about a subject has taken place.

Effective writing amounts to talking on paper or a computer screen. Effective writers make their points clearly, using ordinary language that is familiar to the people they are trying to reach. Your writing should read well—sound good to the ear when read aloud. As you write, say what you are writing to yourself. When polishing your writing, read it aloud to catch any awkward phrases or sentences, and any disconnected or unclear thoughts.[47]

Writing effectively is not easy. But you can make it a lot less difficult for yourself if you lay a proper foundation before you try to write. First, you should have a specific objective in mind. Next, you should gather your facts (this may involve searching your files or consulting with others). Then, you should make an outline—that is, a simple breakdown of your major points. Expand each major point by writing beneath it the minor ones that you wish to use to support it. Arrange your points in the order best suited for a logical presentation. Then write using simple, familiar, and concrete words.

When you review your writing, be sure that you clearly understand the words you have used. Then ask yourself: "Will my readers understand my words? Will they get the same meaning that I do?" Some words pose little danger of any misunderstanding. For example, the word *book* means much the same thing to all of us. Other words, however, may have wide differences in meaning for various people.

If you want your written communication to have impact, use short sentences. Professional writers know that writing is easier to read and remember if most of the sentences and paragraphs are brief. However, you should not use short sentences all the time, because such writing tends to strike readers as choppy and monotonous. Try to alternate a long sentence with one or two short ones, and try to keep sentences to 15 or 20 words.

Try to limit each paragraph to a single topic. As a rule, start each paragraph with a topic sentence that tells what the paragraph is about. Use transitional devices to tie both your sentences and your paragraphs together. The final sentence in a paragraph can either emphasize the points you wish to get across or lead the reader to your next subject. The introductory paragraphs in a piece of writing tell what the writing is about. The paragraphs that make up the body of a communication state the writer's case (facts, figures, and so on). The closing paragraph or paragraphs recommend an action or summarize the important points of the paper.

Exhibit 5.4 shows an actual memo (Memo A) sent by Jane, a middle manager, to her subordinate managers. Read it first, and then read Memo B, which is a suggested improvement. Do you believe that Memo B carries the basic message intended by the author of Memo A? Which memo would you prefer to receive if you were one of Jane's subordinates?

Two memos compared: Memo A (the original) and Memo B (a revision).   **Exhibit 5.4**

MEMO A

TO: ALL SECTION SUPERVISORS
FROM: Jane Barton

The newly designed personal data sheet—Form 14A—has a necessary, essential, and vital purpose in our organization. It provides the necessary and statistically significant personal data required by the personnel department to be kept on file for future references regarding promotions, transfers, layoffs, and more.

During our recent relocation efforts from the rented facilities at Broad Street to our present location here at Cauley Boulevard, files were lost, damaged, or misplaced, necessitating the current request for replacement of vital personal data on each and every manager in this department. It is also the company's policy to periodically update personal data on file through periodic, personal perusal of one's own records—updating and adding new information as required and deleting obsolete or outdated personal data on file.

Therefore, please complete the attached personal data sheet at your earliest possible convenience but no later than Thursday, May 14, and return it to me by the close of the business day on the 14th.

MEMO B

TO: ALL SECTION SUPERVISORS
FROM: Jane Barton

Attached is our company's revised edition of the personal data sheet. Please fill it out completely and return to me no later than the close of business on Thursday, May 14. Thank you.

The Grapevine

Transmission media or channels of communication can be formal or informal. *Formal* channels are those specifically set up for the transmission of normal business information, instructions, orders, and reports. The organization chart of a business outlines formal channels. *Informal* channels—the **grapevine**—are not specifically designated for use in the dissemination of information, but nearly every employee uses them for this purpose.

Informal channels exist because of the natural desire of employees to be "in the know" and to satisfy their curiosity. Because employees mix and socialize frequently during and outside their normal working relationships, they tend to speculate and invent "information." Often, the less they know about something, the more they invent. At coffee breaks, during lunch, or at social events, people often share things they have heard and seen even though they may not have a complete story to tell.

The grapevine can give managers a clue about what is bothering their people and where the need for immediate or future action lies. Although it is generally a means by which gossip and rumors about the company are spread, managers should be tuned in to it. Do not, however, use the grapevine for disseminating orders or instructions to your people. It is no substitute for formal channels.

Gossip can sometimes serve you in your role as a supervisor by acting as an early warning system. When you hear a rumor, ask yourself what you would do if it were true. Gossip also alerts you to where the leaks are and who may be letting confidential communications get into circulation.

grapevine
informal channels at work that transmit information or misinformation

The grapevine is the channel of communication for informal groups. Informal groups form at lunch, after work, or any time coworkers get together on a casual basis.

To prevent the grapevine from yielding a crop of sour grapes, satisfy your people's need to know what is happening in their department by applying the following rules to your daily situation:

1. Tune in on their informal communications.
2. Combat rumors and gossip with the facts.
3. Discredit people who willfully spread improper information.
4. Be available to and honest with your people.
5. Know when to remain silent.

By applying these rules, you create in your subordinates a feeling of confidence about what is true and what is not true. You also strengthen your personal reputation as a source of sound information, and you foster better morale and cooperation. As a result, you can lessen resistance to change and soften its impact.

Instant Replay

1. The major goals of the communication process are to be understood, to gain understanding, to gain acceptance for yourself or for your ideas, and to produce action or change.

2. A management information system (MIS) is a formal method for making accurate and timely information available to management to aid the decision-making process and the execution of management and organization functions.

3. Communication barriers interrupt the flow of information and inhibit understanding. Communication efforts should be planned to limit or eliminate the effects of barriers.

4. Delivering a speech or a lecture usually involves providing an introduction, an explanation, and a summary.

5. Listening takes up nearly one half of our days. It is a skill that can be learned and improved by techniques such as anticipating a speaker's next point, identifying the speaker's supporting elements, and making mental summaries.

6. The grapevine consists of the transmission of information or misinformation through informal channels in the working environment.

Questions for Class Discussion

1. Can you define this chapter's key terms?

2. What are the possible goals behind efforts to communicate? Which do you think are part of every effort to communicate?

3. What does a management information system do for (a) managers and (b) the organization?

4. What are the basic components of the communication process? How might the choice in one category influence the choices in others?

5. Suppose you are getting ready to communicate to your subordinates about a change in a safety procedure. What should you do before you attempt to relay your message?

6. What are the barriers to effective communication? Can you give an example of each from your experience?

7. How can you improve your listening skills and your ability to retain more of what you hear?

Incident

Purpose: To help identify ways in which managers and companies use the Internet to facilitate communication.

Your task: Review the Web pages of the companies listed below. Identify the ways in which these Web pages facilitate communication with managers.

> Alcon Laboratories: www.alconlabs.com
> Chubb Corporation: www.chubb.com
> Ford Motor Company: www.ford.com
> General Electric: www.ge.com
> 3M: www.mmm.com
> Motorola: www.motorola.com
> Nokia: www.nokia.com

CASE PROBLEM 5.1 *Is Anyone Listening?*

Four Star Financial operates a national chain of retail loan offices that make loans based on homeowners' equity. The retail loan offices process loan applications, compile documentation of collateral, and then send the applications and documentation to the home office. The collateral section in the home office then verifies the documentation and wires funds for the borrower's loan to the retail offices. After receiving loan documentation from the collateral section, Four Star's treasury department then sells most of the loans to other financial institutions. Victor Lopez, a loan resale specialist in the treasury department, has become concerned about documentation verification practices in the collateral department and has approached his boss, Kim Hoffer, about his concerns.

VICTOR: "Kim, I'm worried that some of the collateral documentation specialists are not verifying all of the information before they send the loans on to us for resale. I've spot checked a few and found lots of missing documents. Some of the borrowers are going to default on their loans and the financial institutions that bought the loans are going to accuse us of misleading them about the quality of the loans."

KIM: "What do you mean they aren't verifying the information? They have loan documentation procedures to follow and the verifiers know what they're doing. Listen Victor, we've got enough problems of our own to worry about."

VICTOR: "I know that they have procedures and that they are easy enough to understand. But they have some people who are cutting corners and don't seem to care about doing good work. If I was a manager I'd do something about their work."

KIM: "I don't think this is a big problem. There are always going to be some loans on which they miss some information. The financial institutions that buy our loans know that a few are going to be bad. We and the banks have good projections of expected default rates and interest rates are set high enough to allow for this."

VICTOR: "But that's what I'm talking about. When the workload gets heavy like it has been this year, some of the collateral people just pass on loans without actually verifying the documentation. They just fill out the check-list like they really completed the verification and send them on. Unless you actually go back and do the work yourself you can't tell if they've actually done the verifications. I've checked a few and have sent them back to collateral, but I don't have time to check them all!"

KIM: "Victor, this isn't the first time we've had a conversation about this subject. I know you have been in this business a long time, but I think you are overstating the seriousness of this problem. Quit worrying so much. Anyway, business is good and the company is making money. You'll probably get a good bonus this year. And you're not the collateral manager, so it's not your problem."

VICTOR: "But business won't always be good, and when some of these loans go bad people are going to find that there isn't good documentation for a lot of these loans. I know that these are high-interest loans, but the extra income won't be high enough to offset a large number of defaults. What are you going to do about the problem?"

KIM: "Well, what would you have me do? The collateral people don't report to me. Why should you be concerned about this? You know as well as I that if I go over to tell the head of collateral verification that we don't think they are doing a good job, we'll just make them mad at us. And that will just make things worse in the future. Listen, Victor, you get too worked up about things. You know what your problem is? You don't know how to go with the flow. If you get loans with inadequate collateral, just send them back. Is there anything else on your mind? If not, I've got a lot of work to do."

Questions

1. How do you think Victor feels about his conversation with Kim?
2. What is the likely impact on Victor's future interactions with Kim? How likely is it that Victor will tell Kim about problems in the future?
3. How could Victor have communicated more effectively? What could he have done to obtain a more favorable response from Kim?
4. How should Kim have responded to Victor's concerns?

Judy Whitmire is a product manager for Baker-Allison Inc., a company based in a town of 9,000 in a midwestern state. Baker-Allison manufactures disposable surgical gowns and drapes that are used in operating rooms. The surgical team wears the gowns, and the drapes are used to cover the patient while the surgery is performed. The company also manufactures a few other products used in medical care. The use of disposable drapes and gowns has become widespread because of concerns about the likelihood of infection when non-disposable materials are reused and the cost of sterilizing reusable materials.

A new line of surgical gowns and drapes, for which Judy is the product manager, provides surgeons and nurses with greater protection from accidental infection from viruses. In addition, its price is very competitive even though the company's profit margin on the line is substantial. As a result, sales of the new gowns and drapes have been exceptionally good and will exceed $40 million this year.

Needless to say, the company's reputation for quality and its high standards for maintaining sterile products are critical to the company's sales. A major factor helping to control costs is the low cost of labor in the rural area in which the company is based. All manufacturing takes place in a clean environment in a new plant built specifically for this purpose. In addition, the gowns and drapes are sterilized with cobalt radiation. Because an exact amount of radiation is required for sterility without excessive radiation effects, the radiation equipment must be certified frequently for proper calibration. State regulations require Baker-Allison to conduct and report self-tests of the equipment on a monthly basis and have the equipment tested four times a year by a certified testing firm. Without such testing, Baker-Allison cannot be confident that its surgical supplies are sterile or that they have not been subjected to too much radiation.

Today when Judy was compiling an internal report, she went down to the sterilizer room to get information about the certification of the radiation equipment. The head of the sterilization section was not in, so Judy picked up the equipment certification logs and began to take notes on the information she needed. Much to her surprise, Judy realized that the latest certification test results appeared to have been falsified. She concluded that it would not have been possible for the certification to be performed on the date indicated. She had been working across the hall during the whole week and was certain that the sterilizer had not been shut down that week. Judy feels that the head of the section probably falsified the self-test records because the test requires the equipment to be shut down for a day and the sterilizer section was under severe time pressures caused by the high volume of production. As a result, the company cannot be certain of the sterility of all of the surgical supplies produced over the past month.

On the other hand, despite the careful regulation and required testing of the radiation equipment, there is only a small probability that the equipment is not properly calibrated. In fact industry-wide test results report that only a few sterilizers need recalibration each year. As a result, several manufacturers have begun lobbying the regulatory agency for more liberal certification requirements. The manufacturers have argued that the equipment needs to be self-tested only twice a year and recertified by an independent testing firm once a year.

There are several potentially negative consequences of the problem that Judy has uncovered. One is the action that the state agency may take when it learns that the certification report filed by Baker-Allison was based on phony test results. Another is the potential danger to surgical teams and patients using Baker-Allison products. Because the gowns and drapes may not have been sterile, Baker-Allison may have liabilities related to any infections caused by their surgical products. The situation is made even more difficult by financial pressures on the company resulting from declining sales of some of its other products that are being undercut by imports. In fact, if it were not for the sales of the new line of products, 375 of the company's 750 employees would have been laid off last month.

Judy was shaken as she walked back to her office. She walked into her office and stared out the window as she thought about what she should do.

Questions

1. What issues should Judy consider when making her decision?
2. What action should Judy take?
3. What issues should she take into consideration in making her decision?
4. Whom should she communicate with about her concerns?
5. How should she communicate her concerns?

References

1. Keenan, Faith, and Hamm, Steve. "The New Teamwork," *Business Week* (February 18, 2002): EB 16.

2. Sprout, Alison L. "Reality Boost," *Fortune* (March 21, 1994): 93.

3. Curtin, Leah, and Simpson, Roy L. "Conveying an Effective Message in Voicemail or E-Mail," *Health Management Technology* (February 2002): 52.

4. Stewart, Thomas A. "Managing in a Wired Company," *Fortune* (July 11, 1994): 44.

5. Ibid.

6. Resnick, Rosalind. "Hitching a Ride into Cyberspace," *Nation's Business* (July 1994): 66–68.

7. Nucifora, Alf. "Virtual Teams Are Viable Under the Right Circumstances," *Fort Worth Business Press* (August 31, 2001): 21. Katzenbach, Jon, and Smith, Douglas, "Virtual Teaming," *Forbes* (May 1, 2001): 48–50.

8. Ibid.

9. Nucifora. "Virtual Teams": 21.

10. Maynard, Roberta. "The Growing Appeal of Telecommuting," *Nation's Business* (August 1994): 61–62.

11. Ibid.

12. Tam, Pui-Wing. "Silicon Valley Belatedly Boots Up Programs to Ease Employees' Lives," *The Wall Street Journal* (August 29, 2000): B1.

13. Ibid.

14. Hall, Cheryl. "An Open-Book Policy," *Dallas Morning News* (June 28, 1998): 1H–2H.

15. Ibid.

16. Weiss, Donald. *How to Be a Successful Manager.* New York: Amacom (1986): 33.

17. Case, John. "Games Companies Play," *Inc.* (October 1994): 46–47.

18. March, Robert M. *Working for a Japanese Company.* New York: Kodansha International (1992): 92–93.

19. Goldsmith, Charles. "Look See! Anyone Do Read This and It Will Make You Laughable," *The Wall Street Journal* (November 19, 1992): B1.

20. Sheridan, John H. "Partnering for Personnel," *Industry Week* (July 6, 1998): 11–12.

21. Schuster, Karolyn. "Speaking the Language," *Food Management* (April 2000): 24.

22. Tannen, Deborah. *Talking from 9 to 5.* New York: William Morrow (1994): 15–16.

23. Maurer, Rick. *Beyond the Wall of Resistance: Unconventional Strategies that Build Support for Change.* Austin, TX: Bard Books Inc. (1996): 153–154.

24. Norton, Rob. "New Thinking on the Causes and Costs of Yes Men (and Women)," *Fortune* (November 28, 1994): 31.

25. Ibid.

26. Bose, Indranil, and Mahapatra, Radha K. "Business Data Mining—a Machine Learning Perspective," *Information & Management* (December 2001): 211.

27. Drucker, Peter F. "The Next Information Revolution," *Forbes ASAP* (August 24, 1998): 47–58.

28. Ibid.

29. *Forbes ASAP.* "America's Best Technology Users" (August 24, 1998): 63–86.

30. Ibid.: 68.

31. Ibid.: 63–86.

32. O'Bryhim, Brendan. "X Internet: The Next E-Wave," *Electrical Wholesaling* (January 2002): 18.

33. Ziegler, Bart. "New Generation of Hand-Held PCs Inches Closer to Ideal," *The Wall Street Journal* (January 29, 1998): B1.

34. Maselli, Jennifer. "Voice Recognition Aims to Lower Call-Center Costs," *Information Week* (October 22, 2001): 63.

35. Hathaway, Patti. "Building Rapport," *Executive Excellence* (July 2001): 13.

36. Ibid.

37. Nichols, Ralph G. "Listening Is Good Business," in *Readings in Management,* ed. Max D. Richards. Cincinnati: South Western Publishing (1982): 111.

38. Rogers, C. R., and Roethlisberger, F. J. "Barriers and Gateways to Communication," in *Fifteen Key Concepts for Managerial Success.* Cambridge, MA: Business Classics, Harvard Business Review (1975): 45.

39. Nichols. "Listening Is Good": 111.

40. Ibid.

41. Hathaway. "Building Rapport": 13.

42. Nichols. "Listening Is Good": 111.

43. Rega, Michael E. "Developing Listening Skills," *American Salesman* (May 2000): 3–7.

44. Rogers, C. R., and Farson, R. E. "The Meaning of Active Listening," in *Active Listening.* Chicago: Industrial Relations Center of the University of Chicago (1990): 3.

45. Ibid.

46. Anderson, Carl R. *Management Skills, Functions, and Organization Performance.* Dubuque, IA: Wm. C. Brown (1984): 202.

47. Weiss, Donald. *How to Write Easily and Effectively.* New York: Amacom (1986): 49–50.

MANAGING CHANGE AND STRESS

6

Objectives

After reading and discussing this chapter, you should be able to do the following:

1. Define this chapter's key terms.
2. Explain how people form their attitudes.
3. List and briefly explain the basic steps you can take to change a person's attitude.
4. List and briefly explain the techniques available to change people's attitudes.
5. Explain how to implement change.
6. List causes of stress on the job.
7. List ways of coping with work-related stress.

Introduction

Because of competition from foreign producers that deliver better, cheaper, higher-quality goods and services at lower costs, U.S. companies in every industry are changing and innovating. While some companies have moved production overseas, many U.S. industries are responding to the challenges of foreign producers by increasing their use of automation and computer-driven machines. They are also redesigning jobs to put more decisions into the hands of those who know the work best, creating teams, and reengineering their processes for greater efficiency.

Because people are the key to better quality and productivity, work attitudes, values, and beliefs are critical to the organization's success.

Attitudes, Beliefs, and Values

This chapter looks at attitudes, beliefs, and values and how they form and influence individuals' productivity in the workplace. It also discusses how you as a supervisor can influence individuals to become or to remain good producers. Finally, it offers advice on how you can manage change and stress in yourself and in others.

ATTITUDES

attitude
a person's manner of thinking, feeling, or acting toward specific stimuli

An **attitude** is a consistent predisposition—either favorable or unfavorable—toward a specific stimulus. While attitudes are very stable, general attitudes are more susceptible to change. Research indicates that the degree to which more general attitudes can be changed is related to phases of adulthood. General attitudes are most stable for people in middle adulthood, while they are more amenable to change in early and late adulthood because people tend to be less self-assured and are more open in these phases of their lives.[1]

Behavior and attitudes influence each other. While it is intuitive to conclude that changes in attitudes drive behavior, research indicates that the reverse is true—changes in behavior drive changes in attitudes. When we get a subordinate to change her behavior we should find that she experiences some movement in her attitudes toward alignment or conformity with her change in behavior.[2]

Examples abound at the Toyota–GM assembly plant (NUMMI) in Fremont, California. The attitude of one team leader, Lee Ledbetter, is that team leaders work for the team members, not the other way around. "Communication between workers and managers and among the workers is the key to NUMMI's success. Good products and a good process are important . . . but it's the ability to correct mistakes, to stop the line that makes for top-quality cars."[3] A key to the success of the NUMMI plant has been the participation of workers in improving production processes. Recently, in one year alone, NUMMI workers made 27,000 suggestions for improvements and 90 percent of their suggestions were put into place. In addition, there is enough trust between the United Auto Workers union and GM that managers can do some of the work at this plant, whereas the union's contracts at other GM plants prohibit such actions.[4]

Motorola is recognized as one of the leading companies when it comes to providing training for its employees. The company, which follows a principle of lifelong learning for employees, provides 40 hours of training each year for its employees. In addition, at Motorola the typical employee who works in information technology receives between 100 and 150 hours of training each year. Motorola faces great challenges in providing timely training because of the fast-paced, rapidly changing nature of the electronics industry. Motorola's operations are also distributed throughout the world—the company has information technology people in business units in more than 50 countries. The geographic dispersion of Motorola employees has prompted the company to conduct some of its training through the Internet and with CD-ROM technology.[5] Quest faces similar challenges in training its technical employees because of their geographic dispersion. The company used a training consulting firm to provide technical training to almost 4,000 employees, who speak 12 different languages, in 31 countries.[6]

BELIEFS

Our work experiences and the people we have worked with have created changes in us at various stages in our lives. Our experiences have taught us our individual sets of beliefs. A **belief** is a perception based on a conviction that certain things are true. Beliefs also are based on what seems to be true or probable in one's own mind. This latter kind of belief is often called an *opinion*. Beliefs shape our attitudes, and our attitudes, when made known to others, display our beliefs.

belief

a perception based on a conviction that certain things are true or probable in one's own mind

When you are confronted with new people or concepts, you are usually not predisposed in any specific way toward them. You lack definite attitudes, opinions, and beliefs about them. It is at this point that you are most open and impressionable about the new contacts. Initially, you try to make your own observations, gain some insights, and draw your own conclusions. Think back to the time when you were seeking employment with your present employer. You probably applied based on its reputation, as relayed to you by others whose beliefs and opinions you respected. A friend who spoke well of the company may have suggested that you apply. You were willing to put your future in the hands of an employer on the basis of another's beliefs. As a new applicant, you made your own observations during the selection process and received answers to specific questions. Your

Your workers' attitudes will be a direct reflection of your attitude toward them. The worker pictured here receives recognition and words of encouragement from his supervisor. Wouldn't you work harder knowing your supervisor really cares about you?

beliefs about your new employer were taking shape, and when you accepted the job, you had probably formed a positive set of attitudes toward both your employer and your new job. Your beliefs, therefore, had a definite influence on your behavior.

VALUES

value

judgment about what is right or wrong and important or unimportant

One set of beliefs that we all have is our values. **Values** include judgments about what are important and acceptable behaviors. Values are often expressed as wants and as worthwhile objectives. Having a high-paying job or working for a respected and admired employer are examples of values. Insights on values may be gained by considering the work values that mentors and their protégés might share. When both hold similar work values there is greater likelihood for a harmonious relationship. The following are examples of work values that are relevant to such relationships: innovation, attention to detail, supportiveness, team orientation, aggressiveness, and decisiveness.[7]

Like attitudes, values are learned throughout life. Usually, values are more difficult to change than attitudes. Unfortunately, people are often quick to make assumptions about a person's or group's values based on the person's or group's ethnic or racial background, religious affiliation, place of birth, gender, or age. Their assumptions, which are often inaccurate, may change as they discover the real values of others through interactions in the workplace. Exhibit 6.1 presents the top work values for workers in the United States and a comparison with those for workers in Germany.

Exhibit 6.1   *Comparison of work values in the United States and Germany.*

	RANK IN U.S.	RANK IN GERMANY		RANK IN U.S.	RANK IN GERMANY
Job interest	1	1	Meaningful work	13	3
Achievement	2	9	Work influence	14	10
Advancement	3	15	Pay	15	12
Personal growth	4	11	Benefits	16	4
Esteem	5	14	Company	17	22
Use of ability	6	8	Coworkers	18	2
Independence	7	7	Organizational influence	19	21
Responsibility	8	20	Work conditions	20	18
Feedback	9	13	Interaction	21	19
Security	10	6	Convenient hours	22	16
Supervisor	11	5	Status	23	24
Recognition	12	17	Contribution to society	24	23

Source: Extracted from Dov Elizur, Ingwer Borg, Raymond Hunt, and Istvan Beck, "The Structure of Work Values: A Cross Cultural Comparison," *Journal of Organizational Behavior,* 12 (1991): 21–38.

While these values are common within each country and differences are observable between countries, they are not universal across all members of the workforce in any country. For this reason it is essential for each supervisor to develop an understanding of the values of each of his subordinates. Greater workforce diversity brings greater diversity in values and a challenge for managers to balance the majority's values "with the need to recognize and value individual differences."[8]

People's Attitudes About Work

Herb Kelleher, former CEO of Southwest Airlines, hired people who had a sense of humor and "who have to excel to satisfy themselves and who work well in a collegial environment. We don't care that much about education and experience, because we can train people to do whatever they have to do. We hire attitudes."[9] Colleen Barrett, an executive vice-president at Southwest Airlines, says her airline is looking for people who have the following traits: "listening, caring, smiling, saying 'thank you' and being warm. . . ."[10] Southwest has been extraordinarily profitable in part because of its legendary customer service. Nonetheless, Kelleher backs up his employees and believes in firing a customer before an employee: "The customer is frequently wrong. . . . We write them and say, 'Fly somebody else. Don't abuse our people.'"[11]

THE WORK ETHIC

People's attitudes about work—their **work ethic**—can be grouped into three areas: the importance of working, the kind of work a person chooses or is required to perform, and the quality of the person's efforts while performing work. As a supervisor, team leader, and team facilitator, you can influence the experiences of your associates and, therefore, help shape their attitudes about work and their individual work ethics. A major auto manufacturer is "looking for workers who show not only aptitude, but the right attitude. Teamwork is a must, along with the ability to use math, computers and statistics to identify, analyze and solve quality and cost problems—without shouting for a supervisor."[12] Although it has no requirement that applicants have high school diplomas, nearly one fourth of its Windsor, Canada, plant's third shift (600 people) have a college degree. Like NUMMI, to stay competitive the company needs teams of empowered individuals committed to quality and productivity improvement.

work ethic

a person's attitude about the importance of working, the kind of work he chooses, and the quality of his efforts while performing work

As a supervisor, you need to be aware of your own work ethic and the work ethic of each of your associates. You need to know why people are working for you and your company, what they think of their work, and the quality of their performance. Only then can you understand them as individuals. Unfortunately, some behaviors are the antithesis of those needed for a positive work environment, occurring more commonly than might be

SUPERVISORS AND QUALITY

Motorola is famous for its emphasis on quality, productivity, and innovation. Its best plant in its Land Mobile Division is in Penang, Malaysia. It is decorated with scoreboards touting a variety of performance statistics and slogans to boost morale. "Opened 20 years ago as a cheap assembly shop for pagers, the facility now has an all-Malaysian research and development team of 200 engineers who help develop next-generation two-way radios and cordless phones."

Among the plant's keys to success are its reliance on employee suggestions for improvement, a firm commitment to cooperation through teams, and each associate's willingness to take the initiative "to identify and act on problems that hinder quality and productivity." Workers are rewarded for spotting trouble and fixing it. Careful screening of applicants (basic command of mathematics, English, and science is a must) leads to selection based on individuals' attitudes toward working in teams. New employees work under the guidance of skilled employees and partake in 48 hours of training a year.

Paramount in all employees' efforts is a continuing drive to stay competitive with other company production units. "Just as the Penang plant had its origins as a source of cheap labor, the workers' fear is that Motorola someday could shift work to an even cheaper locale. So managers are . . . looking for ways to boost efficiency even further. Says Managing Director Ko: 'I constantly tell them that we will lose out to other places if we aren't cost competitive.'" Judging by Marina Osman's performance, the plant has few worries. She is a member of the "100 Club," a group of employees who have recommended 100 or more "cost-saving ideas and had at least 60% of them implemented." Says Osman, "I'm one of the family here, . . . I want to do what is best for the company."

Source: Pete Engardio and Gail DeGeorge, "Importing Enthusiasm," *Business Week* (Special 1994 Bonus Issue, "21st Century Capitalism"): 122–123.

expected. Consider the following examples of behaviors, the type of work ethic they represent, and the impact they are likely to have on the workplace: "talk loudest and don't listen to other people . . . talk behind people's backs . . . over-promise and under-deliver . . . don't help anybody else . . . and take the credit for other people's efforts."[13]

THEORIES X AND Y

Douglas McGregor, a professor of management at MIT, developed two theories about managers' views of human nature and motivation.[14] These theories describe opposing perspectives that seem to provide an explanation of how many managers treat their subordinates. **Theory X** managers tend to have the following views of human nature:

Theory X
a set of attitudes traditionally held by managers that includes assuming the worst with regard to the average worker's initiative and creativity

1. The average person has a natural dislike for work and will try to avoid it.

2. The average person has to be threatened, controlled, coerced, and punished to give a fair day's work.

3. The average person avoids responsibility, lacks ambition, and needs constant direction.

Unfortunately, results from a recent survey revealed that Theory X was alive and well:

> Nearly half of companies monitor E-mail, up from 38% last year, according to a recent American Management Association survey, while Internet monitoring increased to 62.8%, up from 54.1% . . . Another study by the nonprofit Privacy Foundation shows that Internet and E-mail use of one out of three employees is monitored daily. Big Brother is watching more employees, more closely, and more often than in the past.[15]

While monitoring may indicate Theory X assumptions about employees, such as they need to be closely controlled, some electronic monitoring by employers is motivated by concerns about legal liability and the improper use of e-mail and the Internet for sexual harassment.[16]

On the other hand, **Theory Y** managers have views of human nature that reflect the findings of recent research on human behavior and motivation. Theory Y includes the following propositions:

1. The average person desires work as naturally as play or rest.
2. The average person is capable of self-control if committed to a goal.
3. The average person is committed to goals for which achievement is rewarded.
4. The average person desires responsibility and accepts it willingly.
5. The average person possesses imagination, ingenuity, and initiative.
6. The average person is intellectually underutilized in the typical industrial setting.

Team leaders who hold Theory Y beliefs about their associates will take an entirely different approach toward them than will leaders who adhere to Theory X. Theory Y managers assume the best, expect no less, and demand the best from each individual. Theory Y managers also demand the best from themselves. According to management consultant and author Tom Peters: "Front-line people have been secretly champing at the bit for decades: Give them the same information the boss gets. Give them access, at any time, to any kind of training they desire. And then let them have at it. 'They' will respond."[17] Theory Y assumptions about human nature are revealed in the success of Julia M. Garcia and her team members at Frito-Lay:

> [They] are responsible for everything from potato processing to equipment maintenance. To help them devise ways to produce and ship chips more efficiently, Garcia and her teammates receive weekly reports on cost, quality, and service performances [scoreboarding] and are kept abreast of the team's ranking in relation to Frito's 22 other potato-chip teams nationwide. Garcia's group, at the top of Frito's rankings for more than a year, also determines crew scheduling and even interviews potential employees for the department—once the sole domain of management.[18]

Theory Y

a set of attitudes held by today's generation of managers that includes assuming the best about the average worker's initiative and creativity

Countless companies have had similar experiences once they tapped the inherent diversity and willingness to do well in most human beings. Look around you at work. You will probably find many examples of men and women, both in and out of management, who are putting forth a mediocre effort. Such mediocre behavior often occurs because their managers expect nothing more from them. Subordinates learn to give what is expected. A mediocre subordinate is usually the reflection of a mediocre manager.

THEORY Z

Theory Z

set of approaches to managing people based on the attitudes of Japanese managers, emphasizing the importance of the individual and of team effort to the organization

The early 1980s brought a sharp focus on Japanese management practices and techniques. In Japan, input from workers and managers at every level is sought before decisions are made. Supervisors and middle managers seek the input of their subordinates before deciding issues. Japanese workers generally feel more loyalty to their employers than do their U.S. counterparts. These attitudes of loyalty are built, in large measure, on a set of factors that include lifetime employment, emphasis on consensus in decision making, slow rates of promotion, less formal forms of control, more general career paths, and broader concepts of work and family concerns. In contrast, employment in U.S. companies is characterized by shorter terms of employment, individual decision making and responsibility, faster rates of promotion, more formal controls, more specialization in careers, and narrower views of work and family. **Theory Z** is a blend of these characteristics; it holds that high motivation and productivity occur when management develops greater trust in workers and demonstrates greater commitment to them.[19] While Japan has been hurt by a prolonged recession over the past decade, corporations in the United States have benefited from the Japanese approach to industrial management and have borrowed many of its concepts.

The Supervisor's Attitudes

It is often said that supervisors are "caught in the middle" because they are concerned most directly about the welfare of their subordinates and associates and at the same time must share and fortify management's authority. Needless to say, this fence straddling can be uncomfortable and demanding at times, but it is necessary. Truly, supervisors, team leaders, and team facilitators are positioned between the needs of their subordinates and associates and the needs of their superiors. Supervisors must be able to empathize with the perspectives of both their subordinates and upper management. Supervisors get in trouble when they identify too closely with either group and become labeled as having extremely "pro-worker" or "pro-management" attitudes. In such cases supervisors are likely to lose the trust and cooperation of the other group.

Beware of accepting the attitudes or opinions of others as your own. We all have a tendency to fill a void in our knowledge by the quickest means available, but this can be a dangerous practice. When you first became a supervisor, you may have heard from your boss or predecessor, "Watch out for Al; he's a sneak," or "You sure are lucky to have Agnes; she's a peach." Dismiss these "insights" and wait to form your own attitudes and opinions through your firsthand observations.

THE PYGMALION EFFECT

George Bernard Shaw's play, later made into a film, about an English flower girl in the slums who is groomed to become a lady of English society was called *Pygmalion*. From the book and film we have deduced what has become known as the *Pygmalion effect*: Assuming the best about people will often result in their giving their best; assuming less will often yield less in their performance. In short, people learn to give what they are expected to give. Students and trainees often learn in accordance with what their teachers and trainers expect of them.

One real tragedy of Theory X is that it is a self-fulfilling prophecy. If a manager really believes what this theory holds about subordinates, she will treat them in an authoritarian and suspicious manner, threatening them and exercising close control. New

The Pygmalion effect describes the performance effects of self-fulfilling prophecies. Think how motivated you would be if your manager and colleagues had strong beliefs in your ability to perform. What could your subordinates accomplish with your belief in them?

employees who have something fresh and creative to offer will soon learn that their ideas, initiative, and drive are not respected or rewarded. They will learn to behave in the ways the boss expects. Soon the employees will adopt the what's-the-use attitude that their boss assumed existed from the beginning. Then the boss can smile and say, "See, I told you so." What Theory X does not say, but implies, is that only a small minority of people possess the attitudes, values, and beliefs necessary to manage others.

An article by Susan White and Edwin Locke provides us with the following insights and suggestions about the Pygmalion effect:[20]

1. Leaders' expectations of their subordinates' performance have subconscious effects on both the leaders' behaviors toward subordinates and the performance of subordinates.
2. Subordinates' self-efficacy (confidence in one's own ability to accomplish a task) can be improved when their managers set up opportunities for them to have a series of small wins.

3. Studies generally demonstrate that the Pygmalion effect does not work as well with female leaders and with female subordinates, but more research is needed.

4. Leaders should have an orientation that subordinates' mistakes are learning opportunities rather than delays in goal accomplishment.

You should have little doubt that you as a supervisor can help or hinder a new person's adjustment to and success in your company's environment. Your attitudes will soon shape those of your subordinates. They will look to you for respect, guidance, and example. Your expectations of them and the examples you set by your daily behavior determine their attitudes toward you and toward their own work.

PROBLEM SUPERVISORS

Without realizing it, some supervisors may be the primary cause of an employee's difficulties. Through their actions or lack of action, supervisors influence their subordinates' behavior. Supervisors have the ability to aggravate their subordinates' difficulties or help them steer clear of problems. Your people are very conscious of your behavior and see guidelines for their own behavior in yours. How your people perceive you—what they think of you as a person and a boss—is very important to you. You need to recognize that you are seen and heard by many others. Your observers are all unique individuals with different attitudes, values, and experiences. Each will observe you at different times and under different circumstances. Therefore, each person's perception of you will be unique and unlike any other. Consider the checklist in Exhibit 6.2. The items you answered with a "yes" response indicate potential sources of difficulty in your relationships

---

Exhibit 6.2   *Determining subordinates' perceptions of you.*

Yes	No		Yes	No	
○	○	1. Do I like to control my people with threats?	○	○	6. Do I issue conflicting orders and instructions?
○	○	2. Do I like to keep them a little off balance and insecure?	○	○	7. Do I forget to compliment them for work well done?
○	○	3. Are my behaviors and dealings with them unpredictable?	○	○	8. Do I discipline them in public?
○	○	4. Do I make promises that I do not or cannot keep?	○	○	9. Do I carry a grudge?
			○	○	10. Do I play favorites?
○	○	5. Do I betray confidences?	○	○	11. Do I take my subordinates for granted?

with subordinates. Without positive perceptions of you, your subordinates will not trust and respect you. As a result you will lack power to influence them by means other than threats and punishment. In short, you will lack leadership ability.

Your Subordinates' Attitudes

Your people have attitudes about their work, the company, and you as their boss. When you first become a supervisor, your people will adopt a wait-and-see attitude about you and your abilities. They are, for the most part, open and objective, waiting for evidence on which to base their opinions. The attitudes they will eventually adopt about you are almost entirely within your power to mold. Their attitudes will surely influence their performance, their output, and the reputation of the department. One of the most demanding and important tasks for managers (and particularly for supervisors) is to identify improper or unacceptable attitudes—attitudes held by subordinates that interfere with their performance.

GOOD ATTITUDES VERSUS BAD ATTITUDES

Once we recognize an attitude as the source of problems, we are able to change it. But problems arise when we must identify the attitudes of other people. First, we attempt to determine the other person's attitudes through observations of the person's actions or words. Because we cannot "see" attitudes, we can only make assumptions about them on the basis of what we see people do and what we hear them say. Second, we may be too quick to label another person's attitude as bad or improper simply because it differs from our own. Despite the difficulty, as a supervisor you need to understand your attitudes and those of your subordinates, and you need to discover why these attitudes exist.

Suppose, for example, that as a supervisor in a machine shop you observe a subordinate named Joe not wearing his safety goggles while operating a grinding wheel, in violation of safety rules. Ten minutes later you pass him again, and he is still not wearing his safety goggles. At this point, you may ask yourself why. The question should have been asked earlier. If it had been, the second infraction might have been prevented. The answer to the question lies in the worker's attitude toward wearing safety goggles. He believes that his attitude is a proper one, or he would not behave in this manner. As his supervisor, your tendency is to label his attitude bad or improper. At this point, the dialogue might go as follows:

SUPERVISOR: Joe, you know we have a shop rule about wearing safety goggles, don't you?

JOE: Yeah, I know the rule.

SUPERVISOR: Do you want to lose an eye?

JOE: Nope.

SUPERVISOR: Didn't I tell you a few minutes ago to wear your goggles?

JOE: Yep.

SUPERVISOR: Well, why don't you wear them, then?

JOE: The strap's too tight. It gives me a headache.

The lesson should be obvious. People believe their attitudes are adequate and act accordingly. Until they see a need for change or can be shown an alternative that gives them better results, they have no incentive to change. Joe was willing to accept a risk to his eye in order to avoid a headache. Why he did not complain without being asked is another problem. If he has to buy goggles out of his own money, he may be reluctant to buy another pair. If the company furnishes them, the storeroom may be out of Joe's size. There could be a dozen reasons. The point is, that you must ask, what is the person's attitude and why does the person have it? When you know the answers to these questions, you can begin to change the attitudes that are the source of problems.

UNCOOPERATIVE ATTITUDES: WHY PEOPLE RESIST CHANGE

Cooperation means working together to reach common objectives or goals. The primary barrier to cooperation may be your weaknesses, inadequacies, and failure to offer a good example. Look first at yourself and your management practices. If you can honestly say that the barrier to cooperation lies outside yourself, the remainder of this chapter should prove helpful to you.

At the core of a person's non-cooperation is a lack of motivation to cooperate. This means that the person has no desire at present to do so. It falls to you, therefore, to attempt to provide the climate and incentives that will foster a spirit of cooperation in each of your people.

Past Change Efforts and Cynicism

How well people accept changes may depend on how well changes have been introduced in the past. Accordingly, it is important for change to go well, because unsuccessful changes can provide the fuel for greater cynicism about future change. Such cynicism then becomes a self-fulfilling prophecy because successful change depends on how well employees accept and become committed to the change. Lack of information about a change also fuels cynicism. Thus attempts to implement change should be well thought-out and well communicated. In addition, employees can be predisposed toward cynicism. The massive downsizing of the 1980s, 1990s, and 2000s has probably contributed to such cynicism in the United States. The following suggestions may be helpful for minimizing change-related cynicism:[21]

1. Inform subordinates of the when, why, and how of the change.
2. Avoid surprises.
3. Involve subordinates in decisions that potentially affect them.
4. View the change from the employees' perspective to understand their needs.
5. Provide subordinates with examples of successful change.
6. Allow subordinates to ventilate their frustrations about the change.
7. Admit past mistakes and provide atonement for costs incurred.
8. Explain why the change is necessary at this time.

Personal Reasons

If change was handled well in the past, employees should be reasonably receptive to new changes. If not, you can anticipate resistance or opposition to the change. On the other hand, people may resist changes because of the personal advantages they may lose. For example, if people know their jobs well and are successful at them, they have job security. They are using tried and proven methods, and they feel no need to make an effort to learn something new. Success also tends to make some people blind to the need to change. This may occur with individuals higher up the organizational hierarchy: "achieving success and power often encourages a misplaced belief that there is nothing left to learn—a sure ticket to derailment."[22]

Most of us have a built-in fear of change. Nearly all such fear is based on ignorance—not knowing what the changes might mean to us and to our position. We have seen people displaced through advances in technology and traditional skills and crafts eliminated. A change in methods may be viewed as a criticism of our present performance, especially when the change is enforced from outside our department. For all these reasons, the supervisor must plan for change, communicate the need for it effectively, and show subordinates the advantages that will accrue to them as a result of adopting the change.

In addition, some people revert to dysfunctional behavior when it comes to change. Management scholar Morgan McCall calls our attention to this human tendency that sometimes proves to be a major barrier to change. He says this "resistance to change is described in drug treatment as 'doing the same thing over and over again, expecting it to come out differently.'"[23] While the job environment is not drug treatment, some subordinates act exactly as McCall describes—they keep doing the same thing over while expecting different results. As a result, supervisors may need to use some of the techniques described in later sections to get such employees to change.

Social Reasons

As you are well aware, most people in a business do not work by themselves. They are probably members of both informal and formal groups.

Changes proposed or suspected may give rise to a fear that the worker's social relationships may be upset, either by the loss of present associates or by the need to find new ones. An individual may be in favor of a change because he can see personal advantages in the new development. The group to which he belongs, however, may be against the change. The individual can either adopt the group's viewpoint about the change and risk difficulties with the supervisor or favor the change and risk expulsion from the group.

Facilitating Change

John Kotter, a professor at Harvard University, has developed a comprehensive approach for implementing change. While much of his approach is applicable to organization-wide change, some of it applies to supervisors as well. A particularly important step in his approach is to create a sense of urgency for the change. Supervisors can create such urgency through actions like having subordinates obtain feedback from unsatisfied customers. They can refuse to take last-minute heroic action to prevent a crisis when the old ways of doing things are no longer adequate to do the job. Supervisors can also facilitate the change process by providing rewards for short-term wins. When subordinates make incremental progress toward the desired change in behavior, supervisors should reward the behavior.

Examples of three approaches to change are described as follows:

> Three groups of ten individuals are in a park at lunchtime with a rain-storm threatening. In the first group, someone says: "Get up and follow me." When he starts walking and only a few others join in, he yells to those still seated: "Up, I said, and NOW!" In the second group, someone says: "We're going to have to move. Here's the plan. Each of us stands up and marches in the direction of the apple tree. Please stay at least two feet away from other group members and do not run. Do not leave any personal belongings on the ground here and be sure to stop at the base of the tree. When we are all there . . . ." In the third group, someone tells the others: "It's going to rain in a few minutes. Why don't we go over there and sit under that huge apple tree. We'll stay dry, and we can have fresh apples for lunch."[24]

The first approach is one of attempting to force people by use of authoritarian decree. This approach generally does not work well and requires great power on the part of the boss. The second approach is one of micro-management. While it may produce somewhat better results, it is time consuming. In addition, while the manager is busy looking inward in order to issue numerous directives for micro-managing the change, she is not looking outward for environmental forces that may affect the unit. The third approach, and obviously the preferred one, involves communication of a vision for change and the benefits to all for changing. It has the advantage of overcoming many of the forces that act as barriers to change.[25]

CHANGING THE ATTITUDES OF SUBORDINATES

A supervisor can bring about a change in a subordinate's improper attitude through a four-step process. After you have observed improper behavior that appears to be driven by an attitude, you should take the following steps:

1. Identify the improper attitude or behavior.
2. Determine what supports it—opinions and beliefs (root causes).
3. Weaken or change whatever supports it (root causes).
4. Offer a substitute for the improper attitude.

Consider the following example, contributed by a student. Mike was a supervisor of 30 assemblers in an electronics plant in Chicago. It was his practice to turn each new employee over to an experienced worker for training until the new person adjusted to the job and became capable of meeting both quality and quantity standards on his own. One day, Mike hired a young, recent immigrant from India named Ehri. Ehri was placed under the direction of Dave, an experienced and willing worker–trainer. However, once he was on his own, Ehri's production was marked by an unacceptable level of rejects.

Step 1: Identify the Improper Attitude or Behavior

When you determine that a subordinate's behavior is improper, you must look for the attitude behind it and state it in precise terms.

Mike went to Ehri and observed him at work. Ehri was working at an almost frantic pace. Mike assumed that this was the reason for the large number of rejects and asked Ehri to slow his pace and concentrate on quality, not quantity.

Often, just by investigating the action, showing concern, and giving corrective instructions, you will be able to solve the problem. The worker may realize at this point that her behavior is unacceptable and change it to meet the demands of the supervisor. This did not happen with Ehri.

Mike had failed to identify the attitude that supported the fast pace of work. Instead, he simply identified an action, which he attempted to stop with orders and instructions. He had dealt with the symptom of an attitude, not with the opinions or beliefs that were causing the problem.

Step 2: Determine What Supports It

On the basis of your investigation and analysis, see if you can spot the roots of the attitude—the primary beliefs that both support and feed the attitude in the employee's mind. The best way to do this is to get the employee talking about his true feelings. Some frequent root causes that support and nurture incorrect attitudes include group pressures, faulty logic, and misunderstood standards.

SUPERVISORS AND ETHICS

U. S. companies practiced widespread downsizing during the 1980s and early 1990s. Reports of downsizing came so frequently that they were almost daily features in the business press. Some downsizing was necessary because it enabled U. S. companies to become extremely efficient and helped to ensure their survival. On the other hand, downsizing frequently did not deliver anticipated cost savings. Some companies that were profitable also downsized. When employees see no compelling need for downsizing, it is more difficult for them to accept the changes related to downsizing, such as increased work loads for survivors. In addition, the consequences of downsizing to those who lose their jobs can be devastating.

Al Dunlop, a CEO who acquired a great deal of notoriety because of his extensive use of downsizing, became known as "Chainsaw." His exploits as a CEO were chronicled in an autobiography entitled *Mean Business.* During his career he downsized extensively at Lily-Tulip, a disposable cup maker; eliminated 11,000 jobs (approximately one third) at Scott Paper; and eliminated approximately one-half of the jobs at Sunbeam. In 1998 Sunbeam's stock declined from $53 in March to $11.25 in June. "In addition, shareholder suits alleged that Sunbeam had pumped up its winter-time sales by selling grills to retailers on attractive terms, with the understanding that they would be delivered later" (Pollock and Brannigan, p. A8). In June 1998 Chainsaw Al received a dose of his own medicine when he was fired as the Sunbeam CEO. In August 1998 Sunbeam's stock declined to $5.13.

Sources: Martha Brannigan and James R. Hagerty, "Sunbeam, Its Prospects Looking Ever Worse, Fires CEO Dunlap," *The Wall Street Journal* (June 15, 1998): A1, A14. Allan Sloan, "Chainsaw Massacre," *Newsweek* (June 29, 1998): 62. Ellen Joan Pollock and Martha Brannigan, "Mixed Grill: The Sunbeam Shuffle, or How Ron Perelman Wound Up in Control," *The Wall Street Journal* (August 19, 1998): A1, A8.

Mike thought the problem had been solved. After all, when a supervisor lays down the law, especially to a new worker, the subordinate should respond. Ehri's production, however, continued to yield an unacceptable number of rejects. Next, Mike and his boss both talked with Ehri. They again emphasized quality and included an implied threat that unless the situation reversed itself, Ehri's job was in jeopardy. But still the problem persisted because Mike had not uncovered the root cause. Even though he was armed with the additional authority of his boss, Mike was still treating a symptom of the attitude. He had not yet uncovered the attitude and its root causes.

Finally, it occurred to Mike that the problem might have originated in Ehri's training. He approached Dave and related the problem of too much quantity and too little quality. After stating that Ehri's job was at stake, he asked if Dave knew how this situation might have evolved. Dave became somewhat embarrassed, and on further questioning, Mike discovered that Dave had told Ehri that quantity was all management really cared about, regardless of what they said to the contrary. Mike had finally struck pay dirt. He now knew what Ehri's attitude was and the root cause for it—misunderstood standards.

Step 3: Weaken or Change Whatever Supports It

Once the root causes are known, they can be analyzed and their vulnerabilities noted. A program of action can then be developed to change beliefs through the use of reason. One way is to point out flaws in the employee's assumptions or how the basis for these assumptions has changed.

Mike instructed Dave to go to Ehri and explain that he had been misinformed. Dave apologized to Ehri and made it clear that he had only been kidding about quantity over quality. Dave had the reputation of being a practical joker, and he really had meant no harm by what he did. He was only taking advantage of a novice who was naive to the ways of a skilled worker like Dave. Ehri had a language difficulty with English and tended to take things literally. Thus he had been easy prey for a joker. Dave felt certain that once Mike talked to Ehri, Ehri would realize that he had been had. When Dave understood that Ehri had not responded to Mike's talk, he was most eager to help correct the problem.

Step 4: Offer a Substitute

Dave had no trouble persuading Ehri to change his thinking, because Ehri had received quite a bit of pressure by that time. Once Ehri realized (as a result of the statements of both Dave and Mike) that his attitude was based on misinformation, he became a superior worker.

You may be able to change behavior by constant harping and criticism, but like the action of water in wearing away rock, it may take too long and leave scars. In general, people will change only if they see that their behaviors are no longer worth maintaining. Threats and orders usually only suppress a natural and observable behavior and drive it underground. The person becomes sneaky and does what you say only when you are there to police your order. When you are absent, the old behavior pattern resurfaces. You must identify the root causes of the behavior and encourage the individual to question the position. Only then will you be able to initiate a permanent change in that person's behavior.

TECHNIQUES FOR OBTAINING CHANGE

Fortunately, many tried and proven methods are available for reducing resistance to change and instilling a desire to cooperate. These methods depend on your understanding of the previous chapters and your ability to apply what you have learned. The basic techniques at your disposal for introducing changes and resolving conflicts include:

- Force-field analysis
- Effective communication
- Persuasion techniques
- Participation techniques

- Training programs
- Organizational development activities

Force-Field Analysis

force-field analysis

a method for visualizing the driving and restraining forces at work within an individual so as to assess what is needed to make a change in a person's behavior

Kurt Lewin, a social psychologist, developed the technique of **force-field analysis.** It is a useful device for visualizing subordinates' resistance to change. Force-field analysis tells us that individuals' behavior with regard to any issue is affected by driving forces and restraining forces. Driving forces encourage us to change, whereas restraining forces encourage us to resist change. Whether we are predisposed toward a change in a negative way or in a positive way depends on the nature and quantity of these forces. If the forces are balanced, we are in a state of inertia. If a change is to take place, driving forces must outweigh restraining ones, the restraining ones must be reduced, or a combination of these must take place. Exhibit 6.3 illustrates this concept.

| Exhibit 6.3 | *Representation of force fields.* |

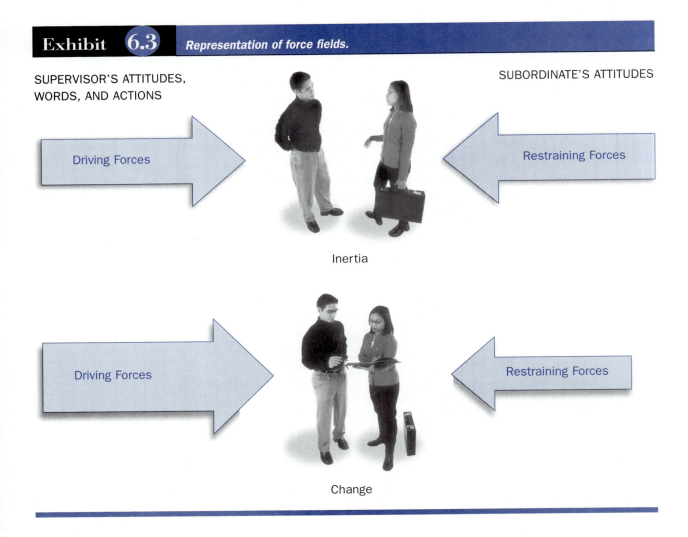

SUPERVISOR'S ATTITUDES, WORDS, AND ACTIONS

SUBORDINATE'S ATTITUDES

Driving Forces

Restraining Forces

Inertia

Driving Forces

Restraining Forces

Change

To understand more clearly this type of analysis, let us consider an example. Assume that you want Barbara, one of your graphics specialists, to work overtime on a special project. Since overtime is never mandatory in your company, Barbara has a choice. Let us assume that you have asked her, and she has refused. The situation might appear as follows:

DRIVING FORCES

1. Barbara will receive additional pay at overtime scale.
2. She wants to please you.
3. She enjoys the type of graphics work in this project.

RESTRAINING FORCES

1. She will be unable to attend a play for which she has expensive tickets.
2. She is concerned about personal safety when traveling home late at night.
3. She needs to leave the deposit for a new apartment at the leasing office.

At this point, there appears to be a standoff. You cannot order her to work, so you must try to reduce her restraining forces or increase the driving forces. Before attempting to do either you will need to understand the forces as Barbara perceives them. In this case we can assume that Barbara is aware of the driving forces but that they are inadequate to overcome the restraining forces. You could increase the driving forces by offering double overtime or making a personal plea for her assistance. Such approaches are sometimes relatively unimaginative and may add to your subordinate's stress level.

On the other hand you may obtain a more predictable outcome by reducing the restraining forces, and you will not add to the stress Barbara experiences. For example, in this situation you may have discretionary funds that will allow you to obtain tickets for her for another night. You also could arrange for someone to escort her safely home, such as a company driver, or you could use company funds to reimburse her for the use of a private limousine service. Alternatively you could arrange to have a courier service deliver the deposit for her apartment to the rental office. These approaches should have a high probability of gaining the behavior you need.

Effective Communication

Chapter 5 dealt with the fundamentals of communication that are essential to every manager. Regardless of the form of communication used, you must lay the groundwork for change and communicate its advantages before you can obtain commitment from your people. A company that is now part of Anadarko Petroleum provides a good example of an organization that used effective communication to facilitate change. The company, which changed its culture to be more responsive to competitive conditions, had a very extensive communications program. Employees were heavily involved in meetings in which action plans were developed for changing the company's culture. Furthermore, detailed timetables of the change process kept everyone informed as to when each component of the cultural change would be initiated and completed.[26]

Persuasion Techniques

Each of the following persuasion techniques works well in certain situations. Which one you choose depends on your understanding of the people and events involved in the particular situation you face. Become familiar with all of them so that you will always carry with you one or more techniques that can be applied to any set of circumstances.

1. *Explain why.* Let your people know the reason behind the proposal or change. Put it in their terms, and tailor your message to each individual.

2. *Show them how.* Explain how the change will affect them, how it will help them, and how it will be implemented. Appeal to their individual needs.

3. *Tell them the truth.* If the change will be painful, let them know it. If they are to be displaced, provide truthful assurances about the company's relocation services or its willingness to retrain them for new positions. See Exhibit 6.4 for an example of how to gain a person's acceptance of more work with no increase in pay—a continuing reality in today's downsized organizations.

You will find that you must often use persuasion techniques to get your subordinates to cooperate. Always remember to put yourself in your subordinates' shoes. Treat them the way you wish to be treated.

4. *Try a compromise.* You may not have foreseen all the possibilities, and people who disagree with you may have some good points on their side. In fact, skilled persuaders often incorporate the suggestions of those they are attempting to persuade into solutions that combine their views. This has a positive impact on the process because the persuader's willingness to adapt the solution to the needs of others builds trust and greater receptivity to sacrifices for the mutual good.[27]

5. *Give an example of a past accomplishment.* Tell your people about similar situations and the positive results that followed. Explain how each person benefited as a result of the change. Professor Jay Conger says that "it is critical to identify your objective's tangible benefits to the people you are trying to persuade."[28]

It's a fact of today's downsized corporate life: At some point, most managers will need to ask an employee to take on more work without raising her pay. The secret to running this negotiation smoothly is to make the employee see what's in it for her. Since the alternative may be unemployment, you can even present the increased work load as good news. Point out that while others are losing their jobs, she's making herself more valuable to the company. If she's already a prized employee, see if you can reward her increased productivity through other means—a better title or larger office, training in new skills, more vacation time. If she's not that essential, you should just get across the point that this is a take-it-or-leave-it deal. (The manager's words are marked in blue; the employee's, in black.)

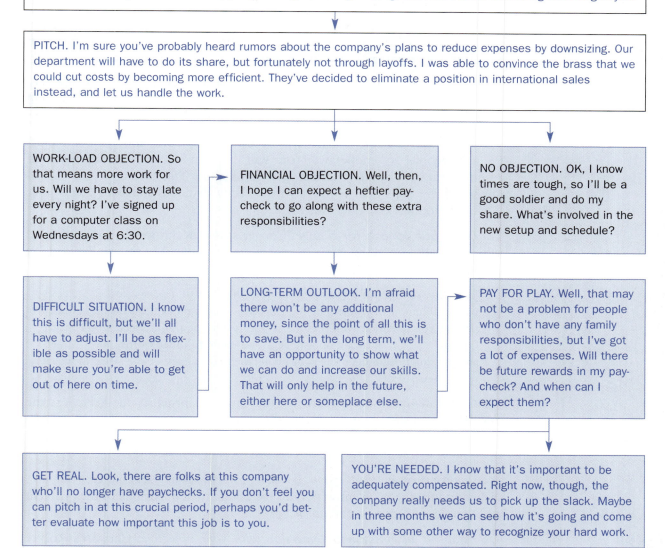

ICEBREAKER. I've just come from a day-long strategic planning meeting, and I have some reassuring news to give you.

PITCH. I'm sure you've probably heard rumors about the company's plans to reduce expenses by downsizing. Our department will have to do its share, but fortunately not through layoffs. I was able to convince the brass that we could cut costs by becoming more efficient. They've decided to eliminate a position in international sales instead, and let us handle the work.

WORK-LOAD OBJECTION. So that means more work for us. Will we have to stay late every night? I've signed up for a computer class on Wednesdays at 6:30.

FINANCIAL OBJECTION. Well, then, I hope I can expect a heftier paycheck to go along with these extra responsibilities?

NO OBJECTION. OK, I know times are tough, so I'll be a good soldier and do my share. What's involved in the new setup and schedule?

DIFFICULT SITUATION. I know this is difficult, but we'll all have to adjust. I'll be as flexible as possible and will make sure you're able to get out of here on time.

LONG-TERM OUTLOOK. I'm afraid there won't be any additional money, since the point of all this is to save. But in the long term, we'll have an opportunity to show what we can do and increase our skills. That will only help in the future, either here or someplace else.

PAY FOR PLAY. Well, that may not be a problem for people who don't have any family responsibilities, but I've got a lot of expenses. Will there be future rewards in my paycheck? And when can I expect them?

GET REAL. Look, there are folks at this company who'll no longer have paychecks. If you don't feel you can pitch in at this crucial period, perhaps you'd better evaluate how important this job is to you.

YOU'RE NEEDED. I know that it's important to be adequately compensated. Right now, though, the company really needs us to pick up the slack. Maybe in three months we can see how it's going and come up with some other way to recognize your hard work.

6. *Plant a seed.* Give your subordinates an idea, and let it germinate in advance of the change. For example, converse with them about "How nice it would be if . . ." or "Have you guys thought about . . ." Then nurture that idea with the proper care and feeding. Your subordinates may come to you with the very suggestion you anticipated. Even better, they may think it is their own idea.

7. *Ask questions.* Ask questions to which the answers will yield support for a change or remove the cause of a possible conflict. When properly presented, questions can lead subordinates to the responses you desire.

8. *Offer a choice.* The choice you present is not *whether* to do something or reject it but rather *when* or *by whom* it will get done.

9. *Offer a challenge.* Present the idea as a goal to be reached or a standard to be surpassed. Portray the change as a test of the team's abilities and skills. Turn the event into a game or contest—a way of probing their potential.

10. *Make a promise.* If possible, give your promise that if the idea is not successful or does not yield the desired results (given an honest effort), you will retreat from your position and withdraw the directive.

11. *Try making a request.* Instead of ordering compliance and being autocratic, ask people to cooperate. You will be amazed at the difference in responsiveness to requests rather than commands. This technique has special appeal to the individual who feels insulted by demands but who bends over backward to meet an appeal for help.

12. *Use subtle appeals for change.* Conger says that autocratic, up-front hard sell approaches or "John Wayne" techniques often lead to failure. Instead, he proposes the following:

> In reality, setting out a strong position at the start of a persuasion effort gives potential opponents something to grab onto—and fight against. It's far better to present your position with the finesse and reserve of a lion tamer, who engages his "partner" by showing him the legs of a chair. In other words, effective persuaders don't begin the process by giving their colleagues a clear target in which to set their jaws.[29]

13. *Give a demonstration.* Show by your own performance the behaviors the new system calls for, how it will work, and how it will benefit the group or individual. Introduce the change with a planned and carefully executed tryout, and the doubts will fade in the light of reason. Seeing is believing.

14. *Involve them in the decision.* Using a problem-solving session, get your subordinates into the problem with both feet. State the dimensions of the problem and then lead them to a consensus.

15. *Establish an emotional connection with your objective.* Chrysler's Robert Marcell helped persuade Lee Iacocca and other Chrysler executives to build the sub-compact Neon in the United States rather than overseas by showing pictures of his hometown, Iron River, Michigan. The pictures showed deserted homes

and boarded-up buildings, such as Marcell's high school. The town's economy had been devastated when manufacturers shifted their purchases of raw materials to foreign mining companies. The consequences to a small city of the loss of employment established an emotional connection with Marcell's objective.[30]

Before you decide to use any of these techniques for persuasion, put yourself in your subordinates' shoes. Identify with their needs, concerns, and attitudes. Then set your course to deal with their driving and restraining forces. By eliminating forces that restrain desired behaviors or by adding incentives that drive people toward such behaviors, you will increase the likelihood of successful change.

Participation Techniques

As we have seen throughout this chapter, people need to be in the know about the things that affect them. Managers must use various means to involve their people in decision making and to allow them to participate more fully in the work of the department.

One means for increasing employee participation is to share one's formal authority. By delegating authority to responsible subordinates, a supervisor can expose her subordinates to the complexities of her job. Such delegation also facilitates the development of her subordinates.

Another approach for increased participation is the formation of worker teams to assist in identifying and solving problems. "At a time when companies are looking for ways to streamline operations and cut costs, managers . . . have gotten measurable results that show the best answers can come from asking those who know best—the workers."[31] We discuss problem-solving sessions in detail in Chapter 9, and this chapter's *Supervising Teams* box tells about one company's successes with worker-run problem-solving teams.

A third method of enlisting participation depends on your style of supervision. A democratic management style promotes a feeling of shared responsibility and a voice in what happens. Such a style places trust in the workers and makes the supervisor more dependent on them. The workers know this and usually act accordingly. No one wants to betray the trust of another. For the most part, people want to live up to the expectations others have of them, provided that they have the abilities and skills to do so. Chapter 10 explores in some detail different styles of management and their advantages and disadvantages.

Training Programs

Training programs are formal ways in which you and your organization can teach employees skills, knowledge, and attitudes that they need to perform their present tasks. For example, when you teach one of your subordinates how to operate a piece of machinery, you impart the information he needs to understand the machine's performance capabilities. Through practice, the operator

SUPERVISING TEAMS

The Reynolds and Reynolds Company has achieved significant improvements in one of its plant's methods, quality, and productivity through two primary efforts: forming worker-run problem-solving teams and implementing cross-training. One of the company's plants repairs computer systems components. The plant was having problems coordinating between repair and distribution units. The 45 non-union employees seemed, at times, to be acting at cross-purposes. The managers in charge of repair and distribution decided to form a five-person team made up of volunteers—"two employees each from the distribution and repair sides and one from internal engineering." The team's first goal was to improve formal communications.

The team began with a meeting of all non-management employees. Suggestions were made and criticized. Workers worried that management might not approve of their ideas and that membership on teams might hurt their individual performance ratings. Over the following months, the team members sent their ideas to supervisors, and the team decided to rotate its membership, allowing others who wanted to a chance to serve. Among the time- and money-saving ideas that were generated were proposals to cross-train repair persons so that they could vary the kinds of repair work they performed, prepare weekly schedules specifying which products were to be repaired, and share information through a network with all technicians.

The results were truly significant. Parts repaired per month rose from 4,800 to 6,500. Backlogs on orders were reduced from 5 to 1.3 percent. Waiting time for parts repairs decreased from two weeks to one day. The need to handle returned parts more than once was eliminated. All these improvements were accomplished without increasing the workforce and with minimal investments in capital equipment. It took supervisors a while to see the importance of letting the workers take ownership of problems, but the bottom-up approach to solving problems proved its worth at Reynolds and Reynolds.

Source: Raju Narisetti, "Bottom-Up Approach Pushes Plant's Performance to the Top," *Chicago Tribune* (November 29, 1992): sect. 7, 13.

gradually gains the manual dexterity required for efficient operation of the machine. Finally, you impart the proper attitudes about safe operation, proper operating procedures, and appropriate maintenance. You teach it all simultaneously and with equal emphasis. Chapter 12 covers training in greater detail.

Organizational Development Activities

organizational development
a planned, managed, systematic process used to change the culture, systems, and behavior of an organization to improve its effectiveness in solving problems and achieving goals

Organizational development (OD) has been defined by the Conference Board, a nonprofit research group, as "a planned, managed, systematic process [used] to change the culture, systems, and behavior of an organization in order to improve the organization's effectiveness in solving problems and achieving its objectives." This process involves efforts in education and training that eventually affect everyone in an organization.

Organizational development requires that an organization identify its strengths and weaknesses, define its objectives, identify its problem areas, establish OD goals, set up programs for achieving those goals, and evaluate progress toward improvement. Outside consultants and experts usually conduct research into the organization's operations. They then recommend and teach the implementation of OD programs for change. If OD efforts are to succeed, the commitment of top management to them is essential. Organizational changes, if they are to be lasting, must begin at the top.

Organizations that adopt organizational development programs must set specific goals for their entire operation and its various divisions and subunits. The total organization may have the following goals: (1) to improve the organization's productivity, profitability, and human resources and (2) to improve the organization's efforts at communicating, promoting intergroup cooperation, and preparing for and coping with change.

As a supervisor, your goals will be influenced by those of your boss and your unit or division. One goal might be to reduce waste and scrap by 10 percent. Another might be to improve the communication skills of the personnel in your department. You can then design specific programs to accomplish your goals.

OD programs include those designed to assess employee attitudes, to improve employee cooperation, and to build team spirit. OD activities need your commitment if they are to succeed. You, like all the managers above you, must be committed to them, and you must be willing and able to sell them to subordinates who will participate in them. Change can mean security for those who know it is coming and are prepared for it. It can mean insecurity for those who do not. You can do a great deal to reduce insecurity and stress among your people by supporting change.

An example of wide-scale organizational development has been taking place at Levi Strauss and Company, which has historically been one of the better-managed U. S. organizations and has gone through difficult times in recent years. The company's delivery of its products had become slower than competitors and it had been losing market share. To turn the situation around, Levi dramatically changed the organization and its processes. A large task force of key employees was given the task of designing new processes for getting products to the market quicker. The task force also designed new jobs to make Levi more competitive. Employees then had to apply for these new jobs.[32] To gain employee commitment to doing things differently, Levi tried creative tactics such as the following:

> In May, employees at Levi Strauss & Co. were baffled when a giant red cube appeared one morning outside the company's San Francisco headquarters. Gossip ensued about the contents: A bundle of jeans? A memorial to the firm's recently replaced ad agency? Or was it just new art? Several days later, at a company-wide meeting, the box popped open to reveal . . . nothing. "The point," a top executive told the denim-clad staff, "is from this day on, we want you to think outside of the box."[33]

Stress

stress

worry, anxiety, or tension
that accompanies situations
and problems we face and
makes us uncertain about
the ways in which we should
resolve them

Changes, the passage of time, and threats (real or imagined) can cause stress among the members of organizations. **Stress** occurs in people when they face situations in which they are powerless or uncertain about what to do. All of us experience stress on and off the job. When we attempt to learn new skills, meet new people, or are asked to chair a committee or run a meeting, we are usually somewhat uncertain about exactly what we should do. When we face a series of stress-inducing activities or situations, such as role conflict or role ambiguity, our peace of mind and our health can suffer. Among the most serious health threats associated with stress are migraine headaches, depression, skin problems, ulcers, high blood pressure, and heart trouble. People who face continual stress, such as air-traffic controllers, physicians, and surgeons, can become victims of chronic depression that sometimes leads to dependence on drugs.

With today's emphasis on cost-cutting, layoffs, and outsourcing, workers and managers are facing new realities in their workplaces, many of which are sources of stress. People working for U. S. corporate giants such as IBM, Sears, and General Motors have discovered that job security is no longer a reality. According to John Simmons, a consultant on employee involvement plans, workers feel betrayed and less willing to contribute since their employers seem to worry more about cost-cutting than they do about increasing worker responsibilities.[34]

The International Labor Organization (ILO) of the United Nations issued a report on stress around the world. In it, the ILO states that job stress is rapidly increasing around the world and is affecting nearly every job category. The report indicates that in the United States about $200 billion is lost "annually from compensation claims, reduced productivity, absenteeism, added insurance costs and direct medical expenses for related diseases such as ulcers, high blood pressure and heart attack."[35] The leading causes of stress are usually identified as workplace monitoring, conflicting personal and job demands, difficult coworkers, machine-paced work, too much work, uncomfortable environmental conditions, low wages, the lack of control over one's job, incompetent supervisors, and fear of losing one's job. According to Debra J. Lerner of the New England Medical Center:

> Job strain, broadly defined as being responsible for doing a lot of work with little control over how it's done, not only can make people sick, it can also make them feel lousy about their lives. A national survey of 1,319 working men and women found that job strain was associated with lethargy on and off the job, a decreased social life, and more depression. . . . Previously job strain had been associated with an increased risk of heart disease and other physical ailments.[36]

Working Woman magazine surveyed its readers and discovered that 71 percent were experiencing stress linked to inadequate pay and "working long hours."[37] A different survey of 100 major companies by Pitney Bowes Management Services revealed the following:

Workers at three-fourths of firms that have carried out reengineering actions . . . [defined as] simplifying jobs, performing jobs in a logical order, combining jobs and contracting out support work to other firms . . . were more fearful about losing their jobs. . . . Likewise, 55 percent of the firms said their employees felt overburdened by their assignments after the changes. At the same time, 71 percent of the companies said their initiatives led to greater employee productivity, 61 percent reported cost-efficiency increases and 40 percent saw profit increases.[38]

Furthermore, studies by other economists at the U. S. Bureau of Labor Statistics confirm that some people are working longer hours, which probably relates to the amount of job-related stress they experience. The percentage of employees (nonagricultural) working 49 hours or more per week increased from 13.0 percent in the 1970s to 18.5 percent in the 1990s. Managers work particularly long hours, are being asked to do more work as a result of downsizing and lean staffing, and have less job security than in the past. They spend more time traveling as a result of the globalization of the economy. Furthermore, they now share power with teams, which can add to their stress levels, and the status that they used to receive from perks is not as evident now that workplaces are more egalitarian.[39]

It is clear that the work load for managers can be a contributor to stress. In addition, a large number of people have two jobs—5.7 percent of those employed in May 2000 had multiple jobs. Nonetheless, although some people are working more hours, the U. S. Bureau of Labor Statistics reports that the number of hours worked overall remained relatively constant between 1964 and 1999, with only a .5 percent decline in average weekly hours.[40]

Some employer practices are also creating additional stress for employees. One is increased management efforts to keep tabs on their people. As noted earlier in this chapter, a large proportion of employers search their employees' e-mail. Intrusive actions are more possible now with advanced electronic communication and surveillance technology, and more firms are now monitoring their workers through electronic monitoring and surveillance. With the addition of security cameras to the list of monitoring techniques, the proportion of companies conducting such monitoring increased even further.[41]

As a result of such sources of stress, managers must reduce their own stress as well as help their employees cope with it. The next section discusses strategies for coping with stress.

COPING WITH STRESS

Some stress is healthful and necessary for performance. It gets us motivated and raises our energy levels. Excessive stress, however, has to be recognized and the causes eliminated or brought under control. Stress can and does cause both physical and psychological harm. Courts and juries are awarding significant damages to employees who suffer both kinds of harm due to stress, and the workers' compensation boards of many states will let workers recover damages for psychological injuries. Exhibit 6.5 presents several

<table>
<tr><td colspan="2">**Exhibit 6.5**   *Stress in the workplace.*</td></tr>
<tr><td>**SOURCES OF STRESS**</td><td>**MANAGEMENT ACTIONS FOR STRESS REDUCTION**</td></tr>
<tr><td>Competition and Change</td><td>Plan and implement changes with greater concern for employees</td></tr>
<tr><td>Technological Change</td><td>Decrease expectations for the contributions of new technology, offer training for new technology</td></tr>
<tr><td>Increasingly Diverse Workforce</td><td>Provide help and understanding when mistakes at the cutting edge are made; promote professional networks, mentoring, and buddy systems for minorities and women; provide diversity training</td></tr>
<tr><td>Downsizing</td><td>Provide early warning of potential downsizing, outplacement services, layoff/severance packages, retraining services</td></tr>
<tr><td>Employee Empowerment and Teamwork</td><td>Encourage teamwork, be approachable for discussion, be part of the team, cooperate with other teams, treat team members fairly, build in team recreational activities</td></tr>
<tr><td>Work/Home Conflict</td><td>Implement flexible work schedules, telecommuting, family leave, sabbaticals</td></tr>
<tr><td>Elder and Child Care</td><td>Provide family care leave, child care centers</td></tr>
<tr><td>Violence in the Workplace</td><td>Implement referral programs for troubled employees, conflict resolution programs</td></tr>
</table>

Sources: Richard S. DeFrank and John M. Ivancevich, "Stress on the Job: An Executive Update," *Academy of Management Executive* (August 1998): 55–66. Daniel C. Feldman and Carrie R. Leanna, "Managing Layoffs: Experience at the Challenger Disaster Site and the Pittsburgh Steel Mills," *Organizational Dynamics* 18(1) (1989): 52–64. R. Roosevelt Thomas, Jr., "From Affirmative Action to Affirming Diversity," *Harvard Business Review* (March–April 1990): 107–117. David A. Thomas and Suzy Wetlaufer, "A Question of Color: A Debate on Race in the U. S. Workplace," *Harvard Business Review* (September–October 1997): 118–132. Catherine Petrini and Rebecca Thomas, "A Brighter Shade of Team Building," *Training & Development* (November 1995): 9. Stuart Klein, "Teams Under Stress," *IIE Solutions* (May 1995): 34–38. Chris Wood, "Dealing with Tech Rage," *Maclean's* (March 19, 2001): 41–42.

causes of stress in the workplace and ways that supervisors and managers can help reduce such stresses.

Managers at every level of an organization have a legal and moral duty to identify causes of stress, to work to reduce its impact on employees, and to identify and try to help employees who have trouble handling stress. If the cause seems to be an inability to perform duties, training may be the cure. If the stress comes from other sources, your company may have an employee assistance program (EAP) that can help. Many organizations have the following types of EAPs to assist their employees:

- Facilities for exercise, such as health club memberships, jogging tracks, exercise instruction, and weight-training rooms

- Courses to teach people how to handle stress through such means as meditation, proper nutrition, time management, and conflict management
- On- or off-site confidential counseling opportunities to explore such stressors as financial problems, marriage difficulties, and psychological problems
- Flexible work schedules, job sharing, daycare, and telecommuting to accommodate individual needs
- Substance abuse counseling and treatment
- Time off for coping with family and other emergencies

The 1993 Family and Medical Leave Act requires unpaid leave for up to 12 weeks for employees who have worked for a covered employer for at least one year and for 1,250 hours over the previous 12 months, for any of the following:

1. To care for the employee's child after birth or adoption or foster care
2. To care for the employee's spouse, son or daughter, or parent who has a serious health condition
3. For a serious health condition that makes the employee unable to perform his or her job

Psychologist Bryan E. Robinson recommends the following techniques for "combating an out-of-control work life":[42]

- Make a conscious effort to slow down the pulse and rhythm of daily life—eating, talking, walking, and driving.
- Learn to say no when you are overcommitted and you have a choice about new assignments.
- Delegate work to competent people.
- Avoid unrealistic deadlines or self-imposed time limits on important tasks.
- Build time cushions into your schedule. One way is to allow more time for each appointment during your day.
- Avoid making important decisions in haste. Take time to think about them carefully.

Psychologist Jude Miller adds that people can cope with stress by "being assertive and clarifying problems appropriately with coworkers or supervisors—and get out of the building and walk once a day."[43] In addition to taking these steps, try getting enough rest, and eat a proper diet to build up your resistance and stamina. Try to play as hard as you work, and separate your work from your family and social life. This chapter's *Incident* feature contains a checklist to help you identify the stress-inducing conditions that exist in your workplace.

TECHNOSTRESS

With today's highly technical society, a new kind of stress is emerging: technostress. The introduction of new machines and technology often brings new stressors to an organization and its people. Managers need to plan for the selection, introduction of, and adaptation to new machines and equipment to reduce the stress on employees as much as possible. People must be consulted and trained before any new equipment is introduced. With new technologies come new demands on both associates and supervisors. All may fear higher quotas, workforce reductions, and being asked to learn new skills.

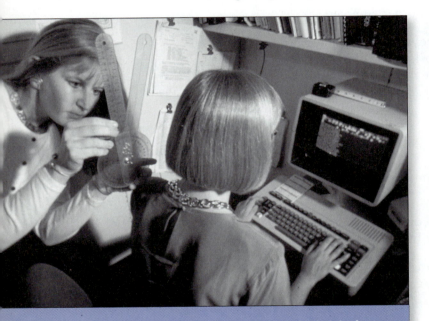

The physical stress of repetitive work can be alleviated with the help of ergonomics. Here an ergonomics consultant observes a worker. By learning how the worker does her job, the ergonomics expert can make modifications to reduce stressful movements.

In addition, various kinds of adverse health effects have emerged with the introduction of computers and computerized workstations. The most harmful effects are operator fatigue, eyestrain, exposure to radiation and electromagnetic fields, and carpal tunnel syndrome. This last-mentioned effect is the result of repetitive wrist–hand, hand–fingers motions, such as those made by a computer data entry clerk. These repetitive movements irritate nerves and tendons, causing pain, numbness, and swelling. The proper design of workstations and training of operators can help eliminate and counter these harmful effects.

For help with office and workstation arrangements, consider the services of an architectural interior designer. Interior office design professionals are practitioners of *ergonomics:* the successful blending of people, equipment, and machines. Pay attention to the complaints of people who must use the equipment and spaces. Additional advice from the federal government's Occupational Safety and Health Administration (OSHA) for avoiding these problems includes the following:

- Positioning equipment to avoid glare from windows and overhead lights on computer displays
- Using adjustable screens with adjustable contrast and colors
- Using detachable and adjustable keyboards (height and tilt)
- Establishing breaks in place: operators refocus their eyes for several minutes each half hour

- Establishing regular hourly breaks, allowing operators to move away from their workstations

Several cities have passed or are considering legislation that implements most if not all of these guidelines.

If you and your employees face continual stress, your attitudes about work, your employer, and your coworkers are bound to be affected. Since stress is a result of uncertainty, you can usually do various things to give your people more certainty. Training is one way to give people the level of skills and the knowledge of procedures that can help alleviate their stress. Unqualified individuals may be transferred to jobs that they can handle. Professional help may be available through your company's human resources office, your company's health and workers' compensation insurers, and various EAPs such as counseling, psychiatric treatment, and drug interdiction programs.

Instant Replay

1. Our experiences help shape our individual beliefs.
2. Our beliefs help shape our attitudes.
3. When supervisors observe undesired behaviors, they must act to change them.
4. To change attitudes, we must identify the supports for them, weaken those supports, offer a substitute, and sell it.
5. Techniques for changing behaviors include force-field analysis, effective communications, persuasion techniques, participation techniques, training programs, and organizational development activities.
6. Stress is worry, anxiety, or tension that accompanies situations and problems we face. Stress can distract us from our work, adversely affect our attitudes, and injure our health unless we learn to cope with it or remove it from our workplace.

Questions for Class Discussion

1. Can you define this chapter's key terms?
2. How do you form an attitude about a person, place, or thing?
3. What kinds of attitudes held by workers need changing? How would you go about changing a subordinate's attitude?
4. What are the techniques or tools described in this chapter that can help you change your own or other people's attitudes?
5. What are the major causes of stress in the workplace?
6. What are the ways in which a person can cope with work-related stress?

Incident

Purpose: To identify stressors in your work or school environment.

Your task: Read the checklist that follows, and mark those items that you find in either your work or school environment. Note that those items marked "absent" are potential stressors.

Present Absent

○ ○ 1. Open communications exist between managers and workers.

○ ○ 2. Employees are adequately trained before taking on new tasks.

○ ○ 3. Employees are adequately recognized and rewarded for achievements.

○ ○ 4. Employees are trained in how to handle stress.

○ ○ 5. Employee privacy is respected.

○ ○ 6. Employees are encouraged to take risks.

○ ○ 7. Employees are notified in advance of pending changes.

○ ○ 8. Employees believe that their pay and benefits are fair.

○ ○ 9. Employees are encouraged to take advantage of EAPs.

○ ○ 10. Major reorganization or reengineering has not taken place in the recent past.

○ ○ 11. Major reorganization or reengineering is not planned for the near future.

○ ○ 12. The work climate or environment is pleasant.

○ ○ 13. Employees may work flexible hours and schedules.

○ ○ 14. In general, employees feel that there are enough employees to perform the work.

○ ○ 15. Employees have access to and are trained to use the technology they need.

CASE PROBLEM 6.1   *New Database Software*

Lupe Mendoza spotted Cecilia Hunter at the other side of the cafeteria and walked over to sit down at her table. Lupe said, "Have you heard the latest? We're going to change database software."

Cecilia said, "Who told you that? This isn't another of those rumors, is it? I've just recovered from the last change in software."

Lupe said, "I have a friend, Joanne Branson, who used to work in this section. She moved over to corporate purchasing a couple of years ago. Anyway, last week she saw contracts for new database software."

Just then Martin Cowan and Greg Youngblood walked up to the table. Cecilia said, "Have you heard that we're changing database software again?"

Martin groaned, "Not again! I've still got a few files that I haven't converted from the previous software. Most of us have only recently learned the present software well enough to feel comfortable. How are we going to learn all of this new stuff while we take on these new accounts from the merger?"

Greg said, "I heard about this new software from a friend whose company implemented it last fall. It's so complex that it takes almost a year to really learn it well. In fact, at my friend's company a couple of people quit their jobs because of the software."

Lupe said, "This is going to be a disaster. The last time we switched software the whole system was messed up for months. The worst problem was when we found errors in the conversion and people had to go back and trace through the data to do corrections."

As the four of them walked back to their office they ran into their boss, Tommy Lance. Martin said, "We've heard rumors that we're going to change database software. Are they true?"

Tommy said, "I had hoped to keep this quiet until I could announce the change to everyone at once. Yes, it's true. The new software is much more powerful than what we're currently using and it has new features that will really help us in the future. Besides, we're getting a good price on the software because we'll be among the first in our industry to make the changeover."

Lupe said, "But isn't it bad to be among the first to use new software? Don't some companies like to let other companies experiment first and then adopt it after it appears that everything works okay?"

Martin said, "Lupe's right. One of our old vice-presidents who left for a big promotion said that it's better to be safely behind the leading edge of information technology. One of the wags around here likes to say we're on the bleeding edge of technology."

Tommy said, "This isn't leading-edge software. It's been out for a year now and lots of companies in other industries are using it. We need to get on with the change and quit dragging our heels. This software will be the new standard and we'll be better off making the change now rather than waiting until our competitors change over."

Greg said, "I agree with Cecilia. New software always sounds great on paper. But I've heard that when you start to work with the new software, the new features just make your computer run slower. And, the added features are kind of a waste because most people never use them."

Tommy said, "Listen, you can complain all you want, but it's not going to change anything. Just get used to it. We're going to have to make the change, and I think it's a good move. Telling doom-and-gloom stories about the new software isn't going to help. You need to adopt a positive attitude and embrace the new change. You'll see that we'll be better off with this new software. Besides, it's useless to try to resist new technology. I'll send out a memo about the change next week. I've got to run to a meeting with the vice-president."

After Tommy left, Greg said, "Do any of you know why we have so much security around the mainframe room? Back in the 1980s one of the employees got so frustrated with the company that he dumped a bucket of water in one of the mainframe computers. Can you imagine how frustrated he was? I heard that when the police took him away he was mumbling something about changes in software."

Questions

1. Why do you think Tommy's subordinates are so resistant to the new software?
2. Explain how the change could have been managed more effectively.
3. How can Tommy help get his people to accept the change?
4. Why do you think Tommy did not involve his subordinates in the decision?

CASE PROBLEM 6.2   *Another Reorganization*

Betty Cooper couldn't believe the e-mail from Vice-President Larry Kendall: "Effective immediately the workers' compensation claims unit and the long-term disability claims unit will be moved to the 24th floor to be located with the health insurance claims unit. All three units will report to Hal Murdoch, assistant vice-president for claims. Office assignments are posted on the bulletin board in the health insurance break area. The physical relocation of files and office equipment will take place the day after tomorrow. If you have any questions about this change, consult your supervisor." Betty thought to herself, "I am a supervisor and I don't have a clue about what's going on!" She looked up and saw her boss, Libby Wilkerson, standing at the door.

Libby said, "Betty, Vice-President Kendall just called and wants us to come up to his office. In case you haven't heard, we're going to reorganize and he wants to give us the specifics. I don't know anything more about this than you do, except that the whole thing came together very quickly at the senior executive level."

At the meeting in Vice-President Kendall's office, Betty learned that Libby was being transferred to underwriting and that indeed, Hal Murdoch would be her new boss. She had worked with Hal before and had a good relationship with him. She also learned that all three claims processing units were going to be organized in teams and that a team-based compensation system was going to be implemented. After the meeting Hal said, "What a surprise! I just found out about the reorganization myself two days ago. But let's focus on the task ahead of us. Claims processing costs have skyrocketed and senior management has told us that they want us to try teams and team-based compensation in order to improve efficiency. You'll have to get your people on board with this change in order for us to make this work."

The next day Betty Cooper brought her subordinates together to explain the reorganization. She outlined what she had learned at the meeting about the reorganization. She explained that they would be working in teams and that they would be compensated on the basis of team performance. She then asked for questions.

Joanne Moore said, "Why do we have all of these reorganizations? One of the reasons costs are increasing is that they keep moving us around all of the time. We've had so many reorganizations around this place that if it weren't for the telephone book I couldn't tell where anyone works anymore. And where did this stuff about teams come from?"

Carolyn Hudson said, "Between the reorganizations and downsizing, the only people who have any job security around here are the people who do the moving for us. But aside from the move, I don't understand the need for teams or the team-based compensation. That sounds like a bad idea to me."

Jim Harper, who seemed to be upset, said, "Why do they think teams will be the answer to increasing costs? And while I respect the people in this unit, I'm not sure my pay should be determined by how well they perform as a team."

Sandy Barry said, "How big are the teams going to be and how are we going to decide who's going to be on each team? Can we pick who we want to be on our team? Has anybody in this company actually tried to do this?"

Carolyn Hudson said, "What happens to those people who don't get picked for a team? Can we kick someone off our team if they don't perform?"

Betty said, "Hold on, we're getting way ahead of ourselves. These are good questions for which I don't have any answers at this time. And I certainly understand your concerns. Nonetheless, I would like for us to come up with our own approach to this and then get Hal's support for what we want to do."

Joanne Moore said, "Why should we waste our time trying to come up with rational ways to organize with teams? I'll bet that one of the senior executives will tell us what we're going to do regardless of what we decide. So why don't we just save a lot of time and wait for another e-mail from Vice-President Kendall?"

Questions

1. What are the likely barriers to successful implementation of the changes in this case?
2. What mistakes have already been made?
3. What should Betty do to increase the likelihood of successful change?
4. What factors will help Betty implement these changes?

References

1. Kreitner, Robert, and Knicki, Angelo. *Organizational Behavior,* 5th ed. Boston: Irwin McGraw-Hill, 2001.
2. Burke, Warner. "Organization Change Is Not a Linear Process," Presentation to the Academy of Management Annual Meeting, Washington, DC (August 6, 2001).
3. Nauman, Matt. "Job Well Done," *Chicago Tribune* (September 18, 1994): sect. 17, 3.
4. Chappell, Lindsay. "GM Missed Early Lessons of NUMMI," *Automotive News* (June 7, 1999): 26.
5. Kosan, Lisa. "Training Spans the World," *eWeek* (January 29, 2001): 54–57.
6. Ibid.
7. Lee, Felissa K.; Dougherty, Thomas W.; and Turban, Daniel B. "The Role of Personality and Work Values in Mentoring Programs," *Review of Business* (Spring/Summer 2000): 33–37.

8. Jamieson, David, and O'Mara, Julie. *Managing Workforce 2000.* San Francisco: Jossey-Bass (1991): 27–29.

9. Peters, Tom. "'Fountain of Youth'—And Low Fares," *Chicago Tribune* (September 26, 1994): sect. 4, 5.

10. Ibid.

11. Ibid.

12. Muller, Joann. "Assembling a New Auto Worker," *Chicago Tribune* (May 29, 1994): sect. 8, 1.

13. Browning, Guy. "How to Get Ahead by Being a Bastard," *People Management* (November 25, 2001): 154.

14. McGregor, Douglas. "The Human Side of Enterprise" in *Classics in Management,* Harwood F. Merrill, ed. New York: American Management Association (1970): 461–475.

15. Swanson, Sandra. "Beware: Employee Monitoring Is on the Rise," *Information Week* (August 20, 2001): 57.

16. Ibid.: 57–58.

17. Peters, Tom. "Nobody Knows Nothin', So Go Ahead, Take Those Risks," *Chicago Tribune* (August 29, 1994): sect. 4, 3.

18. Zellner, Wendy. "Team Player: No More 'Same-ol'—Same-ol'," *Business Week* (October 17, 1994): 95–96.

19. Ouchi, William G. *Theory Z: How American Business Can Meet the Japanese Challenge.* Reading, MA: Addison-Wesley, 1981. Pascale, R. T., and Athos, A. G. *The Art of Japanese Management.* New York: Simon & Schuster, 1981. Ouchi, William G., and Jaeger, A. M. "Type Z Organization: Stability in the Midst of Mobility," *Academy of Management Review* (April 1978): 305–314.

20. White, Susan S., and Locke, Edwin A. "Problems with the Pygmalion Effect and Some Proposed Solutions," *Leadership Quarterly* (Fall 2000): 389–415.

21. Reichers, Arnon; Wanous, John P.; and Austin, James T. "Understanding and Managing Cynicism about Organizational Change" in *Academy of Management Executive* (February 1997): 48–59.

22. McCall, Morgan W., Jr. *High Flyers: Developing the Next Generation of Leaders.* Boston: Harvard Business School Press, 1998: 164.

23. Ibid.: 163–164.

24. Kotter, John P. *Leading Change.* Boston: Harvard Business School, 1996: 67.

25. Ibid.

26. Franklin, Ann. Address to the Metroplex Human Resource Planning Society, Las Colinas, TX (Spring 1997).

27. Conger, Jay A. "The Necessary Art of Persuasion," *Harvard Business Review* (May–June 1998): 84–95.

28. Ibid.: 91.

29. Ibid.: 87.

30. Ibid.

31. Narisetti, Raju. "Bottom-Up Approach Pushes Plant's Performance to the Top," *Chicago Tribune* (November 29, 1992): sect. 7, 13.

32. Scheff, David. "Levi's Changes Everything," *Fast Company* (June–July, 1996): 65–78.

33. Bounds, Wendy. "Inside Levi's Race to Restore a Tarnished Brand," *The Wall Street Journal* (August 4, 1998): B1.

34. Franklin, Stephen. "For Workers and Their Employers, It Was a Wonderful Life," *Chicago Tribune* (December 22, 1992): sect. 3, 3.

35. *Chicago Tribune.* "World Faces Epidemic of Job Stress" (March 23, 1993): sect. 1, 3.

36. Kotulak, Ron, and Van, Jon. "Job Strain Sickens People and Also Demoralizes Them," *Chicago Tribune* (November 6, 1994): sect. 5, 4.

37. McHenry, Susan. "Jobs We Love to Hate," *Chicago Tribune* (November 1994): 12.

38. *Chicago Tribune.* "Execs, Workers Clash over Redefined Jobs" (October 11, 1994): sect. 3, 3.

39. Rones, Phillip L.; Ilg, Randy E.; and Garnder, Jennifer M. "Trends in Hours of Work Since the Mid-1970s," *Monthly Labor Review* (April 1997): 3–14. "Overworked and Overpaid: the American Manager," *Economist* (January 30, 1999): 55–56.

40. Kirkland, Katie. "On the Decline in Average Weekly Hours Worked," *Monthly Labor Review* (July 2000).

41. Diederich, Tom. "45% of Big Firms Monitor Workers," *Computerworld Online News* (April 20, 1999).

42. *Chicago Tribune.* "Bringing Your Work Life Under Control" (September 19, 1994): sect. 4, 3.

43. *Chicago Tribune.* "If You're Reading This, Odds Are Good That You're Stressed" (November 21, 1994): sect. 4, 3.

HUMAN MOTIVATION

Objectives

After reading and discussing this chapter, you should be able to do the following:

1. Define this chapter's key terms.

2. List and give examples of the common needs that humans share.

3. List and give an example of each of Herzberg's maintenance factors.

4. List and give an example of each of Herzberg's motivational factors.

5. Describe the expectancy theory of motivation.

6. Describe the reinforcement theory of motivation.

7. Describe the equity theory of motivation.

8. Discuss how supervisors can improve quality and productivity.

9. Explain how failure to manage diversity can decrease motivation.

Introduction

> The greatest motivational act one person can do for another is listen.
>
> —ROY E. MOODY

People are the most complex, difficult-to-manage resource that any business has. We bring our hopes and ambitions to work, along with our problems and defects. Most of us want our jobs and careers to provide us with many things. Some of us view our jobs as a source of the money we need in order to live the kind of life we feel is important. Some of us want a challenge, work that we can take pride in, and a sense of progress and accomplishment.

Most employers recognize that their employees are complex creatures who expect more than a paycheck from their employment. Employers know that dissatisfied, unhappy workers are generally poor performers. They know that satisfied workers often produce above the standards set for their jobs. Knowledgeable employers recognize, therefore, that it is in their best interests to attempt to provide their employees with the kinds of satisfaction they seek on the job.

This chapter explores human needs and their relationship to our behavior. It introduces you to popular theories of human motivation and describes what you and employers can do to help others get more from their jobs than simply a paycheck. Finally, it links motivation with the all-important concepts of quality and productivity.

Motivation Defined

motivation

the drive within a person to achieve a goal

Motivation is the drive within a person to achieve a goal. It is an internal process that takes place in all human beings, influenced by their perceptions and experiences as well as external variables. People are motivated by a variety of causes that can and do influence their behaviors. For example, Jamal's wife is expecting a baby. Consequently, he has become very eager to work all available overtime hours to earn more income. Maria is asking for additional duties from her supervisor and has returned to school to enhance her chances for a promotion. But as soon as both people achieve their objectives, their behaviors will usually cease to be motivated by these objectives.

As a supervisor, team leader, or team facilitator, your primary responsibility is to influence behaviors in order to increase the effectiveness and efficiency of your employees and operations. You must maintain an environment that supports your subordinates' motivated behavior. To achieve this, supervisors have to make sure that their diagnosis of performance problems is accurate before they attempt to increase the motivation of their subordinates. The following incident involving legendary football coach Bear Bryant illustrates such a misguided attempt:

Worker recognition enhances self-esteem. Here, a supervisor at Xerox presents a service award based on length of service. The presentation is held in front of coworkers to enhance self-esteem.

The University of Alabama was playing the University of Arkansas. Coach Bear Bryant was in a rage because the game was scoreless at halftime. In the locker room he went from player to player, telling them they were playing like dogs. When he came to player Henry Clark, he grabbed him by the shoulder pads, lifted him up, shook him, put him back down, and said, "Henry, you ain't playing worth a damn." Clark looked up and said, "Hell Coach, I ain't even been in the game yet."[1]

As author and consultant Tom Peters puts it: "The average person, age 18 or 58, comes to the workplace fully endowed with motivation. Our primary role as 'leaders' is to clear the silly B.S. out of the way—and let the troops get on with the job."[2] Terry Neill, a management consultant, believes that "Genuine empowerment . . . is not the things you do to or for people: it's the impediments you take away, leaving room for folks to empower themselves."[3]

This chapter examines several basic, interrelated theories about motivation—why people do what they do. All will help you visualize and interpret the causes behind your own and your subordinates' behavior.

Human Needs

When people work for subsistence-level wages, as most Americans did until the late 1940s, they concentrate on surviving. Their primary concern is for employment that will give them the money to furnish themselves and their families with the necessities of life. They live in fear of losing their jobs and, therefore, tolerate nearly any kind of working conditions and environment. People who observed the industrial economy of the United States in the early years of the 20th century found little joy in its workers' hearts. While it is difficult to grasp the severity of the Great Depression, which left most Americans at a subsistence level, some indication is provided by the fact that the stock market's Dow Jones industrial average declined 90 percent between 1929 and 1932.[4] Unsurprisingly, many companies and their managers believed that people worked primarily for money, and they were partially correct in those beliefs. Theory X (Chapter 6) had many disciples.

THE HAWTHORNE STUDIES

Since the 1920s, businesses have studied their employees in efforts to find out more about them. Probably the most important study—one that launched intense interest about and research into employee behavior and motivation—was the Western Electric Company's study in the 1920s. In 1927, engineers at the Hawthorne Plant of the Western Electric Company near Chicago conducted an experiment with several groups of workers to determine the effect of illumination on production. When illumination was increased in stages, the engineers found that production increased. To verify their findings, they reduced illumination to its previous level. Surprisingly, even after illumination was reduced, production increased again! Perplexed, they called in Elton Mayo and his colleagues from Harvard to investigate.

The First Study

The Harvard researchers selected several experienced women assemblers for an experiment. Management removed the women from their formal group of assemblers and had them work in another area. The women were compensated on the basis of the output of their group and received no direct supervision as they had before, only indirect supervision from several researchers in charge of the experiment. Next followed a series of environmental changes, each discussed with the women in advance of its implementation. For example, breaks were introduced and light refreshments were served, the normal six-day week was reduced to five days, and

SUPERVISING TEAMS

Methods for motivating teams are provided in the following examples from three very different companies: General Motors–Cadillac Division, Mary Kay Cosmetics, and Motorola.

General Motors–Cadillac Division

At General Motor's Cadillac engine plant in Livonia, Michigan, productivity and quality improved after all employees were assigned to groups of eight to fifteen people called "business teams," which meet at least once a week and energize employees in the following ways:

- They are highly autonomous, with responsibility for their own scheduling, training, problem solving, and other activities.
- They develop their own quantitative performance indicators.
- They employ a pay-for-knowledge system (employees are paid more if they learn more) to encourage employees to learn *all* plant jobs.
- Awards for suggestions are given to teams as a whole, encouraging people to work together.
- Performance appraisals emphasize support for the business team.

Mary Kay Cosmetics

At Mary Kay Cosmetics in Dallas, teams are now a way of life and employees are energized by having their ideas and

suggestions heard and seriously considered. Creative action teams (CAT) were instrumental in launching Mary Kay Cosmetics in Japan, in planning the company's 30th anniversary celebration, and in developing a savings plan for sales directors. "They listen to you in the CATs," says Southwest distribution supervisor Tina Lynch. "Nothing gets thrown out. Everything is weighed. It may be a crazy idea or it may be a time-consuming idea, but they really do listen."

Motorola

One of the most impressive examples of empowered teams that we have seen was in our visit to a Motorola microchip-making plant in the Philippines. With team names such as the Last Maverick, Path Finder, Revival X, and Be Cool, the Filipino teams have been consistent finalists (appropriately referred to as the "Magic 10") in Motorola's worldwide team recognition program, the Total Customer Satisfaction (TCS) showcase. Winning teams are flown, all expenses paid, to locations such as Disney World in Florida to display and discuss examples of how they achieve breakthrough results. Team accomplishments are regularly reported in an in-house quarterly magazine. As a result of this "publicity," teams at other Motorola facilities around the world can learn about and incorporate these valuable team ideas.

Sources: Cadillac and Mary Kay Cosmetics sections excerpted from Bob Nelson, *1001 Ways to Energize Employees.* New York: Workman Publishing (1997): 80. Motorola section excerpted from Bradley L. Kirkman and Benson Rosen, "Powering Up Teams," *Organizational Dynamics* (Winter 2000): 54–55.

the workday was cut by one hour. Each of these changes was accompanied by an increase in the group's output.[5]

To verify the assumptions that the researchers made, the women were returned to their original working conditions. Breaks were eliminated, the six-day week was restored, and all other conditions that had prevailed before the women were isolated were reinstated. The results were that production again increased!

In the extensive interviewing that followed, Mayo and his group concluded that a team spirit had been created, quite by accident, when management singled out these women to be the study group and then consulted with them before making each change. The women felt that they were something very special, both individually and collectively. Their isolation as a group and their proximity at work provided an environment for the development of close personal relationships. The formal group had been transformed into an informal one—a clique.

The Second Study

To test the researchers' findings, a new group of workers was selected and isolated. This time the researchers chose a group of men. Several of them were involved in wiring equipment, whereas others soldered the wired connections. Several important events happened in this formal group. The men eventually split into two separate informal cliques because one group felt its work was more difficult than the other's and its members adopted a superior attitude. This left the remainder of the workers to form another clique. Both cliques included wirers, solderers, and an inspector, and each group also engaged in setting standards of output and conduct. The members of the group that considered itself superior mutually agreed on production quotas. As intergroup rivalry developed, the output of the other group began to decline. The superior group became superior in output also, which caused additional condescending behavior and a still greater decrease in morale and output in the other group. Even though each man was to share in a bonus based on the formal group's total output, informal group conflict resulted in a decline in production.

These two experiments revealed that people work for a variety of reasons—not just for money and subsistence. They seek satisfaction for more than their physical needs at work as they also seek to satisfy their social and esteem needs.

A HIERARCHY OF NEEDS

The Hawthorne studies and many more that followed have given us a much wider view of why people work and what they expect from work. Well-known psychologist Abraham H. Maslow identified five universal human needs that act as fuel for our internal drives to change or achieve. Exhibit 7.1 shows this hierarchy of needs as levels or steps in an upward progression from the most basic to the highest psychological need.[6]

Exhibit **7.1** *A. H. Maslow's hierarchy of human needs.*

SELF-REALIZATION NEEDS	JOB-RELATED SATISFIERS
Reaching Your Potential	Involvement in Planning Your Work
Independence	Freedom to Make Decisions Affecting Work
Creativity	Creative Work to Perform
Self-Expression	Opportunities for Growth and Development

ESTEEM NEEDS	JOB-RELATED SATISFIERS
Responsibility	Status Symbols
Self-Respect	Money (as a measure, for some, of self-esteem)
Recognition	Merit Awards
Sense of Accomplishment	Challenging Work
Sense of Competence	Sharing in Decisions
Sense of Equity	Opportunity for Advancement

SOCIAL NEEDS	JOB-RELATED SATISFIERS
Companionship	Opportunities for Interaction with Others
Acceptance	Team Spirit
Love and Affection	Friendly Coworkers
Group Membership	Team Inclusion

SAFETY NEEDS	JOB-RELATED SATISFIERS
Security for Self and Possessions	Safe Working Conditions
Avoidance of Risks	Seniority
Avoidance of Harm	Fringe Benefits
Avoidance of Pain	Proper Supervision
	Sound Company Policies, Programs, and Practices

PHYSICAL NEEDS	JOB-RELATED SATISFIERS
Food	Pleasant Working Conditions
Clothing	Adequate Wage or Salary
Shelter	Rest Periods
Comfort	Labor-Saving Devices
Self-Preservation	Efficient Work Methods

THE NEEDS–GOAL MODEL OF MOTIVATION

Human needs provide the basis for our first theory of motivation. Our definition of motivation—the drive within a person to achieve a goal—tells us that motivation is an internal process. It is something we do within ourselves, not something we do to others. The term *drive* in our definition denotes a force that is fueled by human needs common to all of us. These needs, both physical and psychological, provide motives for our actions and behavior. To achieve our goals, we must take actions. Our actions toward achievement are efforts, both mental and physical, that we feel are necessary to attain our goals.

human needs

physiological and psychological requirements that all humans share and that act as motives for behavior

Our goals may be tangible or intangible. We may want a new car or a job with higher status. The specific forms our goals take are a result of our personal makeup and desires at given moments in time. They are shaped in part by our experiences, individual perceptions, and current environments.

According to the needs–goal theory of motivation, a person who is motivated is in a state of unrest because she feels or believes that something is lacking—the goal. It is the unfulfilled need that creates the state of unrest. And since our needs can never fully be satisfied, we are continually setting goals. It is in our nature to want more—to continually strive to progress, to improve our conditions, and to acquire something new. As a result we engage in courses of action to achieve these goals, which result in satisfaction. Failure to achieve these goals results in frustration.

Supervisors who wish to understand the drive to work may wish to consider the following assertions about human needs and motivation:

- An unsatisfied need is a strong motivator.
- People can be influenced by more than one unsatisfied need at any given time.
- Needs can never be fully satisfied. They may cease to motivate behavior for a time, but they can and will return to act once again as motivators.
- People who seek satisfaction in one need area and do not find it will experience frustration and may try to compensate by overemphasizing another need.
- The perception of what we need at any given time is shaped in part by our experiences, by external influences on us, and by our capabilities to change our situations.

TYPES OF HUMAN NEEDS

Physiological Needs

Physiological or bodily needs are at the base of the need hierarchy. Unsatisfied physiological needs can influence behavior, whereas satisfied physiological needs are not motivators. For example, when we are hungry, we desire food of a type and in a quantity necessary to satisfy our hunger. Once we have eaten our fill, our hunger dissipates and no longer motivates our actions. New needs surface and take over as motives for our actions. But as we all know, hunger will return.

Safety Needs

The second level of human needs—safety needs or physical security—is our next concern. Having satisfied our physiological needs for the moment, we are concerned about providing for their satisfaction in the future. Once we have achieved an economic position that provides the means necessary to secure our physical maintenance, we want to protect this condition. A person who gets a job is anxious to keep it. He is concerned with preventing its loss and the accompanying loss of the ability to provide for physical needs. The person may, as a result, join a union to gain this kind of security. Like his physical needs, the person's need for security will weaken as a motive for actions once the individual reaches an adequate degree of satisfaction. But if his job is threatened, the need for security may once again become an active motivating force.

Social Needs

With the satisfaction of safety or security needs, the desire to satisfy social needs may become preeminent. These needs include a desire for human companionship, for affiliation with people and groups, for love and affection, and for a sense of belonging. Once we have achieved an adequate measure of satisfaction, our social needs begin to wane, and the fourth level of need stimulates our behavior.

Esteem Needs

The need for esteem is two-sided. First, we wish to be appreciated for what we are and for what we have to contribute—to be respected by others. Second, we need to have a feeling of self-esteem—to know we are worth something to ourselves and to others. We need a positive self-image. From this need comes the desire for praise and for symbols that reflect our self-approval and others' appreciation of our efforts. We seek prestige and status positions among our peers. We behave in ways that are pleasing and acceptable to others whose opinions we value. We wish to master the tasks given us, thus becoming competent performers. We want fair and equitable treatment from others.

Self-Realization Needs

Finally, our need for self-realization (sometimes called self-actualization) takes over when we achieve some measure of satisfaction in the previous four levels. We begin to experience a need to fulfill our potential and to be creative. To some, this means striving for higher levels in company management and obtaining the added authority and prestige that such positions provide. To others, it means being the best machinist, computer programmer, violinist, or supervisor that they have the potential to become. The need for self-realization causes people to pursue interests and knowledge for their own sake and for the joy of the pursuit.

All these needs are common in all of us to some degree. At any given moment, one or more of them are active, while the others lie dormant. When we feel satisfied in one or more areas, those areas will cease for a time to motivate our behavior. However, enough satisfaction for some may be too little or too much for others. In general, no need is ever completely satisfied, and none can ever cease completely to be a motivator. It is the unfulfilled need that is the strongest motive for human behavior.

McClelland's Acquired Needs Theory

All I want is a warm bed, a kind word and unlimited power.

—ASHLEIGH BRILLINT

In addition to the needs described above, D.C. McClelland has identified three important needs that commonly serve to motivate employees: *achievement, power,* and *affiliation.* McClelland says that employees acquire such needs from their experiences in life. Because the strength of these needs varies across employees, supervisors must determine the dominant needs for each employee in order to understand how to motivate her. Interestingly, he found that achievement is a dominant need for only 10 percent of the U.S. population.[7] Although such individuals constitute only a small proportion of the workforce, they are important for company performance. Supervisors need to know how to channel their need for achievement through valuable work activity.

McClelland's work also provides good insights into the motivations of managers, particularly in the area of needs for power. McClelland found that most good managers have a strong need for power that is oriented toward the institutions they serve, where they want to have influence and make an impact. Interestingly, managers with high needs for power and who have high inhibitions (high self-control) often use their power in an altruistic manner on behalf of others. McClelland developed the term **institutional managers** for those managers who have high needs for this type of power, are high on inhibition measures, and have low needs for affiliation. He found that institutional managers feel responsible for their organizations, like to work, tend to sacrifice some of their own interests for the good of the organization, and have high regard for justice in the sense that they want employees to be rewarded for their hard work and sacrifices.[8]

Institutional managers provide a dramatic contrast to managers McClelland calls **personal power managers.** These managers have stronger needs for power than affiliation but, in contrast to the institutional managers, they have low inhibition (low self-control) and their power is often

institutional manager
a manager who has a high need for power, high inhibitions, and low need for affiliation

personal power manager
a manger with strong power and affiliation needs and low inhibition

directed toward self-gratification. Personal power managers exhibit a number of unfortunate behaviors, such as being rude to others, engaging in sexual exploitation, and surrounding themselves with symbols of their power, such as big offices and fancy cars. McClelland also identified a third type of manager as **affiliative managers,** whose affiliation needs are greater than their power needs. Unfortunately, affiliative managers, who have a strong desire to be liked, are the least effective of the three types of managers. These managers often disregard organizational procedures, and their subordinates do not feel personal responsibility and do not take pride in their work groups. They also do not know how their managers feel about them.[9]

affiliative manager
a manager with affiliation needs greater than power needs

Strong needs for achievement are not necessarily consistent with good management. McClelland describes the relationship as follows:

> While it sounds as if everyone ought to have the need to achieve, in fact, as psychologists define and measure achievement motivation, the need to achieve leads people to behave in ways that do not necessarily engender good management. For one thing, because they focus on personal improvement and doing things better by themselves, achievement-motivated people want to do things themselves. For another, they want concrete short-term feedback on their performance so that they can tell how well they are doing. Yet managers, particularly in large, complex organizations, cannot perform by themselves all the tasks necessary for success. They must manage others to perform for the organization. And they must be willing to do without immediate and personal feedback since tasks are spread among many people.[10]

In a later section we explore how managers can apply their knowledge of needs in order to obtain motivated work behavior.

Supervisors and Human Needs

What does all this mean to you as a supervisor? A major goal for every organization is to help individual associates reach their goals while they help the organization reach its goals. You know that our common needs provide the motives for human behavior and that each person's personal goals may be quite different from those of her peers. As a supervisor, you are in a unique position to assist your subordinates and to provide them with some of the satisfactions they are seeking. You can be most helpful with regard to their safety, social, and esteem needs, as we shall now see.

When your subordinates joined your department, chances are that you assessed their strengths and weaknesses and got to know as much about them and their abilities as possible. Then you determined their specific needs for training so that they might improve their performance and skills. The end result is that you provided them with the knowledge, skills, and attitudes they needed to keep their jobs. You increased their sense of security and helped them remove some of their initial fears. You taught and enforced safety on the job (the focus of Chapter 16). Your actions helped them achieve a measure of satisfaction for both their physical and safety needs.

You also helped your subordinates with their need for affiliation when you introduced them to their new jobs and work groups. Your effort to know them has made you aware of their individual needs for affiliation and has enabled you to identify those subordinates who are satisfied and those who are frustrated with regard to social needs. You did all you could to help the isolated individuals gain acceptance by fostering a team spirit and by making them all feel part of a larger group. The process of turning individuals into team players is difficult and time consuming. People need to learn a variety of skills to make the transformation, and teams are not for everyone or for every task. But where they do apply and when they function properly, they provide satisfaction for team members' need for affiliation as nothing else at work can.

In regard to your subordinates' esteem needs, you have several key roles to play. When you do performance appraisals you provide the raw material they need for self-insight and improvement. You pass out praise if they deserve it and note the specific areas they must work on to gain your continued praise and acceptance. You also have authority that, if delegated, can enrich their feelings of importance and give them a way to learn certain aspects of your job. They know that this is an important sign of your faith and confidence in their abilities. When one of your people makes a good suggestion, you use it and give the credit to the source of the suggestion. If the idea is not suited to the operation, you tell the subordinate the reason, improving his understanding of the operation.

Various incentive systems can encourage employees to submit suggestions. Haworth Inc., an office furniture manufacturer, has reinvigorated suggestion systems by eliminating a common flaw in such systems—dismissal of the suggestion by the employee's supervisor. At Haworth, supervisors may make comments but are not allowed to dismiss suggestions because employees submit their suggestions for evaluation by a committee.[11] Keys to successful suggestion systems are quick acknowledgment of the suggestion and a timely response indicating whether the suggestion will be adopted or the reason why it will not be adopted. At American Axle and Manufacturing, Inc., 50 percent of employees now submit suggestions and in a recent six-month period the company saved $37,000 and paid employees $73,000 for their suggestions.[12]

General Motors, once the efficiency laggard among auto manufacturers, is also using employee suggestions to make its plants more productive. Aside from employee self-esteem needs served by the suggestion system, significant financial awards are available for teams of workers that make valuable suggestions. The suggestion system has generated a great deal of interest among employees: in a recent quarter the company received 44,000 suggestions. The savings produced by the suggestion system have been substantial. For example, employee suggestions in GM's Metal Fabricating Division enabled the company to save $10 million in a recent year. Interestingly, many observers thought that GM's large size and lack of flexibility would prevent it from catching up with the efficiency of its competitors. Nonetheless, management improvements such as the suggestion system and technological innovations have enabled GM to make huge strides.[13] As one author puts it, "Here's one more suggestion for GM's competitors: 'It's time to admit that the fat man is tap dancing'."[14]

As pointed out earlier, a small but important percentage of the U.S. population is motivated by the need for achievement. Achievement needs for such individuals can often be fulfilled by placing them in sales work or in positions in which they can act as entrepreneurs. Interestingly, while the need for achievement is high for managers, it tends not to be dominant for them.[15]

Supervisors can also provide greater responsibility to employees who are motivated by their need for power. For example, supervisors can allow such individuals to plan and exercise greater self-control over their work.[16] An example of expanding control would be to allow the workers to do the final inspection of their own work. A newspaper advertisement for machinists in the Miami facility of Rolls-Royce included such an inducement by stating that "Selected applicants will work in an innovative environment and be responsible for inspection and superior quality of all products they help manufacture."

You may become frustrated when you attempt to discover which need is a conscious concern to each individual subordinate at any given time. This is difficult knowledge to gain because when you observe your people, you do so in a fragmented way. You see them at work under the influence of many forces from within and outside the company. Even if you know each of your people well, you can be fooled by your observations. In observing the actions of others, we seldom see the motives for them. You, like your associates, tend to play roles at work that mask your true feelings and motives. Yet every supervisor, team leader, and team facilitator must attempt to determine what needs are most important to herself and her subordinates.

Maintenance and Motivation

We can understand motivation better by examining the contributions of Frederick Herzberg, whose work on motivation in business demonstrated some applications of Maslow's hierarchy of human needs. Herzberg and his associates found that two sets of factors must be provided in the working environment to promote motivation.

MAINTENANCE OR HYGIENE FACTORS

maintenance factor
a factor that can be provided in order to prevent job dissatisfaction

First, Herzberg argued that there is a set of factors he labeled **maintenance factors** or hygiene factors. These conditions or factors are *extrinsic*—not connected to the work we do—and will not cause employee motivation in the great majority of people. But a lack of them can cause dissatisfaction, thus preventing or inhibiting motivation. Herzberg argued that these environmental conditions, when provided in the right mix, can only prevent dissatisfaction and remove barriers to motivated behavior. The best a business can hope for by providing these factors is that the average employee will put forth an average commitment in time and effort at his job. Maintenance factors Herzberg identified are:[17]

1. Economic—wages, salaries, fringe benefits, and the like
2. Security—grievance procedures, seniority privileges, fair work rules, company policy, and discipline
3. Social—opportunities to mix with one's peers at work and at company-sponsored events such as parties, outings, and the like
4. Working conditions—adequate heat, light, ventilation, and hours of work
5. Status—privileges, job titles, and other symbols of rank or position

Herzberg viewed money as a maintenance factor because, for the majority of people he studied, it is extrinsic to one's job and of little help in satisfying our higher-level psychological needs—esteem and self-realization. When people are working in jobs they hate, or under conditions that hurt psychologically or physically, money cannot make them work with a personal commitment to excel. (We include economic incentives such as bonuses and suggestion awards in the category of money.) Money or the promise of it can motivate us in the short term, but once obtained, it ceases to motivate. When people feel that they have enough money it becomes less important to acquire more. (For each of us this is an individual perception.)

The quest for money often masks a search for what money cannot buy. "If your workers are complaining about their pay, it's usually a sign that something else is missing. . . . People will work for less (not less than a fair wage . . .) if they enjoy their work and feel as if they're being treated fairly."[18] For most people, money cannot offer intrinsic satisfactions—those directly connected to work and the performance of it. Consider, for example, *Fortune*'s 2001 listing of the 100 best companies to work for in the United States. Beginning with the top, these companies are The Container Store, SAS Institute, Cisco Systems, Southwest Airlines, Charles Schwab, TDIndustries, Fenwick & West, Synovus Financial, Edward Jones, and Plante & Moran.[19] The role of money in the overall scheme of things is illustrated by the answers employees gave for turning down offers from other companies in one of *Fortune*'s recent rankings:

[The employees'] answers vary—cutting-edge technology, exciting work, the chance to change careers within the same company, a shot at a challenging overseas assignment, the promise of promotion from within, flexible or reduced work hours that still keep you on the fast track, truly terrific benefits. But here's the part that may surprise you: Nobody mentioned money. That is not because the 100 Best companies necessarily pay better than their peers. Rather, it's that—pay being equal—most humans seem to need a better reason to get up in the morning. You no doubt dimly recall this concept from Psychology 101: Once people reach a certain level of material comfort, they care more about self-actualization, or in plain English, being interested in what they actually do all day.[20]

According to psychologist C. J. Cranny, "the most important factor in creating an atmosphere that workers find satisfying is whether employees find their work 'intrinsically interesting.'"[21] This can only happen through what Herzberg called *motivation factors*.

MOTIVATION FACTORS

motivation factor

a factor that has the potential to stimulate internal motivation to provide better-than-average performance and commitment from those to whom it appeals

Motivation factors, the second set of factors, are *intrinsic*—directly related to the work we do. For the great majority of us they provide the incentive to make a better-than-average commitment to our efforts. Motivation factors provide the means by which individuals can achieve greater job satisfaction. When provided in the proper quantity and quality, they have the potential to satisfy employees' needs and cause an increased commitment of time and energy. Herzberg identified seven motivation factors:[22]

1. *Challenging work.* The average person wants to view his job as offering an avenue for self-expression and growth. Each person needs something to tax his abilities.

2. *Feelings of personal accomplishment.* The average employee gets a sense of achievement and a feeling of contributing something of value when presented with a challenge that she can meet.

3. *Recognition for achievement.* The average employee wants to feel that his contributions have been worth the effort and that the effort has been noted and appreciated. Money awards, for some, help here.

4. *Achievement of increasing responsibility.* The typical employee wants to acquire new duties and responsibilities, either through expansion of her job or by delegation from the supervisor.

5. *A sense of individual importance to the organization.* Employees want to feel that their personal presence is needed and that their individual contributions are necessary. Higher-than-average compensation can help here for some people.

6. *Access to information.* Employees want to know about the things that affect them and their jobs; they want to be kept in the know.

7. *Involvement in decision making.* Today's employees desire a voice in the matters that affect them and a chance to decide some things for themselves. They need freedom to exercise initiative and creativity.

Exhibit 7.2 provides several examples of specific ways in which jobs can be made more challenging and interesting.

Several of these seven factors, such as those involving increased responsibility and greater involvement in decision making, can be designed into the structure and operations of a business. When companies make the commit-

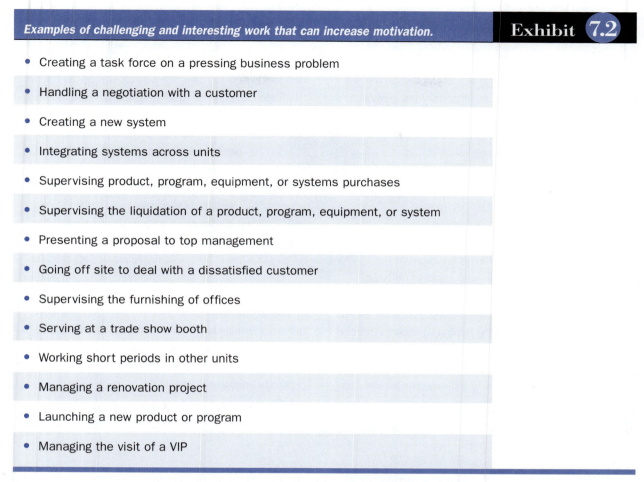

Examples of challenging and interesting work that can increase motivation.

Exhibit 7.2

- Creating a task force on a pressing business problem

- Handling a negotiation with a customer

- Creating a new system

- Integrating systems across units

- Supervising product, program, equipment, or systems purchases

- Supervising the liquidation of a product, program, equipment, or system

- Presenting a proposal to top management

- Going off site to deal with a dissatisfied customer

- Supervising the furnishing of offices

- Serving at a trade show booth

- Working short periods in other units

- Managing a renovation project

- Launching a new product or program

- Managing the visit of a VIP

Source: Extracted from Bob Nelson, *1001 Ways to Energize Employees.* New York: Workman Publishing (1997): 68, 69, 70.

ment to empower employees, they give individuals and teams the authority to make their own decisions, solve their own problems, and achieve greater control over their work. In short, associates and colleagues achieve greater autonomy—a key motivating factor in Herzberg's research. Pollsters and other researchers have discovered that associates feel empowered when they have the authority to do the following:[23]

- Stop work in progress to correct problems (Saturn employees can do this)
- Intervene on a customer's behalf (Marriott associates have this power)
- Rework a product or redo a service (Motorola employees have this duty)
- Make an exception to procedures (autonomous teams have this ability)
- Replace merchandise or grant refunds (most discount chains grant their store managers this power)

SUPERVISORS AND QUALITY

Motivated service associates are the key to customer satisfaction in most businesses, especially the hospitality industry. No one knows this better than the committed and enthusiastic employees of Marriott International's Schaumburg Marriott in Illinois. Tony Prsyszlak, a community college graduate, is a prime example. He greets guests as they arrive: "But please don't call this gregarious 23-year-old a doorman. He is now a multitalented 'guest service associate'—GSA, for short." Prsyszlak is just one of five GSAs who can handle your check-in; all wear several hats—doorman, bellman, front-desk clerk, and concierge. And all are self-managing. The GSAs are a select few—10 percent of the applicants show the necessary flexibility and steadiness under pressure.

More than ever before, "companies are scrambling to hire, train, and hang on to ordinary mortals who can perform feats of extraordinary service. . . . [I]n an era of flattened hierarchies and heightened expectations, [what is needed are] people who are resilient and resourceful, empathetic and enterprising, competent and creative—a set of skills, in short, that [were] once demanded only of managers." To find these extraordinary people takes patience and careful screening, considering not so much formal education and experience as "personality and psychology." Once found, these valuable human beings must be carefully trained and empowered. After an initial eight hours of training, all new hires are given a "buddy" or mentor to help them through their next 90 days. Refresher training is provided at the end of each month. The results of Marriott's new approaches have led to more motivated associates, delighted guests, and a decline in employee turnover.

Source: Ronald Henkoff, "Finding, Training and Keeping the Best Service Workers," *Fortune* (October 3, 1994): 110–111, 114, 116, 118, 120, 122.

Some employees do not desire all or even a few of these factors and the opportunities they represent. This may be true because, for the moment at least, they lack ambition and do not feel the need to change. Still others, because of mental or emotional limitations, may lack the potential to take advantage of these factors and to master higher job responsibilities. For those who, in the manager's opinion, can take advantage of these factors but do not do so, some standards and goals must be set to prod them to keep growing. The manager should make it clear to these employees that more is expected of them and that they can receive more rewards in return for an increased effort. In short, the supervisor, team leader, or team facilitator must try to get such employees oriented toward making progress.

A Gallup Poll asked workers how important various characteristics of the job were to them. It discovered an interesting and nearly equal mix of Herzberg's maintenance and motivation factors. Among the major characteristics listed as "very important" were:[24]

- Over three-fourths of those surveyed listed good benefits, interesting work, and job security (in this order).

- 62 to 68 percent listed the opportunity to learn new skills, one week or more of vacation time, working independently, and recognition from coworkers (in this order).

- 58 percent listed regular hours, having a job in which they could help others, and limits to job stress.

- 52 to 56 percent listed high income (11th on the list), working close to home, work that is important to society, chances for promotion, and contact with many people (in this order).

We point out that Herzberg's theory has limitations in that a substantial number of people may not be motivated by the factors he identified as motivators. Still, his work provides the basis for the concept of job enrichment, which is discussed later in this chapter.[25] Thus, for subordinates who have the potential and the drive to achieve something greater, supervisors have a duty to provide a work environment that contains the motivation factors. If they are made available, like different kinds of fine foods on a buffet, the "hungry" people in any group will select among them according to their needs. Furthermore, Herzberg's theory builds on some of Maslow's theory in that hygiene or maintenance factors generally help us satisfy our physical, safety, and social needs, while motivation factors generally help us satisfy our esteem and self-realization needs.

Unfortunately, Maslow's and Herzberg's work has caused some misunderstanding about the role of money in motivation. When used inappropriately, such as when employees feel that they are being bribed or manipulated, money can undermine motivators or intrinsic aspects of work.[26] Nonetheless, research by Jason Shaw and Nina Gupta shows that properly designed compensation systems are not incompatible with intrinsic factors that underlie job enrichment.

> Our meta-analysis explored whether the relationship between financial incentives and performance was stronger for *extrinsic* (i.e., dull and boring) tasks than for *intrinsic* (i.e., challenging and interesting) tasks. Presumably, if financial incentives erode intrinsic motivation, we would find them to be negatively related to performance for intrinsic tasks. The data show otherwise. It doesn't matter what kind of work people are doing—incentives improve performance. . . . Taken together, then, the hard data are unambiguous—financial incentives improve performance quantity; they *do not* erode intrinsic motivation.[27]

Additional Theories of Motivation

EXPECTANCY THEORY

The development of expectancy theory is credited to Victor Vroom, a renowned management scholar at Yale University. Expectancy theory goes beyond the identification of needs and describes the process by which workers make decisions about motivated behavior. Accordingly, many management scholars call expectancy theory a *process theory.* Expectancy theory explains that workers are concerned about three important questions:[28]

1. How much effort, diligence, care, etc. should I devote to my work?
2. If I perform well as a result of my effort, diligence, care, etc. will I obtain desired outcomes to satisfy my needs?
3. Does my employer provide work outcomes that satisfy my needs?

The first question is important to supervisors because it means that their associates should expect to be high performers if they exert high effort. If, on the other hand, their associates do not have the necessary skills for the job or, for example, the supervisor fails to provide the proper materials to perform the job, they will not expect to be high performers regardless of their efforts. One's belief that efforts will result in productivity is called **expectancy.**[29] Therefore, supervisors must provide training and coaching so that their associates will have a strong expectancy of high performance given high effort.

The second question also is important because it deals with reward systems and associates' perceptions of reward systems. In other words, if associates perceive that high performance is not rewarded with desired outcomes, such as promotions, they will not perceive performance as *instrumental.* The perceived linkage between performance and desired outcomes is called **instrumentality.**[30] Supervisors need to examine the rationality of the reward system when their associates have low perceptions of the instrumentality of performance. For example, the supervisor would need to determine whether promotions are based on performance or on the basis of political factors such as friendship with the boss. Even if promotions are actually based on performance, if associates *perceive* that they are based on politics there will still be low instrumentality and low motivation to perform. In such situations the supervisor will need to communicate the real reasons for promotions and do a better job of explaining promotion procedures.

The third question also is important because it assesses the attractiveness of the potential outcomes that an associate might obtain. The attractiveness of outcomes, such as promotions or raises, varies across

expectancy
belief that effort will result in performance

instrumentality
belief that performance will result in desired outcomes

According to expectancy theory, when training a subordinate in a task, you must communicate exactly what, how, when, and where you want it done. Reaffirm that the worker understands what to do before delegating the task.

associates because they have different needs. The attractiveness of outcomes is called **valence**.[31]

The usefulness of expectancy theory is that it tells supervisors that high motivation is likely only when subordinates perceive that (1) high effort will lead to high performance (high expectancy), (2) high performance will lead to outcomes (high instrumentality), and (3) outcomes are highly desirable (high valence).[32] Expectancy theory provides supervisors with a diagnostic tool for assessing the motivation potential of the work situation for each of their subordinates. Thus, expectance theory tells us that people will do what their supervisor wants them to do if she makes sure the following conditions exist:[33]

1. knows what outcomes her employees value,

2. has identified the behaviors that she wants from her subordinates,

3. provides sufficient training and facilitates the work so that her subordinates can reach desired levels of performance,

4. arranges the work such that high effort produces outcomes large enough to be motivating, and

5. examines the reward system periodically to make sure inequities are eliminated.

As a supervisor, you can influence all of these conditions directly. However, in regard to motivation and rewards, the individual's perception of the desirability of the reward is largely beyond your ability to influence in any meaningful way. Research has demonstrated that supervisors need to consider more factors, such as individual personality differences, in order to determine whether a subordinate is likely to be motivated in a given situation.[34] We look next at the ways in which you can apply expectancy theory.

Enhancing Perceived Expectancy

You must spell out in as much detail as possible what you want people to do. Your subordinates must have a clear understanding of the task, the standards that will be used to evaluate their performance, and the level of quality expected. In a team, team leaders and team members have a say in all these things. Subordinates or team members must also feel that they are capable of performance. If not, it is likely they will turn down or at least resist the assignment. Here are some ways of influencing your associates' perceptions about their capabilities to perform:

- During the hiring process and when forming teams, try to match the person's experiences and skills to the needs of the job and team.

- Provide training for the skills needed for a task before assigning it.

- Try to redesign the job so that subordinates will be asked to perform only those tasks that they feel capable of performing. After a person has self-confidence and a feeling of competence he will be willing to tackle bigger and more demanding tasks.

valence
the value or attractiveness of an outcome

When you have a subordinate who knows what is being asked of her and feels capable of performing to the level expected, then outcomes or rewards become critical.

Enhancing Perceived Instrumentality

Supervisors need to be certain that rewards are given to high performers and not to employees who deliver less. If a person works hard, delivers the level of performance called for, and gets no significantly greater reward than that received by mediocre performers, instrumentality will be low. You will have an unhappy, unmotivated employee on your hands. This is one reason companies are shifting their compensation focus to rewarding based on results, not simply seniority and increases in the cost of living. In addition, make sure that the performance being rewarded is under the complete control of the employee and is not dependent on some factor over which the person has no control. Control over performance, fair evaluations, and rewards can stir people out of complacency and into a motivated state.

REINFORCEMENT THEORY

Reinforcement theory has its foundation in research performed by B. F. Skinner. This theory holds that one can encourage desired behaviors by focusing on the consequences of those behaviors.[35] Simply stated, desired behaviors should be rewarded while undesired behaviors should not be reinforced. If a manager or a company wants to modify employee behavior, timely and appropriate rewards should be provided.

Positive reinforcements should occur as soon as possible after the desired behavior, so that such behavior will be connected with rewards. Good performance can be rewarded through praise, pay increases, promotions, and special favors within a manager's power to dispense. When it is followed by positive reinforcement, rewarded behavior tends to be repeated.

Negative reinforcement involves withholding a punishment if the subordinate engages in a desired behavior. In this manner it rewards desired behaviors. For example, you may tell a subordinate that if her work is completed according the production schedule you will not engage in micro-management.[36]

Punishment attempts through fear and sanctions to discourage repeat performances. Punishment may include denial of privileges, reprimands, and loss of pay or opportunities. As with positive reinforcement, the quicker the punitive action occurs and the more appropriate it is, the greater will be its impact. Unfortunately, a disadvantage of punishment is that its results are less predictable because employees learn only what *not* to do. They still do not know what they should do. Punishment may also lead to revenge and other undesired consequences.[37]

Certain performances need no reinforcement. Actions that are undesirable but have small (if any) consequences may often be ignored. Temporary, non-serious misbehavior may simply be noted and go unpunished. Supervisors are often required to make a judgment about the cause of the behavior and the intent behind it. Most people lose their tempers now and then, and all of us make minor mistakes fairly regularly. Save your punishment for serious offenses, and punish people in private. Pass out your rewards publicly and take time to help celebrate positive contributions.

As a supervisor, team leader, or team facilitator using this theory, keep the following points in mind:

1. Keep your people aware of what is expected and of the consequences for failing to meet expectations.
2. Rewards and punishments must be tailored to the behavior they are intended to reward or punish. Consider the consequences, intent, and seriousness of the behavior.
3. Don't reward mediocre or poor performance.
4. Don't punish inconsequential instances of misbehavior.
5. Don't fail to reward desired behavior.
6. Don't fail to punish behavior you want eliminated.

Companies fail sometimes because their leaders fail to walk like they talk. They emphasize in words certain concepts and then contradict them with their actions. "They preach the importance of teamwork—then reward individuals who work at standing out from the crowd. They encourage risk taking—then punish good-faith failures. . . . Corporate leaders can scuttle a reengineering effort quite quickly if they pump up their own bonuses and order a new fleet of company jets while telling the troops to tighten belts."[38] When your walk contradicts your talk, your associates label you a hypocrite and take their example from your walk.

EQUITY THEORY

Our final theory considers motivation from each person's unique perspective. Equity theory holds that people contribute or withhold their contributions based on individual perceptions of their equity ratios. People compare the ratio of their rewards (outcomes) to their contributions (inputs) with the ratios of relevant comparison groups, to determine the equity of their work situations. Such comparisons may include coworkers or people at other companies. The ratio of outcomes divided by inputs yields a psychological perception of the equity or fairness at work.

When your subordinates perceive that their equity ratios are smaller than the ratios of others, they will experience *negative inequity* and will be dissatisfied with how they are being treated. Common responses to such perceived inequities with comparison groups are to reduce inputs, such as effort or quality of work, and to attempt to change outcomes, such as by seeking a pay raise. Other potential responses include cognitive distortion of the inputs or outcomes of others or changing comparison groups. It is possible to experience *positive inequity*, in which your ratio of outcomes to inputs is more favorable than those of people you use for comparison. In cases of extreme overpayment, individuals sometimes increase their inputs in order to restore their perceptions of equity.[39]

How people perceive their ratios is more important than how their managers or facilitators perceive them. When people lose their enthusiasm and appear to be slacking off, supervisors should consider subordinates' perceptions of their equity ratios. Sit down and discuss their perceptions with them. Ask if they believe anything in the working environment is inequitable or unfair. Quite often you will find a misconception. Sometimes you will find that subordinates have untrue information or that other unmotivated people are influencing them. In such cases, you must do what you can to remove their feelings of inequity.

Managing Motivation

In Chapter 6, we discussed the importance of employees' beliefs, attitudes, and values. These affect how they perceive their world and the demands that are made on them. All of us look for jobs that offer a fit between what we want from work and what our organizations want from us. The closer the fit, the more likely it is that we will find job satisfaction and the means to achieve our personal and professional goals. As Herzberg's theory tells us, job satisfaction comes from the work itself, not from things external to it. Without job satisfaction, we will find it difficult if not impossible to become or to stay motivated—to give our best effort to our performance at work.

Employees become dissatisfied for a variety of reasons. They may enter a job expecting too much. In other cases people may be hired for jobs that are too difficult or too easy. Applicants for employment are often desperate and take the first job offer that comes their way because they need money. Once on the job, people find boredom, unsafe conditions, inadequate training, and uncooperative coworkers. All these situations add up to problems for the new employees and their employers. Most job dissatisfaction can be prevented, but both employees and employers have to work at prevention.

A question frequently asked is whether high morale or happy workers result in improved financial performance. Although this question has been the subject of numerous studies, the evidence is not clear. There are obvious counterexamples in which a company's economic environment prevents good financial performance regardless of the fact that it has satisfied or happy workers.[40] On the other hand, if managers treat talented employees so badly that they leave or refuse to exert themselves, then high performance is impossible.

On balance do happy workers improve corporate performance? The Gallup Organization recently surveyed 55,000 workers in an attempt to match employee attitudes with company results. The survey found that four attitudes, taken together, correlate with higher profits. The attitudes: Workers feel that they are given the opportunity to do what they do best every day; they believe their opinions count; they sense that their fellow workers are committed to quality; and they've made a direct connection between their work and the company's mission.[41]

Nonetheless, while many factors such as involvement and empowerment impact performance, the reward system must be rational before we can expect performance to be sustained at high levels. And while behavior and rewards must be linked, the cost of rewards does not have to be high. Steve Kerr, a noted management scholar, makes the following comments about rewards and performance:

> Distributing rewards without regard for how well people have performed makes little sense in general, and has a particularly negative impact on high performers. Rewards are among the most powerful tools an organization has to thank high performers for past efforts; noncontingent rewards don't do this. Rewards can also play a major role in stimulating future performance; noncontingent rewards don't do this either . . . Twenty years of studying reward systems has convinced me that there is virtually no relationship between the power of rewards and their cost.[42]

QUALITY

In Chapter 1, we defined quality and noted its link to the customer or user of a product or service. Quality, in the final analysis, is measured by the ability of a product or service to meet the needs of the internal or external customer. An internal user may be any person or group in the company who receives output from another employee or group. Exhibit 7.3 highlights four major dimensions of quality.

When a company decides to emphasize quality, it often adopts a *total quality management* (TQM) approach.

Dimensions of quality. **Exhibit 7.3**

1. *Performance characteristics.* A product's operating features and the final outcomes that they produce.

2. *Users' perceptions.* The ways in which a product feels, looks, and performs—its fit and finish.

3. *Useful life.* The length of time that the product can be expected to deliver performance that is in line with user expectations.

4. *Serviceability.* The manufacturer's willingness and ability to furnish quick and reliable repairs—how well the producer backs up the product and its users.

TQM involves the application of quality management principles to all aspects of the business, including customers and suppliers. Total quality management requires that the principles of quality management should be applied in every branch and at every level in the organization. It is a company-wide approach to quality, with improvements undertaken on a continuous basis by everyone in the organization. Individual systems, procedures, and requirements . . . will pervade every person, activity and function of the organization [and will] . . . require a broadening of outlook and skills and an increase in creative activities . . . The spread of the TQM philosophy would also be expected to be accompanied by greater sophistication in the application of quality management tools and techniques and increased emphasis on people.[43]

six sigma

a quality approach having a goal of no more than 3.4 defects in a million units

Six sigma programs, which have a goal of no more than 3.4 defects per million units, are an outgrowth of TQM and require suppliers to also pursue high-quality approaches. The high emphasis on training in both the TQM and six sigma approaches is evident in the black belt and green belt titles that are bestowed on managers and employees who have acquired expertise in six sigma methodology.[44] TQM and six sigma mean a never-ending quest by every member of an organization to improve people and processes. Everyone must be committed to and participate in the effort to improve quality. Your job as a supervisor is to instill this concept into your people and teams. Make a commitment to quality your personal philosophy. Unless you and your people see quality as your responsibility, such approaches will not work.

Quality leaders such as Toyota, Caterpillar, Dow Chemical, GE, Honeywell, and the Dana Corporation recognize that quality is a never-ending journey, not a destination.[45] Providers who are in close touch with their customers create high-quality products and services—they know what customers want and need. These producers design quality into their end products and processes and set precise performance standards for all of their component parts. From the product design teams to the engineering and production teams, concern for quality dominates the efforts of all concerned. Once the suppliers are chosen (in part for their reputations for and commitment to quality), contracts are drafted. Close contact is then maintained to ensure that all the parts produced meet standards. Cross-functional teams are sometimes used, with members from marketing, production, and design, as well as vendors, working on the projects from beginning to end. The Honeywell Corporation provides an example of this approach—creating a cross-functional team to facilitate communication and participation at all levels of the organization.[46]

PRODUCTIVITY

Productivity is usually expressed as a ratio measure of outputs divided by inputs, yielding a *productivity index* (PI). A PI can be calculated for most clerical or production activities. Inputs may be tons of materials, hours of machine time, dollars of invested capital, or hours of labor invested to pro-

SUPERVISORS AND ETHICS

Reengineering preaches that you can tinker with and fine-tune an existing system or process just so long before a replacement is required. Instead of continually replacing and rebuilding components of existing systems, companies must continuously focus on redesigning their structures and processes—adopting newer, faster, more efficient models for nearly everything they do. But what good will this do if your efforts leave fearful, unmotivated employees in their wake?

"In too many companies, reengineering is corporate code for firing about a third of the workforce. And it's not something you do once and for all. It is a tool, and a powerful one, for reshaping your company continuously." Reengineering, "executed ruthlessly, . . . can corrode the esprit de corps vital to teamwork. Listen to US West's Jerry Miller, whose team of billing clerks in . . . Minnesota, got downsized out of existence: . . . 'When we first formed our teams, the company came in talking teamwork and empowerment and promised we wouldn't lose any jobs. It turns out all this was a big cover. The company had us all set up for reengineering. We showed them how to streamline the work, and now 9,000 people are gone. It was cut-your-own-throat. It makes you feel used.'"

But it does not have to work this way. The Allina company in Minnesota operates not-for-profit hospitals, clinics, and medical transportation services. The company, which has over 22,000 employees, began its reengineering efforts by focusing on changing worker attitudes and creating mutual trust between union employees and management. A team of management and union people was created and empowered to make changes. "For instance, it found a way to close one of Allina's hospitals without leaving employees stranded. The team set up an employment center that placed 95% of the closing hospital's employees elsewhere in Allina or in other companies. Not only did this gesture raise morale and save the company $8 million in severance costs, but more importantly, it also showed that management was serious about working with labor."

Sources: Nancy K. Austin, "What's Missing from Corporate Cure-Alls," *Working Woman* (September 1994): 19. Brian Dumaine, "The Trouble with Teams," *Fortune* (September 5, 1994): 92. Allina Internet website (2002), www.allina.com/ahs/home.nsf

duce the output. Outputs are the units realized through the investment or application of inputs. The value of such indexes is in their comparisons over time. By continually calculating a PI for each of your people, teams, and operations, you can measure progress or setbacks.

THE QUALITY, PRODUCTIVITY, AND PROFITABILITY LINK

Quality and productivity are two sides of the same coin. Improvements that lead to better quality also must lead to increased productivity. When this occurs, profitability will increase as well, thus assuring the continued existence of the organization. W. Edwards Deming—the man who taught Japanese companies and many in America much of what they know about quality—believed that when quality improves, costs decrease.[47] Companies have less need to scrap materials and rework their outputs. With less waste and fewer mistakes, productivity improves through the more efficient use of resources. Customers are satisfied, more jobs are provided and companies ensure their future.

> It's no secret that many manufacturers have succeeded in linking cost-cutting with quality improvement. Toyota, for instance, expects a 3% reduction in costs each year from its supplier firms, says Dan Cavanaugh, plant manager at Dana Corp.'s automotive frame plant in Stockton, Calif....Workers at the plant, which performs 115 ft. of welds on each 300-lb. frame, are constantly looking for ways to improve quality and reduce costs. Each worker is expected to come up with three ideas per month, and in a recent month the average was 3.8, Cavanaugh says.[48]

Most efforts to improve quality also will help increase productivity. As with quality improvements, productivity gains begin with a commitment from top management to make improving productivity a priority. The efforts required for productivity must be funded. Goals need to be stated and corporate environments must be modified to take on the new challenges and changes required. Standards must be set, gains and losses measured, plans created, tools and techniques chosen and used, and people rewarded for their efforts.

Productivity can be improved by producing the same outputs with fewer inputs or by increasing outputs with the same or fewer inputs. Either approach implies more efficient use of resources. People are a main ingredient in the constant search for improvements in productivity. The more motivated and satisfied the individuals, the more productive they are likely to be. On the other hand, people suffering from job stress and job dissatisfaction tend to produce less than their satisfied, low-stress counterparts.

A look at the symptoms typically exhibited by dissatisfied workers should tell you how they affect productivity in a negative way. The typical symptoms are tardiness, absenteeism, delayed work, shoddy work, and time lost to gripes and complaints about their station in life. There also may be theft and shrinkage, or employees may actually damage company property or engage in sabotage simply to vent their frustration. Over time, dissatisfied employees may become emotionally and physically ill, further reducing their productive capacities. If they decide to leave, their replacements will need training and production time will be lost.

The Property and Casualty Division of United Services Automobile Association puts its philosophy about productivity this way:

> Productivity improvement isn't just working harder, it's working smarter. It means devising a method to get the best return on our investment in people, facilities, equipment and other resources. . . . Improving productivity . . . means finding better ways to do more with the resources we have. . . . In short, we need to provide quality products through distribution systems that are customer-convenient and operator-efficient.[49]

Note that the company, though discussing productivity, makes clear references to quality.

People are both the cause and the cure for problems in quality and productivity. Today's emphasis on empowering workers requires them to be proficient in the four Rs—reading, 'riting, 'rithmetic, and responsibility. Ritz-Carlton hotels empower all employees, without higher approval, to "spend up to $2,000 to fix a guest's problem. . . . [Its] new focus on employee involvement has helped cut turnover from 80% to 45%, saving nearly $12.5 million."[50] When you and your company give people more authority, you are asking them to think and decide more—to depend more on their own abilities and judgment than they have in the past. "As long as you let everybody in on the facts—budgets, cost data, customer-satisfaction feedback—these independent decisions will usually be good ones."[51] Exhibit 7.4

| Suggestions for improving both quality and productivity in your operations. | Exhibit 7.4 |

1. Be committed to improving quality and productivity. Constantly demonstrate your commitment in every action you take.

2. Once you have defined a problem, seek suggestions from subordinates closest to the problem about how to solve it. Diverse people yield diverse suggestions.

3. Give your people all the information they need and the reasons for changes in procedures before you attempt to implement them. You need your people's cooperation and support to make the changes effective and efficient.

4. Whenever possible, show and demonstrate rather then simply tell people why changes are necessary.

5. Keep the trust and respect of subordinates, and do what you can to break down any barriers to effective communication and cooperation.

6. Encourage your people to look for ways to improve everything they do and to share their ideas with you and their coworkers. Then reward them when they do so.

7. Let subordinates and team members know why quality and productivity are important to them and their organization. Explain and demonstrate with real examples the costs of poor quality and lagging productivity—for example, how a defective product lost a customer and wasted resources.

8. Make it clear that each person is accountable for quality and productivity gains. Make employee quality and productivity improvements part of each employee's regular evaluations.

9. Share productivity and quality improvements with other supervisors and get them to share their discoveries with you.

offers some suggestions to help you and your people improve your organization's quality and productivity.

This chapter has covered several useful models that help you understand how to motivate your associates. With appropriate motivation, good training, and a TQM approach, managers can expect high quality from productive associates. Nonetheless, the manager's own behavior can undermine otherwise favorable conditions for high motivation. The following excerpt explains—in contrast to mere lip service—how a manager's actions have real impact:

> If the employees believe in you, they reward you with superior efforts. If you fail to meet their expectations, they punish you with substandard quality and efficiency. . . . Show me an organization with a high absentee rate, problems with expense accounts, or a cover-your-butt mentality, and I'll show you a manager who is secretly leading the pack in every one of those deficiencies. . . . Managers reap what they sow, sweet and sour. . . . One of the big management myths is that employees really are influenced by memos and speeches. . . . Every manager's best remembered teachings come at unexpected times—a compassionate hand on a shoulder; a supportive comment when the politically safe course is silence; a word of encouragement when criticism might easily be justified; a selfless distribution of credit in front of people who make a difference.[52]

QUALITY OF WORKING LIFE

quality of working life
a general label given to various programs and projects designed to help employees satisfy their needs and meet their expectations from work

Improvements in the **quality of working life** (QWL) may be obtained through a variety of programs. Typical QWL programs include a variety of EAPs, training programs, team-building activities, labor–management committees, flexible work schedules, and pay for performance. These programs attempt to "give employees greater opportunities to participate and a larger say in decision making."[53] Such programs are most effective when every manager, team leader, and team facilitator is committed to their success and when those they are designed to serve play a meaningful role in their design and implementation.

WORKER PARTICIPATION TECHNIQUES

Many organizations have discovered that the best way to improve operations is to empower employees, both individually and in teams. "To empower people is to make them virtually autonomous, to inform them, to invest them with authority and then trust them to use it."[54] Giving people access to needed information is vital to making empowerment succeed. Many companies use a variety of techniques to do so: general information-sharing sessions, various kinds of scoreboarding activities, company newsletters, computer training, and committees for dealing with a variety of work-related issues.

MOTIVATION AND JOB DESIGN

Job Rotation

The term **job rotation** is used in two ways. In one type of job rotation, people are moved to different jobs, usually on a temporary basis, to give them additional experience, understanding, and challenges. It is most frequently used to cross-train people and to give them a better appreciation for the importance of jobs and their interrelationships. Employees who participate in job rotation are usually more valuable to themselves and to their employers because they can perform competently in more than one job. From this, supervisors gain more flexibility and can deal with absences more effectively. In another type of job rotation, employees rotate the performance of tasks on a relatively short cycle, such as every set number of hours or days, in order to relieve the boredom of repetitive tasks. This is a common practice in production line settings to prevent boredom from affecting motivation.

job rotation
movement of people to different jobs, usually for a temporary period, in order to inform, train, or stimulate cooperation and understanding among them

Job Enlargement

Job enlargement increases the number of tasks a job includes or the amount of output expected from the jobholder. It does not increase the number of responsibilities or the level of personal involvement the jobholder experiences. It usually requires people to do more of the kinds of tasks they are already doing regularly. Since job enlargement can add challenges for some, it can aid motivation and spark a renewed interest and enthusiasm for work. And for some, a sense of competence can arise from being able to produce more, both in quantity and quality.

job enlargement
increasing the number of tasks or the quantity of output required in a job

Job Enrichment

Today, manufacturers are turning many highly specialized, hazardous, and routinized assembly-type tasks over to robots. In contrast, for human workers, the emphasis now is strongly on **job enrichment**—enriching a job by providing the jobholder with variety, greater autonomy, and an increased amount of responsibility and challenge. Essentially, job enrichment attempts to build in more of the motivators that Herzberg found.[55] Job enrichment establishes client

Workers develop organizational commitment and identify more closely with the organization when they participate in group activities.

job enrichment

providing variety, deeper personal interest and involvement, greater autonomy and challenge, or increased responsibility on the job

relationships for the jobholder, includes more responsibility (vertical loading), forms natural work units, combines tasks, and opens feedback channels. Those employees respond best in enriched jobs who have a stronger desire to grow or develop skills on the job.[56] However, as we discuss later in this section, job enrichment is not for everybody. While job enrichment has many benefits, many production-line workers prefer their repetitive, specialized tasks. Their reasons are many. Some do not want a challenge and the additional effort it represents. Others are working to their capacities with their jobs the way they are and could not adjust to more duties. Still others do not like the new responsibilities or the ways in which their jobs will be enriched.

Managing Diversity

According to a U.S. Labor Department report, the number of female and minority managers has increased significantly in U.S. companies. Simultaneously, the differences between men's and women's salaries have shrunk. In addition, women and minorities now hold leadership positions at high levels of the U.S. government. At the end of the 20th century, women served as the U.S. Attorney General, the Secretary of State, and the Secretary of Health and Human Services. There were also two women justices on the U.S. Supreme Court. Still, we have far to go in the area of diversity. Minorities make up only 6.3 percent of the boards of directors for the largest companies in the United States. In 1998 Frank S. Jones, a minority board member of the Cigna Corporation, stepped down from the board because of dissatisfaction over the company's progress toward greater diversity. Upon leaving the board, Mr. Jones recommended that Cigna retain the services of an independent third party to assess the company's progress toward greater diversity. Of particular concern was the underrepresentation of minorities in fast-track positions.[57]

Taylor Cox has identified a number of organizational practices that may cause bias or serve to limit the career progress of women, minorities, or disabled individuals.[58] As you read the list of these practices in Exhibit 7.5, ask yourself how such practices have the potential to limit the progress of certain people.

Instant Replay

1. The Hawthorne studies of the 1920s demonstrated the social and esteem needs that people have and the natural tendencies of workers to form their own groups or cliques.

2. Abraham Maslow ranked human needs in a hierarchy that progresses from physical needs through four psychological needs. Each can act as a motive for human behavior.

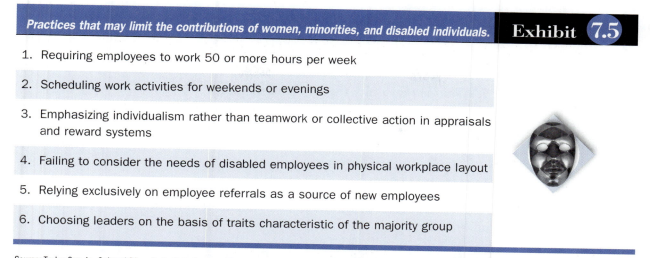

Practices that may limit the contributions of women, minorities, and disabled individuals. **Exhibit 7.5**

1. Requiring employees to work 50 or more hours per week

2. Scheduling work activities for weekends or evenings

3. Emphasizing individualism rather than teamwork or collective action in appraisals and reward systems

4. Failing to consider the needs of disabled employees in physical workplace layout

5. Relying exclusively on employee referrals as a source of new employees

6. Choosing leaders on the basis of traits characteristic of the majority group

Source: Taylor Cox, Jr., *Cultural Diversity in Organizations: Theory, Research, and Practice.* San Francisco: Berrett-Koehler, 1993.

3. Managers and their organizations have the power to assist employees in their search for satisfaction in every need category.

4. Herzberg identified two sets of factors that can either prevent dissatisfaction or promote motivation in employees. These are called, respectively, maintenance factors and motivation factors.

5. Expectancy theory holds that people will exert effort if they believe that performance is likely and that performance, in turn, will lead to desired outcomes.

6. Reinforcement theory states that desirable behavior will be repeated if rewarded and that undesirable behavior can be discouraged through withholding rewards or administering punishment.

7. Equity theory states that individuals' perceptions of equitable treatment are based on comparisons with relevant people and groups. Inputs are compared with outputs to determine if equitable treatment exists.

8. Productivity and quality go together. Efforts to improve one must also act to improve the other. Efforts to improve both must never end.

Questions for Class Discussion

1. Can you define this chapter's key terms?

2. What are the needs we humans have in common? What are some examples of satisfactions that are available to us through our work?

3. What are the motivation factors identified by Herzberg? What is their purpose in an organization?

4. What are the maintenance factors identified by Herzberg? What is their purpose in an organization?

5. What is the expectancy theory of motivation? How has it been demonstrated in your own experience?

6. What is the reinforcement theory of motivation? How has it worked in your own experience?

7. What is the equity theory of motivation?

8. What can supervisors do to promote improvements in both quality and productivity?

Incident

Purpose: To assess the motivational climate at work for both you and your subordinates.

Your task: Take the following quiz. Tally your responses as follows: for each "yes" response, 2 points; for each "no" response, 1 point. A score of 14 or higher indicates that you work in a highly motivating climate. Let your subordinates or team members take this quiz. The results may help you create more stimulating environments and jobs for subordinates.

Yes	*No*	
◯	◯	1. My boss knows me as an individual.
◯	◯	2. I have access to the people and information I need to perform my job.
◯	◯	3. Company incentives encourage my intellectual growth.
◯	◯	4. I have served or am now serving on a team.
◯	◯	5. I have taken advantage of one or more company EAPs.
◯	◯	6. I am proud of my company and share that pride with outsiders.
◯	◯	7. I receive regular feedback on my performance at work.
◯	◯	8. My company allows time to deal with family and personal problems.
◯	◯	9. I recommend my company to outsiders as a great place to work.
◯	◯	10. My pay is linked to my performance.

CASE PROBLEM 7.1   *Lighting a Fire Under the Sales Force*

Kelly Morton owns a small chain of shoe stores. The stores sell medium- to higher-quality shoes for both men and women, and the sales force is paid on commission. Over the past six months sales have been flat. Kelly has brought in the store managers for a group meeting in order to seek their advice on how to get the sales people to generate more sales. Because the stores are relatively small, the store managers are the direct supervisors of their sales people. Kelly started the meeting by reviewing sales figures and then asked the store managers how to improve sales.

Lou was the first to speak. Lou said, "I think the solution is simple. We've always done well with commissions. Because we pay straight commission we get good sales people and they tend to stay with us. Our sales people make more than those at other stores who get paid an hourly wage. I think we're getting some competition from the larger retailers that are beginning to carry lines of shoes similar to some of our higher-quality merchandise. We need to bite the bullet and increase the percentage for commissions. It'll cost more but we'll make up for the extra cost with volume."

Chris spoke up next. "I disagree with Lou. We've always paid commissions, but sales are still flat. Something has changed and it's not just the competition from big chains. That tells me that we need to add something else. Let's have an awards dinner where we give out plaques to our top sales people. We can post their pictures in each store. You know, sort of a Wall of Fame. And we could have a professional athlete come in and make a motivational speech that will fire everybody up for next year. Money is not the answer because these people already make good money. What's a bigger commission or a cash award going to mean to them? I think that people want to see themselves standing up in front of their peers receiving the top sales person award for the year and hear the applause. They can visualize that and it's real to them."

Lou said, "I disagree. Plaques don't mean much because everybody gets them. The next time you go to your insurance agent's office look at the line of plaques on the wall. Those insurance people aren't all superstars, but they all have plaques. If we want more sales we need to get out the checkbook."

Cary said, "I think you're wrong, Lou. But I don't know whether an awards dinner is the answer. I try to create a warm environment where the sales people like to come to work. In our store we all like each other and I try to tell people when they've done a good job. This causes the sales people to treat the customers well and we get repeat business. Sure, the money's important, but our sales are flat because not enough of our people know that we appreciate their efforts."

Lynn spoke next. "I don't think praise and pats on the back are going to increase sales. They might work with kids' soccer teams, but they won't work with adults. Why don't we have a contest where the sales person having the highest sales next quarter gets an all expenses-paid trip for two to Hawaii. It will be January then and it will probably be about 5 degrees here with a cold wind blowing off the lake. Our sales people will work harder to try to sell the most shoes because they know they could be sitting on the beach in Maui. My sister is an insurance agent and her company has contests all the time. Last year she got to go to Bermuda because of one of those contests."

Pat responded, "Our sales people are very competitive and like to win at anything they do. It's like a game with them and they keep score of whether they're winning by the dollar amount of their sales. But I disagree with Lynn. People want cash prizes based on their sales instead of trips. Lots more people could get rewards that way. If we only send the top sales person on a trip to Hawaii and we have 50 sales people, there is only a two percent chance of winning. I don't think our sales people are going to connect hard work with a trip. As a result most of them are going to blow it off. Why work hard if only one of us is going to get a trip?"

Lou said, "Look, I don't think we need any fancy gimmicks to make sales increase. Everybody knows how it works. If you work hard you make money. My go-getters work hard and generate sales. The lazy people who don't work hard don't make much money and they leave after a few months. There are two kinds of people in this world: the go-getters and the couch potatoes. The go-getters are going to work hard because they can make good money, and it's not worth our time dealing with the lazy people because they aren't going to change. All we have to do is pay more for commissions. Selling is becoming harder and we need to pay more."

Finally Kim spoke up. "Look, I hate to be negative, but we're going to waste a lot of money with all of these ideas. I think we simply have some people who need to be reminded that everybody has to sell hard if they want to keep their jobs. Let's give everybody a sales quota and then rank everybody by sales at the end of the next quarter and fire the bottom 10 percent. They'll get the point."

Questions

1. What theories of motivation are represented in the different store managers' comments?

2. If you were Kelly Morton, what would you do?

3. What does this case reveal about human motivation?

CASE PROBLEM 7.2 *Slow Motion*

Fernando, Morrie, George, and Isaac were standing next to the service manager's office as a woman drove her car out of the shop. Fernando, the service manager, turned to Morrie, the shop supervisor, and said, "She's the third customer this week who has complained about the work we did on her car. She said that we took twice as long to fix the car as we promised. It seems like we are either too slow or don't do good work. Other times we can't even figure out what's wrong with the car. I don't know how many people are bringing their cars back multiple times before we get them repaired correctly, but it's a lot. Why can't we fix the cars right before they send them out?"

Morrie said, "Cars are a lot more complicated today than they were 20 years ago. The mechanics have to know how to use computer diagnostic equipment, and they have to be able to repair the computers and electronics on the cars. They have to be able to fix cars that have a lot more moving parts than the old ones. We used to be able to keep someone's car longer to fix it, but now customers really get upset if we have to keep their cars overnight. Another problem is that it's really hard to find and keep good mechanics. Many of our people are inexperienced and turnover is high. And you wouldn't believe the number that apply but flunk the drug test."

George, one of the best and most experienced mechanics, said, "I think some of the younger mechanics don't care about their work like we used to. It used to be that when you worked in a garage you saw the customer and knew whose car you worked on. Now I don't even know who owns the car. There's just a number on the windshield and I never see the customer. When I started doing this work in the 1970s sometimes a customer would come back and say "thanks." That made me really feel good. Other times they would come back and tell you that their car wasn't fixed right. You could see that you had really let them down if their car broke down on the road after you worked on it. I really learned something from that. But now I just work back here in the shop and don't see anybody but mechanics all day long. Sometimes I feel like I'm just working in a factory."

Isaac, a well-trained young mechanic, said, "George, you old guys always think that things were better in the old times. But seriously, I'll bet you didn't have to work under so much pressure. We get told to do it right, but the customers always want us to do the work in less time than we really need. And we're supposed to be learning how to use the latest diagnostic computers just to keep up with the new cars. Why bother? Some of the guys are just taking their time to do the jobs. I try to work hard in order to get the car out quickly. But then one of the runners will bring back another car and I'll start working on it while the other guys are still working on the same car. I'm taking courses at the community college at night in bodywork and am saving my money so that I can open my own body shop some day. That's where the real money is."

Morrie said, "I think that's part of the problem. We're losing too many guys like Isaac. And the guys like George are going to be retiring someday. Most of these young mechanics don't take any pride in their work anymore. I think most of this younger generation doesn't care about doing a good job. George is right, things were better in the old days."

Fernando said, "These young people tell me that they don't want to be mechanics. They want white-collar jobs even though they may not make more money than good mechanics or plumbers. I understand, though, because I used to be embarrassed when people asked what I did for a living or when people would see grease under my fingernails. I used to feel like Rodney Dangerfield—no respect. But now it doesn't bother me anymore. Besides, I just do paperwork now and deal with the customers. But if I lived in Germany I would go back to being a mechanic because I could work on those great cars all the time. Those German mechanics are really good. And they get to wear those uniforms that say BMW or Mercedes. I'd really like that."

George said, "Do you think they pay mechanics in Germany with an incentive for fixing more cars or a monthly salary? That would make a difference to me. I like to get paid on an incentive basis like we get paid here. But these younger guys don't seem to respond to it. Most of them are just slow, dumb, and sloppy."

Fernando said, "Well I still don't know what to do. Maybe I should ask the owner of the garage to hire some more mechanics."

Questions

1. What is causing the problems in the shop? Will hiring more mechanics help?
2. What motivational theories seem to apply to this case?
3. What would you do to improve the situation?
4. Are age differences relevant to the problems?
5. What else could be causing the problems? What motivates Fernando, Morrie, George, and Isaac?

References

1. Martin, Don. *TeamThink*. New York: Penguin Books USA (1993): 96. Herskowitz, Mickey. *The Legend of Bear Bryant*. New York: McGraw-Hill (1987): 95–96.
2. Peters, Tom. "To Be the Best You Can Be, Forget About the Boss," *Chicago Tribune* (December 5, 1994): sect. 4, 2.
3. Peters, Tom. "Managers Need Surprise Tactics, Front-Line Thinking to Rout Competition," *Chicago Tribune* (October 3, 1994): sect. 4, 5.
4. Franklin, Stephen. "90% Collapse of 1929–32 Was Worst U. S. Bear Market," *Fort Worth Star Telegram* (September 1, 1998): A9.
5. Mayo, Elton. *The Social Problems of an Industrial Civilization*. Boston: Division of Research, Graduate School of Business Administration, Harvard University (1945): 68–86.
6. Maslow, Abraham H. *Motivation and Personality*, 2d ed. New York: Harper & Row, 1970.
7. Marx, Robert; Jick, Todd D.; and Frost, Peter J. *Management Live: The Video Book*. Englewood Cliffs, NJ: Prentice Hall, 1991.
8. McClelland, David C., and Burnham, David H. "Power Is the Great Motivator," *Harvard Business Review* (January–February 1995): 126–139.
9. Ibid.
10. Ibid.: 126.
11. DuPont, Dale K. "Eureka! Tools for Encouraging Employee Suggestions," *HR Magazine* (September 1999): 134–138.
12. Ibid.
13. Corbett, Brian. "Getting It Right," *Ward's Auto World* (January 2002): 46–47.
14. Ibid.: 47.
15. Marx, Jick, and Frost. *Management Live*.
16. Ibid.
17. Herzberg, Frederick. "One More Time: How Do You Motivate Employees?" in *Business Classics: Fifteen Key Concepts for Managerial Success*. Boston: Harvard Business Review (1975): 13–22.
18. Caggiano, Christopher. "What Do Workers Want?" *Inc.* (November 1992): 101.
19. Levering, Robert, and Moskowitz, Milton. "The 100 Best Companies to Work For," *Fortune* (January 8, 2001): 148–159.
20. Fisher, Anne. "The 100 Best Companies to Work for in America," *Fortune* (January 12, 1998): 69–70.
21. Caggiano. "What Do Workers Want?"

22. Herzberg, "One More Time."

23. *Inc.* "So This Is Empowerment?" (July 1994): 96. Schneider, Benjamin; Brief, Arthur P.; and Guzzo, Richard A. "Sustaining a Climate and Culture for Sustainable Organizational Change," *Organizational Dynamics* vol. 24 (Spring 1996): 7–19.

24. Caggiano. "What Do Workers Want?"

25. Champoux, Joseph E. *Organizational Behavior: Integrating Individuals, Groups, and Processes.* Minneapolis: West, 1996.

26. Kohn, Alfie. *Punished by Rewards: The Trouble with Gold Stars, Incentive Plans, A's, Praise, and Other Bribes.* New York: Houghton-Mifflin, 1993. Kohn, Alfie. "Why Incentive Plans Cannot Work," *Harvard Business Review* (September–October 1993): 54–63.

27. Gupta, Nina, and Shaw, Jason D. "Let the Evidence Speak: Financial Incentives Are Effective!" *Compensation and Benefits Review* 30(2) (1998): 28, 30.

28. Weiss, Joseph W. *Organizational Behavior and Change: Managing Diversity, Cross-Cultural Dynamics, and Ethics.* Minneapolis: West, 1996.

29. Ibid.

30. Ibid.

31. Ibid.

32. Ibid.

33. Kreitner, Robert, and Kinicki, Angelo. *Organizational Behavior,* 5th ed. Boston: Irwin McGraw-Hill, 2001.

34. Kanfer, Ruth. "Motivation," in Cary L. Cooper and Chris Argyris (eds.), *The Concise Blackwell Encyclopedia of Management.* Oxford, UK: Blackwell (1998): 422–426.

35. Skinner, B. F. *Contingencies of Reinforcement: A Theoretical Analysis.* New York: Appleton-Century-Crofts, 1969.

36. Weiss. *Organizational Behavior.*

37. Ibid.

38. Labich, Kenneth. "Why Companies Fail," *Fortune* (November 14, 1994): 52–54, 58, 60, 64, 68.

39. Champoux. *Organizational Behavior.*

40. Grant, Linda. "Happy Workers, High Returns," *Fortune* (January 12, 1998): 81.

41. Ibid.

42. Kerr, Stephen. "Organizational Rewards: Practical, Cost-Neutral Alternatives That You May Know, But Don't Practice," *Organizational Dynamics* (Summer 2000): 66, 70.

43. Barrie, Dale. "Quality," in Slack, Nigel (ed.), *The Blackwell Encyclopedic Dictionary of Operations Management.* Cambridge, MA: Blackwell (1997): 166.

44. Schmitt, Bill. "A Slow Spread for Six Sigma," *Chemical Week* (February 13, 2002): 34–35.

45. Bartholomew, Doug. "Cost vs. Quality," *Industry Week* (September 2001): 34–41. Schmitt, "A Slow Spread for Six Sigma."

46. Boyle, Richard J. "Wrestling with Jellyfish," *Harvard Business Review* (November–December 1992): 14.

47. "William Edwards Demming and TQM," *Workforce* (January 2002): 40.

48. Bartholomew, "Cost vs. Quality," 40.

49. Belcher, John G., Jr. *Productivity Plus.* Houston, TX: Gulf Publishing (1987): 27.

50. Austin, Nancy K. "What's Missing from Corporate Cure-Alls," *Working Woman* (September 1994): 16–19.

51. Ibid.

52. Mullen, James X. "Actions Speak Louder Than Speeches," *The Wall Street Journal* (July 10, 1995): A12.

53. Schuler, Randall S. *Managing Human Resources,* 5th ed. New York: West (1995): 9–10, 676–677.

54. Austin. "What's Missing."

55. Weiss. *Organizational Behavior.*

56. Oldham, Greg R. "Job Enrichment" in Cary L. Cooper and Chris Argyris (eds.), *The Concise Blackwell Encyclopedia of Management.* Oxford, UK: Blackwell (1998): 340.

57. Lublin, Joann S. "Cigna Director's Diversity Challenge Hits a Dead End," *The Wall Street Journal* (June 15, 1998): B1, B8.

58. Cox, Taylor, Jr. *Cultural Diversity in Organizations: Theory, Research, and Practice.* San Francisco: Berrett-Koehler, 1993.

BUILDING RELATIONSHIPS WITH INDIVIDUALS

Objectives

After reading and discussing this chapter, you should be able to do the following:

1. Define this chapter's key terms.

2. List and briefly explain the purposes of human relations.

3. Describe the application of each of the human relations roles to the relationship between supervisors and their subordinates and peers.

4. Describe how a middle manager's job is different from a supervisor's job.

5. Describe how supervisors can create and maintain good human relations with their bosses.

Introduction

This chapter explores how you as a supervisor can build good working relationships with each individual with whom you work. Relating successfully to others is the key to your growth and advancement. Solid individual relationships produce the cooperation and assistance you need to reach your goals.

The development and maintenance of sound on-the-job relationships with associates, peers, and superiors is referred to as **human relations.** From the moment you first meet another person at work, a relationship begins. How you relate to each person with whom you must work is largely up to you. Because none of us works in a vacuum, the quality of your interpersonal relationships will determine just how effective and efficient you will be. We all must depend to some extent on others. Consider the following example of the undesirable outcomes of poor interpersonal relations:

human relations
the development and maintenance of sound on-the-job relationships with subordinates, peers, and superiors

Richard Delbridge of the University of Cardiff Business School has made a study of the reality on the shopfloor. Delbridge spent several weeks working in two factories, one a car-parts maker . . . the other a television assembly plant . . . Delbridge notes [workers'] chafing at endless attempts to shave a fifth of a second off some task on the line, and their dislike of being bossed around. Workers in the car-parts company seemed to have kept more control over their life on the line. But that did not stop resentments. A quality inspector thought of as a management lackey was tied up and dumped in a rubbish bin. He was rescued by a security man. But one of his colleagues was put into a bin of parts headed for Birmingham, and found only at a gate inspection.[1]

Obviously, interpersonal relations have reached a low ebb when such activities take place in the workplace. This chapter is designed to help you develop effective working relationships by applying concepts from Chapters 1, 5, and 7. It will carry over to all the remaining chapters in this text as well, for sound working relationships are at the heart of building teams, leading, staffing, training, appraising, and disciplining.

Goals of Human Relations

The wide range of ages, backgrounds, and experiences in many work groups increases the difficulty of building sound human relations. After a brief look at the goals of human relations, we examine some major roles you must play to build relationships on the job. Keep the following goals in mind as you approach the task of building sound human relations:

- To help each individual obtain satisfaction in the work environment
- To increase each individual's effort and commitment to the job and the company
- To foster a spirit of cooperation between you and your subordinates, peers, and boss
- To help each individual be himself or herself while on the job
- To know and understand each person as an individual
- To treat each associate as an individual deserving of respect

Good human relations is now being recognized as one of the critical determinants of success in many successful companies. Richard Branson, the founder of Virgin Atlantic Airways and Virgin Records, emphasizes the importance of treating employees well so that customers will be treated well. Federal Express recognizes the same relationship and emphasizes employee development.[2] The same formula often works in professional athletics. Consider the coaching success of former NBA star Larry Bird. Bird's human relations skills played a role in advancing his team through playoff rounds during his first year of coaching. Bird's actions as a team player provided favorable indications that he would have good human relations skills as a coach (supervisor). While Bird was still playing, Red Auerbach, president and former coach of the Boston Celtics, said the following:

> It's like Larry Bird always says before a big game: "I'll be ready and the other guys will be ready and we're going to win this thing." Not "I'm going to win it." He says, "We're going to win it." Larry Bird gets as big a thrill out of making the pass as he does making the shot.[3]

While Bird coached, these indications proved to be true. The way he related to players is admirable. Indiana Pacers guard Travis Best said:

> It's not what he says, it is how he says it that is making the difference. He doesn't scream at you, he doesn't embarrass you when you make a mistake. He just looks at you, and you get the message. Then when the time is right, he'll talk to you calmly and explain what he wants.[4]

ENABLING WORKERS TO BE THEMSELVES

Allowing employees to be themselves is an important practice of many top-ranked companies. An employee at Southwest Airlines, which has been in the top five of *Fortune*'s top-ranked companies to work for on multiple occasions, said the following: "They treat you with respect, pay you well, and empower you. They use your ideas to solve problems. They encourage you to be yourself."[5] An employee at TDI Industries, number six on the *Fortune* list in 2001, said the following: "This company makes you feel like a human being again."[6] At Microsoft, "Bill (never Mr. Gates) personally answered all e-mail from employees."[7]

Better performance is likely when diverse employees feel that they can be themselves in the workplace. A recent survey by the Society for Human Resource Management and *Fortune* found that 91 percent of respondents felt that their companies obtained a competitive advantage from their diversity initiatives while 79 percent perceived that such initiatives improved morale. In addition, 79 percent believed that diversity efforts improved their company cultures and 77 percent perceived that such efforts facilitated recruitment.[8]

Many companies have achieved greater diversity in their workplaces by hiring more women, particularly in nontraditional jobs. In order to attract talented women to their companies and address their needs (and those of men as well), many companies have added on-site child care facilities. All of the following companies, which have been in *Fortune*'s top 100 companies, have on-site child care facilities: Fel-Pro, MBNA, S.C. Johnson Wax, ACX-IOM, CMP Media, Lucas Digital, Mattel, St. Paul Companies, Quad/Graphics, Amgen, Motorola, Baptist Health Systems, William Beaumont Hospital, and Glaxo Smith Kline.[9]

Diversity efforts are implemented through company policies, sensitivity and conscious-raising programs, diversity training programs, one-on-one coaching, counseling programs, mentoring programs, telecommuting opportunities for single parents, forums for women and minorities, employee assistance programs (EAPs), relocation services, and scholarship programs. In addition, organizational support for diversity efforts has expanded. For example, performance on a diversity dimension now affects the compensation of top executives at Bell South, and at United Technologies an executive is designated as the company's director for diversity, with responsibilities for wide-ranging activities and programs.[10] Another example is provided by ALAGASCO, an Alabama-based utility company, that pays employees $500 for ideas on how to deal with diversity problems in their units.[11]

While progress could always be better, consider the proportion of management positions held by women in two of *Fortune*'s top 100 companies: Merck—31 percent, and Patagonia—more than 50 percent.[12] Tom Peters, management author and lecturer, asks a question: "Wouldn't a corporation that could exploit the uniqueness of each of its 1,000 employees (or 100 or 10,000) be phenomenally powerful?" Consider the potential impact of 1,000 sets of skills and unique approaches, 1,000 sets of ambitions and creative urges, all complementing each other. Apple Computer asks its people to commit to its vision while they are with the company. In return, it gives them the opportunity to exercise their creativity, to pursue their curiosity, and to grow through a variety of experiences. At Oticon, Denmark's hearing-aid maker, all employees are members of one large "talent bank that effectively organizes itself to create and tackle whatever projects need doing."[13] Those who cannot gain support for their ideas or find a project team where they are welcome will not be on the payroll for long.

A diverse workforce makes greater demands on supervisors than a homogeneous one. When a subordinate, peer, or boss has an identity that we do not share, "we are likely to relate to this person based on the stereotypes that we associate with the individual's [religion,] affectional orientation, age, ethnic heritage, gender, physical abilities/qualities, and/or race."[14] While working to overcome these stereotypes, you also must try to perceive individuals as they perceive themselves—as members of diverse groups that influence their attitudes and, therefore, their behavior on the job. Supervisors need to remember that "All workers want to succeed on the job and be accepted by the organization, but they also want to maintain their own senses of identity and have their special perspectives and assets acknowledged and appreciated."[15]

Authors Marilyn Loden and Judy Rosener believe that "most people want more authentic, honest, and respectful relationships with others than they presently have."[16] Exhibit 8.1 explains how people with diverse backgrounds would like to interact more effectively and comfortably. As people with diverse backgrounds have more contact and grow more open, they begin to value and appreciate each other's diversity. Keep these findings in mind as you develop your relationships with others at work.

YOUNGER AND OLDER EMPLOYEES WANT:

- More respect for their life experiences
- To be taken seriously
- To be challenged by their organizations—not patronized

WOMEN WANT:

- Recognition as equal partners
- Active support of male colleagues
- Organizations to address work and family issues proactively

MEN WANT:

- The same freedom to grow or feel that women have
- To be perceived as allies, not as the enemy
- To bridge the gap between dealing with women at home and at work

PEOPLE OF COLOR WANT:

- To be valued as unique individuals, as members of ethnically diverse groups, as people of different races, and as equal contributors
- To establish more open, honest working relationships with people of other races and ethnic groups
- The active support of white people in fighting racism

WHITE PEOPLE WANT:

- To have their ethnicity acknowledged
- To reduce discomfort, confusion, and dishonesty in dealing with people of color
- To build relationships with people of color based on common goals, concerns, and mutual respect for differences

DIFFERENTLY ABLED PEOPLE WANT:

- Greater acknowledgment of and focus on abilities, not just on disabilities
- To be challenged by colleagues and organizations to be the best
- To be included, not isolated

PHYSICALLY ABLE-BODIED PEOPLE WANT:

- To develop more ease in dealing with differently abled people
- To appreciate abilities—in addition to understanding disabilities
- To give honest feedback and appropriate support—without being patronizing or overprotective

GAY MEN AND LESBIANS WANT:

- Recognition as whole human beings—not only as sexual beings
- Equal employment protection—like all other groups have
- Increased awareness among straight people regarding the impact of heterosexism in the workplace

HETEROSEXUALS WANT:

- Increased awareness of lesbian and gay issues
- A better understanding of the legal consequences of being gay in America
- More dialogue about heterosexist issues with lesbians and gay men

Source: Marilyn Loden and Judy B. Rosener, *Workforce America!* Homewood, IL: Business One Irwin (1991): 76–78.

SUPERVISORS AND ETHICS

In the fast-paced world of the Silicon Valley it might be assumed that people do not have sufficient time to ensure that their decisions regarding the treatment of employees, customers, and vendors reflect the highest standards of integrity. Such an assumption would be false for many Silicon Valley companies, and when employees are asked to tell their favorite stories about their companies, the themes of the stories often deal with integrity. Furthermore, integrity is often defined in such basic terms as whether one keeps his word.

One example concerns CenterBeam, a company that specialized in the installation of wireless networks. The firm had been hiring extensively and had made an offer to a candidate. Before the candidate accepted, the firm received a resume from an overwhelmingly impressive individual. When the firm's managers asked CenterBeam's CEO whether they could rescind the offer, the CEO said no. He replied that the firm had to keep its promises in order to be a company that people will trust. In another incident, the firm had received an order of tape drives, but before its engineers unpacked the equipment they found that another vendor could supply the same equipment for a savings of over 18 percent. Some of the engineers asked whether they could send the equipment back to the original vendor so that they could take advantage of the lower prices with the other vendor. CenterBeam's executives said no, but they did ask the original vendor to replace the order with less expensive equipment, which produced a savings of over 8 percent.

A common problem in many startup "dot com" firms was that the companies exaggerated their potential financial performance. When they could not deliver on their extravagant promises, investors became disappointed and stock prices took a dive. The same kind of exaggerations were often used to recruit employees. When employees see their firms present exaggerated promises to outside stakeholders and job candidates, they become cynical and distrustful of their employers. On the other hand, companies that are honest in their promises build reputations of trustworthiness and get positive referrals to other potential customers.

Source: George Anders, "Honesty Is the Best Policy—Trust Us," *Fast Company* (August 2000): 262.

COMMUNICATING SUPPORTIVELY

All of your efforts at developing sound human relations involve communicating by both words and actions with your associates and those outside your immediate sphere of influence. The ways in which you communicate can cause others to be open and honest or closed and defensive. If your words and deeds are supportive of the feelings and efforts of others, you encourage open and honest two-way communication. This two-way communication process should firmly bridge your relationships with your associates, peers, and superiors. According to authors Blank and Slipp, all managers must:[17]

- Convey clearly [their] expectations for the work unit, while recognizing group differences in communication and perspective

- Provide feedback [on performances] often and equally to all members of the workforce
- Openly support the competencies and contribution of workers from all groups
- Become comfortable asking questions about preferred terminology or interactions
- Confront racist, sexist, or other stereotypic or discriminatory behavior

Take the short quiz in Exhibit 8.2. Any "rarely" responses indicate a need to improve your communications efforts.

How supportive are you when communicating with subordinates or team members?   **Exhibit 8.2**

Usually Rarely

○ ○ 1. I make time to listen to my people's problems.

○ ○ 2. I greet my people warmly and sincerely express my interest in their well-being.

○ ○ 3. I give my people the information they need to perform effectively.

○ ○ 4. I encourage my people to come to me with their ideas and suggestions.

○ ○ 5. I am slow to criticize any idea given to me and try to look for its good points first.

○ ○ 6. I use humor when appropriate in my communications.

○ ○ 7. I share any praise I receive when part of it is due to the efforts of my subordinates or team members.

○ ○ 8. I take the chance, whenever possible, to talk with my people, one on one.

○ ○ 9. I express sincere interest in my people's families, inquiring as to their health and well-being.

○ ○ 10. I consider my people's feelings and circumstances before attempting to judge or criticize their actions.

○ ○ 11. I take every opportunity to compliment people for any job that is well done.

○ ○ 12. I give quick feedback to my people on all matters that are of importance to them.

○ ○ 13. I try to keep people from waiting on me.

○ ○ 14. I offer explanations for my actions and decisions.

Developing Sound Working Relationships with Subordinates

You should have a personal commitment to do what you can to help all of your associates and teams reach their potential. The ideal on-the-job relationship should result from your understanding, mastering, and executing four fundamental roles. These roles relate to and depend on one another.

1. Educator—a builder of skills and developer of potential
2. Counselor—an adviser, director, cheerleader, and coach
3. Judge—an appraiser, mediator, and dispenser of justice
4. Spokesperson—a message carrier for both associates and superiors

YOUR ROLE AS EDUCATOR

Your role as an educator is usually the first one you play in relation to a new associate. Before new associates arrive, you have assessments of the training they need in order to adjust to their duties. This initial training is vitally important; it communicates the manager's expectations, the company's standards for performance, and the skills, knowledge, and attitudes required in the individual. Through training, new employees discover what the company stands for (its core values), and they become more closely aligned with the company.

> [P]eople bring their best to their work only if they can involve their whole selves. They must feel free to talk about the things they are passionate about, to explore opposing points of view. These discussions create deeper relationships if people feel connected by a shared desire to have their organization succeed. Leadership that relies on such characteristics as relationship building, trust, nurturance, intuition and letting go is the leadership of the future.[18]

Training, when properly planned and executed, does much to remove the initial fears we all have as we begin something new. It convinces trainees of our interest in and concern for them. They should emerge from training with a clear understanding of what is expected of them and how they are supposed to achieve it. Through training, team leaders, team facilitators, and supervisors demonstrate their commitment to

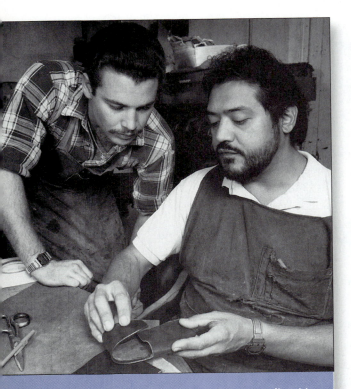

In your role as educator, you demonstrate your commitment to helping your subordinates reach their potential. After your training sessions, workers should understand what is expected of them and how they can achieve it.

SUPERVISING TEAMS

The decision to create teams in the workplace is not made lightly. Teams are not for every company and not appropriate for many tasks. Route sales people and executives' secretaries are not candidates for team membership. When determining whether teams should be used, managers need to ask whether the purpose can be best achieved by a team. Is the goal or purpose suited to a team, as opposed to a broader organizational purpose, or one individual's purpose (e.g., the leader's)? If so, a carefully selected team may be the answer, if given time to meld as a unit.

For best results, members need a clear, shared understanding of the task to be done. Other needed qualities: "A strong personal desire to complete the task," the "right mix of . . . technical or functional expertise," problem-solving and decision-making skills, and interpersonal skills required to investigate and analyze problems and implement solutions. Finding the right mix of skills usually means finding the right mix of people—those who possess what is needed or those who can acquire such skills in a reasonable amount of time. The result will usually be diversity in membership with corresponding differences in approaches to reaching solutions. Then the team members must be encouraged and allowed "to invest the time early in the process to plan their task, build teamwork, and acquire the knowledge they need."

Sources: Jon R. Katzenbach and Douglas K. Smith, *The Wisdom of Teams.* Boston: Harvard Business School Press (1993): 47–48, 62–63. "Setting Up Successful Company Work Groups," *Nation's Business* (August 1994): 10.

helping trainees perform well and reach their potential. This chapter's *Supervising Teams* feature notes the importance of skill development and managing diversity in teams.

There is a second phase to your role as an educator. You will recall from Chapter 4 that the definition of the directing function includes educating subordinates. To educate means to foster subordinates' intellectual development.

Enlightened employers like General Electric, Motorola, and Allied Signal [now Honeywell] have discovered that a key ingredient for getting employees to acknowledge and embrace organization change is compensation. . . . [T]hese companies reward teamwork, measurable quality improvements, and employee's acquisition of new skills. "Getting the rewards right and steadily raising the goals [stretch goals] is how a company communicates its values and direction to its work force."[19]

Now that workers are taking on more activities of a managerial nature, team leaders and facilitators also have additional responsibilities. According to James Treece they now need to do all of the following:[20]

- Instill commitment in subordinates rather than rule by command and control
- Become coaches who train workers in necessary skills, making sure they have resources to accomplish goals

- Provide broader perspective by explaining links between a job and what happens elsewhere in the company
- Give greater authority to workers over scheduling, priority-setting, and even compensation
- Use new information technologies to measure workers' performance, possibly based on customer satisfaction or the accomplishment of specific goals

Workers must also be empowered for greater decision making and must learn how to do the following:[21]

- Become initiators, able to act without management direction
- Become financially literate so that they can understand the business implications of their actions and decisions
- Practice group interaction skills, including how to resolve disputes within their work group and how to work across functions
- Acquire new math, technical, and analytical skills in order to deal with the increased information component of their jobs

By understanding your role as an educator, mastering the knowledge and skills you wish to teach others, and executing this role in accordance with established training principles and procedures (Chapter 12), you will be well on your way toward promoting your own success by fostering success in others.

YOUR ROLE AS COUNSELOR

counselor

the human relations role in which a supervisor is an adviser and director to subordinates

When performing the **counselor** role well, good supervisors want to know the subordinate's individual needs, aspirations, and desires. They listen and sometimes provide advice on how realistic the person's thinking is. Sometimes they suggest solutions to problems. They do not suggest solutions to personal or emotional problems; instead they may suggest that talking with a specialist—an authority trained to help in that particular area.

One of the critical requirements of being a good supervisor is that employees must feel that their supervisor notices them and that she really cares about them. Taking the time to coach employees sends a strong message that you are aware of subordinates and that you have their welfare in mind. While supervisors are always pressed for time, good supervisors find the time to coach their subordinates. Here is a three-step approach for coaching in relatively short amounts of time on a day-to-day basis:[22]

Recognize: Notice what the employee likes and dislikes, when he looks excited about his work and when he looks like he's bored silly. Has he recently shown a new skill or interest? Has he asked for your feedback on a task he has done? Is he having trouble with some aspect of his job? Has he indicated that he is interested in changing or expanding his responsibilities?

Verbalize: Strike up a conversation. Let the employee know that you notice. If he has demonstrated a new skill, you might say, "Hey, do you really like doing that? What do you like about it? Would you like to do more of it?" Establish rapport. Show your interest in his current job satisfaction, and help him explore ideas for his long-run career development.

Mobilize: All the talk in the world does no good if you are not prepared to take action. An employee who talks to you about his job is not just seeking sympathy. He wants advice, guidance, and the opportunity to pursue his goals. How can you help him find those opportunities within his current job? How can you help him prepare for future challenges? Show the sincerity of your support by helping to remove obstacles that prevent his further development.

On the other hand, you should help solve problems or recommend solutions when problems are job-related and beyond the capability of subordinates. Nonetheless, you should not solve all problems, as this may retard the development of the problem-solving skills of your subordinates. When problems must be resolved at higher levels, ensure that they are referred to the correct authority. Follow up by checking on their disposition, and make sure that your subordinate is informed of the decision. Even if the results do not satisfy the individual, you have tried to help. You have done the best you could, and a subordinate will know it. You will have passed a major test.

Staying aware. Many supervisors ignore counseling until a problem arises. Then they call a hasty conference and belittle, berate, or chew out the subordinate who is in trouble. Very soon subordinates get the message that the only time they see or hear from the boss is when she is unhappy or upset about their performance. Some supervisors claim that they do not have the time or that the time spent on counseling could be better spent on other things. The plain fact is that if supervisors do not counsel their people, they will have plenty of fires to put out and very little time for counseling. But if they invest the time necessary to touch base with each person periodically, they will be able to spot potential difficulties and prevent future problems or the necessity of corrective measures such as discipline or punishment.

To be effective in your role as counselor, you must practice active listening. When you have discussions with subordinates, do more listening than talking.

Doing something. If you are going to do something about a subordinate's problem, you should conduct a formal interview. The four basic principles that apply to a problem-centered coaching interview are as follows:

> The first principle of successful coaching is to get your subordinate involved. The more active a part the subordinate can take in appraising the problem for himself, and in outlining possible courses of action, the more committed he will be to the solution. And, the more enthusiastically he will work for its success.
>
> The second principle is that you encourage him to participate actively in the interview. Your role in the coaching interview is not to tell your subordinate what to do or how to do it, but rather to help him develop for himself a plan of action for dealing with the problem at hand. You can raise key questions which will help him find a solution, but don't lead him by the hand unless it is absolutely necessary.
>
> The third principle is to make sure you both understand the meaning of what is being discussed and said. The only sure way of doing this is to get your subordinate to express his views in his own words. You should restate those views, in different words, to see if you can reach agreement. Otherwise, the two of you could come away from the coaching conference with entirely different ideas of the issues discussed and decisions made.
>
> Finally, the fourth principle is to force yourself to do more listening than talking. Even if you say relatively little during your meeting, the interview can prove of considerable value—provided you listen. If he is upset, you give your subordinate a chance to let off steam. You also give him an opening to try out his ideas on you for a change.[23]

The value of learning from mistakes is a point we have touched on before, and it applies to coaching as well. Good coaching can come from team members as well as the team leader. The former director of the British Athletics Federation stresses the importance of coaching by team members and has made the following observation: "One person's experience is a learning opportunity for the team. What is the point of making a mistake if no one is going to learn from it?"[24]

An analogy can be drawn between the supervisor's role in the motivation of subordinates and the theater director's role in bringing out the best in actors. A director, like a supervisor, knows that the actor's motivation comes from within and many influences can interfere with a superior effort. But the director knows that she can do much to provide the climate and incentives that may spark an inner drive within the actor. She may remove distractions that interfere with concentration, make certain that the actor has done the necessary homework, and confer with the actor to determine his perceptions of the role. The director also is able to set the stage with props and lighting that will allow the actor to perform to the best of his ability. Last, throughout the rehearsals and the performances, the director offers advice and criticism. Coaching and sincere concern often provide the spark the actor needs to give a superior performance. By sensing the actor's needs, strengths, and weaknesses, the director can provide advice and trigger the actor's commitment to excel.

YOUR ROLE AS JUDGE

Serving as judge successfully involves being proficient at four important tasks:

1. Enforcing company policies and regulations
2. Evaluating each subordinate's performance
3. Settling disputes between your people and teams
4. Dispensing justice

Enforcement. To enforce company policies and regulations, you must first be aware of them. You have to know what they say, as well as their proper interpretation. Consistency of enforcement is the key to gaining acceptance of company policies and management decisions. You must do the same with regard to your department's procedures and practices. Do people know about them? Do they understand them? Are they following them? All these questions are usually answered through various controls you design into your operation. Proper induction and training should go a long way toward ensuring that the department's procedures and practices are properly interpreted and utilized.

Evaluation. Evaluating subordinates is one of your most important and time-consuming tasks as a supervisor. You must use the performance criteria of the standards for each job and make objective and honest evaluations of each person's output and contributions. Is he meeting production standards? Is he correcting or trying to correct deficiencies noted in previous appraisals? Is he cooperative? Do his behaviors interfere with the efforts of other workers in the department?

Appraisals take place daily. In routine visits with your people, you have an excellent opportunity to note their successes and question their deficiencies. This will allow you to catch an error when it first appears and take corrective action. At the same time, you are letting your people know regularly how they stand with you. Your being with them routinely gives them the opportunity to ask questions and to clear up misunderstandings. When the time finally rolls around for a formal semiannual or annual review, there should be no surprises. You have kept your people informed on a daily basis.

Your day-to-day coaching and less frequent performance appraisals blend nicely with your role as a counselor. When your observations tell you that a worker's attitude probably causes a deficiency in her output or conduct, try to find the real causes for the behavior. You will recall that it is only when people see their attitude as improper that they are willing to reject it. Chapter 6 deals with attitudes and Chapter 13 probes more deeply into the appraisal process.

Settling disputes. Part of your role as a judge is to act as a peacemaker. People problems are the most persistent and frequent problems you have to deal with each day. Inevitably, two or more individuals or groups of subordinates will do battle with each other. Sometimes the causes are hidden from your view and only surface under stress with an open display of hostility. When you witness such disturbances, begin an investigation to uncover the causes on both sides. Analyze your evidence, and make a decision. Try to avoid treating the symptoms, but concentrate your energies on the disease. When you have reached a conclusion about the merits on both sides, confront the participants with your findings. Work toward a reconciliation that will not leave any scars as lasting reminders of the battle. Avoid any emphasis on who was at fault (chances are, both sides share the blame), but point out why the problem got started and how it can be avoided in the future.

Conflict between team members and teams is another source of concern. Sources of conflict include disagreements over members' or teams' roles and authority, perceptions of unequal treatment, stereotypical thinking about diverse members, and competition for scarce resources. Your job is to manage conflict by creating "a climate in which healthy debate can occur."[25] People who find it hard to work together can be reassigned. Members and groups can hold meetings to determine their own solutions, redefining their purposes or ways of interacting. Rules and procedures are useful ways of managing conflict because they outline orderly ways for allocating resources and using resources or facilities.[26] However, the supervisor should not attempt to suppress all conflict because it is often needed to provide the stimulus for improved procedures and better ways of doing things.

Dispensing justice.   Justice, in a supervisory sense, means seeing to it that each of your subordinates gets what she deserves. When your people are doing a good job, they deserve your praise. When they break a rule or violate a procedure, they must be shown the error of their ways. Rest assured that people want to know the limits of what they will be allowed to do. Once these limits are explained, people expect them to be enforced and usually anticipate some admonishment for each of their infractions. This admonishment may simply be a verbal warning, but in the case of repeated offenses, it may take the form of some other disciplinary action.

Improper or unacceptable conduct on the job cannot be tolerated. To prevent it, your company installs you as its chief enforcement officer in your department and gives you power to discipline violators. To many people, discipline simply means punishment. This is the negative side of a much broader concept. The positive side is the one that emphasizes informing organization members ahead of time about acceptable conduct. It places the emphasis on self-control and mutual trust. When new employees are hired, you should inform them of the rules on the very first day. You should clarify the meaning of acceptable and unacceptable behavior and performance. Soon after you become the supervisor of a section you should inform your associates of your standards and expectations. When rule infractions occur, take action. To do otherwise would ultimately undermine your formal authority and your integrity. You will find that it is much better to start out tough than to try to become so later. It is difficult and unpleasant to impose discipline for infractions of rules that you failed to explain.

When punishment is necessary, you must be certain that it fits the offense. Quite often, when dealing with unionized workers, the manager's disciplinary powers are limited by the union contract. Be certain that you have the power to take a specific action before you do so. And keep in mind that subordinates expect you to act equitably—to be impartial and fair. An example of the importance of being impartial is provided by Texas Tech basketball coach Bobby Knight. While some of his actions have been the subject of substantial controversy, he gets high marks in the area of discipline. Knight has demonstrated courage in disciplining his players. Probably the most difficult test for Knight, while he coached at the University of Indiana, was when he removed his own son from the team for rules violations.[27]

Chapter 14 deals in more detail with the tasks involved in disciplining.

YOUR ROLE AS SPOKESPERSON

Your superiors expect you to represent management's point of view adequately to your subordinates. You are the only manager who can translate management's plans into action. Your boss, in particular, is counting on you to defend and to reinforce management's position. But you must be a **spokesperson** for your work group as well.

You must back up your subordinates when they are right—or when they are wrong because they executed your orders. If they believe that a policy or regulation is unfair, relay their feelings to those in a position to change it. You can do much to protect your people from harassment and from getting shortchanged. Just as you hope for their loyalty, they need yours. In addition, as the spokesperson for your team or unit, you must keep higher authorities informed of your team's progress.

You must respect the confidences of both your superiors and your subordinates. Sometimes your people will request an answer to a question, and you know the answer, but you may not be able to disclose it. Information given to you in private with a request for your silence must be respected. If you betray a confidence, you will soon find yourself ostracized from the group or excluded from opportunities to obtain information.

As a team leader or team facilitator, your spokesperson role also

spokesperson

the human relations role through which a supervisor represents management's views to workers and workers' views to management

In your role as spokesperson, you represent management's point of view to your subordinates and keep higher authorities informed of your team's progress.

involves interacting with staff to acquire the appropriate support for your team. You may obtain such support by networking with your team's internal and external customers and suppliers. You also have information needs that may be served by interactions with external sources in your spokesperson role. Finally, as your unit's spokesperson, you arrange for cross-training to expand your team's skills and understanding of the needs and functions of others.

If you properly execute your role as spokesperson, your superiors and your subordinates will learn to trust you and to rely on you more in the future. This will strengthen your relationships with them and promote harmony and cooperation in your department. Take the quiz in Exhibit 8.3 to assess how well you are playing your four human relations roles with subordinates.

MAINTAINING YOUR RELATIONSHIPS WITH SUBORDINATES

So far we have discussed how to build a sound relationship with your individual subordinates. How can you preserve such relationships once they are established? The answer lies in persistence. When we talked about personality formation, we agreed that it was a continuous process. So it is with on-the-job relationships. Like any other living thing, human relations need constant attention. Each day brings about changes in the parties involved, so that what worked well yesterday may not today. Recognition of this dynamic aspect of people and their relationships dictates the need for maintenance. Establishing a sound relationship with each person is only a beginning. If the relationship is to grow and be mutually beneficial, maintenance must be scheduled and performed.

The relationship between supervisor and subordinate advocated in this chapter is distinctly different from the relationship between two people called *friendship*. At the base of sound human relations are common interests (effective and efficient operation of the department, for example), mutual respect, and a concern for the other person's welfare. This is or should be true about your relationships with your friends, as well. But you should try to prevent a true friendship from emerging out of sound human relations with your subordinates.

If you allow a friendship to form between yourself and a subordinate, you do so at your own expense. How easy is it to give orders to a friend? Do you appraise your friend's performance and freely offer criticism? How about the times when you have to pass out an occasional dirty job? Would you consider your friend objectively as a candidate for it? You cannot form friendships with all of your subordinates, so aren't you opening yourself to criticism about playing favorites?

Your honest answers to these questions should alert you to the inherent dangers of friendship with subordinates. The subordinate you befriend is open to criticism, too, and that person's relationships with peers may be in jeopardy. Choose your friends from among your peers.

EDUCATOR ROLE

Usually Rarely

  ○   ○   1. I make certain that my actions do not contradict my words and instructions.

  ○   ○   2. I carefully construct a program for training my people, being certain to set specific objectives.

  ○   ○   3. I make certain that my people have the information and resources they need to do first-class work.

  ○   ○   4. I assign work to people based upon their willingness and their abilities to perform it.

  ○   ○   5. When I find an attitude in a subordinate that is interfering with performance, I work on changing it.

JUDGE ROLE

Usually Rarely

  ○   ○   1. I look for causes behind any failures by my people to meet the standards set for their performance.

  ○   ○   2. I withhold any criticism until I have all the facts and am aware of all the circumstances surrounding an issue.

  ○   ○   3. I try to discipline without emotion.

  ○   ○   4. I recognize that circumstances should temper any approach to discipline.

  ○   ○   5. I know that it is better to forewarn and forearm subordinates about the expectations I and the organization have for them than to punish their failing to meet standards.

COUNSELOR ROLE

Usually Rarely

  ○   ○   1. I make time for anyone who wishes to see me about a personal or work-related problem.

  ○   ○   2. I make certain that any counseling I do is in private and free from interruptions.

  ○   ○   3. I give the person seeking my help my undivided, sincere attention.

  ○   ○   4. I recognize that I cannot solve every problem and should not try to give people all the answers.

  ○   ○   5. When I cannot help someone solve a problem, I will try to refer him to another person with more expertise.

SPOKESPERSON ROLE

Usually Rarely

  ○   ○   1. I take seriously every complaint or gripe I hear from subordinates.

  ○   ○   2. I listen carefully to subordinates' suggestions and ideas and try to use them.

  ○   ○   3. When I cannot solve any problem my people give me, I take it to a higher authority for resolution.

  ○   ○   4. When my people experience success, I make certain others higher up hear about it.

  ○   ○   5. I try my best to reflect management's points of view accurately, defending them and enforcing their decisions.

Each "rarely" response indicates that you need to improve your conduct.

Getting Along with Staff Specialists

Probably dozens of times each week your department is affected by the actions or policies of staff specialists. A large percentage of the e-mail replies, forms, and reports you generate are destined for them. The advice and service you receive from staff specialists can save you hours of agony and independent research. These people form an invaluable group of counselors on professional matters. Do everything you can to take advantage of their labors and to foster a cooperative and receptive atmosphere. At times, they may appear to you as prying eyes or fifth wheels. But over the long run, your success as a supervisor—as well as that of all other managers—depends on your seeking and using their advice. And as the concept of functional authority suggests, you may have no choice.

Developing Sound Human Relationships with Peers

Your peers are the other managers on the same level of the management hierarchy. You work more closely with some than with others, but situations can change rapidly in business. The most important reasons for establishing good human relations with your peers are these:

- To know and understand them as individuals
- To approach and cooperate with them as individuals
- To assist them in achieving satisfaction from their jobs
- To foster a spirit of cooperation and teamwork among them
- To tap their diverse base of knowledge, skills, and experience

Your success as a manager is linked to your peers and what they think of you as a person and as a supervisor. Your personal and professional reputation with them is important for a number of reasons. If they think highly of you, they will expend their time and energy on your behalf and help you with advice. How you measure up with them and how they react when your name is mentioned are factors that may influence your boss as well. When your boss looks at his subordinates—you and your peers—for someone to delegate responsibility to or to train for a higher position, he will compare you to them. If you cannot get along with or are avoided by your peers, your boss will know it.

Your peers represent an enormous pool of talent and experience that is yours to tap and to which you can contribute. For this reason, if no other, it is to your advantage to cultivate their friendship. In many ways, you need each other, and all of you stand to benefit from a partnership or alliance based on mutual respect. If you are off in your own little world and are unwilling to share your knowledge, you deny yourself the advice and experience your peers are ready to provide. You may be branded as uncooperative or antisocial and destined, at best, for a career as a supervisor. Higher positions have no need for isolates. You will find, if you have not already done so, that the more you give of yourself, the more you will receive from others.

YOUR ROLE AS EDUCATOR

The two-way nature of your role as educator includes assisting your fellow supervisors in their growth and development and enlisting their help on your own behalf. You have a great deal to give your peers. You have talents and skills that may be developed to a greater degree in you than in some of them. You have knowledge about human nature, your job, and management in general that can be beneficial to others. You have attitudes and a personality that can be the basis for friendship and that can sustain a fellow supervisor when she needs help.

Most people have experienced the joy that comes with helping a less experienced person solve a problem. Besides the momentary joy you feel when you share your knowledge and your tricks of the trade, you get something much more lasting: a good reputation. Psychologically, all of your peers who profit through your efforts on their behalf are in your debt. They may not always show overt appreciation (and you should not always expect it), but they will find it hard not to reciprocate, to share what they have with you. When you need a favor, a bit of advice, or a helping hand, your colleagues will respond if they are able to do so.

Your peers' advice and know-how cannot be found in books. In a relatively short span of time, you may receive (if you are wise enough to ask) what might take you years to discover on your own. Which is easier and more fun: reading about how to do something difficult or having someone who knows how to do it show you? Your peers probably feel the same way about this as you do. The better your peers know you, the greater the quantity of help available to you. Give what you have, and take advantage of what others have to give. Do not bury your talents, and do not let others bury theirs.

YOUR ROLE AS COUNSELOR

Counseling involves mutual exchange of ideas and opinions. Counselors are people to whom you go for advice and to try out your ideas. They provide you with guidance and a plan in the absence of one of your own. The key to counseling your peers is empathy—the intellectual and imaginative understanding of another's feelings and state of mind. From this develops a mutual respect and appreciation.

As with subordinates, just being available and favorably predisposed toward your peers may give them what they need at precisely the moment they need it—a sympathetic ear. By listening to others who have difficulties, you provide emotional first aid. By responding when asked and when qualified to do so, you may give people the support they need to resolve their difficulties.

When a friend asks you for advice and you have empathy for that person, speak your mind freely. Without empathy (which usually means without friendship), you should confine your guidance to work-related matters. Steer clear of personal advice unless you know the person well.

For the give and take of counseling between friends and associates to work, we must have open communication channels. Do your best to avoid arguments and displays of temper with your associates. Do not burn any bridges so that you cannot return to a pleasant relationship once a momentary storm passes. If for a time you alienate a peer, stand ready to apologize when you have been in the wrong. Be quick to forgive a colleague who has injured you. You do not have to call all of your peers your friends, but you should not call any of them enemies. By sharing the successes of others, you enrich the returns to them. By sharing the sorrows of others, you capture their friendship. So it is also when they reciprocate.

YOUR ROLE AS JUDGE

The role of judge is closely allied with the counseling role in human relations. You have four specific duties to attend: enforcement, settling disputes, evaluation, and criticism.

Enforcement. The duty you have to enforce company policies and regulations affects your peers as well. There is an urgent need for all supervisors to be uniform in both the interpretation and the application of these policies and regulations. You probably have experienced the unhappy situation that results when one supervisor is lenient and another is severe. Imagine a situation in which you are trying to get your workers to arrive and leave on schedule, whereas the supervisor in the adjacent department allows his people to come and go as they please. How much more difficult has this supervisor made your job? Where two managers interpret or enforce the same regulation or policy in different and conflicting ways, a wedge is driven between them. This wedge acts as a barrier to both communication and cooperation.

Settling disputes. When you find yourself at odds with a peer over an interpretation of policy or of how to enforce a rule, get together with that individual and work it out between you. A meeting and a polite discussion are all that it takes to resolve the difficulty. If you two cannot work the matter out, get together with your bosses. Do not let the conflict continue any longer than necessary. Take action as soon as you are aware that a problem exists.

Periodically, you may be called on by circumstances to serve as a peacemaker. For example, two of your associates are engaged in an argument,

SUPERVISORS AND QUALITY

Are you tenacious? Do you have the technical skills to run the business and produce the product? Do you believe in your own ability? These are questions that assess a person's ability to become an entrepreneur. According to Jon P. Goodman, Director of the University of Southern California's Entrepreneurship program, successful business startups are the product of passion and perspective. Entrepreneurs have traits that any supervisor, team leader, and team facilitator would do well to acquire. Empowered teams and work groups need inspired leaders and members. Such people demonstrate a true commitment to a vision and values.

They then keep their associates focused on both and inspire them to produce quality outputs.

Entrepreneurs see problems as opportunities, crises as challenges, and failures as learning experiences. They "have imagination, the ability to envision alternative scenarios. . . . Successful entrepreneurs act out of choice. They are never victims of fate." When you adopt these perceptions, you become a role model for others. Your enthusiasm and commitment will become infectious, leading to the ability to inspire others to give quality performances.

Source: Jon P. Goodman, "What Makes an Entrepreneur?" *Inc.* (October 1994): 29.

and their emotions have taken over. As a witness to the dispute, you may be able to intervene with a calmness and logic that the others lack. Do so when you find yourself in such a situation. It does managers no good to squabble, especially in public. Workers read all kinds of things into such events. You may save a friend or associate from the embarrassment of looking foolish.

Evaluation. Study your peers for an understanding of their management techniques. All of them have their unique characteristics and methods. Hold your standards up to theirs, and see how they compare. Where you discover significant differences, make every effort to determine which is the better set to follow. Both your and their techniques could prove to be inferior to yet another set of standards.

Your peers make excellent working models to observe and evaluate. Try out your theories and applications on your associates, and get their reactions to them. Watch how they handle themselves in difficult as well as routine matters. Test your attitudes against theirs, and see if you can refine your viewpoints and pick up some of their methods.

Criticism. When you observe a peer engaged in improper or forbidden conduct, you owe a bit of friendly correction. Others, especially workers, who observe a supervisor's improprieties draw conclusions that inevitably harm that supervisor's reputation and your own. You are all in this together.

When a peer's actions and objectives are contrary to yours, you must confront her with your observations. Let her know, in a tactful and sincere manner, what you know. After all, if you know what she is up to, it is quite likely that others also know—including the boss. Of course, you must still discuss the matter in private. You may find more often than not that a peer is unaware that she is doing anything wrong and will appreciate your drawing attention to the matter.

You, in turn, must stand ready for constructive criticism. We all need it occasionally and, in fact, stop growing without it. Contentment and smugness creep in, and a false sense of security takes over. We begin to believe that we are consistently right and gradually close our minds to the new and different. The strongest kind of friendly correction you can exert is your own good example. By promoting the things you believe in and by opposing the things you believe to be wrong, you take a stand and exhibit principles for others to see and admire.

We all tend to cover for a friend or peer in trouble. But in the long run, you stand to lose far more than you could ever gain. You will identify yourself as an ally of improper conduct and demonstrate wholly unacceptable attitudes for any manager to hold. You do not hold a position of power and trust in order to shield your friends from earned discipline. Nor should you punish; that is a middle manager's duty. You need not inform on a peer since, in time, things have a way of surfacing and getting to those who should know. However, if a peer is violating the law or a policy that places the company at risk, senior management needs to be informed. Confront your peer with the information you have. If your suspicions are confirmed, give the person a short time to inform senior management. If he fails to notify senior management, then you have an obligation to do so. Do not compromise your own position of trust and personal integrity to help anyone.

YOUR ROLE AS SPOKESPERSON

You owe loyalty to your peers, but only when they are in the right. Allegiance to someone is a precious gift, not to be given lightly. It must be earned as well as respected. Loyalty implies mutual trust and confidence. When these things are not mutual, they cannot persist.

You should never spread a rumor about anyone. But when you hear one, it is your job as a spokesperson to refute it if you can. If you cannot, ask the other person to substantiate the statement. Inquire about the source. The person will know what you are thinking—that he is spreading gossip. When this bit of gossip relates to a peer, let that individual know its content and its source.

When an untrue rumor pertains to you, and you view its content as serious—such as an attack on your character—defend yourself. Trace it to its originator, and confront that individual with your knowledge. Control your temper, but make your point as forcefully as you feel is necessary. Then bury the incident, and try not to carry a grudge. If a rumor is minor and not related to your character, let it go. You do not have the time to track down all rumors, nor should you try to do so.

Respect legitimate demands for your silence, as when you converse about personal matters with a friend. Information revealed to you by a peer that pertains to that person alone should not be a topic of conversation with others. If you reveal a secret or break a confidence, your peer is sure to find out about it. What will happen to your reputation then?

The role of spokesperson also pertains to spreading good news or praising the ideas, contributions, and accomplishments of your peers. Giving credit where it is due and expressing your appreciation for benefits received, especially in public, is a pleasant duty one manager or friend owes another.

Finally, remember that you are also a spokesperson for your subordinates. When another supervisor interferes with them or their work, make it clear that the interference is inappropriate. Such an action challenges your authority. You must shield your subordinates and yourself from outside interference and conflicting orders or instructions.

COMPETITION WITH YOUR PEERS

Keep in mind that although you should maintain good relations with your peers and develop cooperation with them, you are still in competition with them. In much the same manner as a professional athlete, you have to maintain a balance between individual displays of talent and ability and the need for team play. All great athletes achieve their greatness in this way. You must be willing to take a back seat now and then and let another manager's talents come through. The best way to maintain good human relations is to develop yourself into the best person and manager you have the potential to become. You will gain expert and charismatic power in so doing, which will draw people to you. Use the checklist shown in Exhibit 8.4 as a guide to evaluate your human relations efforts in dealing with your peers. Any "rarely" responses indicate a need to make an adjustment.

Getting Along with Your Boss

Before we get into specifics about your relations with your boss, we will discuss how your boss's job resembles yours and how it differs.

Since you are a supervisor, your boss is a middle manager. He is accountable for your actions. Your boss is similar to you in that he is both a follower and a staff or line manager. He executes all the functions of management and is evaluated on the basis of his subordinates' performances. Your boss, like you, must develop sound working relationships with subordinates, peers, and superiors. He probably served an apprenticeship as a supervisor, so you can probably count on him to understand your situation.

| Exhibit | 8.4 | *Evaluate how well you are playing your human relations roles with peers.* |

Usually Rarely

○ ○ 1. I carry my own weight.

○ ○ 2. I lend a hand when and where needed.

○ ○ 3. I have the best interests of my peers in mind.

○ ○ 4. I am loyal to my peers.

○ ○ 5. I respect the privacy of things told to me in confidence.

○ ○ 6. I refrain from engaging in negative gossip.

○ ○ 7. I share my expertise and experiences with peers.

○ ○ 8. I try to earn the respect of peers.

○ ○ 9. I show my peers common courtesies and respect.

○ ○ 10. I share information with peers.

○ ○ 11. I avoid passing the buck.

○ ○ 12. I am a team player.

○ ○ 13. I defend my peers' actions in their absence.

○ ○ 14. I do not bear any grudges.

○ ○ 15. I try to avoid making any enemies.

Any responses of "rarely" indicate a need for improvement.

Compared to a supervisor, however, a middle manager has more differences than similarities. As the following list shows, your boss has a number of duties and interests that are unlike yours. Your boss:

- Directs the work of other managers
- Exhibits strong pro-management attitudes
- Spends more time on planning than you do
- Spends less time with subordinates
- Spends more time with peers and superiors
- Is more of an adviser than a director
- Has more freedom of action and flexibility

- Has more information and a broader perspective
- Is less concerned with procedures and tactics and is more concerned with planning and strategy
- Is more concerned with tomorrow than with today
- Is more concerned with the organizational impact of management actions than individual effects

As to the last item on this list, supervisors and subordinates often evaluate a management decision on the basis of its effect on them. Suppose that higher management has recently reduced the plant budget for overtime. This decision is translated at your level into less overtime and production flexibility for the department and less income for the workers. Your people see this as a reduction in their potential earnings. Your boss probably participated in the decision and the objectives it was designed to achieve. For instance, lower overtime expenses may conserve income, allow your company to price its line more competitively, and reduce overall expenses. Your boss sees the decision as logical and supports it. Once you know the reasons behind a decision, you should support the decision as strongly as your boss does. Give what facts you can to your subordinates to soften the blow. Emphasize that the conservation of income may prevent layoffs and save jobs. You must be flexible enough to meet rapidly changing situations such as this.

Employees with disabilities must be treated with respect and dignity. They often have superior productivity and attendance records. Here a supervisor at Dell Computers confers with an employee who is visually challenged.

YOUR BOSS'S EXPECTATIONS

Most middle managers expect their subordinate managers to be loyal followers. Your boss, like you, needs the respect and support of subordinates. She must be able to count on your willingness and ability to enforce company policies and standards. She is relying on you to carry out decisions with the proper attitude. Do not let any of your actions or remarks jeopardize your boss's reputation.

Your boss expects you to get along well with your peers and with the company's various staff specialists as well as with your subordinates. If you are able to resolve your disputes on your own, without arguments and displays of temper, you are demonstrating resourcefulness. Initiative is another extremely important characteristic for any manager to possess. Are you the kind of manager who waits for orders or instructions before acting? If you do, you lack this essential quality. When you have the authority to act in a situation and know what must be done, you must not be afraid to respond.

Finally, your boss expects you to keep her informed. Share your knowledge about essential operations with your boss. Nothing can injure you quite as effectively as for the boss to be surprised—to find out about something secondhand. You can make your boss look bad if you fail in your duty to keep her abreast of developments. Share what information you have with your boss, without betraying any confidences.

WINNING YOUR BOSS'S CONFIDENCE

If you meet your superior's expectations, you are well on your way toward gaining his confidence. In addition, try to learn from your mistakes, as each one may have a lesson to be learned. Study your errors to avoid repeating them. Bring your efforts at self-development to your boss's attention. The courses you take in school and recent articles or books you have read that have been helpful in your work are all worthy topics of conversation with your boss. Additional ways to improve your supervisory abilities are described below.

Finding a Better Way

As a manager, you should give methods improvement a high priority. No matter how smoothly an operation is running, there is usually room for improvement. Turn your attention to the costliest operations first. That is where you stand to realize the greatest savings. Then systematically work your way through the rest of your operations. Five magic words related to methods improvement have proved to be valuable to many supervisors and those aspiring to supervision. All are related to reengineering: (1) combine, (2) eliminate, (3) rearrange, (4) reexamine, and (5) simplify. Look at a plan, program, procedure, or practice with these words in mind.

Do not keep your successes to yourself. Share them with your peers and superiors. Others can profit from your innovations. The time, effort, and money that can be saved are important, but the effect on your reputation and career is also important. Just be certain that an idea is yours before you take credit for it. Where you receive help, give credit to that individual.

Keeping Your Promises

A can-do attitude is great if you really can do what you promise. Before making a promise, be as certain as possible of the resources at your disposal and the limits on your operations. If, in your best judgment, you have what it will take to get the job done, commit yourself and your people to the endeavor. It is better to be a little bold than to be too cautious. If circumstances change dramatically for reasons beyond your ability to foresee, let your boss know. He will understand, and adjustments can be made. However, if you should have known about or suspected the changes, your reputation will suffer.

Speaking Positively or Not at All

Whatever the topic of conversation, be sure that what you say is positive. Resist the temptation to engage in gripe sessions and to put another person down. Such displays are clearly negative and completely without redeeming qualities. If your gripe is justified, reveal it to those who can act on it. If the person you wish to criticize is a subordinate, approach that person in private, and keep your comments constructive. No one, especially not a boss, benefits from associating with a person who is always negative. Few activities are as futile as gripe sessions. Names are dropped and things are said that all too often you later wish you could retract or forget. If you have nothing positive to say, you are better off saying nothing.

Constructive criticism, whether of an individual or of an idea, is not negative, and you are perfectly right to engage in it as long as the environment is correct. When an argument is put forth that favors a course of action and you see a disadvantage to it, you must air that point if the advocate of the proposal fails to do so. When the boss or anyone else puts forth a proposal in your presence, she wants your honest reactions.

Taking a Position

You must be a contributing member of the management team—carrying your own weight and standing ready to help teammates. If you want the respect of others, you must have convictions. These convictions or beliefs tell others who you are and where you stand. However, before you take a stand on an issue, make sure that you think it through and anticipate the possible drawbacks, as well as your supportive arguments. Then prepare your defense.

When you take your stand and find it untenable, do not be reluctant to yield to superior forces. Bullheadedness is not a quality that endears you to anyone, while reasonableness *is* such a quality. You want to be thought of as a person of principle—one who thinks things through and fights for what he or she believes. The corollary to this is equally important: You must oppose things you believe to be improper or wrong.

Involving Your Boss in Major Decisions

Just as you stand ready to help a subordinate or peer with a problem, your boss is ready to help you. When you have a problem with which you have wrestled but to which you have no certain solution, set up a meeting with your boss, explaining in advance what you wish to discuss. Assemble your research and facts. Construct a list of alternatives you have considered. What the boss wants most is to see that you have considered the matter and given it your best effort. She will not make your decisions for you, except when you have reached an impasse. Even then, most bosses offer only suggestions and direct your attention to additional items you may have overlooked. That method may be a little frustrating, but the learning experience is invaluable to you.

Each contact you have with your boss should be as professional as you can make it. Be yourself, but be prepared.

OBTAINING SOME OF YOUR BOSS'S AUTHORITY

Learn your boss's needs, ambitions, strengths and weaknesses. You can learn from a strong boss and may be able to help a weak one. The boss, like you, is probably looking for subordinates who can attend to time-consuming details and assume routine tasks. By delegating them, the boss creates time for more important tasks—the ones he alone must tackle. Your boss also gains time to take on a larger portion of his own boss's duties and thus prepares for advancement. So it goes from supervisor to chief executive. Through delegation, each trains another. A manager who has not trained a subordinate to take her place may be unable to advance. Her lack of mobility acts as a ceiling on those with ambition and ability below.

Your boss will begin to delegate duties to you when you have proved that you are worthy of respect and confidence. You will get details and routine tasks at first. If you handle them well, you can look forward to increased responsibilities. The increased duties may become yours permanently, enlarging your job description and serving as justification for increases in pay, status, and a possible change in title.

If your boss is reluctant to delegate, you should urge him to do so. First, you must free yourself from your details and routines in order to make time available. Then go to your boss with time on your hands and a plea for additional duties. You may not be successful at first; old habits die slowly. But you have planted a seed, and a good manager will not let it die. Your boss will be disturbed by your idleness and impressed by your initiative. If you persist, your boss will respond.

Do not assume any of your boss's duties or anyone else's without consultation. There is a tendency for a bright and eager young supervisor to spot something that needs doing and do it. This is fine as long as you have jurisdiction over the matter. But when the duty you perform belongs to another, you are guilty of grabbing power from that person. This will be interpreted to your disadvantage.

Do not get yourself into a position where your boss becomes too dependent on you. If the boss views you as indispensable, she may consciously or unconsciously restrict your chances for advancement. She will fear losing you, through promotion or transfer, and the corresponding disruption of the status quo this may represent. Your best defense is to train a successor. When the opportunity arises and the time is right, you can then point with pride and confidence to that subordinate as your logical and well-trained successor.

YOUR EXPECTATIONS OF YOUR BOSS

Besides mutual respect and trust—which are prerequisites for a working relationship—your boss should provide you with the following:

- Constructive criticism
- Fair evaluations
- Essential guidance
- A constant flow of necessary information
- Recognition for jobs well done
- An appropriate management style
- Training for growth and development
- A good example

Where one or more of these items is lacking, look first at yourself for the cause. Something in you or your performance may be missing. If you do not give respect or loyalty, you have none coming. If you do not respond well to criticism, you may not receive it. If you do not think your boss's evaluations of your performance are fair, why did you accept them without protest? You may not be receiving guidance because you have not asked for any. Is the guidance you seek really essential? If you do not get information, maybe it is because you cannot keep a secret or have no need to know. If your boss's management style with you is not to your liking, have you discussed it with him? You may find, as many management students do, that the more you learn about management principles and practices, the more critical of people in authority you become. If this is happening to you, do not be alarmed. You are experiencing what all children growing up experience: the realization that the adult who occupies a position of trust and authority is really just a human being.

The beauty of all this is that you will know when something goes wrong and why. How you react to your new knowledge and act on it determines whether you remain always a freshman or become a senior and graduate. Knowledge is power, and power needs controls on its use. As you mature, you will discover flaws where you saw none before. An inadequate manager often provides a better learning situation than a real professional does. When things run smoothly, you often do not know why they do. But when things go sour, you have a chance to ask and determine why. That goes for your own mistakes as well as for those of the boss. Your analysis of your boss's shortcomings can prevent them from plaguing your own efforts. Most of the cases in this book (and in every other management text) portray managers with flaws and inadequacies for just this reason.

According to a study by professors and psychologists Robert Hogan and John Morrison, the average subordinate thinks that her managers are competent between 60 and 75 percent of the time. In another study done by Personnel Decisions Inc. of Minneapolis, a human resource consulting firm, 56 percent of the 800 people surveyed thought their bosses were "top-notch"; only 8 percent thought that their bosses treated them unfairly.[28]

Exhibit 8.5 provides some suggestions for maintaining a good relationship with your boss.

| Exhibit **8.5** | *Suggestions for managing your boss.* |

1. Analyze your boss's job, leadership/operating style, and needs system to gain a better feel for where he or she is coming from.

2. As a consequence of this analysis, you should understand the boss's aspirations, goals, and plans, concerns, problems, and priorities, and so perform to increase the likelihood of your boss's success.

3. Recognize that the boss is a human being and thus has need for support, encouragement, attention, and sincere praise, as well as for the expected technical assistance. Avoid backing him into a corner with possible loss of face.

4. Keep the boss fully informed as to progress on and problems with assignments and, above all, avoid embarrassing the boss with surprises.

5. Present solutions to problems as opposed to merely highlighting the problems.

6. Function in a positive and facilitating manner, but don't hesitate to challenge the boss and offer constructive criticism when needed.

7. Ensure that the boss gets the credit for success and thus is made to feel and look good.

8. Should you get a new boss, show him or her how indispensable you are and that you intend to remain so.

9. In all transactions involving the boss, ask yourself: "Will my action strengthen or weaken my boss's perception that I am an understanding and supportive subordinate?"

10. To the extent possible, develop strategies to cope with the less attractive aspects of the boss's behavior.

11. Use "I messages" when it is essential to confront your boss regarding behaviors you find inconsiderate or possibly punishing.

12. Use positive "self-talk" to bolster your feelings about your supervisor, avoiding self-sabotaging messages ("can't," "don't know how," "it's too hard"). A good verbal guide: "What you say is what you get!"

13. Change yourself because your ability to change your boss, who has the power, is necessarily limited. *Example:* Assume your boss is a slow decision maker. Shift your self-talk from "That guy dreads making a decision," to "Hey, this gives me a lot of freedom to fill that void."

Source: Julius E. Eitington, *Winning Manager: Leadership Skills for Greater Innovation, Quality, and Employee Commitment.* Houston, TX: Gulf Publishing Company (1997): 27.

Instant Replay

1. Human relations involves the development and maintenance of sound on-the-job relationships with subordinates, peers, and superiors.

2. Supervisors must relate to people at work by perceiving them as they perceive themselves—as members of diverse groups that influence their attitudes and behaviors.

3. Building human relationships requires you to play fundamental roles as educator, counselor, judge, and spokesperson.

4. As an educator, you share your knowledge, skills, and experiences with others.

5. As a counselor, you provide advice, service, direction, and a sympathetic ear.

6. As a judge, you evaluate the performance of subordinates, enforce rules and standards, settle disputes, and dispense justice.

7. You win your peers' respect by lending a hand when and where you can and by being a friend.

8. As a spokesperson, you represent subordinates to higher authority and management to subordinates.

9. You win your boss's respect and confidence by meeting expectations and by playing your roles as they are prescribed.

10. You learn your boss's job by creating time in which to help perform some of the boss's tasks. You train your replacement through delegation of duties.

Questions for Class Discussion

1. Can you define this chapter's key terms?
2. What are the major purposes of human relations?
3. How should a supervisor play the basic human relations roles with subordinates? With peers?
4. How is a middle manager's job different from a supervisor's?
5. What is involved in creating and maintaining a good working relationship with one's boss?

Incident

Purpose: To help you identify cultural differences between yourself and others.

Your task: For each aspect of culture listed, record a summary statement for yourself and another person at work or in your class who is different from you in some major way. Then discuss the similarities and differences.

You	Another Person	Aspect of Culture
○	○	1. Importance of being on time
○	○	2. Command of the English language
○	○	3. Openness to meeting new people
○	○	4. Conversational style
○	○	5. Age
○	○	6. Educational background
○	○	7. Work ethic
○	○	8. View on importance of family
○	○	9. Gender
○	○	10. Favorite foods
○	○	11. Willingness to conform
○	○	12. Respect for others

CASE PROBLEM 8.1 *Short in Stature*

Kirby walked into Nancy's office and said, "I need to talk to you." He then closed the door and said, "I didn't appreciate it when you challenged my new production scheduling plan in the meeting a while ago. If you had real concerns, why didn't you wait to talk to me in private? It is embarrassing to have someone trash my ideas, and I don't want it to happen again."

Nancy, taken by surprise by Kirby's response, replied, "Well, I'm sorry if I embarrassed you. It was certainly not my intention. I just have some strong feelings about the schedule and simply said what I felt. It looked to me like at least two others felt the same way, because it seemed to me like they were really biting their tongues when you outlined the plan."

Kirby said, "I don't think that's true. You were the only one who objected to the schedule. Besides, your tone of voice indicated that you were dismissing the plan as ridiculous. You're not going to get away with being disrespectful to me."

Nancy then said: "I'm sorry you feel that way. You really caught me by surprise with the plan for a new production schedule."

Kirby then responded: "I will not let you undermine my attempts to improve the way we do things around here. Nancy, you've got a bad attitude and you need to change it. If you're that unhappy around here, then you need to leave. We can't tolerate any people who aren't cooperative." Kirby then opened the door and left.

Nancy couldn't believe what had just happened. She felt terrible about Kirby's reaction. Just then, Irene stuck her head in the door. She said, "I'm sorry, but it looks like little Napoleon had another temper tantrum. Was he in here chewing you out?"

Nancy said, "Yes, that's what happened. I should have known better than to challenge his ideas in the meeting. I just feel awful."

Irene said, "I know it was no fun for you, but I really appreciate the fact that you shot down his idea. Everybody knows that his proposed new schedule would be a disaster. Besides, he's so insecure that even the slightest objection by anybody gets misconstrued as a personal attack. People are afraid to say anything."

Nancy said, "I don't know what to say anymore. We all have more experience than Kirby and have a pretty good idea about what will work with our production facilities. These meetings never go well anymore because we can't disagree with anything Kirby wants to do."

Just then Cary walked in and said, "Wow! I just saw Little Napoleon walking down the hall from this direction. What did he say to you?"

Nancy described the conversation again and Cary said, "That sounds like him. I think that you'd be a great supervisor, but this organization is so male-dominated that even someone like Kirby is tolerated. I know you're upset, but thanks for saying what you did. This new scheduling plan of Kirby's sounds about as bad as the rest of his ill-conceived ideas. Because we've been a good unit in the past and still care about this place, we perform in spite of his incompetence. So it's not clear to me that upper management knows how bad he is."

Thirty minutes later Kirby went to see his boss, George Master. "George, I've had it with Nancy. She's really got a bad attitude and is poisoning the well with her negativity. Every time I try to introduce a new change, I've got to deal with her. I want to start laying a paper trail to get rid of her. She's got some friends in the department and they tend to take her side on most things. If we get rid of her the rest will fall in line."

Questions

1. How should Kirby have attempted to gain acceptance of his plan for a new production schedule?

2. How should Kirby handle his differences with Nancy? With some of the other associates?

3. What do you think George Masters will want to know about the situation?

4. What advice do you have for Kirby? For Nancy? For George?

Feedback from the Boss	CASE PROBLEM 8.2

Sandy had asked Ed, one of eight project managers who reported to her, to come by to talk about issues related to the project Ed's group had just completed at Blue Valley Manufacturing.

SANDY: "Ed, thanks for coming by. I wanted to share some feedback from the last project your group just completed. You're just starting your group's next project and there's some information that may be helpful. We received some feedback from Francis Drummond, the contract manager at Blue Valley, that they were a little dissatisfied with the amount of cooperation they received from your group."

ED: "I'm not surprised to hear that Francis complained. He seemed to be determined, even from the first day, not to like anything we did for them."

SANDY: "Why didn't I know about any problems you were having with Francis? You didn't tell me about any difficulties."

ED: "Well we never really worked with Francis very much except for the first week of the project. After a week, two other people at Blue Valley took his place as contacts for our group and he faded into the background. They were good people to work with, although I gather that they were taking a lot of abuse from Francis for various things. Evidently he's one of those people who is never satisfied with anything, and I understand that he is not well-liked over there."

SANDY: "Francis said that you and your group were difficult to work with and that he had serious reservations about ever working with us in the future."

ED: "I don't know why he would say that. We did good work for them, and their people were delighted with the inventory system we installed."

SANDY: "I know that you and your group do good work. Your group is one of our best, and we've received good feedback from clients in the past. But Blue Valley is an important client to us. They have work for us to do and there is a lot more competition now. In the future, whenever your group is having any difficulty with a client, I need to know about it."

ED: "Well, we really never had a problem with the anyone except Francis, and he seems to be such a grouch that their people provide a buffer between him and outside contractors."

SANDY: "I understand your point about Francis, but I didn't know there were any problems at Blue Valley."

ED: "Well, I didn't think there *were* any problems. Our guys work well with everyone. They're the most congenial group around. The clients we work for are always asking us to do more jobs because they like us and the work we do."

SANDY: "Ed, I don't think you're hearing what I'm trying to tell you. I just found out this morning that it will be difficult to get more jobs with Blue Valley because Francis is unhappy with us, and I didn't know anything about it."

ED: "There are always some minor issues with any job. I always thought that as the project manager I would be trusted to deal with them. I dealt with them and we got the job done. Furthermore, we got along really well with the people we worked with over there. It seems to me that we always do good work, our jobs are never late, and we're never over budget."

SANDY: "Ed, I appreciate the good work you and your group do. I just need to be informed any time there's a problem. That's all I'm asking for. Just keep me informed better on the next job."

ED: "Sandy, I've got to tell you. I'm really surprised by your reaction to whatever Francis told you. We really knocked ourselves out on that job. We made money for our company and we worked around a real jerk to get the job done. And the feedback I seem to be getting is not 'thanks for doing a tough job.' Instead I'm being told that you don't trust my judgment in dealing with clients. Do you want us to call you all of the time with everything that comes up on the job?"

SANDY: "That's not what I'm saying, Ed. All I'm asking you to do is to tell me when there is a problem with the client."

ED: "Look, I feel really bad that Francis is saying that Blue Valley isn't going to give us any more business. But Francis is a jerk and everybody over there knows it. Our guys really took a lot of guff from him during that first week. He was really abusive to our people. Finally I told him, in a calm and quiet manner, that he had to quit abusing our people if he wanted us to get the job done. I was very professional in dealing with him and he has no reason for dissatisfaction. It just surprises me that you don't seem to believe what I'm telling you."

SANDY: "One more time, Ed, and listen closely. Tell me when there are problems with any client in the future."

Questions

1. What is the likely outcome of this session between Sandy and Ed?
2. How could Sandy have done a better job of providing feedback to Ed?
3. What do you think of how Ed handled the feedback from Sandy?
4. How well is Ed managing his relationship with Sandy?

References

1. *Forbes.* "Labor Relations," citing *The Economist* (July 27, 1998): 32.
2. Martin, James. *Cybercorp: The New Business Revolution.* New York: American Management Association, 1996.
3. Bennis, Warren. *Leaders on Leadership: Interviews with Top Executives.* Boston: Harvard Business School Press (1992): 56–57.
4. Associated Press, "All Talk," *Fort Worth Star Telegram* (January 16, 1998): D2.
5. Levering, Robert, and Moskowitz, Milton. "The 100 Best Companies to Work for in America," *Fortune* (January 12, 1998): 84.
6. Levering, Robert, and Moskowitz, Milton. "The 100 Best Companies to Work for in America," *Fortune* (January 8, 2001): 148–159.
7. Ibid.
8. "Diversity Programs Support Recruitment, Retention, and More," *HR Focus* (January 2002): 3.
9. Levering and Moskowitz. "The 100 Best": 84–95.

10. Raphael, Todd. "Diversity Lives at Bell South," *Workforce* (January 2002): 18. Gale, Sarah Fister. "Companies Find EAPs Can Foster Diversity," *Workforce* (February 2002): 66–69.

11. Levering and Moskowitz. "The 100 Best": 84–95.

12. Ibid.

13. Peters, Tom. "Tapping Worker Curiosity Can Electrify Company," *Chicago Tribune* (October 26, 1992): sect. 4, 6.

14. Loden, Marilyn, and Rosener, Judy B. *Workforce America!* Homewood, IL: Business One Irwin (1991): 62.

15. Blank, Renee, and Slipp, Sandra. *Voices of Diversity.* New York: Amacom (1994): 192–195.

16. Loden and Rosener. *Workforce America!*

17. Blank and Slipp. *Voices.*

18. Wheatley, Margaret J. "Quantum Management," *Working Woman* (October 1994): 16–17.

19. Richman, Louis S. "The New Work Force Builds Itself," *Fortune* (June 27, 1994): 70.

20. Treece, James B. "Breaking the Chains of Command," *Business Week*, Special 1994 Bonus Issue, "The Information Revolution" (1994): 112–113.

21. Ibid.

22. Chase, Nancy. "Coaching on the Run," *Quality* (September 1999): 80.

23. American Hotel & Motel Association, Educational Institute. *Training and Coaching Techniques.* East Lansing, MI (1976): 75.

24. "Catch the Coach at Least 8 Times a Year," *People Management* (November 9, 2000): 18.

25. Holt, David H. *Management Principles and Practices,* 3rd ed. Englewood Cliffs, NJ: Prentice Hall (1993): 497.

26. Ibid.

27. Martin, Donald E. *Team Think.* New York: Penguin Books USA, 1993.

28. Winokur, L. A. "Well, They Say There Are Lies, Damn Lies, Statistics and Bosses," *The Wall Street Journal* (January 10, 1991): B1.

CHAPTER 9

SUPERVISING GROUPS

Objectives

After reading and discussing this chapter, you should be able to do the following:

1. Define this chapter's key terms.

2. List and briefly explain the forces that shape a group's personality.

3. Describe the duties of a meeting's chairperson before, during, and after a group problem-solving session.

4. Describe the duties of a group's members before, during, and after a group problem-solving session.

5. Describe errors in team decision making.

6. List and briefly describe the group-serving and self-serving roles played by members of a group problem-solving session.

7. List the types of cliques, and give an example of each.

8. Describe how group behavior can be affected by internal group competition—what happens to the winning side and what happens to the losing side.

Introduction

Groups are formed when two or more people come together for the purpose of achieving some mutual goal or benefit. More specifically, a **group** is two or more people who are consciously aware of one another, who consider themselves to be a functioning unit, and who share in a quest to achieve goals or obtain some common benefit. When we say that the members are aware of each other, we mean that they know something about each other, are clear about why they are together, and recognize the need to cooperate. There are two basic kinds of groups in organizations: *formal groups* that are

group

two or more people who consider themselves a functioning unit and share a common goal

created by management and *informal groups* created by members of the organization. This latter type of group allows its members to associate with others who share their values and interests. As a supervisor, you must learn to work with both kinds of groups.

Teams in U. S. factories and offices are having a tremendous impact on quality and the productivity of their organizations. The value of such teams is flexibility for management and motivation to excel for team members. For example, at Goldman Sachs, an enormously profitable Wall Street firm, a professional observed that "Team work here is better than on any professional sports team I've ever even seen."[1] It is no surprise that Goldman Sachs was number 15 on *Fortune*'s 2001 list of the best 100 companies for which to work.[2] Similarly, furniture maker Herman Miller, an early innovator with work teams, has been on *Fortune*'s list.[3] Teams can accomplish incredible feats. For example, teams of astronauts have repaired the Hubble telescope while it orbited the earth. The astronauts worked as a team while sharing ideas for improvement during training. The team's members helped each other and wanted each to perform with perfection.[4]

The role of the supervisor also is changing because of team structures. Supervisors may be elected members of such teams, serving on a rotating basis, or they may become more like coaches than traditional managers. This chapter focuses on how groups form and how you can effectively manage and get along with groups at work.

Collective Entrepreneurship

Many modern companies that compete successfully in today's global economy have one major thing in common. They have managed to create a team spirit in their employees that translates into high levels of innovation, adaptability, and financial success. Employees at all levels come to believe in common goals and in united efforts to achieve them. Talent and energy then are pooled into what former Secretary of Labor Robert Reich labeled *collective entrepreneurship*. Employees feel a real partnership and commitment to the company's future because they feel that they *are* the company. Rewards and praise flow to teams of employees, not to individuals. Technology is looked on as a means to aid workers and managers, to cut routine, and to give them more opportunities to use their imagination and insight for their company.[5]

For workers, collective entrepreneurship means "accepting flexible job classifications and work rules; agreeing to wage rates linked to profits and productivity improvements; and generally taking greater responsibility for the soundness and efficiency of the enterprise."[6] For managers, collective entrepreneurship means "continually retraining workers for more complex tasks; automating in ways that cut routine tasks and enhance worker flexibility and creativity; diffusing responsibility for innovation; taking seriously labor's concern for job security; and giving workers a stake in improved productivity through profit linked bonuses and stock plans."[7]

The Personality of Groups

A group, like the people who compose it, has a personality as unique and subject to change as any individual's. The group's personality is partially a composite of the personalities of its members. We say "partially" because a group is always something more than the sum of its parts. That some-thing more comes about because of the interaction of group members, which creates energy and qualities that may not be possessed by any of the individual group members. An example would be a basic training group in the military. Individually, its members may not have the desire or the will to excel and may not know their capabilities. But in group situa-tions, the pressure to conform and the feeling that "If they can do it, so can I" will dominate. If 20 trainees were dispatched on a 20-mile hike, one at a time at intervals of 10 min-utes, very few (if any) would complete the march. When all 20 embark on the hike together, most will finish, even if their buddies have to carry some of them. Combat units often exhibit tremendous courage that individuals would not show without the support of and the commitment to their comrades.

All groups—even formal ones—have personalities. Group personalities are the sum of individual personalities, plus the synergy that is created when those individuals work together.

There is a term for the fact that groups often produce at greater levels than the sum of their individual members: **synergy.** Common table salt is a chemical combination of two poisons—sodium and chlorine. Alone each is dangerous; together they are beneficial and take on properties that neither has alone.

The term *synergy* applies to any combined operation or action; thus it can be either positive or negative. Satisfied groups or group members can exhibit greater positive action or forces for change than the individuals within the group could do on their own.

synergy
cooperative action or force of two or more elements pulling together that yields a result greater than the sum of the results that could be achieved separately by the elements

Formal Groups

A **formal group** may be defined as two or more people who come together by management decision to achieve specific goals. Your company, your department, your shift, and the various management committees are but a few of the many formal groups you encounter each day. Any individual, especially a manager, may belong to more than one formal group simulta-

formal group
two or more people who come together by manage-ment decision to achieve specific goals

SUPERVISORS AND ETHICS

"There is an inherent conflict in considering workforce diversity because of the need to see each worker both as an individual and as a member of a group. . . . A key to supervising an individual worker effectively is knowing as much as possible about that worker. . . . [A] worker's membership in a particular group, that is, his or her group identity . . . is simply another factor—and often an important one—in helping a manager understand an individual employee's behavior and perspective."

Stereotypes exist for both individuals and groups. Care must be taken to avoid identifying an individual through any stereotype based simply on one or more aspects of the person's background, heritage, or group membership. "When group identity is recognized, it is often in terms of stereotypes—categorizing individuals only by their group identity—rather than seeing group identity as one part of a complex individual."

Just as people change over time, so, too, do the groups to which they belong. What may have been true about a certain group last year is not true today. Whereas some group members exhibit many of their group's characteristics, others exhibit only a few. Some members may identify strongly with their groups; others may have only a casual affiliation. And most members of any group belong to and identify with other groups, further compounding their uniqueness and complexity.

The only safe harbor for any of us is to try to get to know people by their walk and talk. The answers to why they walk and talk as they do are found in part in their experiences, inherited traits, and group memberships. Therefore, these become valuable reference points for both understanding each other and for building various human relationships.

Source: Renee Blank and Sandra Slipp, *Voices of Diversity*. New York: Amacom (1994): 6–11.

neously. For instance, you are an employee of a company, working in a particular functional division and within a specific department. You are a member, therefore, of at least three formal groups. If you serve on a committee, you belong to a fourth formal group.

Formal groups may be temporary or permanent. An *ad hoc* committee—one set up to solve a particular problem and dissolved when the solution is determined—is an example of a temporary formal group. Most formal groups in your company are permanent, although even whole divisions can be dissolved or merged into others on occasion, as the needs of the business may dictate. Formal groups may be true teams if they consist of "a small number of people with complementary skills who are committed to a common purpose, performance goals, and approach for which they hold themselves mutually responsible."[8] "The teams most popular today are of two broad types: work teams, which include high-performance or self-managed teams, and special-purpose problem-solving teams. . . . While problem-solving teams are temporary, work teams, used by about two-thirds of U.S. companies, tend to be permanent."[9]

Every formal group has a leader. The heads of most formal groups are managers who have been installed for just that purpose. The leader of a self-

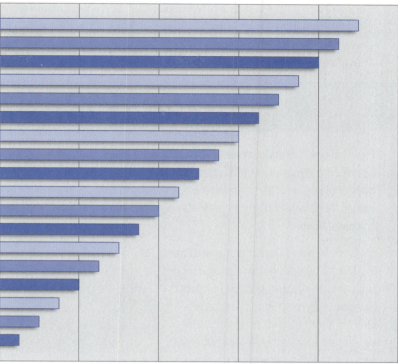

Exhibit 9.1

A continuum of empowerment for groups and teams.

RESPONSIBILITY/AUTHORITY

- Making Compensation Decisions
- Disciplinary Process
- Team Member Performance Appraisal
- Product Modification and Development
- Budgeting
- Facility Design
- Equipment Purchase
- Choosing Team Leaders
- Vacation Scheduling
- Cross-Functional Teaming
- Hiring Team Members
- External Customer Contact
- Managing Suppliers
- Continuous Improvement
- Quality Responsibilities
- Equipment Maintenance and Repair
- Training Each Other
- Housekeeping

AMOUNT OF EMPOWERMENT/AUTONOMY

Source: Adapted from Richard S. Wellins, William C. Byham, and Jeanne M. Wilson, *Empowered Teams.* San Francisco: Jossey-Bass (1991): 26.

managed team may be elected or appointed by the team's members, and leadership may be rotated among the members over time. Either way, the formal group's leader has varying degrees of formal authority at her disposal. Exhibit 9.1 shows a continuum of empowerment. The higher a team climbs on the continuum, the more autonomy it has. Management teams usually have the highest degree of autonomy.

MANAGEMENT TEAMS

Teams of managers may be permanent or temporary. Characteristics of such teams are that they usually:

> make decisions by consensus in areas affecting the entire operation—resource allocation, funds distribution, facility design, budgeting, hiring—subject to the approval of top management. . . . [A] team effort yields better decisions, protects . . . from arbitrary or careless actions, and, above all, strengthens team

members' commitment to [the company's] goals. . . . [A] boss cannot obtain by decree the creativity, initiative, and dedication needed to do a job properly; such allegiance can come freely only from people who have a sense of "ownership" [entrepreneurship] of the organization's goals.[10]

As a manager, you will serve on several teams. The fact that you are a manager makes you a member of management, which is a team of decision-

SUPERVISING TEAMS

Organizations may utilize several different types of teams, for different purposes. The following are some common types of teams. Note that some of the types of teams may overlap. For example, a project team may also be a cross-functional team.

Project Teams. Project teams are formed for the special purpose of completing a project, such as developing a new product. However, they also may be assembled for projects such as to facilitate the implementation of a new enterprise software system, to develop a new training program, or to establish standards for databases. These teams are formed only for these special-purpose projects and are disbanded after the project has been completed. Some organizations also refer to project teams as *task forces,* which are created to examine a particular problem or to institute change. At GM's Saturn Division, the 15-member machine maintenance team set out to decide the least expensive way to sharpen cutting tools used on transmission parts. They decided that an outside source would be best, thus taking the work away from their own in-house operations. (At Saturn, foremen are called work unit module advisers and are selected through the combined efforts of the division's management and union leaders. Workers at other GM facilities elect foremen.)

Quality Assurance Teams. Quality groups are created to make certain that a company's products and services meet the needs and expectations of customers. A quality assurance group may ask its dealers, clients, and suppliers to serve as group members or consultants, and its members maintain constant contact with these people. At Saturn, Annette Ellerby helps her 15-member team check electrical systems on the company's subcompacts.

Cross-Functional Teams. Cross-functional teams may be made up of members from various functional groups—marketing, production, finance, and so on—and they may cross-train their members in each other's areas of expertise. Cross-functional teams regularly investigate problems and processes that affect two or more functional areas and work to find mutually agreeable solutions. Their membership and focus keep shifting as issues are resolved and new ones emerge. At Saturn, "each team regulates personal calls on its phones. Some use an honor system, while others make team members use a personal credit card."

Product Development Teams. Product development teams are a particular kind of cross-functional team. They bring together all functional areas involved with creating new products—engineering, production, research and development, marketing, purchasing, and so on—along with key representatives from suppliers.

Sources: Bradford McKee, "Turn Your Workers into a Team," *Nation's Business* (July 1992): 36–38. David Woodruff, "Where Employees Are Management," *Business Week,* 1992 Bonus Issue (January 19, 1993): 66. Thomas P. Flannery, David A. Hofrichter, and Paul E. Platten, *People, Performance, and Pay: Dynamic Compensation for Changing Organizations.* New York: The Free Press, 1996.

makers. As a traditional supervisor, you head a formal unit within a formal organization—your work group. When you serve on a committee, head a true team, or act as a team facilitator, you are a linking pin, connecting the group with others. You benefit from such connections by gaining a better understanding of others in your organization.

The automotive parts supplier A. O. Smith Corporation has created teams that give its seven unions a voice in planning and decision making. It has problem-solving committees on the shop floor, plant-wide advisory committees with union representatives, and union officials on the top management strategic planning committee.[11] Most major corporations have product design teams that include engineers, market researchers, production managers, and representatives from suppliers. The multiple perspectives represented within the team ensure, from the very beginning, that the product created is what the consumer wants and can be manufactured efficiently and with quality. Another kind of management team is the crisis team—a group of managers from various departments that can act swiftly in the face of any crisis the company may face. Such teams plan their actions before crises actually occur.

According to experts, "the task of setting up work teams among employees should begin at the top."[12] Several conditions must exist before organizations can successfully implement teams. The first is that they must have the expertise needed to form teams and a willingness to share problem solving with team members. The second is that it must be possible to change the way things get done—procedures, processes, traditions, and habits. The third is that there must be sufficient commitment in money and time to prepare people for team roles and to continue training efforts. Typical subjects of team training include decision making, how to run meetings, communication skills, handling conflict, implementing change, using quality tools (benchmarking, statistical controls, and scoreboarding), evaluating team and team members' performances, and reengineering concepts. Before GM's Saturn Division produced any cars, "workers got 300 to 700 hours of schooling, covering basic skills such as conflict management and problem solving. That has been followed by ongoing training in specific areas, such as interviewing techniques."[13] This chapter's *Supervising Teams* feature contains a synopsis of Saturn's teams.

WORKER TEAMS

Ideally, you should be concerned with molding your people into a **team** or group of teams that feels an owner's concern for the organization and its goals. A true team leader or facilitator is much more than the head of a group of workers and must have both a mature personality and a sense of security.

Maturity is required so that emotions can be controlled when dealing with people who may be less mature. Security is required so that the leader does not fear sharing management authority with others and does not fear being challenged. Managers who are new to team leadership have much

team

a work group in which members feel a compelling need for team work, assume joint responsibility for accomplishment of the team's goals, and hold each other accountable for results teaching and learning to do. They must master a participative style of supervision and be willing to teach problem solving and decision making to team members. They also must be proficient in interpersonal skills and be able to take the time necessary to deal with delays that group approaches often involve. The qualities of patience, tact, and enthusiasm are essential. "Typically, a team leader still spends time actually performing various production or service tasks. . . . Often the team leader serves as a spokesperson for the team, coordinates team activities with other departments or teams, and devotes time to training new team members."[14]

One of the keys for good team dynamics is a solid foundation for relationships within the team. Such a foundation should include a clear mission, explicit values that are accepted by team members, ground rules that are agreed upon, and an understanding of the limits of the team's empowerment and the decisions that will be made by management. A second key is to hold face-to-face meetings periodically instead of relying too much on more sterile forms of communication, such as e-mail. Another key is to facilitate conflict resolution by training members to engage in healthy discussions of differences, to listen actively, and to avoid finger pointing and blame placing. In addition, it is important for team members to recognize that there may be gender differences that affect group dynamics, such as in how men and women listen. A final key is that the team needs recognition in order to sustain high performance in the long term.[15]

Organizing your subordinates into worker teams presents new challenges to supervisors, such as mastering the participative style of supervision.

Team facilitators (sometimes called *team advisers* or *group leaders*) "frequently play a coordinating and facilitating role. They help teams communicate with one another and serve as a conduit for information that flows from teams to other organizational departments and from these back to the teams."[16] As a leader of teams, you must learn that your major tasks are to help each team define its goals, set the limits for each team, help obtain the resources each team requires, and mold a cooperative and committed spirit in each team. The team facilitator has a blend of traditional supervisory and middle management responsibilities. Both team leaders and team facilitators often have wide spans of control—numbers of subordinates. "For example, AT&T Operator Services in Richmond, Virginia, moved from a span of control of one leader for each 12

members to one leader for each 72 members. As teams mature, it is not uncommon for six or more teams to report to a single group leader."[17]

An example of successful team work is provided by ABC Rail Products Corporation's Chicago Heights factory. The factory was losing money, and managers and union workers were not cooperating. One hundred twenty-five jobs were on the line when the chairman and CEO, Donald W. Grinter, met with union leaders: either the two would work to save the plant or it would be closed. Management shared financial data, and union representatives and plant managers met to discuss their options. "Organizational lines began to blur as workers and management formed quality management teams to address problems as part of a formal total-quality system."[18] The company worked with vendors to tighten control and quality over supplies, and a new management team was installed. Gradually, the losses diminished, profits returned, and backorders resulted. Says plant general foreman, Bill Dutrizac, "Now all that inventory is computerized, it's well organized. You ask somebody to do something extra now, they do it."[19] Says Don Grinter about the turnaround, "It was a thousand little things adding up."[20]

Toyota's automobile manufacturing operations in the U. S. have established a reputation for excellent teamwork. However, the U. S. operations of other Japanese automobile manufactures also display excellent teamwork. For example, Honda of America provides extensive training for its employees in both problem solving and teamwork. The purpose of such training is to improve efficiency and quality by harnessing the suggestions and creativity of its teams. Honda also provides opportunities for team recognition by having the teams make presentations every six months on their quality circle results. Judges evaluate the presentations on the teams' problem-solving processes.[21]

An example of superb teamwork by Southwest Airlines ground crews is presented in Exhibit 9.2. Southwest's ground crews work with the precision of an Indy race-car pit crew. Interestingly, Southwest is one of the most highly unionized companies in the United States, with over 84 percent of its employees represented by unions. Obviously Southwest Airlines has a very different relationship with its unions than many other companies. One difference is how the company invests in relationships. This is reflected in negotiations: Southwest's CEO James Parker says the company tries to work with a goal of determining the most that it can pay employees rather than the least.[22]

In addition to teamwork in manufacturing plants and on the flight line, teams of knowledge workers also work in office environments. Unfortunately, the layout of existing office space often detracts from both teamwork and personal space. To address the intensive information requirements for knowledge workers and their need for collaborative efforts, IBM and Steelcase have developed a new, highly personalized computerized office environment called BlueSpace. The BlueSpace environment, which facilitates collaborative efforts while retaining personal space, has cubicles with such innovations as sensors that automatically adjust the temperature in spaces to individuals' preferences as they arrive and touch screens that enable team members to instantly determine members' locations and their availability.[23]

Exhibit 9.2	*Teamwork by ground crews at Southwest Airlines.*

Minute by Minute at LAX

2:45 P.M. Like a finely honed pit crew waiting for that Indy car to arrive, Rudy Guidi, Calvin Williams, Kirkland Howling, and Ricardo Perez prepare to spring into action. Rudy and Calvin go over the bin sheet, which tells the team how much baggage, freight, and mail is on the aircraft, while the rest of the team makes sure the equipment is in position to turn the plane. The ground crew is joined by First Officer Ken Brown, who is there to do a preflight check on the aircraft.

2:46 P.M. The aircraft is in sight, and Ricardo jumps up on the back of the tug to guide the plane into the jetway. Rudy and Calvin each start up a belt loader and begin to move toward the plane as it approaches the gate.

2:47 P.M. The aircraft comes to a complete stop at the gate. The jetway is already moving toward the door of the aircraft. The baggage bins of the Boeing 737 fly open. A fueler pulls up to the aircraft while crew members off-load bags.

2:48 P.M. Ken pauses for a moment from his preflight check to help Kirkland connect the pushback to the nose gear of the airplane. Provisioning crew members race through the rear door of the aircraft to stock ice, drinks, and snacks and to empty trash. Passengers begin to deplane.

2:49 P.M. The freight coordinator pulls up in his tug to ensure freight labeled NFG (Next Flight Guaranteed) makes the next flight.

2:50 P.M. First officer completes his preflight check. Flight attendants move through the cabin of the aircraft to reposition seat belts and pick up trash.

2:51 P.M. All bags are off-loaded. Ramp agents begin loading bags for new passengers. Provisioning is complete. Current flight crew (pilots and flight attendants) is relieved by new flight crew. Operations agent makes initial announcement calling for preboarders. Several adults with children and a person on crutches make their way to the plane. Fueler is pulling the hose out of the wing of the aircraft.

2:52 P.M. Operations agent begins boarding customers in groups of 30. Bags are loaded and fueling is complete. Most of the ground crew move to another gate to prepare for the arrival of the next aircraft.

3:00 P.M. Passenger boarding is complete; operations agent gives weight and balance sheet to pilot. Pilots trim the aircraft according to the load. Ramp agent connects the communication gear to talk to the pilots from the tarmac.

3:01 P.M. The jetway pulls back and the door of the aircraft closes. Pushback maneuvers the plane onto the tarmac and turns the plane toward the runway. Ramp agent unhooks the pushback from the aircraft and the plane taxis toward the runway.

Here is what this ground crew of four accomplished in 15 minutes: There was a complete change of flight crew; 137 customers came off the plane and another 137 boarded; the ramp agents unloaded 97 bags, 1,000 pounds of mail, and 25 pieces of freight weighing close to 500 pounds. The ramp agents then loaded 123 bags and 600 pounds of mail (no freight), while the fueler pumped 4,500 pounds of jet fuel into the wing of the aircraft. It's an impressive spectacle. People come out of nowhere and the entire area around the plane is abuzz. Then, in a mater of minutes, their jobs complete, the swarm of people disappears and the plane pulls away.

Building Group Effectiveness

Recent research has identified three variables that affect a group's effectiveness: task interdependence, outcome interdependence, and potency. *Task interdependence* relates to the degree to which a group member is concerned with or involved in the work of other group members. Teams dealing with quality improvement have a high degree of task interdependence, whereas scientists engaged in basic research and development often have a low degree of it.[24]

> Outcome interdependence exists when task accomplishment by a group yields consequences that are important to and shared by some or all group members— for example, pay, time off, and recognition. The "outcomes" are bestowed by people other than group members, usually a supervisor or senior manager. They may be rewards or punishments; they may include pay, promotion, skill acquisition, exposure, or survival . . . [and] do not include any benefits derived from within the group, such as social interaction. . . . Potency is the collective belief of group members that the group can be effective. This belief depends on group members' sense that they have what they need to succeed—for example, training, skills, talented members, money, time, access to key organization members, and feedback about group performance. Potency tends to be closely linked to performance. . . . Additionally, task interdependence and potency are linked.[25]

For groups to succeed and be effective, they need outcome interdependence, a minimal belief in their own effectiveness (potency), and a degree of interaction that is right for the task (enough opportunities for interaction must be provided). The more successes the group has, the greater its sense of potency. The more meaningful the rewards and the more equally they are distributed, the greater the group's effectiveness.[26] These are the hallmarks of a "learning organization," one that "values—and thinks competitive advantage derives from—continuing learning, both individual and collective."[27] Here is a case in point. Fred Simon, project manager for the development of a new Lincoln Continental, brought the car to market faster, cheaper, and with less intergroup infighting than ever before at Ford. His engineering teams learned to work together instead of jealously guarding their respective turfs.

> Simon found that the engineers who designed the air conditioning, the headlights, the power seats, and the CD player, all working separately, had each made their component such that when used simultaneously they would drain the car battery. . . . Because Simon's engineers understood [the value of working in a learning organization] they put their heads together and came up with a solution: Raise the car's idle to increase the battery's charge. Of course, that lowered fuel efficiency, and the engineers in charge of that didn't particularly like making such a sacrifice. The difference this time was that the problem got solved quickly and because it was clear the change was made for the good of the car, no one felt like a loser.[28]

Team leaders or supervisors in charge of teams need rewards to help keep teams moving in the right direction. They also need to be able to reinforce behaviors that make for good teamwork. In some organizations the process of putting the interests of the team ahead of individual interests is such a foreign concept that it has been humorously referred to as an "unnatural act." While the ability to provide financial reinforcements is important in all work organizations, we know that many of the reinforcements are non-financial. The following are a few suggestions for non-financial rewards:[29]

- Give out formal recognition for exceptional individual achievement, like "Living the Teamwork Values" awards for team members who have been caught "walking the talk" of the company's and/or team's explicitly stated values.

- Take video shots of your team's working experiences and create a video production for use and distribution at key organizational meetings. (Another alternative is a photo collage or a slide show, either of which could be computerized and distributed on disk or made accessible online.)

- Take team photos and either write to or ask the company's Public Affairs department to profile the team in a corporate publication or an industry/trade journal.

- Invite senior management and key stakeholders to attend team meetings and functions in order to "showcase" the team and its members at work. (Note to senior management and key stakeholders: Make the time to attend.)

- Take a photo of the team, or a team member, with a corporate executive or distinguished external VIP, and have it framed for all the team members and/or the VIP. Include the photo in a public recognition event, publication, or other type of "visibility vehicle."

As a group's supervisor, you need to be a facilitator. You must clearly define the group's goals, listing the essential tasks and the degree of quality you wish to see in its performance. You also must structure the group to provide sufficient interaction among group members, monitor its performance, and when necessary, offer leadership and coaching. Finally, you must be certain that the group perceives the fact that important group outcomes depend on both individual and collective performance.[30]

Building a team requires that you give the intended members a "common approach and a common language for addressing management concerns. . . . The best method for coordinating the inputs of managers and employees with different functional skills is to provide simple, common, sensible guidelines and procedures. These guidelines should be used jointly to carry out responsibilities without inhibiting individual contributions."[31] One typical way to begin is to teach a common approach to solving problems and making decisions. Once team members participate in group training sessions and begin to focus on common objectives, they get to know one another. They see the advantages of many minds concentrating on a common problem and the value of compromise and cooperation.

SUPERVISORS AND QUALITY

The role of team leader on a self-directed work team boils down to being an active participant and facilitator—removing obstacles by providing training that allows team members to execute the processes and tasks that accomplish their purposes and goals. Specifically, facilitators' roles include the following:

1. Provide training and tools essential for maintaining and improving quality. Team members should be able to:

   - Identify and define internal and external customers' needs and requirements
   - Establish quality standards for the team's and team members' performance
   - Measure all performances and identify deviations from set standards
   - Investigate and remove the sources of deviations from standards
   - Make all improvements standard operating procedure
   - Continue to search for evolutionary and revolutionary (reengineering) changes to improve quality

2. Provide training and tools essential for team interaction and collaboration. Team members should be able to:

   - Exercise effective communication skills when conducting meetings, resolving conflicts, reaching agreements, and engaging in feedback activities
   - Navigate through the various stages of team building
   - Appreciate the uniqueness of each team member and value the contributions and participation of each

3. Provide training and tools essential for team members to obtain and improve work-related skills and experiences. Team members should be able to:

   - Operate equipment and machinery effectively and efficiently
   - Maintain equipment and machinery properly
   - Engage in safe work habits and practices
   - Execute tasks effectively and efficiently

INFLUENCE WITHOUT AUTHORITY

Team leaders and team members have the ability to get things done or exert influence even when they have little or no formal authority. They can exert influence by providing services and other things of value to other associates or managers that create an obligation to reciprocate or return a favor. These services or things of value can serve as currencies. Currencies requiring no authority may be task related, position related, or relationship related. Task-related currencies include information sharing of both technical and organizational varieties, providing assistance, doing undesirable tasks, and various forms of cooperative behavior such as quick responses. Position-related currencies include access to personal contacts or networks and inclusion of another person as an important insider. Relationship-related currencies include such things as acceptance or inclusion in the group, friendship, personal support, and understanding.[32]

A CONTRARY VIEW OF TEAMS

Teams are not the answer for all management problems or a silver bullet for improved performance. Unfortunately, the term "teamwork" is often misused. Sometimes it is used as a euphemism for suppressing legitimate disagreement with the manager's viewpoint or submitting to the will of others at all costs. Donald G. Smith has pointed out a number of problems with this common but dysfunctional view of teamwork.

> Positive-thinking gave business . . . the idea of the *team player,* which is a wonderful euphemism for someone who looks the other way when the Cossacks plunder the village. . . . When I entered corporate America directly out of college, I was given some invaluable advice by an older employee . . . [management] did not want to see boat rockers, and such people were immediately marked with an indelible stamp and considered unpromotable. The basic idea was to swallow one's integrity during business hours and to be a part of the "team." . . . I participated in programs that cost twice as much as they should have because of mismanagement, and I slavishly followed the orders of some of the most incompetent and mentally deficient human beings I have ever encountered.[33]

The points of this discussion are that supervisors should avoid misusing the term "teamwork" and that they should not stifle constructive dissent for the purpose of teamwork. In addition, some employees do not want to take on some of the responsibilities of self-managed teams. While self-managed teams are the means by which many companies have empowered their employees, some people find that they do not fit the system. For example, self-managed team members give each other feedback. Some employees find this very stressful because other team members pay great attention to how they do their jobs.[34] In addition, with self-managed teams some employees feel that they have many bosses instead of one boss. At Eaton's plant in South Bend, Indiana, one employee said the following:

> "They say there are no bosses here," says Randy Savage, a long-time, devoted employee, "but if you screw up, you find one pretty fast." Indeed, with everyone watching everyone else, it can feel like having a hundred bosses. . . . Worker mishaps that might hamper production or tarnish the plant's reputation are considered an affront to everyone and prompt a sort of communal confession.[35]

In addition to these concerns, some team members do not like to give negative feedback to other team members and find that their communication or interpersonal skills are inadequate for such functions. For example,

> Similarly, some workers refuse to speak at meetings called to point out problems with a coworker's performance. . . . And others say they would never go in front of the rest of the workforce to apologize for a mistake . . . With workers expected to sort out problems among themselves rather than have managers intervene, strong interpersonal skills are vital. . . . But Mr. Gordon [team member] didn't like the frequent meetings on communication. For instance, new workers are required to give speeches before new employees and managers and to attend training seminars about saying

"we," never "I" or "you," when being critical to avoid sounding accusatory.[36]

GROUP DECISION TECHNIQUES

In this section we will first discuss two techniques for generating new ideas: brainstorming and the nominal group technique. An important feature of both techniques is that they prohibit evaluative comments or criticism of members' offerings during the idea elicitation phase because criticism tends to reduce the amount of new ideas put forth.[37]

Teams often make decisions through consensus. However, achieving consensus is often a challenging task. Exhibit 9.3 provides some suggestions for reaching consensus.

We will conclude this section with a discussion of general processes of group decision making.

Work teams at Saturn take responsibility for reaching quality and production goals. Because they are given decision-making tasks, workers on participatory teams often have greater self-esteem and work harder.

Techniques that facilitate team consensus.

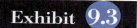

Exhibit 9.3

- Ask people for the rationale behind an opinion or perspective.

- Don't let people change their minds or drop out just to avoid conflict.

- Don't let the group slip into one-person subgroups, majority-rule votes, or horse-trading, unless the group consciously decides to do that.

- Don't let the group get polarized on positions or stuck in either/or decisions. Look for alternatives.

- Look for areas of agreement or common ground first, then move on to issues of disagreement.

- Ask people who are not in consensus with the majority: "What alteration of this position *could* you accept or support?"

- Poll people to determine their initial position. (Use a fist for "no support," high five for "full support," and three fingers for "needs modification.")

- After consensus has apparently been reached, ask each person individually: "Will you endorse this decision with key stakeholders when you leave this room?"

Source: From Lynda C. McDermott, Nolan Brawley, and William W. Waite, *World Class Teams: Working Across Borders.* New York: John Wiley & Sons, Inc. (1998): 168.

Brainstorming

brainstorming

group idea generation processes in which creativity is encouraged while evaluation is limited to a separate phase

In **brainstorming** sessions, individuals are given a statement of a problem that requires their input. Members are asked to offer suggestions in the form of ideas or potential approaches that they think will be useful. Wild and unusual ideas are sought since they tend to open new directions of thought and to bring forth more new ideas. The group leader discourages criticism of the offerings in the idea-elicitation phase but allows modifications or combinations and lists them as they are put forth. Each person is encouraged to speak out on each item. Members are chosen for their ability to offer constructive and meaningful contributions. This technique is used to create advertising slogans, new uses for existing products, new products, and new approaches to existing procedures. It is also used to spark creative thinking and creative thinkers.

Nominal Groups

nominal group

group idea generation process in which members develop their ideas individually and then the leader elicits all ideas for group consideration

Nominal groups are a variation of brainstorming. Group members are given a problem and instructed first to work alone to develop a list of ideas in writing. The group leader then goes around the group in a round-robin manner and elicits the first idea from each member. Typically the group leader writes these suggestions on flip charts to disassociate the idea from the person who provided it. After all ideas are listed the group then proceeds to the evaluation phase in which each idea is evaluated individually. Because each idea is disassociated from its contributor, the idea's originator is less likely to become defensive if the idea is criticized.[38]

Group Problem Solving

Group problem solving is usually used for problems affecting the group. It works best in a discussion format—one that allows members to participate actively under the skillful direction of the leader. The following steps are involved in group problem-solving sessions:

1. Identify and define the problem(s).
2. List possible solutions.
3. Evaluate the positive and negative features of each solution.
4. Choose a solution or solutions.
5. Assign responsibility and authority for implementing the solution(s).

While there are advantages of group problem solving, such as involvement of your people, there are also some associated dangers. For example, if you have never included your subordinates in your decision-making process in the past, they may be suspicious of your attempt to do so now. Furthermore, participants bring to the meeting their particular interests and attitudes, which are affected by their informal groups. (We discuss informal groups later in this chapter.) Informal group leaders will be part of the meeting too, so their attitudes may well affect the quality and quantity of ideas of their followers. Such leaders can promote open participation or dominate and inhibit participation. As the formal group leader, you may find your ideas and attitudes challenged openly for the first time. You may be subjected to group criticism and find yourself pitted against the informal leader or leaders.

All these problems and more can be prevented or minimized through proper planning. One point to consider during planning is whether your group is equipped to solve the problem. For example, it should be able to solve problems relating to the reduction of waste or scrap, health and safety, housekeeping, and methods improvement. By soliciting concrete suggestions and taking advantage of your subordinates' involvement in these problem areas, you will be sharing your authority and enlarging your perspective.

ERRORS IN TEAM DECISIONS

Unfortunately, groups and teams are prone to a number of decision-making errors of which supervisors, team leaders, and team members need to be aware. One error, called the *Abilene paradox,* results from failures of team members to communicate their real wants. Because of members' desire to get along with the group, they sometimes decide to pursue alternatives that no members really want. Thus a group might make a decision to take an automobile trip to Abilene although no one really wants to go, as was the case in the original paradox.[39] One of the authors refers to an insightful colleague who helped his department avoid bad group decisions by making timely announcements that "It looks like we're on our way to Abilene." A similar error is called *self-censorship.* This error occurs in cohesive groups in which individuals do not critically examine various alternatives because they do not want to rock the boat.[40]

Another error caused by pressures for group conformity is called *groupthink.* Conditions leading to groupthink include high pressure for conformity, strong desire to remain in the group, punishment of individuals who offer deviating input, and the presence of individuals within the group who are perceived to have extraordinary expertise. Groupthink among presidential advisers has been cited as the cause of the escalation of the Vietnam War and the disastrous Bay of Pigs invasion of Cuba. In these examples the groups were comprised of intellectual superstars who did not want to be excluded from their high-powered groups. As a result, they did not vigorously challenge the group even when they disagreed. This form of "collective dumbness by smart people"[41] also occurs in business. For example, groups of smart people made the decision to produce the Cadillac Allanté, a beautiful and expensive car that turned out to be a commercial failure. Such groups also approved NBC's rigging of crash tests for a sensational exposé about explosions of General Motors trucks in collisions.[42]

Several conditions cause group members to avoid critical thinking or self-limit their input when it deviates from the developing position of the group. Professors Paul Mulvey, John Veiga, and Priscilla Elsass have found that the following conditions make groupthink more likely:[43]

1. Perceptions of great expertise attributed to one or more individuals
2. A compelling argument
3. Individuals' lack confidence in their potential contributions
4. Decisions perceived as unimportant
5. Pressures for conformity
6. Disorganized and unproductive meetings

In order to offset such conditions, these researchers make a number of suggestions for reducing pressures for conformity. These include using smaller decision-making groups, minimizing status differentials among group members, clarifying the purpose of the group, emphasizing the importance of the decision, and describing the procedures to be used in the decision-making process.[44]

GROUND RULES FOR MEETINGS

If the problem-solving session is to accomplish meaningful results, rules and procedures must be established and agreed on in advance by all concerned. Imagine playing a sport in which each participant had her own set of rules. Chaos would be a certainty. Most sports need an umpire or referee whose job it is to enforce the rules and prevent infractions. This role is yours to play as the supervisor.

Essential rules are described below. Using this list as a guide while planning and conducting your meetings should prevent most problems from occurring—or at least prevent any serious conflicts.

Before the Meeting

When you have a specific problem to be solved, communicate it to the group members in advance of the meeting. Be as clear as you can be in defining the problem and in specifying the goals you want the meeting to achieve. Be certain that limits such as time, company policy, and the amount of authority the group will have are clear to the group. Is the group empowered only to recommend solutions or actually to choose them? In the latter case, you must delegate some of your formal authority to the group. If you alone have the power to decide, tell them so.

Give your members all the relevant data you have accumulated and any boundaries on solutions, such as resource limitations, imposed by management. This information will help the group adopt a realistic point of view. Let them know the order (the agenda) in which the group will consider the various issues and the time and duration of the meeting. All who have been chosen to attend should be made aware of their responsibilities to prepare for the meeting. Specifically, each member should make the following preparations:

1. Read the agenda, and prepare a list of questions that he should answer, before facing the group.

2. Gather the information, materials, visuals, and so on that she will be responsible for presenting or disseminating to the group.

3. If a group member should be unable to attend the meeting for any legitimate reason, he should relay his input to the chairperson.

During the Meeting

Provide name tags and assign seating when necessary. Start the meeting promptly, direct the discussion, stick to the agenda and time limits, draw out each member, list the alternatives, and summarize frequently. Maintain order, and keep the meeting on the subject. Normally, you should make your comments only after other members in order to avoid inhibiting the group. In some instances you may want to avoid making your opinions known so that the group will take greater ownership of the decision.

During each meeting, the group members have specific responsibilities that should be communicated to them in advance and briefly repeated to them at the start of each session. If the meeting is to be beneficial to all concerned, each member should be prepared to do the following:

1. Be an active participant by listening attentively, taking notes, following the discussions, seeking clarification when confused, and adding input if the group member has the expertise or experience to do so.

2. Promote discussion and input from all members by respecting their right to their opinions and attitudes and by avoiding discourteous or disruptive behavior. (The chairperson should not hesitate to call on quiet members, using specific questions and asking for opinions.)

3. Practice group-serving roles (described in the next section). From the alternatives listed and analyzed, bring the group to one mind about the best alternative or combination of alternatives to endorse. If the solution is to work, the majority must be behind it. Be ready to compromise in order to break any impasse.

Assign tasks to those affected, if need be, and put the solution into operation as quickly as possible. At the close of each meeting, the participants should be made aware of any specific duties or assignments they will have as a result of the meeting. The chairperson should not allow the members to leave until each of them is clear about her new tasks. In addition to the specific duties each person may receive, all participants have the following general obligations:

1. When the meeting concerns sensitive matters, preserve the confidentiality of the discussion.

2. Relay decisions and changes to those for whom the group member may be responsible and whom they will affect.

3. Carry out promises made and assignments received as quickly as possible.

After the Meeting

After a problem-solving meeting, check on the results and on the group reactions. Follow up on individual assignments.

GROUP MEMBER ROLES

At a meeting, members of the group may play various roles; some of these will be helpful to the attainment of the meeting's goals, whereas others may hinder the group's attempts. Two broad categories of roles are *self-serving* and *group-serving*.

Self-Serving Roles

Self-serving roles can have either positive or negative effects on the meeting and on group members. For example, suppose that as a group leader, you block another participant by not recognizing his raised hand. If you do so in order to get another person to speak who until then has been withdrawn, you have a positive motive and effect on the group. But if you do so in order to promote your own ideas at the expense of others' (a selfish motive), the action can have a negative effect on the group.

As chairperson, you may decide that it is best to withdraw—that is, become an observer—when one of the members begins to criticize another's suggestions. In this way, a participant may be forced to justify her proposal, new information may emerge, and others may be persuaded of the validity of an idea more readily. Why not let a participant tell her peers what you want said?

Dominating involves pushing a special interest; it may include blocking by continuing to talk and not allowing another to get into the conversation. Whether these roles go unchecked and exhibit a positive or negative influence is up to the chairperson to determine. Use your good sense and listen intently. Try to get at the motive behind the role a member is playing. If, in your judgment, the motive is positive, let him continue; if not, take action.

Group-Serving Roles

Group-serving roles are almost always positive in their effects. No matter who practices them, their purpose is to draw members together and shed light where there was darkness. They all promote unity and harmony, and each is essential in order to reach a consensus. They tend to keep a meeting on track, while systematically separating the unimportant from the relevant.

Fortifying is the process by which a member adds encouragement and insights to already aired ideas. It helps members elaborate and interpret what has been said. *Initiating* introduces ideas and major points in order to get the reactions and contributions of group members. *Orienting* tells the members where they have been and where they are at present. It may serve to add emphasis or to clarify ideas, and it keeps people from traveling again over the same ground or going around in circles. *Researching* involves fact-finding and introducing background material pertinent to the discussion so as to remove smoke from people's eyes and substitute facts for fiction.

Observe and label these activities in your group encounters. You will see various positive and negative applications of all these roles in your classes at school, as well as in meetings at work. Study your instructor and the various roles she plays. You will pick up some valuable examples of each of these roles, most of which you will be able to use at work when you find yourself a group leader or participant. Exhibit 9.4 summarizes the various roles played in groups.

PITFALLS OF MEETINGS

Problem-solving sessions may not work well if leaders fail to enforce the ground rules listed above. In addition, other major pitfalls or traps can cause a meeting to be a sheer waste of time.

The Hidden Agenda

A member's hidden agenda consists of his personal feelings toward the subject discussed, the group itself, and the individuals who make up the group. We all have such an agenda whenever we attend a group session, whether with our formal or our informal group. Critical remarks toward group members or their ideas are often motivated by a dislike or distrust of those persons and

Roles played by group members.	Exhibit 9.4

SELF-SERVING ROLES	GROUP-SERVING ROLES
Attention-getting	Coordinating
Blocking	Fortifying
Criticizing	Initiating
Dominating	Orienting
Withdrawing	Researching

their intentions—not their ideas. You must recognize that, as chairperson, you have the duty to see behind the words and get to the motives. Often, you can nullify the hidden agenda's effect simply by explaining that another person or department does not necessarily have to gain at someone else's expense.

A Competitive Spirit

Competition is fine on the athletic field, but it has no real purpose among members of the team. Watch for the remark that attempts to build one person's reputation at the expense of another's. Nothing can ruffle feathers so quickly or create defensive reactions more effectively. A quick review of the second Hawthorne study should refresh your memory about intergroup competition and its dangers.

Chapter 7 discussed the now-famous experimental studies conducted in the late 1920s at Western Electric's Hawthorne plant. The second study uncovered the formation of two informal cliques—one quite strong and the other somewhat weak. Both influenced their members in significant ways. They offered proof that workers' cliques can be positive or negative factors with respect to company standards, policies, and regulations. If they view management favorably, they are capable of achieving standards of output even higher than management may expect. If they feel negative toward management, the informal group will generate much less production than expected. If the supervisor practices sound human relations and relates positively to her group of subordinates, she can influence their behavior and productivity.

Talkative Members

Have you ever tried to carry on a conversation with someone who only stopped talking to think about what to say next? It is quite a frustrating experience. Your voice only fills the gaps between his remarks. Listening is not one of that person's virtues. Members in meetings can quickly fall in love with their own voices and viewpoints. It is the chairperson's job to prevent this. Make sure that everyone has a say and that each person's views are duly noted. Chairpersons find that it is sometimes useful to avoid recognizing a talkative member's request to speak.

Sabotage

Group members sometimes carry on their own conversations while another is speaking; others may attempt to sidetrack the issue. These and similar tactics represent efforts to render a meeting useless. The subversive's motivation may be that failure to reach a decision will maintain the status quo. Disruptive behavior will weaken the will of the group to reach a decision and interest may wane. The chairperson must assess the motives and effects of conscious or accidental sabotage and must act to block it or to confront the saboteur directly. The meeting must be pulled back to its proper focus. Exhibit 9.5 gives you some alternatives for dealing with a disruptive group member.

Some tips for dealing with problem group members.	Exhibit 9.5

1. Try a one-on-one meeting. Schedule a meeting for just the two of you. Confront the person with your observations about how he is disrupting the group's efforts. Listen for all the reasons and perceptions that unfold. See if you can turn disruptive behaviors around with force-field analysis in the meeting or afterward.

2. Let the group confront the individual. Let the individual face the group members directly. Let the members air their grievances about the problem member's behaviors. Talk about the effects those behaviors are having on the group. Avoid personal attacks. Describe the behaviors that have negative consequences.

3. Place limits on the problem member's participation. Let the group leader prescribe the level of participation allowed. For example, the leader may want to deal directly with the individual after each meeting, not during it. Or the leader may not allow the problem member to participate in group discussions when disruptive behaviors occur.

4. Separate the problem member from the group meetings. Let the individual contribute, but on an individual basis, away from the other group members. Assign work that will help the team indirectly.

Informal Groups

Two or more people who come together by choice to satisfy mutual needs or to share common interests are considered an **informal group.** The feature that distinguishes formal from informal groups is the matter of choice. Informal groups or cliques form because of the mutual social needs of people. Formal groups can also be informal groups, provided that all members freely choose to associate with one another on and off the job. Every informal group has a leader. Unlike her counterpart in the formal group, the informal leader derives power through the informal means discussed in Chapter 3. Formal leaders of formal groups seldom have cliques of their own subordinates. This is as it should be. As we pointed out in Chapter 8, a manager's friends should be his peers.

informal group
two or more people who come together by choice to satisfy mutual needs or to share common interests

JOINING A CLIQUE

Once a new employee is hired, he is placed in a specific job, which makes him automatically a member of several formal groups that constitute the business enterprise. If the design of work and the working relationships permit them, informal groups or **cliques** will have been formed as well. The newcomer, like those who have preceded him, will naturally desire the companionship of one or more coworkers on a more or less regular basis, both during working hours and while on his own time.

clique
an informal group of two or more people who come together primarily on the basis of social rationales

The problem confronting the new arrival is that he is initially outside the existing informal groups and, although he desires membership in one of them, is not certain about which one to choose. He needs time to assess the values, attitudes, and reputation of each group. The groups in turn are

Informal groups often form when workers share the common interest of achieving a task.

going to be evaluating the person for prospective membership. In this sense, the new employee is similar to a person seeking admission to a fraternity or sorority. He has to look at what it stands for and get to know its members, while, in turn, its members look the applicant over.

You as a supervisor can do a great deal for new employees. If you know your people well and understand their groups, you can do all in your power to help newcomers gain admittance to a group of subordinates that will exert a constructive influence on them. You hope that all the informal cliques in your section are working with management and not against it. But if one or another is not, do your best to steer the new arrival away from that clique and into more beneficial surroundings. We cover this topic further in Chapter 11.

Before the individual on the outside of a clique can truly become a participating member of the clique, she must go through three separate but related stages of induction: observation, transformation, and confirmation.

Stage 1: Observation. Observation is the initial stage we all find ourselves in as newcomers. By necessity, we must remain neutral toward all the informal groups we encounter until we have time to know them. As time goes on, neutrality becomes increasingly difficult to maintain, as we feel pressure to make a decision or choice. We may begin a kind of trial membership period, wherein we are invited to participate with a group. While meeting with each clique, we are somewhat passive and open to group members' opinions and attitudes, preferring to listen rather than to speak our mind.

Stage 2: Transformation. The next step is for us to decide which group we like best. If the group honors our choice, we begin to confine our socializing almost exclusively to the new group. We mask any personal opinions that are contradictory to those the group holds as essential, and we begin to mouth agreement to these essential attitudes. Like a parrot, we begin to remember and repeat the sacred beliefs even though we may not agree with them. Without this stage, we can never really become an accepted member in a strong informal group.

Stage 3: Confirmation. The confirmation stage is complete when we actually abandon attitudes we once held that are in direct opposition to those of the group and adopt the group's values as our own. We give up our individuality while with the group, though we may retain it on our own. The group has changed us and our attitudes in much the same way as was discussed in Chapter 6. The difference is that several people may have been at work on us here instead of only one.

From this point on, the group has more influence over our behavior than any other force at work. We now weigh the relative merits of proposals against the group's willingness to accept them. If the group vetoes the action, each member feels bound to support that veto.

Not long ago, one of the authors' students relayed the following story. At the start of the business day one Friday, two of George's more able workers presented him with a petition signed by all 26 of his subordinates. It requested that the workday begin and end one-half hour earlier. George was quite concerned, since such a request was not in his power to grant, and he felt that the plant manager would not buy the suggestion. Wisely, he refrained from giving an immediate answer but assured the workers that he would consider the matter carefully.

Over the next two weeks George interviewed every worker to determine just how committed each of them was to the proposed change. The results were amazing. Two men were solidly in favor of the change—the same two who had confronted George with the petition and had initiated it. Eight workers were neutral but willing to go along with the others. The remaining 16 were clearly against it. After George announced his findings, the demand was dropped, and only two people were really unhappy with the decision.

What made the other workers sign? The two men were strong personalities, and one was an informal leader of a large clique. Beginning with his clique members, starting with the weakest, the informal leader got one signature after another until nearly two thirds of the workers had signed. The others fell into line when confronted with the sheer weight of numbers. Not wishing to obstruct the will of the majority, the few remaining holdouts also signed up.

YOU AND YOUR INFORMAL GROUP

The informal group that that you choose or that chooses you will have a dramatic and lasting impact on your reputation and your future. Choose any informal group with the same caution you would exercise when choosing a friend. Pick out the ones that will have the greatest positive effect on your growth and the ones that have the most to offer. As a result, some of their luster and brilliance will rub off on you. You are judged in part by the company you keep, so avoid groups bent on self-destruction.

One of the hazards inherent in membership in an informal group is the restrictions it places on your contacts with others. Once you have reached either the transformation or confirmation stage of induction, you probably have begun to confine your socializing at work to a specific few individuals. In time, you may become rather narrow and cut off from differing opinions. You may be denying yourself the valuable companionship and variety that others have to offer. Do not take yourself out of circulation. Break your routine on occasion, and mix and maintain contacts with others of similar rank.

COPING WITH SUBORDINATES' CLIQUES

Several important principles can help you minimize group conflicts and tensions and maximize group cooperation and contribution:

1. *Accept your subordinates' cliques as a fact of life.* Just as you belong to one or more, so it is with them. Consider their informal groups as allies and additional forces to be won over and brought to bear on mutual problems. The trick is to learn to work with them—not to fight them or try to eliminate them.

2. *Identify and enlist the cooperation of the informal leaders.* They represent a force with which to reckon. Many of them have the potential to be tomorrow's managers. The informal power they have over others can work for you both. Practice sound human relations with them as you would with anyone in your charge. Share with the best of them (whenever you can) some of your formal authority through delegation. They are usually perfect candidates for leadership roles. They also are ambitious people who recognize the advantages that management has to offer.

3. *Prevent intergroup competition and the occurrence of a win–lose situation.* Groups in conflict tend to tear at each other and to reduce the organization's overall effectiveness. Hold out standards to be achieved and surpassed. Use past performance records as targets to hit and scores to beat. These abstract enemies are harder to visualize but easier to beat.

4. *Do not force your people to choose between you and their group.* If you put it to them on an "either/or" basis, they will usually pick their group. Their loyalty to and membership in a clique does not have to be at your expense. They can be loyal and unopposed to you if you are predictable and loyal to them.

5. *Adopt a coach's attitude toward your group(s).* Foster a team spirit, and nurture the comradeship that cliques promote. Play fair, and demand that your subordinates do the same. Team players know the value of rules and team play. Enlist their participation as a group, and protect their self-image.

6. *Appeal to each group member and to each group's sense of competence.* We all have the urge to be good at what we do and to know that others think we are. Give your people a series of challenges that, when met, will give them a sense of accomplishment and pride.

7. *Use appropriate levers to influence people in specific situations.* Examples of levers include positive reinforcement such as incentives, group acceptance,

satisfaction of psychological needs, appeals to pride, and agreed-upon goals. The effectiveness of most of them has to do with your competence in interpersonal and intergroup relations.[45] By setting goals and helping your subordinates set their own, you will be providing incentives for excellence and ways for them to build confidence.

One example of this point involves assembly-line workers on a Corvette assembly operation. They were installing fiberglass parts provided by an outside supplier. These parts had rough edges in their openings that were designed to take dashboard instruments. The rough edges had to be filed clean before the instruments could be inserted. The supplier should have done this, not the assembly-line workers. To deal with the growing sense of frustration and irritation among the assembly workers, General Motors' supervisors arranged a meeting with the supplier's workers at the GM plant. The workers responsible for the rough-edged moldings witnessed firsthand how their sloppy work affected their counterparts. Moldings quickly began to arrive with smooth openings. All now knew why their work was necessary and what would happen at the other end when it was not done properly.

Group Competition

We have seen that intergroup competition at Hawthorne caused ill will and declining productivity within the formal group. Edgar H. Schein, a professor at MIT, has added much to our understanding of what happens within and between competing groups. Whether we are dealing with formal or informal groups, the following apply. Each competing group tends to:[46]

- Exhibit greater togetherness and cohesion
- Become more organized and highly structured
- Expect greater loyalty and conformity from its members
- Accept autocratic supervision willingly
- Become more task oriented and less concerned with the needs of individual members

All these results, at first glance, may appear to be desirable. But as we consider what happens between competing groups, the picture becomes less attractive. In Schein's words:

1. Each group begins to see the other group as the enemy, rather than merely a neutral object.

2. Each group begins to experience distortions of perception—it tends to perceive only the best parts of itself, denying its weaknesses, and tends to perceive only the worst parts of the other group, denying its strengths; each group is likely to develop a negative stereotype of the other. ("They don't play fair like we do.")

3. Hostility toward the other group increases while interaction and communication with the other group decrease; thus it becomes easier to maintain negative stereotypes and more difficult to correct perceptual distortions.

4. If the groups are forced into interaction—for example, if they are forced to listen to representatives plead their own and the others' cause in reference to some task—each group is likely to listen more closely to its own representative and not to listen to the representative of the other group, except to find fault with his presentation. In other words, group members tend to listen only for that which supports their own position and stereotype.[47]

If this intergroup competition—whether between informal or formal groups—results in one group's emerging as the victor and the other as vanquished, the problems compound dramatically. To paraphrase Schein, the winning group behaves in the following way:[48]

- Keeps its cohesiveness
- Tends to become self-satisfied
- Loses its task orientation and reemphasizes individual needs
- Becomes reassured that its self-image must be correct and loses the incentive to question its perceptions

On the other hand, the losing group:

- Becomes initially unrealistic about its perception of why it lost, tending to transfer blame to some external cause
- Tends to lose its cohesiveness
- Becomes more dedicated to tasks and winning
- Experiences less intra-group cooperation and less concern for individual needs
- Eventually reexamines its beliefs and self-image and becomes more realistic in its perceptions

It should be clear to you that intergroup competition has more disadvantages than advantages. The loser may improve, whereas the winner declines. This is not to say that competition is wrong—only that competition between groups within a company is dangerous. Competition can be a powerful tool to muster greater output and cohesiveness among your department's members, if the enemy is not a group of coworkers but rather some outside force or group. If the thing to be beaten is a standard or a past record of output, the group can muster its forces in a cooperative spirit to excel and exceed its previous record.

Outsiders and Insiders

You are affected each day at your workplace by many factors, some of which are outside your company and some of which are inside it. The same is true for your subordinates.

OUTSIDE FACTORS

When was the last time you went to work with a personal family problem so much on your mind that your performance suffered? Your family is but one of many outside groups that can influence your efficiency. Your academic classes in management may be another example. Sometimes what you learn will bring you into conflict with your traditional beliefs or with those of your boss, putting you at odds with him when you attempt to act on your new knowledge. You may find that you know more about a particular task and the best methods for dealing with it than your boss does. The problem will then be one of your selling your idea to your boss and getting permission to implement it.

Customers and competitors can place demands on the business, in turn directly affecting your operations. Their requests, threats, and innovations may be translated into new products, service methods, or procedures for your department. New schedules of production may be the result, with added pressures and tensions for you and those under you.

INSIDE FACTORS

The groups within the company that directly or indirectly affect your performance are your superiors, your peers, and your subordinates. Superiors construct the programs, policies, and regulations that you must enforce and translate to action. Your peers place demands on you for conformity, cooperation, and uniform approaches to problems. They form the nucleus of your friendships and place demands on your time and talents. Your subordinates, as members of your formal groups and as members of their own informal cliques, ask a great deal from you. How you cope with these groups and their demands directly relates to how well you can adjust to tension and frustration. You will be faced with many conflicts between what you think you should do and what others ask you to do. Often you must yield completely to the demands of others. On occasion, you must work out compromises.

Instant Replay

1. A group is two or more people who are aware of one another, who consider themselves to be a functioning unit, and who share a quest for a common goal or benefit.

2. In group problem solving, the roles that group members play may affect the group either positively or negatively, depending on the member's motivation.

3. Various pitfalls can undermine group meetings and their results. Being aware of them and acting to render them negligible is the job of every group leader.

4. Competition has both positive and negative effects on groups. Negative effects of intergroup competition can include hostility, lack of cooperation, and outright sabotage.

5. Supervisors must recognize that informal groups exist and can wield positive or negative power. Their leaders possess strong personalities and are potential management material.

Questions for Class Discussion

1. Can you define this chapter's key terms?

2. As a problem-solving group's chairperson, what should you do before, during, and after a session?

3. As a participating member of a problem-solving session, what should you do before, during, and after the session?

4. What are the group-serving and the self-serving roles played by group members in meetings?

5. What happens to the winning group in intergroup competition? To the losing group? Between the groups?

Incident

Many people work outside the office and factory. Some, such as outside sales people, must be with clients and customers regularly. Others work at home, linked to their boss and coworkers by e-mail, fax machines, telephones, and voice mail. Such an arrangement offers many advantages to both employee and employer. The employee can stay at home with children in need of day-care and avoid the time and expense of commuting to work. The company can operate in smaller spaces, providing less office furniture and equipment. But what about a team spirit linking the telecommuter to his coworkers and others at work?

Purpose: To consider team spirit issues for groups that include telecommuters and outside sales people, who normally work outside of the office or plant.

Your task: List as many ways as you can to include home-working employees in a group's efforts and activities at work. What would you do to instill the absent employees with a real spirit of teamwork?

CASE PROBLEM 9.1   *Team Punishment*

The module 986 motherboard team at the plant was holding a meeting to decide what to do about Theodore, one of their team members. Theodore loaded the wrong supply of resistors into the machine that assembles the boards before they are soldered. As a result, defective boards were produced for three entire days before the mistake was found. All of these boards had to be scrapped and the mistake caused a 10 percent decline in quality and productivity results for the month.

TRICIA: "Let's leave Theodore alone. He's got a lot on his mind and just made a mistake. He feels badly enough about his mistake and we all have good days and bad days. None of us is perfect and we shouldn't be punitive to someone who makes an honest mistake."

CAL: "No, we have to take action to let people know that we're serious about these performance standards. We don't have a boss looking over our shoulders anymore, and we won't have one as long as we manage the team ourselves. I don't like to be the bad guy either, but we're accountable for this team's performance."

CECIL: "Well, what should we do? Should we fire Theodore? This was a serious error. If we don't fire him he's got to know that he has to really concentrate on his job when he loads those components into the assembler. After the boards go through the wave-soldering machine there's nothing we can do."

MARGE: "Let's have a team meeting tonight and vote on whether we keep Theodore or fire him. Glen's not here now, but he'll be back after lunch. He feels strongly about this and can be sort of a prosecutor and argue why we should fire Theodore. Tricia can act as the defense and tell why we shouldn't fire him. That way we'll get both sides just like in a court and we can decide what to do. As long as Theodore gets more than half of the votes he gets to stay."

JAN: "Wow, that sounds like a really awful thing to do to someone. I don't like this at all. Do you people realize what you are saying? How would you like to be treated this way?"

CHRIS: "Jan, we've got to do something. Nobody likes to do this, but we can't have these kinds of quality and production screw-ups. Now, let's get back to the solution we were talking about. What happens if we vote to keep Theodore? How are we going to make sure that he doesn't make the same mistake again?"

RICH: "Well, we'll make Theodore wait out in the hall while we vote. If he wins the vote we'll go get him. Then, Theodore will have to stand up in front of us and read a formal apology. He can then tell us what he is going to do to avoid a similar mistake in the future. Now, let's decide if this is the procedure we should follow."

The team decided to return at 5:00 P.M. and vote on whether to keep or fire Theodore.

At 5:00 P.M. the team assembled to vote on Theodore. As Rich suggested, if the vote was in Theodore's favor, he would have to come into the room, read an apology, and tell the team how he would avoid making the same mistake in the future. If he lost the vote or refused to read the public apology he would be fired.

Just as the team prepared to vote on Theodore, Julio said: "We all used to get along together before we worked with this self-directed team stuff. Now Theodore thinks that he is being picked on because of prejudice. It looks to me like he's got a point. Of the two people disciplined by this team in the past, one was an African American and the other was Hispanic. It doesn't take much imagination to see a pattern here where most of the team is Caucasian and it's forcing higher standards on the minority members of the team. I didn't like the old boss we had either and really got tired of her micro-managing us, but at least she wasn't biased."

MARGE: "There's nothing discriminatory about this. Theodore made a really costly error. If anyone else makes such a mistake like that we'll vote on whether to keep him just like Theodore. Let's stop wasting time and vote."

Source: This case incorporates some ideas from an article by Timothy Aeppel, "Not All Workers Find Idea of Empowerment as Neat as It Sounds," The Wall Street Journal *(September 8, 1997): A1, A13.*

Questions

1. What will be the likely long-term consequences of this team's actions?
2. How do you think the team should enforce its standards?
3. Why do you think the team is taking this approach?
4. How should the team deal with diversity issues?

CASE PROBLEM 9.2   *Unhappy Returns*

Linda Carson is the supervisor of returns at a home improvement and building materials store. Yesterday she asked her associates to attend a meeting today before the store opens.

TOSHIRO: "I hope we're not going to have a long meeting today. Why are we meeting? I hate these early morning meetings."

LINDA: "The store manager asked us to come up with a way to reorganize the way we do returns in order to cut down on costs. Does anybody have any ideas?"

MICAELA: "Why do they want to cut down on costs in returns? Are our costs out of line with other departments?"

LINDA: "I don't know, the store manager didn't say. I don't think we need to know why or whether our costs are out of line. We're just supposed to do what the store manager asked us to do. Winfield, you've been here longer than anyone else. Do you have any ideas?"

WINFIELD: "No, but I'm flexible. I'll go along with what everyone else in the group wants."

BETSY: "I think turnover is too high."

TOMMY: "Wow, Betsy, where'd that idea come from? How's that going to cut costs? They're only paying us a little more than the minimum wage anyway. Who cares how much turnover we have?"

TOSHIRO: "Why don't we make it easier for customers to return merchandise? Right now we have to examine their receipts and then have them fill out a form that asks for lots of information. Then we have to check the form for completeness. With an easier return policy all we would have to do is give customers their money back or give them store credits."

MICAELA: "Oh, sure, we're just going to give customers their money back. Paul, what makes you think that would work? You should have seen this guy who came in yesterday. He was trying to return this smashed electric drill because he said there was a fault in it when it was manufactured. I could see tire tracks on it where someone had run over it with a truck. So Paul, should we give money back to people who try to rip us off?"

TOSHIRO: "Well, Katy, how many great ideas do you have?"

TOMMY: "Paul's right. What does it matter if some of these people rip us off as long as overall costs go down? Right now it is costing us more to process all of the paperwork than the cost of giving some guy a new electric drill or returning his money."

MICAELA: "Do you realize how many guys would come in here every day with bogus claims on broken tools if we made our return policy that easy? Get serious."

GINGER: "Linda, why should we help the company come up with ideas to save costs? We don't get paid very much anyway. Doesn't management get paid the big bucks to solve problems like this? What's in this for us if we come up with a good answer?"

LINDA: "Well, I didn't ask the store manager. I doubt that there will be anything except an opportunity to set things up like we want."

MICHELLE: "Well, I think the problem is that it takes too long to get anyone from the departments to come to the return counter to answer our questions. They just ignore us. Why doesn't anyone do something about that problem? Some of those guys are just worthless out there. I've called ten or more times with no response on several occasions."

MICAELA: "Yeah, I hate that. Linda, why don't you get the store manager to do something about that? Why don't we fix that problem? We've complained about that before but nobody ever does anything."

BETSY: "Hey, that's unrelated to the problem. Let's get back to my ideas about cutting down on turnover."

MICAELA: "Let's just vote on an idea and get it over with. How many in favor of Michelle's ideas about getting quicker answers from the departments?"

WINFIELD: "What are we voting on?"

LINDA: "We're not voting yet. Now, does anybody have any new ideas?"

BETSY: "I still think that turnover is the problem because there aren't enough of us who have much experience with returns."

TOMMY: "Betsy, nobody supports your idea about turnover. We're never going to reduce turnover because the work here is stressful and they don't pay us enough to stay very long. Why don't you quit talking about turnover and let someone else come up with a new idea?"

BETSY: "Linda, I think we could cut down on turnover if we could pay everybody 30 percent more."

LINDA: "Thanks, Betsy. Paul, do you have any ideas?"

TOSHIRO: "I don't like anything I've heard so far."

LINDA: "Winfield, you've been pretty quiet, what do you think?"

WINFIELD: "I can't think of anything."

LINDA: "It looks like we're running out of time. When shall we meet again?"

GINGER: "Are you kidding? You want us to meet again?"

LINDA: "I think so. Okay, until we meet again, be thinking of some ways to lower costs."

WINFIELD: "Linda, I just thought of a suggestion. Can you get the store manager to pay for some donuts next time we meet?"

Questions

1. What steps of the problem-solving process do you see in this case?
2. Evaluate how Linda has managed the meeting and the group.
3. How should Linda handle the next meeting?
4. What are the barriers to successful problem solving in this case?

References

1. Levering, Robert, and Moskowitz, Milton. "The 100 Best Companies to Work for in America," *Fortune* (January 12, 1998): 85.

2. Levering, Robert, and Moskowitz, Milton. "The 100 Best Companies to Work for," *Fortune* (January 8, 2001): 148–159.

3. Levering and Moskowitz. "The 100 Best Companies" (1998).

4. Martin, James. *Cybercorp: The New Business Revolution*. New York: American Management Association, 1996. Lozano, Juan. "Space Shuttle Captures Hubble Telescope," *Associated Press Newswires* (March 3, 2002).

5. Reich, Robert B. "Entrepreneurship Reconsidered: The Team As Hero," *Harvard Business Review* (May–June 1987): 77, 81, 82–83.

6. Ibid.

7. Ibid.

8. Katzenbach, Jon R., and Smith, Douglas K. *The Wisdom of Teams.* Boston: Harvard Business School Press (1993): 45.

9. Dumaine, Brian. "The Trouble with Teams," *Fortune* (September 5, 1994): 86–88.

10. Kizilos, Tolly, and Heinisch, Roger P. "How a Management Team Selects Managers," *Harvard Business Review* (September–October 1986): 6.

11. Hoerr, John. "The Cultural Revolution at A. O. Smith," *Business Week* (May 29, 1989): 66, 68.

12. McKee, Bradford. "Turn Your Workers into a Team," *Nation's Business* (July 1992): 37.

13. Woodruff, David. "Where Employees Are Management," *Business Week,* Bonus Issue (January 19, 1993): 66.

14. Wellins, Richard S.; Byham, William C.; and Wilson, Jeanne M. *Empowered Teams.* San Francisco: Jossey-Bass (1991): 135–138.

15. Thoman, Steven. "Roadblocks to Effective Team Dynamics in the IPPD Environment," *Program Manager* (July/August 2000): 104–108.

16. Wellins, Byham, and Wilson. *Empowered Teams.*

17. Ibid.

18. Maclean, John N. "Rail Equipment Company Learns ABCs of Success," *Chicago Tribune* (November 6, 1994): sec. 7, 1, 4.

19. Ibid.

20. Ibid.

21. Olberding, Sara R. "Site Visit," *Journal for Quality and Production* (May/June 1998): 55–59.

22. Freiberg, Kevin, and Freiberg, Jackie. *Nuts! Southwest Airlines' Crazy Recipe for Business and Personal Success.* Austin, TX: Bard Press, 1996. Gittell, Judy Hoffer. "Investing in Relationships," *Harvard Business Review* (June 2001): 28–29.

23. Ricadela, Aaron. "Office of the Future: A New Way to Work," *Information Week* (January 28, 2002): 42–47.

24. Shea, Gregory P., and Guzzo, Richard A. "Group Effectiveness, What Really Matters," *Sloan Management Review (28)* 3 (Spring 1987): 25–26.

25. Ibid.

26. Ibid.

27. Dumaine. "The Trouble with Teams."

28. Dumaine, Brian. "Mr. Learning Organization," *Fortune* (October 17, 1994): 147–148, 150, 154–157.

29. McDermott, Lynda C.; Brawley, Nolan; and White, William W. *World Class Teams: Working Across Borders.* New York: John Wiley & Sons, Inc. (1998): 168.

30. Shea and Guzzo. "Group Effectiveness."

31. Reich, Robert B., Bittel, Lester R., and Ramsey, Jackson E. (eds.), *Handbook for Professional Managers.* New York: McGraw-Hill (1985): 218.

32. Cohen, Allan R., and Bradford, David L. "Influence Without Authority: The Use of Alliances, Reciprocity, and Exchange to Accomplish Work," *Organizational Dynamics* (Winter 1989): 5–17.

33. Smith, Donald G. *The Joy of Negative Thinking.* Philadelphia: Delancey Press (1994): 93.

34. Aeppel, Timothy. "Not All Workers Find Idea of Empowerment as Neat as It Sounds," *The Wall Street Journal* (September 8, 1997): A1, A13.

35. Ibid.

36. Ibid.

37. Schuler, Randall S. "Brainstorming," in Nigel Nicholson (ed.), *The Blackwell Encyclopedic Dictionary of Organizational Behavior.* Oxford, United Kingdom: Blackwell. (1995): 35.

38. Ibid.

39. Mulvey, Paul W.; Veiga, John F.; and Elsass, Priscilla M. "When Teammates Raise a White Flag," *Academy of Management Executive* (February 1996): 40–49.

40. Ibid.

41. Feinberg, Mortimer, and Tarrant, John J. *Why Smart People Do Dumb Things.* New York: Fireside, 1995.

42. Ibid.

43. Mulvey, Veiga, and Elsass. "When Teammates Raise."

44. Ibid.

45. Sasser, Jr., Earl W., and Leonard, Frank S. "Let First-Level Supervisors Do Their Job," *Harvard Business Review* (March–April 1980): 119–120.

46. Schein, Edgar H. *Organizational Psychology,* 2nd ed. Englewood Cliffs, NJ: Prentice Hall, 1970.

47. Ibid.

48. Ibid.

LEADERSHIP AND MANAGEMENT STYLES

Objectives

After reading and discussing this chapter, you should be able to do the following:

1. Define this chapter's key terms.

2. List and give examples of this chapter's principles of leadership.

3. Briefly define the contingency model of leadership.

4. Briefly explain the leadership concept of blending concern for production with concern for people.

5. List and give situations in which each of the management styles would be appropriate.

6. Explain the steps involved in charismatic leadership.

7. List and briefly explain the leadership indicators.

Introduction

In Chapter 3, we defined authority as the right to give orders and instructions. Power was defined as the ability to influence others—to get them to subject their wills to yours. In this chapter, we will see that leadership is based on both power and authority but depends most heavily on power. Although all managers need authority—the ability to punish and reward that rests in their formal positions—manager–leaders need both power and authority. It is possible to be a manager and yet not be a leader. Exhibit 10.1 relates these two concepts. On the left, we find managers having only management ability, who rely solely on formal authority to influence people. On the right, we find non-managers who possess leadership ability and have power from other sources to influence people. In the middle, we find manager–leaders—those managers who couple their formal authority with their personal power.

Exhibit **10.1** *The relationship between managers and leaders.*

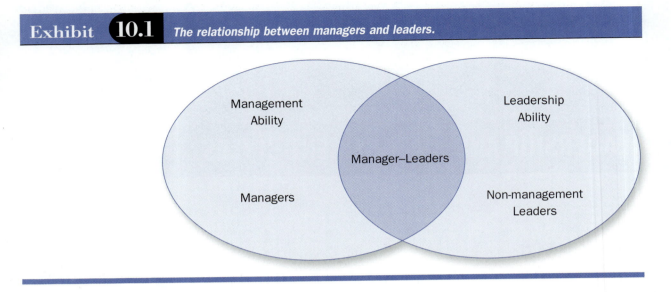

Exhibit 10.2 shows the differences between leadership and management in a different way. It contrasts the traditional roles of a manager with the traditional ways in which leaders handle the same functions. Notice the emphasis given to the leader's role in regard to change. Harvard professors John P. Kotter and James L. Heskett have studied companies that went through major cultural changes and the roles that their manager–leaders played in making those changes. They have found that the primary duties of leaders of change are to sense when change is needed, create a vision of what is needed and a strategy for change, sell the vision and the strategy to followers, and see to it that meaningful changes take place. Author John Huey adds:

> As the power of position continues to erode, corporate leaders are going to resemble not so much captains of ships as candidates running for office. They will face two fundamental tasks: first, to develop and articulate exactly what the company is trying to accomplish, and second, to create an environment in which employees can figure out what needs to be done and then do it well. . . . They are confident enough in their vision to delegate. . . . And they are careful to "model," or live by, the values they espouse.[1]

Chapter 3 pointed out that power comes from one's position. As a manager, you have the right to punish and reward. Power also originates in your personality, competencies, interpersonal relationships, and reputation at work. People look up to authorities who have the expertise they lack. People respect others who are fair and honest. They want to be with and work for others whom they can trust. But trust must be mutual. If you don't trust your people, they will find it difficult to trust you. Trust in your people comes from knowing them well—their abilities, goals, and values.

	Exhibit 10.2
The differences between management and leadership.	

MANAGEMENT	LEADERSHIP
Planning and Budgeting—establishing detailed steps and timetables for achieving needed results, and then allocating the resources necessary to make that happen	**Establishing Direction**—developing a vision of the future, often the distant future, and strategies for producing the changes needed to achieve that vision
Organizing and Staffing—establishing some structure for accomplishing plan requirements, staffing that structure with individuals, delegating responsibility and authority for carrying out the plan, providing policies and procedures to help guide people, and creating methods or systems to monitor implementation	**Aligning People**—communicating the direction by words and deeds to all those whose cooperation may be needed so as to influence the creation of teams and coalitions that understand the vision and strategies, and accept their validity
Controlling and Problem Solving—monitoring results versus plan in some detail, identifying deviations, and then planning and organizing to solve these problems	**Motivating and Inspiring**—energizing people to overcome major political, bureaucratic, and resource barriers to change by satisfying very basic, but often unfulfilled, human needs
Produces a degree of predictability and order, and has the potential of consistently producing key results expected by various stakeholders (for example, for customers, always being on time; for stockholders, being on budget)	Produces change, often to a dramatic degree, and has the potential of producing extremely useful change (for example, new products that customers want, new approaches to labor relations that help make a firm more competitive)

Source: John P. Kotter, *A Force for Change: How Leadership Differs from Management,* New York: The Free Press (1990): 6.

You demonstrate it in what you say and do each day. The example you give sets the tone for your interrelationships and encourages others to use it as an acceptable model for their own behavior. Buck Rodgers, a former vice-president at IBM, puts it this way:

> The people you're trying to motivate have to believe that you have more leverage in the company than they have. They have to accept you as an authority figure whose influence can help or hurt them . . . but they must respect you for your integrity and your ability, and that doesn't come with a title—it has to be earned. If your people see you as a person who can get things done—one who will deliver as promised, who can be trusted, and who can be relied on to help them—you are a leader in their eyes and according to their perceptions.[2]

The following excerpt provides a powerful example of leadership by example. It describes an incident during World War II in which Brigadier General Norman Cota of the U. S. Army found infantrymen stalled by hostile fire from a farmhouse. Cota asked the officer in charge what the problem was:

"Sir, the Germans are in there, shooting as us," the captain replied.

"Well, I'll tell you what, captain," said Cota, unbuckling two grenades from his jacket. "You and your men start shooting at them. I'll take a squad of men and you and your men watch carefully. I'll show you how to take a house with Germans in it."

Cota led his squad around a hedge to get as close as possible to the house. Suddenly, he gave a whoop and raced forward, the squad following, yelling like wild men. As they tossed grenades into the windows, Cota and another man kicked in the front door, tossed a couple of grenades inside, waited for the explosions, then dashed into the house. The surviving Germans were streaming out the back door, running for their lives.

Cota returned to the captain. "You've seen how to take a house," said the general, still out of breath. "Do you understand? Do you know how to do it now?"

"Yes, sir."

"Well I won't be around to do it for you again," Cota said. "I can't do it for everybody."[3]

Leadership

leadership

the ability to get work done with and through others while winning their respect, confidence, loyalty, and willing cooperation

Leadership is the ability to get work done with and through others while winning their respect, confidence, loyalty, and willing cooperation. The first part of our definition is true of management as well. It is the second half of the definition that distinguishes a leader from a non-leader. It is likely that though you may be a leader to some of your subordinates, you may not be to others. The goal is to be a leader to all of your subordinates. Leadership is an art that can be acquired and developed by anyone with the motivation to do so.

LEADERSHIP PRINCIPLES

Established principles or guidelines should govern the exercise of your informal and formal authority. Exhibit 10.3 lists 11 principles of leadership.

Each of these principles provides sound advice for leaders in any position. They serve as concise reminders and as a checklist to which you should frequently refer. They constitute a handy guide to help you assess your practice of management and the exercise of authority over others. If you understand their meaning and make an honest effort to act in accordance with their wisdom, you can avoid many errors and problems.

You should note a similarity between the leadership principles identified in Exhibit 10.3 and the technical, conceptual, and interpersonal skills discussed in Chapter 1. Principles one, six, and ten relate to your development and use of technical skills. Principles three, four, five, and six relate to your interpersonal skills. Principles seven, nine, and ten relate to conceptual skills. All the traits mentioned earlier relate in some way to each of the principles.

| Principles of leadership. | Exhibit 10.3 |

1. Be technically proficient.

2. Know yourself and seek self-improvement.

3. Know your people and look out for their welfare.

4. Keep your people informed.

5. Set the example.

6. Ensure that each task is understood, supervised, and accomplished.

7. Train your people to work as a team.

8. Make sound and timely decisions.

9. Develop a sense of responsibility in your subordinates.

10. Employ your resources in accordance with their capabilities.

11. Seek responsibilities and accept accountability for your actions.

Source: U. S. Army.

LEADERSHIP TRAITS AND SKILLS

Since the early 1900s, attempts have been made to discover a list of traits that would guarantee leadership status to their possessor. The U. S. Army surveyed all levels of soldiers exiting the service in the late 1940s to determine what traits were possessed by the commanders who were perceived to be effective leaders. Although a list of 14 traits emerged from the survey, no commander had all the traits listed, and many famous commanders lacked several.

A list of leadership traits and skills appears in Exhibit 10.4. Because the list is extensive, it is unlikely that any manager–leader would possess all of them. Research has failed to give us a final list of traits that guarantee leadership status to those who possess them. Certain traits may be considered indispensable, whereas others may be a plus but not essential. All the traits and skills listed can be developed and perfected through developmental programs emphasizing education, training, and leadership experiences.

FUNDAMENTAL PRACTICES OF LEADERSHIP

In contrast to the lists of traits in Exhibit 10.4, recent research on leadership has identified five fundamental leadership practices (behaviors) that

Exhibit 10.4 — Traits and skills commonly associated with leader effectiveness.

TRAITS	SKILLS
Adaptable to situations	Clever (intelligent)
Alert to social environment	Conceptually skilled
Ambitious and achievement oriented	Creative
Assertive	Diplomatic and tactful
Cooperative	Fluent in speaking
Decisive	Knowledgeable about group task
Dependable	Organized (administrative ability)
Dominant (desire to influence others)	Persuasive
Energetic (high activity level)	Socially skilled
Persistent	
Self-confident	
Tolerant of stress	
Willing to assume responsibility	

Source: LEADERSHIP IN ORGANIZATIONS, 1/E by Yukl, Gary. © 1981. Adapted by permission of Pearson Education, Inc., Upper Saddle River, NJ.

are necessary for exemplary leadership. Contradicting some of the leadership literature of the past, this research finds no support for the notion that leaders should be charismatic or that the position of leaders is lonely. Instead, the research indicates that exemplary leaders are heavily involved with their followers, about whom they care deeply and to whom they are committed. Exhibit 10.5 lists the five leadership practices and 10 commitments of leadership.

It is important that leaders demonstrate to their followers that they care about them. The following suggestions can help leaders increase their interaction with subordinates and communicate caring:[4]

- Walk the halls at least 30 minutes each day, stopping to talk with people who aren't on your daily calendar.
- Forget the chain of command: strike up conversations with colleagues, customers, suppliers, shareholders, and the person next to you in the elevator.
- Don't eat alone at your desk; go out to lunch with people from other functional areas.
- Leave your office door open (if you have one).
- Move your desk onto the factory floor.
- Sip a cup of coffee in everyone's favorite gathering place.
- Put a popcorn machine outside your work area.

| | Ten commitments of leadership. | **Exhibit** **10.5** |

PRACTICES	COMMITMENTS
Challenging the Process	1. *Search out* challenging opportunities to change, grow, innovate, and improve. 2. *Experiment,* take risks, and learn from the accompanying mistakes.
Inspiring a Shared Vision	3. *Envision* an uplifting and ennobling future. 4. *Enlist* others in a common vision by appealing to their values, interests, hopes, and dreams.
Enabling Others to Act	5. *Foster* collaboration by promoting cooperative goals and building trust. 6. *Strengthen* people by giving power away, providing choice, developing competence, assigning critical tasks, and offering visible support.
Modeling the Way	7. *Set the example* by behaving in ways that are consistent with shared values. 8. *Achieve* small wins that promote consistent progress and build commitment.
Encouraging the Heart	9. *Recognize* individual contributions to the success of every project. 10. *Celebrate* team accomplishments regularly.

Source: James M. Kouses and Barry Z. Posner, *The Leadership Challenge: How to Keep Getting Extraordinary Things Done in Organizations.* Copyright © 1995 by Jossey-Bass. This material is used by permission of Jossey-Bass, Inc., a subsidiary of John Wiley & Sons, Inc.

LEADERS OF DIVERSE WORKFORCES

Leaders routinely rely on a participative leadership style. But leading a diverse workforce calls for leaders who truly value diversity. Pluralistic leaders help create work environments that invite everyone's involvement by promoting cooperation and mutual respect.[5] Here are two suggestions to help you become a pluralistic leader.

First, uncover barriers. You need to know what problems, if any, exist for the individuals under your influence. Do company policies, customs, rituals, ceremonies, and procedures block their progress? Do they ridicule or ignore anyone's ethnic background or personal condition? If so, what can be done to eliminate the barriers? Are diverse individuals and groups able to communicate and work in harmony with one another? If not, why not? Is your company's management really committed to valuing diversity and empowering women,

the differently abled, and minorities? You should examine your own attitudes for any biases, values, stereotypes, and actions that inhibit your ability to value and lead people who are different from you. You can use personal interviews, group meetings, an anonymous survey, or a combination of these to help you.

Second, make personal commitments. You need to have an honest commitment to encourage two-way communication between you and individuals different from you. Through such communication you gain new knowledge and perceptions that help you better understand each individual for whose working life you are responsible. You must have a personal commitment to eliminate unequal and unfair treatment based on an individual's age, sex, sexual orientation, physical limitations, race, nation of origin, or religion. Make a commitment to train, coach, and empower your diverse subordinates to draw the best from them. "It's not enough to hire for diversity; you must also plan for the development of your nontraditional workers."[6] When an organization cannot keep its diverse employees, it usually means that the organization is sending clear signals that success is not possible for those people.

MEN, WOMEN, AND LEADERSHIP

A study of 456 executives (355 women and 101 men) reveals some interesting differences between the ways in which both sexes approach the leadership role. Women respondents tend to be interactive—encouraging others' participation, making people feel part of the organization, and making them feel good about themselves and their contributions. Female respondents also made frequent references to their efforts to include others by sharing power and information. Interactive leaders:

> try to instill . . . group identity in a variety of ways, including encouraging others to have a say in almost every aspect of work, from setting performance goals to determining strategy. To facilitate inclusion, they create mechanisms to get people to participate and they use a conversational style that sends signals inviting people to get involved.[7]

The men in the survey described their styles as being a set of "transactions with subordinates—exchanging rewards for services rendered or punishment for inadequate performance. The men were are also more likely to use power that comes from their organizational position and formal authority."[8]

Both the men and the women claimed to have an equal mix of traits considered to be feminine (understanding, compassion, sensitivity, dependency), masculine (dominance, toughness, assertiveness, competitiveness), and gender neutral (adaptability, tact, sincerity, efficiency, and reliability). Some men lead with participation and inclusion, and some women lead by exercising their formal authority. While one style may be optimal under a specific set of circumstances, it may be ineffective in another. Thus the lesson is that good leaders adapt their styles to the specific context.[9] Both styles of leading can be effective, depending on the circumstances. Both men and women have much to learn from each other's styles.

SUPERVISORS AND QUALITY

Older workers bring years of experience and skill to a job and an organization. They also bring stereotypes. Terry A. Barclay heads Operation Able, a Michigan-based nonprofit training and counseling agency for persons age 45 and older. According to Barclay, "The stereotype in our culture is that older workers are resistant to change. The reality is all of us are resistant to change. . . . I have yet to encounter an older worker who wasn't just as capable as a younger worker of learning a new skill."

To bring out the best in every associate, regardless of age, an environment that encourages learning and risk-taking while making people feel secure and valued is a must. Helen Dennis, author of *Fourteen Steps in Managing an Aging Work Force,* observes that "An older worker may have more to lose than a younger worker. The chances of finding a comparable job with comparable salary and benefits at age 55 are not high." Managing a diverse workforce requires training that encourages people to learn "at their own pace . . . in a nonthreatening, noncompetitive environment." It also requires supervisors, team leaders, and team facilitators to uncover their associates' motives and goals. "Sometimes older workers want different things from work than younger ones," says Dennis. "[T]hey

want a chance to be creative, to mentor, to solve problems, to feel they've made a difference. One of the worst feelings is to leave the work force after 35 years feeling like you haven't made a difference. A lot of older workers want to leave a legacy, to pass on their knowledge."

Michelle Gaggini, at age 23, practically began her career as a supervisor of older employees. "Older workers have a lot of experience, often a lot of loyalty. They can offer qualities to the company that younger workers don't have yet." To gain their commitment and support, Gaggini tries "to give them assignments that make them feel successful, perhaps asking them to lead a group project that will benefit from their experience." She avoids making employment decisions based solely on age; such decisions may result in charges of age discrimination.

Instead, she works hard at building older workers' self-confidence and building in chances for early success. To guarantee quality decisions and performances, Gaggini tries a variety of approaches; she consults with and listens to her people. She allows them a certain degree of personal freedom but believes it is important to "have agreement on the essentials . . . and harmony on the nonessentials."

Source: Charles E. Cohen, "Managing Older Workers," *Working Woman* (November 1994); 61–62. Copyright 2002 © by WMAC, Inc. Rights reserved. Used with permission of Working Mother Media.

LEADERSHIP BEHAVIORS

Extensive research by Gary Yukl and his colleagues reveals 19 categories of leader behavior. These categories, along with definitions and examples, are presented in Exhibit 10.6. The categories clearly label what leaders do and help us recognize these behaviors in our own daily lives. Since these behaviors are quite specific, they can help you identify how to be a better leader. As you study the 19 categories, rate yourself on how many of them you put to use regularly. Try to link each behavior to the skills and traits in Exhibit 10.4. Then try to relate each to your knowledge of human motivation and to the various theories we examined in Chapter 7. Finally, consider how each ties in with your roles as educator, counselor, judge, and spokesperson.

Exhibit **10.6** *Yukl's 19 categories of leader behavior.*

1. **Performance Emphasis:** The extent to which a leader emphasizes the importance of subordinate performance, tries to improve productivity and efficiency, tries to keep subordinates working up to their capacity, and checks on their performance.

   EXAMPLE: My supervisor urged us to be careful not to let orders go out with defective components.

2. **Consideration:** The extent to which a leader is friendly, supportive, and considerate in his or her behavior toward subordinates and tries to be fair and objective.

   EXAMPLE: When a subordinate was upset about something, the supervisor was very sympathetic and tried to console him.

3. **Inspiration:** The extent to which a leader stimulates enthusiasm among subordinates for the work of the group and says things to build subordinates' confidence in their ability to perform assignments successfully and attain group objectives.

   EXAMPLE: My boss told us we were the best design group he had ever worked with, and he was sure that this new product was going to break every sales record in the company.

4. **Praise–Recognition:** The extent to which a leader provides praise and recognition to subordinates with effective performance, shows appreciation for their special efforts and contributions, and makes sure they get credit for their helpful ideas and suggestions.

   EXAMPLE: In a meeting, the supervisor told us she is very satisfied with our work and said she appreciated the extra effort we made this month.

5. **Structuring Reward Contingencies:** The extent to which a leader rewards effective subordinate performance with tangible benefits, such as a pay increase, promotion, more desirable assignments, a better work schedule, and more time off.

   EXAMPLE: My supervisor established a new policy that any subordinate who brought in a new client would earn 10 percent of the contracted fee.

6. **Decision Participation:** The extent to which a leader consults with subordinates and otherwise allows them to influence his or her choices.

   EXAMPLE: My supervisor asked me to attend a meeting with him and his boss to develop a new production schedule, and he was very receptive to my ideas on the subject.

7. **Autonomy–Delegation:** The extent to which a leader delegates authority and responsibility to subordinates and allows them to determine how to do their work.

   EXAMPLE: My boss gave me a new project and encouraged me to handle it any way I think is best.

8. **Role Clarification:** The extent to which a leader informs subordinates about their duties and responsibilities, specifies the rules and policies that must be observed, and lets subordinates know what is expected of them.

   EXAMPLE: My boss called me in to inform me about a rush project that must be given top priority, and she gave me some specific assignments related to this project.

9. **Goal Setting:** The extent to which a leader emphasizes the importance of setting specific performance goals for each important aspect of a subordinate's job, measures progress toward the goals, and provides concrete feedback.

   EXAMPLE: The supervisor held a meeting to discuss the sales quota for next month.

10. **Training–Coaching:** The extent to which a leader determines training needs for subordinates and provides any necessary training and coaching.

    EXAMPLE: My boss asked me to attend an outside course at the company's expense and said I could leave early on the days it was to be held.

11. **Information Dissemination:** The extent to which a leader keeps subordinates informed about developments that affect their work, including events in other work units or outside the organization, decisions made by higher management, and progress in meetings with superiors or outsiders.

> EXAMPLE: The supervisor briefed us about some high-level changes in policy.

12. **Problem Solving:** The extent to which a leader takes the initiative in proposing solutions to serious work-related problems and acts decisively to deal with such problems when a prompt solution is needed.

> EXAMPLE: The unit was short-handed due to illness, and we had an important deadline to meet; my supervisor arranged to borrow two people from other units, so we could finish the job today.

13. **Planning:** The extent to which a leader plans how to efficiently organize and schedule the work in advance, plans how to attain work unit objectives, and makes contingency plans for potential problems.

> EXAMPLE: My supervisor devised a shortcut that allows us to prepare our financial statements in three days instead of the four days it used to take.

14. **Coordinating:** The extent to which a leader coordinates the work of subordinates, emphasizes the importance of coordination, and encourages subordinates to coordinate their activities.

> EXAMPLE: My supervisor had subordinates who were ahead in their work help those who were behind so that the different parts of the project would be ready at the same time.

15. **Work Facilitation:** The extent to which a leader obtains for subordinates any necessary supplies, equipment, support services, or other resources; eliminates problems in the work environment; and removes other obstacles that interfere with the work.

> EXAMPLE: I asked my boss to order some supplies, and he arranged to get them right away.

16. **Representation:** The extent to which a leader establishes contacts with other groups and important people in the organization, persuades them to appreciate and support his or her work unit, and uses his or her influence with superiors and outsiders to promote and defend the interests of the work unit.

> EXAMPLE: My supervisor met with the data processing manager to get some revisions made in the computer programs, so they will be better suited to our needs.

17. **Interaction Facilitation:** The extent to which a leader tries to get subordinates to be friendly with each other, cooperate, share information and ideas, and help each other.

> EXAMPLE: The sales manager took the group out to lunch to give everybody a chance to get to know the new sales representative.

18. **Conflict Management:** The extent to which a leader restrains subordinates from fighting and arguing, encourages them to resolve conflicts in a constructive manner, and helps settle conflicts and disagreements between subordinates.

> EXAMPLE: Two members of the department who were working together on a project were having a dispute about it; the manager met with them to help resolve the matter.

19. **Criticism–Discipline:** The extent to which a leader criticizes or disciplines a subordinate who shows consistently poor performance, violates a rule, or disobeys an order; disciplinary actions include an official warning, reprimand, suspension, or dismissal.

> EXAMPLE: The supervisor was annoyed that a subordinate kept making the same kinds of errors and warned him to make a more concerted effort.

Source: LEADERSHIP IN ORGANIZATIONS, 1/E by Yukl, Gary. © 1981. Adapted by permission of Pearson Education, Inc., Upper Saddle River, NJ.

The Contingency Model of Leadership

Fred E. Fiedler and others have speculated that the effectiveness of a group or organization depends on two main factors: (1) the leader's personality and (2) the leadership situation. As a consequence of their personalities, leaders tend to be either task oriented or relationship oriented. The situation determines the leader's authority and power and places limits on his ability to get things done through others. Fiedler's situational factors include leader–member relations, task structure, and the leader's positional authority to punish or to reward.[10]

LEADERSHIP PERSONALITIES

According to Fiedler's contingency model (sometimes called *situational leadership)*, leaders are primarily motivated by their tasks or their interpersonal relationships with their followers. Whether one or the other is an appropriate focus depends on the leader's situation. Task-oriented leaders seek accomplishments that fortify their sense of self-esteem and competence. Relationship-oriented leaders seek the admiration and respect of their followers to meet their social and esteem needs. Both types of leaders need to be able to play both kinds of roles. The task-oriented leader may, as the need arises, adopt the relationship orientation. A relationship-oriented leader may focus on getting the job done when a crisis arises and time is short. But each will then return to her former orientation. This flexibility marks a true leader who is destined to achieve higher authority. Not all people have this flexibility.

THE LEADERSHIP SITUATION

According to Fiedler's contingency model, a leader's situation has three variables: (1) the degree to which the leader is or feels accepted by followers, (2) the degree to which the task to be accomplished is structured or defined, and (3) the extent of the leader's power—her job description and the influence over others in the organization. The greater the leader's power and acceptance by followers, and the more highly structured the task, the easier it is for the leader to control a situation.

The interaction of these variables is shown in Exhibit 10.7. At the bottom of the figure are eight combinations of the three variables, each describing a possible work situation. In position III, for example, the manager enjoys good member relations, the tasks of the subordinates are unstructured, and the leader possesses a strong organizational power base.

In the upper half of the figure are the two orientation styles: employee orientation and task orientation. In position I—where leader–member relations are good, the task is structured, and leader position power is strong—the manager should employ a task-oriented approach. In position IV—where leader–member relations are good, the task is unstructured, and leader position power is weak—employee-oriented behavior would be more appropriate.

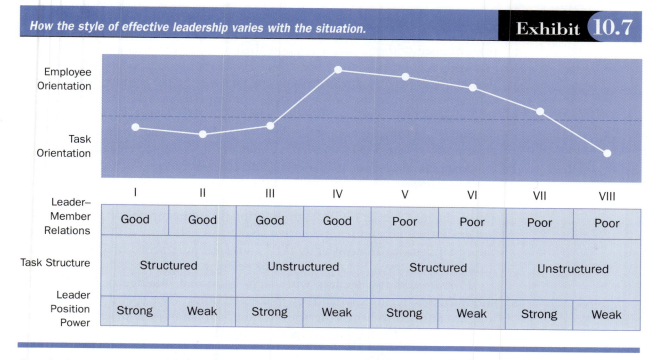

How the style of effective leadership varies with the situation.

Exhibit 10.7

	I	II	III	IV	V	VI	VII	VIII
Leader–Member Relations	Good	Good	Good	Good	Poor	Poor	Poor	Poor
Task Structure	Structured		Unstructured		Structured		Unstructured	
Leader Position Power	Strong	Weak	Strong	Weak	Strong	Weak	Strong	Weak

Research into the contingency model shows that task-oriented leaders perform best when they have either high or low concentrations of power, control, and influence over their situations. Relationship-oriented leaders perform best with moderate power, control, and influence. Leaders should be matched to the situation that calls for their favored approach or orientation. Instead, organizations often require managers to adjust to a variety of situations calling for different approaches.

Emotional Intelligence

Daniel Goleman has developed a concept called *emotional intelligence,* which appears to be a critical characteristic of effective leaders. Goleman has found that there are five components of emotional intelligence: self-awareness, self-regulation, motivation, empathy, and social skill. *Self-awareness* essentially refers to one's understanding of how pressures and influences from others affect one's own behavior toward others. For example, leaders with high self-awareness who know that they may react poorly toward others when facing a tight deadline focus on preparation and lead-time to avoid the pressures of deadlines. Another example is that they ask for help when overloaded.[11]

Self-regulation pertains to controlling one's emotions. For example, when a team the leader is supervising has performed poorly, she would not lash out at the team or engage in a display of anger and bad temper. Instead, the leader would calmly and carefully provide feedback regarding the poor performance without judgment and then analyze the reasons for the poor performance, including her own role. The leader would assemble the team, describe the performance, provide an analysis of the causes, and offer a solution or involve the group in development of a solution. Self-regulation is in stark contrast to the impulsiveness of leaders whose fiery temper and outbursts are sometimes described as components of charismatic leadership. Goleman's research has found that such impulsiveness typically limits the effectiveness of leaders at higher organizational levels.

Motivation in terms of emotional intelligence means that the leader has a greater desire to achieve than to obtain an impressive title, big salary, or status. Instead leaders with high emotional intelligence have a passion for the work they do and want creative challenges. They are also committed to the organization. Interestingly, they enjoy keeping score of how they are doing and continually raise the bar of performance.

Empathy allows leaders with high emotional intelligence to factor in subordinates' feelings when they make decisions. They spend time listening and are attuned to how others are feeling. Goleman provides the following strong support for the importance of empathy:

> In what is probably sounding like a refrain, let me repeat that empathy doesn't get much respect in business. People wonder how leaders can make hard decisions if they are "feeling" for all the people who will be affected. But leaders with empathy do more than sympathize with people around them: they use their knowledge to improve their companies in subtle but important ways.[12]

The final component of emotional intelligence is *social skill,* which enables leaders with high emotional intelligence to maintain good interpersonal relationships. Such skills enable leaders to find common ground with a variety of people, establish rapport, and understand others.

Level Five Leaders

Jim Collins and his research team studied companies that made the transition from being only good to great. They classified companies on the basis of their stock returns over a period of 30 years and identified 11 companies that met the criterion of reaching a transition point after which they obtained stock returns at least three times the level of the market for a period of 15 years. When they examined the difference between a comparison group of companies and great companies, they found that outstanding leadership was one of the factors that made the difference in their success. As a result of their studies of great companies, they developed a concept called *Level 5 Leadership*.

Collins and his team found that Level 5 leaders are characterized by personal humility, in that they are modest and not boastful; they attribute their company's success to other people and not to themselves. They also have fierce resolve and a quiet determination. Their determination has been described as "an unwavering resolve to do whatever must be done to produce the best long-term results, no matter how difficult."[13] They motivate others with high standards instead of personal charisma. When things go wrong they look in the mirror to assign blame, but when they assign credit for successes they look out the window toward others. Their ambition is typically manifested in a desire for the company to flourish in the future, instead of personal ambition. Examples of Level 5 leaders include Alan Wurtzel, former CEO of Circuit City, and the late Darwin Smith, a previous CEO of Kimberly-Clark.[14] The research results of Collins and his team illustrate the importance of having the right people in place. Their results indicate that Level 5 leaders started with getting the right people in place instead of beginning with a vision or strategy:

> We expected that good-to-great leaders would start with the vision and strategy. Instead, they attended to people first, strategy second. They got the right people on the bus, moved the wrong people off, ushered the right people to the right seats—and then they figured out where to drive it.[15]

Management and Leadership Styles

Four main styles of management are available to you: bureaucratic, autocratic, democratic, and spectator. All but the bureaucratic style are leadership styles. Each can have either a positive or a negative impact on your subordinates, depending on their characteristics and the situation. As we will see, each has its place and, when used appropriately, can help you motivate people and create an environment that fosters both quality and productivity. As a leader–supervisor, you must be able to use all three leadership styles as the need for each arises.

With the autocratic style managers hold most of the formal authority. The manager–leader may announce a decision or ask for feedback on it before it is implemented, but the decision is made by the manager–leader. A manager who takes the middle position, the democratic style, asks subordinates to play a part in making the decision. They may be asked to help define a problem, come up with alternatives, or evaluate alternatives. Finally, with the spectator style the manager delegates to subordinates the authority they need to make their own decisions, individually or through teams.

THE BUREAUCRATIC STYLE

The **bureaucratic style** is typified by the manager's reliance on rules, regulations, policy, and procedures. To him, they represent authority and certainty. It is management by the book. Through the exercise of this style, the manager adopts the posture of a police officer religiously enforcing rules and depending on superiors to resolve problems not covered in the manual.

Unlike the other three styles, the bureaucratic style cannot really be a leadership style, because managers who practice it are not really directing

bureaucratic style
a management style characterized by the manager's reliance on rules, regulations, policies, and procedures to direct subordinates

The bureaucratic style of management is appropriate in organizations where strict rules and regulations are required. Although bureaucratic managers must adhere to these rules, they must also show empathy toward their subordinates who must obey those rules.

their people in a personal way. Instead, they are directing them through regulations, procedures, and policies.

Prerequisites. There are three major prerequisites for the use of the bureaucratic style:

1. All the other styles must be inappropriate for use.
2. Subordinates subjected to this style must need it.
3. There is no latitude in decision making or in deviations from procedures.

Limitations. This style is appropriate for some governmental agencies, some military services, and some nonprofit enterprises such as public hospitals. It has a very little value in businesses, and if used improperly it can be devastating to anyone with ambition and creativity who is subjected to it.

Employee reactions. This style does little to build motivation in subordinates. Employees tend to adopt an indifferent attitude toward their peers and their work. The supervisor becomes rather unimportant to subordinates and is perceived by them as a watchdog rather than a manager.

THE AUTOCRATIC STYLE

autocratic style
a management and leadership style characterized by the retention by the leader of all authority for decision making

Leaders of the **autocratic style** keep power to themselves and do not delegate to their subordinates. The making of a final decision is reserved for the leaders alone. They keep their subordinates dependent on them for instructions, and they allow their subordinates to act only under their direct supervision.

Prerequisites. The necessary prerequisites for using the autocratic style are the following:

1. You are an expert in the practice of management, as well as in the handling of your subordinates' jobs.
2. Your subordinates need this approach.
3. You wish to communicate primarily by means of orders and detailed instructions.

Limitations. In general, you should restrict your use of this style to the following situations:

- When you are dealing with new employees who are unfamiliar with the tasks and methods they are expected to perform
- When time is short or when there is an emergency situation that does not allow you to explain the reasons for your orders
- When you are directing a stubborn or difficult subordinate who does not respond favorably requests or the other styles of supervision
- When your authority is directly challenged

You should restrict your use of this style of supervision to the situations outlined. If you lack the prerequisites, you cannot use it effectively. Once the situation changes, you should shift to another leadership style. Keep in mind that the autocratic style is both a management style and a leadership style.

The autocratic style of management lends itself to situations where you need short-term, high-quantity production out of your staff. Supervising repair and damage from a ruptured storm drain in New York City is one such situation.

Employee reactions. People subjected to the autocratic style will generally be high-quantity producers, but only for the short run. They will tend to be tense and somewhat fearful of you. If the style is used too long—that is, after the need for it has ceased—employees will become resentful and withhold their normal contributions to the job. It is not a style that builds team players or encourages strong ties among the workers. It also causes subordinates to become dependent on their leaders.

THE DEMOCRATIC STYLE

Managers of the **democratic style** adopt a "we" approach to their work and to their subordinates. They play the role of coach, drilling their teams on fundamentals and sharing decision-making authority with them. They make frequent use of problem-solving meetings, as outlined in Chapter 9. They delegate freely to subordinates who have earned their confidence, as well as to members of the group in general. They attempt to build a strong team spirit and to foster mutual respect with members of the team and with peers.

This style of supervision often goes by other names, such as the consultative, general, or participative style. It is a leadership style very much in use today.

democratic style
a management and leadership style characterized by a sharing of decision-making authority with subordinates

If you supervise using the democratic style of management, you will share decision-making responsibility with your subordinates. This style works well with highly skilled or experienced workers.

Prerequisites. The following conditions are needed before you implement the democratic style:

1. You should have support from your boss to use it.
2. You should be willing to accept a certain number of mistakes and delays in the early stages of its implementation.
3. You should have a personal commitment to this style and a strong belief in its ability to motivate people. Once you extend this style to your subordinates, you will find it difficult to shift to a different style.
4. You should have carefully prepared your subordinates by means of initial delegations of some of your authority and be willing to consult with your subordinates on small matters during early use of the new style.
5. You should have a high degree of patience and time for group decision-making meetings.
6. You should be prepared to accept less-than-optimum solutions to problems.

Some supervisors may feel threatened by this style. If so, they should not attempt to use it until they have been trained in its use. An employee who has never before been asked for the time of day, let alone an opinion on new procedures, might become suspicious at sudden attempts to obtain her participation in matters affecting the department.

Limitations. This style is best used in the following situations:

- When your workers are highly skilled or highly experienced at their jobs
- Where time is sufficient to permit subordinates to participate as individuals or as a group
- When preparing groups or individuals for changes
- When attempting to solve problems common to the group, and when group support is needed to implement solutions
- When attempting to air gripes or otherwise relieve workers' tensions

Employee reactions. The great majority of today's workers are educated enough for the democratic style of leadership. They can achieve and sustain a high quality and quantity of output for extended periods when supervisors are democratic. Supervisors who use this approach are employee centered rather than work centered, and employees know it. They appreciate the trust and freedom that the supervisor gives them. This style strongly promotes cooperation and group spirit, and gives morale a corresponding boost. Under the democratic style, workers tend to understand the contributions of their peers to a greater degree, and they get to know each other better than under the other two styles.

The transition at the Levi Strauss & Company plant in Murphy, North Carolina, points out the value of both democratic and spectator styles. The plant moved from a traditional, top-down autocratic style of management to a team-based mix of democratic and spectator styles.

> Tommye Jo Daves, a 58-year-old mountain-bred grandmother . . . is responsible for the plant which employs 385 workers and turns out some three million pairs of Levi's jeans a year. . . . [Through management training] . . . two lessons stuck with Daves: "You can't lead a team by barking orders, and you have to have a vision in your head of what you're trying to do." . . . She and her line supervisors have since been converting their plant . . . to team management, in which teams of workers are cross-trained for 36 tasks instead of one or two and thrust into running the plant, from organizing supplies to setting production goals to making personnel policy. Now Daves and her mostly female management crew get lots of direction from the ranks but much less from above.[16]

The results? She and her team reduced the company's policy manual from 700 pages to 50. Quality and customer-response time improved, whereas costs and rejects declined. Nonetheless, the transition was not an easy one. Says Daves, "sometimes it's real hard for me not to push back and say, 'You do this, you do that.' . . . Now I have to say, 'How do you want to do this?' I have to realize that their ideas may not be the way to go, but I have to let them learn that for themselves."[17]

THE SPECTATOR STYLE

The **spectator style,** sometimes called the *free-rein style,* is characterized by treating subordinates as independent decision-makers. The manager or manager–leader develops a strong independent spirit in individual subordinates and teams and relies on their skills, knowledge, experience, and initiative. Subordinates, individually or in teams, perceive themselves to be professionals—that is, experts in their specialties.

spectator style
a management style characterized by treating subordinates as independent decision-makers

The supervisor becomes a facilitator, coach, and consultant. He remains available to subordinates and will intervene when asked to do so or when it is deemed necessary. Supervisors are generally physically removed from direct and frequent contact with subordinates, but continue to stay in touch through meetings, reports, and records of output. This style of leadership is usually the last phase in the evolution of the supervisor's approach to handling subordinates. This chapter's *Supervising Teams* feature and the life-cycle theory of leadership discussed later both emphasize this point.

Prerequisites. The prerequisites of the spectator style of leadership are as follows:

1. Since workers are treated as experts, they must be highly experienced and skilled in their crafts.
2. Controls other than direct and frequent observations must be established to monitor the performance and interactions of both individuals and teams.
3. Workers, individually and collectively, must possess pride in themselves and their abilities as well as the qualities of endurance and initiative.

Limitations. The use of the spectator style should be restricted, as a rule, to the following groups or situations:

- When your subordinates are highly skilled, experienced, and educated
- When you are using outside experts, such as staff specialists, consultants, or temporary skilled help
- When you as the boss are new at your job or lack personal experience in the work being performed by your subordinates

Employee reactions. Workers who work under the spectator style perceive themselves as being in business for themselves; that is, they adopt a somewhat independent air and see their boss as a kind of staff assistant who stands ready to help if needed. This style generally promotes high levels of individual output for indefinite periods. It fosters pride and morale better than the other styles. But if the boss becomes too remote or inaccessible, insecurity may set in, along with resulting stress, fears, and frustrations. All the workers are pretty much on their own and strongly feel the need to prove themselves to their boss and their peers. Consequently, people working under this style need constant reassurance that they are performing up to standard and that they are appreciated.

As a supervisor, team leader, or team facilitator, you must be familiar with all four management styles. You will be faced with subordinates, associates, and situations at one time or another that will call on you to use each of these styles.

During the training of a new employee, you should probably rely

The spectator style of management is useful when your workers are experts in their field and enjoy working independently. Lab technicians are one such example. What could you do as a supervisor to motivate such workers?

SUPERVISING TEAMS

In traditional American organizations, it was not unusual for managers and supervisors either to ignore the emergence of . . . subgroups or to actively discourage this natural process for fear that such groups would constitute cliques whose informal leaders would represent a challenge to formal authority.

Today's supervisors are being taught to encourage the formation of teams and to transform workers into leaders and members of self-managing teams. Supervisors tend to pass through several phases, moving from the traditional planner, director, and controller focused on individual subordinates to a "team resource person." The first phase has the supervisor recognizing or forming—on her own or through higher management edict—one or more work-unit teams. The supervisor is at the center, managing and initiating, encouraging team member interaction, and beginning the process of sharing "control and problem-solving duties with group members."

The second phase begins as the supervisor moves away from traditional methods of managing and begins to share leadership roles and functions with team members. The supervisor becomes a "coordinator," managing "the group primarily through coordination of their skills and activities, and using their resources as fully as possible." Training and power sharing continue while the supervisor increases contacts with other individuals and teams outside her unit or specific teams.

Phase three transforms the supervisor into what Carl Bramlette labels a "team boundary manager," leaving daily decisions and activities in the hands of willing and competent team members. Teams continue to report to the supervisor. "He or she collects data and gives the group feedback on its performance based upon such measures as production, quality, cost, or customer satisfaction." The supervisor acts as a facilitator, getting the resources needed for each team and acting as a mediator between the groups and outsiders. The supervisor may intervene when a group has a problem it can't resolve.

Finally, the supervisor becomes a "team resource person." Teams now have accountability for their own work and determine their own leadership. The team resource person provides any assistance the team may require or arranges for it to be provided by others. Eventually, the team resource person may be phased out.

Source: Carl A. Bramlette, Jr., "Free to Change," *Training and Development Journal* (March 1984): 62–70.

on the autocratic style, the bureaucratic style, or a blend of the two. Once the newcomer has been placed in his job and is performing up to standard, you should switch to one of the other styles of leadership. If you do not, your worker may rebel, and you will have contributed to his eventual termination.

If you try to use a style that is wrong for a specific subordinate, she will probably let you know it. Changes in an associate's attitudes and behavior are the first sign that you may be using an improper style of leadership. Selecting the proper style for individual workers is easy once you acquire some experience as a supervisor, but it may involve a bit of trial and error. Do not hesitate to switch if the style you are currently using fails to get the desired results. And don't forget that a lot of help is available to you through the advice and counsel of your peers and your superiors.

You may not be entirely free to select your own styles of leadership. Your boss may frown on the use of one or another of them. You also may feel inadequate in your understanding of how to implement one or more of the styles. Your tendency might be to use the one with which you feel most comfortable for all of your people. This is almost always a mistake. You should stand ready to offer the style each subordinate needs. Practice and study can enable you to feel confident enough to use all four styles successfully.

The Life-Cycle Theory

People need different styles of supervision and leadership at different times. Paul Hersey and Kenneth Blanchard have given us a theory that explains the importance of adapting one's leadership approach to differences in employee experience. The life-cycle theory, detailed in Exhibit 10.8, shows that the new employee (block 1) needs a high task focus. As the employee acquires new knowledge and skills and demonstrates competence, she requires a high-employee–high-task focus (block 2). With employees who have matured in both tenure and capabilities, the supervisor can move from a high-direction to a low-direction focus, as required (block 4—the experienced, secure employee).[18]

Exhibit 10.8   *Adaptation of Hersey and Blanchard's life-cycle theory.*

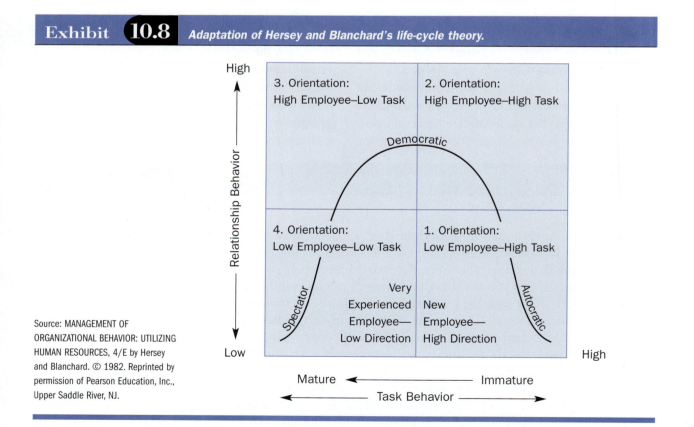

Source: MANAGEMENT OF ORGANIZATIONAL BEHAVIOR: UTILIZING HUMAN RESOURCES, 4/E by Hersey and Blanchard. © 1982. Reprinted by permission of Pearson Education, Inc., Upper Saddle River, NJ.

Charismatic Leaders

Leaders may be classified by whether they are charismatic or non-charismatic, although effective leaders do not have to be charismatic. *Charismatic leaders* have special qualities that enable them to move their followers beyond the status quo toward radical change. Leadership researchers Jay Conger and Rabindra Kanungo have found that there are three stages in the charismatic leadership process. In stage 1, charismatic leaders assess the status quo in order to identify areas in which major changes are needed. They also determine the extent to which their followers' needs are being satisfied by the status quo. After examining resources and constraints, they develop long-term goals for improvement and advocate radical change from the status quo. In contrast to charismatic leaders, *administrators* either maintain the status quo or make only incremental changes.[19]

In stage two, charismatic leaders formulate their vision of what the situation will be like after the radical change. The manner in which charismatic leaders communicate their vision of the future often inspires their followers to action. Conger and Kanungo offer the following rich description of how leaders communicate their vision:

> Using expressive modes of action, both verbal and non-verbal, they manifest their convictions, self-confidence, and dedication to materialize what they advocate. In the use of rhetoric, words are selected to reflect their assertiveness, confidence, expertise and concern for followers' needs. These same qualities may also be expressed through their dress, their appearance, and their body language. Charismatic leaders' use of rhetoric, high energy, persistence unconventional and risky behavior, heroic deeds, and personal sacrifices all serve to articulate their high motivation and enthusiasm, which then become contagious among their followers.[20]

In stage three, charismatic leaders show their followers the tactics and behaviors that will enable them to achieve the vision. They work also to build trust with their followers. For example, they take great personal risks such as by putting their own wealth at risk, taking risks of being fired, or making personal sacrifices on behalf of their followers. Greater trust is established when leaders make greater personal sacrifices. Other important criteria for building trust are that the leader must be willing to work tirelessly on behalf of the vision and must be perceived to have great expertise in the area.[21]

Leadership researchers Robert House, James Woycke, and Eugene Fodor have used evaluations of historians to classify U.S. presidents into charismatic and non-charismatic categories. Those categorized as charismatic leaders include the following: Jefferson, Jackson, Lincoln, Theodore Roosevelt, Franklin Roosevelt, Kennedy, and Reagan.[22]

Unfortunately, there also is a dark side to charismatic leadership. The charismatic leader's total commitment to the vision may prevent the leader from recognizing problems that can derail its accomplishment. Because of their personal commitment of time and energy to the fulfillment of the vision, charismatic leaders sometimes become blind to better ways of accomplishing desired change. In essence the charismatic leader's remarkable commitment to the vision can become his Achilles heel. Charismatic leaders then become less effective because they dismiss valid criticisms or reject good suggestions provided by others.[23] Jay Conger points out how even Thomas Edison's strengths became a source of weakness:

> Thomas Edison, for example, so passionately believed in the future of direct electrical current (DC) for urban power grids that he failed to see the more rapid acceptance of alternating power (AC) systems by America's then-emerging utility companies. Thus the company started by Edison to produce DC power stations was soon doomed to failure. He became so enamored of his own ideas that he failed to see competing and, ultimately, more successful ideas.[24]

Becoming a Leader

CHANGING LEADERSHIP STYLES

Mort Myerson, a well-known and highly capable executive, helped Ross Perot build EDS into a giant of the information systems industry. In the 1980s, EDS merged with General Motors, and eventually Perot and Myerson left EDS. Several years later, Perot formed Perot Systems and asked Myerson to take over as CEO. Myerson found, after returning to a high-level leadership position, that his views on leadership had changed since leaving EDS and that the leadership environment had changed as well.[25] Myerson explained the change as follows:

> What I realized after I left was that I had also made a lot of people very unhappy. Our people paid a high price for their economic success. Eighty-hour weeks were the norm. We shifted people from project to project and simply expected them to make the move, no questions asked. . . . In terms of priorities, work was in first place; family, community, other obligations all came after. . . . We asked people to put financial performance before everything else, and they did. They drove themselves to do whatever was necessary to create those results—even if it meant too much personal sacrifice or doing things that weren't really in the best interests of customers.[26]

Myerson held extensive conversations with employees and customers during his first six months at Perot Systems and found examples of leadership such as the following:

> I listened to some of our senior leaders talk about how they handled people on teams who didn't perform. I heard talk of "drive-by shootings" to "take out" nonperformers; then they'd "drag the body around" to make an example out of them.[27]

As a result of what he learned, Myerson became determined to change leadership at Perot Systems. He and his colleagues worked to change managers who were abusive of their subordinates and coached them toward improvement. Those who could not make the change were asked to leave. Myerson and his colleagues also concentrated on making the organization more humane and encouraged their employees to spend time on community programs and causes. They worked to develop greater concern for the welfare of both their employees and their customers. Myerson himself led by example by being accessible to employees and established honest, open, and direct communications.[28]

Another example of Myerson's leadership at Perot Systems and the values he displayed are illustrated in an incident related to the company's annual Christmas party. The Christmas party became an issue when Myerson realized that the company would be spending $360,000 for the party. When he asked about the rationale for the expenditure, he was told that employees enjoyed dressing up in tuxes and having a good time. Myerson's response was a directive to cancel the party:

> "Now, since I'm Jewish, that wasn't too . . . it wasn't received well—I'll put it that way. I said, 'Look, this has got nothing to do with being Jewish or Christian, this has got to do with the spirit of the holidays. I hereby cancel the party, and here's what we'll do.'
>
> "I said, 'We'll take the $360,000 and buy food and clothes and toys, and we will get our employees to take those things personally and deliver them to the inner city, to people who don't have anything'—which we did.
>
> "The result was, first, outrage that we canceled the party, then depression, then recognition that we were doing something different, and then elation for those who actually took those things."[29]

DEALING WITH MISTAKES

The manner in which leaders deal with their associates' mistakes reveals much about their style and the kind of persons they are. Similarly, the way organizations deal with mistakes speaks volumes about their cultures and the value they place on their employees. While supervisors and organizations may claim to value their employees, mistakes provide a critical test of leadership and fundamental supervisory values. In addition to the impact on the employee making a mistake, other employees observe the consequences of mistakes, and their future behavior is affected by their perceptions of the events.

An incident personally reported to one of the authors provides a good example of how mistakes should be handled. This incident involves a mistake by a plant manager in a leading company. The plant manager had been pressured by the higher-level corporate sales staff to make a million-dollar shipment of one of its products before he was absolutely certain of its quality. Unfortunately, the plant manager gave in to the pressure and shipped the product before he had sufficient assurance that all quality standards had been met. The shipment turned out to be flawed and had to be recalled, causing a million-dollar loss.

The plant manager's superiors decided that, although the company's financial performance for the year would be adversely affected, the manager had potential to develop in the future. Therefore, his bosses decided that they would not terminate or penalize him. They advised him of the seriousness of his mistake and stressed that he had to stand firm even when pressured by others in the organization. In the future he would have to make decisions that he knew were right. This incident, and the leadership demonstrated by the plant manager's superiors, have become part of the folklore of the company. As an interesting aside, the plant manager's superiors have said that they did not terminate him because the company had just invested one million dollars in his development! This investment paid off; the manager became one of the company's best plant managers.

This example shows how the values of the company's leaders guide their decisions about how to deal with a mistake. The leaders were convinced that the plant manager would learn from his mistake and that he deserved another chance. The plant manager's treatment undoubtedly increased his loyalty to the company and to his superiors. Perhaps more importantly, other employees in the organization became aware of the manner in which the mistake was handled. As a result, they have more confidence that they are valued by the organization and are more likely to feel that they will be treated fairly when they make mistakes.

The manner in which leaders handle mistakes also has an impact on the speed with which mistakes are reported to superiors. Some supervisors have a reputation of "shooting the messenger" who bears bad news. A railroad executive told one of the authors of an incident involving a train wreck. In this incident, lower-level employees knew of a correctable problem that could lead to a train wreck. Because the lower-level employees feared executives' reactions to bad news, they did not report the problem. Unfortunately, such examples are all too common, and in some instances such behavior may be representative of how employees perceive the organization's leaders and its culture.

When employees fear leaders' reactions to mistakes, they are less likely to admit their mistakes, request timely assistance, or call attention to problems. Mistakes are then more likely to be covered up or hidden. As a result there will be less opportunity to correct problems in a timely manner. Consequently, the costs of dealing with the results of mistakes may become more severe. Poor leaders spend too much time placing blame for mistakes when their efforts should be focused on determining how such mistakes can be avoided in the future. Blaming subordinates may also lead to perceptions of unfair treatment because in some instances the fault for the mistake may lie squarely with the supervisor as a result of a failure to provide adequate instruction or training. There is a great deal of wisdom in the adage that leaders should reduce their efforts to "fix blame" and spend more time on "fixing problems." This does not mean that when subordinates repeatedly disregard established procedures, and make mistakes as a result, that there should be no adverse consequences. In such cases the supervisor must use progressive discipline, which is discussed in Chapter 14, to change the subordinate's behavior, with termination being the final step if improvement is not forthcoming.

Supervisors should consider the following suggestions when dealing with mistakes. The most important is that the supervisor should focus on determining how the mistake can be avoided in the future. This requires an accurate diagnosis of the situation and answers to several questions. Were circumstances within the control of the employee? Did the employee have adequate instruction? Was the employee adequately trained? If the supervisor's diagnosis reveals that the employee's mistake occurred because the organization's reward system encouraged the wrong behaviors, then supervisors must work to make the system consistent with desired behaviors.

Supervisors have to recognize that employees are human and that even the best employees occasionally make mistakes. However, when supervisors fail to confront mistakes, other employees may view their failure to act as evidence that procedures, product quality, customer service, etc. do not matter. Honest mistakes may be handled in a number of ways. One of the core ideologies of 3M, a highly effective, visionary company, is toleration of honest mistakes.[30] It is important that confrontations about mistakes occur in private. There is wisdom in the U.S. Navy's guideline that one should "praise in public, penalize in private."[31] Employees may be embarrassed or humiliated if coworkers overhear such discussions. Furthermore, coworkers may be embarrassed by the discussion and therefore feel that they have also been punished. Group admonishments should also be avoided because they punish the innocent.

THE BASIC STEPS TO BECOMING A LEADER

Based on his experience as an IBM marketing manager, Buck Rodgers offers the following nine steps for becoming an influential manager:[32]

1. *Establish who's in charge.* Each person in a unit within an organization must be clear about her authority, responsibility, and accountability.

2. *Know what you want to accomplish.* Define your goals, short and long term. Map out your priorities for each day. Monitor your use of time, and check on your progress regularly.

3. *Know what you want each person you manage to accomplish.* Set specific goals for a person to achieve, and let that person know the quality of performance expected. Judge performance on achievements, not on style.

4. *Let the person know what you expect.* Don't let people guess at what you want from them or about how they are doing. Communicate regularly with each individual about what you expect and about what will happen when those expectations are met, exceeded, or not met.

5. *Find out what your employee wants for himself.* Insist that each subordinate spell out goals, aspirations, and expectations.

6. *Find out what your employee expects of you.* What is expected in terms of help—more frequent or less frequent contact with you? More responsibility?

7. *Take being a role model seriously.* Subordinates do as you do more often than they do as you say they should do. Your example provides the psychological and performance models for your group.

8. *Expect others to be self-motivated, but don't count on it.* People have their peaks and valleys. You may need to intercede on occasion, helping subordinates to improve, grow, and prosper.

9. *Understand that the quality of your leadership is determined by the methods you use to motivate others.* What you use and apply to others will be used and applied to you. Open, honest, and sensitive communication builds mutual trust and respect.

ASSESSING YOUR LEADERSHIP ABILITY

You can rely on four major indicators as you attempt to determine the effectiveness of your leadership with your people: morale, group spirit, proficiency, and self-discipline. Each of these can help you measure the impact you are having on your formal group members, individually and collectively.

Morale

People's attitudes toward all the individuals, things, and events that affect them at work constitute their morale. *Morale* can be defined as an individual's state of mind with regard to his job, supervisor, peers, and company. Through the actions and statements of people, you can effectively measure their morale. If your subordinates are positive individuals who take pride in their work, they reflect favorably on you and your group. If they are absent frequently, fail to attend to their duties, or dwell on negative factors, you can assume that your leadership needs improvement.

Group Spirit

What are the major attitudes reflected by the members of your formal group and any informal groups associated with it? Are they positive and supportive, fostering teamwork and harmony, or are they negative and destructive? Both individual and group attitudes are shaped in large measure by your human relations efforts.

Proficiency

How good are you at your job? How good are your subordinates? Are you making an effort to improve both your own level of competence and theirs? Are you aware of any efforts of theirs to seek a higher level of competence? Are you fostering their growth and development? This indicator is tied

SUPERVISORS AND ETHICS

Ray is a traditional supervisor of a toy department in a major chain of discount stores. After the store closed last night, he spent two hours setting up discount signs on various "specials" throughout his department that offered customers up to 25 percent discounts on several very popular items. The discounts he posted were faxed to him yesterday by company headquarters and were to remain in effect for the next seven days.

Shortly after opening the store this morning, one of his cashiers notified Ray that a customer was complaining about the scanner's price not matching the store's sale price for an item. Ray scanned the item and discovered that the new sale price was not recorded. Instead, the older, higher price was still in the computer's memory. Ray immediately told his cashier to honor the sale price and reported his finding to the store manager, Ukare Shimito.

Ukare seemed somewhat unconcerned, dismissing the problem as an "oversight" on her part, and told Ray that the sale price would be entered shortly. She gave Ray this advice: "If the customer discovers a price difference at checkout, honor the sale price you posted by the merchandise."

Throughout the day, cashiers notified Ray of several other price differences. All but one was in the store's favor; prices were higher than the sale placards advertised. By closing time, the sale prices still had not been entered into the computer.

What do you think of the store manager's response to Ray? If you were in Ray's position, what would you do now?

directly to morale and group spirit. If these are below normal or negative, your subordinates will usually demonstrate low levels of proficiency.

Self-Discipline

Can your shop or office function in your absence? Do your people respond promptly and positively to your instructions? Do they readily accept honest criticism? Have you had to reprimand more often than praise? Do your people know the reasons behind what they are expected to do? Can they be trusted? If not, what are you doing about these problems?

You can rate yourself by using these indicators at any time. Chances are that your boss is doing so regularly. If you are placing the kind of emphasis that you should on your human relations, you should experience little difficulty in these general areas.

Instant Replay

1. Leadership is based on a person's formal authority and other sources of influence, such as one's personality, skills, knowledge, and personal relationships with others.

2. Not all leaders are managers, and not all managers are leaders. People who can get work done through willing followers who respect them are leaders.

3. Leaders vary in their traits, such as enthusiasm, tact, and endurance. No one set of traits is common to all leaders.

4. The contingency model of leadership holds that the effectiveness of a group or organization depends on the leader's personality and the leadership situation.

5. In general, the degree to which leaders should focus on tasks or people depends on their own abilities, their subordinates' abilities, and the situation they face at any given time.

6. Charismatic leadership is often required to implement radical change.

7. The manner in which leaders deal with subordinates' mistakes reveals much about their style and the effectiveness of their leadership in the long run.

8. Leadership effectiveness may be evaluated by assessing the morale of individual followers, their levels of proficiency, their self-discipline, and team spirit.

Questions for Class Discussion

1. Can you define this chapter's key terms?
2. What are the components of the contingency model of leadership?
3. What are the four basic management styles? Which is not a leadership style? Why?
4. What style of supervision would you use in each of the following situations, and why would you use it?

   a. A new employee with two years' experience in a similar job

   b. An old-timer who appears to be an informal leader of one of the cliques in your department

   c. A neurotic employee, with a good deal of experience, whose neurosis is interfering with job performance

   d. An employee, with many more years experience than you have, who resents you and your authority

Incident

Purpose: To emphasize the differences between leadership and management.

Your task: Read each listing, and indicate if it is unique to management (M) or leadership (L).

Ⓜ Ⓛ   1. Creating a vision for the company or company unit

Ⓜ Ⓛ   2. Engaging in day-to-day planning

Ⓜ Ⓛ   3. Sensing the need for and producing the strategies for change

Ⓜ Ⓛ   4. Setting the path for reengineering the company or its units

Ⓜ Ⓛ   5. Setting up an organization structure

Ⓜ Ⓛ   6. Controlling and problem solving

Ⓜ Ⓛ   7. Inspiring and energizing people to overcome barriers

Ⓜ Ⓛ   8. Producing a degree of predictability and order

Ⓜ Ⓛ   9. Creating policies and procedures

Leadership at Malden Mills

CASE PROBLEM 10.1

Malden Mills, a family-owned textile company employing approximately 3,000 employees, is located in Lawrence, Massachusetts. During the early 1980s, the 90-year-old company went through bankruptcy but then recovered by placing heavy emphasis on research and development. Research efforts resulted in the development of two new textile products, Polartec and Polarfleece. These products, which are used in coats sold by such retailers as L. L. Bean and Patagonia, enabled the company to become profitable again. Unlike most of its competitors, Malden Mills retained its production facilities in the U. S., paying approximately $11 per hour for wages ($15 including benefits) versus $2 to $3 per hour it could obtain with production in lower-wage countries. The company's high-tech products and equipment set it apart from labor-intensive textile manufacturers, and its emphasis on quality provides a competitive advantage. The company's CEO, Aaron Feuerstein, says that "The quality of our product is paramount . . . and it's the employee who makes that quality. If the quality slips, the employee is in a position to destroy your profit."[33]

On December 11, 1995, the company had a fire that destroyed most of its production facilities. "Structural losses were enormous: 750,000 sq ft of manufacturing and office space in three buildings were destroyed . . ."[34] Feuerstein, who was 70 years old at the time, could have retired and collected the insurance money. Instead of retiring, he did the unthinkable and paid wages totaling almost $15 million. Two days after the fire Feuerstein gave each employee a $275 Christmas bonus, and then he paid the entire workforce a full month's pay for December. In January he paid employees again, even though the plant was still unfinished. And then he paid the employees again for a third month. Employee reactions to Feuerstein's actions were as follows:

> "When he did it the first time, I was surprised," said Bill Cotter. "The second time was a shock. The third . . . well, it was unrealistic to think he would do it

again." Nancy Cotter finished her husband's thought: "It was the third time that brought tears to everyone's eyes."[35]

A majority of the company's workforce was back at work on a full-time basis by March. Incredibly, productivity reached 230,000 yards per week only a few weeks after the fire—it had produced 130,000 yards per week prior to the fire. Feuerstein explained that "Our people became very creative. They were willing to work 25 hours a day."[36] A few months later, 85 percent of the workforce was back on the job, although 400 others were still not on the job. Feuerstein covered their health insurance costs and promised employment with the company in 1997 after the company's new plant became operational. By 1997 all but 70 employees had been re-hired and the company's production facilities have been expanded to include state-of-the-art equipment.

Mr. Feuerstein, a deeply religious individual, said the following:

> I have a responsibility to the worker, both blue-collar and white-collar. . . . I have equal responsibility to the community. It would have been unconscionable to put 3,000 people on the streets and deliver a death blow to the cities of Lawrence and Methuen. Maybe on paper our company is worth less to Wall Street, but I can tell you it's worth more. We're doing fine.[37]

These actions related to the fire are not the only ways in which Feuerstein has demonstrated concern for his employees. He has a reputation for looking out for the interests of his people, such as by enabling employees to obtain heart bypass operations and by providing free soft drinks on the production lines when temperatures get too high.

Finally, there were other positive developments after the fire:

> Another type of loyalty figures in the Malden story: fidelity of the retail customer. In the first weeks after the fire, more than 10,000 letters poured in from retail customers vowing to buy Malden's products and nothing else. Brand identification, an integral part of Malden's rise to success in recent years, remains a driving force after the fire.[38]

Malden Mills Update[39]

Malden Mills filed for Chapter 11 protection from its creditors in November 2001. The fire at the company's facilities kept it out of the fleece market for two years, which allowed competitors to enter and take a sizeable share of the market. Unfortunately, some of Malden Mills' customers did not return after the company went back into production. A contributing factor to the company's financial difficulties was the general slowdown of the economy. Aaron Feuerstein emphasized that he is still convinced that paying his employees after the fire was the right thing to do.

Sources: Michael Ryan, "They Call Their Boss a Hero," Parade Magazine *(September 8, 1996): 4–5. John McCurry, "Loyalty Saves Malden Mills,"* Textile World *(February 1997): 38–42. All Things Considered.* National Public Radio *(November 30, 2001).*

Questions

1. What aspects of leadership do you see in the actions of Aaron Feuerstein?

2. Why did productivity at Malden Mills increase after the fire?

3. Why don't more leaders act like Aaron Feuerstein?

| Winston Churchill | CASE PROBLEM 10.2 |

Successful leaders often have the experience of prevailing in the face of adversity and learning from earlier failures. Leaders' skills also must match the circumstances. Winston Churchill's career provides a classic example.

Churchill began his remarkable political career in 1901 when he became a member of the House of Commons at the age of 26. Prior to his entry into Parliament he had seen combat as a cavalry officer in India, Cuba, and the Sudan and was awarded several medals for valor.[40] He rose quickly in politics and governmental service, becoming the First Lord of the Admiralty (civilian head of the British Navy) in 1911. One of Churchill's decisions about deployment of naval forces in 1915 during World War I resulted in failure and marked the end of his fast-track career. Churchill returned to combat, serving as an infantry officer in 1917. After World War I Churchill returned to public office but was essentially relegated to the sidelines of politics. His calls for rearmament, warnings about the intentions of the Nazis between 1933 and 1939, and criticisms of the government's attempts to appease the Nazis were ignored. When things looked the worst in May 1940, the country turned to the 65-year-old Churchill for leadership as Prime Minister.[41] It is said that Churchill "stood out as the one man in whom the nation could place its trust."[42]

In June 1940 Britain had been at war with Germany for a year. British soldiers had been driven out of France and narrowly escaped capture through an evacuation from Dunkirk. France surrendered on June 22, and the United States had not yet entered World War II. The Battle of Britain, which involved heavy bombing of Britain's major cities, was about to begin, and it appeared that Germany would invade Britain. The outcome looked bleak.[43] In June 1940, Winston Churchill made the following speech to the British Parliament:

> I have, myself, full confidence that if all do their duty, if nothing is neglected . . . we shall prove ourselves once again able to defend our island home, to ride out the storm of war, and to outlive the menace of tyranny, if necessary for years, if necessary alone . . . we shall not flag or fail. We shall go on to the end, we shall fight in France, we shall fight on the seas and oceans, we shall fight with growing confidence and growing strength in the air, we shall defend our island, whatever the cost may be, we shall fight on the beaches, we shall fight on the landing grounds, we shall fight in the fields and in the streets, we shall fight in the hills; we shall never surrender.[44]

Aside from speeches such as this, Churchill's hats, cigars, and two-fingered "v" for victory signs were distinctive, as well as symbolic, and endeared him to his followers.[45] There were other qualities about Churchill as well that made him well-suited for the challenges of leadership during these difficult times. Two specific examples of his personal risk-taking are described as follows:

> Churchill as Prime Minister frequently and deliberately ran terrible personal risks. But the people admired him for it, and loved his offhand disregard for danger. Once, when a German bomb landed near his car and nearly tipped it over, he joked, "Must have been my beef that kept the car down"—a reference to his pudginess.[46]
>
> Winston Churchill was another who liked to leave his underground air-raid shelter in Whitehall for the streets the moment bombs began falling. Attempts were made to stop him, because the risk of getting one's head blown off or losing a limb from shrapnel was great.... I'll have you know," thundered Churchill, "that as a child my nursemaid could never prevent me from taking a walk in the Green Park when I wanted to do so. And, as a man, Adolf Hitler certainly won't."[47]

At the end of World War II in 1945, Churchill lost his bid for reelection because he was unresponsive to the needs for social change after the war. He returned to office again as Prime Minister from 1951 to 1955, but his performance was limited by age and health problems. In general, his service as a peace-time Prime Minister did not measure up to his service during war time.[48]

Sources: John Keegan, "Churchill," Time *(April 13, 1998): 114–118. Leonard Mosley,* The Battle of Britain. *Alexandria, VA: Time-Life Books, 1977. C. L. Mowat, "Sir Winston Leonard Churchill," in the* World Book Encyclopedia, *Vol. 3, Chicago: Field Enterprises Educational Corporation (1960): 424–426. "Four of the Century's Greatest Speeches,"* Time *(April 13, 1998): 118. Brian L. Blakeley, "Sir Winston Leonard Spencer Churchill,"* Encarta Encyclopedia, *Vol. 97. Microsoft Corporation, 1996.*

Questions

1. What aspects of charismatic leadership were displayed in Churchill's speech to the Parliament?

2. Categorize Churchill's specific leadership actions in terms of the three stages of charismatic leadership described in this chapter.

3. Which of the leadership theories presented in this chapter explains why Churchill was a better leader during wartime than during peace? Explain.

4. Explain how Churchill was prepared to take on the leadership challenges of serving as Prime Minister.

References

1. Huey, John. "The New Post-Heroic Leadership," *Fortune* (February 21, 1994): 44, 48.

2. Rodgers, Buck, with Levey, Irv. *Getting the Most Out of Yourself and Others.* New York: Harper & Row (1987): 122.

3. Ambrose, Stephen E. *Citizen Soldiers.* New York: Simon & Schuster (1997): 40–41.

4. Kouses, James M., and Posner, Barry Z. *The Leadership Challenge: How to Keep Getting Extraordinary Things Done in Organizations.* San Francisco: Jossey-Bass (1995): 172.

5. Loden, Marilyn, and Rosener, Judy B. *Workforce America!* Homewood, IL: Business One Irwin (1991): 180–194.

6. Nelton, Sharon. "Winning with Diversity," *Nation's Business* (September 1992): 18–22, 24.

7. Rosener, Judy B. "Ways Women Lead," *Harvard Business Review* (November–December 1990): 119–125. Sharon Nelton, "Men, Women, and Leadership," *Nation's Business* (May 1991): 16–22.

8. Ibid.

9. Ibid.

10. Fiedler, Fred E. "The Contingency Model—New Directions for Leadership Utilization," *Journal of Contemporary Business* Vol. 3, No. 4 (Autumn 1974): 65–80.

11. Goleman, David. "What Makes a Leader?" *Harvard Business Review* (November–December 1998): 93–102.

12. Ibid.: 101.

13. Collins, Jim. "Level 5 Leadership: The Triumph of Humility and Fierce Resolve," *Harvard Business Review* (January 2001): 73.

14. Ibid.: 67–76.

15. Ibid.: 71.

16. Huey. "Post-Heroic Leadership."

17. Ibid.

18. Hersey, Paul, and Blanchard, Kenneth H. *Management of Organizational Behavior: Utilizing Human Resources,* 4th ed. Englewood Cliffs, NJ: Prentice Hall (1982): 88–91.

19. Conger, Jay A., and Kanungo, Rabindra N. "Behavioral Dimensions of Charismatic Leadership," in Jay A. Conger, Rabindra N. Kanungo and Associates, *Charismatic Leadership: The Elusive Factor in Organizational Effectiveness.* San Francisco: Jossey-Bass (1988): 78–97.

20. Ibid.: 87.

21. Ibid.

22. House, Robert J.; Woycke, James; and Fodor, Eugene M. "Charismatic and Noncharismatic Leaders: Differences in Behavior and Effectiveness," in Jay A. Conger, Rabindra N. Kanungo and Associates, *Charismatic Leadership: The Elusive Factor in Organizational Effectiveness.* San Francisco: Jossey-Bass (1988): 98–121.

23. Conger, Jay A. "The Dark Side of Leadership," *Organizational Dynamics* Vol. 19, No. 2 (1990): 44–55.

24. Ibid.

25. Myerson, Mort. "Everything I Thought I Knew About Leadership Is Wrong," *Fast Company* (April–May 1996): 71–79.

26. Ibid.: 72.

27. Ibid.: 72.

28. Ibid.

29. Colvin, Geoffrey. "Value-Driven: Think About This As You Don Your Tuxedo," *Fortune* (December 18, 2000): 74.

30. Collins, J. C., and Porras, J. I. *Built to Last: Successful Habits of Visionary Companies.* New York: HarperCollins, 1994.

31. Ricks, Thomas E. "Deep Trouble: A Skipper's Chance to Run a Trident Sub Hit Stormy Waters," *The Wall Street Journal* (November 20, 1997): A6.

32. Rodgers. *Getting the Most.*

33. Ryan, Michael. "They Call Their Boss a Hero," *Parade Magazine* (September 8, 1996): 4–5.

34. McCurry, John. "Loyalty Saves Malden Mills," *Textile World* (February 1997): 38–42.

35. Ryan, p. 4.

36. Ryan, p. 5.

37. Ibid.

38. McCurry, p. 41.

39. *All Things Considered.* National Public Radio (November 30, 2001).

40. Keegan, John. "Churchill," *Time* (April 13, 1998): 114–118; C. L. Mowat. "Sir Winston Leonard Churchill," in the *World Book Encyclopedia,* Vol. 3, Chicago: Field Enterprises Educational Corp. (1960): 424–426.

41. Keegan. "Churchill." Brian L. Blakeley. "Sir Winston Leonard Churchill," *Encarta Encyclopedia,* Vol. 97, Microsoft Corp., 1996.

42. Keegan, p. 116.

43. Mosley, Leonard. *The Battle of Britain.* Alexandria, VA: Time-Life Books, 1977.

44. "Four of the Century's Greatest Speeches," *Time* (April 13, 1998): 118.

45. Mowat. "Sir Winston Leonard Churchill." Mosley. *The Battle of Britain.*

46. Mosley, p. 60.

47. Ibid.: 148.

48. Keegan. "Churchill." Blakeley. "Sir Winston Leonard Churchill."

SHAPING YOUR ENVIRONMENT

 art III includes four chapters directly concerned with how well you as a supervisor will be able to influence the productivity of your subordinates. This section deals specifically with the proper ways to bring in new people, get them ready to perform to standards, appraise their results, and correct their deficiencies. Through the successful application of the principles in these chapters, you will exercise effective leadership to influence the performance of your subordinates.

Chapter 11 explains the difficult but necessary processes of selecting and introducing new employees. The primary emphasis is on the supervisor's role in hiring and welcoming new people into work groups. The chapter discusses legal restraints and pitfalls to help you hire the best people and to start them off on the right foot. You will learn what to do, how to do it, and what not to do while performing these two vital activities.

Chapter 12 explores the ways in which you can impart new knowledge, skills, and attitudes to workers. Through training, you prepare each worker to perform to standards, excel, and stay out of trouble. You enhance workers' chances for advancement and for increased earnings by training them in accordance with certain important principles. Along with the principles, the chapter discusses various training methods in order to help you select the one that is most appropriate for your training programs.

In Chapter 13, we explore the leader's role as judge—the process through which you evaluate your subordinates' performance. Appraisals help you determine the effectiveness of your training efforts and give you the backup you need to reward and punish.

Chapter 14 examines both positive and negative aspects of discipline. If you are to discipline effectively, you must stress prevention along with correct action. The principles and pitfalls of disciplining subordinates are explored in detail.

SELECTION AND ORIENTATION

Objectives

After reading and discussing this chapter, you should be able to do the following:

1. Define this chapter's key terms.
2. Describe the role of the supervisor in the selection process.
3. Describe the assistance in selection normally provided by a human resources department.
4. List and briefly describe selection devices and procedures.
5. Describe what a supervisor should do to prepare for a selection interview.
6. List and briefly explain pitfalls of the selection process.
7. List the basic goals of an orientation program.
8. List the basic goals of an induction program.
9. Describe what takes place during a new employee's socialization process.
10. State basic questions new employees want answered.

Introduction

Selection is a human resource management function that determines who is hired by an organization and who is not. It is the process by which applicants are evaluated so as to determine their suitability for employment. The basic aim of the selection process is to find the number and kind of employees required by a company to meet its needs for personnel at competitive cost levels. Selection begins with a description of the kind of knowledge and skills needed to fill a vacancy and ends with the decision to hire a particular person.

Selective hiring is a hallmark of successful companies.[1] Since employees are the only real source of competitive advantage for most companies, it is important that they hire and retain the best employees possible.

selection

the human resource management function that determines who is hired

Careful selection practices help companies keep employee turnover at low levels as well. Simply selecting employees who have the right skills is not enough at many companies. Selecting employees who fit the organization is also important for maintaining an organizational culture in which employees work effectively in teams, cooperate with each other, and provide good customer service. For example, at MBNA, one of the largest credit card companies, the most important selection criterion is "People who like other people."[2]

After you have recruited, interviewed, tested, and hired new employees, you must begin to prepare for their arrival and initiation. Some groundwork for this procedure is laid during the selection process. The applicant is informed of the nature of the job, the company's operations in general, and the wage and fringe benefits that go with the job. The remaining tasks involve planning and implementing an effective introduction of the employee to the company, the job, the supervisor, and the working environment.

This chapter looks at these extremely important functions from a supervisor's viewpoint. In some companies, the supervisors have little involvement in hiring new workers. They are told that new people have been assigned to their departments, and they must accept that decision. This is not as it should be. Therefore, we shall turn our attention to the kind of selection process in which supervisors play a significant role.

The Process of Selecting Employees

ADVANTAGES OF SUPERVISOR INVOLVEMENT

If adequate selection is to take place in a business, the decision to hire new workers should be made by the people who will become their bosses. This is because the managers have firsthand knowledge about their departments, the workforce, and the jobs that must be filled. They are best equipped to assess each applicant's suitability and potential both for performing the duties he will inherit and for getting along with the existing workforce. It makes a great deal of sense, therefore, to involve supervisors in the selection process and, in particular, to give them the power to make the final decision to hire a new employee.

Before you select a person for your department, you will probably look over all the applicants carefully in order to select the best from among the many individuals you interview. Since the person hired is someone you have chosen, you will feel a personal commitment to her that otherwise would be missing. You will want her to succeed because a failure will adversely affect you, your department, and the new employee. Part of your success and that of your department will be riding on your choice.

In many companies, teams are involved in the selection process. This chapter's *Supervising Teams* feature shows how such companies share or delegate their hiring decisions.

SUPERVISING TEAMS

Supervisors can empower their teams by making them responsible for a number of functions. Here are some ways that teams can be empowered through external leadership, production/service responsibilities, human resource management, and their social structure:

External Leader Behavior

1. Make team members responsible and accountable for the work they do.
2. Ask for and use team suggestions when making decisions.
3. Encourage team members to take control of their work.
4. Create an environment in which team members set their own team goals.
5. Stay out of the way when team members attempt to resolve work-related problems.
6. Generate high team expectations.
7. Display trust and confidence in the team's abilities.

Production/Service Responsibilities

1. The team sets its own production/service and standards.
2. The team assigns jobs and tasks to its members.
3. Team members develop their own quality standards and measurement techniques.
4. Team members take on production/service learning and development opportunities.

5. Team members handle their own problems with internal and external customers.
6. The team works with a whole product or service, not just a part.

Human Resource Management System

1. The team gets paid, at least in part, as a team.
2. Team members are cross-trained on jobs within the team.
3. Team members are cross-trained on jobs in other teams.
4. Team members are responsible for hiring, training, punishment, and firing.
5. Team members use peer evaluations to formally evaluate each other.

Social Structure

1. The team gets support from other teams and departments when needed.
2. The team has access to and uses important and strategic information.
3. The team has access to and uses the resources of other teams.
4. The team has access to and uses resources inside and outside the organization.
5. The team frequently communicates with other teams.
6. The team makes its own rules and policies.

Source: Bradley L. Kirkman and Benson Rosen, "Powering Up Teams," *Organizational Dynamics* (Winter 2000): 56.

THE SELECTION PROCESS

Exhibit 11.1 outlines the selection process as it occurs when a supervisor and the company's human resources department work together. In most medium to large firms, the supervisor places a request for a new worker with the human resources department as soon as the need arises. To ensure that both the supervisor and the human resources department know what kind of person they will be looking for, an up-to-date description of the job

Exhibit **11.1**   *A typical selection process.*

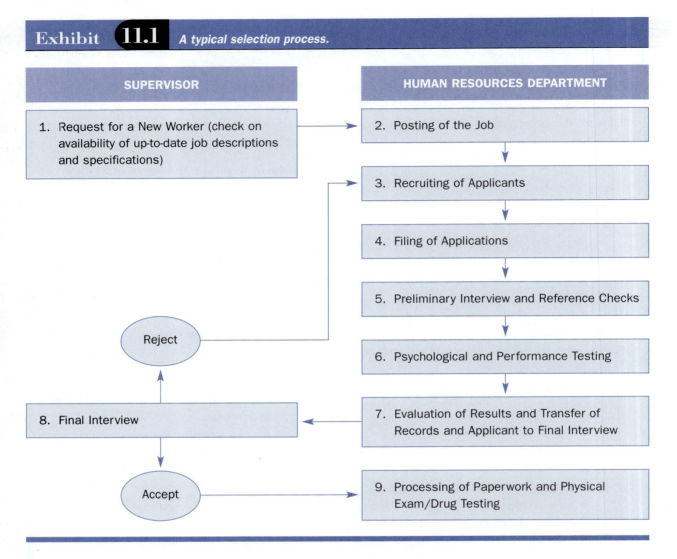

and its duties, as well as a detailed listing of the knowledge, skills, and abilities required of the jobholder, must be prepared. These two documents are called the *job description* and the *job specification,* respectively.

Job Description

job description
a formal listing of the duties that make up a position in the organization

A **job description** is a listing of the duties (tasks and activities) and responsibilities of a job or formal position in an organization. All jobs you supervise should have such a listing. Reference to this document proves helpful in assigning work, settling disagreements, appraising subordinates, and filling vacancies. Exhibit 11.2 consists of a job description for a secretarial position. You will note that nothing in it deals with the personal characteristics desirable in the job holder. These are detailed in the job specification.

Job description for personal secretary.

Exhibit **11.2**

Title: Secretary   Job No. C-10   Grade 4

Effective Date: 2/03

General   Perform clerical and secretarial duties involving keyboarding, correspondence and report preparation, filing, maintaining records, scheduling appointments, distributing mail. Handle confidential information regularly.

Specific Duties   Compose and keyboard routine memos and business correspondence.

Compile and keyboard routine reports.

Send and forward e-mail daily.

Send, sort, and distribute mail and faxes daily.

Maintain and set up files of memos, letters, and reports.

Obtain data and information by telephone, computer, or personal contact on behalf of supervisor.

Receive visitors.

Schedule supervisor's appointments.

Answer phone and take messages.

Handle confidential files.

Equipment   Personal computer, printer, fax, photocopier, and scanner.

Analysis by: _____   Approved by: _____

Job Specification

Exhibit 11.3 shows the **job specification**—knowledge, skills, and abilities a person must have in order to fill the position—for the position described in Exhibit 11.2. Such factors as keyboarding speed, clerical and secretarial experience, and formal education are listed. You need this information when selecting someone to fill a job, assigning work, and determining promotions. As jobs change with the passage of time, the job descriptions and specifications must be revised accordingly. It is standard practice to update these documents at least once every two years.

job specification
the personal characteristics and skill levels that are required of an individual to execute a job

Job Posting

Steps two through seven in the selection process (as illustrated in Exhibit 11.1) are usually performed for you by your company's human resources

Exhibit **11.3** *Job specification for the secretarial position shown in Exhibit 11.2.*

Title: Secretary   Job No. C-10   Grade 4

Effective Date: 2/03

Education   High-school graduate or equivalent

Experience   Secretarial, including word processing

Training Period   1 month

Dexterity   Precise movement of hand and fingers required to operate keyboard at no less than 60 words per minute

Adaptability   Must be able to adjust to frequent changes in duties, such as keyboarding, filing, composing letters, handling telephone

Judgment   Must be able to follow existing procedures and establish new practices where necessary. Must be able to compose business letters, establish filing systems, and receive visitors

Specific Skills   Must have knowledge of Word, Excel, Access, PowerPoint

Contact with Others   Frequent contacts with visitors, vendors, and company managers

Physical Demands   Lifting requirements: under 10 pounds

Analysis by: _____   Approved by: _____

department. Job openings are posted so that present employees will be aware of them. Posting is also a requirement in many union contracts or the employer's affirmative action program. Posting allows existing employees to apply for the vacancy and can result in promotions and transfers that will create new vacancies. In order to make sincere efforts to attract minority and female applicants, the company should advertise vacancies on a regular basis.

Initial Selection

After receiving and processing the paperwork that results from steps four through seven, human resources will usually send you two or more applicants for a final employment interview. As a rule, human resources will send you only applicants who qualify for and have the potential to succeed on the job. You must select the person you believe is the best qualified of the applicants you interview. Then you turn the applicant over to the human resources department for final paperwork.

Exhibit 11.4 lists and briefly describes the federal statutes and executive orders that prevent discrimination in the selection process. In the discussions that follow, the effects of these federal laws are examined as they relate to each of the selection steps or devices. They may be summarized briefly as follows:

Federal anti-discrimination statutes and executive orders relating to selection.   Exhibit **11.4**

STATUTE OR EXECUTIVE ORDER	PROHIBITED SELECTION CRITERIA	EMPLOYERS COVERED
Title VII of the Civil Rights Act of 1964 (as amended by the Equal Employment Opportunity Act of 1972 and Civil Rights Act of 1991)	Race, color, religion, sex, or national origin	Employers having 15 or more employees, unions, employment agencies, and governments
Age Discrimination in Employment Act (ADEA)	Protection for applicants of age 40 or more	Employers having 20 or more employees, unions, employment agencies
Pregnancy Discrimination Act of 1978 (amendment to Title VII)	Pregnancy	Employers having 15 or more employees
Americans with Disabilities Act of 1990	Physical and mental disabilities when job duties can be performed with reasonable accommodation	Employers having 25 or more employees, unions, and employment agencies
National Labor Relations Act of 1935 (as amended by the Labor Management Relations Act of 1947)	Union status—except where pre-hire or hiring agreements are permitted	Employers have $50,000 or more annual input or output across state lines. Retailers having $500,000 or more in annual sales.
Executive Order 11246	Race, color, religion, sex, or national origin	Federal contractors and subcontractors
Rehabilitation Act of 1973	Physical and mental disabilities	Federal contractors and federal government

Sources: Charles R. Greer, *Strategy and Human Resources: A General Managerial Approach,* 2nd ed. Englewood Cliffs, NJ: Prentice Hall, 2001. James Ledvinka and Vida G. Scarpello, *Federal Regulation of Personnel and Human Resource Management.* Boston: Kent Publishing Company, 1991. Robert D. Gatewood and Hubert S. Feild, *Human Resource Selection,* 4th ed. Fort Worth, TX: Dryden Press, 1998. Herbert G. Heneman and Robert L. Heneman, *Staffing Organizations.* Middleton, WI: Mendota House, 1994.

1. It is unlawful for an employer to fail or refuse to hire or to discharge an individual because of race, color, religion, sex, age, national origin, disability, pregnancy, or union status.

2. It is unlawful for an employer to limit, segregate, or classify an employee or applicant for employment in any way that would tend to deprive the individual of employment opportunities because of race, color, religion, sex, age, national origin, disability, pregnancy, or union status.

Title VII of the 1964 Civil Rights Act requires discrimination complaints to be filed within 180 days of the alleged violation and provides for remedies of reinstatement and recovery of lost pay. The Civil Rights Act of 1991 amended the act by allowing punitive damages when a company engages in discriminatory practices with malice or with reckless indifference to the law.

States and local governments also have similar statutes that cover many employers that are too small for federal coverage. In addition, many states and cities have statutes that prohibit discrimination on the basis of sexual orientation.[3]

Recruiting

There are two sources of supply for personnel: internal and external labor markets. Companies may fill vacancies internally by promoting someone, transferring a person from one job to another (usually a permanent job change), recalling a laid-off worker, or using job rotation to fill a vacancy on a temporary basis. Consider posting your employment needs with your company's other divisions and partners.

People currently employed at your company have friends, neighbors, and relatives who might make good employees. Employee referrals are such a good source of applicants that during periods of low unemployment leading companies such as Cisco Systems, Deloitte & Touche, and Texas Instruments have paid employees for referrals who are hired.[4] Because people tend to refer people similar to themselves, if women and minorities are under-represented in your workforce, you will need to use more than employee referrals as a source of new employees. In such cases external recruiting efforts will be required. The Equal Employment Opportunity (EEO) policy may also provide guidelines for recruiting representative numbers of **minority** members and women.

minority

according to the EEOC, a member of one of the following groups: Hispanics, Native Americans, African Americans, Asians or Pacific Islanders, Alaskan natives

Typical external sources of employees include unsolicited applications, employment agencies (both public and private), referrals from existing employees, schools, colleges, universities, temporary help agencies, unions, trade associations, and solicitation through help-wanted advertising. Employers may advertise through various electronic media, including radio and cable television programs devoted to helping local employers find workers. As noted in Chapter 2, Internet job sites are a common avenue for listing or advertising vacancies. *E-recruiting,* the practice of using Internet sites to recruit, has become an important tool for finding job candidates. E-recruiting provides a number of benefits, such as lower costs through elimination of recruitment agency fees, speed, and access to large numbers of candidates. Unsurprisingly, the number of companies using the Internet to recruit increased 40 percent between 2000 and 2001. Because of the high volumes of resumes that employers often receive, automated application evaluation tools allow employers to screen applications and resumes quickly.[5] While human resource departments usually handle such recruiting tasks, e-recruiting may be very useful for supervisors in smaller companies who may need to do their own recruiting. Exhibit 11.5 ranks recruiting sources according to their effectiveness in improving job performance and turnover/job survival.

AFFIRMATIVE ACTION PROGRAMS

The U.S. government requires companies to develop Affirmative Action programs (AAP) under the following circumstances: (1) they have been found guilty of discriminatory practices, or (2) they do contract work for the federal government (valued at $50,000 or more) and employ more than 50 employees. They also may develop an AAP when they recognize that they need to improve their employment record with regard to women and minorities. One important part of an AAP is a stated goal and timetable for hiring more women and minorities.

Effectiveness of recruitment sources.   Exhibit **11.5**

MOST EFFECTIVE

- Referrals by current employees

- In-house company postings

- Rehired former employees

SLIGHTLY LESS EFFECTIVE

- Walk-ins

LEAST EFFECTIVE SOURCES

- Newspaper ads

- School placement centers

- Employment agencies

Source: Michael A. Zottoli and John P. Wanous, "Recruitment Source Research: Current Status and Future Directions," *Human Resource Management Review* 10 (2000): 353–383.

EEO/AFFIRMATIVE ACTION AND VALUING DIVERSITY

Equal employment opportunity and affirmative action are legal concepts initiated and mandated by the federal government and reinforced by numerous state and local laws. They tend to be quantitative and focus on the problem of getting employers to build and maintain workforces that are truly representative of the population from which they draw employees. In contrast, efforts to pursue diversity for cultural, moral, and economic purposes are purely voluntary, and begin where EEO and Affirmative Action efforts end. These are proactive efforts designed to bring change and stimulate creativity while creating working environments that welcome and utilize the unique skills of every employee. They seek to truly integrate, not assimilate. Valuing diversity means acceptance and co-existence for different cultures and values of various ethnic and social groups.

REVERSE DISCRIMINATION

Affirmative Action programs are pursued when a case of prior discrimination has been established or when an employer has a significant under-representation of minority and female employees. Determinations of under-representation take into consideration the relevant labor markets from which employers can be expected to hire employees for various jobs. "Generally, minority/female promotion or hiring over white males will not be considered reverse discrimination if the company has not met its affirmative action goals."[6] On the other hand, when race or gender becomes a factor in conducting layoffs, the courts may find reverse discrimination. For example, in 1986 the U.S. Supreme Court ruled, in *Wygant v. Jackson Board of Education,* that the school board's actions were unconstitutional. The school board "attempted to preserve the racial balance of the teaching staff by laying off more senior white teachers rather than less senior black teachers."[7]

RECRUITING WOMEN

More and more qualified women are entering what were once male-dominated professions. For example, Carly Fiorina has risen to the position of CEO at Hewlett-Packard.[8] However, such successes do not guarantee that women are adequately represented in the full range of jobs in all organizations. As a supervisor in charge of hiring new workers, you must seek to recruit women from whatever sources you can. Furthermore, it may be necessary to offer childcare facilities and flexible working hours to attract some women. Another issue in recruiting women involves pregnancy. Over the next decade, more than 20 million pregnancies are anticipated among working women in the United States.[9]

As noted in Exhibit 11.4, employers cannot discriminate against women on the basis of pregnancy. As one employment lawyer says, "if pregnant workers must be reassigned because they aren't able physically to perform a job, they mustn't be treated any worse than employees with other disabling conditions."[10] Nonetheless, in 1997 3,977 pregnancy-bias complaints were filed

SUPERVISORS AND ETHICS

Internet recruiting has rapidly become a major source of job candidates for many employers and provides great opportunities for matching applicants with jobs. The large Internet job sites, which host resumes and job listings, provide a valuable matching service to both employers and job seekers. Unfortunately, in recent years there have been also been abuses of the Internet in the area of recruiting, particularly in times of low unemployment in high-demand areas such as engineering and information technology. Because some of the best job candidates are already in the workforces of competitor companies, recruiters often target companies in their recruiting efforts. In order to find such potential job candidates, unethical recruiters hack into the private areas of company websites, where they can gain access to employee directories and home pages.

Some of the biggest abusers of Internet recruiting are freelancers who get paid by the head for quickly locating scarce talent. Since their fees are sometimes as much as 30 percent of the annual salary of the candidate, there are strong financial incentives to resort to unethical tactics. The demand for ethically borderline search skills has become so great that a few firms even provide expensive seminars that teach techniques for hacking into employers' websites. One such firm has advertised that its seminars enable one to "drive your bus right through your source company's website—loading up candidates as you go." An example of one of the techniques is flipping.

Flipping is used to find Web pages that are linked to a specific site, allowing a search within those links. This can be used to find people who create links from their home pages to their colleges, associations to which they belong, and the companies that employ them.

Unethical recruiters can use flipping techniques to enter an employer's private intranets, where they can gain detailed information about company personnel. Other similar techniques are used by unethical recruiters to obtain information from company websites not intended for public use. Because of such abuses, companies should avoid putting too much information on their websites and should build in firewalls to keep hackers from getting into information unintended for the public.

In addition to unethical recruiting practices that rely on Internet technology, there have been more traditional abuses. For example, some unethical recruiters use false identities to gain access to company sources of potential job candidates. The following example describes such a practice:

> "I know a recruiter who has called companies saying he's with the Larry King Show. He says, 'We'd like your CFO to be on our show, can you spell his name?' It's amazing, but he gets all the information he needs. And the CFO's secretary would probably send you her boss's fourth-grade report card if she thinks you're from Larry King."

Other examples of abuse include paying employees for copies of company phone directories or conning receptionists and mailroom clerks out of information on company personnel. To counter such tactics, companies need to train people in these areas to verify identities of callers and the legitimacy of their requests for information.

Source: Eilene Zimmerman, "Fight Dirty Hiring Tactics," *Workforce* (May 2001): 30–34.

with the EEOC, up 6 percent from the previous year. The National Association of Working Women cites pregnancy discrimination as one of the top five concerns of people who call in on its hotline.[11] Supervisors must ensure that pregnancy is not used as a reason for rejecting qualified women applicants.

RECRUITING MINORITIES

Minority recruiting involves development of a strategy for increasing the pool of applicants who have an interest in your job openings. Neighborhood associations, churches, community action groups, state employment offices, ethnic newspapers, and current minority employees may be able to help you, along with search firms that specialize in recruiting minorities. Schools that have large enrollments of minorities are also good sources of applicants, and the number of minority college graduates is increasing. Black people age 25 or older accounted for 13 percent of college graduates in 1995, up from 6 percent in 1975. Over the same time period the proportion of graduates who were Hispanic men increased from 8 to 10 percent, and the proportion of Hispanic women among graduates increased from 5 to 8 percent.[12] Special programs designed to increase the number of minority graduates, such as the minority engineering program at the University of Arizona, may help you find candidates. In addition, for higher-level jobs there are professional associations such as the National Association of Black Engineers and the National Black MBA Association. Internet sites also are good sources of potential applicants, as they often list resumes.

Before minorities are introduced to a workforce, current employees must be encouraged to cooperate with the company's affirmative action efforts. As with all new employees, every effort must be made to find the best qualified candidates and to ensure their early success on the job.

THE SUPERVISOR'S ROLE IN MINORITY HIRING

New minority employees, like everyone else, want an even chance for success. For those minorities who come from disadvantaged circumstances and have gaps in their educational backgrounds, be prepared to provide extra training. Minority employees want and need to be respected and appreciated for their good points and potential. They also want to carry their own weight. Supervisors must realize that in some circumstances new minority workers may arrive expecting the worst: resentment, rejection, hostility, and isolation. As a result they may seem hypersensitive. What a non-minority worker might brush aside, a minority member may consider an insult or personal attack. Until all of your subordinates feel that they are being treated as individuals, you can expect a measure of discontent. Evaluate people on their merits, avoiding stereotypes and generalities. Get to know each person as a unique individual.

There may be a few workers, however, who try to take advantage of the situation. Some may be looking for special privileges. They may want to use the fact that they are women or minorities as a lever in an attempt to gain favored treatment. This inequity, although clearly understandable, must be prevented.

RECRUITING THE DIFFERENTLY ABLED

The differently abled or disabled are those individuals who: (1) have a physical or mental impairment that substantially limits one or more major life activities, (2) have a record of such an impairment, or (3) are regarded as having such an impairment. Two major laws protect people with disabilities: the Americans with Disabilities Act of 1990 (ADA) and the Rehabilitation Act of 1973. ADA has basically replaced the Rehabilitation Act, although earlier court cases on the latter provide current guidance for ADA interpretation.[13] Under Section 1630.4 of the ADA, employers may not discriminate against a qualified person with a disability when they recruit, hire, determine pay and benefits, make job assignments, and grant leaves of absence. Qualified persons are defined as those who are capable of performing a job's "essential functions."[14]

ADA protects individuals with disabilities from employment discrimination based on current or past physical and mental conditions. Examples of those protected include people with a history of cancer, heart trouble, or a contagious disease, providing that their conditions do not pose a significant risk to coworkers or render them unable to perform their work. In addition, ADA protects people who have undergone or who now are undergoing rehabilitation for alcohol or drug dependencies.

Under both laws, employers must make reasonable accommodations that will allow employment of the disabled. Examples of inexpensive accommodations include providing wheelchair ramps, installing handrails, replacing revolving doors, installing speech-recognition aids, and lowering elevator controls.[15]

Under ADA physical examinations may be administered only after the applicant is given a conditional offer of employment. When the physical examination is conducted it must be a regular part of pre-employment procedures. Furthermore, the employer can use only job-related physical conditions to deny employment. It should be noted that drug tests for illegal substances are not considered to be physical examinations under ADA.[16]

Fortunately, many employers have rejected old biases and recognize the value of the differently abled. One of the authors and two colleagues recently interviewed the vice-president of human resources for a Fortune 500 company. The interview lasted over an hour while the executive outlined his views on the future of human resources and how companies can benefit from the function's evolving role. He looked at each of us, listened to our questions, and kept us spellbound with his intellect and enthusiasm. At the end of the interview, he walked us out of the departmental offices, took us down the hall to the elevators, pressed the

As supervisor, you play a major role in the success of minority or differently abled subordinates. With the labor force now coming from diverse groups, your company's success rests on your ability to help all employees reach their potential.

button to summon an elevator, took us down to the main floor, escorted us to the security desk and told the guard that we were leaving. He then shook hands with us and said goodbye. This remarkably talented man is truly an asset to his organization, and he is differently abled because he is blind.

Applicant Screening Procedures

Steps four through eight listed in Exhibit 11.1 deal with several selection tools or screening devices: the application, the preliminary interview, various kinds of tests, and the final interview. These devices, like recruiting, are governed in some ways by federal, state, and local anti-discrimination legislation.

Your best defense against accusations of discrimination or bias in hiring is to be certain that any employment practice or device adheres to the following:

- It is job-related—it is predictive of success or failure on a specific job
- It is a business necessity—the company must do what it does to provide for its continued existence
- It acknowledges a *bona fide occupational qualification* (BFOQ)—for example, a licensing or age requirement
- It honors a *bona fide seniority system* (BFSS)—a seniority system established and maintained that does not have the intent to illegally discriminate[17]

THE APPLICATION

The application is your primary method for obtaining the key facts about a candidate for a job. The information it obtains can help you weed out unqualified people and avoid unnecessary interviews. Some companies are now using computers and sophisticated software, such as Restrac or Resumix, to scan resumes in order to eliminate unqualified applicants. Companies that use computer systems to screen resumes include Coca-Cola, Sony, IBM, Avis Rent A Car, Pfizer, Microsoft, and Shell Oil. Job applicants now are realizing that it is important that their resumes contain the key words for which such systems search, and that they must prepare their resumes in scanable formats.[18]

An application "should state that your company is an Equal Employment Opportunity Employer and that you do not discriminate on the basis of race, color, religion, national origin, age, sex, [sexual orientation where prohibited by state or local laws], marital status, or handicap." For employees who are not represented by a union, the statement that your company hires "at will" indicates that the person is not guaranteed any specific period of employment.[19]

Examine your employer's application form. If it contains any of the inquiries discussed in Exhibit 11.6, you should be on guard. Evaluate the need for each question, and eliminate those that are not closely related to job performance or to predicting success on the job for which the applicant will be considered.

Age, date of birth? Since state and federal laws prohibit discrimination, do not use the answer to this question illegally. Requesting the applicant's age is generally permissible as long as the information is not used for a discriminatory purpose.

Arrests? Since an arrest is no indication of guilt and minorities are arrested disproportionately, this question should be avoided because it is discriminatory.

Convictions (other than traffic violations)? This question is not advisable on a general basis, but it may be appropriate for screening candidates who have been convicted of certain offenses and are under consideration for certain kinds of jobs. The same applies to less than honorable military discharges. If this information is necessary, exercise care in how these records are used in order to avoid possible discrimination.

Available for Saturday or Sunday work? While employee work scheduling is an important issue, this question may discourage applications from members of certain religious groups. If this question is necessary because of business requirements, indicate that an effort will be made to accommodate the religious needs of employees.

Age and number of children? Arrangements for care? While the intent of these questions is to explore a source of absenteeism or tardiness, the effect is potentially discriminatory against women.

Citizenship? Unless required by national security, this question should be avoided because it creates a potential for discrimination on the basis of national origin.

Credit record? Own a car? Own home? Unless required because of business, these questions should be avoided because of potential adverse effects on minorities or women.

Eye color? Hair color? Eye and hair color are not related to job performance and may serve to indicate an applicant's race or national origin.

Fidelity bond? Since a bond may have been denied for an arbitrary or discriminatory reason, use other screening considerations.

Friends or relatives? This question implies that the company prefers to hire friends or relatives of employees and is potentially discriminatory because such a preference is likely to reflect the demography of the company's workforce.

Garnishment record? Federal courts have held that wage garnishments do not normally affect a worker's ability to perform effectively on the job.

Height? Weight? Unless height or weight is directly related to a job requirement, this question should not be listed on the application form.

Maiden name? Prior marriage name? Widowed, divorced, separated? These questions are not related to job performance and may be an indication of religion or national origin. These inquiries may be appropriate if required for identification purposes in pre-employment investigations or security checks.

Marital status? A federal court has held that refusal to employ a married woman when married men occupy similar jobs is unlawful sex discrimination.

Sex. State and federal laws prohibit discrimination on the basis of sex except where sex is a bona fide occupational qualification necessary to the normal operation of business.

Note: If certain information is needed for post-employment purposes, such as Affirmative Action plans, it can be obtained after the applicant has been hired. Maintain this data apart from information that is used in the hiring decision process.

The best general guideline to follow on employment application forms is to ensure that the information elicited is related to qualifications for effective performance on the job.

Source: Illinois Department of Employment Security.

INTERVIEWS

interview

a two-way conversation under the control of one of the parties

The **interview** can be defined as a conversation between two or more parties that is under the control of one of the parties and that has the goal of accomplishing a special objective. It must be carefully planned and skillfully executed if its special objective is to be achieved. As a supervisor, you will be using interviews to screen and hire new employees. Effective interviews require a quiet environment and extensive use of open and closed questions.

The major purpose of a selection interview is to fill in the gaps in information obtained from other selection procedures and devices such as the application, resume, and test scores. Interviews are useful for assessing whether the applicant will fit in well and can provide a good indication of an applicant's communication and interpersonal skills.[20] Human resource experts generally agree that the interview should not be used to collect factual data since it can be obtained more quickly and economically from an application, resume, etc.[21]

To encourage the interviewee to talk you should use open-ended questions that cannot be answered with a yes or no. Open-ended questions start with such words as *why, what, when, where, which, who,* and *how.* Closed-ended questions start with such words as *can, is, do, have,* and *shall.* The interviewer must always listen attentively, never interrupt, and in general refrain from expressing opinions or making snap judgments.

The employment interview has two primary purposes: to evaluate the qualifications and suitability of the applicant to fill the job opening and to give the applicant the information necessary to make an intelligent decision about accepting an offer of employment, should it be given. Be honest about the working conditions, the chances for advancement, and the type of duties you will expect the new employee to perform. Review the job description and the job specification in advance, and have them handy for reference during the interview.

Avoid asking questions that could open you and your employer to accusations of employment discrimination. Exhibit 11.7 gives you precautions to follow when conducting the interview. In addition to these, conduct all of your interviews in the same manner, using the same format and questions. When the same questions are asked of each applicant the interview is said to be a *structured interview.* With such interviews you are not trying to compare apples with oranges since all applicants are asked the same questions. Adding structure is one of the best ways to increase the predictive power or validity and reliability of an interview.[22] (Validity is discussed later in this chapter.) In addition, the use of multiple interviewers, such as a tag team approach, increases the predictive power of interviews. Questions about how applicants handled issues in their past experience, such as conflicts within teams, also increase the predictive power of interviews.[23] The use of such questions is called *behavior-based interviewing.* This interviewing technique is used by companies such as S. C. Johnson Wax, Merck, Steelcase, and Procter & Gamble.[24]

| *Questions to avoid in conducting an employment interview.* | **Exhibit** 11.7 |

- Do not ask any questions of a female applicant that would not be asked of a male candidate (such as inquiries pertaining to child care, marital status, birth control methods, or hindrances to travel or working weekends).

- Do not ask questions of applicants of one race that would not be asked of another (such as questioning one's ability to work in a location with members of another racial group).

- Do not ask the birthplace of an applicant nor require that the applicant submit proof of birth. Since birthplace may indicate a person of foreign origin, it is better to avoid this question than to risk a discrimination charge on this basis.

- Do not ask questions that tend to identify the age of the applicant when age is not related to successful job performance.

- Do not ask a person's religious affiliations.

- Do not ask about an applicant's type of military discharge from general military service. You may ask about job-related experience in the U.S. Armed Forces.

- Do not ask questions on the general physical or mental condition of an applicant.

Source: Illinois Department of Employment Security.

Directive interviews. The **directive interview** is based on a format of specific questions set down in advance (structured) and followed exactly. The questions should ask for the information the interviewer considers most essential. Here are some examples: "What did you do between your job with the ABC Company and your employment at XYZ, Incorporated?" "Why did you leave the ABC Company?" Generally, the interviewer will ask the set of questions (questions she has written down in advance) in the order in which they are listed. Certain questions may be more important than others since they may reveal more valuable information. Make sure that the applicant knows the nature of the job for which he is being interviewed and that he also has an opportunity to ask questions.

This type of interview works best when you are dealing with applicants for routine production or clerical positions. It allows you to obtain the maximum amount of job- or performance-related information in the minimum amount of time.

Non-directive interviews. The **non-directive interview** also is planned, but it is generally less structured and more flexible. Questions may be written down, but they are designed to be open or loose in order to allow applicants more freedom in their responses and to reveal the attitudes behind their words.

directive interview
an interview planned and totally controlled by the interviewer

non-directive interview
an interview planned by the interviewer but controlled by the interviewee

As a supervisor, you need to make job candidates feel at ease. You need to listen carefully. Most important, leave your biases out of the process—pick the most qualified candidate.

Typical questions that might be asked include the following: "Why did you apply for this job?" "Of the jobs you have held, which did you like best (least) and why?" The object of these open questions is to let the applicants talk so that their aspirations, goals, and preferences can come out.

The interviewer is not bound to a rigid format with this indirect approach. One question can lead to others, with the applicant's responses determining the direction and flow of the interview. Quite often you will find out a great deal from an applicant's detailed explanations and will uncover much more than you would in a directive interview. People left to talk on their own will say more than they normally would because they are not sure how much you want to know. They will seize the opportunity to speak their minds if they are relaxed and encouraged to speak up. Nonetheless, even with the non-directive interview, you should ask the same general questions of all applicants so that you can make valid comparisons.

behavioral interview

an interviewing technique in which job applicants are asked to describe how they handled critical incidents in their prior experiences

Behavioral interviews. In a **behavioral interview,** the interviewer asks the applicant about how she dealt with a critical situation in the past. For example, an applicant might be asked to explain how he dealt with a conflict with a subordinate. Other examples might be to ask the applicant how she coached a work team so that it could meet its goals or how he handled an employee who made a critical mistake. The rationale of behavioral interviews is that past behaviors provide good predictions of how candidates will act in the future. In addition, since interviewees are asked about their past experiences, the information is more reliable than responses to questions posing hypothetical situations. By asking the same questions of all applicants, the interviewer can structure the interview, which helps make it more valid and reliable.[25]

Work sampling. The job for which you are attempting to hire employees may require skills that can be tested with a work sample or work performance test. For example, you could let the applicants demonstrate their ability to run a machine, meet close tolerances, file correspondence, keyboard, and the like. If your human resources department has not included such tests in the selection procedure, you should work with its selection specialists to develop work sampling or performance tests that can be included as components of the selection process.

Preparing to Interview

Like any other type of interview—whether for counseling, for sharing your evaluations, or for interrogation and fact finding for disciplinary actions—the employment interview should be held in private and in an environment as free from interruptions as you can make it. Since you usually know well in advance when an applicant is due to report, set aside enough time to do the kind of interview you prefer, and do your homework before the meeting. Read the candidate's application thoroughly and review the job description and specification. Prepare a brief checklist of the essentials you wish to cover so that you do not waste time or overlook an important area.

Conducting the Interview

No matter what type of interview you choose, you should observe the following basic procedure:

1. *Put the applicant at ease.* Keep in mind that the applicant will probably be a bit nervous. A comfortable chair, a quiet room, good ventilation, a cup of coffee, and a smile along with your handshake will go a long way toward relieving his tension.

2. *Stick with your schedule.* If you have planned your questions and prepared an outline to follow, stay with them. You must resist the temptation to wander from essential areas and talk about whatever arises. You have certain points to cover, and you do not usually have the luxury of unlimited time.

3. *Listen.* By now you are probably sick of reading about listening, but it is of the greatest importance to the communication process—especially when you are engaged in a discussion. If you do all the talking, you will learn nothing. If you use the time between your questions simply to plan for what you will cover next, you will miss the applicant's answers. If you are not attentive to the applicant, you will cause her to stop talking. Summarize your thoughts about the applicant periodically, in writing, as time and discussion lags permit.

4. *Remain neutral.* Mask your reactions, whether favorable or unfavorable. If the applicant senses your feelings one way or the other, he will begin to tailor responses to your reactions. You will receive what you have indicated you want to hear, not what the applicant wants to say. Try to uncover the applicant's way of looking at things. You will gain a perspective on the individual and her attitudes that otherwise would be denied to you. If an applicant's attitudes or feelings are contrary to yours, simply ask yourself if it really matters. Will those opinions keep the applicant from a successful job performance? If not, forget them.

5. *Avoid asking leading questions.* Questions formulated to lead a person to the answer you want to hear will do just that. An example is "You got along with your boss, didn't you?" If a person answers no, he is pretty stupid. These questions simply waste time. They tell an applicant where your values are, but you will not learn the applicant's values.

6. *Give the applicant a specific time by which she will have your final decision.* Then stick to that time limit as best you can. If you delay your decision too long, you may lose your prospect. You may be surprised to hear the applicant tell you that he is not sure and wishes to examine other opportunities. If you really want that person, set a time by which he should give you a definite answer.

TESTS

Under federal guidelines, tests are any paper-and-pencil or performance measure used as a basis for any employment decision, including selection and hiring. Such measures include interviews, applications, psychological and performance exams, physical requirements for a job, and any other device that is scored or used as a basis for selecting an applicant. The tests you use should attempt to measure only the performance capabilities that can be proved to be essential for success in the job to be filled.

Disparate or Adverse Impact

disparate impact/ adverse impact
the existence of a significantly different selection rate between women or minorities and non-protected groups

Federal guidelines say that selection devices must have no disparate or adverse impact. **Disparate** or **adverse impact** exists when a significantly different selection rate exists for women or minorities than for other groups. Adverse impact may be determined by several criteria, such as the following guideline:

> A selection rate for any race, sex, or ethnic group which is less than four-fifths (4/5) (or 80 percent) of the rate for the group with the highest rate will generally be regarded by the Federal enforcement agencies as evidence of adverse impact.[26]

For example, if an employer hires 60 percent of white males who apply but less than 80 percent of that figure (less than 48 percent overall) of women and minorities, the selection procedures being used have an adverse impact. As a result, the employer will have to demonstrate that the selection procedures are job-related or valid and reliable. Because of potential challenges to hiring decisions and requirements of the Equal Employment Opportunity Commission (EEOC), accurate records of all those interviewed and hired must be kept. All applicants, whether hired or not, must be classified by sex, race, and ethnic group, including whites.

Some screening criteria or devices that may lead to disparate or adverse impact include tests, educational requirements, height and weight requirements, preferences for relatives of employees, and reference checks. Unless a screening device can be shown to be job related, a business necessity, or a BFOQ, it should not be used. Examples of such business necessity-related qualifications include state-mandated licensing requirements, language abilities, and apprenticeship training for skilled crafts positions.

Validity

Validity is the degree to which a selection criterion or a device measures what it is supposed to measure. With respect to testing for employee selection, the term often refers to evidence that the device is job related—that the device is a valid predictor of future performance on a job. There are several kinds of validity; the ones most relevant to supervisors are *criterion validity* and *content validity*.

Criterion validity involves the demonstration that those who perform well on the test will have high evaluations of actual job performance. Content validity means that the test provides a fair sample of the content of the job. Content validity is established by having experts identify the knowledge required for a job. Test items are then written for various aspects of that knowledge.

validity

the degree to which a selection device measures what it is supposed to measure or is predictive of a person's performance on a job

SUPERVISORS AND QUALITY

One evening, the plant maintenance engineer contacted the company president at her home and asked if she was aware that employees were using drugs on the job. She replied that she was not and asked how he knew this to be a fact. The engineer replied that he had found drug paraphernalia—syringes, rubber straps, and unidentified pills in various trash containers throughout the work areas. The president immediately contacted the company's attorney and asked for his help.

Together, the president and the attorney worked up a program to deal with possible drug abuse on the company's premises involving company employees. The program involved three distinct phases: education, testing, and rehabilitation opportunities. It was initiated with a two-hour education session on drug abuse, its effects on the workplace, and its costs in both dollars and human

terms. The employees were informed that they would be tested for drugs through urine sampling (the most common form of testing) on the following Monday at a nearby testing lab. Employees were assigned a report-in time and given the entire day off with pay. Persons testing positive were required to enroll in a rehabilitation program before being allowed to return to work. Those refusing to be tested or to join the rehab program were fired after explanations and warnings. Each year, all employees would be randomly tested at least once.

This company's policy is typical of a sound approach. It makes no exceptions, it forewarns, it offers treatment, and it is not punitive for those who avail themselves of the opportunity to get straight. Its primary motivations are to prevent injuries and losses and to keep good people on the job.

An example of a criterion-based or predictive validation follows. To construct a valid physical test, a state agency decided to study the physical demands made on troopers during the execution of their daily duties. A test was developed, made up of a short run with full weight of equipment and a drag-and-carry test simulating the extraction of accident victims. The test was given to recruits but was not used to hire them. After the recruits were selected and had their job performances rated by their superiors, the test results were compared to their ratings. A good relationship was found, and the test was then considered a valid selection device. It simulated with accuracy the physical demands that were made on troopers, and the test included major examples of their daily requirements.

Pre-Employment Drug Testing

Nearly all companies have some employees who have had substance abuse problems. Substance abusers frequently cause injuries to themselves, as well as others, and damage to property. According to a survey by the American Management Association, 56.7 percent of "companies with sales of less than $50 million . . . carry out drug testing on job applicants."[27] As a supervisor, the extent of your involvement in drug testing will probably be limited to getting the results after the offer of employment has been made and the test(s) given. Offers of employment are usually conditional on successful completion of physical exams and drug tests. Nonetheless, you should have some rudimentary understanding of drug testing procedures.

There are many potential difficulties with drug testing. First, there is the potential for error, as not all drug tests are 100 percent reliable. Many experts also agree that common over-the-counter drugs can lead to a positive test result. Because of the legal liabilities and concerns for accuracy, employers routinely use qualified laboratories to process samples. In order to avoid charges of discrimination, employers must be careful to test all applicants instead of only selected ones. In addition, two-step processes are common requirements for drug testing. The first step in the process is a screening test. Screening tests are relatively economical but not as reliable as other tests. For all positive results, a more reliable but more expensive type of test, called a confirmatory test, is also conducted. Drug tests are controversial because of concerns about privacy. However, pre-employment testing is much less controversial.[28]

AIDS, HIV, and Hiring

About one million Americans are currently believed to be HIV positive—infected with the virus. The majority "are young adults between the ages of 25 and 44, the age category that contains half the nation's workers."[29] The Supreme Court has ruled that simple fear of contagion by any virus—without any medical assessment that the fear is well-founded—cannot justify firing an employee with any contagious disease. Through this decision, those who test positive for HIV and AIDS (along with others who suffer from contagious diseases) have been placed under the protection of the 1973 Vocational Rehabilitation Act and the 1990 Americans with Disabilities Act or ADA. Thus under the provisions of ADA, AIDS or HIV cannot be the basis for refusing to hire an applicant. In addition, under the provisions of ADA, employers must make "reasonable accommodations" for those with HIV or AIDS and must comply with confidentiality requirements.

Fear of AIDS is a reality in the workplace requiring education for all employees. As a result, many employers have formulated effective and humane policies and training programs to deal with this issue. Many companies have also adopted the guidelines recommended by the American Red Cross and the National Leadership Coalition on AIDS. We will discuss this issue further in Chapter 16.

Screening by Polygraph

The polygraph, sometimes called the lie detector, was used by 10 percent of U. S. companies to screen job applicants before being banned by federal law in 1988. The Employee Polygraph Protection Act states that private employers may not require, request, or suggest that employees or prospective employees take lie detector (polygraph) tests, except when conducting in-house investigations. Employers may then request employees to take lie detector tests under strict conditions.

Screening by Paper-and-Pencil Integrity Tests

Paper-and-pencil integrity or honesty tests, written and graded by vendors, are used to eliminate applicants who are likely to steal from the company. There is substantial evidence that such tests can be valid predictors of tendencies for theft and other undesirable work behaviors. Integrity testing is restricted in only two states: Massachusetts and Rhode Island.[30] The following provides a good summary of the status of paper-and-pencil integrity tests:

> The results of this work [previous research] consistently indicate that these tests are valid in reference to criteria that include theft, detrimental behaviors, and overall job performance. This validity may be demonstrated in spite of attempts by applicants to distort their responses and to appear more honest than they in fact are. Also, integrity tests can add to the prediction of job performance in selection programs that consist of cognitive ability and personality measures. Finally, little data exist that indicate these tests are at variance with any of the laws that govern selection.[31]

The Immigration Reform and Control Act

The Immigration Reform and Control Act of 1986 requires most employers to hire only American citizens and aliens who are authorized to work in the United States. When you hire, you must verify the employment eligibility and identity of each employee and complete and retain the one-page federal form I-9. In general, you must complete Form I-9 for persons employed for three days or more by the end of the third business day following the hire. For people employed for fewer than three days, you must complete the form by the end of the first day of employment. Once Form I-9 is completed by both the employer and the new hire, the documents used to verify identity and employability should be photocopied and kept on file with the Form I-9 for three years after the date of employment, or for one year after the date the employment is terminated, whichever is later.

Pitfalls

In employee selection, as in most of your duties, a number of pitfalls may snare you if you are not aware of them. Since there is a strong similarity between appraisals of subordinates and appraisals of applicants, some of the same pitfalls discussed in Chapter 13 apply here as well.

1. *The halo effect.* This occurs when you let one outstanding good characteristic in an applicant influence your overall assessment.

2. *The rush job.* If you are inadequately prepared for an interview, how can you find out all you need to know about an applicant?

3. *Failure to follow the principles of sound interviewing.* After you have completed this chapter, you should have a good grasp of what these principles are.

4. *Overselling your company or the job.* By overstatements, puffed-up generalizations, and inaccurate or untruthful information, you might be sowing the seeds that eventually frustrate the new person and lead him to quit. The person may accept the job with false hopes as a result of your inaccurate promises.

5. *Omitting pertinent information.* If you leave out vital facts with regard to the applicant's duties or working conditions, she will be forced to make a decision on the basis of incomplete information. Give the facts as clearly as you can, leave out the sugar coating, and be complete in your description of the job.

6. *Neglecting sound public relations.* If your decision at the close of your interview is a negative one, and you have not left the person with a good impression about your company, you will be promoting unfavorable public opinion about your organization. Such unfavorable opinions could cause a decline in job applicants and even in sales. You want to make an honest but favorable impression so that, no matter what happens, when the visit is over both parties will leave with positive impressions.

7. *Asking discriminatory questions.* Companies can find themselves in major difficulties with federal and state governments if they seek discriminatory information on application forms and during interviews.

8. *Hiring friends and relatives who don't qualify.* Pressures from these two groups can be tremendous. Nonetheless, members of these groups must be subjected to the same screening devices and procedures that apply to all other candidates.

Welcoming and Inducting New Employees

When you have offered the job and the applicant has accepted, you must now begin your planning to welcome the new arrival. As a result of the interview, you should have a fairly good idea of training needs. If you know that some training will be needed, map out your plans, and get the program organized in a way that allows you to begin as soon as possible. Prepare your department or team for the new person by communicating positive information about him. Plan to make that first day a truly positive experience—one that will tell the applicant that his decision to work for you was a good one.

ORIENTATION

Orientation includes the planning and conduct of a program to introduce the new employee to the company, including all policies, practices, rules, and regulations that will immediately affect the employee. Orientation programs are usually conducted by members of the human resources department and typically occur within the first few days after the new person arrives. Typically materials such as handbooks on company policies, descriptions of benefits, rights under various laws, and disciplinary procedures will be distributed and explained.

orientation
the planning and conduct of a program to introduce a new employee to the company and its history, policies, rules, and procedures

Most orientation programs give employees a broad overview of the entire organization, with a special emphasis on how and where the new person fits in with the rest of the organization. The goals usually include the following:

- To instill a favorable first impression with regard to the company, its products, its leadership, and its methods of operation
- To familiarize the new people with the policies, procedures, rules, and benefits that are initially most important
- To outline in detail the specific expectations that the company has for its employees with regard to on-the-job behavior
- To explain the various services that exist for all employees and describe how one can take advantage of them

INDUCTION

induction

the planning and conduct of a program to introduce a new employee to his or her job, working environment, supervisor, and peers

Induction includes the planning and conduct of a program to introduce your new person to his job, working environment, supervisor, and coworkers. As the supervisor, induction is your responsibility. You should begin to plan the induction activities of your new subordinate soon after the acceptance of an employment offer. Tailor the induction activities to fit the needs of the subordinate, set specific goals, and work out a timetable to achieve them.

In Chapter 6, we discussed the Pygmalion effect. You will recall that a manager's assumptions about their new people can affect his treatment of them. You must assume the best about your new person and demonstrate trust until your assumptions are proved to be incorrect. You also must have confidence in the person's ability to learn new responsibilities. It is essential to get a new employee started with a positive set of experiences from the first day on the job. Have all materials ready so that she can get right to work. A warm welcome and immediate successful experiences will foster motivation, reassure the new person, and help allay the insecurity or anxiety that comes with a new job. Induction becomes a very important program that can increase the short- and long-term performance of new employees. When done poorly, however, it can sow the seeds for early failure and employee turnover. Accordingly, it is important to shield your people from negative initial experiences by introducing them to successful employees and experiences. Try to keep malcontents away from them until they have firmly established their attitudes and mastery over their tasks.

Induction Goals

Among the typical goals for induction are the following:

- To instill favorable impressions and attitudes about the work section, its operations, and its people
- To remove as many sources of anxiety as possible by helping the new person meet his needs for security, competence, and social acceptance
- To design and provide initial experiences that foster motivation and promote early success
- To begin to build a human relationship that is based on trust and confidence

Exhibit 11.8 contains a checklist that may prove useful to you as you plan your program.

Making Arrangements

You must contact the human resources department and procure the necessary forms, passes, booklets, and so forth so that they are available on the first day. As noted in Exhibit 11.8, the person's work area must be prepared so that the basic inventory of tools, equipment, supplies, and materials is on

Checklist for planning your induction program.	**Exhibit**	**11.8**

Yes No

○ ○ 1. Are tools, equipment, supplies, and other things on hand for the newcomer's first day?

○ ○ 2. Have you reserved time with coworkers and others that the newcomer should meet during his induction?

○ ○ 3. Have you planned to give the newcomer a really positive experience the first day?

○ ○ 4. Have you planned a systematic introduction of the new person's duties to her?

○ ○ 5. Have you talked with the newcomer's coworkers, paving the way for a friendly welcome?

○ ○ 6. Have you reserved enough time to spend with the newcomer in the first few days on the job?

hand. Everything must be in its place and in working order so that there are no surprises waiting for the new person or for you.

Make arrangements for the new person to join one or another of the formal groups of workers in your department. It is a good idea to get someone to act as the new employee's mentor—a guide and tutor who will be available to answer questions and provide help once you have finished your induction activities. A mentor should be a volunteer who knows the ropes and whose judgment and abilities you respect. This person can provide immediate acceptance and social companionship on and off the job.

THE FIVE BASIC QUESTIONS

As soon as the new employee arrives, the induction or initiation procedure begins. The typical induction answers the following five basic questions for the new worker:

1. Where am I now?
2. What are my duties?
3. What are my rights?
4. What are my limits?
5. Where can I go?

Where Am I Now?

After greeting the new arrival warmly, you should explain in words and graphic form just where he fits into the entire company's operations. By starting with a copy of the company's organization chart, you can move from his slot in your department all the way up the chain of command to the chief executive. Explain the jobs performed in your department and in the departments adjacent to it. Name the personalities involved in each, with particular emphasis on those the new employee is most likely to encounter. Give the newcomer a good idea of how his job and department relate to the ultimate success and profitability of the company.

This initial explanation can be followed by a tour of the department and a look at the work area. Introduce the person to his coworkers and mentor, and give them a chance to chat. Next, familiarize the new person with the facilities within the department and the adjacent areas that he will need to use, and explain the functions of each.

Introduce the newcomer to people you meet along the way in such a manner as to demonstrate your enthusiasm and pride in having him join your operation. Something like this should do the trick: "Sharon, I'd like you to meet Howard Kramer. Howard, this is Sharon Watkins. Howard has just joined our team, and we are lucky to have him." This gives your new worker a chance to know your true feelings about his decision to come aboard. The newcomer will quickly begin to sense that he is respected and well thought of, as well as needed. Howard will not remember the names of all those to whom he has been introduced, but he will remember your enthusiastic welcome.

During your walk through the company, you should have an excellent opportunity to review the company's history and to reinforce its orientation program. By sharing knowledge of the company, you will give the new person the sense of being an important part of a successful organization. There is tremendous value in this since we all like to feel we belong to groups that are bigger and more powerful than ourselves. Review the company's line of products or services, and point out the major events in the company's history that have contributed the most to its present position. Pass on positive information so that the new employee develops an attractive but honest image of the company, its people, and its future.

What Are My Duties?

Give a copy of the job description to the new person, and go over each duty. Explain the details implied by the general listing, and check his understanding of each. Wherever you can, demonstrate each duty—either by performing it or by giving specific examples. By answering questions for your new worker, you will be helping to accomplish all the goals of your induction program.

What Are My Rights?

Explain the pay periods and how pay is calculated. Also, explain fringe benefits such as group life and health insurance plans, the company's profit sharing plan, paid holidays, incentive awards, the suggestion plan, and the like. In particular, communicate the eligibility requirements (where they exist) for each benefit. Review the overtime procedures you follow, and explain how workers become eligible for overtime. Go over the appraisal process, and specify what will be rated in it. If there is a union, explain the grievance process and how to file a grievance. Cover all the areas that you know from experience have been sources of misunderstanding in the area of workers' rights. For instance, workers often confuse sick days with personal-leave days.

If there is a union, be certain to introduce the steward and explain the rights employees have in regard to union membership. Where this is voluntary, say so. Do not give your views about unions. Simply advise the newcomer of what he needs to know.

What Are My Limits?

Your first and most important duty regarding discipline is to inform each employee about the limits or boundaries on his conduct and performance (see Chapter 14). Discipline starts with the induction and orientation of each person. The do's and don'ts that you intend to enforce should be explained, along with the penalties attached to each. Pay particular attention to the areas affecting safety. Each worker should know not only the rules but company policy as well. If safety equipment is needed, be sure that it is issued or purchased, whichever is required. Then be certain to emphasize safety throughout the newcomer's training. Instill respect for safe working habits and conduct right from the start. Enforcement then becomes easier.

Where Can I Go?

This question involves the opportunities for advancement that exist for each new person. Explain the employee's eligibility for training and advanced programs that increase both work skills and the opportunities for promotion. State the criteria you use for making promotion and transfer decisions. People need to know what is required of them in order to advance. Finally, explain the standards they must meet in order to qualify for a raise.

FOLLOWING UP

Plan a follow-up interview to talk with the newcomer about the first day's experiences and answer any questions that may have accumulated. See if you can get a handle on how he really feels.

At the end of the first week, schedule another informal meeting with the new person, and determine if he is making an adequate adjustment to the new job. Your personal daily observations should tell you if he and the group are getting along and if any personal problems are beginning to surface. Watch for warning signals such as fatigue, chronic complaints, lack of interest, or sudden changes from previous behavior patterns. If you spot any of these signals, be prepared to move swiftly to uncover the causes.

You must be prepared for the possibility that the new person may not be cut out for the type of work that has been assigned. If your observations and his responses seem to indicate this, get together with your boss and discuss the matter. You may be able to work something out, such as a transfer to a different job within or outside your section. It may also be possible to redefine duties to compensate for the difficulties. You want to try your best to salvage the new arrival and to avoid costly termination and replacement proceedings.

After the new employee's questions are answered, a **psychological contract** forms between employer and employee that summarizes what both are expected to give and receive from each other. Although unwritten, it should be understood by all concerned. The terms of the contract evolve as time passes and experiences increase. Both parties must feel that the changes are necessary and fair. Each party must believe that the other is living up to his commitments.[32] As you participate in orientation and induction programs and activities, make certain that you know what is likely to happen to the new person once she is on the job. Be honest, and clear up any misconceptions that you sense. Don't promise or let your company promise more than you know it can deliver.

psychological contract
an unwritten recognition of what an employer and an employee expect to give and to receive from each other

The Socialization Process

When people enter a new organization to take a new job, they go through a number of experiences that familiarize them with their new environment—its people, goals, processes, and systems. **Socialization** is the process through which both the new person and the organization learn about each other. Ultimately, this leads to an understanding by which both parties can live. Through socialization, new employees discover their place in the environment, the restrictions on their freedom, and how to succeed.

socialization
the process new employees undergo in the first few weeks of employment through which they learn how to cope and succeed

All you have to do is treat the new person like a guest in your home whom you wish to impress favorably. Through adequate planning, a warm welcome, a constructive induction program, and conscientious follow-up, you will be doing all that you can do or are expected to do.

Instant Replay

1. A proper selection procedure usually involves the supervisor in the interviewing process.

2. Selection devices include any interview, form, test, or other instrument that will be used in making the decision to hire.

3. Selection devices and procedures should not adversely affect minorities and women, and they must be valid.

4. The selection process involves both obtaining and giving information. Selection errors can be expensive in terms of both litigation expenses

involved with discrimination charges and replacement costs for a person who should not have been hired.

5. Orientation programs are usually conducted by the human resources department and are designed to welcome new employees to the enterprise as a whole.

6. Induction programs are usually conducted by the supervisor of the new employee and are designed to welcome new employees to a specific job, working environment, and peer group.

7. Studies show that the first few days on a new job are extremely important and largely determine the future performance and careers of newcomers.

8. The supervisor of a new person, more than any other factor at work, can mean the difference between success and failure on the job.

Questions for Class Discussion

1. Can you define this chapter's key terms?
2. What is the proper role for a supervisor to play in the process that will select a new subordinate?
3. What will a human resource management department normally do during the selection process?
4. What are the major selection devices used in a typical selection process?
5. How should you prepare to give a selection interview?
6. What are the goals of a good orientation program?
7. What are the goals of a good induction program?
8. What happens to an employee who passes through the socialization process?
9. What are the questions that new employees want answered?

Incident

Purpose: To test your knowledge of the application of federal human resource laws.

Your task: Agree or disagree with each of the following statements. Do not consult the key that follows until you have checked each question.

Agree   Disagree

○   ○   1. It is illegal to hire an alien for a job.

○   ○   2. Every employer is required to have an Affirmative Action plan.

Agree   Disagree

○   ○   3. The Americans with Disabilities Act does not protect job applicants who have HIV or AIDS.

○   ○   4. Employers may use polygraph tests during selection activities.

○   ○   5. An I-9 form must be completed before an applicant is hired.

○   ○   6. Affirmative Action programs specify exact numbers of people to be hired.

○   ○   7. Paper-and-pencil integrity tests have low validity for selection purposes.

○   ○   8. People who have been discriminated against cannot sue for punitive damages.

○   ○   9. Unstructured interviews have more validity than structured interviews.

○   ○ 10. Drug testing is not a common practice in hiring.

(Key: All are false.)

CASE PROBLEM 11.1   *Revolving Door Employment*

Winston walked into Lichelle's office, collapsed into the chair and said, "Have you heard the news? Joan just gave two weeks notice. Seems that her husband just got transferred to a job in Milwaukee. With all of these talented women who work here, why is it that they always follow their husbands when these guys get new jobs? Why don't some of the husbands follow their wives when they get new jobs? I just feel like we're totally at the mercy of the husband's job situation and that it has nothing to do with how well we manage around here. Joan really liked it here and was doing a great job!"

LICHELLE: "What do you mean by saying that the women always follow their husbands? I'm here and I haven't left to follow my husband someplace!"

WINSTON: "Well, you know what I mean. Our turnover rate for women is really high and a lot of it has nothing to do with us. We must have had six or seven women who left this year because their husbands or boyfriends got transferred. And the costs of losing these people are really high. We lose their skills and have to suffer through the learning period for their replacements."

LICHELLE: "I know what you mean. We really fell behind when Julie left last month. What do you think we should do?"

WINSTON: "Perhaps we should try to hire more guys since they seem to stay on the job longer."

LICHELLE: "I don't think we can do that legally. Besides, we've got some women here that have been with the company longer than any of the guys. In addition to being illegal, it wouldn't be fair. I don't like that idea at all."

WINSTON: "Yeah, I know. I hate anything related to hiring that sounds like discrimination. But it doesn't seem fair to us either when all of these women leave for reasons that have nothing to do with how well we treated them. This turnover is really going to hurt our profitability this year."

LICHELLE: "I know. This is really bad but I don't know what to do."

WINSTON: "Maybe we should start asking women applicants about the job status of their husbands. You know, how likely it is that they are going to be transferred or take a new job in the next three or four years? It's job-related because if they leave it costs us real money."

LICHELLE: "I don't think you can ask questions like that."

WINSTON: "Okay, why don't we ask the same question of both women and men?"

LICHELLE: "That might be better. But I don't see how asking personal stuff like that could ever be job-related. I don't think you can ask questions like that. I think our hands are tied because of the EEO laws."

WINSTON: "Well, let's check with the HR people on that issue. Here's a related issue. It seems to me that we're also losing lots of women because of pregnancy. Why don't we ask women applicants if they plan to get pregnant in the next two or three years. We won't discriminate against women, we just won't hire the ones that are going to quit because of pregnancy."

Questions

1. If the turnover rate of women is higher, can gender become a job-related selection factor? Explain.
2. Who is right about Winston's proposal to ask both men and women about the likelihood that their spouse will be transferred, Winston or Lichelle? Explain.
3. Would Winston's proposal to ask about pregnancy be legal? Explain.

Youth Movement	CASE PROBLEM 11.2

Scott looked at the new advertising campaign that had just come from the ad agency. He had the task of hiring and supervising five new sales people to promote the new malt liquor product using the new ad campaign. The ads had lots of pictures of young, attractive people in their early 20s to mid-30s. Most of the posters involved sports themes such as rock climbing, beach volleyball, and surfing. A major component of the sales strategy was to have the sales people promote the malt liquor by distributing paraphernalia such as caps and T-shirts at sporting events, rock concerts, festivals, and at sports bars. The company had identified people in their 20s and 30s as its primary consumer group, and this segment was expected to account for 80 percent of sales. As Scott finished going though the materials, his boss, Eric, walked into his office.

ERIC: "Well Scott, what do you think of the campaign?"

SCOTT: "I think it's great. This promotional stuff is really going to appeal to these young people who are going to buy our malt liquor."

ERIC: "Yeah, I think so too. The strategy has really worked well for other companies. Do you have a set of applicants to interview for the five sales jobs?"

SCOTT: "Wow, that was a tough job. I had over 125 applications to look through. But I've trimmed the list down to 25."

ERIC: "That's great. But you can't interview 25 people and still get your other work done."

SCOTT: "Yeah, I know. Would you take a look at the 25 applications and help me narrow it down some more?"

ERIC: "Sure. Let's take a look and trim it down to about 10 or 12." Eric then took a few minutes to look through the stack of applications.

SCOTT: "Well, what do you think?"

ERIC: "These look pretty good. I can see why this was a tough job. But I would eliminate the three guys in here that don't seem to fit."

SCOTT: "Which ones are those?"

ERIC: "Well, they're the older guys. There is one who is 48, another who is 53, and one is 56."

SCOTT: "But they have good solid sales experience and all of them have done sales in the beverage industry."

ERIC: "You're right, but can you see these guys relating to our customers at rock concerts and at beach volleyball tournaments? It's not going to happen."

SCOTT: "Will there be any problems with doing this given that they appear to be the most qualified in terms of sales experience?"

ERIC: "Nah, even if they could do the job they'd just want too much money. So you can just eliminate them on that basis."

Questions

1. Do you agree with Eric's recommendations? Why or why not?

2. Are Eric's recommendations legally acceptable? Explain.

3. How would you attack Eric's argument?

4. What should Scott do if he disagrees with Eric?

References

1. Pfeffer, Jeffrey. *The Human Equation: Building Profits by Putting People First.* Boston: Harvard Business School Press, 1998.

2. Levering, Robert, and Moskowitz, Milton. "The 100 Best Companies to Work for in America," *Fortune* (January 12, 1998): 84.

3. Leonard, Arthur S. "Sexual Orientation and the Workplace: A Rapidly Developing Field," *Labor Law Journal* vol. 44, No. 9 (1993): 574–583.

4. Martin, Justin. "So, You Want to Work for the Best. . . ," *Fortune* (January 12, 1998): 77–78.

5. Seminerio, Maria, "E-Recruiting Takes Next Step," *eWeek* (April, 23, 2001): 51–54.

6. Pell, Arthur R. *The Supervisor's Handbook.* New York: McGraw-Hill (1994): 102.

7. Lee, Barbara A. "Reverse Discrimination," in Lawrence H. Peters, Charles R. Greer, and Stuart A. Youngblood (eds.), *The Blackwell Encyclopedic Dictionary of Human Resource Management.* Oxford, United Kingdom: Blackwell (1997): 294.

8. Taylor, Chris. "HP's Fierce Face-Off," *Time* (March 4, 2002): 46–48.

9. Shellenbarger, Sue. "Recent Suits Make Pregnancy Issues Workplace Priorities," *The Wall Street Journal* (January 14, 1998): B1.

10. Ibid.

11. Ibid.

12. Yavarkovsky, Judith. "College Graduates Age 25 and Older, by Sex and Race: United States, 1975, 1985, and 1995," *Statistical Bulletin—Metropolitan Life Insurance Company* Vol. 78, No. 3 (1997): 33.

13. Gatewood, Robert D., and Feild, Hubert S. *Human Resource Selection,* 4th ed. Fort Worth, TX: Dryden Press, 1998.

14. McKee, Bradford. "The Disabilities Labyrinth," *Nation's Business* (April 1993): 18–23.

15. Greer, Charles R. *Strategy and Human Resources: A General Managerial Approach,* 2nd ed. Englewood Cliffs, NJ: Prentice Hall, 2001.

16. Frierson, James G. "An Employer's Dilemma: The ADA's Provisions on Reasonable Accommodation and Confidentiality," *Labor Law Journal* Vol. 43, No. 5 (1992): 308–312. Postol, Lawrence P., and Kandue, David D. "An Employer's Guide to the Americans with Disabilities Act," *Labor Law Journal* Vol. 42, No. 6 (1991): 323–342.

17. Schuler, Randall R. *Managing Human Resources,* 5th ed. New York: West (1995): 261–262.

18. Pollock, Ellen Joan. "Sir: Your Application For a Job Is Rejected; Sincerely, Hal 9000," *The Wall Street Journal* (July 30, 1998): A1, A12.

19. Half, Robert. *On Hiring.* New York: Crown (1985): 67.

20. Heneman, Herbert G., III, and Heneman, Robert L. *Staffing Organizations.* Middleton, WI: Mendota House Inc., 1994.

21. Gatewood and Feild. *Human Resource Selection.*

22. Heneman and Heneman. *Staffing.*

23. Lancaster, Hal. "Making a Good Hire Takes a Little Instinct and a Lot of Research," *The Wall Street Journal* (March 3, 1998): B1.

24. Martin. "So, You Want to Work."

25. Kleiman, Carol. "True to Life: Behavioral Interviews Focus on Experience," *Fort Worth Star-Telegram* (February 20, 2000): Careers Section.

26. Equal Employment Opportunity Commission. *1978 Uniform Guidelines on Employee Selection Procedures,* 1978.

27. *Inc.* "And Whose Syringe Might This Be?" (August 1994): 104.

28. Osterloh, John D., and Becker, Charles E. "Chemical Dependency and Drug Testing in the Workplace," *Western Journal of Medicine* Vol. 152, No. 5 (1990): 506–513. Rothstein, Mark A.; Knapp, Andria S.; and Liebman, Lance. *Cases and Materials on Employment Law,* 2nd ed. Westbury, NY: Foundation Press, 1991.

29. Noble, Barbara P. "At Work: AIDS Awareness Goes to the Office," *The New York Times* (December 6, 1992): 25.

30. Gatewood and Feild. *Human Resource Selection.* Bernardin, H. John, and Cooke, Donna K. "Validity of an Honesty Test in Predicting Theft Among Convenience Store Employees," *Academy of Management Journal* Vol. 36, No. 5 (1993): 1097–1108.

31. Gatewood and Feild. *Human Resource Selection:* 637.

32. Schein, Edgar H. *Career Dynamics: Matching Individual and Organizational Needs.* Reading, MA: Addison-Wesley (1978): 94–97.

TRAINING

Objectives

After reading and discussing this chapter, you should be able to do the following:

1. Define this chapter's key terms.
2. Explain the advantages that a supervisor gains from training a subordinate.
3. Explain the advantages that a trainee gains from training.
4. List the basic requirements that a trainer must satisfy in order to train.
5. List the basic requirements a trainee must satisfy in order to learn.
6. List and briefly describe the principles that govern training.
7. Briefly describe the training cycle.

Introduction

This chapter is concerned with how you can help your subordinates acquire new skills, improve their existing ones, and improve their abilities to handle their jobs. Training becomes necessary by the very fact that you have subordinates. Whether they are old-timers, newcomers, or a mix of the two, you must continually see to it that they are functioning effectively. If they are not, training is in order. Whether you train or rely on others to help you with training, you are responsible for seeing to it that your people are properly trained.

American corporations spend in excess of $55 billion on training each year.[1] The ability to attract, develop (train), and retain employees is one of the criteria *Fortune* uses to select its annual list of the world's most admired companies. Examination of *Fortune*'s list reveals that top-ranked companies historically place a great deal of emphasis on training. For example, GE, which has ranked first on numerous occasions, takes pride in being a meritocracy in which developmental opportunities enable employees to reach the top regardless of the schooling they had prior to joining the company.

Wal-Mart, which also ranks high on the *Fortune* lists, has shifted its emphasis to training and development of its existing workforce rather than simply emphasizing hiring.[2] Such investments in training provide attractive rates of return for the companies' investments. "Motorola [also a leader in training] calculates that every \$1 it spends on training delivers \$30 in productivity gains within three years."[3] Consider also the following description of specialty firms that specialize in training employees to use computer software.

> CBT Group PLC . . . emigrated from its Irish birthplace to Silicon Valley and built a market capitalization of nearly \$2 billion—close to Apple Computer Inc.'s current value—in the three years since its initial public stock offering. The reason? Surging demand for instruction in the use of personal-computer technology. CBT isn't alone. Training specialist Learning Tree International is suddenly valued at nearly \$600 million, while rival Computer Learning Centers Inc. has a market cap of \$544 million. . . . New instructional software from CBT and others is sharply boosting the productivity of computer-based education, which schools and universities have tried with mixed success since the 1970s. Training companies are adding multimedia graphics, exploiting the Internet and linking training to payoffs like increased revenues. They are also helping to demonstrate what instruction is best conducted on PCs, and which requires live teachers.[4]

The Subjects of Training

Training imparts attitudes, knowledge, and skills. It is an ongoing process governed by basic principles and provided by people with the aid of machines and methods specially suited to the subjects to be covered and the persons to be taught. Training, like daily living, increases our knowledge and understanding of the people and things that surround us.

ATTITUDES

We have already said much about attitudes, and all of it is related to the training process. You must remember that when you train, you are attempting to instill positive attitudes—either as replacements for improper ones or as useful additions—in the minds of your trainees. Attitudes are taught primarily through your own example and secondarily through your words. Workers learn an attitude by observing what you do. If you talk about safety but act in an unsafe manner or lightly skip over safety during the training period, your workers will adopt the same casual attitudes.

KNOWLEDGE

Knowledge is the body of facts, ideas, concepts, and procedures that enable people to see or visualize what must be done and why. If trainees can understand the whole job and its relationship to the work of others, they have a better chance to master their own jobs. They must understand the theory (fundamental principles and abstract knowledge) that governs their work before they can adequately perform their own tasks. Then with your help they must translate theory into practice through training. Knowledge is important but applying knowledge is even more critical.

SKILLS

The best way to teach a skill is to involve the trainees as quickly as possible in performing the skill. Practice and more practice are keys to the successful acquisition of motor skills. Trainees first develop an in-depth understanding of the tools, equipment, or machinery and then move to an actual working knowledge of the trade or craft. In this manner they gain controlled exposure to both the technical side and the manipulative side of their jobs.

Early successes are essential in the early phases of training. Accordingly, you must build in opportunities for small positive accomplishments. It is also important to prevent trainees from developing improper work habits. Often you may have to ask the trainees to unlearn certain procedures or habits acquired from earlier experiences before you can substitute the

In an effort to improve their workforce, many large companies offer basic education programs. Literacy classes, such as the one shown at Aetna Insurance Company, teach workers the skills they need to succeed on the job.

proper methods. This is a difficult and time-consuming task that requires a great deal of patience from both you and your trainees.

Tom Peters, author of many management books, offers several suggestions to managers who want their companies to survive in today's business climate. He says workers must be trained to accomplish the following goals:[5]

- Learn many jobs (20 to 30).
- Perform many tasks (maintenance, repair, budgeting, and quality control).
- Perform many skills (problem cause-and-effect analysis, listening, interpersonal dynamics—team problem-solving skills).
- Function as a member of a business team, with team leadership rotating among its members.

A major barrier to training is that about 20 percent of current and new employees lack the basic literacy skills they need to succeed in their jobs.[6]

According to the American Management Association, 24 percent of major U. S. employers are conducting basic remedial training programs to enable their employees to cope with their present and future job demands.[7] R. J. Reynolds invested about $2 billion in automating its factory in Winston-Salem, North Carolina, before discovering that its workforce lacked the reading skills necessary to operate and maintain the new equipment. Of its 6,000 workers, 1,300 had to be put through a basic literacy program. Finally, IBM offered a free college-level course in algebra to its employees but discovered that only 30 out of 280 workers who signed up were able to read and calculate at the 12th-grade level—a prerequisite for taking the course.[8]

Advantages of Training

ADVANTAGES FOR THE SUPERVISOR

How do supervisors benefit from training a subordinate? The following are but a few of the many benefits you receive when you train your people properly:

1. *You get to know your subordinates.* When you are dealing with new employees, you hasten the process of learning about their needs, wants, and potentials. With your other subordinates, you get a chance to update your knowledge of each person. This knowledge facilitates decision making about personnel decisions such as recommendations for promotions, raises, and transfers.

2. *You further your own career.* As each individual increases his efficiency and effectiveness, the whole group benefits. As your subordinates perform and feel better, they enhance your reputation as a supervisor and leader. As we have stated before, your reputation is largely a product of their performance.

3. *You gain more time.* As a result of training, your people become more self-sufficient and confident. Their improvements in performance reduce the time you must spend on corrections and deficiencies. You then gain more time for planning, organizing, controlling, and coordinating. You may be able to shift from an autocratic style of supervision (so necessary during the training) to a less time-consuming style. A striking example of effective delegation and time management is provided by General George Marshall's leadership during World War II. "Gen. George Marshall ran World War II and still took a daily nap after lunch and went home by 4:30."[9]

4. *You promote good human relations.* One of your primary roles in developing good human relations with your people is that of educator. They gain self-confidence, pride, and security through their training, which promotes cooperation and respect for you. Many will see you as the cause of their improvement and will rely on you more for advice and direction in the future.

5. *You reduce safety hazards.* By engaging in safe behaviors, emphasizing safety rules, and conveying safety-oriented attitudes, you reduce the likelihood of violations and the resulting accidents and injuries. How tragic it would be to

SUPERVISORS AND ETHICS

If companies expect their employees to think and act ethically, they must create "organizational integrity . . . based on the concept of self-governance in accordance with a set of guiding principles. From the perspective of integrity, the task of ethics management is to define and give life to an organization's guiding values, to create an environment that supports ethically sound behavior, and to instill a sense of shared accountability among employees." Guidance and examples from the top form the foundation of an ethical corporate culture and environment. In addition, training and incentives for fostering ethical behavior are required. Finally, ethical training efforts and results must be audited and either rewarded or corrected.

According to the executive director at Carnegie Mellon University's Center for the Advancement of Ethics, ethics training involves two related areas: compliance training, which alerts people to policies, regulations, and laws that establish acceptable behavior within a company, and cognitive thinking exercises, which develop skills to allow people to think through various "moral mazes" they may be confronted with in the workplace.

Ethics training can take some interesting and unusual formats. Citicorp uses "an ethics board game, which teams of employees use to solve hypothetical quandaries. General Electric employees can tap into specially designed interactive software on their personal computers to get answers to ethical questions. At Texas Instruments, employees are treated to a weekly column on ethics over an international electronic news service." The key seems to be to make ethics training realistic and connected to one's personal situation in life and at work. A company is limited only by its ethics trainers' creativity and imagination.

Sources: Lynn Sharp Paine, "Managing for Organizational Integrity," *Harvard Business Review* (March–April 1994): 111. Kenneth Labich, "The New Crisis in Business Ethics," *Fortune* (April 20, 1992): 167, 168, 172, 176. *Human Resources Management: Ideas & Trends in Personnel* 273. Chicago: Commerce Clearing House (April 15, 1992): 60.

have to live with the knowledge that a subordinate's injury might have been prevented if you had done all that you should have in the area of safety.

ADVANTAGES FOR SUBORDINATES

Training gives your workers many advantages, including the following:

1. *They increase their chances for success.* Through training, workers gain new knowledge and experiences that help reduce the risks of personal obsolescence and increase their value to themselves and to the company. By exposure and practice, workers learn new techniques that enhance their abilities and their enjoyment of work. By successfully completing training, workers confront change, meet challenges, overcome their fears, and gain self-confidence.

2. *They increase their motivation to work.* Through successful training experiences and proper guidance, individuals experience a greater measure of achievement. They find ways to reduce fatigue, increase contributions, and

expend less effort to accomplish their tasks. These accomplishments tend to fortify a desire to work harder. We all need a sense of competence.

3. *They promote their own advancement.* As workers become more proficient, they earn the right to receive additional duties, either through delegation or through a job change. By proving themselves through the learning process, they justify the investment of additional company time and money in their development. They become more mobile members of the organization.

4. *Their morale improves.* Mastery of new responsibilities inevitably leads to new prestige and importance. This newfound pride can be translated into higher earnings, a greater commitment to the company, and a renewed self-image. Workers see themselves as necessary and more valuable parts of the whole and as greater contributors to the group's success.

5. *Their productivity increases.* Subordinates perform their jobs with less wasted effort and lower scrap rates, which results in higher-quality production and a greater return to themselves and the company.

Some or all of these benefits will accrue to everyone who takes part in training. Training tells your people of both your company's interest and your personal interest in their welfare and development. Just be sure to let trainees put their training to use as soon as possible after its completion.

Requirements of Training

REQUIREMENTS FOR TRAINERS

Ideally, you as the supervisor should plan and execute the essential function of training. However, there are times when you cannot train subordinates. You may lack either the time or the firsthand knowledge of the job to be taught. In such cases, you may have to delegate the training duties to a subordinate or rely on the various staff specialists your company can provide. Either way, you are accountable for their actions and the results. Therefore, it would be wise for you to assist in the planning of the training and to check up on its execution periodically.

Regardless of who does the training, that person must be proficient in the subject matter or skills to be taught and possess a working knowledge of the ways in which people learn. More specifically, she should understand the principles that govern training, and the different training methods, along with their respective advantages and disadvantages. Every trainer must recognize that her actions will teach as much as, if not more than, the words spoken during training. Here are a few basic suggestions for trainers that are applicable to almost any training situation:[10]

- *Be enthusiastic.* If you are enthusiastic about training it is easier for your subordinates to become enthusiastic about or at least receptive to the training experience.

SUPERVISORS AND QUALITY

Jack Welch initiated the "work-out" process at GE in order to fix problems and to move decision making to the level of workers. The process requires a manager to stand in front of an assembly of subordinates and respond to their proposals for doing things differently. During this process the manager's boss stands behind the manager but, the manager cannot look to his boss for guidance. Managers are allowed three answers for each proposal: yes, no, or more information is needed. During the day-long sessions a manager might handle more than 100 proposals. Here is an example of a worker's proposal and the manager's response:

"I've worked for GE for over twenty years, I have a perfect attendance record. I've won management awards. I love this company. It's put my kids through college. It's given me a good standard of living. But there's something stupid that I'd like to bring up."

The man operated a valuable piece of equipment that required him to wear gloves.

The gloves wore out several times a month. To acquire another pair he had to call in a relief operator or, if none was available, shut his machine down. He then had to walk a fair distance to another building, go to the supply room, and fill out a form. He then had to walk around the plant to track down a supervisor of sufficient authority to countersign his request. Only after he had returned the signed form to the supply room was he given a new pair of gloves! Frequently he lost as much as an hour of work.

"I think it's stupid."

"I think it's stupid too," said the general manager in front of the room. "Why do we do that?" At that point everyone in the room was dying to hear the answer. Finally, from way back in the room came the answer: "In 1973, we lost a box of gloves."

"Put the box of gloves on the floor, close to the people," the manager ordered.

As this example indicates, over the passage of time operational and managerial changes make many operational policies obsolete and counterproductive. It is important that managers and supervisors listen to their subordinates so that they can respond to suggestions for doing things better or more quickly. As this example indicates, experienced workers are often subjected to mindless and demoralizing policies that dampen productivity. Properly trained subordinates can make many decisions that enable them to perform their work better and more efficiently. Delegation of decision-making authority also enriches workers' jobs.

Source: Robert Slater, *Jack Welch and the GE Way: Management Insights and Leadership Secrets of the Legendary CEO.* New York: McGraw-Hill, 1999.

- *Simplify.* Focus on fewer points that can be learned well rather than try to cover too much material that will not be learned.
- *Be sensitive to body language.* The body language of your subordinates can indicate whether you need to speed up or slow down in covering the material or make it more interesting.
- *Provide feedback.* Show your subordinates what they have learned and where they need to acquire more knowledge.
- *Provide reinforcement.* Provide positive reinforcement to your subordinates as they make progress in mastering the skills or knowledge to be acquired.

- *Expect occasional failures.* Very few training approaches work every time for every subordinate as people tend to respond differently to different training approaches.

REQUIREMENTS FOR TRAINEES

In general, people who are about to go through training should meet the following requirements:

1. They should be informed about what will be taught and why.
2. They should recognize the need to learn the material.
3. They should be willing to learn what is to be taught.
4. They should have the capability to learn what is to be taught.

Given capable trainers and trainees who meet these preconditions, genuine learning and meaningful improvements in performance are possible. Learning theory tells us that without motivation or the incentive to learn, no real learning will take place. When learning does take place, motivated trainees and trainers are the central reason for it. The principles that follow will enable you to design and execute a successful training program.

The Principles of Training

You should keep in mind several principles while planning and conducting a training program. Use these principles as a checklist to make certain that you have not overlooked anything important. To remember them, think of the mnemonic MIRRORS:

- Motivation
- Individualism
- Realism
- Response
- Objective
- Reinforcement
- Subjects

These principles are interdependent and interrelated.

MOTIVATION

motivation
the training principle that requires both trainer and trainee to be favorably predisposed and ready to undergo training

The trainee's **motivation** is often a problem. While new employees are usually anxious to get through training successfully so as to gain some level of independence and security, more experienced employees may be less enthusiastic. Experienced employees often do not see the need to learn skills or they have fears about their ability to learn.

Remember that training imparts a sense of competence. If people know what is expected of them, believe that they are capable of mastering those expectations, see the rewards that lie ahead, and desire those rewards, then they should be motivated.

INDIVIDUALISM

The principle of **individualism** states that the training you prepare and present must be tailored to meet the needs and situations of individuals. To do this, you must know what skills and knowledge people already possess so that you can start from there in designing your program. By building on what they already know, you can use their experiences as a frame of reference. For instance, if people already know how to operate a particular piece of machinery that is similar to but not the same as the one they must now operate, begin by pointing out the similarities, and then show the differences or exceptions.

Finally, this principle states that you must vary your presentation of material to fit people's ability to assimilate it. Let the trainees advance at a comfortable rate, and do not present too much material in large chunks. If you overload them with information, you will only frustrate and confuse them.

You probably already have some experience working with older employees. When older employees go through training, you can individualize your approach by relying on thoroughness rather than speed. Use older employees' backgrounds and experiences as connecting links to the new information or methods. By providing constant feedback to keep them abreast of their progress, you help overcome some of the fear of failure that older workers may have when facing the new and different.

When you train your workers, both your technical expertise and attitude are important. Training is a perfect time to instill motivation in a subordinate.

individualism
the training principle that requires a trainer to conduct training at a pace suitable for the trainee

REALISM

Make the learning process as close to the real thing as you can. In most training situations, you should teach people on the job, using their actual equipment, tools, or machinery. In the case of office or clerical employees, use the actual computer software, procedures, and practices. Such **realism** is not always possible. For example, equipment may be unavailable for training because it is being fully utilized in current production. When you cannot train on the job, or deem it wiser not to do so, set up conditions that are as close to actual working situations as possible. Use examples and situations that accurately reflect actual problems the worker is likely to encounter. Then move from the simulated conditions to the actual environment as soon as possible.

realism
the training principle that requires training to simulate or duplicate the actual working environment and behavior or performance required

A medium-size manufacturer in the Midwest provides a good example. The company was reluctant to purchase the latest manufacturing equipment because it lacked skilled workers who could operate and maintain it. The solution was to find a community college that had the computer-integrated equipment and then send a select group to learn the equipment. After the group was trained, the workers returned to train others in the plant on the equipment that was then being installed.

RESPONSE

response
the principle of training that requires feedback from trainees to trainers and vice versa

The principle of **response** reminds you to check regularly on the trainees' receptiveness and their retention of material. Involve the trainees in a two-way conversation. Ask questions and encourage them to do the same. Response also includes the concept of evaluation. Besides oral questions and answers, you can evaluate or measure the trainees' progress by conducting performance tests or written quizzes. Involve the trainees in feedback throughout the training process and share the results of regular evaluations with them. One member of a corporate training program put it this way: "I like the daily quizzes my instructor gives. They let you know right away how well you have caught on to the material covered. It keeps you on your toes and forces you to review each night. I need this course. It means another 25 dollars per week."

OBJECTIVE

objective
the training principle that requires trainers and trainees to know what is to be mastered through training

The principle of the **objective** states that trainees and trainers should always know where they are headed at any given point in the training process. As a trainer, you have to set goals for the training program and for each of the individual training sessions you conduct. These goals must be communicated to the trainees so that they know where they are headed.

The goals of trainees should be realistic, specific, and within the trainees' ability to achieve. They tell employees that their training is planned and professional. We will discuss objectives further in this chapter.

REINFORCEMENT

reinforcement
the training principle that requires trainees to review and restate knowledge learned; also refers to rewards for correct responses

According to the principle of **reinforcement**, if learning is to be retained it should involve as many senses as possible and be accompanied by rewards such as verbal compliments. When you first explain an idea, you may involve both sight and hearing, using a demonstration coupled with an explanation. Then you can let the trainees try out their understanding by repeating the demonstration and explanation in their own words. They will then be using sight, touch, and hearing. They will also be reviewing the concepts as well. By using frequent summaries and by reviewing key points, you will be practicing reinforcement. Reinforcement also includes rewarding correct responses. By repetition, practice, and rewards for correct responses you lend emphasis and greatly increase retention.

SUPERVISING TEAMS

SRC Holdings (formerly Springfield Remanufacturing Corporation) in Springfield, Missouri, has relied on trained, committed team members since its management bought the first business from International Harvester in 1983. The company specializes in rebuilding used engines. But as CEO Jack Stack puts it, "Our real business is education. We teach people about business. . . . When people come to work at SRC, we tell them 70 percent of the job is disassembly—or whatever—and 30 percent of the job is learning."

Worker training focuses on teaching the basics about how a business operates. Employees are taught how to read financial statements—cash flow, balance sheet, sources and uses of funds—everything workers need to know to keep score and follow the evolution of what Stack calls "the great game of business." The company offers classes and tutorials, allowing people to learn as much as they care to and to advance as far as they wish. The more they learn, the more they realize how dependent they are on one another and the more they understand what is needed for the survival of their company.

SRC gives individuals the responsibility for their own futures and job security. It asks people to think about where they want to go and how things can be done better, faster, and cheaper. By giving employees a share of the profits and making continual training available, SRC is building a flexible, organic organization that can respond rapidly to change and customer demands. The employees feel and act like owners because they have been given the incentives and tools (bonuses, weekly meetings, training, and so on) to do so. The company shares all the information it has with employees. It relies on all of its employees to spot what needs to be done and how to do it. All employees have the same goals and depend on one another to reach them. Thus the whole company acts as one—a team committed to finding the most efficient and profitable ways to run SRC.

Source: Jack Stack with Bo Burlingham, *The Great Game of Business.* New York: Doubleday/Currency, 1992. "No More 'Etch A Sketch' Planning," *Inc.* (December 31, 2001): 110–111.

Try to put the knowledge and skills that must be learned to work in a real situation as soon as possible. Studies reveal that we retain about 50 percent of what we hear immediately after we hear it and about 75 percent of what we experience immediately after the event. As time passes without further reference to our knowledge or to the application of our skills, our retention of them diminishes still further. More than one training supervisor knows the truth behind the adage "Tell them what you are going to tell them; tell them; and tell them what you told them."

SUBJECTS

The principle of **subjects** is two-sided: You must know as much about the trainees as possible, and you must have a mastery of the subject to be taught. If you are preparing to teach an entire job, you will want to consult the job description and its corresponding job specification. Next, you will need to know the job holder's relevant skills and knowledge. To determine the subjects to

subjects
the principle of training that requires trainers to know the subject being taught and to know the trainees' needs

teach to your current subordinates, consult their most recent performance evaluations, your current observations, and the workers themselves. Disciplinary actions and records also may point out the need for training. So may the results of exit interviews conducted with employees who quit. Common complaints may signal problems that can be eliminated through training.

A company that switched computer software provides a relevant training example. After a week, the quality of work began to decline. It became obvious to the division manager that many departments were having trouble with the new software. On investigation, the division chief discovered that several supervisors were unable to teach the new software because they themselves had not learned it. Several other supervisors knew the software but seemed unable to teach it to their team members. The division chief worked with the director of training and developed two courses. One course trained supervisors how to train, and the other trained them on the new software.

The Training Cycle

Exhibit 12.1 shows the four parts of a successful training effort. Training, like planning, demands that you know your destination before you plan your trip. The first step is to identify where training is needed. Once areas are identified, the next step is to write objectives specifying what is to be taught, under what conditions, and how the learning can be verified. Unless all persons undergoing the training have no knowledge of what is to be taught, a pre-test may be needed to determine their levels of knowledge. You can then construct a training plan to answer the questions *who, when, where, how,* and *how much.* Then the program is conducted and the results are evaluated. A post-test may be used for comparison to determine the success of the program and areas that need more improvement or repetition.

PART 1. IDENTIFYING TRAINING NEEDS

You know that your people need training when things are not as they should be. Your efforts at control and supervision should tell you when performances are not meeting expectations or standards. Training is always needed to some degree with new subordinates, new equipment, and new procedures.

Let's assume that you are a restaurant manager faced with the arrival of a new employee who must be trained to be a waiter. How would you start to determine what should be taught? It would make sense to turn to your copies of the waiter's job description and job specification. You have these, they are up to date, and you have already used them to conduct your recruiting and interviewing prior to your decision to hire. They contain a list of duties and tasks, as well as a list of the personal qualities demanded of a waiter. The task of greeting customers cordially after the host seats them requires language and interpersonal skills. The task of serving customers their orders requires manual dexterity and coordination—mental as well as

The four basic components of the training cycle. **Exhibit 12.1**

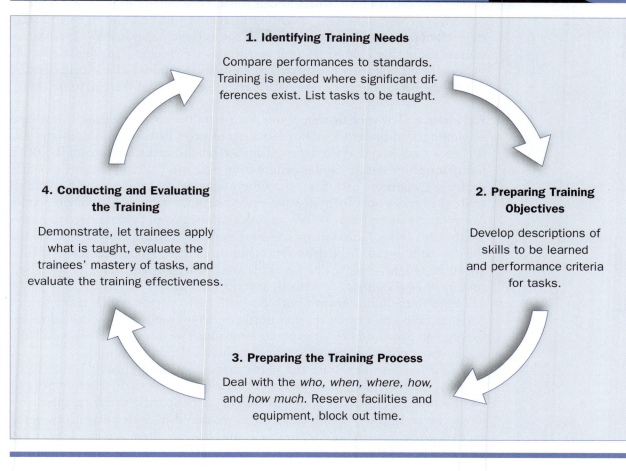

1. Identifying Training Needs

Compare performances to standards. Training is needed where significant differences exist. List tasks to be taught.

2. Preparing Training Objectives

Develop descriptions of skills to be learned and performance criteria for tasks.

3. Preparing the Training Process

Deal with the *who, when, where, how,* and *how much*. Reserve facilities and equipment, block out time.

4. Conducting and Evaluating the Training

Demonstrate, let trainees apply what is taught, evaluate the trainees' mastery of tasks, and evaluate the training effectiveness.

physical. Once you know what types of performance are expected of the waiter, you have the raw material necessary to assess training needs. If the new person is experienced, you will probably have to teach your particular restaurant's methods.

The day has arrived. Ben, your new waiter, has two years of experience with the job. Your earlier and present contacts with Ben will tell you the areas in which he needs training. After induction, you show Ben the job description and talk through each of the duties with him, making sure to point out any differences that may arise between what Ben has been doing elsewhere and what he will be expected to do for you. Now that Ben is familiar with his tasks, you are ready to try him out on each and to monitor his performance. But before monitoring, you must have a clear understanding of each task, of the conditions that surround its performance, and of the criteria by which you will judge the quality of performance. These three items constitute what is called a **training objective.**

training objective
a written statement of what the trainee should be able to do, the conditions under which the trainee is expected to perform, and the criteria used to judge the adequacy of the performance

PART 2. PREPARING TRAINING OBJECTIVES

Before you can train or a person can learn, both parties must have common objectives. These should be in writing to avoid confusion and to ensure mastery. All objectives should state three things as clearly as possible: (1) what the trainee should be able to do (the performance expected); (2) the conditions under which the learner is expected to do it; and (3) how well the task must be done—the performance or criteria.[11] Let's look at each of these in more detail.

Performance. The specific things you want a trainee to do are usually outlined or summarized under the major headings of tasks listed in a job description. But each task may have a series of minor related tasks. For example, Ben's job description states, "Takes orders from patrons." What subtasks or other duties are connected to this one? One might be that the waiter be able to write the orders on a form in a prescribed manner so that the kitchen people can properly interpret it. Before an order can be taken, patrons need to know what is available. Consequently, menus must be distributed and specials for the day announced. All these subtasks must be understood and stated if they are to be taught. Finally, certain skills are connected with these tasks. They, too, must be identified, described, and (in some cases) taught.

Your immediate concern with Ben will be to decide which tasks he can perform, and you cannot do that until you have listed all the detailed tasks. Before you can train Ben or evaluate how much he already knows, you have to possess a complete list of required tasks, skills, and attitudes.

Objectives usually state the performance needed by using active verbs such as *construct, list, identify,* and *compare.* These specified behaviors can be observed or evaluated fairly easily. The more specific the duty, the easier it will be to find out if the trainee has mastered it. Stay away from verbs such as *know, understand, appreciate,* and *believe;* these actions are far too vague to be taught or evaluated with precision.

Conditions. Objectives should list the items needed by the trainee to execute the performance and any limits or constraints that will be placed on performance. In our example of Ben, you already know that he will need the restaurant's prescribed order forms, a writing instrument, and a knowledge of the kitchen staff's shorthand for taking orders from patrons. But there is a time restraint as well at your restaurant. Ben must take the order within a fixed period after patrons are seated or, if they are undecided at his first visit, he must return to the table within five minutes of his first contact (at which he announces the specials of the day).

When preparing to write the conditions for a task, you need to address the equipment, materials, and time restraints.[12] Conditions usually begin with the word *given.* For example, "Given the restaurant's order form, a ballpoint pen, and a working knowledge of the restaurant's order shorthand, the waiter should be able to. . . ." Each learning objective at the beginning of each chapter in this text begins with a specification of the conditions that are considered necessary for a student to demonstrate each performance listed.

The two conditions are to read and to discuss each chapter. Only then can a student be expected to perform each objective. In a business setting, some objectives may begin with a statement about what will be denied to a trainee. For example, "Given no direct supervision. . . ." or "Without the aid of tools, the trainee should be able to. . . ." Such a condition is understood to exist when you as a student take most of your tests. You understand that you are to answer the questions without the aid of notes or the text.

Each major task listed on Ben's job description can be broken down into subtasks. A performance and condition for each can then be written. For example, the subtasks related to "taking a customer's order" may break down as follows:

1. Visit the table.
2. Greet the customer cordially.
3. Introduce yourself and the specials of the day.
4. Offer to take the customer's order.
5. If the customer is undecided, leave and return to take the order.
6. Write the customer's order.
7. Deliver the order to the kitchen.

Each of these subtasks is involved in the major task of taking a customer's order. Each has an attached condition or two. Including your restaurant's policies and procedures in the first performance subtask will give you a complete statement:

1. Visit the table within one minute after the customer is seated by the hostess, armed with the restaurant's order forms, a ballpoint pen, a knowledge of the kitchen shorthand and daily specials, a clean uniform, and a smile on your face.

The performance expected is to visit the customer's table. The conditions surrounding that performance include a one-minute time limit, possession of equipment and knowledge, and a warm and friendly demeanor. Each of the other six subtasks may be given conditions as well. If they are all to be taught together, the conditions in number one will be understood to exist in numbers two, three, four, and six. A new time limit may be required for number five.

The key to writing descriptions of conditions is to be detailed enough to ensure that the desired performance will be executed in the way you want. Add as much description as you feel you must to communicate your intent to the trainee. When in doubt, describe. With detailed lists of tasks and their conditions, both you and the trainee can progress in an orderly manner, leaving little to chance.

Criteria. Criteria state the standards that a trainee must meet in order to give a satisfactory performance. When speed, accuracy, and a quality of performance can be stated, they should be made a part of the training objective. Criteria need not always appear in a training objective. Sometimes they are part of the conditions. Ben's first performance required him to visit a table within one minute of the customer's being seated. In this case, time is both a limit and a criterion for evaluating Ben's performance.

Some criteria are best demonstrated or shown. You as a trainer can do this, pointing out the quality of performance you desire through personal demonstrations or by using behavior modeling techniques employing videotape. Nothing needs to be written into the training objective in this case.

As long as you and the trainee know what makes a performance acceptable, you have met the requirement for including criteria in your training objectives. If you cannot find some words or ways to determine acceptability of performance, perhaps you should reconsider its importance to you and to your trainee.[13] It may be of such minor importance that it should not be treated formally in training.

PART 3. PREPARING THE TRAINING PROCESS

You have determined the needs for training. You have identified the tasks to be taught and have written solid training objectives. These answer the questions "Why should there be training?" and "What will be taught?" The rest of your training program will answer questions relating to *who, when, where, how,* and *how much.* These questions are addressed in Exhibit 12.2. The questions of how and how much are more complicated.

Determining *How*

In what order will the objectives be taught and by what methods? Priorities and a training schedule must be constructed to guarantee that all items are included in an order of presentation that makes sense to the trainee. Many techniques can be used to deliver your training. Exhibit 12.3 lists the major techniques.

Exhibit **12.2**	*Checklist to help you plan your training program.*
The Who:	Who will do the training? Who will receive it?
The When:	What times will be set aside for training?
The Where:	What specific physical areas and equipment will be needed to conduct the training?
The How:	In what chronological order will the tasks be taught? What methods of instruction are best for each task?
The How Much:	How much money will be needed to ensure a successful training effort? How much time and equipment will be needed to teach all the objectives?

Apprenticeships	Apprenticeships are formal on-the-job training programs conducted over relatively long periods of time in order to develop high levels of skill. Typically they involve a minimum of several months and sometimes may require several years, as in the case of union apprenticeship programs. Apprentices typically pay for much of their training by working for lower wages during training.
Coaching	Coaching involves informal feedback and suggestions that supervisors provide on a day-to-day basis. Supervisors help subordinates learn how to perform tasks better and facilitate the acquisition of skills and knowledge.
Computer-Based Training	Computers are used to generate learning material, often in the form of questions or problems, to which students respond. The computer provides positive reinforcement for correct responses and diagnostic information for incorrect responses.
Computer-Aided Instruction	This term is more general than computer-based training. It refers to the use of computers to augment traditional training.
Internships	Internships are similar to apprenticeships. In most business settings internships are less formal and of shorter duration than apprenticeship training.
Job Rotation	With this form of job rotation employees learn and perform various jobs for a relatively short amount of time. Where teams are employed, team members train each other in the various jobs and rotate jobs on a regular basis.
Lecture	Lectures provide a means for quickly disseminating information on new techniques and procedures. A disadvantage is that employees do not gain actual experience. Accordingly, it cannot be assumed that they will be able to apply knowledge acquired from lectures without other forms of training.
Mentoring	In mentoring, supervisors provide career guidance, reassurance, protection, and opportunities for visibility that are useful for career advancement. Mentors often help employees learn the subtleties of how things are done within the organization.
Role Playing and Simulations	Role playing allows trainees to develop skills while dealing with hypothetical situations. For example, an employee may play a role in which she must deal with a difficult customer. Role plays and simulations allow employees to practice skills in realistic but risk-free environments.
Vestibule Training	New employees practice production work using the same equipment as in the real production environment. However, the work product is not used for actual production. As a result there is less fear of making a mistake and learning is facilitated.
Video Tapes	Subordinates can observe the performance of actual job tasks in technical work. For non-technical training, such as how to make a sales call, employees can watch experts perform the task.

Sources: Charles R. Greer, *Strategy and Human Resources: A General Managerial Approach,* 2nd ed. Englewood Cliffs, NJ: Prentice Hall, 2001. Sulaiman Al-Malik in Lloyd L. Byars and Leslie W. Rue, *Human Resource Management,* 3rd ed. Homewood, IL: Richard D. Irwin, 1991. Kenneth N. Wexley and Gary P. Latham, *Developing and Training Human Resources in Organizations,* 2nd ed. New York: HarperCollins, 1991. Irwin L. Goldstein, *Training in Organizations: Needs Assessment, Development, and Evaluation,* 2nd ed., Monterey, CA: Brooks/Cole, 1986.

Bob Eichinger, consultant and former PepsiCo executive, explains that more companies are using a unique training technique that appears especially well suited for developing subordinates for future positions as supervisors. In this technique, promising employees are asked to perform assignments at which they are the worst. Eichinger calls these developmental assignments "going against the grain" (GAG) assignments. By having subordinates work through tasks that they do not perform well, they overcome critical weaknesses that would otherwise limit their upward potential.[14]

Buddy systems. The buddy system is a person-to-person or one-on-one method of training. It may also be known as the teacher–pupil method or the master–apprentice method. Whatever it is called, this method utilizes one trainer and one trainee; a person who knows the job teaches someone who needs to know it. Instruction usually takes place on the job, using the actual workplace, tools, and equipment during regular working hours. When the person doing the training is properly prepared, the buddy system has the following major advantages:

1. *It is flexible.* Learning can take place in a classroom, in a laboratory, or on the job. Changes can be introduced quickly. The system can be tailored in pace and content to meet the individual needs of the trainee.

2. *It allows immediate feedback.* The teacher/trainer works directly with the trainee and can quickly evaluate progress or lack of progress, offering corrections and reviews to improve retention and mastery.

3. *It is personal.* It humanizes the training process and allows for questions and answers, reviews, and additional drills or practices at any time. Personalized corrections may be made, and personalized instructions may be given throughout the duration of training. The system frequently helps the trainees satisfy some of their social needs.

The primary disadvantages of the buddy system are the following:

1. *It is costly.* The salary of wages of the trainer go to pay for the training of just one trainee during any training sessions. Expensive equipment and machines are tied up and used by only one trainee at any given moment.

2. *Extensive preparation is required.* If the real advantages of the buddy system are to be realized, the instructor must adequately assess the needs of the trainee, tailor the instruction to meet those needs, and avoid passing along poor mind-sets, prejudices, and improper shortcuts.

Machine-based systems. Computer-based or programmed instruction methods are referred to as *machine-based systems of training* because they rely heavily on a machine to relay information and evaluate trainee responses. Computers and machines that use videotapes and audio tapes can enhance the learning environment and enrich the training that takes place.

All machine-based instruction requires people (1) to prepare the materials, (2) to monitor the training process by keeping track of time, maintain equipment, and handle questions, and (3) to evaluate the progress of each trainee. This method is more often used to supplement other types of training than to substitute for them. It works well when used to complement other methods.

The advantages of machine-based or computer-based training include the following:

1. *It is uniform.* It ensures that the same material is presented in exactly the same way to each trainee.

2. *It is flexible.* It can be adjusted, or can adjust itself, to fit the needs and pace of the trainees. It involves the learners in the learning process. It frees trainers for other duties and allows them to handle more than one trainee per session.

3. *It is inexpensive.* The costs of computers and instructional software can be spread over dozens or hundreds of trainees. In addition, software vendors often provide machine-based training, trainers, and free or low-cost instructional materials.

Disadvantages of machine-based training include the following:

1. *It is impersonal.* Computers cannot fully replace the need for human interaction. They cannot provide the warmth of a smile and a compliment from an instructor for a job mastered in training. They cannot sense an employee's fear or frustration or the lack of comprehension of a video or verbal message.

2. *It requires expertise.* Learning materials demand a great deal of money, know-how, and time to prepare. To be economical, instructional materials must not require frequent changing or become obsolete in a short time.

3. *It can be boring.* For trainees with short attention spans, for those who learn quickly, and for those who already know a significant portion of the material, the training can become frustrating and boring.

4. *It needs to serve many trainees in order to be economical.* Computer programs and videotapes cost too much to prepare if only a few trainees are to use them.

5. *It may not teach some behaviors.* General Motors found that it had to supplement computer-based training with classroom instruction when it attempted to get GM dealers to use its computer system. Because many of the dealers' sales people and secretaries had little familiarity with computers, GM had to both develop computer skills and change people's mind-sets.[15] An indication of the magnitude of the task is provided by the following: "One person held the mouse up to the screen and tried to use it like a remote control. . . . Another put it on the floor and tried to use it like a sewing machine pedal."[16] The CEO of

Learning Tree reinforces the importance of supplementing computer-based training with classroom instruction: "I'm not convinced that a computer-based course can come anywhere near a classroom in changing people's behavior and mind-set."[17]

Most training requires you to interact with employees. However, technical training, such as learning new computer software, can be done on computers. When you assign computer-based training, be sure to follow up on a personal basis.

Group sessions. Lectures, conferences, and role-playing sessions can be quite effective methods of training more than one person at each session. Lectures present basic principles and individual points of view, and they can be used to introduce or summarize. Conferences and discussions can inform, solve problems, clarify situations, and help participants critically evaluate their opinions, attitudes, and methods. Role-playing allows people to act out a situation to what they see as its logical conclusion. Participants see one another in a different light and have a chance to evaluate others' solutions while trying out their own solutions on the group.

Group training can be useful also for developing cooperation and teamwork among your subordinates. Such training often involves the completion of a group task requiring participants to work together. Consider the following example:

FCC National Bank of Wilmington, Del., sent seven of its senior managers to a one-day program at a Manhattan cooking school. After a morning of discussion guided by a management consultant, the executives were turned loose in the kitchen with instructions and ingredients for a gourmet lunch. "It really did simulate a work situation," said Fay Dadzie, vice-president of human resources. "Sometimes, we'd find ourselves working separately when we should have been working together to get the meal done on time." The task was humbling, said Roland Ridgeway, vice-president of community relations. "Only a couple of people had really ever cooked," he said. "They had to be willing to step back so the rest of us could learn." Ultimately, "we determined that we needed to improve on giving and accepting feedback," Ms. Dadzie said, "and I think we have."[18]

The major advantages of the group-sessions method are the following:

1. *It is uniform.* Two or more people are exposed to the same material in the same way at the same time.

2. *It is inexpensive.* Compared to other training methods, group sessions offer savings in hours and salaries for training purposes.

The major disadvantages of the group-sessions method are the following:

1. *It is impersonal.* It does not allow for individual differences or close involvement in the training.
2. *It magnifies errors.* The impact of each mistake or bit of misinformation is magnified by the number of trainees.
3. *It does not overcome a lack of trust.* In addition, group training is not a silver bullet solution for dysfunctional teams or for building trust with individuals who have serious character flaws.[19] The following comments by Craig Cantoni, president of Capstone Consulting Group, explain the problem:

> "But they [group training programs] are totally useless—even harmful—for a dysfunctional team." Distrustful employees may work well with their boss in a rock-climbing exercise, because if they don't, someone will get injured. "But back in the office, he's still a snake," Mr. Cantoni said.[20]

It is important to recognize the differences among adults regarding how they learn and, therefore, the necessity of adapting to their individual learning styles. For example, some of your subordinates may be tactile or bodily–kinesthetic learners who master material better when they can handle the materials or use a hands-on approach. Others may be logical–mathematical style learners who acquire knowledge better through problem solving. Other subordinates may require demonstrations and some form of interaction before they learn the material. Supervisors should be prepared to train their subordinates using approaches that fit these varying learning styles. In addition, evolving technology is making lifelong learning a necessity; thus it is important to use approaches that match the learning styles of employees who may have completed their formal education many years ago.[21]

Exhibit 12.4 presents a model to help you conduct your training programs.

In designing your training program, try to utilize more than one method of training. For most types of training, a single method will not do. A blend or mix will probably suit your purposes better. When you know what has to be taught and what human and material resources are available, think about which methods should work best for you and your trainees.

Determining *How Much*

This question needs two answers. You must determine how much time you will need for training and how much money you will have to spend. Break the training into learnable units—units small enough to be effectively taught and absorbed in one session. If the units are too big, the trainee will be unable to digest them. It is far better to have less material—leaving ample time for review and practice—than to have too much. A good rule of thumb is to attempt to teach no more than three performances in every 60-minute session.

Exhibit 12.4 *A four-step outline for conducting training.*

STEP 1: PREPARATION OF THE LEARNER

1. Put the learner at ease—relieve the tension.

2. Explain what is being taught, and why.

3. Create interest, encourage questions, and find out what the learner already knows about his or her job or other jobs.

4. Explain the rationale for the whole job and relate it to some job the worker already knows.

5. Place the learner as close to the normal working position as possible.

6. Familiarize the worker with the equipment, materials, tools, and trade terms.

STEP 2: PRESENTATION OF THE OPERATION

1. Explain quantity and quality requirements.

2. Go through the job at the normal work pace.

3. Go through the job at a slow pace several times, explaining each step. Between operations, explain the difficult parts, or those in which errors are likely to be made.

4. Again go through the job at a slow pace several times, explaining the key points.

5. Have the learner explain the steps as you go through the job at a slow pace.

STEP 3: PERFORMANCE TRYOUT

1. Have the learner go through the job several times, slowly, explaining to you each step. Correct mistakes, and if necessary, do some of the complicated steps the first few times.

2. You, the trainer, run the job at the normal pace.

3. Have the learner do the job, gradually building up skill and speed.

4. As soon as the learner demonstrates ability to do the job, let the worker begin, but don't abandon him or her.

STEP 4: FOLLOW-UP

1. Designate to whom the learner should go for help if he or she needs it.

2. Gradually decrease supervision, checking work from time to time against quality and quantity standards.

3. Correct faulty work patterns that begin to creep into the work. Show why the learned method is superior.

4. Compliment good work; encourage the worker until able to meet the quality/quantity standards.

Source: PERSONNEL/HUMAN RESOURCE MANAGEMENT, 5/E by Dessler, Gary. © 1991. Reprinted by permission of Pearson Education, Inc., Upper Saddle River, NJ.

PART 4. CONDUCTING AND EVALUATING THE TRAINING

Training should begin with the following introductory steps:

1. Put trainees at ease.
2. State the objectives to be achieved during the session.
3. Point out the advantages they will receive from the training.
4. Explain the sequence of the events they are about to follow.

You should stress the fact that when you and the company take the time and make the effort to train workers, it is positive proof of concern for the workers and an expression of confidence in their abilities. If eligibility for training was competitive, let each trainee know of your pride in his selection. Let your trainees know that there is no harm in making mistakes. In fact, we learn more by analyzing our mistakes when we discover their causes and can prevent their recurrence.

Demonstration. During the demonstration phase of your training presentation, you have the opportunity to show and tell. You can perform as your objective specifies or let experienced employees demonstrate the tasks. In Ben's case, you may want to call on your skilled wait staff to demonstrate. Or you may videotape performances and let the trainee view the video, commenting on what is being shown and asking and answering questions. If your trainee has no questions, ask some of your own. Check on Ben's understanding of each critical task. Remember that training involves communication, and communication requires feedback.

Application. The application phase of training asks the trainee to get his feet wet. In this case, Ben will be asked to duplicate the performance that he has just witnessed. You may want to show Ben more than one performance before asking him to repeat it. However, don't try to include too many behaviors before you let the trainee try them. By mixing the demonstration with applications, you provide the trainee with immediate feedback and highlight both what he has mastered and what he has not. You will be applying the principle of reinforcement, as well as providing the early and measured successes that are so important to the mastery of performances and the motivation of the trainee. You may wish to videotape the performance and use the tape for review or to examine progress.

Evaluation. In the evaluation phase you determine if the trainee has mastered task performance and if the training effort was successful. The basic question here is whether the trainee can perform, under the prescribed conditions, all the essential tasks at the required level of quality. Evaluation may take place at any point in a demonstration or during a trainee's application of lessons. Performance tests, written or oral quizzes, and the trainer's own observations are the most frequently used devices for evaluating performance.

The effectiveness of training can be measured by four criteria:[22]

1. Trainee reactions to the training—whether subordinates like it
2. Learning—whether subordinates have learned the material
3. Behavior—whether subordinates' behaviors change as a result of the training
4. Results—whether performance in terms of productivity, scrap rates, etc. improves as a result of training

After evaluation, provide trainees with frequent and immediate feedback. Let them know when they are correct, and ask them to spot their own mistakes. Let them examine the product of their efforts and try to find any defects. Once they discover an error, explain, or get them to explain, just how it can be prevented from happening again. Point out how one error—the one just made, for example—can lead to others. Use each mistake as a point for review and then conduct a critique to summarize the entire lesson.

Through evaluation, you can quickly ascertain the need for repeating a training segment. You also will realize how fast you can place people on their own, free from your strict supervision and control. Usually one should gradually reduce the level of supervision and control rather than cause trainees to feel that they will face an abrupt sink-or-swim situation. Be available to them, but simply make your visits and observations less frequent as each person demonstrates an ability to perform to standards. Your follow-up should tell you whether lasting effects have been achieved or whether an individual needs additional training.

Training for Valuing Diversity

Training that promotes the value of diversity takes many forms. Workshops and seminars—conducted in-house or at training centers by insiders or outsiders—can provide unique approaches and lessons learned by others that enlighten participants and stimulate dialogue. Many companies have created advisory teams or committees to implement diversity training programs. Mentoring programs assign people to sponsor those who differ significantly from themselves. For example, an African-American female may be assigned to mentor a Korean-American male, while a white male is assigned to mentor a Mexican-American female. These efforts, once begun, usually remain part of annual training efforts and may evolve to take on new challenges.

Within these general approaches is a variety of methods and tools that aid diversity training. Some training efforts let participants listen to presentations from individuals representing diverse groups; others show video episodes portraying diverse people in various situations. These then become discussion starters, engaging participants in a give-and-take on the issues presented. A variation on this technique is the interactive video, which stops the action periodically and lets the participants enter the presentation with their own thoughts and suggested outcomes for the situations portrayed. Each episode is a case study or simulation of a real event. Burlington Northern Santa Fe uses this approach followed by group discussions. Shell Oil Company uses an "interactive video . . . in which a learner, using a computer terminal interfaced with a videodisc player and a touch screen, works alone through a self-paced lesson."[23] Folger Coffee Company, a division of Procter & Gamble, uses role-playing exercises to get trainees to empathize with each other. Events are scripted, and participants play roles that are unfamiliar to them.

The purposes of all these efforts are to learn how we form our attitudes and perceptions of others, in what ways people differ from one another, how those differences can give individuals and organizations specific advantages, and how to improve the way we interact with people who differ. As King-Ming Young, head of Hewlett-Packard's Professional Development Group, puts it, "Managers today must demonstrate a larger repertoire of behaviors to get the most out of each employee."[24]

In addition to placing value on diversity, it is also important to facilitate the movement of minorities and females into higher-skill jobs and managerial jobs. Unless minorities and females are fully represented in these jobs the full value of diversity will not be attained. Many companies are assigning promising minorities and females to line management jobs very early in their careers in order to build up their level of experience.[25]

Pitfalls

Besides violations of any of the aforementioned principles of training, the following are the major pitfalls:

1. *Leaving it to others.* When you delegate training or use the assistance of staff specialists, you must remain sufficiently involved to ensure that proper training will take place. Remember that you must participate enough in both planning and actual training in order to know whether goals are being achieved.

2. *Making assumptions.* A trainer sometimes makes the mistake of assuming that because trainees are told to read about a concept, they will understand it on their own—or that because the trainer presented the material, all of it has been assimilated. Rely on facts and observations for a proper evaluation of the program and its effectiveness, not on assumptions.

3. *Fearing a subordinate's progress.* Some people fear the successes and increasing abilities of others because they view them as threats to their own security. Managers sometimes refuse to train subordinates out of fear that they may be able to replace them. Keep in mind that unless you have a trained successor, you are locking yourself into your present position. Training is the job of every manager who has subordinates. By failing to train subordinates you neglect an important duty.

4. *Getting too fancy.* Trainers may get too caught up in methods and training aids and lose sight of what it is they must teach. There may be too much flash and too little substance. Have you ever listened to a speaker or lecturer who talked for hours and said nothing?

5. *Substituting training for proper selection processes.* Training is not a substitute for proper selection procedures. Selection (Chapter 11) involves trying to hire the best available person to fill a vacancy. It requires skills in such areas as interviewing, testing, and recruiting. Some employers treat selection as an unimportant activity and rely on the training of new employees to impart the skills required to perform a job properly.

Instant Replay

1. Training is the supervisor's responsibility. It may be delegated, but the supervisor is accountable for it.

2. Training imparts skills, knowledge, and attitudes needed by trainees now or in the near future.

3. Training benefits you, your trainees, and your employer. Be certain that trainees know what they are to learn and why.

4. You are judged on your performance and on the performance of your subordinates.

5. The training cycle asks you to identify your training needs, to prepare performance objectives, to create a training program, and to conduct the training.

6. The central purpose of training is to improve performance and productivity.

Questions for Class Discussion

1. What are advantages that a supervisor receives when she trains a subordinate?

2. What are advantages that a trainee receives through training?

3. What are the basic requirements that a trainer must satisfy?

4. What are the basic requirements that a trainee must satisfy in order to get the most out of training?

5. What are the principles of training and what does each mean to a trainer?

6. What are the major steps in the training cycle?

7. What are the major pitfalls of which a trainer should be aware?

Incident

Purpose: To create and conduct a brief training program, following the four basic parts of training as shown in Exhibit 12.1.

Your task: Create a training program through which you teach another person your way of performing any skill you possess, such as building a model or kneading dough. After you have created your learning objective(s), chosen a method, reserved a location, and gotten a volunteer, write down each step, noting the standards you wish to teach and use to evaluate the learner's performance. Set a time limit, and conduct your training session in class, following the steps outlined in Exhibit 12.4. When you have taught the lesson, evaluate your efforts through the learner's and the class's comments. Don't be surprised if the learner or the class comes up with a better way to do things.

North Star Airlines

CASE PROBLEM 12.1

Abbie Kirkwood is the supervisor of the reservations center at North Star Airlines. As Abbie walked through the rows of cubicles where reservations agents were busy handling calls, Cory Summers, one of the lead persons for the first shift, waived to her and motioned for her to come over to her cubicle. Cory, and the other lead persons, Roberto Garza, Jill Gaither, and Sue Kincaid, were looking at one of the computer screens.

CORY: "We're having some problems with this new upgrade to the system. Several times during the past two weeks we've made errors by booking people in the same seats."

JILL: "We've also had lots of confusion on fare choices since the special fares were introduced over the weekend. In addition, this new ticket-less system is really driving us crazy. Since no ticket is issued when we make a mistake on the confirmation number, the passengers have no way of proving that they have a reservation."

ROBERTO: "Most of our agents don't know how to enter the new codes for special fares and now we're starting to get complaints from our ticket agents in several airports. I thought that things would calm down after a couple of days but that's not happening. We're getting a continuous stream of problems and complaints."

ABBIE: "I've received a few calls too. Maybe we should start tracking the number of errors each agent makes. We could start scoreboarding and post each agent's performance on the wall here by the coffee machine for everyone to see. We could start offering things like free movie tickets and dinners for people who have the fewest errors. For those that make lots of errors, we could write them up and lower their performance evaluations."

JILL: "I'm not sure that our agents can learn these new features on their own. Some of the new features of the upgrade are really complex. The help screens make it a little easier, but it looks to me like we're going to have to do some training."

ABBIE: "I'm not sure that training is the answer. If people are really motivated they can learn anything on their own. Some software vendors charge a lot for training and our people aren't doing anything productive while they're in training."

SUE: "I agree with Jill. Our agents need some training. We really need to do something and fast. Otherwise we're really going to have a problem when reservations for the holiday start to come in."

ABBIE: "Okay, why don't we each just pick out the people we think are having trouble with this software and send them through the training? Each of you can pick out five of your agents that are making the most errors and we'll make them stay late and go through training."

ROBERTO: "Why don't we have everybody go through the training during the regular work week?"

ABBIE: "We'd have to double staff during the training because someone will have to handle the incoming calls. That would be too expensive. Besides, the smarter agents will learn this upgrade without training. Here's what we'll do. We'll ask the vendor to send a software developer out here to train the agents who are making most of the errors. We'll also include some of our best agents from the first shift and have them go through the training as well. They can learn how to do the training. It will be sort of a 'train the trainer' approach. Then we'll have these agents from the first shift train the weaker agents from the other two shifts. They'll have to come in early or stay late in order to overlap with the second and third shifts to do the training. While they do the training they'll get a little overtime."

ABBIE: "Cory, why don't you call the vendor and ask for one of their software developers to conduct the training? They've got some sharp people who ought to be able to explain the upgrades to our agents."

CORY: "What shall I tell the vendor to include in the training?"

ABBIE: "Oh, they'll know what we need. After all, they designed the upgrade and they're the experts. Just tell them to put on the standard dog and pony show for our first shift people after work on Monday, Tuesday, and Wednesday."

ABBIE: "Roberto, you notify everyone where the training will be conducted."

ROBERTO: "What room do you want to use? Do we want to rent a projector for the instructor's computer?"

ABBIE: "We'll just have them do the training in the cafeteria. It's always available late in the afternoon or evening. I don't think we'll need a projector. The vendor's expert can just talk us through the changes. Sue, make sure that we have a separate group of tables and chairs for the training. All of you need to send e-mail to notify those you pick for training. Tell them that they'll need to stay late for a couple of hours of training on each of the three nights next week starting with Monday. Any questions?"

Questions

1. What problems do you see in Abbie's approach toward training?
2. What do you think of Abbie's suggestion for scoreboarding? Selection of trainees?
3. How do you think the agents will react? How would you feel?
4. What is the likelihood that the training will be successful?
5. If you were the supervisor, how would you deal with the problems described in the case?

BK Custom Products

CASE PROBLEM 12.2

Jim Brookshire, the training supervisor for BK Custom Products, had received funding to conduct management training for the production supervisors. The training would start today and he was excited about the opportunity to get the production supervisors up to speed on management techniques. Several months ago he told Bernice Hernandez, the plant manager, that some basic management training would be necessary with the company's recent expansion and promotion of several employees to supervisory positions. Last month Bernice acknowledged that several new supervisors, as well as some of the more experienced ones, were struggling with their duties and told Jim to go ahead with the training. They both agreed that, because there had been no supervisory training in the past, all supervisors—both new and experienced—would receive the training.

Jim then proceeded with the development of the training program. He developed a set of supervisory subjects to be taught and found a management trainer, Mark Harper, a management professor at the local university, who agreed to conduct the training. Jim was impressed with Mark's informal manner and down-to-earth approach and was pleased that he would be doing the training.

Because of the volume of production, Bernice had told Jim that the supervisors could not be away from the plant for the whole day. Accordingly, Jim arranged for the training to be conducted on the job site during working hours. The sessions were scheduled for three hours in the afternoon on Tuesdays and Thursdays for six weeks.

It was the first Tuesday of training and the participants were all seated around a U-shaped table arrangement in the break room. Jim introduced Mark Harper and told the participants that he was a professor from the local university. Mark then started into the first training module. About 20 minutes into the session one of the participant's pagers started beeping. It was Harold Miller's. Harold looked down at the number on the pager and said, "I'm sorry, but I've got to go make a phone call," and left the room. About 20 minutes later a production worker came into the room and motioned for Mary Ferguson, another of the participants, to come to the door. Mary got up and walked around the table to confer with the worker. She then said, "Something's come up in the plant and I've got to leave for a few minutes."

During the first two hours of the training, six of the 20 participants had been in and out of the room for similar interruptions, and two did not return at all. During the last hour of the session Mark had assigned the participants to one-on-one role plays of employee coaching situations. Since many of the participants were in and out of the room, the role players had to be moved around and there was a great deal of confusion.

On Thursday, only 12 of the supervisors showed up for training and the same interruptions continued as on Tuesday. Mark, who was obviously concerned about the interruptions and lack of attendance, said, "Jim, what's going on here? I thought we were going to have 20 people to work with and my exercises will have to be changed. People are being pulled out of the training, and it looks like something's come up today, because eight of the participants aren't here. This is going to be a disaster if you don't get this situation straightened out!"

As Jim was walking back to his office he met Bernice Hernandez in the hallway. Bernice said, "How's the training going?" Jim said, "Not well. The supervisors are continually interrupted and today one third of them didn't even show up! I know we're really busy and there's a real need for the supervisors on the shop floor, but we've got to keep them in the classroom." Bernice said, "Yeah, I know it's a busy time and it's always hard to work in training. By the way, what are you covering in there? One of the department managers said the training was a bunch of 'touchy feely' stuff. Who's this guy Mark Harper? Does this guy know anything about the real world? Do the best you can. I'm counting on you to make this work."

Questions

1. What mistakes do you think Jim has made in his approach to the training?
2. What does Jim's conversation with Bernice Hernandez tell you?
3. What should Jim do in order to turn around the situation?
4. What should he tell Mark Harper?

References

1. Bassi, L., and Van Buren, M. E. "Training Investment Can Mean Financial Performance," *Training and Development* (May 1998): 40–42.

2. Kahn, Jeremy. "The World's Most Admired Companies," *Fortune* (October 11, 1999): 267–275. Stein, Nicholas. "The World's Most Admired Companies." *Fortune* (October 2, 2000): 182–184.

3. Henkoff, R. "Companies That Train Best," *Fortune* (March 22, 1993): 62–65.

4. Carlton, Jim, and Clark, Don. "Teaching Tech Pays Off for Training Firms," *The Wall Street Journal* (February 26, 1998): B8.

5. Peters, Tom. "Bosses Must Keep the Ball Rolling to Stay on Top of Their Competition," *Chicago Tribune* (August 10, 1987): sect. 4, 7.

6. Grossman, Ron. "The Three R's Go to Work," *Chicago Tribune* (October 29, 1989): sect. 4, 1.

7. Godin, Seth, ed. *1995 Information Please Business Almanac and Sourcebook*. New York: Houghton Mifflin (1994): 289.

8. Grossman. "The Three R's."

9. Ricks, Thomas E. "Army's 'Baby Generals' Take a Crash Course in Sensitivity Training," *The Wall Street Journal* (January 19, 1998): A1.

10. Morgan, Rebecca L. "Getting Into Corporate Training—What Does It Take?" *American Salesman* (October 2000): 25–29. Caudron, Shari; Redmon, Marsha; Suleiman, Anver S.; Kaplan-Leiserson, Eva; McDermont, Lynda; and Wagner, Stacey. "Executive Summaries," *Training and Development* (October 2001): 82–83. "20 Teaching Tips to Make Your Training Lessons Stick," *HR Focus* (October 2000): 13. Cone, John W., and Robinson, Dana G. "The Power of E-Performance," *Training and Development* (August 2001): 32–40.

11. Mager, Robert F. *Preparing Instructional Objectives,* 2nd ed. Belmont, CA: Pitman Learning (1984): 21, 51, 86–87.

12. Ibid.

13. Ibid.

14. Eichinger, Bob. Presentation to the Metroplex Human Resource Planning Society (April 1994), Plano, Texas.

15. Carlton and Clark. "Teaching Tech."

16. Ibid.: B8.

17. Ibid.: B8.

18. Associated Press. "Workers Get Insight from Guided Play," *Dallas Morning News* (September 13, 1997): 2F.

19. Ibid.

20. Ibid.

21. Rajsky, Gregory. "Adult Learning," *Products Finishing* (February 2002): 90–91.

22. Cascio, Wayne F. *Applied Psychology in Personnel Management,* 4th ed. Englewood Cliffs, NJ: Prentice Hall, 1991.

23. Jamieson, David, and O'Mara, Julie. *Managing Workforce 2000*. San Francisco: Jossey-Bass (1991): 83–91.

24. Ibid.

25. Eichinger. "Presentation."

THE APPRAISAL PROCESS

Objectives

After reading and discussing this chapter, you should be able to do the following:

1. Define this chapter's key terms.
2. List the major purposes for appraising your subordinates.
3. Explain why clear objectives and standards are needed in order to prepare proper appraisals.
4. List and give examples of appraisal methods.
5. List and give examples of pitfalls in the appraisal process.

Introduction

A primary duty for both supervisors and self-managing teams is to periodically conduct performance appraisals of their subordinates. In the **appraisal process,** supervisors evaluate each subordinate or team member's job performance. Skill levels and potential also may be appraised as a part of the process. The appraisal process is usually referred to as performance appraisal, performance evaluation, or performance review. In most organizations, performance appraisal is formalized—put in writing and made a matter of record—once or twice each year. It provides needed feedback to all employees, letting them know what their superiors, or sometimes even their peers, think of their performance. The day-to-day coaching in which supervisors critique a subordinate's performance, make suggestions for improvement, or provide praise for good work provides the groundwork for the formal appraisal.

appraisal process
periodic evaluations of each subordinate's on-the-job performance as well as skill levels, attitudes, and potential

Goals of Appraisals

Here are the major goals of employee appraisals:

- To measure employee performance

- To measure employee potential
- To analyze employee strengths and weaknesses—providing recognition for the former and ways to eliminate the latter
- To set goals for the improvement of performance
- To substantiate decisions about pay increases and eligibility for promotion, transfer, or training programs
- To eliminate hopelessly inadequate performers

If the appraisal process is to accomplish these goals, it must be objective and accurate. It must also comply with company policies and the constraints of moral, ethical, and legal conduct. Throughout the remainder of this chapter, we deal with the appraisal process from the supervisor's perspective. When team leaders or team members perform appraisals, the process generally remains the same.

What to Appraise

Appraisals can focus on (1) outcomes, such as the results of effort, or (2) work processes or work-related behaviors, such as the actions of subordinates. The first approach focuses on the end product, with quantity and quality measures. The second focuses on how the work is performed, as it appraises the behaviors involved in the work. Appraisal or work behaviors often include measures of intangibles such as cooperation, initiative, team spirit, and the relative difficulty of tasks being performed. Most appraisal programs try to measure both outcomes and behaviors.

As a supervisor or team leader, you will be appraised on the work results of your subordinates as well as on the quality of the processes or behaviors by which you manage—decision making, planning, communicating, and problem solving. As a team facilitator, you will be appraised by the teams you serve on how well you aid their efforts.

Your company's appraisal procedures and appraisal forms will dictate what you appraise. Look at the forms and determine their emphasis on outcomes and behaviors. The best producers from among your subordinates should be the ones

As a team leader, you may visit clients periodically to gather feedback on service and quality. As with any appraisal, you must be as objective and accurate as possible.

SUPERVISING TEAMS

Changes in performance appraisal methods may occur with the introduction of teams into the workplace. Business journals identify three generic approaches currently in use. One or a combination of them may be just right for your teams.

Peer Reviews

Because the nature of teams makes each member dependent upon the performance of others, teammates are asked to evaluate each other's contributions. Peer reviews work best when each member cares about the other members, knows how to perform other members' jobs as a result of cross-training, and has been taught to make honest, valid, and candid appraisals using precise performance standards. In self-managing teams, members hire, discipline, reward, and terminate team members. They usually have the authority to act on their appraisals by identifying those in need of help, and they work with members to improve their performance. If needed improvements do not occur, team members may recommend the termination of poor performers.

Client Reviews

A team's clients are any individuals or groups receiving its output. Clients are found inside and outside the team's department and organization. The team needs to know about dissatisfied clients. Various methods for gathering client input are available. Team leaders may visit clients regularly and interview them, in person or by use of surveys, to gather feedback on performance. Typical questions are: "What are we doing well?" "What are we doing poorly?" "What can we do for clients that we are not now doing?" The answers provide goals for the future.

Self-Assessments

Each team member conducts an evaluation of his own performance as both an individual worker and a team member. This evaluation can then be compared to peer reviews. Any variances may require a meeting with the affected parties to gain understanding of differing perspectives. When disputes and disagreements occur, the team leader or a supervisor may be called on to adjudicate and negotiate solutions.

to receive the greatest financial rewards you have to distribute. Those who demonstrate weaknesses should be counseled and scheduled for training to improve their weaknesses.

STANDARDS

Whether you are appraising outcomes or behaviors, you must do so with well-defined, specific, realistic, measurable, and mutually understood criteria or **standards.** You will recall from Chapter 12 that training objectives require such criteria so that both trainer and trainee can tell when a behavior is being demonstrated with sufficient mastery. Appraising people in different job categories may require the use of different work factors and criteria. Regardless of the forms you use for appraisals, be certain that the

standard

a quantity or quality designation that can be used as a basis for judging outcomes and behaviors descriptive words on them have clear and precise meanings to you and to those being rated. Ambiguity in these measures can provide the basis for legal challenges of the use of performance appraisals.[1]

Be certain to inform your subordinates or team members of the standards by which their work performance will be appraised. Keep in mind that standards will vary in proportion to the employee's time on a job and to the training received. You should not expect the same output from a new person that you expect from a seasoned veteran. Consider the following guidelines when selecting performance standards or criteria:

1. *Relevance.* Standards must relate directly to successful performance on a specific job.

2. *Freedom from contamination.* When comparing the performance of production workers, for example, the appraiser must allow for differences in the equipment they are using. Similarly, a comparison of the performances of field sales representatives will be contaminated if territories differ in sales potential. Since diverse employees have diverse styles, the appraisal should focus on the results they achieve. You must exercise care to avoid making judgments on the basis of stereotypes, biases, or an employee's deviation from an approach typical of your company's dominant culture.

3. *Validity.* To avoid charges of discrimination, employees in each job category must be evaluated by the same standards and methods.

4. *Acceptance.* Regardless of the criteria and methods used, the appraisal system will succeed only if those subjected to it accept it as being valid, fair, and understandable. If you are stuck with an appraisal system in which you and your people do not believe, get together with your peers who feel as you do and work with higher authorities to change things. If an appraisal system has no support from either the appraisers or the appraisees, it will be worthless and will create negative results for all concerned.

APPRAISALS AND DIVERSITY

When evaluating diverse employees, supervisors have to consider the fairness and applicability of various standards of performance. Companies on the cutting edge of the management of diversity have discovered that efforts must be made "to distinguish style from substance—so that many styles and approaches can be accommodated without sacrificing effectiveness within the organization." They do not hold employees to a "homogeneous ideal." Such inflexibility has a discriminatory impact and may exclude diverse groups from positions of leadership, particularly minorities and women. "By shifting the focus away from style to performance results, . . . organizations are enlarging the range of acceptable behavior for diverse employees while remaining focused on quality performance."[2]

Some companies have improved their management of diversity by adopting new philosophies, policies, programs, and operating procedures for hiring, promoting, and appraising employees. Such actions often change the company's culture to one that accepts (not simply tolerates) the existence of subcultures and taps into their unique strengths and contributions. These companies recognize that diverse people have diverse needs and expectations. Training can then focus on meeting these expectations so that these types of employees can survive and prosper in the organization. Support for diverse employees may include support networks, mentors, skills training, and encouragement for self-development. At the same time, all employees should be encouraged to be themselves and to act in ways comfortable for them that accomplish the company's goals.[3]

In some companies, performance standards are developed with input from diverse groups of employees "who understand the organization's needs and also recognize the untapped talent that those outside the mainstream can offer."[4] After all, empowering people means delegating authority and granting autonomy. Once people are trained to perform their duties, they must be given the latitude to do so effectively. Rewards for outstanding performance should be varied as well. Just as people work for differing motives, it takes different incentives to entice and satisfy diverse individuals. One size will not fit all.

Some practical guidance seems in order on the issue of diversity and performance appraisal. For example, what should be done when the performance appraisals of the only three women or minorities are the lowest in the unit? While low performance obviously justifies such appraisal results, it would be prudent to examine the potential reasons for such results and seek advice from human resource staff members.[5] For example, other than the possibility of bias on your part, there could be historical differences in opportunities for training that need to be eliminated or differences in informal mentoring that need to be addressed. Consulting with your boss and staff experts in human resources allows you to work through the potential reasons for these ratings and conclude whether the ratings are warranted.

THE SUPERVISOR AS AN APPRAISER

Effective appraisals require supervisors to have the following attributes, information, and skills:[6]

1. Willingness to communicate performance standards and to obtain employee input and agreement on appropriate personal goals for the period.

2. Knowledge of the key job-related behaviors, objective outcomes, and goals on which the evaluation is based.

3. Sufficient objectivity to focus on the behaviors and outcomes while recognizing that some subjective dimensions of appraisal, such as employee cooperation, are critical.

4. Willingness to provide informal performance feedback and coaching at regular intervals throughout the year.

5. Communication skills to provide respectful and timely feedback that subordinates internalize.

6. Familiarity with the appraisal instrument and knowledge of the meaning of the ratings.

7. Courage to provide honest appraisals to subordinates and to seek such feedback from superiors.

If you feel uncomfortable when it comes to appraising subordinates, try to determine the source of your discomfort. When it is inadequate firsthand knowledge about their performance, it may mean that you do not spend enough time with them, you fail to record observations of their performance, or you do not oversee their work as much as you should. If you need training as an appraiser, you should ask for it. Appraisals are far too important to be done improperly.

Unless you oversee the work of self-managing teams, you will usually not share appraisal duties with subordinates. With or without self-managing teams, the appraiser has the responsibility to keep results confidential and share them only with those who are approved to receive appraisal results.

AVOIDING THE BLAME GAME

Blame placing is not the purpose of performance appraisal. Although organizations may want to assign blame for mistakes, you will most probably have to continue to work with the blamed person. At the same time, that person will have to continue to work with you and his or her coworkers. The purpose of appraisal is to reinforce the positive, identify areas in which improvement is needed, and map out actions for commitment to improved performance in the future. An appraisal goes well if it rewards good performance and helps the individuals involved to learn from errors.

On the other hand, while placing blame for mistakes and poor performance is counterproductive, it is important that supervisors use the appraisal to address poor performance. When supervisors fail to address poor performance they tend to reward mediocrity and demoralize high performers. Some of the best-managed companies, such as Intel, Microsoft, and GE, are adamant about the need to confront poor performance and to deliver bad news to poor performers. Top performers appreciate a work environment that emphasizes excellence and eliminates non-contributors.[7]

Legal Issues and Third-Party Reviews of Performance Appraisals

Federal, state, and local laws deal with employment discrimination. The federal laws discussed in Chapter 11 have some applicability to the appraisal process. The following laws apply: Equal Pay Act of 1963, Age Discrimination in Employment Act of 1967 (as amended), and Title VII of the 1964 Civil Rights Act (as amended in 1972 and 1991). Guidelines for protecting the performance appraisal process from charges of discrimination include the following. Appraisals should:[8]

- be in writing.
- contain specific procedures.
- include specific instructions for supervisors.
- provide for training supervisors how to evaluate employees.
- utilize standardized forms for related groups of employees (e.g., one form could be used for appraising supervisory employees, another for appraising hourly employees).
- be thoroughly communicated to employees.
- be given at least once each year.
- evaluate specific work behavior, not personal traits.
- be continually monitored by equal employment opportunity experts for impact on protected groups.
- include reviews of subordinates' appraisals by persons more senior than the appraisers.
- avoid comments about why an employee is behaving in a certain manner.

Performance appraisals also need to convey an overall description of the employee's performance so that decision-makers have confidence in their value. One of the common problems of performance appraisals is that supervisors do not express what they really think about their subordinates' performance. In other instances the performance appraisal process simply fails to capture critical aspects of job performance that differentiate between excellent, average, and poor performance.

One of the authors is familiar with a situation in which the performance appraisal system really did not serve its intended purposes. In this situation a unionized company was downsizing its workforce and the contract allowed the company to use performance as one of the layoff criteria. When the company's managers attempted to determine which employees to lay off, they realized that the performance appraisals the company had been using for many years did not provide useful performance information. Because the managers wanted to lay off the worst performers, they essentially ignored the appraisals in the employees' files and conducted new appraisals. It was almost as if the mangers were saying, "We really didn't mean what we said in your previous performance appraisals, but this time we're serious." After performing the new appraisals, the managers used them for the layoff decisions. Unsurprisingly, the union filed a large number of grievances over the layoffs on the basis of the new appraisal process and won many of its cases in arbitration. Needless to say, a company is putting itself at risk when it sets aside several years of performance appraisals, which presumably tell employees that their performance is satisfactory, and then ignores those appraisals when it is time to actually use appraisals for important decisions.

Appraisal Methods

Your company probably makes use of several performance appraisal methods. Each has advantages and disadvantages, and none is adequate for all employees or groups. Company policy will typically dictate the appraisal method or combinations of methods that will be used. The methods must be valid and standardized, have no disparate impact on minorities and women, be based on current and objective job-related standards, and be conducted in conformance with the preceding legal guidelines.

360-DEGREE REVIEW PROCESS

The 360-degree review process involves multiple performance appraisers. The individual is appraised by subordinates, peers, and superiors, and also performs a self-appraisal. In some companies, customers are asked to provide appraisals.[9] The rationale for the 360-degree performance review or 360-degree feedback is that a supervisor's performance should be appraised from all directions. Traditional top-down appraisals offer no direct way of determining the quality of supervision from the subordinate's perspective. Furthermore, when peers contribute to the evaluation the supervisor has more incentive for cooperating with them on a regular basis.

The 360-degree feedback process offers a number of potential benefits. For these reasons, many companies, such as Levi Strauss, AT&T, and General Motors, are using 360-degree feedback and multi-rater assessment.[10] Other companies using the process include Exxon Mobil, General Electric, Tenneco, Caterpillar, TRW, Bank of America, and Mass Mutual Insurance. Furthermore, for the past 20 years IBM has had subordinates evaluate their superiors.[11] The following describes some of the 360-degree evaluation process:

> Are you crisp, clear, and articulate? Abrasive? Spreading yourself too thin? Trustworthy? Off-the-cuff remarks may be gathered too. A week or two later you'll get the results, all crunched and graphed by a computer. Ideally, all this will be explained by someone from your human resources department or the company that handled the questionnaires, a person who can break bad news gently. You get to see how your opinion of yourself differs from those of the [raters]. . . . The results won't necessarily determine your pay, promotions, or termination. At least, not yet. The technique as it's now applied doesn't work well for that. . . . What's most interesting about [the] feedback . . . is the huge variety of unpredictable comments—and potential learning—that it delivers. Most people are surprised by what they hear. Only a fraction of managers have a good grasp of their own abilities.[12]

This performance feedback or review system gives supervisors an usually objective and diverse look at how others perceive them. Managers learn of their annoying traits as well as supportive ones. "Many companies are using feedback for cultural change, to accelerate the shift to teamwork and employee empowerment. Bosses who charged up the corporate ladder by controlling everything and barking like a drill sergeant often get an earful from eagerly

SUPERVISORS AND QUALITY

Watson Wyatt, a national consulting firm, has found that bosses "don't listen, . . . don't give [subordinates] a chance to make a difference on the job and [they] don't help them see where their future might be. 'Companies score low on listening and acting on employee suggestions,'" according to a Wyatt consultant. About two-thirds of surveyed workers say that their bosses don't seek and follow up on their suggestions. About the same number of managers believe they are good at giving workers involvement in decisions that affect them. But only 25 percent of workers agree with them. "Most managers said the biggest barrier to change within their companies is their employees. Most employees said the major problem is their bosses' lack of skills and support."

In what ways do the Wyatt surveys reflect the need for 360-degree evaluation programs? How do you explain the differences between managers' viewpoints and those of their subordinates?

Source: Stephen Franklin, "Nobody Listens Around Here," *Chicago Tribune* (December 14, 1994): sect. 3, 3.

critical underlings."[13] When the system was used at Du Pont for providing feedback to some 80 research scientists and support personnel, it strengthened their abilities to work in teams. In other companies the 360-degree evaluation process has been expanded to include suppliers as evaluators of employees.[14] The key factor for successful application of the feedback system is to "pick a small number of shortcomings to fix and decide on a few concrete remedies."[15]

Robert D. Rockey, Jr., president of North American operations for Levi Strauss, is evaluated through his company's 360-degree review process. Based on the feedback he received from his superior, peers, and subordinates, Rockey decided to "loosen up somewhat, to command less, to listen more."[16] Unsurprisingly, appraisees appear to obtain more value from the written comments than the ratings on the scales. Raters also favor the use of their evaluations for developmental feedback rather than for personnel decisions such as raises. In addition, it appears that appraisals should be anonymous, because when raters have to sign their evaluations they rate their managers higher.[17]

GRAPHIC RATING SCALE METHODS

One of the most common appraisal methods is the graphic rating scale. Supervisors rate their subordinates on several graphic rating scale items, such as the one shown in Exhibit 13.1. Typically, the performance of employees is appraised on several factors or dimensions of the job. Examples of common factors include effort, knowledge, cooperation with others, and quantity of output. The person's performance on each factor is then measured on a scale. With graphic rating scale items, each interval on

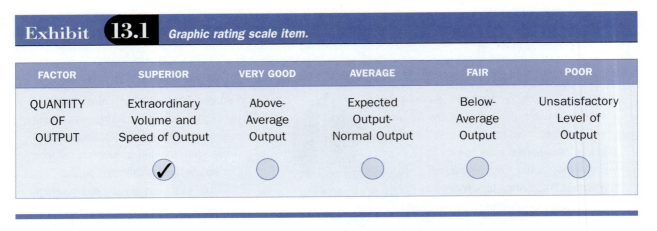

Exhibit 13.1 *Graphic rating scale item.*

FACTOR	SUPERIOR	VERY GOOD	AVERAGE	FAIR	POOR
QUANTITY OF OUTPUT	Extraordinary Volume and Speed of Output	Above-Average Output	Expected Output-Normal Output	Below-Average Output	Unsatisfactory Level of Output
	✓	○	○	○	○

the scale often has a descriptive phrase for the specific level of performance. In Exhibit 13.1, the factor is quantity of output. The rater must decide and mark where the person's performance is on this scale, such as very good, average, fair, etc. After all items are completed, the numerical values are then totaled for an overall performance score.

RANKING AND FORCED DISTRIBUTION METHODS

Because leniency bias and rater inflation are common errors in performance appraisals, your company may require you to complete a *ranking* of your subordinates. With this method, you will be required to rank your people from the most productive to least productive or from the most valuable to least valuable. You may be required to make a simple list of your subordinates, ranking one over another on their abilities and contributions.

The *forced distribution* method provides another remedy for leniency errors or rater inflation. With this approach, no more than a certain percentage of your people may be ranked in each of the performance categories. Performance categories often approximate the percentages of a normal distribution or bell curve. Exhibit 13.2 illustrates a forced distribution approach. When all of your subordinates perform identical tasks, the ranking and forced distribution methods are appropriate. However, when your subordinates perform different jobs the rankings are less valid because the system requires you to compare apples and oranges.[18] Unfortunately, this same criticism applies to many performance appraisal methods. In addition, supervisors usually complain about ranking or forced distribution methods because they often feel that they have a disproportionate number of above-average (or below-average) performers. They argue that the arbitrariness of the forced distribution method makes them give invalid ratings to some of their subordinates.

A limitation of the ranking and forced distribution methods is that, by themselves, they provide very little information of value for providing feedback in a performance appraisal session.[19] For example, a supervisor would find it difficult to conduct a meaningful performance appraisal session if all

Exhibit **13.2**

Forced distribution method of worker appraisal.

Instructions to Rater: List your subordinates by their overall rating in one or another of the categories below. Use their complete initials and do not exceed the percentages listed.

Percentage	Category	Subordinate(s)
5%	Superior	GBH
12.5%	Above Average	SAB, RFL
65%	Average	PTC, BCT, LH, NPB, SDO LMR
12.5%	Below Average	GSW, TFM
5%	Unacceptable	PBC

she could tell the subordinate is that his rank is 8th out of 12. However, because such methods are typically used in conjunction with other appraisal methods, they can make a valuable contribution. Ranking and forced distribution methods force you to make a choice and to evaluate your people in a new way. It is conceivable that performance appraisals may become the criterion for making layoff decisions at some point in the future. If supervisors have failed to distinguish between the performance levels of their employees, the appraisals will not be useful. Unlike the citizens of Garrison Keillor's fictitious Lake Wobegone, where all the children are above average, all of your subordinates cannot be ranked above average with forced distributions.

PAIRED COMPARISON METHOD

The *paired comparison* method requires supervisors to compare subordinates in a pair-wise manner. The supervisor counts the number of times a subordinate is picked as the better of the pairs and a numerical total is obtained. This technique has the advantage of providing a realistic framework of comparison. It is easier for most evaluators to decide whether one subordinate is better than another than it is to decide whether she fits in the average, above average, good, etc., categories of a graphic rating scale. However, paired comparison methods become unwieldy with large numbers of subordinates because of the very large number of comparisons that must be made. They also provide only limited information for the performance appraisal session.[20]

Exhibit 13.3 provides an example of the paired comparison method.

Exhibit 13.3 *Paired comparison method.*

Compare the overall performance of each of your subordinates on a pair-wise basis with every one of your other subordinates. Assign a value of 1 if the first subordinate is better than the second for each pair of subordinates:

PAIRED COMPARISONS:

Rick vs. Jay	1	Jay vs. Alice	1	Josie vs. Jay	1
Rick vs. Alice	1	Jay vs. Felicia	1	Josie vs. Alice	1
Rick vs. Felicia	1	Jay vs. Rick	0	Josie vs. Felicia	1
Rick vs. Josie	1	Jay vs. Josie	0	Josie vs. Rick	0
Rick's Score = 4		Jay's Score = 2		Josie's Score = 3

Alice vs. Jay	0	Felicia vs. Jay	0
Alice vs. Felicia	1	Felicia vs. Alice	0
Alice vs. Rick	0	Felicia vs. Rick	0
Alice vs. Josie	0	Felicia vs. Josie	0
Alice's Score = 1		Felicia's Score = 0

OVERALL RANKING (4 = BEST, 0 = WORST):

Rick	4
Jay	3
Josie	2
Alice	1
Felicia	0

ESSAY, NARRATIVE, AND CRITICAL-INCIDENT METHODS

The most flexible method, but clearly the most demanding method of appraisal, is the *essay* or *narrative* method. In this method the supervisor describes the subordinate's performance in written comments that address all of the relevant performance dimensions of the job. This method offers the maximum degree of expression for precise and informative evaluations and is valuable for conducting an appraisal session. This method applies well to highly educated professionals and to managers who are rated by other managers. However, narratives and essays are time consuming to prepare.

With the *critical-incident* method, the rater records personal observations about both positive and negative occurrences in order to dramatize the particular point under examination. In this method, the supervisor refers to specific situations—critical incidents—that highlight or illustrate a worker's performance. These incidents are of great value in discussing a subordinate's performance in appraisal sessions because they deal with specific observable behaviors. The disadvantage is that critical incidents can only come from frequent observations and recording. Supervisors may not have sufficient opportunities for observation and collection of critical incidents when subordinates work at remote locations. Sales people, construction workers, research people, and staff specialists are a few examples of workers who are often based at different locations. In their cases, comments from the people they serve may provide examples of critical incidents. Exhibit 13.4 provides examples of critical incidents.

BEHAVIORALLY ANCHORED RATING SCALES

The *behaviorally anchored rating scale* (BARS) method of appraisal uses a series of statements that describe performance behaviors ranging from effective through ineffective. The statements are often constructed from critical incidents written by people who have intensive knowledge of the job, such as supervisors or job incumbents.[21] These statements describe behaviors that pertain to a specific dimension of job performance. The statements are then placed on a scale in order of their desirability, and a point value is assigned to each statement. The rater must choose the statement that best describes the ratee's performance for each dimension, then total the points. The following three statements illustrate the use of BARS for rating a trainer's punctuality while conducting training sessions:

- The trainer always arrives 30 minutes early for each training session and makes sure that all equipment is functioning (5 pts.)
- The trainer usually arrives for each training session just before the session is scheduled to begin (3 pts.)
- The trainer is often late for sessions and frequently leaves early (0 pts.)

Critical-incident appraisal.   Exhibit **13.4**

Initiative   Constance requests additional work when she runs out and lends a hand to her less experienced coworkers.

Cooperation   Routinely, she coordinates with coworkers, recognizing that her work is the basis for theirs.

Notice that these statements describe specific observable behaviors that were drawn from critical incidents and that the method requires the appraiser to select one of the descriptive statements. Statements like the ones shown can be constructed for each behavior or dimension considered crucial to successful performance on a job. Input from those who will be rated should be sought during construction of the statements to ensure that a complete list of essential behaviors is included and to help enlist the support of those who will be rated under the BARS method.

A disadvantage of BARS is that the statements are specific to only one job and they are expensive to develop because of the time and statistical expertise required.[22]

CONCLUDING REMARKS ABOUT APPRAISAL FORMATS

The most common approach to appraisal is to combine various formats. For example, a company's standard appraisal form may include several graphic rating scales. It also may require the supervisor to conduct a forced distribution rating of the subordinate's overall performance, e.g. top 10 percent, next 20 percent, etc. The form also may require the supervisor to include three or four objectives developed from an MBO approach. In addition, it may require a short narrative about the subordinate's performance. Use of multiple appraisal approaches enables the company to offset the weaknesses of each and provides a better overall appraisal.

It should be remembered that all appraisal approaches are affected by the personal interests, preferences, and prejudices of the appraiser. No appraisal method will completely eliminate bias. It is up to you, the rater, to be as objective as you can by making every effort to leave bias and personality clashes out of each rating. Your emphasis should be foremost on the subordinate's performance on the job. Try to act like a camera. State as clearly as you can what each person did and how well it was done.

Management by Objectives

In Chapter 4, we introduced you to management by objectives (MBO) as it related to planning. In this chapter, we discuss MBO as a useful method for appraising the performance of teams, team members, and traditional subordinates. Superiors and subordinates agree on the goals subordinates will work to achieve and strategies required to achieve them. The goals may be related to outcomes or behaviors. The primary advantage of MBO as an appraisal method is that people are more committed to achieving goals when they have had a role in setting them.

Effective objectives have the following characteristics:[23]

1. *Specificity.* Objectives identify acceptable behavior and output.
2. *Timeliness.* The deadline for completion or attainment is specified.

3. *Conditions.* Qualifications, boundaries, and limits (schedules, policies, resources) should be specified.

4. *Prioritization.* Objectives are rated by order of importance.

5. *Consequences.* What can be expected for achieving or not achieving is specified.

6. *Goal congruence.* Individual and department goals should fit and not conflict.

In a previous chapter, we discussed stretch goals: "big, athletic leaps of progress on measures like inventory turns, product development time, and manufacturing cycles."[24] Setting and reaching such goals are rapidly becoming ordinary behaviors for individuals and teams. To leap ahead of competition, incremental changes and gradual improvement are not enough. Reengineering demands discarding the old, rethinking everything a company does, and coming up with a whole new effort. Chrysler chose this route with its cab-forward design. "Getting an organization to embrace wrenchingly difficult new goals—particularly in the absence of a crisis—can traumatize employees. Managers who can't stand the relentless new pace quit or get fired."[25] To motivate employees to reach stretch goals, management must explain the urgency and consequences of not reaching the goal. Next, it must convince everyone that the goal is possible and point out, through benchmarking, how others have achieved the goal. Then it must empower people to find their own means and get out of their way.

Stanford professors James C. Collins and Jerry I. Porras have found that long-lasting visionary companies have several common traits. Among them is the continuous setting and achieving of what they call big, hairy, audacious goals (BHAGs). When President John F. Kennedy set a national goal in 1961 to place Americans on the moon and return them safely to Earth by the end of that decade, he was setting a BHAG. In like fashion, when Sam Walton, founder of Wal-Mart, set the goal to become "a $1 billion company in four years (a more than doubling of the company's size)" he was setting a BHAG.[26]

Both stretch goals and BHAGs need little explanation, are "clear and compelling and [serve] as a unifying focal point of effort—often creating immense team spirit. [Each] has a clear finish line . . . is tangible, energizing, highly focused."[27] When working with your teams and subordinates, encourage them to articulate and strive for such goals. The rewards for doing so are incredible for both the individuals involved and their organizations.

As part of the appraisal process, you may need to watch workers perform their jobs. The objective notes you take can be used in your written evaluation.

Appraising with MBO

Approaches to appraising by MBO differ widely, although most efforts begin with implementation at top management levels. Gradually, as the upper echelons gain expertise with MBO, it is used at progressively more levels. If you do not have the permission of your superior to use MBO, you should not use it. Exhibit 13.5 outlines a series of distinct steps that can make MBO work for you. It represents only one of many approaches, but it is a comprehensive method that can prevent some of the major problems others have encountered in their early MBO efforts.

STEP 1: SETTING GOALS

As stated earlier, goals are ends or end states that have to do with a person's or a unit's growth and development. If they are to be meaningful, they should meet the criteria set forth earlier. They must be set through a dialogue or discussion between superiors and subordinates, and both parties must recognize their importance and be committed to them.

STEP 2: IDENTIFYING RESOURCES AND ACTIONS NEEDED

Before superiors and subordinates can agree on goals, they should examine whether the organization and the subordinate have the resources and abilities to achieve them. Resources include human energy, effort, time, money, and materials. Some actions may require the commitment and cooperation of several persons and units.

Exhibit 13.5 *Basic steps in appraising through MBO.*

Step 1. *Setting goals.* Goals must be mutually determined through discussions between supervisors and subordinates. Areas for improvement can be determined from past appraisals, current situations, job descriptions, and the subordinate's ambitions to improve and gain higher responsibilities.

Step 2. *Identifying resources and actions needed.* The amount of time, money, and materials required to reach an objective must be determined. To attain any goal, the efforts of the goal setter and others may be required. Accurate predictions must be made.

Step 3. *Arranging goals in order of priority.* Both the rater and the ratee need to agree as to the importance of each goal and the order in which they should be pursued.

Step 4. *Setting timetables.* Precise times need to be set for the completion of actions and the attainment of goals. These times will allow evaluations of progress and will facilitate appropriate adjustments in either methods or goals.

Step 5. *Appraising the results.* The summary judgment of success or failure that occurs at this step sets the stage for a return to step one. Thus the cycle repeats.

STEP 3: ARRANGING GOALS IN ORDER OF PRIORITY

Which goal should be worked on first, second, and so on? What end state is considered by both parties to be the most essential? One guideline for answering these questions is the level of inefficiency that needs to be eliminated. An attack on the most expensive areas of waste or problems could be placed first on the list of objectives. Lesser areas of waste could be attacked simultaneously or sequentially.

STEP 4: SETTING TIMETABLES

Besides agreeing on priorities, boss and subordinate must agree on the times by which each goal is to be achieved. Time estimates must be made, and calendars must be prepared for future reference. Dates for completion become guideposts and serve as checkpoints to determine progress and problems. As these dates arrive, boss and subordinate coordinate to determine if adjustments are necessary. New times, new approaches, or refinements may be required.

STEP 5: APPRAISING THE RESULTS

At the intervals dictated by your company, you and your subordinates meet to discuss the progress and events that have taken place since the last evaluation. Your appraisal of your subordinates' efforts is not based solely on goal achievement. Your appraisals should consider both processes and behaviors. Additional criteria for use with MBO appraisals are presented in Exhibit 13.6.

Some additional criteria to consider when appraising with MBO.   **Exhibit 13.6**

In addition to the achievement or nonachievement of a goal, consider the following when evaluating performance:

1. How has the subordinate grown as a result of pursuing the goal?

2. Was the subordinate effective? Did she do the right things in a proper sequence?

3. Was the subordinate efficient? Did he use only the necessary amounts of resources?

4. Did the individual help or hinder fellow workers?

5. Were due dates met? Were goals achieved earlier than planned?

6. Were obstacles overcome or circumvented?

7. Were the goals easy or difficult to achieve?

8. Is the subordinate getting better at choosing goals, setting priorities, and establishing timetables?

Appraising by Computer

Some companies are using software to develop more refined measures of the time their employees spend in productive work. For example, British Airways uses software to measure how much time a service representative spends in break time or making personal calls. Such software can also measure performance in resolving customer complaints.[28] Employers may legally monitor the amount of time employees spend surfing the Internet as the Electronic Communications Privacy Act enables employers to monitor employees' e-mail and Internet activity on company computers. A recent survey examined the rationales for companies monitoring their employees. The responding executives cited the following reasons for such monitoring: 31 percent—client interaction quality, 27 percent—productivity, and 20 percent—to detect illegal or criminal activities.[29]

computer monitoring

using computers to measure how employees achieve their outputs by monitoring work as it takes place

Computer monitoring measures how employees achieve their outputs—monitoring work as it takes place—in addition to keeping track of their total output. It counts such things as the number of keystrokes per minute, the use of individual machines per hour, and the number and kinds of items processed by a sales clerk per hour. Computer monitoring allows employers to rate employee productivity and rank employees according to how completely and effectively they use each minute of each working hour. Computer monitoring can provide the specific quantifiable measures of performance needed for meaningful pay-for-performance compensation systems.

Critics of computer monitoring argue that it creates additional worker stress, fatigue, and turnover. Workers fear unauthorized access to and disclosure of highly "personal and private information."[30] From management's point of view, computer monitoring helps control costs, improve security, increase productivity, and obtain more precise information needed for objective appraisals. [Life insurance] "industry representatives also contend that some workers like the monitoring because they view it as a way to prove they are doing a good job and see it as protection in the case of disputes with customers."[31]

Software packages also are used for performance appraisal. Such packages include: 360 on the Net, 20/20 Insight Gold, Employee Appraiser

Using computers to monitor employees is an increasingly popular, but controversial, trend. The computerized checkouts at markets can objectively monitor the productivity of workers.

SUPERVISORS AND ETHICS

A *Macworld* magazine survey of 301 businesses uncovered some disturbing findings about how bosses monitor their employees. Slightly more than 21 percent admitted to "spying" on their employees. Sixty-five percent of managers responding believed that invading an employee's electronic privacy was "philosophically acceptable." Of these, about 22 percent felt it to be "a good tool to verify evidence of wrongdoing," and about 20 percent felt it to be a good way to monitor or enhance employee performance. About two-thirds of the companies surveyed hid their behavior from employees.

What do you think about this issue? Should laws forbid such electronic eavesdropping? Do you think there is a difference between your postman reading your mail before it is delivered and your boss reading your e-mail and computer files?

Source: James Coates, "Computer Privacy? It's Not a Given," *Chicago Tribune* (May 23, 1993): sect. 7, 1.

4.0, Performance Now!, and Visual 360 website: www.lir.msu.edu/hris/database/products.asp.

> [The programs ask] the user to rate an employee in several job areas: Job knowledge, interpersonal skills, customer focus, and so on. . . . Pop-up advice windows in each package provide short but comprehensive tutorials on human resources. At each step during the review-building process, a manager can click on tips for handling employees' defensive reactions to criticism. . . . Each . . . prompts users to support both praise and criticism with examples, and each encourages the managers to enter specifics about their employees during the long stretches between reviews.[32]

Each of the appraisal packages has various legal and consistency checkpoints built in. You should investigate them for their possible application to your situation.

Pitfalls

Be aware of the common types of errors that can be made by raters, and try to eliminate them from your appraisals of subordinates. Committing any one of them will render your rating inaccurate. Some of the pitfalls discussed here also were discussed in Chapter 11 with regard to the selection of new employees.

THE HALO AND HORN EFFECTS

One common rating error is known as the **halo effect.** The rater allows one outstanding positive trait or incident about a person to color the overall rating and image of that subordinate. Because one of your people

halo effect
one positive characteristic, behavior, or incident favorably biases the appraisal

horn effect

one negative characteristic, behavior, or incident adversely biases the appraisal

dresses well and has good manners and bearing, you may tend to let this blind you to other traits or the whole performance record. Conversely, if the most vivid incident you can recall about a person is his commission of a major mistake, you might allow this to obscure other fine qualities and be influenced by the **horn effect.** You must guard against letting isolated events or appearances dominate your total impression and objectivity toward a worker.

RATING THE PERSON—NOT THE PERFORMANCE

There is a strong tendency to give higher ratings if the supervisor and the subordinate get along well and low ratings if they do not. Human nature is such that we have more favorable perceptions of people we like most. On the other hand, a rater's personality and attitudes may clash with those of a subordinate. As a result, the subordinate may receive an unsatisfactory appraisal even though her performance and potential are above average. Your job in appraisals is to rate each person according to his performance in a particular job. Unless an individual's personality traits are interfering with his performance, there is no reason for you to consider them in the appraisal. You may not like an individual, but if a fair appraisal requires that you rank her as superior, you must do so. Leave your biases and prejudices out of the appraisal and avoid personal attacks.

To keep your actual or potential biases in check, you should avoid the following specific behaviors in appraising subordinates:

1. *Stereotyping*—ignoring a person's uniqueness and individuality by assuming that any member of a group must have characteristics that conform to a preformed image of the group. For example, Bill is a sales person, and therefore Bill is . . . , or Jane is Hispanic, and therefore she is. . . . Our perceptions of a member of any specific group may or may not be rooted in fact.

2. *Projecting*—accusing others of the very faults you possess. Examine the anger you feel toward another person, and beneath it you may find that you contributed to the situation.

3. *Screening*—noticing only the negative aspects of a person or his performance, interpreting events in the most negative way possible, recording only events that support a preformed judgment about a person, and ignoring positive contributions.

RATING EVERYONE AS AVERAGE

This error, which often is referred to as the *error of central tendency,* occurs when you rate everyone as average. You may be tempted to do so because you lack sufficient data. Supervisors also commit errors of central tendency because they seek safe, uncontroversial methods of handling appraisals. They may fear that if they rate a person below average, they will face a confrontation at the appraisal session. You will avoid having to justify a below average rating with this approach, but you will also discourage your high performers. Conversely, rating someone high does not make it so. If you falsify subordinates' ratings, they will know it and so will your boss.

SAVING UP FOR THE APPRAISAL

Some supervisors spot a deficiency, record it, and save their discussion of it for the formal appraisal. When this happens, subordinates reasonably feel that they have been treated unfairly. Subordinates should not be surprised by a criticism they receive during an appraisal session. The supervisor should have discussed problems with them at the time when they occurred. The formal appraisal interview should provide a review of past events that exhibits a concern for preventing the recurrence of past infractions, and it should offer a focus for future improvement.

Observe your people on an appropriately frequent basis and make on-the-spot corrections and comments about their work. Let them know where they stand with you on a regular basis. Be open and available—if you are, there will be no shocks or surprises at the appraisal interview. Your informal appraisals will have prepared them for what you will say at the formal appraisal. You also will have the facts to support your appraisal.

THE RUSH JOB

Last-minute hurry-up rating is related to most other appraisal errors. Whether you have two subordinates or 20, you have to give yourself enough lead-time for thinking things through and searching your memory and files for tangible data on which to prepare your appraisals. How would you like it if your boss spent only 15 minutes to appraise your past six months of performance?

Your formal appraisals are important. Your people know that they represent your written opinion of them and their performances. They know that what you say will directly affect their futures and their earnings. They also know that you go on record with your superiors in these appraisals. Give deserved praise and help subordinates to develop programs for improvement. This should be a task that you tackle with great concern and eagerness. You are laying foundations that will have to support future plans and programs. Make those foundations firm and strong.

NOT SHARING THE RESULTS

We have assumed that your formal appraisal of a subordinate will be discussed with him or her. To do otherwise defeats the purpose behind appraising people—to improve their performance individually and collectively. Yet, some organizations have actually prohibited or discouraged the communication of results to the rated individuals. Such policies may be adopted to counter the tendency for the ratings to be more lenient when managers are required to discuss them with their subordinates. Nonetheless, failure to share the results of the evaluation reduces the impact of the appraisal process. If appraisals are not shared in your company, you must realize how this failure affects your subordinates. A sense of fear and distrust is created by this secrecy, and subordinates will be frustrated because they do not know what their boss has said about their performance. If your company has such a policy, work to change it.

LACK OF PROPER TRAINING

All too often, companies sow the seeds for management failures by neglecting to train supervisors in the conduct of performance appraisals. A supervisor who has not been taught how to appraise, how to prepare for an appraisal interview, and how to conduct such an interview will make preventable mistakes. Self-study, conferences with your boss, college courses in human resource management, and management seminars are all good ways to establish or improve your skills in this area.

LACK OF PROPER DOCUMENTATION

When you attempt to criticize an employee's performance, you must be prepared to give specific information. You must have concrete evidence to back up your observations and criticisms. For example, be specific by giving dates and the amount of time missed when noting an employee's tardiness.

Appraisals are used as a basis for decisions about promotions, demotions, raises, and termination. You should appraise specific performances that are essential for good overall performance and document your ratings. Documentation that justifies your ratings is necessary because you may someday find yourself a party to a lawsuit claiming that your appraisal of an employee was discriminatory. In 1998, Ford Motor Company announced its intention to trim the ranks of salaried employees who were either poor performers or average performers who were not expected to be promoted. Although the program was classified as voluntary, Ford managers planned to tell employees that they recommended acceptance of the separation package. In order to limit litigation costs, Ford was expected to do the following:

> But Ford . . . could also be opening itself up to some nasty lawsuits unless it can demonstrate that it has a fair and documented program for appraising employee performance. . . . To minimize lawsuits, Ford is expected to require employees who accept the buyout to sign a legal release prohibiting them from suing the company. Still, for its performance-appraisal system to be viewed as fair, targeted employees will probably have to have been evaluated more than once.[33]

THE ERROR OF RECENT EVENTS

Supervisors often find that recent events inordinately influence their judgment about subordinates, especially if the events are strongly negative or positive. You must guard against letting the most recent events overshadow those of the previous months. The best defense is to keep accurate records of individuals' performances, recording significant events as they occur. Your appraisal should give equal consideration to all that has occurred over the appraisal period.

The Appraisal Session

Your daily contacts should provide you with the facts you need to prepare and support your formal evaluations. The big event for both you and your subordinate is the appraisal session, where you both can discuss the judgments you have made. This meeting should occur in private and without interruption.

Sharing the results of your appraisal efforts takes place in three stages: preparing for the session, conducting the session, and following up on its results.

PREPARING FOR THE SESSION

The session should not just happen. It must be planned with the same thoroughness you would apply to the planning of any important event. Then you can anticipate and prevent problems and misunderstandings that might permanently damage your relationship.

Be certain that you review each appraisal in detail before you attempt to meet with your subordinate. Even though you wrote it, you probably wrote several others at the same time, and it is amazing how easily you can confuse them in your own mind. Anticipate the areas or individual remarks that might give rise to controversy. Be clear in your own mind about why you rated a person below average on a given point and what led you to that conclusion. If you have recorded a failure that the person has overcome and is not likely to repeat, be sure that you state this on the rating. You do not want to put much emphasis on such a situation because most of our learning takes place through trial and error, and we learn best by analyzing our mistakes.

Having analyzed your subordinate's weaknesses as probable points for discussion and questions, construct a list of his strong points. Label what he does extremely well. These points represent excellent introductory material to begin the session. Some managers use what is referred to as the *sandwich approach*. This technique gives the worker a strength, then a weakness, then a strength, and so on. It tends to soften the blows to a person's ego and to promote confidence in the person being rated. Use whatever approach you feel is best for both you and your worker. Watch for a reaction and be ready to adjust your approach as necessary.

Finally, set down a list of goals or objectives that you would like to see the person achieve. The list should relate most specifically to improving performance and growth. Then determine the possible ways in which she might go about achieving each one. For example, suppose that your subordinate has recurring difficulty in making logical and practical decisions. Be ready to get her views on how to improve. Have a suggested plan on hand, and recommend that the subordinate follow it if she does not have a plan. For every weakness, there should be a suggestion for improvement. Let us hope that your subordinate will concur.

CONDUCTING THE SESSION

Make arrangements for adequate time and facilities, and ensure that you will be free of unnecessary interruptions. This is time for just you two, and there should be no distractions. It also is important to remember that you may need to obtain additional information, such as on training programs, that will help a subordinate improve in an area of weakness. You may need to schedule additional sessions to work through developmental plans.

A useful suggestion for supervisors is to focus on behaviors instead of unchangeable employee characteristics or attitudes that you can only presume to exist. As noted earlier, performance appraisal experts often suggest that the appraiser should act like a camera and report what she sees. Supervisors will conduct better appraisal sessions by adhering to the following advice:

> Think about behaviors, not characteristics. Instead of using characteristics to describe employee problem areas (e.g., lazy, slow, bad attitude, not a team player), use descriptive behaviors. Replace "lazy" with "doesn't perform duties in a timely fashion, misses deadlines, does not respond quickly to changing priorities." Or let the employee who doesn't act in the best interests of the team know that he or she "doesn't pitch in to help others when time is available and help is needed." Go from "bad attitude" to "shows unwillingness to support management decisions that he or she may not agree with." Just this simple method of letting the employee know the specific behavior that is creating the problem, as opposed to merely stating that he or she is creating the problem, can let the employee know that you are not being critical or judgmental.[34]

It is important for supervisors to recognize that different employees require different approaches in performance appraisal sessions. In performance appraisal, one approach does not fit all situations. Norman Maier's classic work on performance appraisal sessions identifies three basic approaches. These are the (1) tell and sell, (2) tell and listen, and (3) problem-solving approaches. The *tell and sell* approach is essentially a directive style in which the supervisor describes the evaluation and then outlines the actions needed for improvement in the future. The supervisor then "sells" the evaluation and attempts to obtain the subordinate's commitment to the actions outlined for improvement. This approach works best for younger and inexperienced employees, those who are insecure, and those who are easygoing and unimaginative.

In the *tell and listen* approach, the supervisor describes the appraisal to the subordinate and then allows him to talk through any disagreements with the appraisal. The supervisor practices active listening, notes any inaccuracies, and works through any misunderstandings. This approach tends to reduce defensiveness on the part of the subordinate, which may facilitate acceptance of the appraisal. Unfortunately, with the tell and listen approach, the subordinate may not obtain a clear message about the actions needed for improvement.

For experienced, competent employees, the *problem-solving* approach is appropriate. The supervisor helps the subordinate talk through any performance problems and helps draw out the subordinate's ideas for how to solve the problems. The supervisor helps to channel the subordinate's solutions toward approaches that are consistent with the company's goals or practices.[35]

After making preliminary decisions about the most appropriate style, begin the session by emphasizing that its purpose is to promote improvement in the individual and the department. Then move into the specifics. Be brief and to the point. One good approach is to begin with some rather general questions such as, "Well, Tom, how would you rate yourself on your progress since our last interview?" or, "If you had to appraise yourself for the past six months, what would you say about your performance?" This method gets your subordinate talking and gives you insight into his perception of things. Moreover, it makes the point that this interview is to be a dialogue and an exchange of points of view. Avoid lecturing, and get your subordinate's feelings and observations into the open. Work for mutual agreement and accord.

It usually is better to give your subordinates their written appraisals at least a day before the appraisal session. It also is useful to have subordinates submit a self-appraisal prior to the session, which can be used in the appraisal process. Both help the subordinate to prepare for the session. For each weakness noted, provide evidence of the validity of the rating. Then discuss how the weakness can be overcome. If your subordinate sees no immediate way to improve on the weakness, introduce your thoughts on the matter.

Finally, set some specific short-range goals with your subordinate to remedy the list of shortcomings. These should tackle the questions of what should be done, by what time it should be completed, and how each goal should be reached. You will be instilling hope in each person you work with, and more concretely, you will be showing a way out of the present difficulties. Here again is a chance to convince your subordinate of your honest concern for his welfare and progress.

FOLLOWING UP ON THE RESULTS

After the session and as a part of your normal duties, check on each person's progress toward the goals set in the appraisal session. If Ann said she would brush up on her basic skills, visit with her to see if she has. If Wally said he was going to try a new method, find out how well he is doing. Your people will soon realize, as you do, that appraisals are daily routines that are only periodically summarized through the formal appraisal report and review session. This realization should cause them to give their best regularly and not just at appraisal time.

REWARDS FOR THOSE WHO EXCEL

The extent to which you can provide tangible rewards for subordinates who excel is determined by many factors. These include the degree of your authority, your control over the purse strings through budget requests, and your boss's willingness to delegate to you. Often, all you can do from a dollar-and-cents point of view is to recommend a fixed amount as a raise. A worker who is near or at the top of the salary range may be eligible for only a token increase. Until a worker gets a promotion to a higher pay grade, she will have peaked. The incentive to hasten the promotion may be sufficient to impel that person to work at an above-average pace. Or, if she is trapped by being the least-senior person, it could mean frustration.

You have many intangible awards you can give each person. These include a pat on the back for a job well done and the frequent appreciation you show each person in public and in private. Your demonstration of your dependence on each team player goes a long way toward satisfying his need for esteem and status. You can make your people aware that you understand the value of their individual contributions in a number of ways. For example, you can send a letter of commendation to higher management levels for any exceptional contributions by your people, or you can sometimes grant time off from work. Try to make each reward appropriate for the behavior or outcome. Such rewards have greater impact when they follow quickly on the heels of the event. The appraisal process should make you keenly aware of which subordinates are carrying the load in your department and the extent of your dependence upon them.

Company celebrations of employee contributions vary widely. Most companies stage regular events to honor and celebrate jobs well done. Bonuses, certificates of achievement, induction ceremonies, and peer recognition are but a few of the ways in which companies recognize outstanding performances and behaviors. At 3M,

> The company recognizes success not so much by giving shares or bonuses but by holding events where peers cheer peers. Honorees get a certificate and backpat

from [the CEO] and waves of applause. The top awards come once a year, 3M's Oscar night. With considerable fanfare, three or four eminent innovators are inducted into the Carlton Society, a hall of fame for company immortals. Call it corny but it works.[36]

The Hotel Inter-Continental in Miami started a rewards program it calls "It Pays To Do It Right."

Each month, two of the hotel's 650 full- and part-time hourly employees are recognized for exceptional service. Nominated by guests and managers in two categories, the employee with the most votes in each wins a plaque and $500. Winners are announced at a monthly luncheon that doubles as a pep rally. . . . At an end-of-year party, the grand-prize car and week's vacation in Europe are raffled off among the 24 monthly winners.[37]

Such celebrations create a climate that encourages excellence by providing positive reinforcement for the behaviors the organization values. All of us need regular feedback and positive recognition when we do well. Rewards and ceremonies help satisfy employee needs for recognition and security. John Hooper, managing director of a consulting firm, says that: "Satisfied employees produce satisfied customers, and satisfied customers produce great financial results."[38]

NEGATIVE RESULTS

Just as good appraisals should lead to rewards and tangible improvements, poor appraisals should lead to negative consequences. When performance has been judged to be below standard, requirements for additional training and denials of positive benefits may be in order. It may be appropriate to eliminate raises and bonuses, or to deny promotions. Demotion also may be appropriate depending on management policy or a union agreement. In extreme cases where people can but will not perform, termination may be the only alternative. Inform your people that good and bad consequences are associated with performance appraisals. Be certain that the link between performance and rewards or punishments is clear to each of your subordinates. As with rewards, punishments should be appropriate and timely. Chapter 14 focuses on this difficult area in more detail.

As a summary of the appraisal process review the checklist in Exhibit 13.7. Keep in mind that appraisals can either help or hinder the development of good human relations between you and individuals or groups you supervise. Make appraisals positive experiences in order to cement team spirit and individual morale. Lock away any biases you may have, and stick to the facts. Use observable, measurable job-related standards to rate people on their performances and outcomes. Use your appraisal interview to coach and counsel as well as to praise and to criticize.

| Exhibit | **13.7** | *Checklist to help you prepare for the appraisal process.* |

1. Do I observe my subordinates regularly? If not, I must have a means of obtaining information about their performance and potential.

2. Do I often let them know how they stand with me? Am I honest when I do so?

3. Do I really know each of my people as individuals? If not, how will I develop such knowledge?

4. Can I detail in writing each of their specific duties? Would my list agree with theirs?

5. Do my appraisals emphasize an individual's performance on the job? Am I using established and approved standards for comparison?

6. Can I back up my opinions with facts? With specific incidents?

7. Have I commented on my subordinates' potential?

8. Have I planned to share the results with each person?

9. Have I thought about ways that each person can improve his or her rating?

10. Is this rating something I will be proud to sign?

Instant Replay

1. Efforts to evaluate subordinates take place daily. Formal appraisals usually take place once or twice each year.

2. The appraisal process is too important for a supervisor to delegate.

3. Appraisals look at the rate of personal development and changes in performance capabilities.

4. Appraisals must be based on known standards and linked to definite rewards and punishments.

5. The many approaches and methods of appraising subordinates all have advantages and disadvantages. All are affected to some extent by bias and subjective judgments.

6. If you are aware of the pitfalls of performance appraisal, you can act to prevent them.

7. The real value of appraisals lies in sharing them with the rated individual. Specific problems and achievements can be noted, and plans can be made for improvement.

Questions for Class Discussion

1. Can you define this chapter's key terms?

2. Why do supervisors appraise their subordinates? What in the process will benefit supervisors? What will benefit their subordinates?

3. Why are clear objectives and standards needed in the appraisal process?

4. Which of the appraisal methods described in this chapter would you as a supervisor prefer to use? Why?

5. What are the major pitfalls of the appraisal process?

6. How often are you appraised at work? How often in your management course? Would you like to be appraised more often? Why?

Incident

Purpose: To experience the difficulties connected with the use of vague, general, usually unobservable traits as rating criteria.

Your task: Listed here are traits sometimes used by companies when rating their employees. After each, write a definition of the trait. When you have finished, compare your definitions with those of your fellow students. Then list reasons why rating on the basis of traits is not a valid substitute for rating on the basis of clear, observable, job-related behaviors and standards of work performance.

1. Initiative:

2. Drive:

3. Persistence:

4. Human relations:

5. Promotability:

Virginia's Performance Appraisal   CASE PROBLEM 13.1

Steve Knapp sat down to fill out the appraisal form for his secretary, Virginia Penna. It was a few minutes before he needed to leave for home, but he had forgotten about doing Virginia's appraisal. He had just received a reminder from Human Resources telling him that he needed to complete Virginia's appraisal and turn in the form by tomorrow morning. It had been a hectic day, and Steve had not enjoyed a minute of peace since arriving for work. As he looked at the form, he tried to think about Virginia's performance on each of the rating scale items. There were 10 items on which he had to evaluate her performance: (1) knowledge of duties, (2) accuracy of work, (3) taking initiative, (4) attention to detail, (5) promptness, (6) willingness to take on responsibilities, (7) cooperation with others, (8) effort,

(9) developing new skills, and (10) dependability. There also was an item that requested a global evaluation of her overall performance.

As Steve thought about Virginia's performance with respect to each of the items, he knew that he had a problem. In reality, Virginia's performance over the year had been below average on each of the items except for cooperation. Nonetheless, she had performed better over the past 30 days and was always pleasant and friendly to everyone. Steve knew that if he rated Virginia below average on any of the items, she would be upset. Unfortunately, Virginia was not good at her job, but she had been with the company a long time and was well liked by others as well as himself. He had learned to make up for some of Virginia's weaknesses by doing more secretarial work himself on his personal computer. Nonetheless, he knew that he would be better off with another secretary and that he shouldn't be spending time doing clerical tasks. He wished that Virginia would take a job somewhere else.

Steve looked at the form again. All it required was the completion of the 10 graphic rating scale items. The scales had the following rating categories for each item: needs improvement, below average, average, above average, and superior. Steve knew that he didn't want to have a session with Virginia like he had last year. He had given her two ratings of "needs improvement," and she had started crying immediately after reading the form. As he worked through the form, he told himself that better ratings would help make Virginia feel more confident about herself and that perhaps she would perform better if she received higher ratings this time. Upon completion of the form, he quickly reviewed the ratings. All of the ratings he had assigned were average to above average. Furthermore, he had given Virginia a rating of superior on the item for cooperation with others, and the overall rating was above average.

Steve knew these ratings were higher than Virginia's performance warranted, but he told himself that the appraisal process should be forward-looking. Why dwell on the past since he was powerless to change it? Instead, he told himself that the higher ratings were justified because he expected Virginia to do better next year. He reassured himself that Virginia would be pleased with the ratings. He thought that she also might work harder because of a Pygmalion effect or out of gratitude. Why go through a painful process like he did last year? He had given Virginia low ratings last year, but the appraisal had no effect on her performance. Besides, as a result of an economic downturn, there weren't going to be raises for anyone this year. It wasn't like Virginia's ratings would affect anyone else. As Steve completed the last item on the form, he reached for the phone to ask Virginia to come in for her appraisal.

Questions

1. How do you think Virginia's performance will be affected by Steve's ratings of her?

2. Will his approach to Virginia's ratings affect those he assigns when he rates his other subordinates?

3. What mistakes has Steve made in rating Virginia's performance? How do you think Steve should have approached the appraisal process?

4. What are the likely consequences of Steve's appraisal of Virginia?

Rating Monroe's Performance   CASE PROBLEM 13.2

Liz Jarrell was trying to complete Monroe Moore's performance appraisal. Monroe was one of 12 financial analysts who worked for her. She had been on the job for about two months since being transferred back to the United States from the company's operations in Brazil. Liz had been working on the evaluation for over an hour and was making little progress. The problem was that she simply did not know how to rate Monroe's performance. Monroe did not stack up well with the other people in the unit in terms of completed financial analyses. On the other hand, it appeared that he was highly respected within the department as well as by people in other departments. He seemed to spend a lot of time helping other analysts and was very good at some of the more sophisticated analyses that were becoming more important. It looked like several of the analysts called Monroe when they needed help on difficult issues. In addition, she knew that he had spent a couple of days teaching a workshop for new employees in another department. The other department had requested his assistance, and her predecessor, Peg Flynn, who had retired from the company, had authorized it before her arrival.

As she looked at the ratings on the form, she didn't know whether Monroe's performance should be rated as needs improvement, below average, average, above average, or superior. Liz knew that Monroe had completed 40 percent fewer analyses than any other member of the department and that he was often late with the ones he completed. The records for the rest of the year before she arrived at the department showed a similar pattern of performance. In addition, since her arrival in the department, Liz had emphasized the importance of productivity and timely work.

Questions

1. What rating should Liz assign to Monroe's performance?
2. Explain your justification for the rating.

Source: The underlying concepts for this case are based on a case developed by Development Systems International, located in Studio City, California.

References

1. Schuler, Randall S., and Jackson, Susan S. *Human Resource Management: Positioning for the 21st Century.* Minneapolis: West, 1996.

2. Loden, Marilyn, and Rosener, Judy B. *Workforce America!* Homewood, IL: Business One Irwin (1991): 161–178.

3. Ibid.

4. Ibid.

5. Flynn, Gillian. "Getting Performance Reviews Right," *Workforce* (May 2001): 76–77.

6. Neal Jr., James E., "Doing Performance Appraisals Right," *Credit Union Executive Newsletter* (September 10, 2001): 4. Flynn, "Getting Performance Reviews Right." "How Our Readers Make Performance Management Work," *HR Focus* (October 2001): S1–S3. Fandray, Dayton. "The New Thinking in Performance Appraisals," *Workforce* (May 2001): 36–39. Clarke-Epstein, Chris. "Truth in Feedback," *Training and Development* (November 2001): 78–80.

7. Grote, Dick. "The Secrets of Performance Appraisal," *Across the Board* (May 2000): 14–20.

8. Commerce Clearing House Editorial Staff with George S. Odiorne. *Performance Appraisal: What Three Companies Are Doing.* Chicago: Commerce Clearing House (1985): 31–34. Flynn, "Getting Performance Reviews Right."

9. O'Reilly, Brian. "360 Feedback Can Change Your Life," *Fortune* (October 17, 1994): 93–94, 96, 100.

10. O'Reilly. "360 Feedback."

11. Antonioni, David. "Designing an Effective 360-Degree Appraisal Feedback Process," *Organizational Dynamics* Vol. 25, No. 2 (1996): 24–38.

12. O'Reilly. "360 Feedback."

13. Ibid.

14. Taylor III, Alex. "The Auto Industry Meets the New Economy," *Fortune* (September 5, 1994): 58.

15. O'Reilly. "360 Feedback."

16. Mitchell, Russell. "Managing by Values," *Business Week* (August 1, 1994): 48–49.

17. Antonioni. "Designing."

18. Cascio, Wayne F. *Applied Psychology in Personnel Management,* 4th ed. Englewood Cliffs, NJ: Prentice Hall, 1991.

19. Schuler and Jackson. *Human Resource Management.*

20. Cascio. *Applied Psychology.*

21. Ibid.

22. Ibid.

23. Schuler, Randall. *Managing Human Resources,* 5th ed. New York: West (1995): 329.

24. Tully, Shawn. "Why to Go for Stretch Targets," *Fortune* (November 14, 1994): 145–146.

25. Ibid.

26. Collins, James C., and Porras, Jerry I. *Built to Last: Successful Habits of Visionary Companies.* New York: HarperBusiness (1994): 91–99.

27. Ibid.

28. Conlin, Michelle. "The Software Says You're Just Average: Technology Alters How Performance Is Gauged—and Rewarded," *Business Week* (February 25, 2002): 126.

29. "E-mail: What You Don't Know Can Get You Fired," *The Columbus Dispatch* (May 7, 2001): 01E. "Watching Employees," *USA Today* (February 25, 2002): B.01.

30. Ibid.

31. Ibid.

32. Stewart, Doug. "Employee Appraisal Software," *Inc.* Special Technology Issue Vol. 16, No. 13 (November 1994): 104–105.

33. Schellhardt, Timothy D., and Goo, Sara. "At Ford, Buyout Plan Has a Twist," *The Wall Street Journal* (July 22, 1998): B1.

34. Frankel, Lois P., and Otazo, Karen L. "Employee Coaching: The Way to Gain Commitment, Not Just Compliance," *Employment Relations Today* Vol. 19, No. 3 (1992): 311–320.

35. Maier, Norman R. F. *The Appraisal Interview: Three Basic Approaches.* La Jolla, CA: University Associates, 1976.

36. Loeb, Marshall. "Ten Commandments for Managing Creative People," *Fortune* (January 16, 1995): 136.

37. Barciela, Susana. "Attaboys Pay Dividends in Work Place," *Chicago Tribune* (January 4, 1995): sect. 6, 5.

38. Ibid.

DISCIPLINE

Objectives

After reading and discussing this chapter, you should be able to do the following:

1. Define this chapter's key terms.

2. Differentiate between positive discipline and negative discipline.

3. Explain the role of penalties in the exercise of discipline.

4. List and briefly explain the principles of discipline.

5. List and briefly explain common pitfalls that can affect a supervisor's efforts at discipline.

6. Explain what it means to discipline your subordinates fairly.

7. Describe why supervisors should know themselves and their subordinates well before they attempt to discipline their subordinates.

Introduction

By **discipline,** we mean two distinct and related concepts: education and training to foster compliance with reasonable rules and standards (called *positive discipline*), and the dispensing of appropriate sanctions for wrongdoing (called *negative discipline*). Both approaches are necessary to promote reasonable and safe conduct at work and to sustain acceptable performance.

Nearly everything we have been exploring since Chapter 1 relates to this chapter. Your human relations role as judge requires you to administer discipline. As a supervisor, you are the person closest to your subordinates and are the member of management best suited to deal with them when they violate rules. If you hire new people, you should be thinking about how well they will fit in with the work environment. Your training and appraisals can either prevent problems or be the cause of them. Both can either foster self-discipline or sow the seeds for future performance problems.

discipline
the management duty that involves educating subordinates to foster obedience and self-control and dispensing appropriate punishment for wrongdoing

The Supervisor and Discipline

Subordinates and team members depend on their supervisors, team leaders, and team facilitators to satisfy many of their needs at work. They expect and deserve to be treated ethically and to have their employment rights respected. Employees at all levels need to know the standards that will be applied to their behaviors. They also must be given the training to meet these standards. Finally, all of us need regular feedback to know how we are doing and to help in our efforts to improve. When superiors fail to help subordinates, others stand ready to do so. Unions, cliques, and lawyers are three such groups.

If subordinates, teams, and team members like their jobs and respect their supervisors, leaders, and facilitators, they have the best reasons for avoiding punitive action. Such workers are bent not on disruption but on construction. When people know that their leaders have their best interests at heart, they will not intentionally let them down.

Subordinates and Responsibility

Effective discipline depends on many things, not the least of which is the individual employee's willingness to accept responsibility for his behaviors. Too many organizations rely on controls imposed on the individual to enforce compliance with standards. There is no real substitute in organizations for employee self-control and willingness to comply with standards. When individuals accept responsibility for their own efforts, punitive efforts are seldom needed.

Author Peter Drucker points to three prerequisites that managers at all levels must provide if they expect their employees to take responsibility for their actions: productive work, feedback information, and continuous learning.[1] These three elements show the link between planning and performing work. Although planning and execution are separate sets of activities, they should involve the same people. MBO is but one example of this. Those who perform tasks are fountainheads of information on how to do them best. They want and need to be consulted and to have their suggestions considered. In order to take responsibility, your people need timely information, regular feedback, and occasional guidance.

A Fair and Equitable Disciplinary System

As is the case with appraisal systems, unless your subordinates view the disciplinary system as both fair and equitable, it will cause more problems. Disciplinary efforts must consider a person's dignity, her legal rights, and the union agreement if one exists. A fair and equitable disciplinary system has the following characteristics:

1. It has reasonable policies, rules, and procedures that govern conduct at work. These exist to prevent problems and do not violate any federal, state, or local laws.

2. It communicates the rules and provides prior warning of the consequences that one can expect when guilty of a deliberate violation.

3. It enforces rules, policies, and procedures consistently, and consistently applies sanctions for infractions.

4. It has progressively severe penalties for repeated infractions by the same party.

5. It places the burden of proving guilt on management.

6. It considers the circumstances surrounding an infraction and allows for appropriate mitigation of punishment.

7. It has appeals and review procedures.

8. It has a short memory—it purges memories of wrongdoing after a reasonable time and avoids holding a grudge.

9. It is delivered in a pleasant manner.

Evaluate the disciplinary system you live with by these standards. If you suspect or know that there are problems, get together with your fellow supervisors and go to those who can change things. You cannot expect to enjoy the respect of your subordinates if you have to violate the preceding standards when performing your role as judge.

Understanding diversity comes into play in discipline. When disciplining Hispanic and Korean workers, don't expect them to look you in the eye. In these and other cultures, it is a sign of respect to lower one's eyes to the ground.

AN APPROPRIATE NUMBER OF RULES

A contributing cause of rules violations is that organizations have too many rules. When there are too many rules, employees often find that some of the rules are unreasonable or outdated. They also learn that many rules are simply not enforced. In general, rules are reasonable when they are needed for safety or to promote operational efficiency. Employees tend to obey reasonable rules while they tend not to obey unreasonable rules. When asked whether their organizations have too many rules, supervisors often deny that this is the case. However, when asked if their organizations have any rules that are not enforced, they almost universally agree. They then often change their position and agree that their companies have too many rules. When there are too many rules, employees see that some are not enforced and perceive the inconsistency. As a result, they may not understand which behaviors are tolerated and which are prohibited.

THE HOT STOVE CONCEPT

Professor Douglas McGregor (who gave us Theories X and Y) offers a useful analogy to keep in mind when approaching disciplinary tasks and handing out penalties. Called the *hot stove concept,* it compares the organization's disciplinary system to a hot stove and the employee who has earned punishment to a burn victim. Professor Raymond L. Hilgert from Washington University puts it this way:

> The first element is advance warning: just as everyone knows that if he touches a hot stove he'll be burned, so should every employee know the rules and work standards. Second, the pain should be immediate: the boss shouldn't wait to respond. Third, discipline should be consistent: anytime you brush up against the stove, you get the message. Finally, hot stoves are impersonal, and the boss should be too.[2]

Anyone who touches the hot stove will experience the same result. Initially, the victim will feel anger and hostility toward the stove, but normally this reaction is a result of the realization that the angry person is wrong or has acted incorrectly. The anger fades in time, and the victim learns respect for the stove. The victim's behavior will change in the future. So it should be with your disciplinary actions. They should be immediate when wrongdoers earn them. People should not be in doubt that burns will occur when rules, procedures, standards, and policies are violated. Make sure that they know the stove is hot and that it will burn anyone who fails to respect its heat.

PROGRESSIVE DISCIPLINE

progressive discipline
a system using warnings about what is and is not acceptable conduct; specific job-related rules; punishments that fit the offense; punishments that grow in severity as misconduct persists; and prompt, consistent enforcement

just cause
discipline of appropriate severity for violation of reasonable rules; it follows a warning with consistent rule enforcement and substantial proof

Progressive discipline uses warnings about what is and is not acceptable conduct; specific, job-related rules; penalties that fit the offense; sanctions that grow in their severity as misconduct persists; and prompt, consistent enforcement. Exhibit 14.1 highlights the characteristics of an effective and equitable discipline system in more detail. Many of the requirements for **"just cause"** for discipline are also incorporated in the characteristics presented in Exhibit 14.1. Union contracts universally require just cause or simply cause before employers can discipline employees. Employees protected by civil service rules also have protections similar to the concept of just cause. The specific components of just cause include the following: adequate warning, reasonable rules, fair investigation of the incident, substantial evidence, fair or consistent application of rules, and an appropriate penalty (proportional to the severity of the offense).[3]

Managers lose the respect of employees (and lawsuits in court) when they attempt to enforce vague rules, penalize in an inconsistent manner, fail to follow their own disciplinary procedures, fail to warn employees of rule changes, and fail to warn them of unacceptable conduct. The progressive discipline system is formal; it is familiar to all who are governed by it. It

✳

Characteristics of an effective and equitable discipline system.	**Exhibit** 14.1

- Specific rules

- Reasonable rules (necessary for safety and efficiency)

- Relevance to job

- Clearly defined punishments

- Punishments that fit the severity of the offense

- Punishments that increase with repeated infractions

- Careful investigation

- Prompt enforcement

- When enforcement has become lax, new warnings are provided before any discipline

- Consistent enforcement

- Documentation of offenses committed and punishments given

- Effective communication of standards and what happens when they are violated

- Effective communication during disciplinary meetings

- Disciplinary actions performed in private

- An appeals process

- Follow-up to prevent recurrence and to cement relations

places limits on managers' actions and their flexibility to deal with problem employees. But it must do so in order to be perceived as just and fair. It offers the best defense against accusations of bias and discrimination.[4]

Exhibit 14.2 presents several vignettes of common disciplinary incidents. As you read through these, think about whether discipline was warranted and the severity of discipline that you think is appropriate. Although these vignettes describe disciplinary actions against employees in union environments that were eventually taken to arbitration, a progressive approach to discipline should be used with both unionized and non-union employees. With progressive discipline the intent is not to punish the employee but to correct the employee's problem behavior and to rehabilitate his performance. Accordingly, successively more severe punishments are meted out only if the unacceptable behavior continues. Typically the first

| Exhibit | **14.2** | *Examples of disciplinary action.* |

Evaluate the appropriateness of the discipline applied in each of the following situations and formulate the reasons for your decisions: (*Note:* The arbitrator's decisions appear at the end of this section.)

Repeated Tardiness. A water pipeline mechanic, who had an excellent work record over 19 years at a utilities department, had begun to accumulate tardiness violations. The department's rules, which defined tardiness as being one minute late, imposed discipline for an accumulation of three tardiness violations in 30 days or six violations in a six-month period. The department also had a Constructive Action Plan that would clear violations from the employee's record if there were no more in a six-month period. Because of the employee's seven violations in a 12-month period and three disciplinary actions, he chose to participate in the Constructive Action Plan. (Most of his instances of tardiness occurred for violations of one, two, or three minutes.) During his fifth month in the plan he had another tardiness violation. The last violation occurred when he was 10 minutes late to work on a night call-out for emergency repairs while working on the rotating night shift. During the four-day period leading up to the incident the employee had worked over 19 hours of mandatory overtime with two 16-hour days and little opportunity for sleep. On the night of the incident he was called back less than two hours after working a full eight-hour shift. As a result of this violation, his record of tardiness violations, and the conditions of the Constructive Action Plan, the employee was given a five-day suspension and placed on last chance warning status with one more violation being termination.

Sleeping on the Job. An electrician employed for 11 years at a beverage production facility was assigned the job of repairing a flow meter during the night shift. After diagnosing the problem, he went to a computer terminal to order the part. His supervisor, who found him seated in front of the terminal with his eyes closed and his chin on his chest, concluded that he was sleeping. When confronted by his supervisor the employee denied being asleep. In the two-year period leading up to the suspension the employee had been disciplined six times with two written reprimands, two 1-day suspensions, one 3-day suspension, and a 1-week suspension. As a result of this incident he was suspended for one week for sleeping on the job.

Insubordination. A mechanic who had been employed for nine years at a manufacturing plant frequently used his vacation time to take time off Fridays in order to be off work for three-day weekends. Because this practice caused his coworkers to work more weekends than they desired, the employee, who had a good disciplinary record, began to incur the displeasure of his boss and coworkers. Typically he also would not stay when needed to complete work after his regular shift because he had a second job. In addition, he was sometimes argumentative, disrespectful of management, and uncooperative. Company policy required employees to provide 24-hour advance notice for vacation requests and one-hour notices for sick leave requests. On a day leading up to the incident, the employee called in approximately four hours before he was supposed to report to work and requested vacation time for that day. Although his supervisor denied his request, the employee failed to show up for work and was given a written warning the next week. After receiving the warning, the employee told a coworker that they needed to "get together and get rid of that big-nosed ____ ____ [the supervisor]." Five days after this incident the company terminated the employee for gross insubordination and attempting to discredit a supervisor.

Arbitrator Decisions. Tardiness case: reduced the five-day suspension to a one-day suspension and removed the "last chance" status because discipline was too severe for the circumstances. Sleeping case: denied the grievance because employer's determination of sleeping was credible. Insubordination case: reinstated the employee because of lack of progressive discipline—no back pay for four weeks.

SUPERVISING TEAMS

When companies use self-managing teams, disciplining members may or may not be part of their duties. Some teams discipline their members with subtle group pressures to conform to the group's norms, and others have the authority to pass judgment and deliver punishments. However, more often than not, self-managing teams and their rotating leaders prefer to let traditional managers handle discipline. This is due in part to the unpleasant aspects and complexities of the disciplinary process. The law, union contracts, and company policies govern the process. Furthermore, unacceptable performances must be carefully documented. All this requires training.

Johnsonville Foods in Wisconsin operates almost entirely through employee teams whose members are responsible for defining their jobs, inspecting their output, scheduling their own production, continuing their learning, and disciplining. CEO Ralph Stayer puts it this way: "We believe discipline is the problem of people who have to work with other individuals, peers. We think any work area should set up its own standards and rules and enforce them. It's part of our overall philosophy. People are in charge of their own areas: setting budgets, hiring, firing, training, and discipline."

Companies that have tried team disciplining have found mixed success. In general, people who are made to feel responsible for their work (those who feel they own their jobs) tend to take more pride in performing their duties. More pride usually means fewer problems with their work and between them and their counterparts. In addition, most people take criticism from their peers with greater reluctance than they do criticism from their supervisors. (Think about it. Suppose you make a mistake and a team member turns to you and says, "You sure blew it this time. Look at the problem you caused." How would you feel?) Criticism and sanctions given to a person by friends and peers can change behavior, but few such people are willing to discipline each other. Fewer still can be objective and unemotional, and avoid doing lasting damage to relationships while disciplining peers.

Another problem arises when teams discipline their members. This practice reduces the supervisor's formal authority. This may be appropriate where the supervisor is a facilitator and coach, acting as a supporting agent for the autonomous team. But in general, unless teams or their leaders are responsible for hiring, training, and evaluating team members, they should not have the power to discipline them.

Sources: Ralph Stayer, "How I Learned to Let My Workers Lead," *Harvard Business Review* (November–December 1990): 72–76. Walter Kiechel III, "How to Discipline in the Modern Age," *Fortune* (May 7, 1990): 180.

---

instance of a rule violation or unacceptable behavior results in an oral warning not to violate the rule again. A written warning is given for the second violation. Further violations of a similar type generally result in suspensions of one to seven days. A very serious violation might result in a 30-day suspension if there have been previous suspensions. Most employers do not suspend employees for more than 30 days, and demotions are relatively rare because they seldom produce desired results. After multiple suspensions, a further violation typically results in termination. Another aspect of progressive discipline warrants explanation because it is sometimes misunderstood. While progressive discipline applies to successive violations of the same rule, it also applies to violations of different rules. The progressive requirement is met when an employee been disciplined a number of times for different rule violations and then is terminated for a subsequent violation.[5]

Arbitrators who have been asked to rule on the fairness of a disciplinary action of unionized employees look for progressiveness in the disciplinary actions as well as adherence to a regular procedure for assessing discipline and consistent treatment of employees who receive discipline. (Judges apply some of the same criteria when non-union employees find a way to litigate their terminations.) It should be noted that a few acts of misconduct are so serious that employees may be terminated with the first incident without the application of progressive discipline. These very serious types of misconduct are discussed later in this chapter.

Positive Discipline

positive discipline
the part of discipline that promotes understanding and self-control by letting subordinates know what is expected of them

Positive discipline promotes understanding and self-control. The primary aim of discipline by any manager in the organization should be to prevent undesirable behavior or to change it into desirable behavior. You must communicate what is expected of each individual with regard to her behavior on the job. This process begins with the arrival and induction of each new employee and continues throughout her employment.

The subject of your communication should be the limits placed on individuals by company policies, departmental rules, job descriptions, and the union contract (if one exists). By communicating rules and expectations of acceptable behavior before any infraction occurs, you forewarn your subordinate about the type of conduct you want on the job. If employees stay within these boundaries, they risk nothing, but if they step outside them, they can expect management to react in certain predictable ways. Once established, these boundaries need to be maintained by regular review of their usefulness and by the judicious application of fair punishments.

Employees gain security when they know their jobs and the standards they must meet. They are aware of the degree of freedom allowed and have definite limits that they know they must not overstep. If they cross one or another of these limits, they know that a punishment will follow the violation.

Positive discipline can be illustrated by a police officer traveling in the flow of traffic in a well-marked, easily identifiable police car. She is visible to other motorists, serves as a reminder to obey traffic regulations, and represents a warning that violators will be apprehended and given a penalty. There is nothing sneaky or subterranean about her behavior, and the officer's main purpose is to prevent violations from occurring. Contrast this with an unmarked squad car parked out of the view of passing motorists. In this case, prevention is de-emphasized, and detection and punishment are emphasized.

An example of positive discipline comes from a Florida company, Tampa Electric. The company has a procedure it calls a "discipline-making leave day." When an employee below the rank of top management commits an offense or series of offenses that would ordinarily lead to a suspension, the company gives the employee a one-day suspension with pay. The employee is given that day to think seriously about whether or not he wants to continue to work for Tampa Electric. Since the procedure has been used, attendance problems have been cut in half. Supervisors who had been reluctant to give an earned suspension now see it as a positive step toward improving conditions.[6] Another advantage is that since pay is not withheld for the day off, there is less justification for a disciplinary appeal.

Do not leave your people guessing about the limits imposed on them or about their chances of getting caught in wrongdoing and being penalized. Be visible and obvious, and let them have no doubts about your intentions and your punitive powers. You are not trying to trap anyone. Rather, you are serving to inform them by your actions and words that you wish to promote reasonable behavior and to prevent any unacceptable conduct.

People resent rules that they consider unnecessary or unfair. It often is insufficient to issue prohibitions. People need to know why they cannot do certain things. For example, if employees cannot smoke in department A, the supervisor should explain why they cannot. If your subordinates are not to use company tools at home on a loan basis, tell them why not. Resentment follows from a lack of understanding the need for rules or regulations. Be sure your people have adequate explanations so that their obedience will be based on logic. This should provide an incentive to cooperate.

LEGAL CONCERNS

Chapter 11 introduced you to the various laws that govern the hiring and selection processes. The equal employment opportunity laws also affect disciplinary and dismissal decisions. It is unlawful to discipline, deny employment rights to, or terminate someone because of race, color, religion, sex, national origin, age, or handicap status. Worker compensation laws from the 50 states prohibit discipline and termination of employees who make compensation claims. Similarly, the Occupational Safety and Health Act (discussed in more detail in Chapter 16) protects employees from terminations and other disciplinary actions when they exercise their rights under the act. Labor laws (discussed in Chapter 15) prohibit the disciplining of workers for involvement in efforts to unionize and for engaging in lawful union activities. In addition, some cities have enacted laws that prevent discrimination on the basis of one's sexual preference or orientation.

A number of federal and state laws protect **whistleblowers**—employees who notify authorities of violations of laws by their employers that are contrary to public policy (the good of society). In addition, it generally is unlawful to penalize individual employees in any way for refusing to engage in unlawful activities. Clearly, every organization needs a specialist in the area of the law and discipline. Check with your human resource specialists before you decide to take any disciplinary actions.

whistleblower
an employee who notifies authorities of violations of laws committed by his or her employer that are contrary to public policy

RESOLVING COMPLAINTS

Complaints should be a warning to you that something is not right for your people. Complaints can be symptoms of deep-seated or long-standing problems with work or its environment. If they are not dealt with in a fair and equitable way, they can lead to employee misconduct. For example, a person's job may be so boring and unfulfilling that she seeks conversations with others at work, disrupting their work and taking her away from her own.

When your subordinate or team member comes to you with a complaint, give it a fair hearing. Show sincere interest, and give the person enough time to say what he thinks. Listen without passing judgment. Get the person's perspective. If you can do something to help, do it. If you cannot, find someone who can. If necessary, send the complaint or the complainer to another person for assistance. Let people know that you and the company don't want their employees to be dissatisfied.

Some companies have open-door policies that encourage employees to go beyond their immediate supervisor, all the way to the top if necessary. Others have individuals or committees to allow for a fair hearing and adjudication of disputes. For example, the Red Lobster restaurant chain uses a peer review panel of employees and managers to review disciplinary action. If the panel finds that the discipline is too severe, it can reverse the action. In one case, the panel reversed termination of a waitress who had worked for the company for 19 years. The panel addressed the issue only three weeks after her termination. More companies, such as Marriott, TRW, and Rockwell International, are using these procedures as a means of improving employee relations and reducing litigation.[7]

See this chapter's *Supervisors and Ethics* feature for more on alternative methods for resolving complaints and Chapter 15 for a detailed discussion. Just be sure that the paths created within your organization are understood and used by your people.

Employee assistance programs, such as company-sponsored health clubs, help reduce employee stress. EAPs help employees deal with personal problems that could otherwise hurt productivity.

EMPLOYEE ASSISTANCE PROGRAMS

Programs created to help employees with personal and job-related problems at work are collectively called employee assistance programs (EAPs). A person with a family, health, financial, stress-related, or substance abuse problem may need

SUPERVISORS AND ETHICS

Alternative dispute resolution (ADR) includes any method used, short of a lawsuit, to settle disputes in the workplace. Favored by federal laws such as the 1991 Civil Rights Act and the Americans with Disabilities Act, ADR methods are growing in popularity and are used by some of our nation's largest and smallest companies—Motorola, Travelers Corporation, and Coors Brewing Company to name but a few. ADR methods, often quicker and less costly than traditional lawsuits, may consist of a committee of managers and workers, a panel of neutral third parties, or a single outside neutral party. Procedures may be less formal, as in the case of mediation by an outsider, or more formal, such as arbitration hearings for resolving union–management contract interpretation or disciplinary issues. (These are discussed in Chapter 15.) In addition to union–management issues, ADR deals with accusations of discrimination in employment decisions (promotions, pay, layoffs, and firings), claims of sexual harassment, and disputes over employer evaluations and disciplinary actions.

Four major ethical issues accompany the use of ADR. First, in some instances, arbitration may be the only option when employers require new hires to use arbitration instead of litigation. The choice may be to take the job, giving up the legal right to sue, or to look for work elsewhere.

The second ethical issue arises through the ways in which ADR is administered. In non-union companies with a mandatory ADR, management may set up the committee, designate the individuals who will serve as judges (with the potential of over-representation of some groups and under-representation of others), and prescribe procedures. Employees may or may not have a say in any of these decisions.

The third issue arises when the employer pays for mediation or arbitration, because the persons hired to resolve the issues may be more sympathetic to the employer's views. In arbitration procedures involving management and unions, the parties split the costs, which eliminates pay as a source of bias.

Finally, history teaches that "Employees who win in arbitration generally get lower monetary damages than similar cases tried in federal court and heard by juries." Awards granted may be limited to the actual dollar losses suffered, and arbitrators may ignore or refuse to grant monetary awards for pain and suffering—compensatory damages allowed in federal court cases. "The systems succeed so well for employers that they 'virtually eliminate excessive punitive damages [by juries] for reckless employer conduct,' [says] Martin Payson, a partner in the White Plains, New York, office of Jackson, Lewis, Schnitzler & Krupman. His law firm has set up more than 20 such systems."

Sources: Carol Kleiman, "Unsettling Disputes," *Chicago Tribune* (November 27, 1994): sect. 8, 1. "A Dispute on Company Tribunals," *Chicago Tribune* (December 11, 1994): sect. 7, 8.

immediate help. Exercise, diet, and access to medical professionals offer employees a way to handle a variety of problems, which, if left unattended, can lead them into disciplinary troubles. Drug intervention programs offer substance abusers a way to overcome addictions and to remain employed. People who are unable to cope with their problems will become problems for themselves and others at work. Some of the symptoms of troubled workers are absenteeism, tardiness, implausible excuses, lateness in completing assignments, difficulties in working with others, and turnover.

The hospitality industry suffers from high rates of absenteeism and employee turnover. Some hotels experience as much as 100 percent turnover in a year. The Chicago Hilton and Towers has reduced its turnover rate to about 38 percent thanks in large part to its EAPs focused on wellness: smoking cessation, diet, exercise, training in interpersonal relations, and regular meetings with new hires and staff.[8]

When a subordinate or team member begins to exhibit signs of trouble, follow this advice from human resource managers:[9]

- *Try to pinpoint the problem.* Lack of training? Significant changes in assignments? Changes in the person's personal life? For personal problems, outside expertise may be recommended. Practice your coaching and counseling roles, and talk to the person, one on one.

- *Keep focused on what has changed and what is missing.* Concentrate on what is no longer acceptable performance or behavior and on why a change is needed. Explain options, and offer to do what you can to correct problems.

- *Check for burnout.* People under stress or those who work too much can suffer burnout. They may need time away to recover their energies and commitment. Options include reassigning work and a leave of absence.

- *Consider your own behavior toward the individual.* Are you using the proper leadership style? Have you been available for assistance? Have you neglected to give adequate feedback and appraisals?

- *Show concern for the person's welfare.* Stand ready to assist in any way possible to restore the person's performance to acceptable levels.

Diversity and Discipline

The following guidelines promote positive discipline in any organization by all people regardless of gender, religion, race, age, ethnic background, and physical challenges. They have been culled from the writings of several experts in the area of managing diversity.

- Make certain that individuals know the standards that will be applied to outcomes and behaviors and why those standards are necessary.

- Make sure that people have the necessary resources to succeed.

- Tailor rewards and punishments to fit the circumstances.

- Remove any rewards for poor or negative performances. For example, don't give a poor performer less to do and overburden your star performers as a consequence.

- Remove any punishments for positive performances. For example, don't punish people for exercising their authority and initiative when it results in honest failures. Empowering means the freedom to experiment and fail.

- Encourage all employees to respect and value the individuality and uniqueness of each organizational member and the subcultures to which each belongs.

- Give each person prompt, objective feedback on performance. In particular, make sure that when you have negative feedback for a minority person that you tell him or her in a timely manner. This has been an issue for white supervisors. As one high-level African-American executive has explained, "Frequently, white supervisors are reluctant to give negative feedback to black employees because they are afraid it will end up in a lawsuit or be misinterpreted as racism." It is unfair to deprive your minority subordinates of negative feedback that would help them avoid discipline or assist their development.[10]

Negative Discipline

Negative discipline emphasizes the detection of wrongdoing and punishment. It can become bureaucratic and impersonal, relying heavily on records, rules, and procedures, but it need not be this way. It is sometimes characterized by a lack of trust in subordinates, by demands for blind obedience, and by employees' willful disobedience of rules and regulations. Many employees play a game with their supervisors when they work in such an environment. They become covert and sneaky in their behavior. They deliberately plot to break rules to see if they can beat the system and get away with it or simply to keep management off balance and irritated. They do so because they resent the approach to discipline taken by their employer and supervisors, and they delight in frustrating their efforts. They have not developed the attitudes that support a willing compliance with their organization's rules.

A climate in which negative discipline thrives—one in which the need for penalties is frequent—should be examined and restructured to promote willing compliance and positive discipline. Individual counseling is absolutely essential in order to turn the situation around. Human relationships need development, nourishment, and maintenance. The disciplinary system must be worthy of respect and have the confidence of employees.

negative discipline
the part of discipline that emphasizes the detection and punishment of wrong-doing

PENALTIES

Penalizing wrongdoers is an important aspect of discipline. Sometimes preventive actions fail; then the need for prompt and fair action takes over. Your power to take action in dealing with infractions is probably limited. Typically, most supervisors can issue oral and written warnings on their own. Suspensions generally require approval by the manager of employee relations. Your formal disciplinary power depends on your company's policies, and, if your company has a union, the union contract will spell out many of these responsibilities.

COMMON PROBLEMS

As a supervisor, you will likely face one or more of the problems identified in Exhibit 14.3 during any given year. Rule violations usually carry the penalty of a verbal reprimand for the first offense, a written reprimand for the second, and a suspension without pay for a third violation. Of course, the person's intentions and work history, as well as the circumstances surrounding the offense, must be considered before any punishment can reasonably be given. Illegal activities may require immediate suspension or dismissal as well as criminal prosecution. However, not all illegal or criminal activities that occur off the job provide legitimate justification for discipline. If such activities do not pose a threat to coworkers, repel customers, or interfere with the performance of the job, the employer may lack justification for imposing discipline.

Absenteeism and sexual harassment will account for most of the problems you are likely to run into. Most companies say that absenteeism is their biggest problem, and sexual harassment is a growing concern for many companies. Dealing with these problems effectively requires that you be aware of the causes and your options for responding to them.

Absenteeism

People miss work for a variety of reasons. If the employee has a legitimate excuse, the first time it happens you may just let her know that you are concerned. If there is a possibility that the reason will recur, discuss it with the employee, and try to prevent it from occurring. Suppose that Jill, a single parent, has not been late or absent in the past. Yesterday, she called in with a request to take the day off because her babysitter was not available. Is this

Exhibit 14.3	Common disciplinary problems.
Absenteeism and tardiness	Insubordination
Discourtesy	Off-duty misconduct
Dishonesty	Possession of drugs on the premises
Drinking on the job and intoxication	Safety violations
Failure to follow procedures	Sexual harassment
Failure to pass a drug test	Sleeping on the job
Falsifying records	Substance abuse

Source: BNA Editorial Staff, *Grievance Guide,* 10th ed., Washington, D.C.: Bureau of National Affairs, Inc., 2000.

a legitimate reason? Maybe. But it can recur, and Jill should be working on an alternative to her regular sitter.

Sometimes your company may be to blame for absent employees. Suppose your company offers five sick days each year that cannot be banked and if not used are lost. Suppose employees with legitimate gripes are experiencing job-related stress about which the company has done nothing. At some point, the stress becomes too much to deal with, and the employee feels a real need to escape the source of the stress, at least for a time. Finally, suppose your subordinate has come to you with a plea to enrich his job. If you fail to deal with your worker's boredom and loss of motivation, you may have an absent worker in the not-too-distant future.

Treat all absentees seriously. Talk to each when he returns. Keep an eye open for patterns in absenteeism—for

Sexual harassment destroys the morale and productivity of victims. Subordinates should be trained to know what conduct is inappropriate, and you must take every complaint seriously.

example, Jack is always out the third Friday of every month. Be sure that you are setting a good example through your own attendance before you decide to discipline others for poor records. Remember also that under the Family and Medical Leave Act employees can request up to 12 weeks of unpaid leave per year for serious illnesses; to take care of newly born children or newly adopted children; or to take care of seriously ill parents, spouses, and children.

Stay in touch with all of your people regularly. Greet them warmly when they come in each day. Listen to their concerns, and deal with their problems promptly. Give those who can handle it a larger say in what they do and how they do it. Through thoughtful delegation, you empower people to become more responsible and to take more pride in themselves and their work.

Sexual Harassment

Under Title VII of the Civil Rights Act, **sexual harassment** is defined as:[11]

> unwelcomed sexual advances, requests for sexual favors, and other verbal or physical conduct of a sexual nature when
>
> (1) submission to such conduct is made either explicitly or implicitly a term or condition of employment,
>
> (2) submission to or rejection of such conduct by an individual is used as a basis for employment decisions affecting such individual,

sexual harassment
unwelcomed sexual advances, requests for sexual favors, and other physical and verbal conduct of a sexual nature

(3) such conduct has the purpose or effect of unreasonably interfering with an individual's work performance or creating an intimidating, hostile, or offensive working environment

Although sexual harassment has been illegal since 1980 and Anita Hill's allegations of sexual harassment during Clarence Thomas's Supreme Court confirmation hearings in 1991 brought great attention to the issue, it seems a great deal of such harassment still occurs in the workplace: the number of cases reported doubled between 1991 and 2000. During the same time period, awards to victims of sexual harassment increased sevenfold.[12] An increasing number of sexual harassment cases in Europe indicate that sexual harassment is not a problem unique to the United States.[13] Because of the increasing numbers of men and women working together, opportunity for possible harassment also increases.[14] Furthermore, defending against charges of sexual harassment is tremendously expensive. One New York attorney estimates that it costs her corporate clients $100,000 or more in legal fees when they have to go to court on such cases.[15] In addition, the 1991 Civil Rights Act allows victims to sue for both actual and punitive damages. As a supervisor, you could be named in a sexual harassment suit or complaint, making you liable for damages. If you know about a case of sexual harassment at work (see Exhibit 14.4) and fail to take any action, you are liable for the consequences.

The number of sexual harassment complaints is increasing despite the efforts of companies to deal with the issue and the publicity associated with the problem. The news media was filled with reports of former President Clinton's problems related to the lawsuit of Paula Jones over sexual harassment. Clearly, the repercussions from this incident undermined his effectiveness as the Chief Executive of the United States. Problems continue at the corporate level. Two former employees of an investment company claimed that they were sexually harassed while management ignored their problems. One of the former employees claimed that her supervisor "on several occasions . . . exposed himself to her." The other claimed that her manager "offered to pay her rent if she would become his mistress, asked repeatedly to see her breasts, put his tongue in her ear and bragged to her about his sexual prowess."[16]

Many companies are responding to the need to prevent sexual harassment and minimize a company's legal exposure to charges of harassment with training. Du Pont "maintains a 24-hour hot line that provides advice to employees on dealing with sexual harassment."[17] Ford Motor Company also has a toll-free number for reporting complaints.[18] Many companies bring in outside consultants and conduct workshops and seminars either on or off company premises. According to a survey by the Society for Human Resource Management, "75% of the 292 companies surveyed say they have implemented some kind of sexual harassment prevention program."[19]

When sexual harassment is not as obvious or blatant as in the examples cited earlier, there is room for confusion about what actions constitute sex-

Examples of sexual harassment and responses.

Exhibit 14.4

EXAMPLES

- Unwelcome touching, patting, or pinching

- Sexually offensive language, pictures, or objects

- Derogatory, sexually based humor

- Pressure to engage in sexual activity

- Disparaging remarks to a person about his or her gender

- References to an assumed or desired sexual relationship

- Suggestive references about a person's body or appearance

- Unsolicited, unwanted notes, e-mail messages, graphics, calls, or requests for dates

- Obscene gestures

RESPONSES

- Say no. Sexual harassment is a pattern of behavior that continues after you say no.

- Don't blame yourself. It's not your fault.

- Don't ignore it. The behavior is likely to continue.

- Tell someone.

SUPERVISORY RESPONSES

- Do not ignore the behavior.

- Confront the alleged perpetrator and determine the facts.

- Report findings to superiors.

- Follow up on superiors' decisions.

ual harassment. One of the points of confusion is that companies sometimes set higher standards than the law requires in order to protect themselves against litigation. An example is the so-called Seinfeld case in which the Miller Brewing Co. "fired Jerold Mackenzie for showing somebody a page in a dictionary; he sued to get his job back, and a jury (with, let us note, 10 women on it) awarded him $26 million."[20] Another source of confusion is that no uniform standard exists for sexual harassment, because juries appear to take the environment of the industry or work community into consideration. A final source of confusion is the mixed signals of recent court decisions on the issue.[21]

One woman who provides training in this area for companies gives the following advice:

"When we do sexual harassment training workshops in companies, we ask people to look at different kinds of insensitive or abusive behavior and ask themselves, Is this appropriate for the workplace?" says Betsy Plevan. "Is this something you would want to read about yourself in *The Wall Street Journal*? Would you want your mother to hear about it? In other words, Are you proud of this?" Adds Vladeck: "Even the most thick headed people will suddenly 'get it' if you ask them, Would you like someone to treat your daughter this way?"[22]

Another problem is related to romance in the workplace, a common occurrence in most organizations. Employees are free to become romantically involved, although most companies prohibit one participant from supervising the other. However, when relationships are broken off, problems of sexual harassment sometimes occur in the workplace. One of the authors knew a senior manager who provided the following advice to all managers: "Remember that today's willing participant in an office romance is tomorrow's litigant."[23] Supervisors may have to counsel employees about this problem. It may be helpful to provide the following advice:

An employee does not forfeit her right to protection from sexual harassment if she was romantically involved with a coworker, but she has to make it clear to him that any further sexual advances are unwelcome. The prudent thing in this situation may be to tell everyone, including management and other employees, that the relationship is over, so as to dispel any appearance that she is still welcoming his advances.[24]

A strong, clear stand against sexual harassment must be taken because the company is usually liable for violations it finds out about. It may even be liable for those it should have known about, and it is usually liable for those committed by supervisors that it did not know about. However, the company can take some actions to reduce its liability.[25] In addition to prevention efforts, supervisors must deal with any accusations as soon as they become aware of them. A written company policy spelling out what sexual harassment is and the consequences of harassment must be communicated to all employees. A specific procedure for filing a sexual harassment complaint must be established. The complaint procedure should enable employees to appeal to higher-level managers or an internal authority without going through their supervisors. This cut-out around the immediate supervisor is necessary because in the vast majority of cases the supervisor is the harasser.[26] The importance of having effective anti-harassment policies was emphasized in two 1998 U.S. Supreme Court decisions. The Court ruled as follows:

Among the court's holdings is that an employee who resists a supervisor's advances need not have suffered a detriment, such as dismissal or loss of a promotion, to be entitled to sue the company. But such a suit cannot succeed, the court said, if the company has an anti-harassment policy with an effective complaint procedure and the employee has not used it.[27]

When investigating charges of sexual harassment, the supervisor must be careful not to violate the rights of the accused. Claims of sexual harassment are sometimes false and should be investigated with diligence and discretion.[28] Anyone who feels the need to complain should be allowed to do so in privacy and with dignity. No implied or expressed penalty or fear of retribution should be connected with filing a complaint. See this chapter's *Supervisors and Quality* feature for additional suggestions for creating a viable sexual harassment policy.

BEFORE TAKING ACTION

The actions you take when your subordinates violate rules and regulations should be governed by the following principles:

1. Know each subordinate, his record, and the nature and causes of the offense.

2. Know your powers as laid down in your job description. When in doubt, check with your boss and your peers.

3. Check on the precedents, if any, that governed similar situations in the past.

4. Be consistent. If you have given an oral warning on the first minor offense as a general rule, do so in every like case.

5. Consider the circumstances surrounding the misconduct. Was it willful or accidental? Was the person aware of the limits placed on her conduct? Is this her first offense? Get the facts. Remember that in employee relations, unlike the law, ignorance of the rule *is* an excuse.

6. If a subordinate has made the same mistake more than once, make the sanctions progressively more severe. Generally, you progress from an oral warning to a written reprimand and eventually to suspension.

7. Coordinate with the other supervisors on enforcement. Every manager should enforce every policy, rule, standard, and procedure with equal weight and effort. It is better not to have a rule that is unenforced or unenforceable.

8. Be reasonable and fair.

The most important aspects of fairness involve basing your decisions on the circumstances. What may be an appropriate penalty for one party to an infraction of the rules may not be so for another. For example, suppose that you find two of your people in a shoving match; before you can break it up, one of them hits the other. Both people are guilty of fighting, but can you

SUPERVISORS AND QUALITY

Companies that care about their employees and their bottom line know that a successful attack on sexual harassment begins with education and preparedness. They are proactive and commit the funds needed to prevent as well as deal with harassment on the job. The costs for the company that experiences sexual harassment and its legal aftermath include legal fees and damages awarded to victims, weakened morale and team spirit, injured company reputation, weakened employee loyalty to and respect for management, reduced quality and productivity, and absenteeism and employee turnover.

The best defense is a good offense. The problem needs to be addressed head on—no denials, no foot dragging. Start with the facts:

- 90 percent of harassment cases involve men harassing women; 9 percent involve same-sex harassment; 1 percent involve women harassing men.

- Intentional harassment is an exercise of power, not romance.

- Harassment can and does occur in every kind of organization.

- In cases of harassment, it's what the receiver of a behavior thinks about it that matters, not what the perpetrator thinks.

Next, give guidance through the best means available. Experts teach two guidelines to men who don't want to offend a woman at work: assume that off-color remarks, comments, and sexual gestures are unwelcome at work; and take a person literally when she or he says no.

If you're not certain that your behaviors are acceptable, consider how your spouse, mother, sister, or daughter would feel when witnessing or receiving the behavior you intend.

Now write a policy in line with the following guidelines:

- Start with top management's commitment for both funding and emphasis.

- Get your employees involved in the drafting of a policy.

- Spell out procedures and options for preventing, discovering, reporting, and investigating violations.

- Build in safeguards and protection for all the parties involved.

Finally, when accusations prove to be founded, follow through with appropriate disciplinary procedures and actions to prevent similar occurrences in the future.

Source: Ellen Bravo and Ellen Cassedy, The 9 to 5 Guide to Combating Sexual Harassment. New York: John Wiley & Sons (1992): 66–67, 110.

think of reasons for which justice might dictate coming down harder on one than on the other? Consider the circumstances and the motives underlying the action you observed. Someone started the fight. Shouldn't that person be dealt with more severely than the person who was provoked? What if one of them had done this before, whereas the other had a clean record? Wouldn't these facts influence your decision?

Being fair does not mean treating everyone the same. You are not a machine that operates automatically or in the same manner with everyone. When we talk about precedents, we mean treating similar offenses in a similar manner. But the key word is "similar." Be certain that what you are dealing with and the people you are dealing with are sufficiently similar to warrant concern for precedents.

When you punish, you must look at the person and the circumstances. This does not mean that you do so in order to exercise prejudice or to get even. If you are vindictive or carry a grudge, you are bound to attack people personally. They will know it, even if you do not admit it. You will be basing your actions on a personal dislike for them and not on their actions. As in making appraisals, you must be as objective as you can in order to prevent criticism of your motives or intent. Your job and your reputation are too valuable to risk on immature behavior.

Do not be the cause of your subordinates' mistakes. Set the example, and let them know you mean what you say. Give them the security that comes with knowing what they must do and why.

A man who audited stores for a large retail chain for more than 30 years once told one of the authors that where he uncovered dishonest employees, there was usually a dishonest manager. For example, a dishonest manager would, on the way out of the store each day, help himself to a handful of peanuts or candy. At other times, such a manager might be too lenient in enforcing rules or regulations or deal weakly with dishonest employees. Honest employees began to resent the extras enjoyed by their peers and decided to get into the action, too. It may start with a pen or pencil, but it may not end until there are substantial losses.

Keep in mind that you are not the final voice in matters of discipline. Your company and the union may have procedures providing for review of your decision, since matters of discipline are often considered too important to entrust to any one manager. (Chapter 15 has much more to say on this matter.) If you are wrong, you will be overruled. If not, you should be able to count on your boss for backing. Your subordinates will hear about your disciplinary decisions. Do not jeopardize your relations with them by hasty or irrational actions. Be sure that you have the facts and that you have put them together properly. Consult with superiors before you act.

Consider the case of a supervisor named John and his subordinate, Harry. John has given an oral order to Harry. Harry has failed to respond. Orders are intended to provoke an immediate positive response and usually do if they are not over-utilized, so John immediately assumes that Harry is being insubordinate. Without any further investigation, John suspends Harry for one week while he and the company decide whether or not to fire Harry. But wait a moment. Aren't there legitimate reasons Harry could have had for not following the supervisor's order? Here are but a few:

1. Harry did not hear the order.

2. Harry was told to do something illegal.

3. Harry was told to perform a task outside his job description or beyond his capabilities or training.

4. John was unclear in his order, and Harry did not understand it.

All these and more could get Harry off the hook. If John relies solely on his observations, without any further investigation, he is likely to make an improper decision and be reversed. In that case, Harry will be back at work, with pay for his time off. Meanwhile, John will have damaged his reputation and alienated Harry, among others. It pays to get the employee's point of view.

GIVING THE REPRIMAND

You have studied the case of wrongdoing, gathered your facts, touched base with experts, and reached the conclusion that disciplinary action is necessary. You have chosen the penalty to fit the offense and scheduled a meeting with the offender. Now begins one of the least pleasant parts of being a supervisor. Here are some tips to make the disciplinary session as productive as possible:

- Choose a time and place that ensures privacy and freedom from interruptions.
- Have your facts in writing and your mind clear about the who, what, when, where, and how.
- Be businesslike and serious. The meeting is not the time or place for discussion about anything other than the offense and the consequences of it.
- Adopt a pleasant approach in administering the discipline. The manner in which discipline is administered is important. Empirical evidence shows that when discipline is delivered in a pleasant manner and the supervisor makes an accurate diagnosis of the situation, there is less damage to the relationship and greater likelihood that the discipline will be viewed as appropriate. Emotional reactions to discipline also are less likely when supervisors administer discipline in a pleasant manner.[29]
- Take charge of the meeting. Lay out your case with specifics. Get agreement on essentials, and listen for any new information.
- Be clear about the fact that the behavior is at issue, not the person.
- Try to get a commitment from the offender for improvement and for no repetitions of the offense.

THE DECISION TO TERMINATE

The decision to terminate a person usually rests with the person or persons who have the authority to hire. In most disciplinary cases, this is the last resort, and it should take place only when all else has failed. Some situations, however, usually demand that the guilty party be dismissed immediately. These include the following cases:

1. Gross insubordination, such as refusal to comply with a direct, lawful order

2. Drunkenness on the job
3. Willful destruction of company property
4. Serious cases of dishonesty or theft
5. Bringing a firearm on company premises

Certainly there will be exceptions, even in these extreme situations, and whatever circumstances surround each of these exceptional cases must be considered. It is nevertheless true that a large majority of companies require that the penalty for these infractions be automatic dismissal.

LEGAL CONCERNS

Along with employment discrimination laws and the other federal laws already discussed in this chapter, nearly all the states have some laws that restrict an employer's right to fire anyone for any reason. The courts have added to these restrictions. While the employment-at-will rule from the common law still generally prevails, there are some important exceptions. **Employment at will** means that both the employer and the employee have the right to terminate the employee's employment at any time, with or without just cause.

In 1980, the California Court of Appeals ruled that employers had a duty to deal fairly and in good faith with employees and could be held accountable for discharging employees without having good cause.[30] Since then, more than 40 states have allowed exceptions to the employment-at-will rule under specific conditions. Discharged workers can recover losses and regain their jobs by proving that an implied or expressed contract was violated or that the firing was contrary to public policy.[31] As a result, employers who wish to retain the power to terminate employees at will must refrain from making any promises, guarantees, or covenants that may lead the employee to believe that some right to long-term employment exists.

Puerto Rico has enacted the Discharge Indemnity Act, which details just causes for terminating an employee (see Exhibit 14.5). Several states are now drafting their own laws using Puerto Rico's act as their model.

To summarize, while there are exceptions, employment at will is still broadly applicable, and supervisors must understand that their companies can terminate employees when it is appropriate to do so.

employment at will the common law doctrine that holds that employment will last until either employer or employee decides to terminate it, with or without cause

Pitfalls

As is the case with the pitfalls we discussed in the previous chapters, the major problems you encounter when you attempt to carry out your disciplinary duties can be minimized by an awareness of their causes.

Starting off soft. Supervisors, especially those who are new at the job, are apt to associate being lenient with being liked. They sometimes feel that if they

Exhibit 14.5 *Definition of "just cause" in Puerto Rico's Discharge Indemnity Act.*

Sec. 185b. Discharge without just cause

Good cause for the discharge of an employee of an establishment shall be understood to be:

(a)   That the worker indulges in a pattern of improper or disorderly conduct.

(b)   The attitude of the employee of not performing his work in an efficient manner or of doing it belatedly and negligently or in violation of the standards of quality of the product produced or handled by the establishment.

(c)   Repeated violations by the employee of the reasonable rules and regulations established for the operation of the establishment, provided a written copy thereof has been timely furnished to the employee.

(d)   Full, temporary, or partial closing of the operations of the establishment.

(e)   Technological or reorganization changes as well as changes of style, design, or nature of the product made or handled by the establishment and in the services rendered to the public.

(f)   Reductions in employment made necessary by a reduction in the volume of production, sales, or profits, anticipated or prevalent at the time of the discharge.

A discharge made by mere whim or fancy of the employer or without cause related to the proper and normal operation of the establishment shall not be considered as a discharge for good cause.

Source: P.R. Laws Ann. Tit. 29, Sect. 185a–185i.

look the other way on occasion or mete out less than a deserved penalty for an infraction, they will endear themselves to their subordinates. This is inaccurate. In actuality, their leniency will be the cause of more trouble. If Mary arrives late and you say nothing, she will be encouraged to do it again. So will the others who witness the event and your failure to take constructive action.

It is always easier to start out tough, with an emphasis on the letter of the law. As you gain self-confidence and additional knowledge about your duties and your people, you can shift the emphasis to the spirit of the law as well, tempering your judgment within the framework of your understanding of your people, their personalities, and the group pressures at work on them. This is what justice means. Each person and most events are unique and should be dealt with as such.

If you are soft, those who toe the line will resent you for it. They will see no tangible reward for proper behavior, while they witness some for improper conduct. Your softness will be interpreted as weakness, and you can expect your subordinates to test you further to find the limits. One former stockbroker who decided to run his own small company learned hard lessons about starting out too soft:

> In one recent month, he had to fire four of his staff of about 50 employees, including two who tested positive for cocaine. . . . He has given up on any idea of being a team player. . . . He admits he is partly to blame for his problems. He was lax at first, too friendly. He did things that in retrospect weren't very smart, such as breaking out cold beers for everyone at the end of a shift or granting personal loans. Not anymore. The plant has a zero-tolerance policy toward alcohol in the workplace, and he stopped making loans long ago. Now, his workers feel somewhat betrayed, like children whose parents bend the rules one day and crack down the next. . . . Another tough lesson involved drugs and alcohol. Initially, Mr. Robbins didn't want to spend the money on drug screening. . . .[32]

Acting in anger. How many times have you wished you could take back remarks made to another in anger? If you are like most people, the answer is: too often. With emotions influencing your observations and judgment, you will seldom make a sound decision. Too often you will have to back down and apologize for a demonstration of your lack of self-control. Never attempt to discipline while you or the other persons involved are angry. It helps to move physically away from the situation and the environment of a wrongdoing in order to regain your composure. Tell the persons involved to report to you in your office in a few minutes. This will give you time to recapture your composure and reason.

Disciplining in public. If you have some critical remarks for an individual, make them in person and in private. Each person has a reputation to uphold, both with you and with his peers. He has pride and self-esteem, which need protection. He does not wish to be subjected to ridicule or embarrassment. It may not be penalties that your people fear, but your way of dispensing them. Your methods may make the difference between a constructive and a destructive kind of discipline. Human resource experts say that when an employee is disciplined in public, those who observe the discipline also are punished because most people do not like to observe such actions.

Incomplete research and analysis. Let us assume that you see a man stretched out on a packing crate 30 feet away and, because he has his eyes shut, you jump to the conclusion that he is sleeping on the job or, at the very least, goofing off. You should know by now—from your experience and from this book—that appearances do not always reveal the whole truth. Where discipline is involved, it takes more than one observation to make a sound case. Unless you go to the man (preferably with a witness you can count on) and ask him some questions, you cannot really be sure that your observations are correct.

If you intend to penalize someone, be certain that you have a firm case that will stand up to review by a higher authority. Have the details clearly in mind, and make some notes of your observations for later reference. Memory loses certainty and eliminates details with the passage of time between a disciplinary action and the appeal of that action. Answer questions such as who was there and what was said by each. If all you have is your word against the subordinate's, you will lose the case, especially when a union is involved.

Exceeding your authority. Keep in mind that, like your people, you have limits on your power and conduct. Check with your boss and your peers when you are in doubt about what action to take. There is no legitimate excuse for falling into the trap of exceeding your authority.

 **Being vindictive.** Be sure that your actions and words are not based on personality clashes or personal prejudice. Put your biases aside, or they will shine through with a neon brilliance for all to see. If you single out one person for disciplinary action, and your reasons rest in your personal biases, you certainly will lose your case and face the wrath of those who must review your actions.

Like your subordinates, you have personal preferences. It would not be reasonable to expect you to like all your people. But you are being paid to serve all of them, regardless of their personal feelings toward you or yours toward them. Unless a subordinate's personality is defective and interferes with performance, you cannot in conscience hold it against that individual.

Leaving it to others. Like appraising your people, disciplining them is your exclusive right and duty. You cannot be asked to part with it if you are expected to control and direct your workers properly. Some companies allow the human resource department or some other authority to mete out discipline. This reduces the supervisor's role to that of an arresting officer. Your subordinates will soon realize that you cannot punish but can only report violations. As a result, your status will be reduced greatly. This represents a tremendous handicap to a supervisor. Although some managers prefer this arrangement because it releases them from a difficult responsibility, they fail to see that giving up this power makes them impotent and subjects them to additional and needless harassment from above and below.

Even worse than losing disciplinary powers to a higher authority is giving them away to a top worker or "straw boss"—someone acting with your authority on your behalf. Remember, these people are extensions of yourself and, as such, represent you and your other subordinates. Do not give them the power to cause you and themselves trouble. You are responsible for your people and are accountable for their actions. If your top worker or straw boss made the wrong decisions, you would have to correct them, thus injuring their already difficult position, possibly beyond repair. Most straw bosses do not want such authority. If they do try to assume it, make it clear to them that they cannot have it.

Failing to keep adequate records. To gain and keep a perspective on each of your people, you should keep records of their performance appraisals, reprimands, and needs. These files will prove quite helpful when you face tough personnel decisions. They also come in handy when you want to justify your opinions or take specific disciplinary actions.

Instant Replay

1. Both positive discipline and negative discipline are needed if reasonable and safe conduct at work is to be promoted.
2. When an organization or a supervisor tolerates a poor performer, the organization or the supervisor cannot, in conscience, discipline anyone whose performance exceeds the poor performer's.
3. The best kind of disciplinary system is one based on the individual employee's sense of responsibility for her own work and on each employee's self-control.
4. People need to know what is expected of them and how well or poorly they are doing; they have a right to expect consistent enforcement of rules, policies, and standards.
5. People need to know that good work will be rewarded and that poor performance will earn swift and predictable responses from management.
6. People do not resent punishment that they know they deserve. They do resent being punished for something they did not know was wrong—for not being forewarned.
7. The majority of your subordinates will not need negative discipline if the positive side of discipline has been developed.

Questions for Class Discussion

1. Can you define this chapter's key terms?
2. What is the difference between negative and positive discipline? In what ways are they similar?
3. What is the purpose of punishment in a disciplinary system?
4. What are the basic principles of discipline?
5. What are the major pitfalls a supervisor can fall victim to when carrying out disciplinary functions?
6. What does it mean to be fair when disciplining subordinates?
7. Why should you know yourself and your subordinates well before attempting to discipline or punish them?

Incident

Purpose: To test your knowledge and ability to identify sexual harassment in a work setting.

Your task: After each of the following statements, indicate if you agree or disagree with it. The answers are shown at the end of the exercise. Don't look at them until after you have completed the quiz.

Agree *Disagree*

○ ○ 1. If I don't think I am sexually harassing another person, that means I am not doing so.

○ ○ 2. If no complaints of sexual harassment come to a manager's attention, none is occurring.

○ ○ 3. Same-sex harassment is not covered by the law.

○ ○ 4. Fear can keep people who are harassed from complaining.

○ ○ 5. When a man enters what has been an all-female environment, some behaviors of the women will have to change.

○ ○ 6. Sexually suggestive visual material, when placed in one's private office, cannot be grounds for sexual harassment.

(Answers: 1, 2, 3, and 6 should be marked "Disagree")

CASE PROBLEM 14.1 | *Disciplinary Situations*

Assume that you are the supervisor who must decide what to do with subordinates in each of the following situations. Your options include the following: ask your boss to handle the situation, refer the worker to human resources or an employee assistance program, obtain more information, provide training, administer an oral warning, write up a written reprimand, recommend a suspension of three days, recommend a suspension of 30 days, or recommend termination. Your may also choose combinations of these actions. Be prepared to justify your choices.

Situation 1. A subordinate just sent a sexual joke by e-mail to all members of your department. Within 30 minutes after the joke was sent, two females and a male subordinate come to your office to complain about the joke. Company policy forbids employees from using e-mail for personal use and explicitly forbids the distribution of material of a sexual nature.

Situation 2. You read in the paper before coming to work this morning that one of your subordinates was arrested by the police for a domestic disturbance and suspected spousal abuse. It is the third time that he has been arrested. In the first two incidents, his wife had facial bruises and scrapes, on her arms but she refused to file charges. Later on this morning, you learn that his wife had similar injuries again but refused to file charges, and the police have released him.

Situation 3. Your company sells and installs home security systems. All repair and installation technicians carry pagers so that they can be contacted about emergency work or changes in jobs. In addition, your scheduler maintains a list of service calls each technician is to make during the day. Technicians are required to call in when they arrive at a job, leave the job, and take breaks for more than 20 minutes. One of your best technicians, Richard Titus, could not be located for three hours yesterday afternoon. He did not respond to pages and failed to show up at a job. The dispatcher finally got in touch with Richard by calling the apartment of a friend whom she thought was dating Richard. Richard is married and does not live at this apartment.

Situation 4. You manage a team of heating and air conditioning specialists who install custom systems in large buildings. Every morning you have a conference with all of the team to go over developments that will need special attention. It is essential that the team members exchange information so that they can coordinate their efforts. Cooperation, good relations, and respectful treatment among your team members are vital for economical and efficient installations. At this morning's conference, you were going over a foul-up by one of the team members on the previous day that would require a substantial amount of rework. You and he explained the situation so that the others would know how to conduct the rework. After he finished, one of the other team members said, "What kind of an idiot would make a mistake like this?"

Situation 5. This morning you were making a presentation to other supervisors, support staff members, and the plant manager about new classroom facilities and equipment that will be used for training. The classroom equipment includes a computer with Internet access and a projector that displays the computer images on a large screen. Prior to the meeting, you had set up the computer to display a website about technical manufacturing standards and then left to coordinate other issues. Later, as you were addressing the group, you switched on the projector and there in living color was a pornographic scene from a website. Afterward, you found out that one of your subordinates had set you up by switching the Internet address.

Situation 6. Two customers at the expensive restaurant you manage have come to you with a complaint about one of the waiters. The husband and wife, who were part of a dinner party of eight, are outraged at the waiter's treatment of the wife. According to the husband, the waiter had given their party menus and was taking their orders. When it came time for his wife to order she asked the waiter about a particular item on the menu. The waiter replied that he would not recommend it to her. When she asked why, the waiter said that the item was over her calorie limit. The wife, who was obese, was humiliated by the comment, and the husband was outraged.

Furthermore, they stated that the same waiter had made a similar insinuating remark about his wife's obesity on a previous occasion. The waiter has 20 years' service with the restaurant and also is the maitre d'.

Source: Situation 6 is based on an arbitration case by Samuel Kaynard, "Union Club of New York and Hotel Employees International Union, Local 6," Labor Award Reporter: Summary of Labor Arbitration Awards, Report No. 460 *(July 1997): 6–7.*

Questions

1. Review the options listed at the beginning of these situations. What will you do in each of these situations? Explain your reasoning.

2. Might these incidents be related to the quality of supervision these employees have received?

CASE PROBLEM 14.2 | *Sticky Business*

You are a supervisor in a sugar refinery that processes sugar cane into sugar. Recently the shut-off valve to one of the molasses vats failed to work properly, and approximately 300 gallons of molasses was spilled onto the plant floor. You directed several people to work overtime to help clean up the mess. One of the production workers you ordered to help was a long-time employee of 24 years. He refused to stay, saying the following: "I've got things to do. . . . I've got a life outside this refinery. . . , I've got business of my own to take care of." At the regular quitting time, he clocked out and left the refinery.

The next day you confronted the employee about his refusal to obey your directive to stay and help clean up the molasses. He said that he had left work the previous day instead of helping because he had a personal emergency. Your subordinate stated that he had to help find his teenage daughter who was missing. You told him that you would check out his story and meet with him later.

You talked to several people about the missing daughter excuse and determined that your subordinate was lying. In addition, you reviewed his disciplinary record and found that he had been disciplined twice in the past for similar behaviors, although these incidents occurred over five years ago.

Source: Based on an arbitration case by Diane Massey, "Domino Sugar Corp. and United Food and Commercial Workers International Union, Local 1101," Labor Award Reporter: Summary of Labor Arbitration Awards, Report No. 468 *(March 1998): 6–7.*

Questions

1. What disciplinary action will you take in this situation?

2. What factors influenced your decision? Explain the basis for your decision.

References

1. Drucker, Peter F. *Management: Tasks, Responsibilities, Practices.* New York: Harper & Row (1974): 270–271.

2. Kiechel III, Walter. "How to Discipline in the Modern Age," *Fortune* (May 7, 1990): 180.

3. BNA Editorial Staff. *Grievance Guide,* 10th ed., Washington, DC: Bureau of National Affairs, 2000.

4. Ledvinka, James, and Scarpello, Vida G. *Federal Regulation of Personnel and Human Resource Management,* 2nd ed. Boston: PWS-Kent (1991): 315–325.

5. BNA Editorial Staff. *Grievance Guide.*

6. *Success!* "Disciplining Employees with Dollars" (April 1987): 25.

7. Jacobs, Margaret. "Red Lobster Tale: Peers Decide Fired Waitress's Fate," *The Wall Street Journal* (January 20, 1998): B1.

8. Kleiman, Carol. "Employee Turnover a Bottom-Line Issue," *Chicago Tribune* (October 21, 1990): sect. 8, 1.

9. BBP/Prentice Hall. *The 1993–94 Human Resources Guide.* Englewood Cliffs, NJ: Bureau of Business Practice, a division of Simon & Schuster (1993): 1238–1239.

10. Thomas, David A., and Wetlaufer, Suzy. "A Question of Color: A Debate on Race in the U.S. Workplace," *Harvard Business Review* (September–October 1997): 124.

11. Equal Employment Opportunity Commission. *Guidelines on Discrimination Because of Sex.* Section 1604.11, November 10, 1980.

12. "Anita Hill and Sexual Harassment," *Workforce* (January 2002): 32.

13. "Women in Suits," *Economist* (March 2, 2002): 60–61.

14. Zachary, Mary-Kathryn. "Labor Law for Supervisors," *Supervision* (July 2001): 23–26.

15. Duenes, Deborah, and Hermelin, Francine. "Sexual Harassment Inc.," *Working Woman* (October 1994): 9.

16. Pusey, Allen. "Ex-Mayor Folsom, Companies Sued," *Dallas Morning News* (September 25, 1997): 34A.

17. Campbell, Linda P. "Examining Workplace Behavior," *Chicago Tribune* (October 20, 1993): sect. 3, 1, 3.

18. Felsenthal, Edward. "Rulings Open Way for Sex-Harass Cases," *The Wall Street Journal* (June 29, 1998): A3, A10.

19. Duenes and Hermelin. "Sexual Harassment."

20. Fisher, Anne. "After All This Time, Why Don't People Know What Sexual Harassment Means?" *Fortune* (January 12, 1998): 156.

21. Ibid.

22. Ibid.

23. Greer, Charles R. *Strategy and Human Resources: A General Managerial Approach,* 2nd ed. Englewood Cliffs, NJ: Prentice Hall (2001): 78.

24. Petrocelli, William, and Repa, Barbara Kate. *Sexual Harassment on the Job.* Berkeley, CA: Nolo Press (1994): 2–24.

25. Jacobs, Roger B., and Koch, Cora S. *Legal Compliance Guide to Personnel Management.* Englewood Cliffs, NJ: Prentice Hall, 1993.

26. Greer. *Strategy:* 78.

27. Greenhouse, Linda. "High Court Clarifies Sex Harassment Law," *Fort Worth Star Telegram* (June 27, 1998): A1, A15.

28. Greer. *Strategy:* 78.

29. Greer, Charles R., and Labig, Chalmer E., Jr. "Employee Reactions to Disciplinary Action," *Human Relations* Vol. 40, No. 8 (1987): 507–524.

30. Bacon, Donald C. "See You in Court," reprint of an article from *Nation's Business* (July 1989): 4.

31. Ibid.

32. Aeppel, Timothy. "Losing Faith: Personnel Disorders Sap a Factory Owner of His Early Idealism," *The Wall Street Journal* (January 14, 1998): A1, A13.

SPECIAL CONCERNS

art IV offers an in-depth look at two areas that are of special concern for supervisors: dealing with employee dissatisfaction in both union and non-union environments and protecting against several different kinds of hazards.

Dealing with worker complaints in a union or non-union environment is the topic of Chapter 15. It outlines the major prohibitions on union and management conduct as set forth in the most important pieces of federal labor legislation. A step-by-step process is included to help you deal with worker grievances in small and large organizations. Through the discussion in this chapter, you will find that there are issues on which labor and management have mutual interests. Supervisors can do much to help blend the interests of labor and management in the working environment.

Chapter 16 covers security of physical facilities, as well as preventing and coping with work-related accidents, illnesses, and injuries. Various steps, checklists, and procedures are included to help supervisors carry out these important duties. The essentials of the federal Occupational Safety and Health Act (OSHA) and its inspection procedures are explained in this chapter.

COMPLAINTS, GRIEVANCES, AND THE UNION

Objectives

After reading and discussing this chapter, you should be able to do the following:

1. Define this chapter's key terms.
2. List the steps for handling complaints, and comment about what happens in each.
3. List prohibitions of the Wagner Act.
4. List prohibitions of the Taft–Hartley Act.
5. Compare the roles of supervisors and stewards in labor relations.
6. Outline typical grievance procedures for a large organization and a small organization.

Introduction

This chapter discusses the proper ways of dealing with the complaints of employees. First, we consider how to handle complaints in a company where there is no union. Next, we discuss what unions are and why workers join them. Finally, we learn how complaints are handled in a company where there is a union contract.

Complaints

For our purposes, a **complaint** is any expression of unhappiness with working conditions or on-the-job relationships that comes to a manager's attention. A complaint may be based on a worker's assumption that she has been treated unfairly or inequitably. Complaints often begin with a worker's perception that she has been or is being treated differently from others in similar circumstances.

complaint

any expression of unhappiness with working conditions or on-the-job relationships that comes to a manager's attention

499

A complaint may be a symptom of a very different problem from the one it seems to state. The worker may be complaining about his level of pay or job classification, but the real issue may be dissatisfaction with the job—even though the worker may feel that more pay or a higher job classification would make the job more bearable. If this is the case, even after a careful explanation of why a certain level of pay goes with the labor grade, the worker will likely remain dissatisfied because the real problem has not been resolved.

HANDLING COMPLAINTS: A COMPANY-WIDE SYSTEMS APPROACH

Most companies have a recommended or required set of procedures to follow when a supervisor, team leader, or team facilitator is confronted with employee complaints. Typically, the first step is to identify the nature of the complaint and the problem or challenge it poses for an individual or group. This involves getting the facts and perspectives from all those affected by a complaint. Once a complaint is accurately stated, the causes for it—a rule, policy, people problems, or a change of some kind—need to be discovered. If corrective action is warranted, the complaining employee is asked what he views as an adequate remedy. Alternative courses of action are then considered and evaluated for consistency with company policies and applicable precedents. Prompt action usually is called for, and the results must be evaluated to determine if the complaint has been satisfactorily resolved.

Qualities of an Effective Complaint System

Companies that have designed formal complaint systems usually try to make them accessible, safe, and credible. An *accessible* system gives employees a number of options. Such a system may offer resources such as complaint hotlines, counselors, complaint committees, and in-house surveys and suggestion systems. A *safe* system guarantees anonymous or confidential access to those who can help. It forbids reprisals against complainers and takes punitive action when reprisals do occur. A *credible* system assures complainers of a fair and objective hearing from truly neutral parties who have power to investigate and to recommend possible courses of action and ways to proceed.[1]

The importance of dealing with complaints in an effective manner was emphasized by a U.S. District Court's $171.6 million award to Henry Boisvert, a former supervisor at the FMC Corporation. In previous litigation a jury directed FMC to pay Mr. Boisvert $200,000 for wrongful termination. Boisvert, who worked in testing, blew the whistle on the company about problems with the Bradley Fighting Vehicle. He had initially written a report critical of the vehicle that he wanted to give to the Army, but an FMC manager quashed the report. In 1986 FMC terminated Boisvert because he would not sign a report about the Bradley Fighting Vehicle, which he claimed was falsified.[2] According to Boisvert, the amphibious vehicle had the following problem:

In many circumstances, he charged, the Bradley swam like a rock . . . he had one driven into a test pond and watched it quickly fill with water . . . former FMC welders who worked on Bradleys claimed they weren't given enough time to do their work properly and so would simply fill gaps with putty.[3]

In contrast to FMC's response to Boisvert's complaint, an effective complaint system must provide those who have complaints with a safe, credible, and just hearing as well as an objective resolution. It also must guarantee to the supervisors of complaining employees that higher-ups will support their sensible decisions. In addition, it must provide good supervisors, who seldom make mistakes in such matters, with a means of saving face. The complaint system must remove common sources of employee fears so that the system will be used and function properly.[4]

Be ready to handle worker complaints. Understand that their complaints are very important to them. Be ready to help.

Employees who believe that a complaint will not get a fair hearing, or who fear consequences of complaints, can become negative influences at work. Some turn hostile to management. Others waste time, infect others with negative attitudes, and actively work to harm their companies. Do what you can to eliminate the fears of employees and encourage your people to air their complaints. Accept the complaints of employees as a fact of working life, and use the information they provide to mold better employees and working environments.

The Functions of an Effective Complaint System

Effective complaint systems provide the following functions:[5]

1. *Personal communication with individuals*—anonymous and confidential ways to seek accurate information

2. *Confidential counseling with individuals*—people with authority and professional training who are available to help parties define problems and determine ways to find solutions

3. *Investigation and mediation*—experts who can help determine facts and encourage the parties to reach agreement on what is needed to resolve complaints

4. *Adjudication*—a person or group with the powers needed to render a decision or judgment when the parties to a complaint cannot agree on a resolution

5. *Upward feedback*—people and methods to keep management informed about employee concerns, complaints, and the resolutions of them

Exhibit 15.1 presents the requirements for an effective internal complaint procedure (ICP), which provides a formal alternative to the informal open door policy of dealing with complaints. When a company implements an ICP it is important to communicate to employees that the ICP does not take the place of an open door policy of passing on complaints to managers. Instead it provides a formal alternative that is helpful when previous attempts to use the open door policy have failed to satisfy the employee.[6] In unionized environments the grievance procedure would be used for many of the functions of an ICP.

HANDLING COMPLAINTS: DEVELOPING YOUR OWN APPROACH

If you are not fortunate enough to work in an environment that has instituted the preceding system for handling complaints, you still must deal with them more or less on your own. The following discussion can help you formulate your approach. Keep in mind that you should include as many of the aforementioned qualities and functions as you can.

To begin with, your attitude toward the complaints of your subordinates or team members should be to treat them seriously. Your subordinates think that their complaints have merit; they would not bring them to your attention if they believed otherwise. Complaints may come to your attention indirectly through overheard conversations or through uninvolved third parties. In such cases, an investigation is warranted to determine if the complaints have substance. Watch for any sudden changes in established patterns of behavior; these often indicate the existence of an unexpressed complaint. If complaints are not dealt with as soon as they are discovered, situations worsen and the damage can spread quickly to other persons or teams.

An open-door policy (letting subordinates know that you are available and eager to discuss their problems) can prevent problems from getting out of hand. If your people feel that you care about them, will act swiftly, and will use sound judgment, you will find them willing to air their irritations and observations. However, this can come about only after you have established solid human relations with them on an individual or group basis. If you hear complaints only through the grapevine, your people are probably fearful and at least reluctant to bring their complaints to you directly. This means that they may distrust either your judgment or your willingness to deal with their complaints. Find out what is preventing open, honest communication and then go to work on the problems.

1. Standardized complaint form that collects the following:
   - Background information—complainant's name, work location, and date
   - Issue of the complaint
   - Previous discussions with management representatives on the issue
   - Remedy sought by the complainant
   - In cases of sexual harassment—any previous communication with management
   - In cases of problems with coworkers—any previous attempts to resolve the issue with peers
   - Signature of the complainant

2. Centralized processing with unique complaint tracking numbers

3. Acknowledgment of complaint that provides the following information to the complainant:
   - Complaint tracking number
   - Name of investigator

4. Utilization of competent complaint investigators

5. Discussion of potential remedies
   - Investigator first discusses findings with manager who will make decisions on remedies
   - Investigator may make recommendations about a remedy
   - Result of the investigation and decision on remedy is communicated to complainant

6. Complainant receives written report detailing the conclusions to include:
   - Background information
   - Tracking number
   - Investigator's name
   - Summary of the issues
   - Summary of key facts
   - Summary of investigation outcome (may or may not include details of action taken)

7. Documentation stored at central location to include:
   - Complaint form
   - Acknowledgment letter to complainant
   - Notes and statements of witnesses
   - Investigator's recommendations
   - Detailed account of action taken as remedy

8. Appeal procedure
   - Complainant is informed of procedure for appealing to senior management
   - Appeals should be in writing

9. Sound implementation
   - Managers encouraged to continue with informal open door approaches to complaints
   - Managers and employees informed about the internal complaint procedure
   - Distribution of literature about the program to managers and employees
   - Program described in employee handbook
   - Complaint forms made available

Source: Erin S. Hendricks, "Do More than Open Doors," *HR Magazine* (June 2000): 171–176.

A RECOMMENDED APPROACH

The steps that follow will help you deal effectively with your subordinates' complaints. You should find them useful even if your company does not have prescribed complaint procedures.

1. Listen to the complaint. Determine its causes and the complainer's feelings and motives. Be prepared to give the complaining subordinate your undivided attention. If the complainer's timing is not right, set up an appointment as soon as possible.

Remain calm. If the complainer is agitated and emotional, you should be the opposite. You cannot counsel effectively unless you are in control of yourself and the situation. Try to uncover what the complainer is feeling by allowing him to verbalize his feelings and motives. Avoid passing judgment, because you seek information about the other person's perceptions, not your own. Take notes, and reserve your own opinions and facts for later in the meeting. By listening attentively and drawing people out, you may find that the initial complaint gradually slips away as the real, underlying issue comes to the surface. It may be the first time that the employee has been able to express what was really on his mind. Gradually, all the facts will emerge in your subordinate's words, and the problem will come into focus. Then and only then can it be intelligently resolved.

Remember that people frequently just want to talk with someone about their problems. By talking, they are expressing confidence in you and showing respect for your opinion. Often, employees know that the solutions to their difficulty are beyond either their control or yours. In discussing such a situation, we often find a clarity and perspective that is almost impossible to discover alone. Employees may come to realize that the problem is not as serious as they originally thought, or they may actually discover a solution as they attempt to explain their views.

2. Push for solutions. Once your subordinate has talked about the real issues, ask her for her solutions. What would she do if she were in your shoes? What does she think would be a fair disposition of her complaint? You want to know what she thinks will make her happy. If it is within your power to grant such a solution, and if you believe it to be a wise one, then do so. If you need more information or wish to check out her side of the story, defer your answer, and give a specific time for a response. Seek a win–win situation where no meaningless compromises are necessary and where no one is viewed as a loser.

3. Make a decision and explain it. Before you can make a decision, you need to consider who is best qualified to make it. If it is yours to make and you have all the facts you need, give your subordinate your decision and the reasons for it. If higher authorities are involved, identify them. If rules, policy, or procedures are involved, explain their meanings and their applicability to the situation. Your subordinates may not receive the answers that they were looking for, but they will know that you have done your homework.

4. Explain how to appeal. If your workers are dissatisfied with your decision and want to pursue the matter further, tell them how to do so. Let them know whom they should see and how they can make an appointment. If your workers decide to appeal your decision, you should not hold that action against them, and you should let them know that you do not.

5. Follow up. Regardless of the outcome, it is sound management practice to get back to the people who have made a complaint within a reasonable time after its resolution. Assess their present attitudes, and make it clear that you want your people to come to you with their complaints. Be sure you keep a record of any proceedings for future reference.

By being sincere, listening attentively, asking exploratory questions, and acting on each complaint promptly, you will minimize conflicts and reduce barriers to productivity and cooperation.

Maintaining a Non-Union Environment

Fred K. Foulkes, professor of management at Boston University's School of Management, studied the 26 largest non-union industrialized companies in the United States to determine their common attributes, attitudes, and policies. The results are summarized in Exhibit 15.2. Together they summarize a strong management concern for employees. Managers at every level have more flexibility to try the new and different. There is no adversarial relationship between managers and workers; rather, there is a strong climate of cooperation between the two groups.[7]

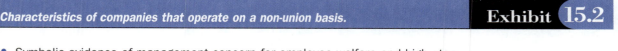

Characteristics of companies that operate on a non-union basis.   Exhibit **15.2**

- Symbolic evidence of management concern for employee welfare and high standards of human resource practices such as job posting, flexible hours, etc.

- Organizational cultures characterized by trust and appropriate plant location and size

- Growth, profitability, and dominant market positions

- Employment security practices

- Promotion from within

- Human resource departments that have influence and representation on the top management team

- Pay and benefit levels at competitive levels

- Management seeks employees' views, such as through regular surveys and interviews

- Careful development of managers with greater emphasis on rewards for longer-term results

Source: Adapted from Fred K. Foulkes, "How Top Nonunion Companies Manage Employees," _Harvard Business Review_ (September–October 1981).

Labor Unions

So far in this chapter, we have discussed handling complaints in companies where there is no union. We now shift to companies that are unionized. Before considering complaint resolution in unionized companies, however, we need to take a brief look at unions in the United States.

union

a group of workers employed by a company or in an industry who have banded together to bargain collectively with their employer

A labor **union** consists of a group of workers (a) who are employed by a company or an industry or (b) who are practicing the same skilled craft and have banded together to bargain collectively with employers for improvements in their wages, hours, benefits, and working conditions. *Craft* or *trade unions* are composed of workers in the same skilled occupation. For example, the International Brotherhood of Electrical Workers (IBEW) is a union organized to represent skilled craftspersons. *Industrial unions* include workers in the same company or industry, regardless of their specific occupations. The United Auto Workers (UAW) and the United Food and Commercial Workers are two examples of industrial unions.

According to the U.S. Bureau of Labor Statistics, 13.9 percent of the workers employed in private and public (government) sectors of the U.S. economy belonged to unions in 1999. The total of 16.5 million union members accounts for 9.4 percent of private sector workers and approximately 37.3 percent of public sector workers. An additional 1.7 million were covered by union contracts but did not have union membership. The overall decline in union members as a proportion of the employed labor force represents a 30.8 percent decline (6.2 percentage points) in union membership since 1983. (Interestingly, actual union membership increased by 265,000 between 1998 and 1999, the largest growth of unions in two decades.)[8] Here are the major reasons behind this decline:

The proportion of the labor force accounted for by traditionally unionized workers has steadily declined as the workforce has grown.

- The proportion of the labor force accounted for by traditionally unionized workers (blue-collar or manufacturing jobs) has steadily declined as the workforce has grown.
- The primary growth areas in the economy are made up of jobs that are traditionally non-union.
- Industry jobs have moved offshore and to the South and Southwest, traditionally non-union areas.

- Workers have shown a trend to decertify their unions, moving from unionized to non-unionized status.
- Many of the foreign-owned companies that have come to the United States to establish production facilities have created non-union workforces.
- Enlightened, people-focused enterprises have created work environments built on trust, mutual respect, and genuine concern for the welfare of their employees, removing major causes for the formation of unions.

UNIONS AND PRODUCTIVITY

Unions are still a political and economic force in our economy. They have achieved some success in replacing their lost blue-collar employees with white-collar, service, and professional employees. Increasingly, unions have become partners with management, working to remove barriers to productivity and to quality. They have done so out of necessity to preserve employment opportunities for their members. They have shown a willingness to trade restrictive work rules and past economic gains for job security.

For example, a few years ago, Detroit Diesel had productivity problems, and relations between the union and management needed improvement. When Roger Penske took over the company, he quickly started building trust with employees and the United Auto Workers (UAW) union. As a result of improved relations and changes in work design, a huge turnaround in labor relations and an increase in productivity took place. The UAW even split the cost of building a new training center for the company's employees.[9]

Because restrictive work practices often have been associated with unionization in the past, it may come as a surprise that a model employer and icon of good management would be heavily unionized. Nonetheless, this is exactly the case with Southwest Airlines: between 84 and 89 percent of the company's employees are represented by unions. Southwest has excellent relationships with its unions. In 1996, the Southwest Airlines Pilots Association (SWAPA)

Workers join unions in an effort to gain bargaining power against management. Union membership is declining because of better management in some companies, a decline in manufacturing jobs, and more legislation designed to protect workers' rights.

agreed to an unprecedented 10-year contract. Obviously, both parties must have had a great deal of trust in each other to enter into an agreement of this length. Early in their relationship, Herb Kelleher, the former CEO of Southwest Airlines, and the lead lawyer for the pilots' union came to an understanding. Kelleher said that if the union's lawyer would not "nit pick" him, he would not "nit pick" the union.[10]

Another unusual feature of labor relations at Southwest Airlines is that the pilots' union tells its members that the name of the game is productivity. This is reflected in the fact that Southwest's pilots fly more hours than pilots do at other major airlines. One of the reasons the pilots' union emphasizes productivity is that the pilots have an incentive to be productive—they receive lucrative stock options. For example, pilots with 10 years of service each receive stock options worth approximately $100,000. The pilot's union tells its members "if you didn't come here to work, you're not going to make it." At a session for approximately 20 newly hired pilots, the vice president of the pilots' union said, this is "Golden Goose Airlines. If you think we're going to let you screw it up you're crazy."[11]

An example of the quick turnaround of Southwest's airplanes was featured in an earlier chapter. The ground crew, who were all union members, worked like a highly coordinated race track pit crew. On a flight on Southwest Airlines, one of the authors observed a Southwest pilot doing his part with a quick turnaround of the plane. He was helping to clean up trash in the passenger cabin while the ground crew did its work.

PUBLIC SECTOR UNIONS

Governmental workers have increasingly turned to unions for representation. In 1999 approximately 42 percent of America's governmental employees belonged to employee associations or unions—a stark contrast to the extent of unionization in the private sector.[12] While we have included the term "employee association," the distinction between unions and employee associations has become blurred and is now largely a matter of semantics. Still, members of employee associations often have a strong preference for the term employer association.

In 1962 federal employees were aided in their attempts to unionize when President Kennedy signed Executive Order 10988. This executive order required federal agencies to recognize and bargain with the associations that represented a majority of their employees, as determined by secret-ballot elections. Executive Order 11491, issued by President Nixon, further encouraged and improved collective bargaining rights for federal employees. Although some public sector unions have occasionally struck in major cities such as New York, Chicago, and San Francisco, they typically do not have the legal right to do so and frequently have been ordered back to work through court orders. In 1999 the largest public sector unions or employee associations were the following:[13]

SUPERVISORS AND ETHICS

The proportion of American working women in unions is around 14 percent, about what it has been for nearly 30 years. Women currently are poorly represented in the ranks of union leaders and organizers, but some 7.2 million members of the AFL-CIO's 14 million members are female.

A report released by a United Nations agency, the International Labor Organization, concludes that women, when given the choice, want to vote for and join unions more than men do. This may be partly because the majority of women are employed in service-sector jobs, which usually pay the least. The report urges unions to organize more women workers and to give them more authority.

During the past two decades, unions have been most successful in organizing businesses that employ many women. According to Susan C. Eaton, author of the UN report, traditional union leadership has long believed that women were "'less organizable' than men—supposedly because they were not committed [to] long-term [employment] or were not full-time members of the labor force." These assumptions are no longer true.

Eaton believes that unionized female employees find a collective voice through their unions that can be used to create change and deal with key issues such as the glass ceiling (policies and practices that inhibit the advancement of protected groups), the disparity between earnings for men and women in similar jobs, and sexual harassment at work.

Source: Wilma Randle, "Study Calls on Sagging Unions to Recruit, Promote Women," *Chicago Tribune* (February 12, 1993): sect. 3, 1, 3.

UNION	MEMBERSHIP IN 1999
National Education Association	2,495,826
American Federation of State, County, and Municipal Employees	1,321,399
American Federation of Teachers	686,518
National Postal Mail Handlers Union	419,987
American Postal Workers Union	315,582
National Association of Letter Carriers	307,761
International Association of Fire Fighters	235,527
American Federation of Government Employees	191,171
American Association of Classified School Employees	166,512

PROFESSIONAL EMPLOYEES

Salaried and professional employees traditionally have resisted attempts to unionize them, but this reluctance has diminished in recent years. In addition to the trend toward unionization noted for governmental workers, other professionals that have gravitated toward unionization include nurses, teachers (most of whom are also government employees), and engineers.

Some of the most interesting developments have occurred with engineers. For example, the Seattle Professional Engineering Employees Association (SPEEA) represents 24,500 of Boeing's engineering and technical employees. In 2000 SPEEA conducted a lengthy strike against Boeing. The strike, which has been termed the first cyber strike, demonstrated the union's technical expertise, as the union utilized the Internet to keep its members unified and informed about the daily progress of negotiations. Airline pilots provide another example of professional employees who have chosen to unionize. The Allied Pilots Association, which represents 11,500 American Airlines employees, also provides an example of a highly sophisticated union of professional employees.[14]

WHY EMPLOYEES BAND TOGETHER

Workers join employee associations and unions for many reasons. They want equity, job security, more pay, and better benefits. By banding together, they improve their bargaining position with employers and are better able to avoid unfair and discriminatory treatment.

Better bargaining position. Compared with their employers, individuals have little bargaining power. A company can simply make an offer on a take-it-or-leave-it basis or make no offer at all. The employee is free to say yes or no. The individual's bargaining power rests on his ability to refuse to accept an employment offer or to quit when dissatisfied. But where all the employees at a company or in a craft or department bargain as one with the employer, the business would have to shut down or operate under severe handicaps if the whole group of workers were to strike.

Fair and uniform treatment. Pay raises, transfers, promotions, layoffs, and eligibility requirements for company training programs can be quite arbitrary without union checks on management's prerogatives. Favoritism and discrimination can influence these decisions, resulting in inequities with little hope for appeal. As a result, unions have pushed for greater reliance on seniority and objective standards. The best man or woman may not always benefit, but the decision will be objective. Unions place great emphasis on job security and constantly try to obtain greater security for themselves and their members' financial futures. Safer working conditions also are a focus of unions, and their efforts have been instrumental in the passage of state and federal safety legislation.

UNION SECURITY PROVISIONS

Unions have fought for years to win recognition from employers. They want to increase their strength by requiring all employees to belong to a union once it is recognized as their legitimate bargaining agent. In an election for certification, a union may win by only a slim majority. Those workers who voted

SUPERVISORS AND QUALITY

Firestone's recall of 6.5 million tires in 2000, mostly from Ford Explorers, and suspicions that defective tires may have contributed to the deaths of 62 people have raised questions about the importance of good labor relations and the implications for quality. Although Firestone, which is Japanese owned, denied that its tires were to blame, a two-year strike by the United Rubber Workers (URW) at the Decatur, Illinois, plant where most of the tires were manufactured is being scrutinized for its role in the defective tires. The union claims that Firestone sought to get rid of the union. "'Firestone's sole purpose was to bust the union,' says union vice president Randy Gordon. 'But we made life miserable for the company.'"

All three parties involved denied that they were to blame. Firestone asserted that the tires were not defective, while Ford maintained that the Explorer is a safe vehicle. On the other hand, the union has speculated that the Explorer has a flaw in its design and that Ford's instruc-tions to its customers incorrectly tell them to under-inflate the tires. Some plaintiffs' lawyers have pointed to the union as the cause of the problem. Plaintiffs' lawyers have assert-ed that employees allowed flawed tires to be shipped from the plant and alleged that replacement workers who worked in the plant during the strike were to blame. Conversely, it has been argued that the strike was not the cause of flaws in the tires, because the plant had quality problems even prior to the strike.

Supervisors need to keep in mind that they are a key to maintaining good relations with the union. They obviously do not have control over larger company policies that affect the quali-ty of labor relations, but they have much influence on the factors at work that can lead to dissatisfaction. Good labor relations and good quality require a continued commitment from both companies and employers over long periods of time. Attempts to take shortcuts around good labor relations typically fail.

Source: Newsweek, "Workers to Ford: Don't Tread on Us" (August 28, 2000): 44.

against it may not be willing to join the union voluntarily. To counter this resistance, unions have tried to enforce various types of *shop agreements*.

With a *union shop* agreement, all current employees must join the union as soon as it is certified as their legitimate bargaining agent. Newcomers have to join after a specified probationary period—normally 30 days. The major-ity of union contracts with employers call for a union shop. The union shop is illegal in the 22 states that have enacted *right-to-work laws*—so named for granting people the right to work with or without membership in a union.[15]

In a *modified union shop*, employees may elect not to join the union that is representing them. Part-time employees, students in work–study pro-grams, and people employed before a specified date may refuse to join.

Employees do not have to belong to the union under an *agency shop*, but they must pay a fee to the union. The reason for this is that union negotiations benefit all employees—members and nonmembers alike. Since all employees benefit, each should pay a share of the costs of win-ning those benefits.

In an *open shop,* membership in the elected union is voluntary for all existing and new employees. Individuals who decide not to join the union do not have to pay any dues to the union.

A *closed shop* requires an employer to hire only union members. This kind of shop is forbidden by the Taft–Hartley Act (described later in this chapter). However, a close relative of the closed shop still exists in the form of *hiring halls.* Hiring halls exist in construction, longshoring, trucking, and any skilled-craft areas. For example, if a construction company needs skilled craftspeople, it will generally contact a union's hiring hall to fill its employment needs. Hiring halls are legal as long as they refer nonmembers for jobs in a non-discriminatory manner.[16]

Labor Legislation

NATIONAL LABOR RELATIONS ACT (1935)

As the Great Depression dragged on, Congress began to analyze its causes and soon realized that the mass impoverishment of so many workers had been a significant factor. To achieve a balance of power between labor and management, the National Labor Relations Act (often called the Wagner Act) was passed as one of the measures of the New Deal. It has often been referred to as organized labor's Magna Carta (great charter or birth certificate) because it guaranteed the right of unions to exist. It gave the individual worker the right to join a union without fear of persecution by the employer. In the words of Section 7 of the Act:

> [E]mployees shall have the right to self-organization, to form, join, or assist labor organizations, to bargain collectively through representatives of their own choosing, and to engage in concerted activities for the purpose of collective bargaining or other mutual aid or protection.

The Wagner Act also listed as unfair practices the following management activities by employers:

- Restraining employees from joining a union
- Contributing financially to or interfering in any way with union operations
- Discriminating in any way against a worker because of union affiliation
- Punishing union members who report management violations of the Act
- Refusing to bargain with a duly elected union of employees

The second and third prohibitions are most significant to supervisors. These provisions have been interpreted as forbidding management from making threats or promises of financial gain to employees who are considering union affiliation or who are about to engage in an election to determine a bargaining agent.

The Wagner Act also established the National Labor Relations Board (NLRB), consisting of five members appointed by the President of the United States. The NLRB is empowered to investigate alleged violations of the Act and to oversee elections to determine a bargaining unit. Its decisions have the power of law and bind both unions and employers. However, as a result of the Wagner Act, another law had to be passed to curb some of the labor excesses it helped create.

LABOR–MANAGEMENT RELATIONS ACT (1947)

During the years between the passage of the Wagner Act and the end of World War II, this country witnessed phenomenal growth in union membership and also in abuses of union power. Organized labor grew from about 4 million members in 1935 to about 15 million (35 percent of the workforce) by 1947. Unions were becoming a powerful force and were exercising financial and economic power that was almost totally unchecked. Postwar strikes threatened the economy.

Congress again felt compelled to balance the two forces. Despite the protests of labor and a veto of the bill by President Truman, it passed the Labor–Management Relations Act, usually called the Taft–Hartley Act. The Act was intended to curb many of the abuses that organized labor had been guilty of in the 1930s. It amended the Wagner Act to include a list of provisions against specific practices by unions:

1. Workers could not be coerced to join or not to join a union.
2. The closed shop was prohibited.
3. Unions (and employers) were required to bargain in good faith.
4. Complex restrictions were placed on certain kinds of strikes and boycotts. The Act prohibited the *secondary boycott*, by which the union forces a company, uninvolved in a labor dispute, to stop dealing with or purchasing from another company involved in a labor dispute. Also prohibited were *jurisdictional strikes*, which were designed to force an employer to give work to one union rather than to another.
5. Unions could not charge their members excessively high initiation fees.
6. Employers were not required to pay for services not performed (featherbedding).

Other provisions allow states to enact right-to-work laws "which make union security agreements, such as union shops and agency shops, illegal."[17] In addition, an emergency provision in the Taft–Hartley Act allows the President of the United States, through the attorney general's office, to seek a court order to stop a strike or lockout that threatens the nation's general health or welfare. The court's order can last for up to 80 days. During this cooling-off period, the federal government attempts to mediate the disputes that are separating the parties. The National Labor Relations Board can hold a secret-ballot vote among the striking or locked-out union members after the injunction is 60 days old to see if the company's latest offer is acceptable.

REPRESENTATION ELECTIONS

The NLRB has established procedures that must be followed by both management and workers when the latter express their desire to be represented by a union. The certification process (the process of getting the NLRB to certify a particular union as the legitimate bargaining agent for employees) begins when at least 30 percent of the workers sign authorization cards calling for a union to represent them. Then the workers can ask the NLRB to schedule a representation (certification) election.

An election will then be scheduled and conducted by NLRB representatives. Once the election is held, the results tabulated, and the disputes settled, the NLRB certifies a bargaining agent. The employer is then obligated to enter into negotiations with the certified union toward a collective bargaining agreement. On average, about 3,000 certification elections are sponsored each year by the NLRB, and about 46 percent are won by unions.[18]

The effort by employees to get rid of their bargaining agent (union) works in the same way as the process of obtaining such an agent. Decertification, as it is called, first requires 30 percent of the bargaining agent's members to call for a decertification election. On average, about 420 decertification elections result in the decertification of unions each year.[19]

THE SUPERVISOR'S ROLE DURING REPRESENTATION ELECTIONS

Your job is the same as any other manager's during employee certification or decertification elections. You should remain neutral and preserve an atmosphere in which workers can express their uninhibited choices. In general, do nothing that is not expressly okayed by higher management. Do not express your opinions—pro or con—toward unions or union membership by your subordinates. Make no threats, and make no promises. Do not give or announce any increases in pay or benefits just before or during representation elections, unless the increases are totally unrelated to the election campaigns.

You may point out to workers the economic costs that are connected to union membership. Such costs include the dues paid to support union officers and activities, the costs of processing employee complaints through the union contract's complaint procedures, and the costs connected with strikes that take people off the payroll. You may also point out that both the union contract and its constitution place restrictions on workers. Rules and punishments are prescribed in both.

SUPERVISING TEAMS

Unions are struggling to find a new identity and to adjust their philosophies to meet several challenges: the rise in white-collar (traditionally non-union) employment along with the decline in traditional union jobs, the threats to their members' wages and jobs from non-union and foreign competition, and their poor public image. Throughout the 1980s, America's largest unions watched their memberships shrink, along with hard-won benefits and wage levels. In response, unions bargained to increase members' employment and job security and gave employers concessions on work rules and monetary issues.

Many unions are shifting from a passive mode and becoming more active. Union leaders realize that they must act in employees' best interests and cooperate to make them more competitive and productive. A recent president of the United Steelworkers of America put it this way: "When it comes to dividing up the pie, we'll be adversaries. But now we have to grow the pie, and that means working together [labor–management cooperation]." The following methods seem to work and are growing in popularity:

1. Loosening of work rules through collective bargaining—more union members can take on more duties, giving them and management more flexibility.

2. Concessions in such areas as overtime and vacation pay.

3. Joint efforts—teams and committees made up of management and worker members—designed to improve quality and productivity and to deal with additional issues. Such groups may not be used in lieu of, or as substitutes for, regular collective bargaining, and worker appointments to these groups are usually under union control.

In exchange, unions want more open communication with management, demanding data on costs and profits. Employment security has become the most important issue for the membership. It is usually guaranteed to some extent for the life of a collective bargaining agreement.

One model for this new labor–management cooperation is the Xerox experience. During the 1980s, the company lost market share to foreign competitors, and it closed factories. Its union met with management and set up teams to find ways to improve productivity and quality. It exchanged concessions on temporary workers and on management's right to fire employees (for excessive absences) for member job security during the life of the then-current labor contract.

The results of these cooperative efforts were outstanding. Absenteeism dropped "from 8.5 percent to 2.5 percent." When 240 jobs were threatened by a proposed closing of a wire harness production facility, workers formed a team that identified means to cut $3.5 million in costs and saved those jobs.

Another team worked up a bid that resulted in the in-house manufacture of parts previously provided by outsiders. These joint union–management efforts allowed the company to add about 1,700 production jobs and made Xerox more profitable and competitive.

Source: Peter Nulty, "Look What the Unions Want Now," *Fortune* (February 8, 1993): 128–130, 132, 135. © 2001 Time Inc. All rights reserved.

Labor Relations

labor relations
management activities necessitated by the fact that the organization has a union that represents its employees

collective bargaining
the process of negotiating a union agreement that covers wages, hours, and working conditions

grievance processing
settling an alleged violation of the labor-management agreement in accordance with the method outlined in that agreement

The area of **labor relations** includes all the activities within a company that involve dealings with a union and its members. Specifically, two main areas are the most important and time consuming: **collective bargaining** (arriving at a contract that covers workers' wages, hours, and working conditions) and **grievance processing** (dealing with complaints that allege violations of the collective bargaining agreement).

COLLECTIVE BARGAINING

Bargaining collectively—the union representatives on one side of the table, management's representatives on the other—is the traditional way in which labor disputes are settled and labor–management agreements are formed. Some time before the expiration date of a labor contract, the two groups begin a series of meetings that ultimately leads to the signing of a new agreement. Bargaining may take place on the local level, where only one local union and employer are involved, or on an industry-wide basis, where the agreement sets the standard for the industry—as in the automotive and trucking industries.

The usual process involves a specialist in labor relations from the company's labor relations department (usually at the vice-presidential level) and the union's negotiating committee. Both sides employ labor lawyers who are well versed in the most recent developments in labor law to help them hammer out specific contract provisions and wording.

Both sides bring a list of demands to the bargaining sessions and, in their own minds, assign to each a priority that will become apparent as negotiations develop. Some demands are made merely to serve as trading material. Negotiations involve give and take, so each side must be prepared to bargain away some of its demands in order to obtain others.

Each side attempts to resolve the many minor issues as quickly as it can, reserving the major issues for the final meetings immediately preceding expiration of the contract. It is then that the pressure for a settlement is greatest. Ultimately, through compromises and trading, a new contract emerges. The agreement is then offered to the union membership, which votes to accept or reject it. A simple majority vote is usually required.

The union contract with management spells out in rather precise terms the rights of workers with regard to wages, hours, and working conditions. It is a formal written document that both managers and union members must thoroughly understand. It can and does limit management's authority.

ENFORCING THE LABOR CONTRACT

Enforcement of the terms of the agreement depends on communication of the contract provisions and of the demands they make on labor and management. Managers must be made aware of their rights and duties. Copies of the agreement are made available to each manager, along with an explanation that is easy to understand. Any questions that may arise in a manager's mind can quickly be answered through consultation with the human resources department or labor relations officials. The union must also make its members aware of their rights and duties. Copies of the contract are distributed to each member, and meetings are held to explain the contract's terms.

THE SUPERVISOR AND THE STEWARD

The **steward** is first of all an employee and a worker. He has the additional responsibilities of a union office because the union members have elected or appointed him. Stewards receive some release time from work to carry out their duties. Exhibit 15.3 lists the responsibilities of supervisors and stewards. More points draw them together than keep them apart.

Just as a supervisor is management's spokesperson, a steward is labor's spokesperson. She has the duty to represent workers in the early stages of

steward
the union's elected or appointed first-line representative in the areas in which employees work

The responsibilities of supervisors and stewards in labor relations.	Exhibit 15.3

SUPERVISORS	STEWARDS
Know the contract	Know the contract
Enforce the contract	Enforce the contract
Look out for the welfare of subordinates	Look out for welfare of constituents
Serve as spokesperson for both management and subordinates	Serve as spokesperson for the union and constituents
Settle grievances fairly (in line with management's interpretation of the contract)	Settle grievances fairly (in line with union interpretation of the contract)
Keep abreast of grievance solutions and changes in contract interpretation	Keep abreast of grievance solutions and changes in contract interpretation
Maintain good working relationships with stewards	Maintain good working relationships with supervisors
Keep stewards informed about management's decisions and sources of trouble	Keep supervisors informed about union positions and sources of trouble
Protect management rights	Protect labor rights

the grievance process. The steward must be able to interpret the contract both to the supervisor and to fellow workers. A worker's complaint usually cannot win the union's backing without the steward's consent.

Stewards, like managers, have a difficult and demanding position. They are workers and must conform to company standards or risk disciplinary action. On the other hand, they have the status of elected union officers who, if they wish to retain their posts, must be effective representatives of their constituents. They may, therefore, feel a good deal of pressure to push complaints to grievance status, even when their own best judgment says they should not. In circumstances where there are few complaints or grievances, some stewards may feel the need to escalate issues or manufacture discontent in order to justify their position and to prove that they are serving a useful purpose.

HANDLING GRIEVANCES

grievance
an alleged violation of the labor–management agreement

When a worker is dissatisfied with a supervisor's disposition of a work-related complaint, she may appeal that decision by filing a formal charge called a **grievance.** A grievance alleges that a violation has occurred of one or another of the provisions of the labor agreement. A complaint that is improperly handled can and usually does become a grievance. Managers should consider every gripe about wages, hours, and working conditions a potential grievance.

If the details of the grievance are not clear to you after you hear the complaining employee's case, ask questions. Conduct your own investigation to determine whether or not the facts presented to you are complete and true. If they are not or if you are uncertain about any of them, gather the evidence needed to clarify the situation. If you are unsure about the proper interpretation or application of the specific language of the labor contract, seek counsel from the labor relations specialists. Exhibit 15.4 provides recommendations to follow while handling grievances.

If you determine that the grievance is without merit, give the worker and the steward your facts, your (management's) interpretation and application of the labor contract provisions, and your specific reasons for denying the grievance. If your verbal answer is accepted by the complaining employee and the union steward, prepare a written record of the complaint and your disposition of it. Be certain that any remedy you grant is within your power to give and has your boss's approval.

On the other hand, your verbal answer to the complaining employee may not be acceptable to him or to the steward. If it is not, your involvement will continue. You will probably be given a written copy of the complaint and will probably have to provide a written response. You will probably be questioned by various labor relations people and union officials during later phases of the grievance procedure.

Normally, grievances are not put into writing until they progress from the first step to the second. This is especially true in large corporations, where the number of grievances is quite large and where the majority are usually solved

| *Do's and don'ts for the supervisor when handling a grievance.* | **Exhibit** **15.4** |

DO

- Begin by assuming that every complaint has merit.

- Give the grieving employee your time and listen carefully to each word.

- Identify the specific contractual wording that the grievance alleges was violated.

- Visually check out the location where the grievance supposedly took place.

- Interview every person who may have knowledge of the grievance, the parties to it, the event, the location, and the circumstances.

- After gathering all your facts, check out all past grievances that have a bearing on this one.

- Hold all your interviews and discussions with concerned parties in private.

- Before giving any answer to the grievance, touch base with your boss.

- Give your answer as completely as you can within any time limit prescribed by the union contract.

- Keep written records of all your findings, your interviews, and your answers.

DON'T

- Settle any grievance outside the terms of the written contract.

- Engage in trading one grievance settlement for the withdrawal of another.

- Engage in bargaining over issues that are not part of the written contract.

- Agree to any changes in the precise wording of the contract.

- Fail to deliver any remedy endorsed by the parties as a settlement for the grievance.

at the level of the steward and supervisor. From this step on, the number of people involved increases, as does the need for precise language.

THE GRIEVANCE PROCEDURE

Where a collective bargaining agreement exists between the company and a union, a formal procedure for handling grievances will be outlined. The following procedure is typical, although one or two intermediate steps may be left out in some agreements:[20]

1. The employee makes a verbal complaint to the supervisor. If the employee (grievant) is unsatisfied with the supervisor's response, the procedure moves to the next step.

2. If the steward feels the grievance is meritorious, the grievance is prepared in written form and signed by the employee. The steward then meets with the supervisor and tries to work out a solution. (Supervisors should research the issue carefully and consult with the labor relations specialists in preparation for this meeting.) If, after hearing the steward's arguments, the supervisor believes nothing new has been added to change the situation, she will stick to the original decision.

3. Union officials meet with the supervisor's immediate superior or a representative from the labor relations department. They examine issues to determine if any precedents from earlier grievance processing apply. If no solution can be agreed on, the grievance advances to the next step.

4. Higher-level union officials meet with the labor relations director or plant manager. Costs and time devoted to the problem are increasing, and both sides will want to solve the issues as quickly and as equitably as they can. If no agreement is reached, the grievance advances to the next step.

5. Arbitration is invoked.

MEDIATION

mediation
the use of a neutral third party in a labor-management dispute to facilitate resolution of the dispute by the parties

Mediation is the attempt to resolve a dispute by using the conflict resolution skills of a neutral outsider who is allied with neither labor nor management. Mediators are asked to bring the two sides together and to facilitate their agreement on a settlement. Mediators have no formal authority and cannot impose a settlement on the parties. Nonetheless, mediators help the parties to reach agreement through a variety of means. They can provide more objective assessments of the costs of disagreement, reestablish communication, clarify the intentions of the parties toward each other, suggest potential solutions (which might be unacceptable if the solution came from the other side), clarify misunderstandings, and help the parties save face.[21] For high-level disputes, such as between large companies and national unions, the mediator may be a distinguished public official, such as a judge, who has a fine reputation and whose insights, wisdom, and power are respected by both sides.

ARBITRATION

arbitration
the use of a neutral third party in a dispute between management and labor to resolve the areas of conflict

In **arbitration** a neutral third party is called in to decide the case. He is a professional arbitrator, selected by the two parties from panels of experts meeting the standards of the American Arbitration Association (AAA) or the Federal Mediation and Conciliation Service (FMCS). In a typical year the FMCS receives between 25,000 and 27,000 requests for panels of arbitrators to rule on grievances that companies and unions are unable to resolve. After requesting arbitration services, however, the parties often settle the cases on their own. FMCS arbitrators issue approximately 4,000 to 5,000 arbitration awards (decisions) each year.[22]

The arbitrator holds a hearing on the grievance. During the hearing advocates for the union and the company present their arguments and evidence. In most cases, lawyers represent one or both sides. At the hearing, the advocates make opening statements on the merits of the case, call witnesses, and conduct direct and cross-examinations of witnesses. The arbitrator is in charge of the hearing and conducts the proceedings in much the same manner as a judge, although with less formality. The hearing may be quite informal depending on the arbitrator's style. Formal rules of evidence are not required, although most arbitrators understand such rules and rely on them to some extent. The arbitrator then writes an award in which the grievance is either sustained or denied. This award or ruling becomes binding on both union and management and can be enforced in federal courts if needed. In addition to resolving grievances, interest arbitration sometimes is used in the public sector to overcome an impasse in collective bargaining, because the parties are usually not permitted to strike.

Instant Replay

1. Complaints are serious matters to be dealt with in a serious way. In a unionized organization, complaints can and often do turn into grievances.

2. Handling complaints requires honesty, sincerity, and an open discussion of all the relevant facts and emotions involved.

3. The grievance procedure begins when you and a subordinate or the union steward meet to discuss a formal complaint alleging a violation of a union contract.

4. When you manage in a union environment, you must know your labor agreement's provisions and how a ruling on a grievance can affect the future interpretation of the agreement.

5. You need to know federal and state laws that regulate your treatment of employees in all matters—not just in labor relations areas.

6. You should develop a cooperative relationship with your steward. Both of you are paid to look out for special interests and to reach accommodations when it is in your mutual interests to do so.

7. Unions exist to serve their members. In many companies, they are a fact of life.

Questions for Class Discussion

1. Can you define this chapter's key terms?

2. How should a supervisor handle complaints?

3. What does the Wagner Act prohibit?

4. What does the Taft–Hartley Act prohibit?

5. In what ways are the supervisor and the steward similar? In what ways are these labor relations roles different?

6. Can you outline a typical grievance procedure for a large organization? What might be left out in a small company?

Incident

Purpose: To get a union member's view about a union—its benefits and drawbacks.

Your task: Interview a union member (family member, classmate, friend, or the like) using the following questions and any others you may wish to add. Compare your results with those of your classmates.

1. Why did you join your union?

2. What are the costs—psychological and financial—connected with your union membership?

3. What direct benefits does your union provide you in the following areas:
   a. Wages and benefits?
   b. Working conditions?
   c. Employee assistance during a strike?

4. Have you ever been involved in a strike?

5. What were the issues that led to the strike?

6. Does your union contract prescribe a grievance process?

7. What is the process?

8. In general, how would you describe the working relationship between management and the union?

9. What do you think your working life would be like if your union did not exist?

CASE PROBLEM 15.1   *Beer Mints?*

Marty Cole, an outside sales representative, was walking through the parking lot to go to his temporary office in the tire manufacturing plant when he noticed a pickup truck with a man sitting in it. The man was drinking a bottle of beer. Marty concluded that there must be a shift change, and he was drinking a beer before driving home. However, when Marty arrived at the plant entrance, he noticed that people were returning from break and that it was not time for a shift change. He then realized that he had seen an employee on break drinking a beer in his pickup. Marty also realized that the pickup had been parked with the back facing the plant entrance. The man had appeared to have been looking in the rear view mirror, and it was now obvious that he had adjusted the rear view mirror toward the plant so that he could see anyone come out and approach in his direction. Marty had approached from the opposite direction and, therefore, had not been seen.

Marty walked back to the security hut and told the supervisor of security what he had seen. He and the security supervisor went out to the parking lot and walked up to the pickup. There was no one in the pickup, but there was a partially opened case of beer on the seat. In addition, there were lots of empty beer bottles in the cargo area of the truck. The supervisor of security returned to the security hut and looked up the license plate of the truck. The owner of the pickup was Buford Collins, one of the tire builders who had worked at the plant for five years. The security supervisor then called Gina Pitts, the director of human resources. Gina came to the security hut, where Marty and the supervisor of security told her what they had seen.

Gina and the two men went to find Buford. The company had a strict policy against drinking on the job specifying that such a violation was grounds for termination. When they found Buford, he was working on the line where the raw tire casings were placed in the hot tire molds. His eyes were runny and his face was flushed and puffy. Gina was convinced that Buford had been drinking and concluded that he looked like someone who drank a lot on a regular basis. Buford, however, denied that he had been drinking and said his face was flushed because of the heat. He explained that he had gone to his truck to get some candy mints but that he had not had a beer. He also explained that he kept mints in his truck and that he liked to go to his truck during his breaks to listen to music and eat mints. Buford's explanation for the empty beer bottles was that he and a friend had been hunting last weekend, and they had put all of their empties in the truck.

Gina told Buford to go home and that he would be on suspension until she and the plant manager decided what to do. Buford then volunteered that he would be willing take a blood alcohol test. Gina told him that it wasn't necessary but that he could do so if he wished. She sent him to the office where a secretary made arrangements for a blood alcohol test. The test was conducted approximately 1 1/2 hours later at a nearby hospital. The test results that came back two days later simply stated, "Negative results. No alcohol detected at the .04 percent level or above." Two days later Gina and the plant manager met with Buford. They told him that he would be terminated for drinking on the job unless he agreed to go through a substance abuse program paid for by the company's employee assistance program. Buford refused. He said that he had not been drinking and would not go through such a program. The plant manager terminated Buford, and the union appealed the case to arbitration. The applicable provision of the union contract says that employees may be terminated only for just cause.

Questions

1. Do you think the discipline of Buford was fair? On what factors do you base your reasoning?

2. What is your opinion of the company's investigation and disciplinary procedure?

3. How strong is the company's case against Buford? Does it have just cause for termination?

4. How do you think an arbitrator will rule in this case?

CASE PROBLEM 15.2 *Downsizing Dilemma*

The order from the CEO was unambiguous. Costs at the plant would have to be reduced by 20 percent. Since labor constituted a high proportion of total costs, it was clear that layoffs would be necessary. The plant manager, director of human resources, production manager, and production supervisors all agreed that the best way to conduct the layoffs would be to first identify the nonessential work activities in each job classification. They would then eliminate a corresponding number of employee full-time equivalents (FTEs) by cutting out these activities in each classification. Although the employees were represented by a union, the contract with the union did not require the company to conduct layoffs according to inverse seniority. The contract only required seniority to be applied when employees had equal ability to perform the job.

The company then conducted an activity value analysis (AVA) of all jobs in order to identify the nonessential activities. Employees wrote out all of the activities they performed each year and the amount of time they devoted to each. Committees of managers then reviewed the activities and decided, on the basis of their essentiality, the number of FTEs to eliminate in each job classification. Because the management team had no confidence in the validity of past performance appraisals, they had teams of three supervisors reevaluate each employee for purposes of the layoff decisions. Employees in each job classification were placed in three categories for purposes of the layoffs: (1) above average, (2) average, and (3) marginal. A point system was used to place employees in each category based on an overall evaluation of ability, skill, and qualifications. The cut-off levels for each category were as follows: 20 or more equaled above average, 10 to 19 equaled average, and 0 to 9 equaled marginal. Employees in the marginal category would be laid off first, followed by the lowest-ranked employee in the average category, next lowest ranked, etc.

When the plant manager and director of human resources reviewed the list of employees who would be laid off by this approach, they realized that the two union stewards, Judy Cooper and Kelvin Hastings, would be laid off. The stewards received point totals of 9 and 6, respectively. Because they felt that the union would find it unacceptable if no union stewards remained on the job, the plant manager and director of human resources decided to add three points to Judy Cooper's evaluation, making her total points 12. They reasoned that Judy had demonstrated leadership on the job by guiding the union to an agreement in the last contract negotiations with the company. Thus Judy Cooper's point total of 12 placed her in the "average" category and one point above Henry Gilbert's total of 11. As it turned out, the company needed to lay off more employees than the number in the marginal category. As a result, it was necessary to go to the lowest-ranking employee in the average category. Thus Henry Gilbert was laid off and Judy Cooper was retained.

The union then filed a grievance on behalf of Henry, contending that he had been unfairly laid off. The union argued that the layoffs were not conducted in accordance with fair procedures equally applied to all employees. It challenged management's use of the special evaluations conducted for the layoffs instead of the regular appraisals Henry and other employees had received on an annual basis for many years. The union requested that Henry be reinstated to his position and paid back pay for the time he was off the job. Approximately eight months later, Henry's case came before an arbitration hearing.

Questions

1. Evaluate the company's layoff procedures. Do they appear to be fair?
2. What is your opinion of the special evaluation procedure used for the layoffs?
3. How do you think the arbitrator should rule in this case? Why?
4. What would you have done if you were making these decisions for the company?

References

1. Rowe, M. P., and Baker, M. "Are You Hearing Enough Employee Concerns?" *Harvard Business Review* (May–June 1984): 130.

2. Gomes, Lee. "A Whistle-Blower Finds Jackpot at the End of His Quest," *The Wall Street Journal* (April 27, 1998): B1, B12.

3. Ibid.

4. Rowe and Baker. "Are You Hearing": 130.

5. Ibid.

6. Hendricks, Erin S. "Do More than Open Doors," *HR Magazine* (June 2000): 171–176.

7. Foulkes, Fred K. "How Top Nonunion Companies Manage Employees," *Harvard Business Review* (September–October 1981): 90.

8. Gifford, Court, ed. *Directory of U. S. Labor Organizations*, 2000 Edition, Washington, DC: Bureau of National Affairs, Inc. (2000).

9. Noe, Raymond A.; Hollenbeck, John R.; Gerhart, Barry; and Wright, Patrick M. Video tape segment, "Detroit Diesel," accompanying *Human Resource Management*. Burr Ridge, IL: Austin Press/Richard D. Irwin, 1994.

10. Menaker, Marvin; Kearns, Gary; Parker, James; and Landau, Ruth. Presentation on Labor Relations at Southwest Airlines, Southwest Academy of Arbitrators, Dallas, Texas (March 1996).

11. Menaker, et al. Presentation on Labor.

12. Gifford. *Directory of U. S. Labor Organizations*.

13. Ibid.

14. Greer, Charles R. "E-Voice: How Information Technology Is Shaping Life Within Unions," *Journal of Labor Research* Vol. 23, No. 2 (Spring 2002): 41–61.

15. Delaney, John T. "Right to Work," in Lawrence H. Peters, Charles R. Greer, and Stuart A. Youngblood (eds.), *The Blackwell Encyclopedic Dictionary of Human Resource Management.* Oxford, UK: Blackwell (1997): 295.

16. Cibon, Partick J., and Castagnera, James O. *Labor and Employment Law,* 2nd ed. Boston: PWS-Kent Publishing Company, 1993.

17. Joel, Lewin G. III. *Every Employee's Guide to the Law.* New York: Pantheon Books (1993): 326.

18. Farber, Henry S. "Union Success in Representation Elections: Why Does Unit Size Matter?" *Industrial and Labor Relations Review* (January 2001): 329–348. Hatfield, Donald E., and Murrman, Kent F. "Diversification and Win Rate in NLRB Certification Elections," *Journal of Labor Research* (Fall 1999): 539–555.

19. Ibid.

20. Miner, John B., and Miner, Mary Green. *Personnel and Industrial Relations*, 3rd ed. New York: Macmillan Publishing Company, 1977. Middlemist, R. Dennis; Hitt, Michael A.; and Greer, Charles R. *Personnel Management: Jobs, People, and Logic.* Englewood Cliffs, NJ: Prentice Hall, 1983.

21. Kolb, Deborah M. *The Mediators.* Cambridge, MA: MIT Press, 1983.

22. Myers, Jewell L. "Arbitration Statistics for Fiscal Year 1996," Unpublished Memorandum from the Federal Mediation and Conciliation Service (December 13, 1996).

SECURITY, SAFETY, AND HEALTH

16

Objectives

After reading and discussing this chapter, you should be able to do the following:

1. Define this chapter's key terms.

2. Outline security measures that supervisors can take to prevent theft by employees.

3. Describe a supervisor's duties in the event of a fire and with regard to fire prevention.

4. Outline procedures open to supervisors to prevent loss from vandalism.

5. Describe the purposes of the Occupational Safety and Health Act.

6. Describe OSHA enforcement procedures and an employer's rights with regard to OSHA inspectors.

Introduction

In this chapter, we are concerned with the supervisor's duties in the following areas:

- **Security**—protecting physical facilities and other resources from loss or damage
- **Safety**—protecting employees and customers from accidents and injuries
- **Health**—preventing employee illness, both physical and emotional, and treating injuries when they occur

Our focus will be on prevention—the ways in which supervisors and others can head off trouble and minimize damage to the company's human, financial, informational, and material resources. We will explore supervisors' responsibilities to protect these resources. Your security and safety duties begin with the screening of new applicants and continue every day as you carry out your managerial functions. Fortunately, staff specialists or

security
efforts at protecting physical facilities and other resources from loss or damage

safety
efforts at protecting human resources from accidents and injuries

health
the general condition of a person physically, mentally, and emotionally; or, efforts at preventing illness and treating injuries when they occur

outside consultants frequently are available to provide assistance in these areas, particularly in larger organizations.

As you provide direction for your employees through training and discipline, you can help to prevent accidents and theft. As a part of organizational efforts, you can build a structure for preventing accidents and enforcing safety rules. Furthermore, as you plan for the future, you can design programs, procedures, and practices that will help workers comply with management policies and state and federal safety standards. You can also develop effective preventive, diagnostic, and therapeutic controls to deal with safety and security problems. Through effective communications, committee action, and peer-group cooperation, you can ensure the coordination of safety and security efforts throughout the company.

Physical Security

The terrorist attacks on the World Trade Center in New York and the Pentagon in Washington, D.C., on September 11, 2001 killed over 3,000 people while they were at work in their offices. In addition, shortly after these attacks anthrax sent through the mail posed hazards for postal facilities.[1] These attacks highlight the vulnerability of workplaces to extraordinary dangers. However, violence has reached a point where homicide is the "leading cause of occupational death for women."[2] Furthermore, it has been estimated that each year 13,000 instances of violence occur in the workplace against women in which the attackers are the targets' husbands or boyfriends.[3] These levels of violence pose serious threats for organizations. In addition to the devastating effects of violence on the workforce, the employer may incur financial liabilities from failing to prevent a disgruntled or terminated employee from attacking others in the workplace.[4]

In order to prevent violence in the workplace, supervisors need to be in close contact with their subordinates and must recognize the indications that an employee is troubled. Employees also must be trained to alert their superiors to potential problems. Employee assistance programs can be helpful in preventing employees from reaching a breaking point, and these programs have much greater utilization when counselors are located on site. In addition, it is important for employees to be assured that they can seek assistance from their EAP on a confidential basis. It is important that the EAP provide other services than substance abuse and depression counseling so that employees who seek EAP assistance will not be associated with such problems simply because their coworkers find out that they are going to the EAP. Better selection procedures can help firms avoid hiring people who have greater potential for violence. For example, the inclusion of a few carefully crafted behavioral questions in selection interviews can help screen out applicants with angry personalities. In addition, the company should make clear policy statements that it will not tolerate threats, harassment, or violence and that it will investigate all reports of such behaviors.[5]

SUPERVISORS AND QUALITY

According to a book published by the National Safe Workplace Institute (NSWI), "some 111,000 acts of workplace violence occur nationwide each year—about 425 per workday." One of NSWI's authors, Dennis Johnson, claims the violence is due in large measure to "an overstressed population; a surfeit of guns; fractured families; . . . and a spreading multiculturalization and gender revolution in the workforce, both of which contribute to the number of scapegoats for anger as well as to mixed signals and differing values that can spark conflict." Workplace liability lawyer Garry Mathiason adds, "20% of all workplace incidents that involve physical injury can be attributed to some type of romantic entanglement. Most often, the victim is a woman."

Workplace assaults and actions that can evolve into violence (stalking, verbal abuse, and employer-directed animosity) are a growing concern and represent millions of dollars in actual and potential liability for employers and employees alike. A convenience store in Texas was held liable for $4.5 million in the case of a murdered employee. The court said that it failed to provide adequate security for the employee. An employment agency in California was held liable for $5.5 million in the death of a winery worker. She was stabbed to death by an employee with a history of violence and a criminal record; the court said that an improper background check was made.

Workplace violence is often "preceded by a string of unheeded warning signs: Some traumatic event, like a layoff or a financial crisis, disrupts the person's life, followed by a period of almost paranoid brooding and escalating, often increasingly specific threats." Companies can take and are taking specific actions to prevent workplace hostilities from escalating into violence. Among the options are:

- Taking a firm policy position that states workplace threats, intimidation, and acts of violence will not be tolerated and will be punished.

- People who have court orders restraining their activities must notify the company of the fact.
- People who cannot get along must be physically separated and not allowed to interact on the job.
- All employees, especially supervisors, must notify proper authorities when they witness or discover serious or potentially serious situations.
  - Potential problem areas—break areas, locker rooms, and parking lots—are kept under surveillance, and a properly trained security staff is on call to deal with problems.
  - EAPs—psychiatric counseling, for example—are in place, and everyone knows how to take advantage of them.
- A specific team is in place and trained for early problem detection and intervention.
- Violence-prevention and dispute-resolution training is provided by consultants or other experts.
- In-depth screening to identify violence-prone individuals is conducted as part of routine screening for applicants.
- Better lighting, having guests sign in, not allowing people to work alone or in isolated surroundings, firing violent employees, and requiring people with demonstrated tendencies toward volatile behavior to get help as a condition of continued employment all further reduce the invitation to violence.

Du Pont is one of several companies that have taken a firm stand and developed policy and programs to deal with these issues. Its Personal Safety Program for employees includes workshops on rape prevention, sexual harassment, domestic violence, and abuse of power in the workplace. "Employees have access to a 24-hour hotline staffed by Du Pont volunteers as well as . . . counselors who can arrange medical and legal assistance."

Source: Tom Dunkel, "Newest Danger Zone: Your Office," *Working Woman* (August 1994): 36–41, 70, 72–73. Copyright 2002 © by WMAC, Inc. Rights reserved. Used with permission of Working Mother Media.

EMPLOYEE THEFT

Each year businesses lose billions of dollars to thefts by customers, employees, and outside criminals. "The International Association of Professional Security Consultants says losses of cash and inventory alone range from $10 billion to $40 billion annually."[6] Thefts of employee property cause suspicion, low morale, dollar losses, and employee turnover. The largest loss to most U. S. businesses results from employee theft. It has been estimated that "sixty to 80 percent of all inventory 'shrinkage' . . . can be blamed on workers. . . . The norm for shrinkage is 2 to 2.5 percent of inventory, although it might run as high as 7 percent in some businesses."[7] "In employee surveys conducted by academics and other specialists, as many as 30 percent of workers interviewed admitted stealing from their employers."[8] According to a Chicago testing company, Reid Psychological Systems, "about 17 percent of applicants admit to stealing from a previous employer."[9]

Employees steal time, money, company assets, and secrets. For money and other motives, employees steal vital information about product designs, marketing plans, customers, finances, and research projects. This information in the competition's hands can do great harm. According to the consulting firm Ernst & Young, "more than half the country's businesses are likely to have suffered financially because of information losses stemming from inadequate computer security measures. And at least some of the financial losses have exceeded $1 million per occurrence."[10] In spite of the size of these losses, only 58 percent of senior managers consider computer security to be very important. "Those who do consider computer security to be very important tend to be in the banking and insurance industries" according to an Ernst & Young survey.[11] Losses of vital information also occur when managers talk too much or to the wrong people, through improper disposal of waste paper, and from uncontrolled access to information by visitors and suppliers.

Electronic thieves working from within companies steal billions of dollars each year through a variety of schemes. Computer criminals can siphon money from business accounts into their personal accounts. They can create phony charges from nonexistent vendors and then authorize payment of those charges. Computer theft may be committed by programmers, computer operators, clerks, bank tellers, executives, and disgruntled or fired employees. Losses to computer thieves tend to be much larger than losses to conventional thieves.

Among the electronic security problems that threaten businesses are: **computer viruses,** bugged facsimile machines, intercepted cellular phone calls, and intercepted Internet or e-mail messages. Computer viruses have become a huge problem, and an entire virus protection software industry has evolved in response. Viruses have changed the way we use our computers, such as by not opening attachments in e-mail from senders we do not know.[12] Facsimile (fax) machines use telephone lines or cellular networks to transmit printed copy. It is possible to tap into a fax machine by making a

computer virus

a rogue computer program that can reproduce itself endlessly or cause other havoc, such as the destruction of stored data secret connection with its telephone line. Thieves can also intercept messages by monitoring cellular calls. Eavesdropping equipment is readily available through most electronics stores.[13]

For controlling theft by employees, "corporate policy and guidelines are the first lines of defense . . . experts say."[14] August Bequai, a Washington, D.C., attorney and author specializing in computer crime, offers five major tips for prevention:[15]

1. *Put out the word.* Managers must warn employees that the company frowns on computer crime, whether it is theft of a floppy disk or information from a database, and that offenders will be prosecuted. When a crime occurs, you must make good on your word.

2. *Name a contact.* Employees should have somebody to talk to if they suspect crimes. If you don't have a security director, you should. This should be a high-level person, reporting directly to the CEO or chairman.

3. *Create a code of ethics and give every employee a copy.* State explicitly what the company regards as computer crime and what it regards as unethical. Tell employees these actions are grounds for dismissal or prosecution.

4. *Educate top management.* Studies have shown that when top executives understand the use and abuse of computer systems, employees commit fewer crimes.

5. *Institute data security.* Your system should have at least three levels of security. Passwords should be changed every 30 days. Don't leave access codes and passwords lying around.

Some companies use various types of tags and coded strips to track assets and to detect the theft of merchandise or unauthorized use of facilities. Software loss-prevention systems enable companies to detect theft by their own employees. Such software, when combined with television surveillance systems, provides a powerful means for controlling theft:

> The marriage of digitalized closed-circuit television (CCTV) systems with POS [point of sale] data mining is enabling retail loss-prevention managers to expose cashier stealing and sweethearting, assemble convincing evidence, and deal with such situations as a matter of routine. The managers simply decide what constitutes suspicious behavior and send their software out to look for it. . . . The system flags POS transactions that are most susceptible to fraud—refunds, credits, discounts, no-sale rings, and the like—and compiles them in a report . . . Instead of fast-forwarding through miles of videotape, loss-prevention managers who want to see what happened can use that information to call up a digitalized video clip of the specific transaction.[16]

Your job also may entail enforcing procedures designed to control access to and use of data. Security software, passwords, access codes, encryption, and virus scanners are but a few of the readily available and inexpensive solutions to computer security. Access to databases can be limited in various ways to keep unauthorized personnel from viewing or working with them. Devices that defend against the bugging of fax machines are available. E-mail and Internet communications software, such as Netscape and Microsoft Internet Explorer, and newer fax machines have encryption features.

SELECTION AND PREVENTION

Preventing crimes committed by employees begins with the selection of each new employee. During the screening process, both supervisors and members of the human resources department should be alert for telltale signs of a potentially dishonest employee (see Exhibit 16.1). In addition to this list of clues, you should check the applicant's lifestyle for any hints that the person is living above his or her level of income. When conducting orientation activities, inform all new employees of your company's policy on dishonesty, and the penalties. Further, many security experts recommend insuring an organization against employee theft through the purchase of fidelity bonds for all those employees who will have access to large amounts of money or valuable goods.

Exhibit 16.1 *Some warning signs of a potentially dishonest applicant.*

1. Gaps in employment	Obtain information about these gaps during the employment interview.
2. Criminal record	A criminal record check must be job-related. The failure to check for a potentially violent criminal background can create employer liability.
3. Lies on the application	Significant falsehoods on an employment application signal future falsehoods.
4. Frequent job changes	Changes that indicate the person does not know what she wants to do (absence of focus or linkage between past jobs) may be predictive of short tenure with your organization.
5. Financial problems	A strong focus on money issues by the applicant may mean over-extension and temptations to profit at others' expense.
6. Overqualification	Someone seeking a job for which he is overqualified may view the job as only a temporary way to make ends meet.

Ask for and verify a recommendation from the applicant's most recent employer. This precaution will not always uncover a person with a history of theft or willful destruction of company property, because many employers simply ask an employee caught stealing to resign. They often do not fire such an employee or prosecute him in the courts because they want to avoid embarrassment or do not want to admit to themselves that they have hired a thief. Few employers provide negative information about former employees because they fear lawsuits for defamation of character. In addition, courts have been notoriously lenient toward white-collar criminals, who often receive only small fines or jail terms of less than a year following convictions for theft amounting to thousands of dollars in cash or goods.

To prevent losses from employee dishonesty, the Council of Better Business Bureaus recommends watching for the following warning signs:[17]

- Accounting personnel who fail to keep their records and billings up to date
- Complaints by customers who claim their statements are inaccurate
- Employees who regularly ask for pay advances, turn down promotions, or fail to take vacations
- Employees who seem to be living a more expensive lifestyle than their pay would permit
- Slow collections and the writing off of an unusual number of bad debts

OFFICE SECURITY

Most companies have tangible assets to protect, such as computer equipment and highly sensitive information. The main problem in protecting office equipment, machines, and sensitive information is preventing access by

Proper security gives employees a feeling of safety where they work. It also reduces losses due to theft.

unauthorized personnel. It should not be possible for someone to enter an office without being screened at the entrance. To make this screening process easier, many offices have only one entrance; it is usually the only non-fire exit as well. Someone should be on hand at all times to greet visitors from the moment the office is opened until it is closed for the day. People who have no legitimate reason to go farther should not be allowed to do so.

SUPERVISORS AND ETHICS

For many years, one of the fringe benefits of working in a brewery was to drink your company's products on the job during lunch and on breaks. The Adolph Coors Company of Golden, Colorado, was such a company until 1994, when one of its employees was killed on company property after smashing his car into a utility pole. He had a blood-alcohol level "three times Colorado's legal limit at the time." At the request of the deceased's family and with input from its employees, Coors developed a new policy that allows employees to drink after work in eating areas. "Consumption is to be modest. By that we mean, not to exceed two 12-ounce beers for half an hour after work," according to a company spokesperson. "The company also plans to beef up educational programs for employees on alcohol use. . . . Coors, the nation's third-largest brewery, is the last major U.S. brewery to ban on-the-job beer consumption." Many breweries continue to give their employees free cases of beer each month or to allow them to purchase cases at a discount.

What is your feeling about the new policy? What about allowing employees to purchase or take home free beer each month?

Source: Chicago Tribune. "Coors Halts On-Job Drinking After Worker's Death" (October 7, 1994): sect. 3, 3.

SHOP SECURITY

Shop or plant security has some parallels to office security. Again, access by unauthorized personnel is the biggest problem standing in the way of safety and security. Similar controls can be exercised over people who attempt to enter the area. Employees may secure their personal belongings in lockers or check them with the company's security personnel on entering the plant or shop.

Plant and office security pose some additional problems, however. Besides protecting property and information from theft, you must be concerned with the prevention of vandalism and fires.

Vandalism is generally considered to be wanton or willful destruction of or damage to another's property. Disgruntled employees and outsiders sometimes vandalize company property. Whoever does the damage, some simple precautions can help prevent or minimize losses.

To begin with, make control over and security for all equipment, machines, tools, and other expensive pieces of company property the responsibility of specified people. Portable pieces of equipment should be issued only on request and should be returned by the persons to whom they were issued. Physical facilities must be kept clean and under observation at regular and irregular intervals. Storage areas require extra security measures if they contain sensitive or highly valuable materials. Closed-circuit television, guards, proximity devices, and alarm systems are popular but expensive prevention and detection measures. Locks remain the primary means of security used by business firms, but they cannot prevent trouble or vandalism if they are not used properly.

vandalism
wanton or willful destruction of or damage to another's property

SHOPLIFTING

Surveys in the retailing industry indicate that shoplifting is a major problem. For example, a 2001 survey revealed that shrinkage in the supermarket industry was equal to 2.26 percent of sales. While shoplifting accounts for 23 percent of shrinkage in supermarkets, 26 percent is accounted for by cashiers.[18] Another survey, focusing on theft, collected data from 30 retail companies having 10,663 stores. This survey provided evidence of widespread shoplifting: 503,860 shoplifters were apprehended in 2000 in these stores.[19] We all lose because stores must raise prices and spend money to prevent thefts by customers. When stores raise their prices, they become less competitive. Dollars lost to theft and spent on security are not available to make businesses more productive and profitable.

Most experts agree that companies can reduce losses by training employees to look out for shoplifters. As a supervisor of retail sales people, you can train your people never to leave a customer alone or out of sight long enough to pocket merchandise. Employees can be trained to catch credit card thieves and users of invalid credit cards by teaching and enforcing proper clearance procedures. Finally, you can enforce anti-theft procedures, such as keeping display cases locked and displaying one item to one customer at a time.

Your employer may offer other remedies and prevention measures as well, such as rewards for catching shoplifters and for recovering stolen or void credit cards. Store detectives posing as shoppers and closed-circuit TVs provide means of monitoring shoppers. Shops can protect merchandise with price tags that self-destruct when tampered with or with tags that only store personnel can remove. Checkpoint Systems Inc., an electronic security firm in New Jersey, manufactures electronic circuits that set off alarms at exits. Such circuits are quite small and can be built into a product's packaging or affixed to a piece of paper and inserted in a product. The cost of installing the system can be recovered in a relatively short time through loss prevention.[20]

Cub Foods in Colorado Springs had a big shoplifting problem until it created and installed two cardboard cops in its aisles. Each is a 6-foot stand-up photograph of a real cop in uniform. The figures are placed in aisles where there have been shoplifting losses. Since their installation, shoplifting is down 30 percent.[21] Wal-Mart's famous senior citizen "greeters" became a fixture in its stores when it became obvious that they reduced store losses to shoplifters.

In addition, the Council of Better Business Bureaus recommends the following deterrents and devices to protect your business:[22]

- Make everyone leaving the store pass through a checkout lane.
- Reduce the number of exits. Unguarded exits can be converted into emergency exits with noise alarms. Unused checkout lanes should be closed and blocked off.
- Make displays symmetrical and organized to make it easier to notice when an item is missing.

- Keep high-cost, high-risk items in locked displays, behind the counters, or on chains.
- Require all packages brought into the store by customers to be checked.
- Be alert for the following: customers who linger in one place, wander aimlessly, and handle lots of merchandise or customers who create distracting situations. They may be creating a diversion for an accomplice who will steal while shop personnel are distracted.

FIRE PREVENTION

Each year, fire departments in the United States are called out to almost 2 million fires. Fires cause approximately 4,000 U.S. deaths and 25,000 injuries each year. In addition, annual property damage from fires amounts to approximately $8 billion.[23]

Although you are not expected to be a professional firefighter, you are expected to minimize the risk of a fire starting in any area over which you have control. A concern for fire prevention begins with the initial training of each employee and continues to be reinforced by fire prevention programs throughout the year. Every department should conduct regularly scheduled inspections. All of your people represent potential causes of fires, just as they can also provide detection and prevention. All employees should be made to feel that fire prevention and detection is a personal responsibility. Such an attitude is instilled through your actions and words and by your responding in a positive way each time a subordinate tells you about a potential fire hazard or takes time to remove one. Exhibit 16.2 is a sample fire prevention checklist.

Be certain that all pieces of firefighting equipment, such as extinguishers and hoses, are visible, accessible, and in proper working order, and make sure that you and your people know where they are and how to use them. Different kinds of fires require different kinds of firefighting equipment. The wrong type of extinguishing agent—such as water used on a grease fire—can spread the fire and increase the likelihood of injuries and property damage. Periodic but unpredictable fire drills will prepare your people for the worst and will reinforce proper evacuation procedures and routes.

Protecting People

Protecting people from illness, accidents, and injuries is not only smart business, it is required by law as well. By law, a business is responsible for injuries suffered by its employees if the injuries occur during or arise as a result of the employee's employment.

accident
any unforeseen or
unplanned incident or event

An **accident** is defined as any unforeseen or unplanned incident or event. An accident does not necessarily result in damage to people or property. Although accidents usually are unforeseen, many are not unforeseeable. Planning and safety programs can and do yield significant

Sample checklist for fire prevention. **Exhibit 16.2**

FIRE PROTECTION

	OK	Needed
1. Are portable fire extinguishers provided in adequate number and type?	○	○
2. Are fire extinguishers inspected monthly for general conditions and operability and noted on the inspection tag?	○	○
3. Are fire extinguishers recharged regularly and properly noted on the inspection tag?	○	○
4. Are fire extinguishers mounted in readily accessible locations?	○	○
5. If you have interior standpipes and valves, are these inspected regularly?	○	○
6. If you have a fire alarm system, is it tested at least annually?	○	○
7. Are plant employees periodically instructed in the use of extinguishers and fire protection procedures?	○	○
8. If you have outside private fire hydrants, were they flushed within the last year and placed on a regular maintenance schedule?	○	○
9. Are fire doors and shutters in good operating condition?	○	○
Are they unobstructed and protected against obstruction?	○	○
10. Are fusible links in place?	○	○
11. Is your local fire department well acquainted with your plant, location, and specific hazards?	○	○

12. Automatic Sprinklers:

Are water control valves, air and water pressures checked weekly? _____

Are control valves locked open? _____

Is maintenance of the system assigned to responsible persons or a sprinkler contractor? Who? _____

Are sprinkler heads protected by metal guards where exposed to mechanical damage? _____

Is proper minimum clearance maintained around sprinkler heads? _____

Source: OSHA Handbook for Small Businesses.

decreases in accidents. In addition, engineering **ergonomics**—the design of work sites, machinery, equipment, and systems to minimize stress and injury on the job—can produce dramatic improvements in accident rates. We will discuss several approaches for providing safer and healthier workplaces in this chapter.

OVERWORK

Downsizing and other lean staffing practices have resulted in overwork for millions of workers in the United States. Overwork has both physical and mental effects. In order to cope with overwork, many workers take unscheduled days off by calling in sick. A survey of 401 companies found a 25 percent increase in such absences in 1997. Another survey found an 11 percent increase in lost time since 1995. Interestingly, workers have apparently adopted rationales for these absences similar to those offered by corporations for downsizing:

> For years, workers have been pressing for more flexibility. Employers have responded with new policies, but slowly. Now, it appears, employees are simply taking the time off when they need it, whether or not their employers formally sanction it. "The American work force has become sophisticated enough to know that the company is going to do what the company has to do to compete globally," including layoffs and restructurings, . . . "What we see now is the individual saying, 'There are some things I have to do, too.'" Increasingly, "it's a two-way street."[24]

PREVENTIVE APPROACHES TO SAFETY AND HEALTH

Although each working environment is unique, each has certain hazards and types of accidents that can be identified and removed or neutralized so that they cause a minimum amount of damage and human suffering. Studies over the years by the Occupational Safety and Health Administration (OSHA) have found the following basic elements in workplaces that have good accident prevention programs and records:

1. The top manager assumes the leadership role.
2. Responsibility for safety and health activities is clearly assigned.
3. Possible accident causes are properly identified and either eliminated or controlled.
4. Appropriate safety- and health-related training is instituted.
5. An accident record system is maintained.
6. A medical and first aid system is ready for possible use.
7. Continued activity is designed to foster on-the-job awareness and acceptance of safety and health responsibility by every employee.
8. People are forewarned about and told how to cope with the hazards they must face on the job.

Many symptoms in the workplace can let you know that you have a problem or will have one in the future. Some obvious signs are accident and injury statistics, employee illnesses that are linked to the workplace, and absentee figures related to these. Not-so-obvious signals include labor turnover, excessive waste or scrap, increases in the number of "near misses" that could have caused injuries or property damage, and the pending receipt of new equipment and new employees. These last two signal a need for safety training.

A rising concern for most employers is the presence of indoor pollution in the plant and office. What has become known as *sick-building syndrome* (SBS) may be caused by one contaminant or by several acting in concert. Indoor locations commonly have chemicals such as asbestos and formaldehyde as well as radon gas. Indoor locations also serve as incubators for various forms of viruses and bacteria with fungal agents, such as molds, that can cause a number of illnesses. Some fungal agents can cause esophageal cancer and deforming arthritis.[25] The EPA has discovered a number of potential cancer-causing substances in offices:

> Many studies conducted by EPA over the last 25 years have shown measurable levels of more than 107 known carcinogens in modern offices. The presence of these volatile organic compounds (VOCs) is due to the change from open windows to energy-efficient living and working environments—modifications made necessary during the energy crisis of the 1970s. Combined with the advent of modern building methodology and products, the result has been energy-efficient offices that contain amounts of known cancer-causing chemicals.[26]

As indoor air pollution becomes a larger problem as more structures are built or renovated to become more energy efficient, it will be important to address these health hazards. Exhibit 16.3 offers advice on avoiding and cleaning up indoor pollutants.

The symptoms of sick-building syndrome include headaches; irritations of the nose, throat, and eyes; skin rashes; dizziness; nausea; frequent respiratory infections; and wheezing and cough. While employees do not always become sufficiently ill to miss work, these health hazards probably detract from their productivity. Ergonomics consultant John Jukes maintains that investments in improving building environments to eliminate such health hazards provide good economic returns in less absenteeism, improved productivity, and better morale.[27]

INSUFFICIENT WORK BREAKS

Insufficient work breaks have become another problem, according to OSHA. In a number of industries, employees simply do not get sufficient opportunities to use the restroom facilities. The following provides some examples:

> An Iowa teacher brings her entire class to the bathroom with her when she needs to go and can't find a substitute. A North Carolina meatpacker had to wait so

| Exhibit | **16.3** | *Avoiding and dealing with indoor air pollution.* |

BEFORE MOVING TO NEW QUARTERS

1. Check the site history. What have been the past uses of the premises? Who have been the tenants/owners?

2. Check with the neighbors. Ask them if there have been any pollution problems in the past with your proposed location and the immediate area.

3. Check with the local city hall. What have been the past zonings for the property? Has there been any problem with the occupants or the facilities?

4. Check the building's plans. Track down the construction drawings and specifications for building materials to spot hidden problems like foam insulation or asbestos.

5. Have the ductwork inspected. Look for mold, fibrous particles, humid conditions, and general state of repair and efficiency of operation.

6. Get a certification of habitability from the owner. Get the landlord or seller to guarantee in writing that the premises are not contaminated.

DEALING WITH YOUR EXISTING POLLUTION

1. Get reliable help. You need professionals to search for and to cure most problems. Find an expert to inspect the premises.

2. Restrict use of the premises to nonsmoking.

3. Provide some means for periodic venting. Periodically air out the indoor areas.

4. Keep all ductwork clean and dry. Bacteria and fungi grow in dark, moist places.

5. Remove and avoid installing anything that gives off unpleasant, irritating odors. An unpleasant smell generally means complications down the road.

6. Provide lots of plants to absorb carbon dioxide and odors. They give off oxygen as well.

long for permission to go that she soiled her clothes. For most people using the toilet at work hardly causes trouble; they just get up and go. But for teachers, factory workers, telemarketers, farm workers and others, meeting this simple need can mean humiliating pleas for permission and even risking the loss of their job. Some try not to drink liquids or go to the toilet all day—habits that court medical problems.[28]

While OSHA regulations mandate that employers have adequate numbers of bathrooms, no requirement for allowing employees to use these facilities existed prior to 1998, when OSHA remedied this situation with a directive for bathroom access.

Employers who treat their employees with such disregard are prime candidates for unionization. The food processing industry has been criticized for poor treatment of employees in this area:

> "Every time I work on a campaign in the poultry industry, this is the No. 1 issue," said spokesman Greg Denier of the 1.4 million member United Food and Commercial Workers International union. "It goes to human dignity."[29]

AIDS IN THE WORKPLACE

AIDS has claimed the lives of 25 million people throughout the world since the disease was identified some 20 years ago. In 2001 it was estimated that 40 million people have AIDS or HIV and that 8,000 die each day from the disease. While there have been breakthroughs in drug therapies that prolong life, the disease remains a terrible threat to life.[30] Unfortunately, employers are sometimes ill prepared to deal with HIV-positive employees or ones with AIDS. Employers must have an AIDS policy and offer an ongoing educational effort to deal with the epidemic.

In their search for guidelines, many companies have taken advantage of a variety of volunteer speakers' programs, such as those offered by the HIV Peer Network in New York, and have adopted as policy the guidelines developed by the Citizens Commission on AIDS of New York and New Jersey. Among these are:

- People with HIV-positive status and AIDS sufferers are entitled to the same rights and opportunities as people with other serious or life-threatening illnesses.

- At the very least, all policies should comply with all relevant laws and regulations, such as the Americans with Disabilities Act (ADA), which protects all persons with AIDS and HIV from discrimination.

- Employers should provide up-to-date information and training on risk reduction for employees.

- Employers should protect the confidentiality of employee medical records.

- Employers should provide education programs for all employees before any problems arise in the workplace.

A manager's kit, which includes posters and pamphlets with guidance on dealing with AIDS in the workplace, is available from the Centers for Disease Control and Prevention in Atlanta. Their AIDS Hotline is 1-800-342-AIDS. Your local chapter of the American Red Cross or the Equal Employment Opportunity Commission's ADA Hotline at 1-800-669-EEOC can provide additional information.

DRUGS AND EMPLOYEES

Employees whose performance is affected by dependency on alcohol or other drugs are a danger to themselves and to others. The drug-dependent employee may steal from the employer or from fellow employees to get the money needed to support a habit. Small mistakes can become major problems and can lead to accidents, injuries, and worse. Consider the following statistics about substance abuse:[31]

- Over 7.4 million U.S. workers use illicit drugs.
- Drug and alcohol use is a contributing cause of 38 to 58 percent of on-the-job injuries.
- The likelihood of injuring oneself or others is 3.6 times higher for workers using illicit drugs.
- The likelihood of filing worker compensation claims is five times higher for employees using illicit drugs.
- Workers who abuse alcohol have 16 more days of annual absenteeism than non-abusers.

To determine if your organization, unit, or team has a substance abuse problem or the potential for developing one, the U.S. Department of Labor suggests the following:

- Look at the statistics on such things as absenteeism, accidents, property losses, security breaches, and workers' compensation claims. Compare them to the past and to national, state, local, and industrial averages for your type of business.
- Consult with all organizational members to get their observations and sense of the extent of the problem. Employees should be part of the investigation and help formulate policy and corrective measures.
- Employees can play various roles to achieve and maintain a workplace free of substance abusers.

Because substance abuse tends to be a hidden problem, many organizations have decided to proceed on the assumption that there may be individuals in the workplace who have or are developing a problem with alcohol or other drugs. The U.S. Department of Labor recommends a five-part workplace substance abuse program that includes:

1. A written substance abuse policy
2. An employee education and awareness program
3. A supervisory training program
4. Access to an employee assistance program
5. An appropriate drug testing program

Step one communicates a clear commitment to creating and maintaining a workplace free of substance abuse. An effective substance abuse policy should:

- State why the policy is necessary and what it is meant to encourage and prevent.

- Define what constitutes an infraction, and describe the consequences.

- Recognize that substance abuse is treatable, and identify company or community resources where employees with problems can obtain help.

- Describe the responsibility of an employee with a substance abuse problem to seek and complete required treatment.

- State the company's position on drug testing and, if testing occurs, the consequences of a positive test result.

- Assure employees that participation in assistance programs is confidential and will not jeopardize employment or advancement. However, you must also inform employees that participation will not protect them from disciplinary action for continued unacceptable job performance or rule violations. It is important to keep the results of drug tests confidential because of the potential for lawsuits over defamation. In such a case, "the truth is not necessarily a defense. Even if the information is true, you can be held liable for telling others 'with malice.' Accordingly, think carefully about whether the people you're passing information to really need to know."[32]

Exhibit 16.4 provides a model for a substance abuse policy.

Step two requires companies to inform employees about drug and alcohol abuse and its effect on the company's safety, security, health care costs, productivity, and quality. Companies must explain their policies and how testing and assistance programs will be utilized. To be truly effective, an education and awareness program must be an ongoing one, not just a one-time effort.

Step three requires supervisors, team leaders, and team facilitators—those most directly responsible for enforcing the policy—to learn how to detect performance problems that may indicate substance abuse. Although supervisors at every level are responsible for observing and documenting unsatisfactory work performance or behavior, they are not responsible for diagnosing substance abuse or treating substance abuse problems. They do need to know the signs that may accompany substance abuse and what to do when they observe them. For example, supervisors may be required to counsel employees and refer them to an assistance program, a company physician, or drug testing program.

Step four specifies ways for dealing with substance abuse. Providing access to a substance abuse EAP communicates a clear commitment by a company (and its unions) that it wishes to save valued employees and help them remain or once again become effective performers. With or without a company or union EAP, all employees should be able to inform coworkers about alcohol and other drugs, confront users with their unacceptable work behaviors, and provide referral information.

These four steps must occur before drug testing can be initiated. Nonetheless, drug testing of new applicants for jobs is rapidly becoming the

Exhibit 16.4 *Sample drug abuse policy statement.*

COMPANY NAME

Street Address, City, State • Phone • Fax • email@company.com

---

DRUG ABUSE POLICY STATEMENT

[Company Name] is committed to providing a safe work environment and to fostering the well-being and health of its employees. That commitment is jeopardized when any [Company Name] employee illegally uses drugs on the job, comes to work under their influence, or possesses, distributes, or sells drugs in the workplace. Therefore, [Company Name] has established the following policy:

(1) It is a violation of company policy for any employee to possess, sell, trade, or offer for sale illegal drugs or otherwise engage in the illegal use of drugs on the job.

(2) It is a violation of company policy for anyone to report to work under the influence of illegal drugs.

(3) It is a violation of company policy for anyone to use prescription drugs illegally. (However, nothing in this policy precludes the appropriate use of legally prescribed medications.)

(4) Violations of this policy are subject to disciplinary action up to and including termination.

It is the responsibility of the company's supervisors to counsel employees whenever they see changes in performance or behavior that suggest an employee has a drug problem. Although it is not the supervisor's job to diagnose personal problems, the supervisor should encourage such employees to seek help and advise them about available resources for getting help. Everyone shares responsibility for maintaining a safe work environment, and coworkers should encourage anyone who may have a drug problem to seek help.

The goal of this policy is to balance our respect for individuals with the need to maintain a safe, productive, and drug-free environment. The intent of this policy is to offer a helping hand to those who need it, while sending a clear message that the illegal use of drugs is incompatible with employment at [Company Name].

If your company is subject to the requirements of the Drug-Free Workplace Act of 1988 (by nature of a grant from or contract with the federal government) you should add the following statement to your drug policy:

As a condition of employment, employees must abide by the terms of this policy and must notify [Company Name] in writing of any conviction of a violation of a criminal drug statute occurring in the workplace no later than five calendar days after such conviction.

Source: President's Drug Advisory Council, Executive Office of the President.

norm. Although routine drug testing for existing employees was controversial in the past and is affected by union contracts and various laws, there is greater clarity today.

> Private employers may screen employees with pre-employment testing, investigate accidents by testing those involved, and conduct random drug tests. Recent litigation has focused not on whether an employer may test but on how the test is done.[33]

The legal environment is more complex, however, than this general statement would seem to indicate. For example, approximately 10 states have laws that regulate drug testing in employment situations. Fortunately, a comprehensive description of state regulations, the *Guide to State and Federal Drug-Testing Laws* has been compiled by the Institute for a Drug-Free Workplace to provide guidance to employers. This publication is available from the Society for Human Resource Management (SHRM) at www.shrm.org.[34]

Organizations doing business with the federal government are covered by the Drug-Free Workplace Act of 1988. These organizations must certify that they provide a drug-free workplace, have a substance abuse policy, conduct ongoing drug awareness programs, and require all employees to notify their companies of any criminal drug statute conviction. They also must notify the federal government of such violations and impose sanctions for an employee convicted of drug abuse violations in the workplace. The U. S. Department of Transportation (DOT) requires drug testing of employees in safety-sensitive positions and drug abuse awareness education for supervisors and employees. In the federal government, routine, random drug testing has been the rule in the armed services for military and some civilian employees since the early 1980s. DOT began urine tests for drug and alcohol use during annual physicals at about the same time and began random testing of air-traffic controllers, aviation and railway safety inspectors, electronics technicians, and employees with top secret clearances in 1987.

As noted earlier, state and local laws tend to limit drug testing of employees. For example, a Connecticut statute allows random testing only in certain highly restricted circumstances. But when drug testing is used selectively, in sensitive work settings, and testing is performed with proper collection and safeguards, the courts have ruled in its favor. The U. S. Department of Labor suggests asking the following questions before testing employees for drugs:

- Who will be tested? (Only applicants? All employees?)
- When will testing be done? (After all accidents? When an employee behaves abnormally? As part of a routine physical? Randomly?)
- For which drugs will testing be done? (Only for illegal drugs? For prescription drugs that may affect work performance? For alcohol?)
- How frequently will testing be done? (Weekly? Monthly? Annually?)

SUPERVISING TEAMS

According to public health reports, smoking costs America over $72 billion each year in health care costs, with losses in productivity accounting for $40 billion of that amount. The public is aware of the consequences of smoking; a Gallup survey found that 94 percent of the survey's American respondents wanted some type of workplace restrictions on smoking. Because of such views of smoking, many state and local governments have implemented regulations that restrict smoking in the workplace, but such regulations vary greatly. Because of the toll of smoking on health, the financial costs associated with smoking, and legal regulations, the number of companies that forbid smoking on the premises has increased dramatically. A survey by the National Cancer Institute found that the proportion of companies that prohibited smoking in offices or common areas increased from 47 percent in 1993 to 65 percent in 1998. The change is even more impressive when today's practices are compared with the mid-1980s, when only 3 percent of companies prohibited smoking on the premises.

Some companies have been aggressive in their attempts to deal with smoking in the workplace. For example, FedEx prohibits smoking in its buildings and aircraft.

CDW Computer Center Inc, which has 1,500 employees, not only prohibits smoking in its buildings, but also in the parking lots. Controls Unlimited also prohibits smoking on the premises and allows employees to smoke outside only on their own time during lunch. In addition, some companies and organizations do not hire smokers. For example, the American Cancer Society does not hire smokers. While there is no law preventing employers from discriminating against smokers, legal issues remain to be resolved. One practical consideration is that even if the company has the right to exclude smokers from being hiring, rejected applicants can still sue the company and it will cost the company to defend itself, even if it has the right to reject such applicants.

Another positive employer practice for dealing with smoking is to provide support for employees who wish to quit smoking. FedEx provides as much as $150 to reimburse employees for Nicorette gum, the drug Zyban (which is prescribed to help people quit smoking), and acupuncture treatments for smoking. The company also has a registered nurse who runs a smoking cessation program for the company.

Source: Grensing-Pophal, Lin, "Smoking Is a Burning Issue for HR Policy Makers," *HR Magazine* (May 1999): 58–66.

- What test will be used, and what procedures will be followed? (How will specimens be collected, identified, and tracked? Will a physician with appropriate training interpret results?)
- What action will be taken if an applicant tests positive? (Refer employees to counseling and treatment after first positive but fire after second?)
- What precautions will be taken to protect an individual's privacy and the confidentiality of test results?

Various organizations and hotlines can give you more information and help you create a drug-free workplace and an employee assistance program. Here are several that you will find eager to help:

- The National Clearinghouse for Alcohol and Drug Information: 1-800-729-6686
- The Drug-Free Workplace Helpline: 1-800-967-5752
- 800 Substance Abuse Line: 1-800-662-HELP
- The American Council on Alcoholism Helpline: 1-800-527-5344

FAMILY LEAVE

As noted in Chapter 14, the Family and Medical Leave Act provides certain protections to employees who have health and other problems. The act affects employers—businesses, nonprofits, and governmental units—with 50 or more employees by granting their employees up to 12 weeks unpaid leave for the birth or adoption of a child; caring for a spouse, child, or parent; or taking care of one's own illness. During the leave, the employer must guarantee that the employee will be able to return to the same or a comparable job. If employees have health care benefits, those benefits must be continued during the term of the leave. Employers may apply employees' accrued sick leave to the leave period. They may choose to exempt employees in the top 10 percent of compensation, those who have not worked at least a year, and those who have not worked at least 25 hours per week or 1,250 hours during the past 12 months. Employees must provide 30 days' notice to their employers for foreseeable leaves.[35]

THE SUPERVISOR'S ROLE

Safety. Nearly all efforts at promoting safety and identifying and getting help to the troubled worker depend on you as the supervisor. Safety programs, regulations, procedures, and committees need your input and enforcement efforts in order to work effectively and efficiently. Exhibit 16.5 outlines your role in efforts at safety promotion and enforcement.

Many sources of help are available to you for identifying problem areas and taking corrective actions. Exhibit 16.6 lists the most important areas to consider when conducting safety and health inspections. When you have identified the hazards, you are ready to set up and implement controls to prevent, eliminate, or deal with each of them. These controls eliminate hazards or reduce their potential to cause harm. Dangerous machines can be eliminated or fitted with proper safeguards. Operators can be thoroughly trained and drilled in safety procedures. Personal protective gear can be purchased, issued, and checked regularly to see that it works and is being used correctly. Access to hazards can be carefully controlled by restricting it to those who are aware of and equipped to deal with hazardous situations.

Substance abuse. Your role as a supervisor is crucial in spotting troubled workers who need special assistance and in getting them started on a program designed to meet their needs. Look for warning signs such as changes

Exhibit 16.5 — *Typical profile of a supervisor with low accident and injury rates.*

THE SAFETY-MINDED SUPERVISOR:

1. Takes the initiative in telling management about ideas for a safer layout of equipment, tools, and processes.

2. Knows the value of machine guards and makes sure the proper guards are provided and used.

3. Takes charge of operations that are not routine to make certain that safety precautions are determined.

4. Is an expert on waste disposal for housekeeping and fire protection.

5. Arranges for adequate storage and enforces good housekeeping.

6. Works with every employee without favoritism.

7. Keeps eyes open for the new employee or the experienced employee doing a new job.

8. Establishes good relations with union stewards and the safety committee.

9. Sets a good example in safety practices.

10. Never lets a simple safety violation occur without talking to the employee immediately.

11. Not only explains how to do a job, but also shows how and observes to ensure continuing safety.

12. Takes pride in knowing how to use all equipment safely.

13. Knows what materials are hazardous and how to store them safely.

14. Continues to "talk safety" and impress its importance on all employees.

Source: U. S. Department of Labor.

in an employee's routine and behaviors. Increases in an employee's tardiness, absenteeism, ineffectiveness, or need for disciplinary action may signal that the employee has a personal or drug-related problem. Employees who suddenly isolate themselves from fellow workers and who become argumentative with their peers are asking for help.

When you think you have a troubled employee on your hands, let the person know what you think, and recommend or refer him to those in your company who can help. Your company's medical department will work with the individual or refer him to an appropriate agency for treatment. Failure to comply with the company's directives may leave the employee subject to disciplinary measures and termination. You need to keep your people aware of the help that is available to them, and your company should have an ongoing educational program to alert employees to the dangers of drug abuse.

Typical scope of a self-inspection program.

Exhibit 16.6

Processing, receiving, shipping, and storage—Equipment, job planning, layout, heights, floor loads, projection of materials, materials handling, storage methods

Building and grounds condition—Floors, walls, ceilings, exits, stairs, walkways, ramps, platforms, driveways, aisles

Housekeeping program—Waste disposal, tools, objects, materials, leakage and spillage, cleaning methods, schedules, work areas, remote areas, storage areas

Electricity—Equipment, switches, breakers, fuses, switch boxes, junctions, special fixtures, circuits, insulation, extensions, tools, motors, grounding, NEC compliance

Lighting—Type, intensity, controls, conditions, diffusion, location, glare and shadow control

Heating and ventilating—Type, effectiveness, temperature, humidity, controls, natural and artificial ventilation and exhausting

Machinery—Points of operation, flywheels, gears, shafts, pulleys, key ways, belts, couplings, sprockets, chains, frames, controls, lighting for tools and equipment, brakes, exhausting, feeding, oiling, adjusting, maintenance, lock out, grounding, work space, location, purchasing standards

Personnel—Training, experience, methods of checking machines before use, clothing, personal protective equipment, use of guards, tool storage, work practices, method of cleaning/oiling/adjusting machinery

Hand and power tools—Purchasing standards, inspection, storage, repair, types, maintenance, grounding, use and handling

Chemicals—Storage, handling, transportation, spills, disposals, amounts used, toxicity or other harmful effects, warning signs, supervision, training, protective clothing and equipment

Fire prevention—Extinguishers, alarms, sprinklers, smoking rules, exits, personnel assigned, separation of flammable materials and dangerous operations, explosive-proof fixtures in hazardous locations, waste disposal

Maintenance—Regularity, effectiveness, training of personnel, materials and equipment used, records maintained, method of locking out machinery, general methods

Personal protective equipment—Type, size, maintenance, repair, storage, assignment of responsibility, purchasing methods, standards observed, training in care and use, rules of use, method of assignment

Source: OSHA Handbook for Small Businesses.

The Occupational Safety and Health Act (1970)

OSHA

the federal agency called the Occupational Safety and Health Administration

In 1970, Congress passed the Occupational Safety and Health Act, which created the Occupational Safety and Health Administration (**OSHA**) "to assure so far as possible every working man and woman in the nation safe and healthful working conditions to preserve our human resources." The law, which became effective in April 1971, applies to all employers engaged in any business affecting commerce and employing people. Its terms apply to all the states, territories, and possessions of the United States as well as to employees of the federal government. The law does not apply to working conditions protected under other federal occupational safety and health laws such as the Federal Coal Mine Health and Safety Act, the Atomic Energy Act, and the Migrant Health Act.

According to OSHA, each employer has the duty to furnish employees a working environment free from recognized hazards that cause or are likely to cause death or serious physical harm. Administration and enforcement of OSHA are vested in the secretary of labor and in the Occupational Safety and Health Review Commission, a quasi-judicial board of three members appointed by the president. Research and related functions are vested in the secretary of health and human services, whose functions will for the most part be carried out by the National Institute for Occupational Safety and Health. The institute conducts research and experimental programs for developing criteria for new and improved job safety and health standards.

OCCUPATIONAL SAFETY AND HEALTH STANDARDS

Various safety and health standards have been issued by OSHA and are available to you through your company or from one of the many local OSHA offices in major cities around the country. Exhibit 16.7 shows a representative OSHA regulation. All help define protective measures or ways in which to deal with an identifiable hazard. We will discuss the activities of OSHA in more detail at the end of this chapter.

It is not enough to warn and instruct employees about safety haz-

Supervisors of workers in hazardous situations need to make sure their employees understand their jobs and are properly protected. Safety of workers is foremost.

Sample OSHA standard dealing with medical services and first aid. Exhibit 16.7

1910.151 Medical Services and First Aid.

(a) The employer shall ensure the ready availability of medical personnel for advice and consultation on matters of plant health.

(b) In the absence of an infirmary, clinic, or hospital in near proximity to the workplace, which is used for the treatment of all injured employees, a person or persons shall be adequately trained to render first aid. First-aid supplies approved by the consulting physician shall be readily available.

(c) Where the eyes or body of any person may be exposed to injurious corrosive material, suitable facilities for quick drenching or flushing of the eyes and body shall be provided within the work area for immediate emergency use.

Source: General Industry Standards, USDOL-OSHA 2206.

ards. Employers are responsible for unsafe behaviors of their employees, such as the failure to wear safety equipment. Thus supervisors also must enforce instructions and remove or eliminate hazards. Supervisors who ignore company or OSHA safety rules and standards can cause a doubling of the OSHA-prescribed penalties if accidents are the result of such behavior. All employers and supervisors are obligated to familiarize themselves and their subordinates with the standards that apply to them.

COMPLIANCE COMPLAINTS

Employees may file complaints about safety and health violations to any local OSHA office. Complaining employees may not be persecuted in any way by their employers. Furthermore, since the *Whirlpool Corporation v. Marshall* case in 1980, workers have had the right to refuse a job assignment or to walk off the job "because of a reasonable apprehension of health [hazards] or serious injury coupled with a reasonable belief that no less drastic alternative is available." This wording and other words in the Supreme Court decision have been interpreted to mean that workers may refuse to perform work that constitutes a clear and present danger, in their minds, to their safety. Employers are not required to pay workers who do not perform such work, but they may not reprimand them in any way.

OSHA INSPECTIONS

OSHA is allowed to select firms for regular inspection visits if they have 10 or more employees, below-average safety records, or employees who have filed complaints. Since the 1979 Supreme Court decision in *Marshall v. Barlow's, Inc.,* employers do not have to admit OSHA inspectors who do not have a search warrant. But all companies (except those with 9 or fewer employees) must keep OSHA records on accidents, illnesses, and employee exposure to potentially toxic materials or other harmful physical agents. Millions of employees have the right to demand information about hazardous chemicals at their work sites. They can demand to know the identities and compositions of chemicals that they are exposed to at work. When OSHA compliance officers (inspectors) call, they may be on a routine inspection, or they may be responding to an employee's complaint. In the latter case, the inspectors need not limit their visits to investigating the complaint.

ON-SITE CONSULTATION

OSHA has developed a free on-site consultation service that is available to any employer on request. An OSHA consultant will visit a business and tour the facilities, pointing out what operations are governed by OSHA standards and how to interpret the applicable standards. The inspector will point out any violations and offer suggestions for how to correct them. No citations are issued, but—as part of the decision to request a consultation—the employer must agree to eliminate, within a reasonable time, all hazards discovered.

State Programs

When the Occupational Safety and Health Act was passed in 1970, many states already had their own state safety laws. Some of these laws were criticized for their weak standards, ineffective administration, and lax enforcement. Others were considered quite acceptable. States have the opportunity to develop and administer their own safety and health programs, provided that they can demonstrate that their programs are "at least as effective" as the federal program. State safety and health programs must be approved by OSHA. About half of the states have developed and are administering their own safety and health programs.

Workers' compensation is another major area of state legislation. Prior to 1910, workers were injured frequently on the job. Their lost wages and medical bills were usually their own problems unless they could prove in a court of law that their employers were the sole force or cause of their injuries. If a worker contributed in any way to the injury suffered or if a worker knew the work to be dangerous, the employer could usually avoid legal responsibility for damages.

Workers' compensation insurance programs compensate employees for medical and disability expenses, as well as for income lost because of an illness or injury. They are state mandated and may be either elective or compulsory. Under elective laws, a company may provide the protection the

workers' compensation
federal and state laws designed to compensate employees for illnesses and injuries that arise out of and in the course of their employment

law requires on its own by insuring itself against worker claims. But employees or their families would then be free to sue the employer for damages for injuries, illnesses, or deaths. "Large employers that self-insure pay these claims out of the corporate kitty, while smaller concerns typically purchase insurance."[36] A worker who suffers an illness or injury on the job can file a claim with the state's compensation board. Benefits are paid to individuals according to schedules stating fixed maximums that may be awarded by compensation boards.

Under compulsory workers' compensation laws, each employer within the state's jurisdiction must accept the application of the law and provide the benefits required. When the company provides the protection required by law through workers' compensation insurance, the employee who suffers an injury or illness may not sue.

The cost of workers' compensation insurance varies, depending on a company's history of worker claims. The more claims filed against a company, and the more benefits paid by an insurance company, the greater the premium charged for workers' compensation protection. Most businesses, therefore, try to insure workers' safety through the latest in safety devices and safety rules. They do this not only to protect their workers from injury but also to protect their profits from the drain of insurance premiums and self-insurance funds.

OshKosh B'Gosh, a maker of children's clothing, had a routine inspection from OSHA and received a citation. Plant operations were at the root of a growing number of cumulative trauma disorders (CTDs) such as carpal tunnel syndrome. According to Pat Hirschberg, the plant's safety chief, "the directive to fix the problem 'was the best thing that could have happened to us.'" A committee was created "to inspect every aspect of production and uncover the sources of injury. It found that most of the worker's problems arose from small, awkward motions that required force and were highly repetitious."[37] Operations caused abnormal use of fingers, wrists, and hands, and neither tables nor chairs were adjustable. The committee presented its findings and recommendations to senior management and convinced them to make several changes. As a result, the company hired engineers to design special equipment to facilitate production operations, introduced job rotation to vary employee activities, instituted training to teach proper equipment adjustment and work positions, and encouraged workers to bring their concerns to management so that changes could be made. The results were as follows:

> The number of claims jumped by a third when the program was introduced, as people began to pay attention to symptoms they might previously have ignored. But because these ailments were caught in the early stages, they never became costly or severe. [Workers' compensation] claims eventually retreated as the company's prevention strategy took effect. [In 1993] comp costs for the firm were down from 1992 by a third, or $2.7 million. That sum alone more than covers the cost of the company's long-term safety investment.[38]

Instant Replay

1. The security of your company's and subordinates' assets is partly your responsibility.

2. Your people depend on you and the company's policies and programs to protect them from recognized and recognizable hazards.

3. Although safety and security are everyone's legitimate concern, your organization depends on you and its other managers for planning, implementing, and enforcing proper programs.

4. Engineering, education (training), and enforcement are the keys to successful safety and security efforts.

5. Supervisors play a critical role in maintaining a drug-free work environment.

6. Supervisors who really care about safety and security listen to their employees, look for hazards, assign responsibility for safety and security, enforce standards and procedures, and discipline violators of safety and security policies.

Questions for Class Discussion

1. Can you define this chapter's key terms?

2. As a supervisor, how would you go about the task of safeguarding your office or shop environment?

3. What are a supervisor's duties with regard to fire prevention? With regard to fighting a fire?

4. How can a supervisor act to prevent losses from vandalism?

5. What are the major purposes of the Occupational Safety and Health Act? When did it become effective in enforcement efforts? How does it enforce its regulations?

6. What are an employer's rights with regard to OSHA inspectors?

Incident

Purpose: To acquaint you with the help available from public and private sources for creating a drug-free workplace.

Your task: Using the telephone numbers provided in this chapter, contact three sources and request their free materials. Summarize the materials, and present your summary to your class. Together with classmates, create a policy for your school or company.

Gerald Haley was the plant manager of the ALU-GULF aluminum smelting plant. As Gerald was reviewing the maintenance schedule for the next week, Del Walsh knocked on his door. Del was a consultant who was advising the company on the installation of new computer controls for the smelter.

DEL: "You're not going to be happy with some news I have for you."

GERALD: "Don't tell me the new controls aren't going to be ready on schedule! We can't take another delay."

DEL: "No, no, that's not it. About 20 minutes ago I went out to take a look at the ducks that are flying in to land on the water out by the pier where the bauxite ships dock. I was walking back from the pier and when I came by the storage warehouse I thought I smelled marijuana smoke. I looked through a small space in the big sliding doors and saw a couple of maintenance guys smoking a joint. I didn't get a good look at who they were, but I thought you ought to know."

GERALD: "You're right, I'm not happy about this. Are they still out there?"

DEL: "I don't think so because a truck pulled up to the doors of the warehouse and they probably slipped out the back door to avoid being seen. There was no way to see the back door from where I was and when the truck pulled in I couldn't see anyone in the warehouse."

GERALD: "Thanks for telling me, Del. We really can't have that stuff around here. As you know, our guys work around dangerous equipment and high voltage all the time. In addition, a lot of the work they do on the power lines to the smelter takes place about 250 feet in the air. There just isn't any room for error or inattention. Because of the danger we have a policy that makes use or possession of drugs or alcohol on the premises a basis for termination."

Gerald called the police, and they responded by sending three officers with drug detection dogs. The police took the dogs through the employees' locker room. The dogs detected no drugs in the locker room, so they shifted the search to the employees' cars in the parking lot. In about 10 minutes, the dogs detected drugs in one of the cars. The police could see what looked like a joint in the ashtray. The police then called in the license tag of the car and obtained the name of the owner. It turned out to be Harry Snider, one of the plant's maintenance workers. Gerald confronted Harry.

GERALD: "Harry, we received a report that two workers were smoking a joint in the warehouse this afternoon. When we brought in the drug dogs they searched the company parking lot and found what appears to be a marijuana joint in your car. As you know, we have a strong policy against using drugs or having drugs on the premises. Do you have anything to say?"

HARRY: "I don't smoke marijuana. If it really is marijuana then somebody else must have left it in there. It's not my dope."

GERALD: "Well, we're going to need a drug test. Are you willing to give us a specimen for a drug test?"

HARRY: "I told you I don't use drugs and that whatever the cops found isn't mine. I'm not going to go through any drug test. I've got some rights to privacy. The answer's no."

GERALD: "I will take your refusal to mean that you have declined the opportunity to establish your innocence. We're going to suspend you until we complete the analysis of the alleged joint and the rest of our investigation."

Three days later, after receiving positive test results on the alleged joint, the company terminated Harry. Harry filed a grievance with the union and the union pursued the case on to arbitration. The union argued that no employee should be fired for mere possession of marijuana and that Harry should be given a second chance.

Source: This case is based on a management brief written by Brian Meiners.

Questions

1. Do you agree with Gerald's actions in this situation? Explain.
2. Do you think Harry has a legitimate argument about privacy rights? Explain.
3. How do you think an arbitrator will rule in this case? What are the critical issues that will determine the ruling on Harry's case?
4. What do you think Gerald should do to prevent another drug incident like this? Why do you think an outsider discovered the marijuana use?

CASE PROBLEM 16.2 *No Chance for a Smoke Break*

Sonny Nygaard had not had a minute's rest all morning. Two shipments had gone out under rush conditions. As he and his coworker Dixy Paxon started the production run for the third shipment, the pulverizer had broken down. Sonny and Dixy had been lucky and could see the burned-out relay as soon as they removed the inspection cover. Unfortunately, it was in a difficult position to replace. While Sonny crawled under the pulverizer to remove the old relay, Dixy left to obtain a replacement. Dixy's departure left Sonny alone in the pulverizer room while other equipment was running. As a result, he had not been able to take his 10:00 A.M. break. Sonny finished removing the relay and crawled out from under the pulverizer. As he stood up, he brushed the dust off his clothes and reached into his pocket for a cigarette. He had just lit the cigarette and taken two puffs when his supervisor, Web Daniel, walked into the pulverizer room. Web saw his lit cigarette and said, "Put that damn thing out before you blow us all to Hell along with the rest of the whole plant! Are you crazy!"

Sonny said, "It just happened sort of automatically. I just didn't think about it. I haven't had a smoke break since we've been so busy this morning and I couldn't leave the area because Dixy left to get a new relay."

Web said, "I don't care what your excuse is. One spark and this place blows sky high. We've given you safety training, plastered this place with no-smoking signs, and enforced the rules. What does it take to get your attention? Go down to the plant manager's office. I'll be down in a few minutes."

Later, at the meeting with Web, the plant manager, and the union steward, Sonny explained that he had not intended to break the rule. He also said that he smoked three packs of cigarettes a day and couldn't go very long without having a smoke. The plant manager reminded him of the extreme danger of smoking in his work area and that violation of the no-smoking rule was grounds for termination on the first offense. He suspended Sonny pending completion of an investigation of the incident and a review of his work record.

Web and the plant manager reviewed Sonny's work and disciplinary records. Sonny had good performance evaluations. Web explained that Sonny was a good, dependable worker, had very low absenteeism, and had worked at the plant for seven years. Nonetheless, the disciplinary record indicated that Sonny had been disciplined on a previous occasion for smoking in an unauthorized area. This incident had taken place two years ago, before Sonny had been transferred into Web's section. Sonny had been suspended for two weeks for the rule violation, but it had taken place in a much less dangerous area than in the pulverizer room. The two managers also interviewed Sonny's coworkers and found that they considered him to be a solid worker. However, one of them came by the plant manager's office after their interviews and said that he had seen Sonny smoking in the pulverizer room on two previous occasions.

The plant manager and Web decided that the appropriate action would be to terminate Sonny. The union's business agent was informed of the pending termination. The business agent said that instead of firing Sonny, the company should first get treatment for his smoking addiction through the employee assistance program. If he smoked in a restricted area after treatment, then termination would be warranted, but not before.

The next day the plant manager called Sonny in and terminated him for violating the no-smoking policy.

Source: Case based on an arbitration case written by Bruce Fraser, "Stone Container Corp. and International Brotherhood of Teamsters, Chauffeurs, Warehousemen and Helpers of America, Local 25," Labor Award Reporter: Summary of Labor Arbitration Awards, Report No. 469 *(April 1998): 4–5.*

Questions

1. Do you agree with the plant manager's termination of Sonny Nygaard? Why or why not?

2. What is the significance of the fact that a coworker had seen Sonny smoking in the pulverizer room before? What is the significance of the fact that he did not report the incident at the time?

3. What is your view of the union business agent's argument that Sonny should first be given an opportunity to get treatment for his smoking addiction?

4. If the case is appealed to arbitration, how do you think the arbitrator will weigh the plant's safety concerns with Sonny's smoking problem, work history, and past smoking violations? Explain.

References

1. Gatehouse, Jonathon. "Terror by Mail," *Maclean's* (November 15, 2001): 22–24.

2. McFarland, Jennifer. "Violence in the Workplace," *Harvard Management Update* (April 2001): 8.

3. Ibid.

4. Mayer, Merry. "Breaking Point," *HR Magazine* (October 2001): 111–114.

5. Ibid.

6. Randle, Wilma. "When Employees Lie, Cheat, or Steal," *Working Woman* (January 1995): 55–56, 76.

7. *Chicago Tribune.* "Employees Top Shoplifters" (December 19, 1994): sect. 4, 3.

8. Emshwiller, John R. "Businesses Lose Billions of Dollars to Employee Theft," *The Wall Street Journal* (October 5, 1992): B2.

9. Ibid.

10. Ziemba, Stanley. "Study Finds Lax Computer Security Is Costing Business," *Chicago Tribune* (November 20, 1994): sect. 7, 5.

11. Ibid.

12. Hayes, Frank. "Secure Your Users," *Computerworld* (September 24, 2001): 70.

13. Cullison, A. E. "Fax Machines an Open Book to Hackers," *Chicago Tribune* (September 9, 1990): sect. 7, 11B.

14. Rochester, Jack B. "Insiders Lead the List of Electronic Thieves," *USA Today* (June 8, 1987): 8E.

15. Bequai, August. "Ethics, Education Key to Crime Prevention," *USA Today* (June 8, 1987): 8E.

16. Weir, Tom. "Caught on Camera," *Supermarket Business Magazine* (November 15, 2001): 11.

17. Council of Better Business Bureaus. *How to Protect Your Business from Fraud, Scams, and Crime.* White Plains, NY: The Benjamin Company (1992): 177–178.

18. Turcsik, Richard, and Summerour, Jenny. "Monitoring Shrink," *Progressive Grocer* (October 2001): 7. Weir, "Caught on Camera."

19. Clark, Ken. "On Guard," *Chain Store Age* (October 2001): 45–48.

20. Reitman, Valerie. "Alarm Sounded on Shoplifting," *Chicago Tribune* (January 28, 1990): sect. 7, 12.

21. Hagedorn, Ann. "It's Why Employees Don't Want the Boss's Portrait on the Wall," *The Wall Street Journal* (November 29, 1990): B1.

22. Council of Better Business Bureaus. *How to Protect.*

23. *FDCH Regulatory Intelligence Database.* "Fire Prevention Week, 2000 by the President of the United States of America: A Proclamation." (October 7, 2000).

24. Shellenbarger, Sue. "Overloaded Staffers Are Starting to Take More Time Off Work," *The Wall Street Journal* (September 23, 1998): B1.

25. Sandler, Howard M. "Microbiologics in the Workplace," *Occupational Hazards* (May 2000): 95–96.

26. Kim, Arnold L. "Sick Building Syndrome Solutions," *Professional Safety* (June 2001): 43.

27. Turner, Toni. "The Phantom Menace," *Director* (September 2001): 90–94.

28. Jackson, Maggie. "Toilet Training for Businesses: OSHA Will Issue New Mandate," *Fort Worth Star Telegram* (March 13, 1998): F1, F4.

29. Jackson. "Toilet Training": F4.

30. *FDCH Regulatory Intelligence Database.* "Statements by HHS Secretary Tommy G. Thompson Regarding World AIDS Day," (November 30, 2001).

31. Fletcher, Lee. "Drug Testing Promoted as Loss Prevention Measure," *Business Insurance* (May 8, 2000): 16.

32. Bahls, Jane Easter. "Dealing With Drugs: Keep It Legal," *HR Magazine* (March 1998): 105–116.

33. Ibid.

34. Ibid.

35. O'Brien, Timothy L.; Gupta, Udayan; and Marsh, Barbara. "Most Small Businesses Appear Prepared to Cope with New Family-Leave Rules," *The Wall Street Journal* (February 8, 1993): B1.

36. Fefer, Mark D. "Taking Control of Your Workers' Comp Costs," *Fortune* (October 3, 1994): 131–132, 134, 136.

37. Ibid.

38. Ibid.

GLOSSARY

accident any unforeseen or unplanned incident or event

accountability having to answer to someone for your performance or failure to perform to standards

affiliative manager a manager with affiliation needs greater than power needs

appraisal process periodic evaluations of each subordinate's on-the-job performance as well as his or her skill levels, attitudes, and potential

arbitration The use of a neutral third party in a dispute between management and labor to resolve the areas of conflict

attitude a person's manner of thinking, feeling, or acting toward specific stimuli

authority a person's right to give orders and instructions to others and to use organizational resources

autocratic style a management and leadership style characterized by the leader's retention of all authority for decision making

behavioral interview an interviewing technique in which job applicants are asked to describe how they handled critical incidents in their prior experiences

behavior modeling a visual training approach designed to teach proper modes of behavior by involving supervisors and others in real-life performances

belief a perception based on a conviction that certain things are true or probable in one's own mind (opinion)

benchmarks performance levels or best practices of the most exceptional companies in an industry

brainstorming group idea-generation processes in which creativity is encouraged, while evaluation is limited to a separate phase

bureaucratic style a management style characterized by the manager's reliance on rules, regulations, policies, and procedures to direct subordinates

career a sequence of jobs that takes people to higher levels of learning and responsibility

career path a route chosen by an employer or employee through a series of related horizontal and vertical moves to jobs of ever-increasing responsibilities

clique an informal group of two or more people who come together primarily on the basis of social rationales

collective bargaining the process of negotiating a union agreement that covers wages, hours, and working conditions

communication the transmission of information and common understanding from one person or group to another through the use of common symbols

complaint any expression of unhappiness with working conditions or on-the-job relationships that comes to a manager's attention

compressed work week a work week made up of four 10-hour days

computer monitoring using computers to measure how employees achieve their outputs by monitoring work as it takes place

computer virus a rogue computer program that can reproduce itself endlessly or cause other havoc, such as the destruction of stored data

controlling the management function that sets standards for performance and attempts to prevent, identify, and correct deviations from standards

counselor the human relations role in which a supervisor is an adviser and director to subordinates

cultural diversity the co-existence of two or more cultural groups within an organization

delegation the act of passing formal or positional authority by a manager to an associate or subordinate

democratic style a management and leadership style characterized by a sharing of decision-making authority with subordinates by the leader

directive interview an interview planned and controlled by the interviewer

discipline the management duty that involves educating subordinates to foster obedience and self-control while dispensing appropriate punishment for wrongdoing

disparate impact/adverse impact the existence of a significantly different selection rate between women or minorities and non-protected groups

directing the supervision or overseeing of people and processes

direction in communication, the flow or path a message takes in order to reach a receiver

diversity differences in people and groups that serve to both unite and separate them from others

employee association a group of workers that bargains collectively or meets and confers with management on behalf of employees but usually lacks the right to strike

employment at will the common law doctrine that holds that employment will last until either employer or employee decides to terminate it, with or without just cause

empower to equip people to function on their own, without direct supervision

ergonomics concern about the design of work sites, machines, equipment, and systems to minimize stress and job-related injuries

ethics a discipline dealing with the rightness and wrongness of human conduct in society

expectancy belief that effort will result in performance

feedback any effort made by parties to a communication to ensure that they have a common understanding of each other's meaning and intent

flexibility the ability of members of a workforce to perform different tasks

flextime a work schedule with flexible starting and ending times

force-field analysis a method for visualizing the driving and restraining forces at work within an individual so as to assess what is needed to make a change in a person's behavior

foreman a supervisor of workers in manufacturing

formal group two or more people who come together by management decision to achieve specific goals

formal organization an enterprise that has clearly stated goals, a division of labor among specialists, a rational design, and a hierarchy of authority and accountability

functional authority the right that a manager of a staff department has to make decisions and to give orders that affect the way things are done in another department

goal the objective, target, or end result expected from the execution of programs, tasks, and activities

grapevine informal channels at work that transmit information and misinformation

grievance an alleged violation of the labor–management agreement

grievance processing settling an alleged violation of the labor–management agreement in accordance with the method outlined in that agreement

group two or more people who consider themselves a functioning unit and share a common goal

groupware software that enables group members to work together without close physical proximity

halo effect one positive characteristic, behavior, or incident favorably biases the appraisal

health the general physical, mental, and emotional condition of a person, and the efforts to prevent illness and treat injuries when they occur

hierarchy the group of people picked to staff an organization's positions of formal authority—its management position authority

horn effect one negative characteristic, behavior, or incident adversely biases the appraisal

human needs physiological and psychological requirements that all humans share and that act as motives for behavior

human relations the development and maintenance of sound on-the-job relationships with subordinates, peers, and superiors

individualism the training principle that requires a trainer to conduct training at a pace suitable for the trainee

induction the planning and conduct of a program to introduce a new employee to his or her job, working environment, supervisor, and peers

informal group two or more people who come together by choice to satisfy mutual needs or to share common interests

information any facts, figures, or data that are in a form or format that makes them usable to a person who possesses them

institutional manager a manager who has a high need for power, high inhibitions, and low need for affiliation

instrumentality belief that performance will result in desired outcomes

interview a two-way conversation under the control of one of the parties

job description a formal listing of the duties that make up a position in an organization

job enlargement increasing the number of tasks or the quantity of output required in a job

job enrichment providing variety, deeper personal interest and involvement, greater autonomy and challenge, or increased responsibility on the job

job rotation movement of people to different jobs, usually temporarily, in order to inform, train, or stimulate cooperation and understanding among them

job sharing splitting the hours of a job between two or more employees

job specification the personal characteristics and skills that are required of an individual to execute a job

just cause discipline of appropriate severity for violation of reasonable rules; it follows a warning with consistent rule enforcement and substantial proof

knowledge worker a highly educated and skilled specialist who has knowledge critical to the success of the organization

labor relations management activities necessitated by the fact that the organization has a union that represents its employees

leadership the ability to get work done with and through others while winning their respect, confidence, loyalty, and willing cooperation

line authority a manager's right to give direct orders to subordinates and appraise, reward, and discipline those who receive those orders

maintenance factor according to Herzberg, a factor that can be provided by an employer in order to prevent job dissatisfaction

management the process of planning, organizing, directing, and controlling human, material, and informational resources for the purposes of setting and achieving stated goals; also, a team of people making up an organization's hierarchy

management by exception a management principle asserting that managers should spend their time on those matters that require their particular expertise

management by objectives (MBO) a management principle that uses performance objectives to guide, evaluate, and reward employee behavior

management by wandering around (MBWA) a leadership principle that encourages supervisors to get out of their offices regularly so that they can touch base with their subordinates and customers

management skills categories of capabilities needed by managers at all levels in an organization

manager a member of an organization's hierarchy who is paid to make decisions; one who gets things done with and through others through the execution of basic management functions

mediation the use of a neutral third party in a labor–management dispute to facilitate resolution of the dispute by the parties

medium a channel or means used to carry a message in the communication process

message the ideas, intent, and feelings that you wish to communicate to a receiver

middle management the members of the hierarchy below the rank of top management but above the rank of supervisor

minority according to the EEOC, a member of one of the following groups: Hispanics, Native Americans, African Americans, Asians or Pacific Islanders, or Alaskan natives

mission the expression in words—backed up with both plans and actions—of the organization's central and common purpose, its reason for existing

motivation the drive within a person to achieve a goal or to be predisposed to perform an activity

motivation factor according to Herzberg, a factor that has the potential to stimulate internal motivation to provide better-than-average performance and commitment from those to whom it appeals

negative discipline the part of discipline that emphasizes the detection and punishment of wrongdoing

networking using one's friends, family, and work-related contacts to help find employment or to advance one's career

nominal group a group idea-generation process in which members develop their ideas individually and then the leader elicits all ideas for a separate evaluation phase

non-directive interview an interview planned by the interviewer but controlled by the interviewee

objective a training principle that requires the trainers and trainees to know what is to be mastered through training

obsolescence a state or condition that exists when a person or machine is no longer able to perform to standards or to management's expectations

open book management the sharing of financial information with employees so that they can make informed decisions and earn a share of increased profits

operating management hierarchy that oversees the work of non-management people (workers)

organizational development a planned, managed, systematic process used to change the culture, system, and behavior of an organization to improve its effectiveness in solving problems and achieving goals

orientation the planning and conduct of a program to introduce a new employee to the company and its history, policies, rules, and procedures

OSHA the federal agency called the Occupational Safety and Health Administration

outsourcing contracting with outside vendors to perform services previously handled within the organization by company employees

peer a person on the same level of authority and status as another

permanent part-time workers employees who wish to work less than 40 hours per week

personal power manager a manager with strong power and affiliation needs and low inhibition

planning the management function through which managers decide what they want to achieve and how they are going to achieve their goals

policy a broad guideline constructed by top management to influence managers' approaches to solving problems and dealing with recurring situations

portable executive a temporary or contingent executive who may fill a position for a period of months to one or two years

positive discipline the aspect of discipline that promotes understanding and self-control by letting subordinates know what is expected of them

power the ability to influence others so that they respond favorably to orders and instructions

procedure a general routine or method for executing day-to-day operations

productivity the amount of input needed to generate a given amount of output

program a plan listing goals and containing the answers to the who, what, when, where, how, and how much of the plan

progressive discipline a system using warnings about what is and is not acceptable conduct; specific job-related rules; punishments that fit the offense; punishments that grow in severity as misconduct persists; and prompt, consistent enforcement

psychological contract an unwritten recognition of what an employer and employee expect to give and to receive from each other

quality the totality of features and characteristics of a product or service (or process or project) that bear on its ability to satisfy stated or implied goals (requirements of producers and customers)

quality of working life a general label given to various programs and projects designed to help employees satisfy their needs and meet their expectations from work

realism a training principle that requires training to simulate or duplicate an actual working environment and behavior or performance required of the trainee

receiver the person or group intended by transmitters to receive a message

reengineering fundamental changes in how work is performed that eliminate unnecessary activities, minimizes hand-offs of work, and combines jobs

reinforcement the training principle that requires trainees to review and restate knowledge learned; also refers to rewards for correct responses

response the principle of training that requires feedback from trainees to trainers and vice versa

responsibility the obligation persons with authority have to execute their duties to the best of their abilities

resume an employment-related document submitted by an applicant, containing vital data such as the person's name, address, employment goals, and work-related education and experiences

role ambiguity uncertainty about the role that one is expected to play

role conflict a situation that occurs when contradictory or opposing demands are made on a manager

role prescription the collection of expectations and demands from superiors, subordinates, and others that shapes a manager's job description and perception of his or her job

rule a regulation on human conduct at work

safety efforts at protecting human resources from accidents and injuries

sanction negative means, such as threats or punishments, used to encourage subordinates to play their roles as prescribed by superiors or the organization

scoreboarding providing feedback on individual and team efforts to reach goals

security efforts at protecting physical facilities and other resources from loss or damage

selection   the human resource management function that determines who is hired

sexual harassment   unwelcomed sexual advances, requests for sexual favors, and other physical and verbal conduct of a sexual nature

six sigma   a quality approach having a goal of no more than 3.4 defects in a million units

socialization   the process a new employee undergoes in the first few weeks of employment through which he or she learns how to cope and succeed

span of control   the number of employees over which a manager has direct supervisory control

spectator style   a management style characterized by treating subordinates as independent decision makers

spokesperson   the human relations role through which a supervisor represents management's views to workers and workers' views to management

staff authority   the right of staff managers to give advice and counsel to other managers in an organization in their areas of expertise

standard   a definition of acceptable performance levels for people, machines, or processes

standard operating procedures (SOP)   sets of procedures providing guidance for decision making given different routine circumstances

steward   the union's elected or appointed first-line representative in the areas in which employees work

stress   worry, anxiety, or tension that accompanies situations and problems we face that makes us uncertain about the ways in which we should resolve them

subjects   the principle of training that requires trainers to know the subject being taught and to know the trainees' needs

supervisor   a manager responsible for the welfare, behaviors, and performances of non-management employees (workers)

synergy   cooperative action or force of two or more elements pulling together that yields a result greater than the sum of the results that could be achieved separately by the elements

syntality   a group's "personality"—what makes it unique

team   a work group in which members feel a compelling need for team work, assume joint responsibility for accomplishment of the team's goals, and hold each other accountable for results

team facilitator   a supervisor in charge of teams but who works outside them

team leader   a supervisor working in a team who is responsible for its members

telecommuting   working at home through telecommunications

temporary workers   workers employed by a temporary work agency to provide labor for other employers

Theory X   a set of attitudes traditionally held by managers that includes assuming the worst with regard to the average worker's initiative and creativity

Theory Y   a set of attitudes held by today's generation of managers that includes assuming the best about the average worker's initiative and creativity

Theory Z   a set of approaches to managing people based on the attitudes of Japanese managers, emphasizing the importance of the individual and of team effort to the organization

top management   the uppermost part of the management hierarchy, containing the positions of the chief executive and his or her immediate subordinates

training   the activity concerned with improving employees' performances in their present jobs by imparting skills, knowledge, and attitudes

training objective   a written statement describing what the trainee should be able to do, the conditions under which the trainee is expected to perform, and the criteria used to judge the adequacy of the performance

transmitter   the person or group that sends a message to a receiver

understanding   the concept that all parties to a communication are of one mind regarding its meaning and intent

union   a group of workers employed by a company or in an industry who have banded together to bargain collectively with their employer

valance   the value or attractiveness of an outcome

validity   the degree to which a selection device measures what it is supposed to measure or is predictive of a person's performance on a job

vandalism   wanton or willful destruction of or damage to another's property

value   judgment about what is right or wrong and important or unimportant

vision   a statement of what kind of company the organization wants to be in the future and the direction in which it will go

whistleblower   an employee who notifies authorities of violations of laws committed by his or her employer that are contrary to public policy

work ethic   people's attitudes about the importance of working, the kind of work they choose or are required to do, and the quality of their efforts while performing work

worker   any employee who is not a member of the management hierarchy

workers' compensation   federal and state laws designed to compensate employees for illnesses and injuries that arise out of and in the course of their employment